Church, Faith and Culture in the Medieval West

General Editor: Brenda Bolton

About the series

Church, Faith and Culture in the M[...] ne most
innovative work from this area of cur[...] iew and
upcoming scholars as well as more est[...] es much
new work from the period 400-1500 t[...] om. The
series is primarily monographic but also includes collected essays on themes of
particular relevance and the significance of individuals. All titles will share a
commitment to innovation, analysis and historical accuracy.

In the last generation an important transformation has taken place in the study
of the Medieval Church in the Latin West. This new focus has moved away from a
narrow concentration on single religious themes to introduce a greater cultural
awareness. Recent cross-disciplinary studies on the Church's rules on
consanguinity provide a case in point while other research has benefited from
theological, political or literary perspectives.

About the volume

Reflecting the range of the honorand's interests, the essays in *Ritual, Text and Law*
provide a stimulating exploration of the interrelated fields of medieval canon law
and liturgy, chiefly through the scrutiny of texts and their transmission. The studies
are grouped thematically under the headings of 'Ritual' and 'Text and Law', with
each section having an introduction by the editors, surveying recent developments
in the study of medieval canon law and liturgy. Individually, the contributors offer
new viewpoints on key issues and questions relating to medieval religious, cultural
and intellectual history, particularly of the period c. 900–1200, and especially the
Italian peninsula. Collectively they illuminate the interaction of medieval
Christianity and its rituals, as well as the relationship of the secular and the sacred
as transmitted in liturgico-canonical texts from the time of the early church to the
14th century.

About the editors

Kathleen Cushing is Lecturer in Medieval History at Keele University, UK; and
Richard Gyug is Associate Professor of History at Fordham University, USA.

Church, Faith and Culture in the Medieval West

General Editor: Brenda Bolton

Other titles in the series:

Gillian R. Knight
The Correspondence between Peter the Venerable and Bernard of Clairvaux
A Semantic and Structural Analysis

Richard Kay
The Council of Bourges, 1225
A Documentary History

Edited by Brenda Bolton and Anne J. Duggan
Adrian IV The English Pope (1154–1159)
Studies and Texts

Sylvia Schein
Gateway to the Heavenly City
Crusader Jerusalem and the Catholic West (1099–1187)

Ritual, Text and Law

Roger E. Reynolds

Ritual, Text and Law

Studies in Medieval Canon Law and Liturgy Presented to
Roger E. Reynolds

Edited by

KATHLEEN G. CUSHING
Keele University, UK

RICHARD F. GYUG
Fordham University, USA

Routledge
Taylor & Francis Group

LONDON AND NEW YORK

First published 2004 by Ashgate Publishing

Reissued 2018 by Routledge
2 Park Square, Milton Park, Abingdon, Oxon OX14 4RN
711 Third Avenue, New York, NY 10017, USA

Routledge is an imprint of the Taylor & Francis Group, an informa business

First issued in paperback 2018

A Library of Congress record exists under LC control number: 2004005860

Notice:
Product or corporate names may be trademarks or registered trademarks, and are used only for identification and explanation without intent to infringe.

Publisher's Note
The publisher has gone to great lengths to ensure the quality of this reprint but points out that some imperfections in the original copies may be apparent.

Disclaimer
The publisher has made every effort to trace copyright holders and welcomes correspondence from those they have been unable to contact.

ISBN 13: 978-0-815-39157-9 (hbk)
ISBN 13: 978-1-138-62043-8 (pbk)
ISBN 13: 978-1-351-14992-1 (ebk)

Contents

PART II: Text and Law

List of Plates

List of Tables

List of Contributors

Jonathan Black, Managing Editor, *Mediaeval Studies*, Pontifical Institute of Mediaeval Studies, Toronto.

Uta-Renate Blumenthal, Ordinary Professor of History, The Catholic University of America.

Dr. Martin Brett, Fellow in History, Robinson College, Cambridge.

Virginia Brown, Senior Fellow and Professor of Latin Palaeography, Pontifical Institute of Mediaeval Studies, Toronto.

Dr. Paul De Clerck, Professor at the Institut Supérieur de Liturgie, Institut Catholique de Paris.

Giles Constable, Professor Emeritus of Medieval History, School of Historical Studies, Institute for Advanced Study, Princeton.

Dr. Kathleen G. Cushing, Lecturer in Medieval History, Keele University.

Dr. Linda Fowler-Magerl, Wissenschaftliche Mitarbeiterin, Stephan-Kuttner-Institute, University of Munich.

John St H. Gibaut, Associate Professor, Faculty of Theology, Saint Paul University.

Richard F. Gyug, Associate Professor of History, Fordham University.

Charles Hilken, F.S.C., Associate Professor of History, Saint Mary's College of California.

Susan Ann Keefe, Associate Professor of Church History, The Divinity School, Duke University.

Prof. Dr. Dr. h. c. mult. Peter Landau, University of Munich.

Hubert Mordek, Professor of Medieval History at the University of Freiburg i. Br.

Eric Palazzo, Professeur d'histoire de l'art du Moyen Age à l'université de Poitiers, Directeur du Centre d'études supérieures de civilisation médiévale (Poitiers).

Dr. Herbert Schneider, Monumenta Germaniae Historica, Munich.

Robert Somerville, Tremaine Professor of Religion; Professor of History, Columbia University.

Timothy M. Thibodeau, Professor of History, Nazareth College of Rochester.

Preface

In his distinguished career, Roger E. Reynolds has published extensively on early medieval liturgy and canon law, with special attention to the transmission of texts. The articles in the present volume written in his honour consider such topics under the broad headings of 'Ritual' and 'Text and Law', and touch at many points on the relations between law and liturgy. In Reynolds' publications, teaching and popular lectures, he has pioneered the study of such connections, and provided fresh insights and understandings as a result. Reynolds' expertise in such central topics, plus his fundamental recognition that historians must be willing to dissolve the barriers between sub-specializations, has been a benefit to his colleagues, and especially to his students. In his teaching at Carleton University in Ottawa (1968-77), and subsequently in his courses and mentoring at the Pontifical Institute of Mediaeval Studies and University of Toronto, he has brought a generation of students, who often have had little knowledge of such fields and knew little of their importance, to an appreciation of the centrality of the liturgy to medieval life and the medieval church, and a recognition of the importance of law in interpreting the liturgical evidence.

The authors of these studies in honour of Roger Reynolds include former students, appreciative scholars who have benefited from his guidance and scholarly critiques, colleagues in the field who have shared insights with him throughout his career, and institutional colleagues from the Pontifical Institute of Mediaeval Studies, where Reynolds has been a Senior Fellow since 1977, and the Monumenta Germaniae Historica, with which he has been Corresponding Member since 1987. In each category, the present list of contributors must be considered representative, not comprehensive: the limits of an already very full volume have meant being more restrictive in inviting contributions than we would have wished. That this should be the case is a tribute to Roger Reynolds' wide range of interests, and his selfless dedication to his students, colleagues and the field.

The editors wish to extend our most appreciative thanks to Ashgate for its enthusiastic support of this project, and especially to John Smedley and the series editor Brenda Bolton. We should also like to thank the contributors for their unfailing professionalism, and the promptness and courtesy with which they responded to our questions and deadlines. We also need to acknowledge as a group the individuals—whose names, for practical reasons, cannot be given here—who wished to contribute to this volume, but who were unable to do so for various reasons. Special mention, however, needs to be made of Professor Virginia Brown, without whose persuasion and insistence, the project might never have been undertaken.

KGC/RFG

List of Abbreviations

BMCL, NS	*Bulletin of Medieval Canon Law*, New Series (1971-)
CCSL	*Corpus Christianorum, Series Latina* (Turnhout, 1953-)
CCCM	*Corpus Christianorum, Continuatio Mediaeualis* (Turnhout, 1971-)
CPL	*Clauis patrum latinorum*, ed. Eligius Dekkers and Aemilius Gaar†, 3rd edn (Steenbrugge, 1995)
CSEL	*Corpus scriptorum ecclesiasticorum latinorum* (Vienna, 1866-)
Decretum	*Decretum Gratiani; Corpus Iuris Canonici*, ed. Aemilius [Emil] Friedberg, i (Leipzig, 1879)
GCS	*Die griechischen christlichen Schriftsteller der ersten drei Jahrhunderte*, 53 vols (Leipzig, 1897-1969)
JE/JK/JL	Philippus Jaffé, *Regesta Pontificum Romanorum ad annum 1198*, 2nd edn by S. Lowenfeld, F. Kaltenbrunner, and P. Ewald, 2 vols (Leipzig, 1885-8; 1st edn, 1851; repr. Graz, 1956). Cited from the initial of the editors in the 2nd edn as JK to the year 590, JE for 590-882 and JL for 883-1198.
Mansi	*Sacrorum conciliorum nova et amplissima collectio*, ed. Joannes Dominicus Mansi, cont. Ioannes Baptista Martin, Ludovicus Petit, 53 vols (Florence-Venice, 1758-98; Paris, 1901-27; repr. Graz, 1960-61)
MGH	*Monumenta Germaniae Historica, inde ab anno Christi quingentesimo usque ad annum millesimum et quingentesimum* (Hanover-Berlin, 1824-). The following sections and sub-sections are cited:
	Scriptores: *Scriptores* (in folio: vols 1-30; = *SS*; in quarto: vol. 31-); *Scriptores Rerum Germanicarum, Nova Series* (= *SRG, NS*); *Scriptores Rerum Germanicarum in usum scholarum separatim editi* (= *SRG*); *Libelli de lite imperatorum et pontificum saeculis xi. et xii. conscripti* (= *Libelli de lite*)
	Leges: *Leges* (in folio; = *LL*), *Capitularia regum Francorum*, ed. Alfredus Boretius and Victor Krause, 2 vols (Hanover, 1883-97; repr. 1957) (= *Capitularia*); *Concilia*, including further sub-sections *Capitula episcoporum* and *Ordines de Celebrando Concilia; Constitutiones et acta publica imperatorum et regum*; and *Fontes Iuris Germanici Antiqui*
	Epistolae: *Epistolae* (in quarto), *Die Briefe der deutschen Kaiserzeit, Epistolae selectae*
	Hilfsmittel
	Schriften der Monumenta Germaniae Historica
	Studien und Texte
MIC	Monumenta Iuris Canonici

NA	*Neues Archiv der Gesellschaft für ältere deutsche Geschichtskunde* (1876-1935)
PG	*Patrologiae cursus completus, Series graeca (Patrologia Graeca)*, ed. J. P. Migne, 161 vols in 166 (1857-66)
PL	*Patrologiae cursus completus, Series latina (Patrologia Latina)*, ed. J. P. Migne, 221 vols (Paris, 1841-64)
QF	*Quellen und Forschungen aus italienischen Archiven und Bibliotheken* (1898-)
RB	*Revue bénédictine* (1890-)
RHE	*Revue d'histoire ecclèsiastique* (1900-)
s.v.	sub vocabulo
SChr.	*Sources Chrétiennes* (Paris, 1941-)
ZRG KA	*Zeitschrift der Savigny-Stiftung für Rechtsgeschichte. Kanonistische Abteilung* (1911-)

PART I
Ritual

Introduction

Ritual

Richard F. Gyug

Two papers in the present volume, those of Timothy M. Thibodeau and Uta-Renate Blumenthal, call attention to comments Roger Reynolds has made concerning the role of liturgy during the Gregorian revolution.[1] Reynolds' point, as they note, was that the reformers were as much liturgists as they were lawyers or politicians, monks or bishops, active or contemplative. His conclusion was that any assessment of the period and its character that did not take account of its liturgical legislation, its liturgical framework for moments of historical significance, or its output of liturgical scholarship would be deficient in essential ways. Reynolds' own scholarship has not made that error; instead, he has placed medieval ritual in the middle of a broader understanding of the medieval church and medieval culture, and has charted interdisciplinary paths to explaining the role of sacred rituals. Moreover, it is implicit in all Reynolds' scholarly work—publication, teaching and popular lectures—that interpreting liturgies of the past requires careful attention to their contexts, and that the lessons of distant liturgical ages, such as the eleventh-century Gregorian Revolution, are apt for the present ecclesiastical age.

The fields of Reynolds' publication and teaching programmes have been broad and covered many individual topics, all linked to the central concern of understanding medieval culture and the medieval church. His works on the illustrations of liturgical manuscripts, early medieval canonical collections, Beneventan manuscripts, and especially clerical orders and duties, are only the beginning of a long list.[2] The articles in the present volume address many of the themes considered by Reynolds; in the present section on medieval ritual and liturgy, they include

---

1 Timothy M. Thibodeau, 'From Durand of Mende to St Thomas More: lessons learned from medieval liturgy', 83-94 at 86 n. 11, citing Reynolds, 'Liturgical Scholarship at the Time of the Investiture Controversy: Past Research and Future Opportunities', *Harvard Theological Review*, 71 (1978), 109-24; and Uta-Renate Blumenthal, 'The Collection of St Victor (= V), Paris: Liturgy, Canon Law, and Polemical Literature', 293-308 at 293 n. 1, citing Reynolds, 'The Liturgy of Rome in the Eleventh Century: past research and future opportunities', in *Scientia veritatis: Festschrift fur Hubert Mordek zum 65. Geburtstag* (Sigmaringen, forthcoming).

2 See Reynolds' list of Principal Publications at 309-18 of the present volume. Beyond the rigorous scholarship of his major publications, there is an equally rigorous program of education and public information, through over 200 academic presentations, radio interviews, newspaper articles, and popular lectures.

discussions of angels, orders and clerical formation, liturgical commentaries, the dedication of churches, and the relations between script and liturgical culture. As has Reynolds' work, they contribute to deeper knowledge of the periods they discuss, and, just as Reynolds' program of teaching and writing, provide the rich historical context needed for contemporary debates.

The area in which Roger Reynolds' contribution is most significant is open to debate, because he has worked in so many areas, but his contribution to the study of medieval orders must rank high in any assessment. Much of his work in the area has concentrated on legal history, because it has been through legal sources that Reynolds has been able to move liturgical scholarship in new directions. Nonetheless, the fundamental question has been liturgical, and has developed in parallel with contemporary concerns about ecclesiastical reform and revitalization. While the Second Vatican Council was meeting in Rome, Roger Reynolds was moving from study at Harvard Divinity School to work on his doctorate at Harvard's graduate school of arts and sciences. The topic on which he wrote his doctoral dissertation, 'Sacred Orders in the Early Middle Ages: shifts in the theology of the lower and higher ecclesiastical orders from late patristic antiquity through the early middle ages as reflected in the Ordinals of Christ and related literature' (1968), was later expanded and published in 1978 in the series 'Beiträge zur Geschichte und Quellenkunde des Mittelalters' as *The Ordinals of Christ from their Origins to the Twelfth Century*.[3] The scholarship of the Liturgical Movement, the reforms in contemporary liturgies, and the inspiring vision of theologians such as Odo Casel, whose emphasis on the liturgy as central to Christian churches' relation to Christ, and Christ's acts as central to a meaningful liturgy, made Reynolds' topic very timely. The Ordinals of Christ, seemingly stray tags, redolent of medieval allegory, lost in early medieval canon-law collections, and scorned by theologians for centuries, describe how Christ's acts exemplified the duties of each order; in effect, how clerical orders imitated Christ's sacramental role, and how thus the church carried out its central mission. In other words, these relicts of medieval ecclesiastical culture expressed in their distant way what had become in the mid-twentieth century a burning issue; i.e., the concept of the primarily liturgical function of Christian churches.

Although the reform of the Roman Catholic liturgy that followed the Second Vatican Council was founded on considerable liturgical scholarship, at least some reasoned responses have questioned whether the reformers recognized the values of liturgical tradition even as they were putting new emphasis on the importance of ritual and liturgy in the life of the church. The Oxford Declaration in 1996 called

---

3   For subsequent work, see especially Roger E. Reynolds, *Clerics in the Early Middle Ages: hierarchy and image* (Aldershot, 1999), and *Clerical Orders in the Early Middle Ages: duties and ordination* (Aldershot, 1999), containing earlier works and supplementary studies first published in the volumes.

for future reform to 'proceed ... from a thorough understanding of the organic nature of the liturgical traditions of the Church'; it was an appeal for a more sympathetic study of past liturgies.[4] Reynolds' work has highlighted how important this study is for the concepts of ministries and orders.

In the Roman Catholic church, discussion of the orders and their ministries at the Second Vatican Council led in 1964 to the restoration of the deaconate as a terminal order, and in 1972, to the conversion of the subdiaconate and minor orders into lay ministries. The argument was that these minor orders were transitional and thus indistinct, and were not intended for service at the altar, and thus not part of the essential liturgical role of the church.[5] As Charles Hilken notes in his article on the historical place of subdeacons in the eleventh and subsequent centuries, Roger Reynolds' scholarship shows that the reasons behind the modern change do not reflect the evolving teaching of the medieval church on the subdiaconate.[6] Hilken examines the implications of this in one community, Montecassino, through consideration of the citation of subdeacons in the abbey's necrology or list of names for liturgical commemoration. Compiled 1164/6 from earlier necrologies and updated with new names for centuries, the list of subdeacons in the necrology shows that deacons were indeed a major order from the eleventh century on, as Reynolds has argued, because the role of subdeacons in assisting at the altar exalted their order. But its members could not be chosen as abbots, as they had been in earlier periods, because a new emphasis on the mass as the defining element of liturgical life precluded those who, like subdeacons, could not celebrate masses from holding the highest office.[7]

Although not concerned with orders or institutions, Paul De Clerck's inquiry into the characteristics and history of the concept of an 'angel of peace' is founded on assumptions much like those discussed above: the expression of Christian thought through the ages of the church can explain the meaning and import of

---

4 'The Oxford Declaration on the Liturgy issued by the Liturgy Forum of the Centre for Faith and Culture at Westminster College, Oxford, at the conclusion of the 1996 Conference of the Centre', in *Beyond the Prosaic: renewing the liturgical movement*, ed. Stratford Caldecott (Edinburgh, 1998), 163-5 at 164-5.

5 Paul VI, *Lumen gentium*, constitutio dogmatica de ecclesia, 21 November 1964, c. 29, *Acta apostolicae sedis*, 57 (1965), 5-75; and Paul VI, *Ministeria quaedam*, motu proprio, 15 August 1972, *Acta apostolicae sedis*, 64 (1972), 529-34; for the latter, see Charles Hilken, 'Necrological Evidence of the Place and Permanence of the Subdiaconate', in the present volume, 51-66 at n. 1.

6 'The Subdiaconate as a Sacred and Superior Order', in *Clerics in the Early Middle Ages*, no. IV, 1-39; see also 'Patristic "Presbyterianism" in the Early Medieval Theology of Sacred Orders', *Mediaeval Studies*, 45 (1983; repr. *Clerics in the Early Middle Ages*, no. V), 311-42, for a study of changing perceptions of the relations between priests and bishops, certainly a topic with ecclesiological implications.

7 In the next section, 'Text and Law', John Gibaut's article on sequential ordination ('The Peregrinations of Canon 13 of the Council of Sardica', 141-60) touches on similar issues of the place of individual orders in the medieval ecclesial hierarchy, but approaches the topic from a canonical perspective, and thus reflects a second side of Roger Reynolds' scholarship in the area.

contemporary spiritual concerns. Furthermore, much of De Clerck's exploration is concerned with liturgical evidence. In order to shed light on a reference in the *Deprecatio Gelasii* (492-6) to a prayer directed toward an 'angelum pacis', De Clerck traces references to the angel of peace in the Book of Enoch, through references in eastern liturgies, especially litanies, before noting the functional roles played by angels in western liturgies. In the west, angels appear in the liturgy as purifying agents in baptism, as guardians and protectors in exorcisms, and as sanctifiers and intercessors. The angel of peace appears especially as a companion, whether in death, which is the role of the angel of peace in the *Deprecatio Gelasii*, or on voyages. For De Clerck, exploring the use of a simple term, at once both familiar and cryptic, takes a historian through far-flung sources to arrive at a full, contextualized meaning.

The meaning of the liturgy was explored by medieval liturgical commentators, whose works are rich in materials for understanding medieval culture, but whose formulas and approaches pose nearly insoluble problems for historical analysis. Interpreting such texts and emphasizing their value for historical study have been issues that Roger Reynolds has explored in articles,[8] and especially in his classes on liturgy and liturgical commentary. They are also issues that Timothy Thibodeau considers in his contribution. After reflecting on the meaning of liturgical study for the contemporary academy, Thibodeau describes the transmission and reception of William Durandus' *Rationale divinorum officiorum*, the compendious commentary on the liturgy written between 1294 and 1296, from its enormous diffusion in medieval manuscripts and early printed books to Martin Luther's condemnation of its allegorical method and the critiques of twentieth-century liturgical scholars such as Louis Bouyer, who characterized such allegorical commentaries as accretions and departures from authentic tradition. At the same time, however, as Durandus' approach was being denigrated, more sympathetic readings, such as that of Marie-Dominique Chenu, could place Durandus' 'symbolist mentality' at the centre of a world in which liturgy reflected and encompassed the divine order and salvation history. Thibodeau concludes by describing Thomas More's allegorical reflections on the passion and how complicated and rooted in the liturgical culture of traditional religion even the most exemplary humanists were.

Thibodeau noted Bouyer's dismissal of the medieval liturgical tradition,[9] but the shifts described above, such as the Oxford Declaration's call for more histori-cally informed reforms, point to a new acceptance of the medieval past and its

---

8   See for instance the articles in n. 1 above; also 'Guillaume Durand parmi les théologiens médiévaux de la liturgie', in *Guillaume Durand, Évêque de Mende (v. 1230-1296): canoniste, liturgiste et homme politique*, Actes de la Table Ronde du C.N.R.S., Mende 24-27 mai 1990, ed. Pierre-Marie Gy (Paris, 1992), 155-68; and 'Liturgy, Treatises on', in *Dictionary of the Middle Ages*, ed. Joseph R. Strayer, 13 vols (New York, 1982-9), vii, 624-33.

9   Thibodeau, 'From Durand of Mende to St Thomas More', at 85.

liturgy. Indeed, the study of liturgy and ritual hardly needs defending in the modern academy. In part a result of the post-modern critique of the modernist disdain for ritual, perhaps in part also a result of observing how charged the ecclesiastical debates on liturgy have been, the use of liturgical sources for historical studies has burgeoned, often with analysis indebted to anthropological approaches. As a small indication, from one university press alone, Cornell, between 1990 and 1996 six works on medieval liturgical topics or using liturgical sources were published.[10] In the same period, from the same press, there were at least two works on secular rituals.[11] Overall, historical works using liturgical materials, some as prominent as Miri Rubin's *Corpus Christi* or Eamon Duffy's *The Stripping of the Altars*, have become almost standard fare.[12] Recently, however, in a cautionary study about the analysis of medieval political ritual and the imposition of social-scientific models,[13] Philippe Buc has warned that narrative descriptions in medieval sources, much less normative directives, cannot be accepted at face value as representing events. This is a timely reminder that historical understanding, if possible at all, depends on a profound knowledge of historical materials and an awareness of their associations, a lesson that Roger Reynolds has imparted to a generation of students, and a warning that he has sounded in his reviews.

Eric Palazzo's contribution on hyssop, the aromatic herb used in sprinkling lustral water during the dedication of a church, exemplifies the scholarship and contextual study that Reynolds has brought to interpreting narrative accounts of ritual events. After summarizing the classical, biblical, and medieval uses of the herb, Palazzo applies this knowledge to a text from the life of St Berthe de Blangy. In the incident, a bishop refused to dedicate a church because hyssop had not been provided for the ritual. What elsewhere has been described as the bishop's trivial objection is shown in Palazzo's exposition to have been replete with sacramental meaning: the outward sign of the baptismal-like cleansing of the church was its

---

10 I.e., Frederick Paxton, *Christianizing Death: the creation of a ritual process in early medieval Europe* (Ithaca, NY, 1990); Sharon Farmer, *Communities of Saint Martin: legend and ritual in medieval Tours* (Ithaca, NY, 1991); Lester K. Little, *Benedictine Maledictions: liturgical cursing in romanesque France* (Ithaca, NY, 1993); Megan McLaughlin, *Consorting with Saints: prayer for the dead in early medieval France* (Ithaca, NY, 1994); Mary C. Mansfield, *The Humiliation of Sinners: public penance in thirteenth-century France* (Ithaca, NY, 1995); and Paul Binski, *Medieval Death: ritual and representation* (Ithaca, NY, 1996). Not all have used anthropological models, but all are noteworthy for the emphasis they place on liturgical evidence.

11 I.e., Geoffrey Koziol, *Begging Pardon and Favor: ritual and political order in early medieval France* (Ithaca, NY, 1991); Peter Arnade, *Realms of Ritual: Burgundian ceremony and civic life in late medieval Ghent* (Ithaca, NY, 1996).

12 Miri Rubin, *Corpus Christi: the Eucharist in late medieval culture* (Cambridge, 1991); Eamon Duffy, *The Stripping of the Altars: traditional religion in England, c. 1400-1580* (New Haven, CT, 1992).

13 Philippe Buc, *The Dangers of Ritual: between early medieval texts and social scientific theory* (Princeton, 2001).

lustration with holy water applied by bundled stalks of hyssop, the plant itself carrying the weight of its classical medicinal property of healing the lungs and airways, plus the biblical connotations of its purifying application, both overlaid in medieval allegorical commentaries with penitential and baptismal overtones. Of course, the bishop could not continue, and with Palazzo's exposition in mind, we have a glimpse at the liturgical logic and world-view that the text's author probably expected would give meaning to the narrative.

Jonathan Black's article is also an example of how a close examination of a source can lead to unexpected conclusions, in this case one that qualifies the point of this introduction in stressing the primacy of liturgy in the medieval mind. Quodlibetal questions and theological commentaries in general have many discussions of the sacraments, but relatively few that are liturgical in content. In examining the Quodlibets of Guerric of Saint-Quentin (d. 1245), one of the first masters of theology, Black finds only three questions that could be classified as liturgical by their topics: why orders were conferred on Saturdays in the ember days, why there was no kiss of peace in the Mass for the dead, and why Old Testament and New Testament readings have different formulaic endings. Although these are indeed liturgical topics, the last is not treated in liturgical commentaries at all, and the discussions of the first two by liturgical commentators are dependent on one another, whereas Guerric of Saint-Quentin follows altogether different lines of argumentation. The tantalizing implication is that specialization was clearly a fact in the academies of the thirteenth century. The common liturgical culture did not carry over into a common scholarly understanding.

If a sophisticated analysis of the past depends on a knowledgeable appreciation of its sources and the events described in them, an observation to which all the articles described above bear witness, it is important to note how these methods have been tested and developed in Roger Reynolds' own work. His studies of orders, and his valorization of liturgical studies are perhaps the most prominent aspects of his work, but many of his publications have been marked by an interest in the totality of culture in a locale or region. His numerous studies of the Visigothic clergy and councils are typical of such a regional concentration.[14] In this regard, Herbert Schneider's study and edition of a hitherto-unstudied Visigothic *Ordo in susceptione presbiterorum* is a companion to Reynolds' interests. The ordo gives directions for a three-day meeting in which local priests would come to be examined and instructed by their bishop in the practice of the liturgy, the norms of ethical clerical conduct, and didactic and theological concerns. There is evidence for such meetings elsewhere in the western church well into the Carolingian period. Thereafter, the parallel functions of diocesan synods perhaps supplanted the special

---

14 See most recently 'An Early Rule for Canons Regular from Santa Maria de l'Estany (New York, Hispanic Society of America MS HC 380/819)', *Miscel·lània litúrgica catalana*, 10 (2001), 165-91; and approximately nine earlier articles.

instructional function of the ordo. Even within the early medieval tradition of such meetings, the Visigothic ordo represents a distinctive textual tradition, and corresponds to the particular ecclesiastical situation of the seventh-century Visigothic church.

The ordo studied by Schneider is noteworthy in at least one additional way. Both the manuscripts in which it is now preserved are copied in the Beneventan script, the calligraphic text-hand of southern Italy and Dalmatia that defines the cultural region with which Reynolds' work is most closely identified. In topic after topic, he has found unusual or variant points in southern Italian witnesses, whether the copying of the *Collectio hibernensis*, the persistent use of the Collection in Five Books, the production of an extraordinary Greek mass in Beneventan script, or one of many other discoveries.[15] When E. A. Loew defined this cultural zone in his magisterial study, *The Beneventan Script*, first published in 1914,[16] it appeared to be most significant for its transmission of classical texts. Now, however, Reynolds' re-interpretation of Beneventan as a liturgical script *par excellence* has changed the way in which the region is viewed, and his collaborative contribution to the Monumenta Liturgica Beneventana program has reinforced the new assessment of the script as a marker of a monastic, liturgical culture.

Virginia Brown, one of Reynolds' collaborators in the program, picks up on the theme of a liturgical script in her article. As a by-product of the larger project to catalogue and study Beneventan liturgical manuscripts, Brown has discovered witnesses that extend the script's reach into new regions and periods. In the present study, she develops a topic that she first advanced in 1981 with the discovery of prayer books from Neapolitan religious houses that had been written in Beneventan script but clearly dated to the sixteenth century, over two-hundred years after Loew had first thought the script to have ended.[17] With the present discovery, there are now ten witnesses representing nine codices written in Beneventan in Naples during the sixteenth century. The present manuscript is remarkable not only for its date but also for preserving the first vernacular Italian prayers to have been written in Beneventan. Brown edits these and the other unidentifiable texts in the article, and provides incipits for the remaining identified prayers. In the detailed consideration of the manuscript, its content, and its script and writing practices, Brown argues that it was produced in the first half of the fifteenth century probably at the female Benedictine house of San Patrizia, Naples.

---

15 The Hibernensis and the Collection in Five Books are considered in many articles in Reynolds' lists of publications; for the Greek mass, see Roger E. Reynolds, 'The Greek Liturgy of St. John Chrysostom in Beneventan Script: an early manuscript fragment', *Mediaeval Studies*, 52 (1990), 296-302.

16 E. A. Loew, *The Beneventan Script: a history of the south Italian minuscule*, 2nd edition prepared and enlarged by Virginia Brown, 2 vols. (Rome, 1980; first edition, Oxford, 1914).

17 'Latin and Italian Prayers in a Sixteenth-Century Beneventan Manuscript from Naples', 95-132 at 132 n. 1, for bibliography.

This introduction to the first part of our studies in honour of Roger Reynolds has considered the implications of his work on liturgy and ritual. It is difficult, and surely incomplete, to separate these implications from the way in which he has approached the topics—with careful analysis, rooted in a nuanced understanding of textual transmission, and placed in cultural contexts—and from a second major area of his work, the study of the canonical tradition. The study of canon law has gone through its own revolutions, in theoretical, practical and academic terms, even as liturgical studies have. Roger Reynolds has been an active participant in all three areas: liturgical, textuai and legal studies. Considerations of the last two fields are, however, matters for the second part of this tribute.

Chapter 1

L'ange de paix

Paul De Clerck

Les litanies des liturgies latines anciennes comportent souvent une demande pour la paix: 'pro altissima pace et tranquillitate temporum nostrorum, pro pace ecclesiarum, pro quiete populorum, etc.' Dans la *Deprecatio Gelasii* cependant, attribuée au pape Gélase (492-6), on trouve une demande à la formulation attachante, mais intrigante: 'Angelum pacis et solacia sanctorum, praesta, Domine, praesta'. Qui donc est cet ange de paix? Si on l'entend d'un compagnon personnel, une présence angélique à nos côtés ne peut être qu'agréable. Si la demande vise des situations sociales, voire mondiales, on reconnaîtra aisément son actualité, à tous les âges de l'humanité.

Pour circonscrire la nature et la fonction de cet ange de paix, nous ne nous aventurerons pas longtemps dans les méandres de l'angélologie. Nous explorerons surtout les sources liturgiques, qui constituent l'environnement immédiat de cette prière. Après un bref éclairage sur le monde angélique dans l'Antiquité, nous nous lancerons dans une investigation des sources liturgiques orientales et surtout occidentales, pour tenter de mieux décrire le visage de cet ange mystérieux.[1]

Le monde de l'angélologie

Après une phase d'éclipse, les anges reviennent aujourd'hui à la mode.[2] Ils l'étaient beaucoup plus encore dans le monde antique. Le livre d'Hénoch en est un témoin privilégié.[3] Il s'agit d'un écrit apocalyptique, qui commence par décrire la chute des anges; les chapitres 37 à 64 sont appelés le *Livre des paraboles*; ils contiennent la majorité des renseignements qui nous intéressent. Les anges y sont qualifiés

---

1 Nous utiliserons les documents rassemblés dans notre thèse, Paul De Clerck, *La 'prière universelle' dans les liturgies latines anciennes: Témoignages patristiques et textes liturgiques*, Liturgiewissenschaftliche Quellen und Forschungen, 62 (Münster, 1977). La *Deprecatio Gelasii* y est publiée aux pages 170-3. Pour une vue d'ensemble, voir J. Michl, 'Engel', dans *Reallexikon für Antike und Christentum* (1962), v, 53-322.

2 Voir par exemple Michel Serres, *La légende des anges* (Paris, 1993); Olivier Abel, *Le réveil des anges. Messagers des peurs et des consolations*, Autrement, Mutations, 162 (Paris, 1996), sans compter le nombre de films où interviennent des personnages célestes.

3 Ed. André Caquot, in *La Bible: Ecrits intertestamentaires*, éd. André Dupont-Sommer et Marc Philonenko, Bibliothèque de la Pléiade, 337 (Paris, 1987), 463-625.

diversement: anges de justice, de puissance, des principautés, du châtiment; ils sont gardiens, veilleurs, saints, glorieux, etc. Voici un passage sur les quatre archanges, qui donne bien le ton du livre:

> XL. J'ai vu ensuite les milliers de milliers, les myriades de myriades, innombrables, incalculables, de ceux qui se tiennent devant le Seigneur des Esprits. J'ai regardé et aux quatre côtés du Seigneur des Esprits, j'ai vu quatre personnages différents de ceux qui ne dorment pas. J'ai su leurs noms, car l'ange qui était venu avec moi et m'avait montré tous les secrets me les avait appris. J'ai entendu la voix de ces quatre personnages prononcer des louanges en présence du Seigneur de gloire.
>
> La première voix bénissait le Seigneur des Esprits pour toute l'éternité.
>
> La seconde voix, je l'ai entendue bénir l'Elu et les élus qui sont suspendus au Seigneur des Esprits.
>
> La troisième voix, je l'ai entendue implorer et prier pour les habitants de l'aride et supplier au nom du Seigneur des Esprits.
>
> La quatrième voix, je l'ai entendue repousser les Satans et leur interdire d'approcher le Seigneur des Esprits pour calomnier les habitants de l'aride.
>
> J'ai ensuite demandé à l'ange de paix qui m'accompagnait (et) m'avait montré tous les secrets: 'Qui sont ces quatre personnages que j'ai vus, dont j'ai entendu la voix et transcrit (les paroles)?' Il m'a répondu: 'Le premier est Michel, (l'ange) miséricordieux et lent à la colère; le second est Raphaël, préposé à toutes les maladies et à toutes les plaies des humains; le troisième est Gabriel, préposé à toute puissance; le quatrième est préposé à la repentance (riche) d'espérance pour ceux qui hériteront la vie éternelle, il se nomme Phanouël'.[4]

Ce passage introduit bien dans le monde de l'apocalyptique, qui fourmille d'anges. Il nomme l'ange de paix, qui apparaît déjà dans un de ses traits caractéristiques, comme un compagnon de route, qui guide le non-initié et l'introduit dans un monde inconnu.

La Bible   Ni la Septante ni le Nouveau Testament ne citent l'ange de paix. Mais la Vulgate porte, en Is. 33: 7: 'Ecce videntes clamabunt foris, angeli pacis amare flebunt', et certains Pères de l'Eglise ont commenté le passage en nommant l'ange de paix et son influence protectrice.[5]

Le Nouveau Testament connaît les anges, particulièrement nombreux, bien sûr, dans l'Apocalypse. Ils y apparaissent notamment comme des messagers de Dieu; 'l'ange du Seigneur' ne semble souvent se distinguer du Seigneur lui-même que par

---

4   *La Bible*, éd. Dupont-Sommer et Philonenko, 510-1. Dans ce même genre de littérature, l'ange de paix apparaît encore dans le *Testament des douze Patriarches*, au *Testament de Dan* 6: 5, *ibid.*, 898, et au *Testament d'Aser* 6: 6, *ibid.*, 918: 'Car, quand l'âme s'en va troublée, elle est torturée par l'esprit malin dont elle était l'esclave dans ses convoitises et ses œuvres mauvaises. Mais si elle est paisible, dans la joie, elle fait la connaissance de l'ange de la paix qui l'introduit dans la vie éternelle'. Notons deux traits que nous retrouverons dans nos textes liturgiques: l'opposition entre l'ange de paix et d'autres êtres, ici l'esprit malin, et sa fonction d'introduire dans la vie éternelle.

5   Eusèbe de Césarée, *Commentaire d'Isaïe* 33, PG 24.325C.

l'épaisseur d'un papier à cigarette. Il assure la transcendance divine. Il apparaît tantôt comme un substitut de Dieu, tantôt comme un être personnel, à forme humaine. Mais Dieu n'est pas le seul à être entouré d'anges; saint Paul ne s'écrie-t-il pas que 'un ange de Satan est chargé de me frapper' (2 Col. 12: 7), ou que 'Satan lui-même se camoufle en ange de lumière' (2 Col. 11: 14)? En ses premiers chapitres, l'Apocalypse nomme 'les anges des Eglises'; ils désignent soit leurs ministres, soit, plus probablement, une sorte de personnification de la communauté en question. Bref, les écrits bibliques ne sont guère prolixes en ce qui concerne l'ange de paix.

Le Pasteur d'Hermas Cet écrit connaît de nombreuses catégories d'anges. Par deux fois, le Pasteur est identifié à l'ange de la pénitence et de la conversion (*metanoia*), dans les Visions 5.7 et surtout dans les Préceptes XII, 4.7: 'Moi, l'ange de la pénitence qui triomphe du diable, je serai avec vous. Il peut faire peur, le diable, mais cette peur manque de force. Ne le craignez donc pas et il vous fuira'.[6]

Voici la première qualification d'un ange, outre celui de la paix: l'ange de la pénitence; il aide l'homme à se convertir. On retrouve ici un contexte d'opposition.

Références liturgiques

Les litanies Les liturgistes orientaux désignent souvent par 'l'ange de paix' la litanie secondaire accrochée à une litanie majeure, et qu'ils nomment *aitèsis* à cause du verbe de demande qu'elle comporte (*aitèsômeta*). Ainsi trouve-t-on dans la liturgie byzantine, après la Grande Entrée, une litanie principale qui se conclut par celle de 'l'ange de paix'.[7] Sa première attestation se lit dans les *Constitutions apostoliques*, tant à l'Office du soir que du matin ou qu'à la synaxe.[8] Saint Jean Chrysostome, dans ses prédications antiochiennes, mentionne lui aussi l'ange de paix; il rapporte d'abord la teneur de la prière pour les catéchumènes, puis il les invite à prier eux-mêmes, en utilisant des termes très proches de ceux de la prière elle-même:

> Vous, les catéchumènes, priez l'ange de paix; demandez que toutes vos affaires soient pacifiques, pacifique la présente journée et tous les jours de votre vie; demandez que vos fins soient chrétiennes: ce qui est beau, ce qui est utile, c'est que vous puissiez vous présenter au Dieu vivant et à son Christ.[9]

---

6 Hermas, *Le Pasteur*, éd. Robert Joly, *SChr*., 53bis (Paris, 1998), 145 et 207.

7 F. E. Brightman, *Liturgies Eastern and Western* (Oxford, 1896), 380-1. On trouve la même *aitèsis* dans la liturgie de Saint Jacques, *ibid.*, 39; et dans la liturgie chaldéenne, *ibid.*, 266.

8 *Les Constitutions apostoliques*, VIII, 36.2-3, 38.2 et 6.8: *Didascalia et Constitutiones apostolorum*, éd. Franciscus Xaverius [Franz Xavier] Funk (Paderborn, 1905), 544-6 et 480; éd. Marcel Metzger, *SChr*. 336 (Paris, 1987), 247, 251 et 155. La dernière référence mentionne bien la paix, mais pas l'ange.

9 Jean Chrysostome, *In ep. II ad Cor, hom.*, 2.8: *PG* 61.403; il mentionne aussi l'ange de paix dans son sermon *pour l'Ascension*, I, 1: *PG* 50.443A; et *Contre les Juifs*, III, 6: *PG* 48.870.

Dans son Commentaire de l'épître aux Colossiens, qui date de sa période constantinopolitaine, il commente plus largement:

> Chaque fidèle a un ange ... Ainsi donc, si nous avons des anges, nous devons nous comporter décemment, comme si un enseignant nous accompagnait, car un démon est là aussi. C'est pourquoi nous prions et demandons l'ange de paix, et nous prions pour la paix en tout lieu. Car rien ne lui est équivalent; dans les églises, dans les prières, dans les supplications, dans les salutations: la paix.[10]

Le contexte de ces demandes nous rapproche de ce que nous avons déjà constaté précédemment; la paix s'implore au milieu des troubles, et l'ange de paix lorsqu'on se trouve environné par les démons.

La demande pour l'ange de paix passera en Occident, à l'occasion sans doute de ce que nous avons appelé, dans notre thèse, la seconde vague de textes litaniques occidentaux; ce ne sont plus des traductions de textes grecs, mais des adaptations. Comme nous le rappelions en tête de cet article, la demande pour la paix se retrouve, sous une forme ou l'autre, dans plusieurs de ces litanies; seule la 'prière que le pape Gélase prescrivit de chanter pour l'Eglise universelle' mentionne l'ange de paix. Ce formulaire situe la demande qui nous occupe exactement à la même place qu'en Orient, c'est-à-dire en fin d'une litanie principale; la teneur des demandes n'est cependant pas la même.[11] Voici les dernières demandes de la *Deprecatio Gelasii*:

> Mortificatam vitiis carnem et viventem fide animam
> Praesta, Domine, praesta
> Castum timorem et veram dilectionem
> Praesta, Domine, praesta
> Gratum vitae ordinem et probabilem exitum
> Praesta, Domine, praesta
> Angelum pacis et solacia sanctorum
> Praesta, Domine, praesta.[12]

Les deux premières invocations reflètent un esprit que l'on peut qualifier d'ascétique. La troisième demande une vie au cours agréable et une fin heureuse, tandis que la dernière invoque l'ange de paix et les consolations des saints. Les trois dernières expressions évoquent donc la mort; l'ange de paix semble invoqué comme

---

10 Jean Chrysostome, *In ep. ad Col, hom.*, 3.4: *PG* 62.322.
11 La même structure se rencontre dans le formulaire que l'on trouve dans le Missel de Stowe, *The Stowe Missal*, éd. George F. Warner, 2 vols, Henry Bradshaw Society Publications, 31-2 (London, 1906-15); appelé 'Irl1' dans De Clerck, *La 'priere universelle'*, 145 ss.; ici comme dans la *Deprecatio Gelasii*, la finale change la formulation des demandes par rapport à *l'aitèsis* orientale. Si la teneur des prières occidentales se retrouve en Orient, il ne s'agit cependant pas d'une traduction, du moins par rapport aux formulaires aujourd'hui connus.
12 De Clerck, *La 'prière universelle'*, 172.

un compagnon sûr, destiné à faciliter le voyage, qui se terminera par la réception que réserveront les saints consolateurs.

Pour éclairer la personnalité de cet ange de paix, quittons le domaine des litanies, qui ne nous fournit aucun renseignement à cet effet. Cherchons plus largement dans les textes chrétiens anciens, surtout liturgiques, qui en ont gardé la trace. Précisons d'emblée que nous trouverons bien d'autres qualifications des anges. Outre l'ange de la pénitence-conversion rencontré déjà chez Hermas, nous découvrirons l'ange du baptême, de la lumière, de la prière ... . Un problème se pose dès lors: comment classer ces occurrences? A l'examen, ces désignations des anges ne paraissent pas très rigoureuses, à témoin une bénédiction de l'eau baptismale gallicane qui utilise quatre dénominations différentes, sans modification apparente de sens: 'angelus benedictionis, medicans, pietatis, et veritatis'. Cet état des choses nous fait préférer une présentation des textes par les fonctions attribuées aux anges plus que par leurs désignations.[13]

L'ange du baptême Le témoin privilégié en est le traité de Tertullien sur le baptême. Au chapitre 5 de son livre, il écrit:

> A quoi bon rappeler tout cela? C'est pour qu'on ait moins de mal à croire à la présence sur les eaux du saint ange de Dieu en vue de notre salut, puisque l'ange impur du Malin entretient commerce avec elles pour la perte de l'homme.[14]

'L'ange du baptême' n'est pas encore nommé. Mais on retrouve déjà le contexte d'opposition; si un ange saint intervient au baptême, c'est pour contrecarrer l'influence de l'ange du Malin. Tertullien poursuit:

> Cela ne veut pas dire que ce soit dans l'eau que nous recevions l'Esprit Saint. Mais purifiés dans l'eau, nous sommes préparés par le ministère de l'ange à recevoir l'Esprit. Ici encore la figure précéda la réalité: de même que Jean fut le précurseur du Seigneur préparant ses voies, de même l'ange qui préside au baptême (*angelus baptismi*) trace les voies pour la venue du Saint Esprit, en effaçant les péchés par la foi scellée dans le Père, le Fils et l'Esprit Saint.[15]

---

13 Les monographies les plus intéressantes sont celles de Jean Daniélou, *Les anges et leur mission* (Paris, 1951, 1990²); Erik Peterson, *Le livre des anges* (Paris, 1953); Jean Leclercq, 'Invisible présence. Les anges au baptême', in *idem*, *La liturgie et les paradoxes chrétiens*, Lex orandi, 36 (Paris, 1963), 75-86. Sur la liturgie catholique actuelle, on peut se reporter à Pierre-Marie Gy, 'La place de l'Ange dans la liturgie de Vatican II', dans *Colloque sur l'Ange (26-28 juin 1981)* (Pont-à-Mousson, 1981), 179-86; Pierre Jounel, 'La présence des anges dans la liturgie d'Occident', in *ibid.*, 187-201, repris dans *idem*, *Liturgie aux multiples visages: mélanges* (Rome, 1993), 13-26.

14 Tertullien, *Traité du baptême*, éd. R. F. Refoulé, SChr., 35 (Paris, 1952), 72-4.

15 *Ibid.*, 75.

Rôle extraordinaire: l'ange du baptême prépare la venue de l'Esprit en effaçant les péchés![16]

Aussi ne sommes-nous pas étonné de voir l'ange cité fréquemment dans les textes baptismaux ultérieurs: dans les prières sur les catéchumènes, comme déjà chez Chrysostome, dans les exorcismes, et dans les prières de bénédiction des eaux. Citons le texte gallican auquel nous faisions allusion à l'instant:

> Deus ... descendat super aquas his angelus benedictionis tuae ...
> Respice, Domine, super has aquas,...angelum pietatis tuae his sacris fontibus adesse dignare ...
> Benedic, Domine Deus noster, hanc creaturam aquae et descendat super eam virtus tua, desuper infunde spiritum tuum sanctum paraclytum, angelum veritatis.[17]

La fin de cette prière rejoint le commentaire de Tertullien, mais, fait unique dans notre documentation, l'ange de vérité est ici identifié, par apposition, à l'Esprit Saint. Le texte le plus proche que nous connaissions provient de la liturgie baptismale hispanique: '... ut has simplices aquas tua sanctificatione benedicas; et ex tuis sedibus Angelum tuum sanctum dirigas qui eas sanctificet ...'.[18]

Citons encore une ancienne bénédiction des eaux qui se maintiendra dans le Rituel romain de 1614:

> Domine, sancte Pater, omnipotens aeterne Deus, aquarum spiritalium sanctificator ... et super has abluendis aquas et vivificandis hominibus praeparatas angelum sanctitatis emittas, quo peccatis vitae prioris abluti reatque deturso, purum Sancto Spiritui habitaculum in regeneratis procuret.[19]

La fonction de l'ange de sainteté est ici exactement pareille à celle que décrivait Tertullien: ôter les péchés de la vie antérieure et préparer ainsi la venue de l'Esprit Saint. Aussi n'est-il pas étonnant de voir un ange invoqué dans les exorcismes, comme par exemple celui-ci:

> Deus Abraham ... , qui Moysi famulo tuo in monte Sinai apparuisti, et filios Israël de terra Aegypti eduxisti, deputans eis Angelum pietatis tuae, qui custodiret eos die ac nocte: te

---

16 Notons au passage la note de l'éditeur: 'Nous sommes ici en présence d'une pensée théologique qui se cherche'!, *ibid.*, 75, n. 1.

17 *Missale gothicum*, éd. Leo Cunibert Mohlberg, Rerum Ecclesiarum Documenta, Fontes, 5 (Rome, 1961), n° 256-7.

18 *Missale mixtum*, *PL* 85.468A. Remarquons que l'éditeur écrit le terme Ange avec majuscule!

19 *Sacramentaire gélasien: Liber sacramentorum romanae aecclesiae ordinis anni circuli*, éd. Leo Cunibert Mohlberg, Leo Eizenhöfer et Petrus Siffrin, Rerum Ecclesiarum Documenta, Fontes, 4 (Rome, 1960), n° 606. Ce texte se trouve aussi dans le *Sacramentaire de Gellone: Liber sacramentorum gellonensis*, éd. A. Dumas et J. Deshusses, 2 vols, *CCSL*, 159, 159A (Turnhout, 1981), i, n° 2377; et le *Sacramentaire d'Angoulême: Liber sacramentorum engolismensis*, éd. Patrick Saint-Roch, *CCSL*, 159C (Turnhout, 1987), n° 2002; ainsi que dans le *Rituel romain* de 1614, Titre II, ch. CIII, n° 5, comme un doublet de la grande bénédiction des eaux.

quaesumus, Domine, ut mittere digneris sanctum Angelum tuum de caelis, qui similiter custodiat et hunc famulum tuum N. et perducat eum ad gratiam Baptismi tui.[20]

Les auteurs se sont bien sûr interrogés sur la personnalité de cet ange du baptême. Curieusement, à notre connaissance, aucun n'a relevé la proximité que nous venons de mettre en relief avec le Saint Esprit. B. Neunheuser l'identifie au Christ,[21] ce qui ne correspond pas aux citations que nous avons lues, et a été contesté.[22] A. d'Alès et E. De Backer considèrent l'ange comme le ministre du baptême,[23] ce qui ne semble pas non plus refléter le sens des textes. E. Amann y voyait 'une créature préposée par Dieu à l'exécution des grandes choses qui se passent dans la piscine baptismale';[24] c'est l'expression la plus proche des sources, même si elle paraît en adoucir la portée.

A l'ange du baptême, joignons celui de la *metanoia*, déjà cité par Hénoch et Hermas. Clément d'Alexandrie le mentionne: 'Celui qui s'est approché de l'ange de la pénitence n'aura plus à se repentir, quand il quittera son corps, ni à rougir quand il verra le Seigneur venant avec son armée'.[25]

Encore une fois, c'est dans la perspective de la fin de la vie que l'ange de la pénitence est évoqué. Origène citera aussi cet ange, dans un passage où il renvoie au *Pasteur* d'Hermas.[26] Voyant dans la parabole du bon Samaritain le type de la conversion du pécheur, il écrit encore:

---

20 *Sacramentaire gélasien*, n° 291; *Rituel* de 1614, Titre II, ch. IV, n° 17. L'opposition des démons et de l'ange de paix est clairement exprimée dans un texte du Rituel monastique de Fleury, n° 50: 'sit ad nostrae humilitatis introitum, sanctorum tuorum meritis, fuga demonum et angeli pacis ingressus', éd. Anselme Davril, *The Monastic Ritual of Fleury*, Henry Bradshaw Society Publications, 105 (London, 1990), 96.

21 Burkhard Neunheuser, 'De benedictionis aquae baptismalis', *Ephemerides liturgicae*, 44 (1930), 201.

22 A. Bakker, 'Christ an Angel?', *Zeitschrift für die neutestamentliche Wissenschaft*, 32 (1933), 255-63; Joseph Barbel, *Christos angelos*, Theophaneia, 3 (Bonn, 1941). Dans l'Euchologe de Sérapion, la prière 27 mentionne aussi un 'aggelon eirènikon', en contexte baptismal; s'appuyant notamment sur l'ancienne tradition du Christ-ange attestée chez les Pères, le récent éditeur de l'Euchologe conclut qu'il n'y a pas de raison de ne pas voir le Christ en cet ange de paix; Maxwell E. Johnson, *The Prayers of Sarapion of Thmuis*, Orientalia Christiana Analecta, 249 (Rome, 1995), 193-4.

23 Adhémar d'Alès, *La théologie de Tertullien* (Paris, 1905), 325, n. 4; Emile de Backer, *Sacramentum: le mot et l'idée dans Tertullien* (Louvain, 1911), 163.

24 E. Amann, 'L'ange du baptême chez Tertullien', *Revue des sciences religieuses*, 1 (1921), 209-21.

25 Clément d'Alexandrie, *Quis dives salvetur*, 42; éd. Otto Stählin, *Clemens Alexandrinus*, 4 vols, *GCS*, 12, 15, 17, 39 (Leipzig, 1905-36; réimp. Berlin, 1970-85), iii, 191.

26 Origène, *Sel. Psalm.*, 37; *PG* 12.1372BC. Cf. Karl Rahner, 'La pénitence chez Origène', *Revue des sciences religieuses*, 24 (1950), 80 ss.

Comme (le Samaritain) était sur le point de partir, le matin, il prend deux deniers de son argent et les donne à l'hôtelier, c'est-à-dire à l'ange de l'Eglise, à qui il prescrit de prendre soin du malade et de le conduire jusqu'à la guérison.[27]

C'est le seul texte de notre corpus où est reprise la désignation que l'on trouve dans l'Apocalypse 1: 20-3: 14.

L'ange sanctificateur L'ange, qualifié de saint, est invoqué, nous l'avons vu, dans certaines prières de bénédiction des eaux baptismales, avec parfois une quasi identification à l'Esprit Saint. Nous avons trouvé une mention d'un ange de sanctification: '... oremus ... ut in medio Hierusalem in congregatione sanctorum haec nomina sibi faciat ab angelo sanctificationis in beatitudinem aeterni gaudii recensiri'.[28]

Dans un sacramentaire d'une abbaye limousine, datant du onzième siècle, on trouve, juste avant *l'Orate fratres*, une formule d'épiclèse qui invoque l'ange de bénédiction et de consécration: 'In nomine sanctae et individuae Trinitatis descendat hic sanctus angelus benedictionis et consecrationis super hoc munus et pacis'.[29]

L'ange de la prière Depuis Tobie, on sait que les anges présentent à Dieu la prière des saints;[30] l'Apocalypse le confirme (8: 3-4). Tertullien note qu'il serait irrespectueux de s'asseoir, lors de la prière:

> Si quidem inreverens est assidere sub conspectu contraque conspectum eius, quem cum maxime revereraris ac venereris, quanto magis sub conspectu Dei vivi angelo adhuc orationis adstante factum istud inreligiosissimum est?[31]

La présence des anges lors de la prière sera un thème fréquent de la littérature monastique, en rapport avec le verset du psaume 137: 1: 'Je te chante en présence des anges'. Saint Benoît en conclura au sérieux de la prière: 'Considérons donc comment nous devons nous tenir en la présence de la Divinité et de ses Anges, et conduisons-nous dans la psalmodie de manière que notre esprit concorde avec notre voix'.[32]

---

27 Origène, *Comm. sur Jean*, XXVIII, 8; *Der Johanneskommentar*, éd. Erwin Preuschen, Origenes Werke, 4, *GCS*, 10 (Leipzig, 1903), 399.
28 *Missale gothicum*, n° 365, 'post nomina' de la messe des saints Ferreol et Ferrucion.
29 Cité par V. Leroquais, *Les sacramentaires et les missels manuscrits des bibliothèques publiques de France*, 4 vols (Paris, 1924), i, 155. Le texte provient du manuscrit Paris, Bibliothèque Nationale, lat. 821, fo 6v. Après les mots 'et pacis', l'éditeur écrit: (sic).
30 Tob. 12: 12-15.
31 Tertullien, *De oratione*, 16.6, éd. G. F. Diercks, *CCSL*, 1 (Turnhout, 1954), 266.
32 *Règle de saint Benoît*, 19, éd. Philibert Schmitz (Maredsous, 1962), 86. Benoît spiritualise le verset psalmique, à la différence du Maître qui le prend strictement au sérieux, au point de conseiller aux moines, pendant les oraisons, de cracher par derrière plutôt que par devant, où se trouvent les anges! (*La Règle du Maître*, éd. Adalbert de Vogüé, *SChr.*, 105 [Paris, 1964], 47.23 et 48.7-9).

Mais nous n'avons trouvé la mention d'un ange de la prière que dans un seul texte eucologique, dans une hymne de Synesios de Cyrène, à la fin du quatrième siècle:

> Donne-moi plutôt comme ami, Seigneur, l'ange saint de la sainte énergie, l'ange de la prière où Dieu resplendit, cet aimable bienfaiteur, défenseur de mon âme, défenseur de ma vie, veillant sur mes prières, veillant sur mes actes.[33]

L'ange de paix, le compagnon protecteur C'est dans cet environnement protecteur que nous rencontrons l'ange de paix. Sa qualification la plus coutumière est celle de *comes*, compagnon sur le chemin, que ce soit celui du voyage ou celui de l'existence d'un chacun. On en trouve des citations très générales, comme dans cette introduction au Notre Père de la liturgie hispanique:

> Christe Dei Filius ... eo quod unaquaeque anima ad suum tutamentum custodem habeat Angelum pacis, procul efficiciatur refuga ille quondam Angelus auctor iniquitatis; ut corde et corpore purificati, ad corporis et sanguinis tui sacramenta mereamur accedere beatificandi.[34]

Mais la plupart des références à l'ange de paix proviennent de prières pour les voyageurs; les pérégrinations étant dangereuses, on invoque un compagnon divin, chargé de veiller sur leur chemin. Ainsi déjà dans *l'Euchologe de Sérapion* trouve-t-on une prière pour les voyageurs: 'donne-leur l'ange de paix, pour les accompagner; qu'aucun mal ne leur arrive.[35] Les références abondent; citons entre autres une *Benedictio cum egreditur in itinere*:

> Protegat vos auxilium Domini ut nihil vobis praevaleat scandalum inimici. Per diem vos salutaris Domini umbra circumtegat, per noctem amica quies ipsa gratia relatura confoveat, deducat vos mirabiliter dextera Dei praebeatque ante faciem vestram divinae pacis angelus comes.[36]

Ou, en un lieu liturgique plus curieux, cet *Hanc igitur* d'une messe *Ad proficis-cendum in itinere*:

> Hanc igitur oblationem, Domine, famuli tui *illius*, quam tibi offeret ob desiderium animae suae commendans tibi Deo iter suum, placatus suscipias depraecamur. Cui tu, Domine,

---

33 Synesius, *Hymne*, 4.264, éd. Christian Lacombrade, Collection des Universités de France (Paris, 1978), 66.

34 *Liber mozarabicus sacramentorum et les manuscrits mozarabes*, éd. Marius Férotin (Paris, 1912), n° 972, col. 453.

35 Euchologe de Sérapion, éd. Johnson, *Prayers of Sarapion of Thmuis* (Rome, 1995), n° 27, p. 79 (littéralement: un ange pacifique). Voir aussi Basile de Césarée, *Lettres*, Ep. 11, éd. Yves Courtonne, 3 vols, Collection des Universités de France (Paris, 1957-66), i, 41 (même expression).

36 *Sacramentaire de Gellone*, n° 2098; *Sacramentaire d'Angoulême*, n° 1855. Cf. *Proprium Officiorum Ordinis Praedicatorum. Liturgia horarum* (Rome, 1982), 773-4: benedictio pro itinerantibus.

angelum pacis mittere digneris, angelum tuum sanctum, sicut misisti famulo tuo Tobiae
Rafaël angelum, qui eum salvum atque incolumem perducat usque ad loca destinata ... .[37]

Citons encore cet extrait d'un *Liber precum*:

> Domine sancte ... qui es doctor sanctorum et dirigis itinera sanctorum, dirige angelum
> pacis nobiscum, qui nos ad loca destinata perducat. Sit nobis comitatus jucundus, ut
> nullus viae nostrae subripiat inimicus.[38]

Revient ici la note d'opposition et de crainte de l'ennemi, mais surtout la
confiance en Dieu qui enverra un joyeux compagnon de route! L'ange de paix est le
protecteur par excellence; ce *comes*, c'est celui que la tradition ultérieure appellera
l'ange gardien.[39] Même s'il n'y est pas explicitement nommé, on ne peut manquer de
citer la prière qui a longtemps terminé l'heure de Complies, avant le coucher:

> Exaudi nos Domine, sancte pater, omnipotens aeterne Deus, et mittere dignare sanctum
> angelum tuum de caelis qui custodiat, foveat, protegat, visitet et defendat omnes habi-
> tantes in hoc habitaculo.[40]

Signalons enfin une *collectio ad pacem* gallicane pour la veille de la Nativité: 'Et
dirigere dignare angelum pacis, qui oscula nostra puris sensibus inligata conectat'.[41]
Faut-il voir dans la désignation de cet ange une allusion aux troupes célestes qui, le
lendemain, vont chanter la gloire de Dieu et la paix pour les hommes (Lc 2: 14)?[42]

Identification des anges Nous avons rencontré plus haut le rapprochement fait
entre l'ange du baptême et l'Esprit Saint. On sait que certains auteurs ont vu dans
le Christ un ange. L'épître aux Hébreux affirme clairement la subordination des
anges par rapport au Christ (Héb. 1). Cela n'a pas empêché certains de qualifier le
Christ du terme d'ange,[43] notamment en l'identifiant à l'ange du grand conseil

---

37 *Sacramentaire gélasien*, n° 1317; *Sacramentaire de Gellone*, n° 2794. Autre *Hanc igitur* dans le
    Sacramentarium triplex, éd. Odilo Heiming, Corpus Ambrosiano-Liturgicum, 1, Liturgiewissen-
    schaftliche Quellen und Forschungen, 49 (Münster, 1968), n° 3417. Autres références: *Sacramen-
    taire gélasien*, n° 291, 1594; *Sacramentaire de Gellone*, n° 2793, 2799.
38 *Libellus sacrarum precum*, Orléans, Bibliothèque municipale, MS 184 (161), cité par Edmond
    Martène, *De antiquis ecclesiae ritibus*, IV, c. 34; éd. Venise, 1788, iii, 247; cité en *PL* 101.1414.
39 Il est encore qualifié de 'custos' en *Sacramentaire de Gellone*, n° 1564. Cf. André Wilmart, 'Prières
    à l'ange gardien', dans *idem*, *Auteurs spirituels et textes dévôts du moyen âge latin: études
    d'histoire littéraire* (Paris, 1932; réimp. 1971), 537-58.
40 D'après le *Rituel de Fleury* (cité en n. 20), n° 52. *Le Liber Ordinum en usage dans l'Église
    wisigothique et mozarabe d'Espagne du cinquième au onzième siècle*, éd. Marius Férotin (Paris,
    1904), c. 306, n. 2, le nomme lors du renvoi de la messe.
41 *Missale gothicum*, n°2.
42 Paul Glaue, 'Der "Friedensengel"', dans *Monatschrift für Gottesdienst und kirchliche Kunst*, 22
    (1917), 89 ss., a émis l'hypothèse que le nom de l'ange de paix provient de ce contexte.
43 Voir Justin, *Dialogues*, 56.4, in *An early Christian philosopher: Justin Martyr's Dialogue with
    Trypho, chapters one to nine*, éd., J. C. M. van Winden (Leiden, 1971); Origène, *Contre Celse*, éd.

d'Is. 9: 5.[44] Dans une source gallicane, nous avons trouvé également le terme ange pour désigner Jean-Baptiste: 'Da plebi angelum custodem, qui filium Mariae fide concipiente praedixit'.[45]

L'ange de lumière et l'accueil des âmes au paradis On trouve la désignation d'ange de lumière pour la fonction angélique assez banale de protection; ainsi dans la Vie de sainte Macrine,[46] ou pour la bénédiction d'une maison: '... petamus pro hanc domum adque omnes habitantes in ea, uti eis Dominus angelum pacis, angelum lucis, angelum defensionis adsignare dignetur ...'.[47] Pour la bénédiction d'une maison, encore, dans une source hispanique:

> Benedicere etiam dignare, Domine Deus noster, cibos ac potus quae sumuturi sunt in hac domo cum gratiarum actione ... ut mereantur angelum pacis, castitatis et veritatis, qui eos semper ab omnibus malis custodiat, protegat adque defendat. In nomine sanctae Trinitatis in hoc domicilio habitent angeli salutis et pacis.[48]

Une fonction plus caractéristique de l'ange de lumière est l'accueil des âmes après la mort; ainsi, dans la prière après la communion d'une messe pour des défunts laïcs: 'Praesta quaesumus, omnipotens Deus, ut animam famuli tui *illi* ab angelis lucis susceptam in praeparatis habitaculis deduci facias beatorum'.[49]

Cependant l'ange de paix accomplit lui aussi des fonctions similaires, dans un *ordo* de recommandation du corps défunt:

> Dum hic depositum fuerit corpus commendatum, spiritus quoque eius in patriarcharum sinu receptus, paradisi laetitia perfruatur, et hic angelus pacis ob defensionem e caelis idem semper aspiciat.[50]

Aussi trouve-t-on abondante mention des anges dans les textes de la liturgie des funérailles. Voici, avec la désignation 'ange de l'alliance' que nous n'avons pas encore rencontrée: 'Suscipe, Domine, animam servi tui *illius* revertentem ad te. Adsit ei angelus testamenti tui Michael ...'.[51]

Marcel Borret, *SChr.*, 132, 136, 147, 150, 227 (Paris, 1967-76), iv, 7.25; Cyprien, *Ad Quirinum (Testimoniorum)*, 2.5, éd. R. Weber, dans *Sancti Cypriani episcopi Opera*, CCSL, 3 (Turnhout, 1972); *Constitutions apostoliques*, II, 30.2. Cf. Joseph Barbel, *Christos angelos* (Bonn, 1964²).

44   Voir la *Tradition apostolique*, 4, éd. Bernard Botte, *SChr.*, 11 (Paris, 1968²), au début de la prière eucharistique; et *Constitutions apostoliques*, VIII, 12.6.

45   *Missale gothicum*, n° 103.

46   Grégoire de Nysse, *Vie de sainte Macrine*, éd. Pierre Maraval, *SChr.*, 178, (Paris, 1971), 74-7.

47   *Sacramentaire de Gellone*, n° 2821; *Phillipps: Liber sacramentorum augustodunensis*, ed. O. Heiming, *CCSL*, 159B (Turnhout, 1984), n° 1847. On trouve la même association de l'ange de paix et de l'ange de lumière en *Sacramentaire gélasien*, n° 1565.

48   *Liber Ordinum*, c. 22.

49   *Sacramentaire gélasien*, n° 1665.

50   *Liber Ordinum*, c. 131.

51   *Sacramentaire gélasien*, n° 1621.

Ou la prière conservée dans le Rituel de 1614: 'Deus, ... hunc tumulum bene-dicere dignare, eique Angelum tuum sanctum deputa custodem'.[52]

On est très proche du chant qui a accompagné durant des siècles la sortie du corps vers le cimetière, après la messe des funérailles: 'In paradisum deducant te angeli ...'.[53] N'est-ce pas ce que nous aimerions tous entendre, un jour?

Conclusion

Qui donc est l'ange de paix? Cet être à la belle appellation se range dans une multitude d'autres anges, parmi lesquels nous en avons repéré quelques-uns aux désignations proches. Dès son apparition dans le livre d'Hénoch, l'ange de paix se présente comme un compagnon de route, chargé de mener le voyageur à bon port, particulièrement dans un environnement hostile. Dans les textes liturgiques occi-dentaux, c'est sa qualification de *comes* qui le définit au mieux.

Cependant, dans *l'aitèsis* byzantine qui semble être le prototype de ses usages liturgiques, l'ange de paix est souvent cité en rapport avec le dernier voyage et la fin de la vie. La *Deprecatio Gelasii* est fidèle à son modèle oriental quand elle entoure la demande pour l'ange de paix par celles d'une fin heureuse et de la consolation des saints. Pas étonnant dès lors qu'on le retrouve dans les prières des funérailles, car 'l'ange de paix [est] chargé d'accueillir l'âme à sa sortie du corps et de la conduire au Paradis'.[54]

Espérons qu'il nous y conduira tous!

---

52 *Rituel romain*, Ordo exsequiarum, n° 21.
53 *Ibid.*, n° 11.
54 Jean Daniélou, *Théologie du judéo-christianisme. Histoire des doctrines chrétiennes avant Nicée*, 2 vols, Bibliothèque de Théologie, 5.1 (Paris, 1958), i, 145.

Chapter 2

Priester bei der Prüfung:
Ein westgotischer *Ordo in susceptione presbiterorum* in süditalienischer Überlieferung

Herbert Schneider

In der Familie lateinischer Liturgien zeichnet sich die westgotische durch ihr markantes Eigenprofil aus.[1] Über das ganze 7. Jahrhundert ist ein deutliches Bemühen in der Synodalgesetzgebung auf der iberischen Halbinsel zu beobachten, die Liturgie im gesamten Reich, mindestens aber in den einzelnen Metropolitanbezirken zu vereinheitlichen. Relativ zahlreich sind auch die noch vorhandenen, wenngleich allesamt späteren Handschriften, die uns die westgotische Liturgie als eindrucksvolle kulturelle Schöpfung erscheinen lassen. Zu Recht wurde immer auch die Vielfalt der Anlässe betont, zu denen diese Liturgie rituelle Formen entwickelte, nicht nur auf den sozusagen klassischen Feldern der Meß- oder Sakramentenfeier; sie war auch eine betont 'staatstragende' Liturgie, die den König beim Auszug mit seinem Heer ebenso zur Schlacht begleitete, wie sie ihn bei der Heimkehr auch wieder begrüßte.[2] Dennoch decken die Editionen der mehr oder weniger offiziellen Sammlungen der liturgischen Texte (Liber sacramentorum, Breviarium, Liber ordinum, etc.) nicht alles ab, was die westgotische Liturgie an Riten entwickelt hat. Beispielsweise ist die ganze westgotische Synodenliturgie nicht im Zusammenhang liturgischer Handschriften überliefert, sondern in Handschriften der Rechtssammlungen: der *Ordo de celebrando concilio* für die westgotische Provinzialsynode wie auch der für die Nationalsynode.[3] Das liturgische Repertoire muß außerdem noch umfangreicher gewesen sein, als die erhaltenen Texte erkennen lassen. Von der so wichtigen, weil die Salbung in die

---

1 Als Überblick empfiehlt sich Cyrille Vogel, *Medieval Liturgy: an introduction to the sources*, rev. and trans. William G. Storey and Niels Krogh Rasmussen (Washington, D.C., 1986), 273-80, außerdem der Supplément bibliographique bei Anthony Ward-Cuthbert Johnson, *Marius Férotin, Le Liber mozarabicus sacramentorum et les manuscrits mozarabes*. Réimpression de l'édition de 1912 et bibliographie générale de la liturgie hispanique, Bibliotheca 'Ephemerides Liturgicae', Subsidia, Instrumenta Liturgica Quarreriensia, 4 (Roma, 1995), 41-90.

2 Vgl. den *Ordo quando rex cum exercitu ad prelium egreditur* bzw. die *Orationes de regressu regis* im Liber ordinum 48 und 49: *Le Liber ordinum en usage dans l'église wisigothique et mozarabe d'Éspagne du cinquième aud onzième siècle*, ed. Marius Férotin, Monumenta Ecclesiae Liturgica, 5 (Paris, 1904), 149-55.

3 Synodalordines 2 und 3, ed. Herbert Schneider, *MGH Ordines de celebrando concilio* (Hannover, 1996), 143-7 (Ordo 2), und 205-6 (Ordo 3).

lateinische Liturgie einführenden Königsweihe ist beispielsweise gar kein schriftliches Formular mehr vorhanden.[4]

Die folgenden Beobachtungen gelten nun einem kleinen, bisher offensichtlich unbekannt gebliebenen westgotischen *Ordo in susceptione presbiterorum*, der zur Anwendung kommen sollte bei der jährlichen Versammlung, zu der die Landpriester nach kanonischem Recht zur Überprüfung ihrer Amtsführung beim Bischof zusammenkommen mußten. Er hat sich nur noch in zwei Handschriften der beneventanischen Schriftüberlieferung erhalten und nicht innerhalb einer liturgischen Textsammlung, sondern im Zusammenhang mit frühmittelalterlichen Rechtsammlungen. Möglicherweise ist er deswegen auch von der Liturgiewissenschaft unbemerkt geblieben, aber als liturgischer Text auch von der Kanonistik nicht weiter beachtet worden. Die moderne akademische Professionalisierung der Fachgebiete 'Liturgie' und 'Kanonistik' hat ja zwar jeweils achtungsgebietendes Spezialwissen angehäuft, zum gegenseitigen fruchtbaren Austausch ist es aber nicht immer in wünschenswertem Umfang gekommen—mit rühmlichen Ausnahmen. Zu denen zählt zweifellos Roger E. Reynolds.[5] Insofern kann der vorliegende Beitrag durchaus verstanden werden als eine kleine Bereicherung seiner Bemühungen um die 'Canonistica Beneventana'.[6]

Der Ordo ist überliefert in zwei Handschriften, die miteinander zusammenhängen und in der Kanonistik ebenso wie in der Kunstwissenschaft, bei den Paläographen und auch den Kodikologen gut bekannt sind: Città del Vaticano, Biblioteca Apostolica Vaticana, Vat. lat. 5845, fos 311vb-312rb,[7] und Montecassino, Archivio dell'Abbazia,

---

4   Einen Rekonstruktionsversuch der Salbungsliturgie aus meist chronikalischen Nachrichten wurde unternommen von Férotin, *Liber ordinum*, Appendice II, 498-505, und von Michel Gros, 'Les Wisigoths et les liturgies occidentales', in *L'Europe héritière de l'Espagne wisigothique*. Colloque international du C.N.R.S. tenu à la Fondation Singer-Polignac (Paris, 14-16 mai 1990), ed. Jacques Fontaine-Christine Pellistrandi, Collection de la Casa de Velázquez, 35 (Madrid, 1992), 125-35, hier 132.

5   Roger E. Reynolds, 'Pseudonymous Liturgica in Early Medieval Canon Law Collections', in *Fälschungen im Mittelalter: Internationaler Kongreß der Monumenta Germaniae Historica München, 16.-19. September 1986*, vol. 2: *Gefälschte Rechtstexte. Der bestrafte Fälscher*, MGH Schriften, 33/ii (Hannover, 1988), 67-72, hier 67: 'In fact, it is little appreciated by many liturgiologists that early medieval canon law collections are one of the richest sources for pesudonymous liturgical tracts ..., that their origins are often associated with canon law contexts, and that they owed much of their popularity and diffusion to incorporation within canon law collections'.

6   Roger E. Reynolds, 'Canonistica Beneventana', in *Proceedings of the Ninth International Congress of Medieval Canon Law*, ed. by Peter Landau-Joers [richtig: Joerg] Mueller, MIC Series C, Subsidia, 10 (Città del Vaticano, 1997), 21-40.

7   Vgl. E. A. Lowe [Loew], *Scriptura Beneventana* , 2 vols (Oxford, 1929), i, Tafel XL; E. A. Loew, *The Beneventan Script: a history of the south Italian minuscule*, 2nd edn prepared and enlarged by Virginia Brown, 2 vols, Sussidi eruditi, 33-4 (Roma, 1980), i, 352 und ii, 152. Zu beiden Handschriften existiert eine reiche Bibliographie in bisher 10 Bänden: *BMB: Bibliografia dei manoscritti in scrittura beneventana, 1-10*, 10 vols (Roma, 1993-2002).

Cod. 541, pp. 4-6 (in moderner Paginierung).[8] Beide sind Ergebnisse benediktinischen Schreibeifers. Der Codex Casinensis, die jüngere Handschrift, ist wohl unter Abt Theobald (1022-35) in Montecassino selbst geschrieben worden und enthält die Rechtssammlung des Cresconius[9] und die Collectio Dacheriana.[10] Der *Ordo in susceptione presbiterorum* steht auf den beiden inneren Seiten des ersten Binio, in zwei Kolumnen à 38 Zeilen, die Initialen und auch manche Rubrik sind in roter Farbe hervorgehoben. Der Handschrift fehlt am Anfang mindestens ein Folium, denn das erste Stück, der Ordo für die westgotische Nationalsynode, setzt mitten im Text ein, während es im Vat. lat. 5845 vollständig erhalten ist. Die Casineser Handschrift stimmt in textlichen Einzelheiten mit dem Vaticanus so auffallend überein und ist zeitlich knapp 100 Jahre nach diesem anzusetzen, daß sie in diesem Teil als Abschrift ohne textkonstitutionellen Eigenwert gelten muß; das geht vor allem aus einem kleinen, durch ein Homoioteleuton bedingten Textverlust hervor.[11]

---

8   Friedrich Maassen, 'Bibliotheca latina iuris canonici manuscripta. 1. Theil: Die Canonensammlungen vor Pseudoisidor', *Sitzungsberichte der Kaiserlichen Akademie der Wissenschaften <Wien>. Philosophisch-Historische Klasse*, 53 (1866), 383; Maurus [Mauro] Inguanez, *Codicum Casinensium manuscriptorum catalogus*, 3 vols (Montecassino, 1913-41), iii, 199-203; Hubert Mordek, 'Zur handschriftlichen Überlieferung der Dacheriana', *QF*, 47 (1967), 577 Anm. 15; *idem, Kirchenrecht und Reform im Frankenreich: Die Collectio Vetus Gallica, die älteste systematische Kanones-sammlung des fränkischen Gallien. Studien und Edition*, Beiträge zur Geschichte und Quellenkunde des Mittelalters, 1 (Berlin, 1975), 101 Anm. 15; Loew-Brown, *The Beneventan Script*, ii, 89; Klaus Zechiel-Eckes, *Die Concordia canonum des Cresconius. Studien und Edition*, Teil 1 und 2, Freiburger Beiträge zur mittelalterlichen Geschichte, 5 (Frankfurt a. M., 1992), 323-4.

9   Zur Sammlung siehe Zechiel-Eckes, *Concordia canonum*, und neuere Literatur bei Lotte Kéry, *Canonical collections of the early Middle Ages (ca. 400-1140): a bibliographical guide to the manuscripts and literature*, History of Medieval Canon Law, 1, ed. Wilfried Hartmann-Kenneth Pennington (Washington, D.C., 1999), 33-7. Die von Hartmut Hoffmann vorgeschlagene Identifikation des Büchereintrags *Concordiam canonum* unter den Handschriften des Abtes Theobald in *Chronica monasterii Casinensis/Die Chronik von Montecassino*, MGH Scriptores, 34 (Hannover, 1980), 266 Anm. 18, mit Cod. 541 hat allgemein Anklang gefunden, vgl. Giulia Orofino, *I Codici decorati dell'Archivio di Montecassino*, 2/ii: *I codici preteobaldiani e teobaldiani*, con la collaborazione di Lidia Buono e Roberta Casavecchia (Roma, 2000), 15.

10   Zur Sammlung siehe Hubert Mordek, 'Zur handschriftlichen Überlieferung der Dacheriana', *QF*, 47 (1967), 577; und *idem, Kirchenrecht und Reform im Frankenreich*, Register, und besonders 259-63; Franz Kerff, *Der Quadripartitus: Ein Handbuch der karolingischen Kirchenreform. Überlieferung, Quellen und Rezeption*, Quellen und Forschungen zum Recht im Mittelalter, 1 (Sigmaringen, 1982), 18-20; und Kéry, *Canonical Collections*, 87-92.

11   Siehe unten Edition, Variante g. Eine Textlücke des Casinensis auf Grund eines gleichlautenden Wortes, aus der die Vorgängigkeit des Vaticanus ebenfalls hervorgeht, läßt sich auch im Synodalordo 3 für die westgotische Nationalsynode feststellen, siehe Schneider, *Ordines*, 206. Die behauptete Abhängigkeit des Casinensis vom Vaticanus bezieht sich nur auf die Ordines-Texte; Martina Stratmann, 'Briefe an Hinkmar von Reims', *Deutsches Archiv*, 48 (1992), 37-81, hier 43 mit Anm. 26, sieht im Hinblick auf die Rechtssammlungen (Cresconius, Dacheriana und Quadripartitus) hingegen den Casinensis als Apograph der Handschrift Città del Vaticano, Bibl. Apostolica, Reg. lat. 1347 (aus Reims, zur Zeit Hinkmars); diese Abfolge anhand der Rechtssammlungen unterstreicht auch Reynolds, 'Canonistica Beneventana', 23.

Der Vaticanus, der erst 1619 in die Vatikanische Bibliothek kam, wird paläographisch datiert auf jene Jahre, in denen die Mönche von Montecassino in Capua im Exil lebten, also auf die Jahre 915 bis 934. Die Handschrift überliefert als hauptsächlichen Inhalt die Collectio Dionysiana.[12] Allerdings ist darin auch die Capitulatio der Concordia canonum des Cresconius zu lesen, dann der *Ordo de celebrando concilio* für die westgotische Nationalsynode (fos 308vb-311vb), hier aber ohne Überschrift und mit einer historisch sehr interessanten Vorbemerkung,[13] und in direktem Anschluß der *Ordo in susceptione presbiterorum* (fos 311vb-312rb). Ihm folgt unmittelbar die Collectio Dionysiana mit der Vorrede 'Apostolorum canones qui per Clementem ...' (fo 312rb). Der Text ist in unprätentiöser Buchschrift in zwei Kolumnen zu je 27 Zeilen geschrieben, unterscheidet allerdings manchmal farblich zwischen Rubriken und Gebetstexten und kennzeichnet deutlich den Beginn des einzigen Gebetes mit einem Großbuchstaben.[14]

Inhaltlich regelt unser Ordo nicht eigentlich eine wirklich gottesdienstliche Handlung, aber er regelt eine dreitägige Zusammenkunft der Diözesan-Priesterschaft wie einen Gottesdienst. Die Zusammenkunft der Presbyter bei ihrem Bischof im 'conventus lętaniarum'—offensichtlich eine Zeitangabe, die uns noch beschäftigen wird—beginnt mit einem sonst aus liturgischen Abläufen bekannten Ritual: Die Presbyter versammeln sich im 'praeparatorium' um ihren Bischof samt den Diakonen und dem Archidiakon. Nach Eintritt der Ruhe werfen sich alle auf den Ruf des Archidiakons 'Oremus' zu Boden und schweigen eine Zeitlang. Der Bischof eröffnet eine kleine psalmodische Versikelreihe. Erst dann steht der Bischof auf, um die Oration 'Domine Ihesu Christe, corona iustorum ...' vorzutragen. Es schließt sich ein kleines Leseprogramm an mit dem Pseudo-Clemens-Brief über die Sakramentenspendung, dann eine Lesung geeigneter Kanones, die der Bischof ausgewählt hat und die zur presbyteralen Standesethik passen. Nach solcherart geistig-geistlicher Einstimmung und Belehrung kommt es zum eigentlichen Zweck der Zusammenkunft, der Überprüfung seelsorgerlicher Praxis und entsprechender Korrektion: 'Postinde quid unusquisque in spatio presentis anni profecerit tam in lectionibus quam in officiis sacris, vel quomodo divina officia vel sacramenta ab illis in suis ecclesiis peragantur et perquirendi et instruendi'.[15] Der erste Teil der Prüfung und Korrektur wird sich also

---

12 Zur Sammlung siehe Kéry, *Canonical Collections*, 9-21.

13 Siehe Schneider, *Ordines*, 208 Nr. 1a.

14 Giulia Orofino, 'Considerazioni sulla produzione miniaturistica altomedievale a Montecassino attraverso alcuni manoscritti conservati nell'Archivio della Badia', *Monastica 3: Scritti raccolti in memoria del XV centenario della nascità di S. Benedetto (480-1980)*, Miscellanea Cassinese, 47 (Montecassino, 1983), 131-85, hier 144-5, rückt die Hs. wegen ihres Initialenschmucks in Parallele zum Casinensis 175, der ein Dedikationsbild mit dem noch lebenden Abt Johannes (915-34) aufweist (vgl. Tafel 12). Vgl. auch Valentino Pace, 'La decorazione dei manoscritti pre-desideriani nei fondi della Biblioteca Vaticana', *Scrittura e produzione documentaria nel mezzogiorno longobardo, Atti del Convegno internazionale di studio (Badia di Cava, 3-5 ottobre 1990)*, ed. Giovanni Vitolo-Francesco Mottola, Acta Cavensia (Badia di Cava, 1991), 405-56, hier 412-13 (mit Tafeln 9-12).

15 Siehe unten Edition Nr. 4.

mehr auf die Fortschritte im laufenden Jahr beziehen, wobei die 'lectiones' eher auf ein irgendwie geartetes Fortbildungsprogramm gemünzt scheinen als auf gottesdienstliche Lesungen selbst, denn die sind wohl in die 'officia sacra' mit eingeschlossen, und so könnten mit 'officia sacra' dann auch eher die Kenntnisse über die Riten angesprochen sein, weniger die Riten selbst, denn von denen ist dann ja im zweiten Teil der Rubrik klar die Rede. Der zweite Teil der Prüfung hat deutlich die gottesdienstlichen Verrichtungen selbst und speziell die Formen der Sakramentenspendung im Auge.

Der zweite Tag der Zusammenkunft gilt der Überprüfung der sonstigen Lebenspraxis, vor allem auch des priesterlichen Lebenswandels, hat also ein Thema zum Gegenstand, das sich durch die gesamte Geschichte der klerikalen Standesethik zieht: die Glaubwürdigkeit. Der dritte Tag schließlich rückt die Zusammenkunft in die Nähe des Schulunterrichts: Die Priester müssen mit eigenen Worten das aufsagen, was sie im Unterricht der Trinitätslehre oder sonst passender Lehrstücke auswendig gelernt haben. Die Zusammenkunft endet also damit, wo sonstige synodale Versammlungen gerade des Westgotenreiches, wenigstens die der höheren Ordnung, gerne begonnen haben: mit der Behandlung dogmatischer Themen.[16] Nach den drei 'Litaneitagen' werden die Priester mit dem bischöflichen Segen nach Hause geschickt in ihre 'cellae'.

Kontrolle und Belehrung der Landpriester bei einer jährlichen Zusammenkunft war schon früh die Sorge der gesamten kirchlichen Gesetzgebung. Der erste einschlägige Kanon stammt von der Synode von Auxerre vom endenden 6. Jahrhundert. Mitte Mai sollen alle Priester der Diözese in die (Bischofs-)Stadt zur Synode kommen, die Äbte am ersten November zu ihrem eigenen 'concilium' beim Bischof, ohne daß jeweils ein Zweck dieser Versammlung angegeben ist.[17] Hält man sich aber vor Augen, daß die Äbte schon am Anfang des Jahrhunderts von der Synode von Orléans (511) in Kanon 19 aufgefordert wurden, zu Zwecken der Korrektur jährlich einmal mit dem Bischof zusammenzukommen, darf ohne weiteres geschlossen werden, daß

---

16 Vgl. Toledo IV, Vorrede: '... Et quoniam generale concilium agimus, oportet primum nostrae vocis sermonem de deo esse, ut post professionem fidei sequentia operis nostri vota quasi super fundamentum firmissimum disponantur', *La Colección canónica Hispana, V: Concilios hispanos: segunda parte*, ed. Gonzalo Martínez Díez-Felix Rodríguez, Monumenta Hispaniae Sacra, Serie canónica, 5 (Madrid, 1991), 180 Z. 330ff.-181 Z. 333; Toledo XII, c. 1: '... primi diei synodalis exordio ... habita primum est de sancta trinitate conlatio', *Concilios visigóticos e hispano-romanos*, ed. José Vives, España cristiana, Textos, 1 (Barcelona-Madrid, 1963), 385; Toledo XIII, Vorrede: '... prius de fide sanctae trinitatis sermocinationis nostrae coepit esse principium ...', *ebenda*, 414, und Toledo XVII, c. 1, *ebenda*, 528 (vgl. auch unten Anm. 80).

17 Auxerre (561-605), c. 7: 'Ut medio Madio omnes presbyteri ad synod (!) in civitatem veniant et kalendis Novembris omnes abbates ad concilium conveniant', *Concilia Galliae, A. 511-A. 695*, ed. C. de Clercq, *CCSL*, 148A (Turnhout, 1963), 266; sowie Jean Gaudemet et Brigitte Basdevant, *Les Canons des Conciles mérovingiens (VIe-VIIe siècles)*, 2 vols, *SChr.*, 353-4 (Paris, 1989) i, 82-3.

auch die jährliche Zusammenkunft von Auxerre den Sinn haben sollte, die Amts- und Lebensführung der Priester zu kontrollieren.[18]

Eine jährliche Kontrolle des Landklerus ist vor allem aus den Synoden der Karolingerzeit bekannt.[19] Gleich das erste Konzil nach einer langen Zeit der Dekadenz im Merowingerreich im Jahre 742, das sogenannte Concilium germanicum, gab den Startschuß mit seinem Kanon 3. Danach mußte jeder Presbyter in der Frühjahrsfastenzeit seinem Bischof bei einer 'synodus' genannten Versammlung Rechenschaft ablegen 'sive de babtismo sive de fide catholica sive de precibus et ordine missarum'.[20] Was zunächst im austrasischen Reich Karlmanns gelten sollte, wurde auch von Pippin für Neustrien im Jahre 744 auf der Synode von Soissons in Kanon 4 vorgeschrieben[21] und bald von den Bischöfen des gesamten Frankenreiches übernommen.[22] Karl der Große formulierte eine gleichgeartete Bestimmung in seinem ersten Kapitular,[23] dann auch ausführlicher in der Admonitio generalis von 789 (c. 70).[24] Unter Ludwig dem Frommen wurde die Überprüfung der Landpriester zeitlich von der Abholung der heiligen Öle am Bischofssitz am Gründonnerstag abgelöst, ja es scheint, als ob sich die jährliche Priesterkontrolle überhaupt allmählich abgeschwächt hätte und peu à peu durch andere Institutionen ersetzt worden wäre, wie die Visitation, die sich zeitlich parallel mit dem Klerus-Examen seit dem Concilium germanicum entwickelte, oder das Examen durch spezielle 'missi', vor allem aber durch die Diözesansynode.[25] Von einzelnen Bischöfen des Frankenreiches sind dabei innerhalb der Capitula episcoporum einzelne und manchmal sehr ins Konkrete gehende Bestimmungen zur Priesterkontrolle erhalten, etwa von Theodulf von Orléans, übrigens einem Westgoten, der seinen Priestern vorschreibt, bei der Diözesansynode die liturgischen Gewänder, die Bücher und Geräte vorzuführen, mit denen sie ihren Dienst ausübten.[26]

Daß solche Prüfungen in der frühmittelalterlichen Kirche stattfanden, läßt sich leicht an der synodalen Gesetzgebung ablesen, in welchen Formen dies geschah, an

---

18 Orléans (511) c. 19, *Concilia Galliae*, CCSL, 148A, 4, und *Les Canons des Conciles mérovingiens*, ed. SChr. 353, 490-91: 'Abbates pro humilitate religionis in episcoporum potestate consistant et, si quid extra regulam fecerint, ab episcopis conrigantur; qui semel in anno, in loco ubi episcopus elegerit, accepta vocatione conveniant'.

19 Vgl. zum Folgenden Wilfried Hartmann, *Die Synoden der Karolingerzeit im Frankenreich und in Italien*, Konziliengeschichte, Reihe A, Darstellungen (Paderborn u. a., 1989).

20 *Concilia aevi Carolini*, ed. Albertus Werminghoff, *MGH Concilia*, 2/i (Hannover, 1906), 3. Zum ganzen Themenbereich siehe E. Vykoukal, 'Les examens du clergé paroissial à l'époque carolingienne', RHE, 14 (1913), 81-96.

21 *MGH Concilia*, 2/i, 35.

22 *MGH Concilia*, 2/i, 47.

23 *MGH Capitularia*, i (Hannover, 1883), 45, c. 8.

24 *MGH Capitularia*, i, 59: 'ut episcopi diligenter discutiant per suas parrochias presbyteros, eorum fidem, baptisma et missarum celebrationes ...'.

25 Vykoukal, 'Les examens', 92-6.

26 Theodulf von Orléans, *Erstes Kapitular*, c. 4, ed. Peter Brommer, *MGH Capitula episcoporum*, i (Hannover, 1984), 106.

manchen, allerdings nicht sehr zahlreichen liturgischen Leitfäden. Dabei sind allerdings jene von vornherein auszuscheiden, die eindeutig auf das bischöfliche Sendgericht ausgerichtet sind, bei dem Klerus und Laien einer Glaubens- und Sittenprüfung in der jeweiligen Gemeinde unterzogen wurden.[27] Ein in mindestens fünf Handschriften überlieferter fränkischer Ordo *Qualiter synodus habendus sit ab episcopo cum presbyteris* aus dem 9. Jahrhundert kommt im Anliegen der Priester-Überprüfung beim Bischof unserem *Ordo in susceptione presbyterorum* nahe, ist aber davon in den konkreten Formen ganz unabhängig. Die Terminologie der jeweiligen Veranstaltung ('synodus' bzw. 'conventus') signalisiert schon einen Unterschied, und auch der Ablauf ist ganz verschieden geregelt. Im fränkischen Ordo kommt es nach der brüderlichen Begrüßung durch den Bischof auch zu einer belehrenden Phase: 'Presbyteri cum ad synodum evocati conveniunt, primo post fraternam episcopi salutationem legendum erit in consessu sacerdotali initium et pars aliqua libri curae pastoralis aut certae (!) omelia de evangelio "Designavit dominus" et faciendus ad eos sermo, quo eis ostendatur pondus et poericulum simul officii dignitas sacerdotalis, et demonstranda erit quoque ipsius vocabulum, unde scilicet et qua ex causa presbyteri vel sacerdotis appellatio constet'.[28] Der Lesestoff setzt sich also zusammen wohl aus der Regula pastoralis Gregors des Großen und der 17. Homilie desselben Papstes zum Evangelium Luc. 10: 1-9.[29] Dann erfolgt die Prüfung durch 'magistri et inquisitores', die von den Archipresbytern ausgewählt und zusammen mit diesen und den 'Kardinalpriestern' der Bischofskirche die einfachen Landpreister examinieren. Derweilen überprüft der Bischof mit seinen Chorbischöfen, Diakonen und sonstigen Klerikern den Ruf seiner Presbyter (bei den Laien?), aber auch konkrete Vergehen. Die Landpriester müssen nach erfolgter Wissensprüfung ihre 'libros et vestimenta, missalia reliquumque instrumentum sui ministerii' dem Bischof präsentieren, ganz so, wie es Theodulf von Orléans seinen Priestern beachtet wissen wollte.[30] Die Prüfung war übrigens mit einer echten Qualitätssicherung verbunden: Wessen Wissen für ungenügend befunden wurde, der mußte eine Zeitlang am Bischofssitz bei den 'doctores' nachsitzen—oder wurde gar aus seinem Amt entfernt!

Spätestens um die Jahrtausendwende entwickelte sich in Oberitalien ein *Ordo qualiter in ecclesia ab episcopo synodus agatur*, dessen Schwerpunkt ebenfalls auf der Klerus-Prüfung liegt. Der Ordo wurde zunächst mit dem Dekret des Bischofs Burchard von Worms überliefert, wanderte dann aber in hauptsächlich französische Pontifikalbücher. Die Synode ist zweigeteilt in eine Prüfung des Landklerus und eine

---

27 Vgl. den vielleicht zwischen 860 und 890 zu datierenden *Ordo qualiter synodus per villas caelebrari debet*, der zuletzt ediert ist bei Albert Michael Koeniger, *Die Sendgerichte in Deutschland*, Veröffentlichungen aus dem Kirchenhistorischen Seminar München, 3. Reihe Nr. 2 (München, 1907), 191-4.

28 Zitiert nach Franz Gescher, 'Geschichte und Recht der kölnischen Diözesansynode', Erstesr Teil (mehr nicht erschienen; masch. Diss., Köln 1923), 86.

29 Gregor I., *Regula pastoralis*, PL 77.13-128, bzw. *Homiliae 40 in evangelia*, PL 76.1138-49.

30 Siehe oben Anm. 26.

Prüfung unter Einschluß des Kathedralklerus.[31] Sie wird feierlich mit einem Gebetsteil eröffnet; darauf wird ein nicht genau definierbarer Text der Trinitätsdogmatik ('capitulum Niceni concilii perlegat, ubi de fide catholica plenius tractatur') vorgelesen, dann zur Vereinheitlichung wie zur Kenntnis der Liturgie der *liber officiorum*. Die nur die Landpriester betreffende erste Befragung betrifft das Taufritual, die auf den gesamten Klerus ausgedehnte einen ganzen Fragenkatalog zu Glaube, Liturgie und Disziplin.[32]

Von all diesen Formularen ist unser *Ordo in susceptione presbiterorum* völlig unabhängig. Er hat, wie im folgenden nachgewiesen werden soll, die Verhältnisse einer früheren Zeit und einer ganz anderen Welt im Blick: die westgotische Kirche. Dort sind mit dem vierten Konzil von Toledo vom Jahre 633 Regeln zur jährlichen Priesterkontrolle entwickelt worden, wie sie auch der Ordo voraussetzt. Dieses außergewöhnlich große Nationalkonzil unternahm unter dem Vorsitz Isidors von Sevilla als unbestrittenem Haupt der westgotischen Hierarchie ein umfassendes Gesetzeswerk zur Stabilisierung des ja erst einige Jahrzehnte zuvor katholisch gewordenen Reiches und seiner Kirche. An ihm nahmen alle sechs Metropoliten des Landes teil. Unter den 75 Kanones des Konzils befassen sich mehrere auch mit der Vereinheitlichung der Liturgie und der Sorge um das Standardwissen des niederen Klerus. Kanon 26 schreibt fest, die Priester sollten, wenn sie von ihrem Bischof für die Kirchen auf dem Land ordiniert werden, den 'libellus officialis'—bekannter als 'liber manualis'—in die Hand bekommen, ein liturgisches Ritualbuch, aus dem sie die rechte, also mit dem Bischofssitz übereinstimmende Gottesdienstordnung für die Spendung der Sakramente, speziell der Taufe, ersehen konnten.[33] Wir wissen sogar aus einer Rubrik des Formulars für die Priesterweihe, daß der Bischof am Ende des Weihegottesdienstes nach dem Schlußgebet dem Neupriester das Manuale übergab.[34] Aber die Bücher sollten kein toter Buchstabe bleiben. Derselbe Kanon bestimmte auch, jährlich hätten die Landpriester zum Bischof zu kommen, um ihm Rechenschaft

---

31 Synodalordo 5, ed. Schneider, *Ordines*, 230-57.

32 Synodalordo 5, Nr. 7: 'Post haec autem perquirantur presbyteri, qualiter catecuminos facere, qualiter energuminos exorcizare, qualiter scrutinia et aurium apertiones facere vel eosdem baptizare debeant', bzw. Nr. 9: 'Quibus taliter narratis perscrutandi et inquirendi sunt cardinales sacerdotes et levitae nec non et reliqui videlicet: de credulitate trinitatis et unitatis, de dilectione dei et proximi, de humilitate et castitate, de ieiunio et oratione, de helemosinarum largitate, de officiis ecclesiasticis simul et omnibus cavendis viciis et virtutibus adipiscendis', ed. Schneider, *Ordines*, 250-52.

33 Toledo IV, c. 26, ed. *Colección Hispana*, v, 216.

34 'Hoc explicita, dat [sc. der Bischof] ei [sc. dem Neupriester] manualem, et dicit ei hanc confirmationem', *Liber ordinum*, ed. Férotin, 55 mit Anm. 1 und dem Hinweis, daß in spanischen Bibliothekskatalogen vom 8. bis 11. Jahrhundert häufige Nennungen des 'liber manualis' vorkämen. Vgl. auch Francisco Martín Hernández, 'La formación del clero en la iglesia visigotico-mozarabe', in *Hispania Christiana: estudios en honor del Prof. Dr. José Orlandis Rovira en su septuagésimo aniversario*, ed. Josep-Ignazi Saranyana, Eloy Tejero (Pamplona, 1988), 205. Martín Hernández verfolgt in seinem Beitrag (*ibid.*, 193-213) die Ausbildung der Kleriker hauptsächlich vor ihrer Weihe in bischöflichen Schulen und den Bildungskanon der Priester, übergeht aber die lebenslange institutionalisierte Verhaltenskontrolle der Priester während ihrer Amtsführung ganz.

über ihren Dienst abzulegen. Sie erhielten ihre Bücher laut Kanon 26: '... ita ut quando ad letanias vel ad concilium venerint, rationem episcopo suo reddant, qualiter susceptum officium celebrant vel baptizant'.[35]

Der Kanon hat ein jährlich stattfindendes 'concilium' der Landpriester bei ihrem Bischof zum Ziel, obwohl ein anderer Kanon des IV. Toletanum den Bischof jedes Jahr auch selbst auf Reisen zu den einzelnen Kirchen schickt, um bevorzugt (?) die vermögens- und verwaltungsrechtlichen Probleme kennenzulernen, aber auch die 'vita ministrantium'.[36] Im Suebenreich war die Priesterkontrolle offenbar etwas anders geregelt; jedenfalls bestimmte die Synode von Braga II (572) mit Kanon 1, die Überprüfung bei den jährlichen Visitationen der Bischöfe vorzunehmen: '... per diaeceses ambulantes primum discutiant clericos, quomodo ordinem babtismi teneant vel missarum et quaequmque officia in ecclesia teneant vel quomodo peragantur'.[37] Anders also die Bestimmung von Kanon 26 vom IV. Toletanum. Der Kanon setzt offensichtlich die generelle jährliche Überprüfung des Klerus schon als bekannte Institution voraus, redet jedenfalls nicht davon als von einer neuen Einrichtung, ja verknüpft die Sache schon mit einem wohlbekannten liturgischen Datum: 'quando ad litanias vel ad concilium venerint ...'. Die presbyterale Prüfungssynode scheint sprachlich schon eine solch enge Verbindung mit ihrem Datum eingegangen zu sein, daß man von ihr selbst als von den 'Litaneitagen' reden konnte.

Solche Litanei- oder Bittage prägten in hohem Maße das westgotische Kirchenjahr. Schon vor der Bekehrung König Rekkareds zum Katholizismus war auf der Synode von Gerona (517) bestimmt worden, zweimal im Jahr sollten solche mit Fasten verbundenen Bittage gehalten werden: in der Woche nach Pfingsten von Donnerstag bis Samstag, also drei Tage lang, und ein zweites Mal Anfang November (und falls da ein Sonntag in die drei Fasttage fiel, in der Woche darauf ebenfalls von Donnerstag bis Samstag, an dem das Triduum mit einer Meßfeier abgeschlossen werden sollte).[38] König Chinthila verlangte 636 die Einführung neuer 'Litaneitage' jedes Jahr vom 13. Dezember an, die 'novae litaniae' genannt wurden.[39] Das darauffolgende und besser besuchte, deswegen wohl auch mit höherer Autorität ausgestattete Konzil von Toledo des Jahres 638 schärfte dann nochmals die Beobachtung

---

35 Toledo IV, c. 26, ed. *Colección Hispana*, v, 216.
36 Toledo IV, c. 36, ed. *Colección Hispana*, v, 222f.: 'Episcopum per cunctas dioceses parrociasque suas per singulos annos ire oportet, ut exquirat quid unaquaeque basilica in reparationem sui indiget ... (oder bewährte Presbyter oder Diakone schickt:)... qui et reditus basilicarum et reparationes et ministrantium vitam inquirant'. Möglicherweise sind mit den *ministri* nicht die Presbyter, sondern Kirchenverwalter gemeint.
37 Braga II (572) c. 1, ed. Vives, *Concilios visigóticos*, 81.
38 Gerona (517), c. 2 und 3, *Colección canónica Hispana, IV: concilios galos, concilios hispanos; primera parte*, ed. Gonzalo Martínez Díez-Félix Rodríguez, Monumenta Hispaniae Sacra, Serie Canónica, 4 (Madrid, 1965), 285f.
39 Toledo V (636), c. 1 *De institutione novarum letaniarum*, ed. *Colección Hispana*, v, 277f.; vgl. dazu José Orlandis, Domingo Ramos-Lisson, *Die Synoden auf der Iberischen Halbinsel bis zum Einbruch des Islam (711)*, Konziliengeschichte Reihe A, Darstellungen 1 (Paderborn u. a., 1981), 175.

dieser neuen Litaneitage ein.[40] Darüberhinaus beschloß das letzte westgotische Konzil, von dem noch Akten erhalten sind, das 17. Toletanum vom Jahre 694, ein dreitätiges außerordentliches Bittfasten nach Ende des Konzils ('speciales litaniae') und das ganze Jahr hindurch solche dreitägigen Fasttage ('triduana ieiunia') jeden Monat.[41] Kanon 6 des Konzils gibt vor, solche monatlichen Bittage ('letaniae') seien schon eine 'institutio priscorum patrum', und man wolle jetzt lediglich die Gebetsintentionen genauer definieren.[42] In der Tat verzeichnen die in Handschriften des 11. Jahrhunderts überlieferten mozarabischen Kalender neben dem 'ieiunium' genannten Fasten am Jahresbeginn oder einem vereinzelten 'ieiunium mensuale' Litaneitage für Anfang September.[43] Abgehoben davon werden aber überein-stimmend die 'kanonischen Litaneitage' Anfang November (nach Toledo IV) bzw. Mitte Dezember (nach Toledo V und VI).[44]

'Dies letaniarum' tauchen dann auch im Zusammenhang mit der Synodenliturgie auf. Sowohl der westgotische *Ordo de celebrando concilio* für die Provinzial-synoden[45] wie derjenige für die Nationalsynoden[46] gehen davon aus, daß die ersten drei Tage jeder Synode besonders privilegiert und nur der Diskussion dogmatischer und liturgischer Fragen reserviert sind, und diese drei Tage werden 'dies letaniarum' genannt.[47] Die Privilegierung der ersten drei Synodentage ist übrigens ein Indiz dafür, daß beide Synodalordines in der jetzt vorliegenden Form im Zusammenhang oder kurz nach dem 17. Konzil von Toledo verfaßt worden sind, denn dieses Konzil

---

40 Toledo VI (638) c. 2, ed. *Colección Hispana*, v, 304.

41 Toledo XVII (694), Vorrede und c. 6, ed. Vives, *Concilios visigóticos*, 526 und 532.

42 Toledo XVII (694), c. 6, ed. Vives, *Concilios*, 532.

43 Férotin, *Liber Ordinum*, 449-97, hier 450-51 ('ieiunium observabitur' oder ähnlich), 456 ('Ieiunium mensuale', Codex B), 460 und 466 ('Ieiunium mensualem', in Codex B von 1052), 478-9 ('Letanie celebrande sunt ...', vor dem Fest des Hl. Cyprian). Vgl. die Zusammenstellung der verschiedenen Nennungen bei Férotin, *Liber mozarabicus sacramentorum*, 141-2.

44 Férotin, *Liber ordinum*, 486-7 ('Letanie canonice' für November-Anfang) bzw. 490-91 für Mitte Dezember (Codex B: 'Letanie celebrande sunt tribus diebus'; Codex C: 'Letanie celebrande sunt tribus diebus pro adventu Angeli'; Codex D: 'Litanie tribus diebus ante solemnitate sancte Marie celebrande sunt'; Codex E und F: 'Letanie canonice'). Férotin beschreibt anderwärts einen 'Liber canticorum et horarum', der Lesungen für dreierlei Typen von Litaneien bietet: 'Lectiones de Letanias canonicas, Item in Letanias pro pluvia postulanda' und 'Incipiunt Letanias pro diversitate flagellorum', ed. Férotin, *Liber mozarabicus sacramentorum*, 643, und ebenda 645 wird der Text einer Litanei abgedruckt.

45 Synodalordo 2, ed. Schneider, *Ordines*, 142-86.

46 Synodalordo 3, ed. Schneider, *Ordines*, 205-16.

47 Synodalordo 2 (textgleich mit Synodalordo 3) Nr. 9: '... Nec ad aliud aliquid ante transibitur, quam ista omnia (nämlich die Diskussion des Trinitätsdogmas und der Einheit der liturgischen Riten) explicentur, ita tamen, ut in totis tribus diebus letaniarum nihil aliud agatur nec rectractetur, nisi sola conlatio de mysterio sanctae trinitatis et de ordinibus sacris vel officiorum institus ...'; bzw. Nr. 11: 'Per singulos tamen illos tres dies letaniarum episcopi vel presbiteri cum admonitore primum orationibus prostrabuntur. Sicque collecta a metropolitano oratione consurgent et de divinis tantum, ut dictum est, rebus collationem habebunt. In reliquis tamen diebus cunctis adstantibus oratio colligenda est et sic consedentes causarum negotia colligant', ed. Schneider, *Ordines*, 181-2.

institutionalisiert diesen Brauch in seinem ersten Kanon.[48] Die beiden Konzilsordines haben stillschweigend die ersten drei Synodentage mit offiziellen Litaneitagen identifiziert, aber mit welchen? Denen nach Pfingsten, denen des November-Anfangs oder der Dezember-Mitte? Während noch das 11. Konzil von Toledo (675) den Termin der Provinzialsynoden in die Entscheidung des Königs oder Metropoliten stellte,[49] führte schon sechs Jahre später das 12. Toletanum (681) einen festen Synodentermin ein: die Kalenden des November, und damit kanonische Litaneitage.[50] Für das endende 7. Jahrhundert stand also die Gleichung Litaneitage Anfang November = die ersten drei Tage der Provinzialsynode fest.

Welches aber sind die 'litaniae', an denen der *Ordo in susceptione presbiterorum* seinen 'conventus' ansiedelt? Die synodale Gesetzgebung fällt für eine Datierung völlig aus, denn sie gibt nirgendwo einen Anhaltspunkt für den Termin einer solchen untergeordneten 'Synode', die ja eigentlich noch unterhalb der Ebene einer Diözesansynode liegt und von welcher der Ordo wohl deshalb auch nur von einer 'Zusammenkunft an den Litaneitagen' redet. Oder sollten die 'dies letaniarum' des Ordo gar nichts mit den eingespielten kanonischen Litaneitagen zu tun gehabt haben und unabhängig von diesen, jeder solchen Zusammenkunft den Namen gegeben haben, weil dabei Litaneien gebetet wurden? Das ist ganz und gar unwahrscheinlich, weil der Ordo Gebetstexte vorgibt, aber gerade nirgendwo eine Litanei anspricht—außer eben zur Bezeichnung des Termins.[51] Für die großen Provinzialsynoden waren die Litaneitage des November reserviert—zumindest ab dem 12. Toletanum—, und man kann nicht annehmen, daß dabei die einzelnen Diözesan-Bischöfe ihren Klerus sozusagen neben ihrer großen Provinzialsynode auch noch um sich versammelt hätten—ganz abgesehen davon, daß bei einer solchen Regelung für manchen Landpfarrer der Weg zum Synodenort, also in die Provinzhauptstadt, unverhältnismäßig weit gewesen wäre. Für die Priesterprüfung kämen also nur die kanonischen Litaneitage nach Pfingsten in Frage oder jene des Dezember, die von Toledo V (636) eingeführt wurden.

---

48 Toledo XVII (694), c. 1: 'De tribus diebus, quibus in initio concilii nichil aliud agendum iubetur, nisi tantum de fide rebusque spiritualibus, nullo secularium interposito', ed. Vives, *Concilios visigóticos*, 528.

49 Toledo XI (675), c. 15: '... placuit definire, ut paternis institutionibus obsequentes omni anno ad peragendam celebritatem concilii in metropolitana sede, tempore quo principis vel metropolitani electio definierit, devotis semper animorum studiis confluamus ...', ed. Vives, *Concilios visigóticos*, 366.

50 Toledo XII (681), c. 12: 'Placuit huic venerando concilio, ut iuxta priorum episcoporum singularum provinciarum canonum instituta annis singulis in quaqumque provincia kalendis novembribus concilium celebraturi conveniant', ed. Vives, *Concilios visigóticos*, 400. Diese Bestimmung schärfte das nachfolgende Toletanum mit Kanon 9 dann nochmals ein, *ibid.*, 426.

51 Allenfalls der Psalmvers 32: 22 in der eröffnenden Liturgie der Versammlung wird auch in einem Meßformular *De letanias canonicas* bei der Brotbrechung gesungen: 'Ad confractionem panis.— Antiphona: Fiat misericordia tua, Domine, super nos, sicut speravimus in te', ed. Férotin, *Liber mozarabicus sacramentorum*, 456.

Angesichts der für Reisen unpassenden winterlichen Jahreszeit, spricht allerdings alles für die Litaneitage nach Pfingsten als Termine für die Priesterprüfung.[52]

Diese Litaneitage weisen, unabhängig von ihrer konkreten Datierung, jedenfalls ganz ins westgotische Milieu—aber nicht nur sie. Im Ordo zeigen noch andere Elemente ausgesprochen westgotisches Gepräge, schon gleich eines der ersten Worte. Nach dem Ordo sollen sich alle im 'praeparatorium' zusammenfinden, wo offensichtlich der ganze Konvent abgehalten wird. Dieses Wort ist nicht klassisch lateinisch, aber auch nicht allgemein christlich verbreitet, sondern nur in den mozarabischen Liturgietexten zu Hause, und hier bezeichnet es die Sakristei.[53] In der westgotischen Liturgie finden erstaunlich viele Akte im 'praeparatorium' statt. So wird der Sakristan hier an seinem hauptsächlichen künftigen Wirkungsort ordiniert,[54] wird der künftige Archipresbyter ebendort vom weihenden Bischof erst einmal einer Prüfung unterzogen;[55] dorthin ziehen nach der Gründonnerstagsmesse die Liturgen mit Gefolge, um sich zur anschließenden Fußwaschung zu rüsten,[56] und hier wurde manchmal auch das Fleisch der Osterlämmer an Ostern gesegnet.[57]

Westgotisches verraten auch die biblischen Zitate innerhalb der Liturgie des *Ordo in susceptione presbiterorum*. Gleich zu Beginn der Versammlung stimmt der Bischof den Psalm-Vers 61: 9 an: 'Sperate in eum, omnis conventus plebis meę, effundite coram eo corda vestra'. Das entspricht textlich ziemlich genau der mozarabischen Version des Psalters mit der kleinen Variante 'et effundite coram illo'.[58] Dagegen weichen davon die anderen Psalter-Versionen beträchtlich ab. Das Psalterium Gallicanum, also die vornehmlich in Gallien verbreitete Version, bietet: 'Sperate in eo ['eum', wenige Handschriften] omnis congregatio populi / effundite coram illo corda vestra', die Versio iuxta Hebraeos hingegen: 'Sperate in eo omni tempore populi / effundite coram eo cor vestrum'.[59] Beim konservativen Charakter liturgischer

---

52 Auf die Jahreszeit nimmt zum Beispiel auch Toledo IV c. 3 Rücksicht, wenn es als Termin für die Provinzialsynoden den 18. Mai und die folgenden Tage bestimmt 'quando herbis terra vestitur et pabula germinum inveniuntur', *Colección Hispana* , v, 185.

53 Vgl. Albert Blaise, *Dictionnaire Latin-Français des auteurs du moyen-âge*, CCCM, *Lexicon Latinitatis medii aevi* (Turnhout, 1986), 721. Der einzige angeführte Beleg nach *Bulletin Du Cange-Archivum Latinitatis Medii Aevi*, 2 (1925), 24, aus dem *Liber mozarabicus sacramentorum* läßt sich leicht vermehren; siehe die folgenden Anmerkungen.

54 Férotin, *Liber ordinum*, 42-3.

55 *Ibid.*, 56.

56 *Ibid.*, 191.

57 *Ibid.*, 224.

58 *The Mozarabic Psalter (Ms. British Museum, Add. 30,851)*, ed. J. P. Gilson, Henry Bradshaw Society Publications, 30 (London, 1905), 37.

59 *Biblia sacra iuxta vulgatam versionem*, ed. Robertus Weber (Stuttgart, 1975, zweite verbesserte Auflage), 842-3. Bei Psalm 32: 22 sind die Abweichungen kaum charakteristisch; immerhin sei darauf hingewiesen, daß dieser Psalmvers in einer Votivmesse im Liber ordinum vorkommt, ed. Férotin, *Liber ordinum*, 315: 'Ad confractionem. Fiat misericordia tua, Domine, super nos, sicut speravimus in te'; und wortgleich auch im Meßformular *De letanias canonicas* (in manchen Handschriften eindeutig den Litaneitagen des 1. November zugeordnet), ed. Férotin, *Liber mozarabicus sacramentorum*, 455.

Überlieferung kann das Gewicht solcher Textvarianten nicht hoch genug veranschlagt werden.[60]

Der Ordo zum Konvent an den Litaneitagen ist, strukturell betrachtet, eng verwandt mit jenen Ordines, welche die westgotische Liturgie für die Synoden geschaffen hat, nur etwas vereinfacht, aber in mehreren Elementen durchaus ähnlich, was von der Sache her ja auch nahe lag. Im Folgenden beziehe ich mich auf den westgotischen Ordo für die Provinzialsynoden (Ordo 2 der *Ordines de celebrando concilio*), der, wie anderwärts nachzuweisen versucht wurde, in der jetzigen Form im Zusammenhang mit dem 17. Toletanum (694) oder kurz danach, jedenfalls noch vor 711, formuliert wurde, die älteste Form (Toledo IV, c. 4) weiterentwickelt hat und mit dem zusammen auch der Ordo für die Nationalsynode (Ordo 3 der *Ordines de celebrando concilio*) entworfen wurde.[61]

Schon die Bestimmung, der Konvent habe sich in der ersten Stunde des Tages zu versammeln, setzt beide Ordines in Beziehung zueinander.[62] Dann folgt das Schweigegebot, die Prostration zum Gebet, im einen Fall das stille Gebet, im anderen eine kurze responsoriale Psalmodie, dann das Eröffnungsgebet vom stehenden Bischof, während die anderen noch in der Prostration verharren.[63] Am Ende des jeweiligen Eröffnungsgebetes liest man die eigenartige Rubrik, das Vaterunser (einmal als 'oratio dominica' und das andere Mal als 'oratio paterna' bezeichnet) sei jetzt nicht zu sprechen, die Oratio nur zu 'konfirmieren'.[64] Dazu muß man sich vor Augen halten, daß in der westgotischen Liturgie die Abfolge Oratio-Pater noster-Benedictio sehr häufig anzutreffen ist; wird diese Abfolge unterbrochen und das Vaterunser später gesprochen, findet sich manchmal der Ausfall eigens vermerkt.[65] In unseren beiden Ordines ist eine solche Rubrik eigentlich sinnvoll nur im *Ordo de celebrando concilio*, denn dort wird dann nach dem Schlußgebet das Vaterunser wirklich vor der Benedictio gebetet und also nur an den Schluß des Gottesdienstes

---

60 Erinnert sei an den Beweisgang für die Mit-Autorschaft Theodulfs von Orléans im *Opus Caroli regis contra synodum* (*Libri Carolini*) anhand der westgotischen Bibelzitate von Ann Freemann, 'Theodulf of Orléans and the Psalm Citations of the "Libri Carolini"', *RB*, 97 (1987), 195-224, und Roger E. Reynolds, 'The Pseudo-Hieronymian "De septem ordinibus ecclesiae"', *RB*, 80 (1970), 252, argumentiert ebenfalls mit Hilfe der Verwendung einer westgotischen Bibelversion im mozarabischen Antiphonarium.

61 Siehe Schneider, *Ordines*, 13-19 und 142-86.

62 *Ordo in susceptione*, Nr. 1: 'Hora prima diei ...'; und Synodalordo 2 Nr. 1: 'Hora diei prima ...', ed. Schneider, *Ordines*, 176 Z. 2.

63 Vgl. *Ordo in susceptione*, Nr. 1: '... facto aliquandiu silentio—dicat hanc orationem'; mit Synodalordo 2 Nr. 2: '... sedentesque in diuturno silentio sacerdotes ... dicturus est archidiaconus: Orate, statimque omnes in terra prostrabuntur tam episcopi quam presbiteres et orantes diutius tacite cum fletibus atque gemitibus, unus ex episcopis senioribus surgens orationem palam fundet ad dominum, cunctis adhuc in terra iacentibus, dicens hanc orationem', ed. Schneider, *Ordines*, 176.

64 Vgl. *Ordo in susceptione*, Nr. 2: '... Qua oratione explicita oratio dominica non dicatur, sed ipsa tantummodo confirmatur'; mit Synodalordo 2 Nr. 3: '... In qua oratione oratio paterna non dicitur nec benedictio, sed ipsa solummodo oratio confirmatur', ed. Schneider, *Ordines*, 178.

65 Vgl. Férotin, *Liber ordinum*, 70: 'sic oratio ista colligitur, absque oratione dominica ...'.

verschoben, nicht so im *Ordo in susceptione*; dort kommt ein Vaterunser gar nicht vor.

Die Rubriken, mit denen der Lesungsteil gestaltet wird, ähneln sich in beiden Ordines ebenfalls frappierend. Bei der Priesterversammlung werden der Pseudo-Clemens-Brief zur Eucharistie oder Kanones nach dem Geschmack des Bischofs verlesen, bei der Provinzialsynode eine Reihe Konzilskanones aus der Rechtssammlung und anschließend Kanones nach dem Geschmack des Metropoliten, bevor dann bei beiden die eigentlichen Tractanda angegangen werden.[66]

Zieht man noch in Betracht, daß der *Ordo in susceptione presbiterorum* nicht bloß eine strukturelle Nähe zum Synodenordo aufweist, sondern auch zusammen mit ihm überliefert wird, ja daß der Synodenordo in diesem Strang der Überlieferung redaktionell noch eine ganz ursprüngliche Stufe repräsentiert und sogar noch in das Redaktionsskriptorium zurückzureichen scheint,[67] wird man den Schluß ziehen können: Der Ordo für die Priesterprüfung an den Litaneitagen und die *Ordines de celebrando concilio* 2 (für die Provinzialsynode) wie auch 3 (für die westgotische Nationalsynode) sind einer gemeinsamen Initiative entsprungen oder zumindest auseinander abgeleitet. Für die Synodalordines in der vorliegenden Form ist eine schriftliche Fixierung um das 17. Toletanum (694) sehr wahrscheinlich. So dürfte auch jener kleine Ordo für die Zusammenkunft der Landpriester spätestens gegen Ende des Westgotenreiches verfaßt worden sein. Daß sich seine Spur in spanischen Handschriften verloren hat und er nur noch aus süditalienischer Überlieferung bekannt ist, muß nicht weiter erstaunen. Auch für die frühe Form des Synodalordo 3 gilt, daß sie nur noch in unseren beiden Handschriften erhalten ist und die spanische Überlieferung aus dem 10. Jahrhundert schon einen geglätteten Text aufweist.

Man hat ja nach der muslimischen Eroberung der iberischen Halbinsel nach 711 mit einer regelrechten 'Fluchtwelle' ins restliche Europa zu rechnen, zu beobachten etwa dem Toledaner Erzbischof Sisenand, der beim Papst in Rom Zuflucht suchte, oder dem Erzbischof von Tarragona Prosper, der über Sardinien die Reliquien des Hl. Fructuosus nach Ligurien gerettet hat (San Fruttuoso). Auf diesem Wege sind sicher auch Handschriften über die Pyrenäen gewandert, so nachzuweisen bei einer Klerikergruppe aus dem Kloster Urgel oder wahrscheinlich zu machen an dem berühmten westgotischen *Liber orationum* in Verona.[68]

---

66 Vgl. *Ordo in susceptione*, Nr. 3: 'Deinde leguntur canones, quos legendos episcopalis auctoritas diiudicarit (!), vel aliud, quod congruum moribus vel vitę sacerdotum perspectum fuerit'; mit Synodalordo 2 Nr. 5: '... vel aliud de canonibus, quod metropolitano aptius visum fuerit, ut legatur', ed. Schneider, *Ordines*, 179.

67 Siehe Schneider, *Ordines*, 13-22, besonders 16-17, wo die redaktionelle Priorität der italienischen Überlieferung gegenüber der spanischen dargelegt ist.

68 Vgl. Michel Gros, 'Les Wisigoths' (wie Anm. 4), 133f.: 'Il est très possible que le célèbre *Liber orationum de festivitatibus* de Vérone, certainement écrit à l'usage de l'Église de Tarragone vers l'an 700, ait appartenu à ce groupe'; und *idem*, 'Observacions sobre l'Oracional hispanic de Verona', *Mens*

Edition

Überlieferung:

Hs. 1: Montecassino, Archivio dell'Abbazia, Cod. 541, pp. 4-6 (in moderner Paginierung) (1022-35; Schriftheimat: Montecassino)

Hs. 2: Vatikan, Biblioteca Apostolica Vaticana, Vat. lat. 5845, fos 311vb-312rb (915-34; Schriftheimat: Capua)

Vorbemerkung:

Hs. 1 stellt eine direkte Abschrift von Hs. 2 dar; so wird Hs. 2 der Edition zu Grunde gelegt. Trotzdem werden auch die wichtigeren Varianten von Hs. 1 mitgeteilt. Die Orthographie und Grammatik ist belassen worden, evtl. bei Auffälligkeiten mit (!) versehen. Unsichere Auflösungen von Abbreviaturen stehen in runden Klammern. Die Interpunktion entspricht modernem Gebrauch. Wegen größerer Übersichtlichkeit und leichterer Zitierfähigkeit werden die einzelnen Abschnitte in Nummern eingeteilt. Kursiv-Druck für die gesprochenen oder gesungenen Textteile ist Herausgeber-Zutat, ebenso der Fett-Druck in der Überschrift.

Ordo in susceptione presbiterorum, quando ad conventum lętaniarum[69] occurrunt

1. Hora[a] prima diei[70] residens episcopus in preparatorio[71] circumstantibus universi (!) parrochitanis presbiteris facto aliquamdiu silentio dicat archidiaconus: *Oremus. Et statim episcopi (!) et presbiteri ad orationem[b] prosternuntur.* Sicque iacentes et sub aliquo spatio horarum orantes[c] dicat episcopus cum astantibus diaconibus hunc versum: *Sperate in eum, omnis conventus plebis meę, effundite coram eo corda*

---

a   Der Text schließt in Hs. 1 direkt an die Überschrift an.

b   folgt Rasur von ca. 2 Buchstaben Hs. 1.

c   korr. aus oratio Hs. 1.

---

concordet voci: Pour Mgr. A. G. Martimort à l'occasion de ses 40 années d'enseignement et des 20 ans de la Constitution Sacrosanctum Concilium, ed. J. Dutheil-Claude Dagens (Paris, 1983), 484-8.

69   Es handelt sich bei der Presbyter-Versammlung nicht um eine klassische Diözesansynode, sondern um eine Zusammenkunft zur Überprüfung der Amtsführung der Pfarrer. Der Konvent wurde an traditionellen Litaneitagen des westgotischen Kirchenjahres abgehalten, am ehesten jenen, die vom Konzil von Gerona (517), cc. 2 und 3, ed. *Colección Hispana*, iv, 285 f., auf die Woche nach Pfingsten festgelegt worden waren.

70   Die Zeitbestimmung entspricht den westgotischen Synodalordines, vgl. Synodalordo 2 bzw. 3: 'Hora diei prima ante solis ortum...', ed. Schneider, *Ordines*, 176 Z. 2 bzw. 208 Z. 12. Zu weiteren Übereinstimmungen damit siehe unten Anm. 77 und 79.

71   Der westgotischen Kirche eigentümliche Bezeichnung für 'Sakristei', vgl. Blaise, *Dictionnaire Latin-Français*, 721.

vestra.[72] Respondent presbiteri adhuc iacentes: *Fiad* (!), *domine, misericordia tua super nos, sicut speravimus in te.*[73]

2. Deinde[d] iacentibus illis surgens episcopus dic(at) hanc[e] orationem[f]:

Domine[74] *Ihesu Christę, corona iustorum et perfecta sanctificatio sacerdotum, sanctifica horum fratrum ad nos pertinentem conventum et genuum incurvatione prostratum. Nullum ex*[g] *eis fraudibus consuetis decipiat,*[75] *nullum libidine sauciet, nullum superbia inflet vel qualibet vitiorum contagione commaculet, sed purissima et beneplacita tibi vasa effecta,*[76] *inculpabiliter inhęreant tractare commissa sibi ministeriorum*[h] *divinitus sacramenta. Per.*

Qua[77i] oratione explicita oratio dominica non dicatur, sed ipsa tantummodo confirmatur.

3. Post hęc posito anologio legitur epistola sancti Clementis[78] de tractandis sacramentorum[j] ministeriis. Deinde[79] leguntur canones, quos legendos episcopalis auctoritas diiudicarit (!), vel aliud, quod congruum moribus vel vitę sacerdotum perspectum fuerit.

---

d   Deinde - orationem rubrizieren Hs. 1 und Hs. 2.

e   korr. aus hac Hs. 1.

f   oratio Hs. 1.

g   ex - nullum fehlt Hs. 1 (Homoioteleuton).

h   ministrorum Hs. 1.

i   Qua—confirmatur rubrizieren Hs. 1 und Hs. 2.

j   sacramentum Hs. 1.

---

72   Ps. 61: 9 in mozarabischer Textversion, vgl. *Mozarabic Psalter* (wie Anm. 58), 37.

73   Ps. 32: 22.

74   Die Oratio ist sonst nicht nachzuweisen, dürfte auch speziell zu der Presbyter-Prüfung verfaßt worden sein.

75   Grammatikalisches Subjekt: conventus?

76   Anspielung auf Act. 9: 15 (vas electionis), Rom. 9: 21 bzw. 23 (vas in honorem bzw. vasa misericordiae) oder 2. Tim. 2: 20-1 (vas in honorem sanctificatum)?

77   Der Hinweis auf den Ausfall der oratio dominica (= Vaterunser) erklärt sich nur durch die in der westgotischen Liturgie beliebte Abfolge Oratio-Pater noster-Benedictio. Die Rubrik steht fast wortgleich in den westgotischen Synodalordines 2 bzw. 3, wo sie sinnvoll ist, weil dort das Vaterunser auf das Ende der Liturgie verschoben wird, vgl. Synodalordo 2 Nr. 3 bzw. Synodalordo 3 Nr. 3, ed. Schneider, *Ordines*, 178 Z. 32-3 bzw. 209 Z. 48-9.

78   Gemeint ist wohl Ps.-Clemens, Ep. 2 (JK †11), ed. Paulus Hinschius, *Decretales Pseudo-Isidorianae et Capitula Angilramni* (Leipzig, 1863), 46-52, bzw. *PL* 56.893-6. Wegen des westgotischen Charakters des Ordo muß eine vor-pseudoisidorische Textversion angesprochen sein.

79   Die freie Auswahl von passenden Kanones oder sonstigem Lesestoff entspricht der Rubrik des westgotischen Synodalordo 2 Nr. 5 (nach der Verlesung der capitula de conciliis agendis) bzw. Synodalordo 3 Nr. 9: vel aliud de canonibus, quod metropolitano aptius visum fuerit, ut legatur, ed. Schneider, *Ordines*, 179 Z. 46 bzw. 211 Z. 90.

4. Postinde quid unusquisque in spatio presentis anni profecerit tam in lectionibus quam in officiis sacris vel quomodo divina officia vel sacramenta ab illis in suis ecclesiis peragantur, et perquirendi et instruendi.

5. Alia quoque die de cura laborum et moribus suis beneviventium requirendi sunt.

6. Tertio item die quicquid de trinitatis sanctę misterio[80] memorię commendaverunt, totum verbis propriis recitabunt, sive aliud, quod memorię omni sacerdoti convenerit retinere, ab ipsis totum est recitandum.

7. Sicque expletis letaniarum diebus ad cellas suas cum benedictione[81] episcopi remeabunt.

---

80 Die westgotische Kirche begann nach ihrer Konversion vom Arianismus zur Orthodoxie ihre Synoden bevorzugt mit Diskussionen des Trinitätsdogmas 'more synodi universalis', siehe Orlandis, *Synoden*, 341-3. Die Synode Toledo XVII (694) schreibt in Kanon 1 die (auch schon in Toledo XI von 675 bezeugte) Übung fest, die ersten drei Synodentage zur Diskussion und Belehrung über das Trinitätsdogma zu reservieren, vgl. Vives, *Concilios visigóticos*, 528.

81 Einen eigens für eine Synode formulierten und häufig überlieferten Schlußsegen enthält der Synodalordo 2 Nr. 22, ed. Schneider, *Ordines*, 185-6. Im allgemeinen setzen sich die westgotischen Benediktionen aus drei Gliedern zusammen, die jeweils mit *Amen* beantwortet werden, vgl. M. Ruffini, 'Il ritmo prosaico finale nelle "Benedictiones" dell'Orazionale Visigótico (Cod. LXXXIX della Biblioteca capitolare di Verona)', *Analecta Sacra Tarraconensia*, 31 (1958), 209-58; und *idem*, 'Strutturazione morfologica e sintatica delle "Benedictiones" dell'Oracional Visigótico (ms. LXXXIX della Biblioteca capitolare di Verona)', *Analecta Sacra Tarraconensia*, 32 (1959), 5-29; und Edmond [Eugène] Moeller, *Corpus Benedictionum Pontificalium*, CCSL, 162B (Turnhout, 1973), XXI-XXII und LXII f.

Chapter 3

Le végétal et le sacré:
l'hysope dans le rite de la dédicace de l'église[1]

Eric Palazzo

Dans les études médiévales modernes, l'intérêt pour le monde végétal ne s'est jamais démenti. Si l'on s'en tient seulement au XXe siècle, on ne compte plus les publications qui abordent selon des modes différents le monde végétal du Moyen Age occidental. Parmi ces publications, plusieurs sont consacrées d'une part à l'étude du jardin médiéval,[2] d'autre part au symbolisme des plantes et enfin à leurs vertus thérapeutiques ainsi qu'à leurs multiples utilisations pratiques.[3] Dans ces différents domaines, les auteurs médiévaux sont tributaires de textes de l'Antiquité. Ainsi Franco Cardini a rappelé de façon précise le lien direct existant entre les auteurs de l'Antiquité ayant disserté sur les plantes et leurs vertus magiques—Pline l'Ancien et Isidore de Séville en tête—et les théologiens du Moyen Age qui ont largement suivi leur prédécesseurs à propos de ces vertus.[4] Le monde monastique du haut Moyen Age a largement contribué à faire la synthèse entre l'aspect pratique lié à la connaissance des plantes, notamment pour leur culture, le symbolisme du jardin et les vertus médicinales des plantes. Le célèbre plan de l'abbaye de Saint-Gall du IXe siècle prévoit un espace particulier pour le jardin médicinal, un autre pour le potager puis encore un pour le verger. Dans son *Hortulus* rédigé entre 841 et 842, Walafrid Strabon participe aussi à l'ancrage dans la culture monastique de l'étude des plantes.[5] Dans ce texte, Walafrid décrit avec une relative précision vingt-quatre espèces de plantes pour lesquelles il dit toute son admiration. Pour chacune d'elle, il insiste sur les propriétés médicinales et magiques en même temps qu'il développe un véritable

---

1 Cette contribution a fait l'objet d'une conférence prononcée dans le cadre des Semaines d'études médiévales du CESCM à Poitiers le 25 juin 2001.

2 Parmi la vaste bibliographie consacrée au jardin médiéval, on retiendra: Sylvia Landsberg, *The Medieval Garden* (London, 1998); Michel Cambornac, *Plantes et jardins du Moyen Age* (Paris, 1998); *Le jardin médiéval: colloque, concert, et exposition (mai-septembre 1988)*, Les Cahiers de l'Abbaye de Saint-Arnoult, 3 (Bordeaux, 1990); voir aussi Massimo Miglio, 'Il giardino come rappresentazione simbolica', *L'ambiente vegetale nell'alto Medioevo (30 marzo-5 aprile 1989)*, 2 vols, Settimane di studio del centro italiano di studi sull'alto Medioevo, 37 (Spoleto, 1990), ii, 709-24.

3 Voir par exemple les actes des semaines de Spolète cités à la note précédente.

4 Franco Cardini, 'Le piante magiche', *L'ambiente vegetale*, ii, 623-61.

5 *PL* 114.1121-30.

symbolisme du végétal, non dépourvu d'ailleurs d'une certaine touche poétique. Avant lui cependant, le capitulaire de Willis promulgué par Charlemagne entre 792 et 800 incitait fortement les moines à s'intéresser à l'horticulture et au jardinage. La dimension proprement médicinale attachée à l'étude des plantes au Moyen Age a rencontré un important succès après le haut Moyen Age et en dehors du seul monde des monastères. La médecine médiévale s'est très tôt intéressée aux vertus thérapeutiques des plantes et l'on peut citer, à titre d'exemple, le célèbre manuel de médecine composé par Hildegarde de Bingen au XIIe siècle qui illustre parfaitement cet intérêt des 'médecins' pour les plantes considérées comme les éléments premiers des remèdes.[6] Enfin, le jardin médiéval apparaît très tôt dans la théologie comme une image du paradis où les plantes sont assimilées aux différentes vertus chrétiennes. Cette vision allégorique du jardin se fonde essentiellement sur l'interprétation de certains textes vétéro-testamentaires à propos desquels les théologiens médiévaux ont glosé autour de la notion d'*hortus conclusus*, elle-même porteuse d'une signification ecclésiologique.

La présente contribution souhaite élargir la perception que nous avons du végétal dans le Moyen Age occidental en étudiant le triple symbolisme biblique, exégétique et liturgique d'une plante, l'hysope, utilisée dans le rituel de la dédicace de l'église et de la consécration de l'autel. A plusieurs égards, ce triple symbolisme suggère la compréhension de l'usage du végétal dans la liturgie non plus seulement à partir de considérations pratiques mais aussi sur le plan de la signification ecclésiologique des plantes dans leur utilisation rituelle. D'ailleurs, l'exégèse liturgique du haut Moyen Age ne proposait-elle pas une vision totale du symbolisme du rituel au sein duquel tout élément, du vêtement liturgique aux acteurs de la célébration, en passant par les objets, les lieux et on pourrait ajouter les plantes, était porteur d'une signification théologique. Dans un premier temps, je rappellerai les considérations essentielles relatives à l'hysope et à ses divers usages au Moyen Age, notamment dans le domaine de la médecine. Dans un second temps, je procèderai à une rapide exploration dans les textes bibliques, exégétiques et liturgiques qui construisent la valeur symbolique de l'hysope.

1. L'hysope: présentation de la plante et usages médiévaux

L'hysope appartient à la famille des lamiacées, ou des labiées. Le genre *hyssopus* est représenté par une quinzaine d'espèces dont la plus connue est sans doute l'*hyssopus officinalis*. Il s'agit d'une herbe aromatique qui pousse en buisson sur tout le pourtour méditerranéen et même jusque dans certaines régions d'Orient. Selon les spécialistes,

---

6 Gottfried Hertzka et Wighard Strehlow, *Manuel de la médecine de sainte Hildegarde*, tr. Fr. (Montsurs, 1994).

cette plante vivace est originaire du sud de l'Europe et de l'est asiatique. Elle pousse spontanément sur des massifs rocheux ou sur les murs, mais elle fait fréquemment l'objet d'une culture à vocation thérapeutique et ornementale. D'une hauteur variant entre 15 et 60 centimètres, l'hysope possède une tige portant des feuilles étroites et longues de 1 à 4 centimètres. Ses fleurs sont généralement de couleur bleue foncée ou violacée, et plus rarement roses ou blanches. La floraison a lieu du mois de juin jusqu'en septembre.

Dans les textes médiévaux, l'usage médicinal de l'hysope n'est attestée avec certitude qu'à partir du XIIe siècle chez Hildegarde de Bingen puis au XIIIe siècle chez Albert le Grand. On pense cependant qu'elle fut probablement utilisée dès le haut Moyen Age dans la pharmacopée monastique. Dans ses *Etymologies*, Isidore de Séville au VIIe siècle précise entre autres la principale vertu thérapeutique de la plante: 'Hyssopum herba purgandis pulmonibus apta. Unde et in veteri testamento per hyssopi fasciculos aspergebantur agni sanguine, qui mundari volebat. Nascitur in petris haerens saxo radicibus' (Etym. XVII, 9). Avant Isidore, Hippocrate, Galien et Dioscoride préconisaient l'usage de l'hysope pour lutter contre les inflammations pulmonaires ainsi que les toux ou bien encore afin d'évacuer les mauvaises humeurs. Les médecins de l'Ecole Salerne considérait l'hysope comme un remède efficace contre les problèmes respiratoires en tout genre. Les traités de botanique des XVIIe et XVIIIe siècles reprendront les considérations thérapeutiques à propos de l'hysope développées par les médecins de l'Antiquité et du Moyen Age à propos de l'hysope. Autrement dit, l'hysope était recommandée pour traiter les affections bronchiques, l'asthme et les toux, du fait notamment de ses vertus pectorales et expectorantes. A forte dose, elle devient un hyperexcitant et devient dangereuse car elle peut alors provoquer des manifestations épileptiques. Dans son *Manuel de Médecine*, Hildegarde écrit à propos de l'hysope:

Mangée souvent, elle purifie les écumes fétides et maladives contenues dans les humeurs, c'est-à-dire qu'elle purifie, comme fait la chaleur qui, dans la marmite, dépure par le bouillonnement. Elle est bonne dans tous les aliments. Cuite et pulvérisée, elle est plus utile que crue. Employée comme condiment dans les mets, elle rend le foie plus capable de rendement et purifie aussi un peu les poumons. Qui tousse et souffre du foie, et aussi qui souffre des poumons en haletant, que l'un et l'autre mangent de l'hysope avec des plats de viande ou aussi roussi dans une sauce, et ils iront mieux. Si quelqu'un mange l'hysope en n'y ajoutant que du vin ou que de l'eau, il en sera plus fatigué que soulagé. Si le foie d'un être humain est malade de tristesse, avant que la maladie prenne le dessus, il faut faire cuire des poulets avec de l'hysope, et manger souvent tant l'hysope que la chair de poulet. Mais aussi il faut manger de l'hysope cru, trempé dans du vin, fréquemment, et boire ce vin, parce que l'hysope est plus utile pour celui qui est atteint de cette maladie que pour celui qui souffre des poumons.[7]

---

7   Hildegarde, *Manuel de la médecine*, 229.

Le passage sur l'hysope extrait du *Manuel* d'Hildegarde résume à lui seul les vertus et les usages thérapeutiques de la plante ainsi que son utilisation à des fins culinaires. A ce propos, l'hysope était fréquemment utilisée dans la cuisine de l'Antiquité ainsi qu'au Moyen Age. Apicius la recommandait pour aromatiser les sauces et le sel tandis que divers traités et livres de cuisine médiévaux la citait dans diverses recettes.

Dans la définition de l'hysope donnée par Isidore de Séville, il était certes fait allusion aux vertus médicinales de la plante mais aussi à son utilisation à des fins purificatrices. Pour cette dernière utilisation, Isidore fait référence à des usages de l'Ancien Testament relatant que ceux qui voulaient se purifier s'aspergeaient de sang d'agneau avec de l'hysope. La définition de l'hysope par Isidore informe à la fois sur les vertus thérapeutiques de l'hysope mais aussi sur son usage rituel, en l'occurrence celui de la purification dans l'Ancien Testament. Comme c'est l'habitude chez le maître de l'encyclopédisme antique, à l'explication simple et concrète vient s'ajouter la signification symbolique. En ce sens, Isidore est une fois de plus celui qui ouvre la voie à l'interprétation théologique de l'hysope à partir du haut Moyen Age.

2. L'hysope dans les textes bibliques

Nombreux sont les passages bibliques qui mentionnent l'usage de l'hysope pour des aspersions dans le cadre de rites de purification.[8] L'un des rites de la Pâque juive relate que le hébreux devaient se servir d'une touffe d'hysope trempée dans le sang de l'agneau pascal et en asperger le linteau et les deux poteaux de la porte des maisons:

> Moïse appela tous les anciens d'Israël et leur dit: Allez vous procurer du bétail pour vos clans et égorgez la Pâque. Vous prendrez une touffe d'hysope, vous la tremperez dans le sang du bassin, vous appliquerez au linteau et aux deux montants le sang du bassin et personne d'entre vous ne franchira la porte de sa maison jusqu'au matin' (Ex. 12: 21-2).

Toujours extrait du livre de l'Exode, citons le passage marquant l'inauguration solennelle de l'alliance entre Dieu et son Peuple:

> Moïse vint raconter au peuple toutes les paroles du Seigneur et toutes les règles ... . Il (Moïse) prit le livre de l'alliance et en fit lecture au peuple. Celui-ci dit: 'Tout ce que le Seigneur a dit, nous le mettrons en pratique, nous l'entendrons'. Moïse prit le sang, en aspergea le peuple et dit: 'Voici le sang de l'alliance que le Seigneur a conclue avec vous, sur la base de toutes ces paroles' (Ex. 24: 1, 7-9).

---

8   E. Levesque, 'Hysope', dans *Dictionnaire de la Bible*, 5 vols (Paris, 1895-1912), iii, cols 796-800. Voir aussi les mentions citées dans le *Thesaurus linguae latinae*, 6/ii, cols 3162-4.

Ce passage ne mentionne pas expressément l'hysope mais un verset de l'épître aux Hébreux précise que Moïse a utilisé à cette occasion l'hysope pour sceller par le sang cette alliance avec Dieu:

> Lorsque Moïse eut proclamé à tout le peuple chaque commandement conformément à la loi, il prit le sang des veaux et des boucs, puis de l'eau, de la laine écarlate et de l'hysope, et il en aspergea le livre en disant: Ceci est le sang de l'alliance que Dieu a ordonnée pour vous (Héb. 9: 19).

Des rites d'aspersion à l'aide de l'hysope et visant la purification sont décrits dans le texte biblique. Le chapitre 14 du Lévitique consacré à la description du rituel de la purification des lépreux par un prêtre contient plusieurs passages concernant l'usage de l'hysope dans ce rituel:

> Le prêtre ordonne de prendre pour celui qui se purifie: deux oiseaux vivants, purs, du bois de cèdre, du cramoisi éclatant et de l'hysope (Lév. 14: 4);
> Il prend l'oiseau vivant avec le bois de cèdre, le cramoisi éclatant et l'hysope (14: 6);
> Pour purifier la maison de son péché, il prendra deux oiseaux, du bois de cèdre, du cramoisi éclatant et de l'hysope (14: 49);
> Il prendra le bois de cèdre, l'hysope, le cramoisi éclatant et l'oiseau vivant; il les trempera dans le sang de l'oiseau égorgé et dans l'eau vive; il effectuera sept aspersions sur la maison; c'est ainsi qu'il purifiera la maison de son péché, au moyen du sang de l'oiseau, de l'eau vive, de l'oiseau vivant, du bois de cèdre, de l'hysope et du cramoisi éclatant (14: 51-2).

La purification par l'hysope apparaît encore dans un passage du psaume 51 dont la thématique globale est celle de la purification de David après qu'il fut allé chez Bethsabée:

> Aie pitié de moi, mon Dieu, selon ta fidélité; selon ta grande miséricorde, efface mes torts. Lave-moi sans cesse de ma faute et purifie-moi de mon péché ... Voici, dans la faute que j'ai été enfanté et, dans le péché, conçu des ardeurs de ma mère. Voici, tu aimes la vérité des ténèbres, dans ma nuit, tu me fais connaître la sagesse. Ote mon péché avec l'hysope, et je serai pur; lave-moi, et je serai plus blanc que la neige (Ps. 51: 1-2, 5-7).

3. L'hysope dans les textes liturgiques

Les textes liturgiques médiévaux mentionnant l'usage de l'hysope concernent essentiellement le rite de la dédicace de l'église et de la consécration de l'autel. L'*Ordo romanus* 42, selon la numérotation proposée par l'éditeur des rituels romains anciens, Michel Andrieu, décrit le rite de la dédicace ainsi que celui de la déposition des reliques à Rome (vers 700-50), tandis que l'*Ordo romanus* 41 donne le texte de la dédicace d'une église en pays franc (vers 750-75).[9] Dans ces textes, l'essentiel du rituel est concentré autour de la déposition des reliques des martyrs et de la consécration de l'autel. A côté de cela, on accorde une grande importance aux lustrations. C'est ainsi que l'on voit à plusieurs reprises l'évêque procéder à des aspersions, accompagnées de bénédictions, sur les murs extérieurs et intérieurs de l'église, de même que sur l'autel. Derrière ces gestes, se cache une forte connotation liée au symbolisme baptismal. Dans le rituel romain, ces diverses et multiples aspersions sont réalisées à l'aide d'une branche d'hysope. Les textes des *Ordines* 41 et 42 ont été largement repris dans la compilation liturgique majeure de la seconde moitié du Xe siècle, le pontifical romano-germanique,[10] réalisée à Mayence, siège du pouvoir politique et religieux de l'Empire ottonien, et destinée à doter les évêques de l'Empire d'un instrument liturgique à la mesure de leur rôle dans l'organisation du *Reichskirchensystem*. Dans les pontificaux romains de la seconde moitié du Moyen Age, ces textes ne seront que très peu changés ou retouchés par les liturgistes de la Curie à Rome et le schéma général du déroulement du rite de la dédicace tel qu'il apparaît dans le pontifical romano-germanique est celui maintenu dans le texte des différentes versions du pontifical romain.[11] Voici le début du texte de ce rituel:

> Ordo a benedicendam ecclesiam: In primis erunt preparata in ecclesia quecumque necessaria, id est fasciculus ysopi, de quo fiat aspersorium longum; duo vasa magna cum aqua pro duplici aqua benedicenda, quorum unum ponatur ante fores ecclesie, aliud coram altari.

Plus loin dans le rituel, au moment de la consécration de l'autel, on prévoit que l'évêque exécute les gestes suivants:

> Deinde in dextera parte atque sinistra per quatuor cornua altaris scilicet faciat similiter cruces, repetens in qualibet unctione verba premissa et cum ysopo aspergat et circueat ipsum altare tribus vicibus vel septem canendo antiphonam 'Asperges me … dealbator' (Ps. 51: 9).

Dans le pontifical de Guillaume Durand, de la seconde moitié du XIIIe siècle, d'autres rituels que celui de la dédicace de l'église et de la consécration de l'autel atteste l'utilisation de l'hysope. C'est par exemple le cas du rituel de la visite des paroisses par un évêque qui mentionne: 'Et mox, tradens ysopum alicui sacerdoti

---

9   Michel Andrieu, *Les ordines romani du haut Moyen Age*, 5 vols, Spicilegium sacrum lovaniense, 11, 23, 24, 28, 29 (Louvain, 1931-1961), iv, 339-47 et 397-402.
10 Cyrille Vogel, Reinhard Elze, *Le pontifical romano-germanique du dixième siècle*, 3 vols, Studi e Testi, 226, 227, 269 (Città del Vaticano, 1963-1972), i, 82-9.
11 Michel Andrieu, *Le pontifical romain au Moyen Age*, 4 vols, Studi e Testi, 86, 87, 88, 99 (Città del Vaticano, 1938, 1940, 1941), i, 176-97, et ii, 420-48.

superpellicium et stolam habenti, manum eius osculanti, ut aspergat totum cimiterium, ipse autem, prosequitur dicens …'.[12] Toujours dans le pontifical de Guillaume Durand, il est également question de l'hysope dans un passage de l'*ordo ad recipiendum processionaliter prelatum vel legatum*:

> … Deinde surgit et tunc prelatus vel, eo absente, maior ipsius ecclesie offert sibi ysopum cum aqua benedicta, ut se et circumstantes aspergat, et thus benedicendum in thuribulo ponendum.[13]

L'importance accordée à l'usage de l'hysope dans le rituel de la dédicace de l'église est particulièrement évidente à la lecture d'un passage extrait de la vie de sainte Berthe de Blangy.[14] Après trois tentatives infructueuses pour édifier son église, la sainte réussit enfin à faire procéder à la consécration de l'édifice par onze évêques. Mais, le jour de la dédicace venu, l'évêque diocésain se désole de voir que Berthe n'avait pas prévu d'hysope et prétend ainsi qu'il ne peut procéder aux rites. Face à Berthe, l'évêque prononce ces mots:

> Sans hysope, aucun d'entre nous n'oserait d'aucune manière dédicacer une église, à l'encontre de la constitution transmise à nous par les Pères, pour que l'*ordo* de notre ministère ne paraisse pas négliger ou contredire les constitutions canoniques, et soit pour cela jugé criticable.[15]

Tandis que Berthe priait dans son oratoire pour qu'un miracle se produise, un marchand d'hysope vint à passer par là et le rituel de la dédicace de l'église peut se dérouler normalement non sans que Berthe eut adressé des reproches aux évêques présents. Anne-Marie Helvétius a donné une interprétation de ce passage de la vie de sainte Berthe de Blangy.[16] Selon cet auteur, l'épisode est remarquable non seulement à cause de ce qu'il suppose comme connaissance par la sainte des détails du déroulement de la liturgie—ce qui n'est pas du ressort des femmes—, mais aussi et surtout du fait que l'insistance sur l'oubli de l'hysope apparaîtrait comme une faute mineure, voire insignifiante, qui ne mettrait nullement en question l'exécution du rite. Dans la dernière partie de cette contribution, je vais essayer de

---

12 Andrieu, *Pontifical romain*, iii, 625.

13 *Ibid.*, iii, 627.

14 Dans un passage du *De consecratione*, Suger écrit 'Populus enim pro intolerabili magnitudinis sue impetu foris agebatur, et dum chorus prefatus aquam benedictam extra, hysopo ecclesie parietes virtuose aspergendo …', montrant également l'importance de cet usage dans le récit de la dédicace de l'église de Saint-Denis; Suger, *Œuvres*, texte établi, traduit et commenté par Françoise Gasparri (Paris, 1996), i, 44.

15 Anne-Marie Helvétius, 'Le saint et la sacralisation de l'espace en Gaule du nord d'après les sources hagiographiques (VIIe-XIe siècle)', dans *Le sacré et son inscription dans l'espace à Byzance et en Occident. Etudes comparées*, Byzantina Sorbonensia, 18 (Paris, 2001), 137-61, sp. 151-2, les traductions sont celles de l'auteur.

16 Helvétius, 'Le saint et la sacralisation', 151-2.

montrer que ce détail, l'hysope, prévu dans la dédicace de l'église est au contraire fondamental pour la validité sacramentelle du rite et que l'épisode de la vie de sainte Berthe de Blangy a précisément pour fonction de mettre en évidence le caractère indispensable de la plante pour le bon fonctionnement du rite de la dédicace. Pour cela, il me faut explorer un dernier genre littéraire, les textes exégétiques portant sur la signification théologique de la liturgie.

4. L'hysope dans les commentaires sur la liturgie

Les commentateurs de la liturgie ont dès le haut Moyen Age donné une signification théologique à l'hysope qui s'inspire en partie de l'interprétation étymologique d'Isidore de Séville à laquelle j'ai fait allusion plus haut. Dans sa grande encyclopédie *De universo*, Raban Maur au IXe siècle souligne les vertus spirituelles contenues à travers l'hysope: 'Hyssopus herba humilis, cuius radices saxum penetrant: quod significat humilitatem poenitentiae, sive baptismum, ut in psalterio: Asperges me hyssopo, et mundabor'.[17] D'emblée soulignons la forte connotation purificatrice accordée par le commentateur carolingien aux vertus de l'hysope. D'une certaine manière, on pourrait affirmer que chez Raban Maur, les vertus thérapeutiques de la plante, liées—on l'a vu—aux soins qu'elle permet pour lutter contre les affections respiratoires, donc du souffle, sont également applicables au domaine spirituel. Dans son traité sur la dédicace de l'église, Rémi d'Auxerre, toujours au IXe siècle, ne dit mot sur la signification théologique de l'hysope. Dans la seconde moitié du XIIIe siècle, l'autre grand commentateur de la liturgie au Moyen Age à côté de Raban Maur, Guillaume Durand, insiste également sur le double symbolisme baptismal et purificateur lié à l'usage de l'hysope dans le rite de la dédicace de l'église et de la consécration de l'autel: 'Trina autem interius et exterius cum ysopo ex aqua benedicta aspersi; trinam baptizandi immersionem significat'.[18] On le voit clairement, plus encore que chez Raban Maur, la purification de l'église et de l'autel par l'hysope au moment du rite est étroitement associée à la purification sacramentelle réalisée au moment du baptême. Ceci ne suprend nullement si l'on pense au fort parallélisme établi par les théologiens médiévaux entre le baptême et le rite de la dédicace de l'église, au cours duquel c'est l'édifice qui est baptisé, étant donné l'action purificatrice exercée par les aspersions des murs du bâtiment. Dans ce cadre, l'hysope joue un rôle de première importance étant donné son usage à des fins purificatrices dans les textes vétéro-testamentaires ainsi que ses vertus thérapeutiques également centrées autour de la notion de purification, cette fois corporelle. D'autres théologiens après Guillaume Durand, comme par

---

17 *PL* 111.527-8.
18 *Guillemi Duranti Rationale Divinorum Officiorum I-VIII*, ed. A. Davril et T. M. Thibodeau, 3 vols, CCCM, 140, 140A-B (Turnhout, 1995-2000), i, 68-9.

exemple Jacques de Voragine, reprendront à leur compte la signification de l'hysope donnée par l'évêque de Mende dans son *Rational des Divins Offices*.

A l'ensemble de ces texte, ajoutons les intéressants passages extraits de l'*Hortus deliciarum* du XIIe siècle dans lequel il est question à diverses reprises de l'hysope. Par exemple, à propos de la sagesse de Salomon, le texte rappelle la notion de purification en y ajoutant une dimension nettement pénitentielle:

> Salomon sedens super ligna disputavit a cedro Lybani usque ysopum qui exit per parietem ... Intueamur autem quomodo Christus disputaverit a cedro Lybani usque ad ysopum qui exit per parietem ... Ysopus est herba humilis purgans pectus et pulmonem ... Quis est ysopus, nisi humanitas Christi purgans a peccato et a pena peccati? ... Ysopus enim fuit Christus humiliter mortem gustando, cedrus fuit excellentissime resurgendo. Paries per quem ysopus exit, quem exeundo non corrumpit, est virgo Maria de qua Christus processit, et virginitatis sigillum non fregit.[19]

Conclusion

A l'issue de cette brève contribution destinée à honorer un ami et un grand historien de la liturgie, j'espère avoir montré tout l'intérêt pour le médiéviste de la nécessité de sonder l'histoire de la liturgie du Moyen Age jusque dans ses moindres recoins, là où l'on ne s'attend pas obligatoirement à y trouver le symbolisme le plus profond. Concernant l'hysope, on a pu constater à quel point sa signification théologique, dans le cadre du rite de la dédicace de l'église et de la consécration de l'autel était puissante, tournée à la fois vers les propriétés de la plante dans son usage médicinal et en direction de ses vertus spirituelles purificatrices. A n'en pas douter, d'autres enquêtes de ce genre mériteraient d'être entreprises afin de .préciser mieux encore la manière dont le végétal et le sacré se rencontrent dans la liturgie médiévale.

---

19 Herrad of Hohenbourg [Herrade de Landsberg], *Hortus Deliciarum*, ed. Rosalie B. Green, 2 vols (London, 1979), n° 724.

Chapter 4

Necrological Evidence of the Place and Permanence of the Subdiaconate

Charles Hilken

On the fourteenth kalends of June, **Iaquintus, subdeacon and abbot**, died; and brothers
of our congregation, Albertus priest and monk, [Brother Antonius de Pomaro], Petrus
deacon and monk, Petrus deacon and monk, [Leo subdeacon and monk], Benedictus,
Iohannes, Berardus, Iohannes, Azzo, Petrus, and Iohannes, monks; [in the year
MCCXLVIII, **Bartholomeus subdeacon and chaplain of the lord pope, and
archdeacon of San Germano**]. *Montecassino, Archivio dell'Abbazia, MS 47, fo 291r
(square brackets [ ] denote additions to the necrology; bold indicates names
highlighted or written in red ink).*

The foregoing necrological entry from Montecassino consists of the names of
fourteen monks, three of whom are subdeacons. One of the subdeacons was an
abbot, another a monk, and the last a papal subdeacon and chaplain as well as the
archdeacon of San Germano, the city that lay at the foot of Montecassino. What, if
anything, can be understood by the prominence of the subdiaconate in this liturgical
remembrance of the dead?

The subdiaconate, one of the grades or orders of ordained clergy in the medieval church, no longer exists in the Roman Catholic church which, in modern times,
has reduced the number of orders to the episcopate, presbyterate, and diaconate,
thereby suppressing the subdiaconate and the minor orders of porter, lector, exorcist, and acolyte.[1] In its long history, the subdiaconate inhabited a middle ground
between major and minor orders. The major orders of bishop, priest, and deacon
were marked off in the liturgies of ordination by a laying on of hands; they were

---

1 Paul VI, *Ministeria quaedam*, motu proprio, 15 August 1972, *Acta apostolicae sedis*, 64 (1972),
   529-34, reformed the norms of the sacrament of Holy Orders. The *Code of Canon Law*
   (Washington, D.C., 1983), book 4, title 6, defines Holy Orders. See c. 1008: 'By divine institution
   some among the Christian faithful are constituted sacred ministers through the sacrament of orders
   by means of the indelible character with which they are marked; accordingly they are consecrated
   and deputed to shepherd the people of God, each in accord with his own grade of orders, by
   fulfilling in the person of Christ the Head the functions of teaching, sanctifying and governing';
   and c. 1009: '§1. The orders are the episcopate, the presbyterate, and the diaconate. §2. They are
   conferred by an imposition of hands and by the consecratory prayer which the liturgical books
   prescribe for the individual grades'; c. 230 provides for the establishment of the lay ministries of
   lector and acolyte, which were formerly numbered among the minor orders.

further characterized, at least in the medieval era, by universal celibacy and by ministry at the altar of the eucharist. The rites of ordination for the minor orders did not include the imposition of hands by presiding clerics, but rather only the bestowal of various objects associated with the ministries involved. Clerics in minor orders were not held to the strict rule of celibacy and did not attend at the altar during the eucharist. In the early Middle Ages, the status of the subdiaconate as a major or minor order was unclear. The conferral of office by the laying on of hands was not part of subdiaconal ordination.[2] Subdeacons, however, did approach the altar with the wine and water for the chalice, and the wash-basin and towel for the *lavabo* during the preparation of the offerings. There is also a record, especially in papal decrees, of injunctions of universal celibacy for the subdiaconate. By the pontificate of Innocent III, at the beginning of the thirteenth century, the entire Latin church accorded the subdiaconate the status of a major order.

In his essay, 'The Subdiaconate as a Sacred and Superior Order', Roger E. Reynolds carefully laid out the history of the permanent inclusion of the subdiaconate in the major ecclesiastical orders, a transformation that he proved took place in the eleventh and twelfth centuries. Professor Reynolds studied the liturgical, canonical, and theological literature of the era, and gave special attention to papal and synodal decrees. The intention of this essay is to relate the evidence from historical records in these same centuries to Reynolds' argument.[3]

What are the other sources for the history of the subdiaconate? The diplomatic record is episodic and narrowly focused, for the most part, on political and economic activities. Diplomas reveal activities and offices that went beyond the liturgical, but their passing references to subdeacons as legal actors do not reveal any perspective in particular on the extent of and regard for the subdiaconate itself. Is there a way to get at the fuller picture of the order of subdeacons, the ordinariness of their place in their ecclesiastical communities? Necrologies can be of service here. Ecclesiastical communities, especially monastic ones, produced

---

2 Gaetano Moroni, 'Suddiacono', in *Dizionario di erudizione storico-ecclesiastica* (Venice, 1855), lxxi, 3-24, at 6, knew of evidence of imposition of hands in Spain and Visigothic Gaul.

3 See Roger E. Reynolds, 'The Subdiaconate as a Sacred and Superior Order', in *Clerics in the Early Middle Ages* (Aldershot, 1999), no. IV, 1-39. See also Moroni, 'Suddiacono', at 7 for conclusions worth noting as anticipating those of Reynolds: '1. Che errarano quelli che ad Urbano II, e molto più quelli che ad Innocenzo III riferiscono, siccome ad autore, che sagro addivenisse il suddiaconato; 2. Che tuttavia Innocenzo III fu il primo il quale chiaramente affermasse "Subdiaconatum hodie inter sacros ordines computari"; 3. Che la ragione, per la quale a sagro ordine fu innalzato il suddiaconato, quella stessa fu per la quale Urbano II avea ai suddiaconi conceduto di potere qualche volta col permesso della santa Sede essere promossi al vescovato, cioè "quia et ipsi altaribus administrant"; 4. Che sino al IX secolo non fu il suddiaconato tenuto sagro; 5. Che da quel tempo fu varia intorno a ciò la disciplina della chiesa romana, ma che dopo Innocenzo III costantemente fu per sagro riguardato tal ordine'. Reynolds differed substantially from Moroni's fourth point by demonstrating the great ambiguity of the evidence for the status of the subdiaconate before the eleventh century.

necrologies according to a logic that made them simultaneously remarkably inclusive and exclusive records; exclusive because the community narrowly defined the categories of names remembered, but inclusive in that once the categories were established, communities strove for both completeness and permanence in the building of a necrology. If 'subdiaconus' was one of the titles remembered by communities in the remembrance of the dead—and it was—then the necrology beyond any other historical or liturgical text holds the promise of a fuller picture of the medieval subdiaconate. The present study concerns evidence of the subdiaconate contained in the necrology of Montecassino. The particular merits of the necrology of the great abbey of Saint Benedict are threefold. One is the abbey's proximity to and relations with the see of Peter in Rome. Changes emanating from the papacy, especially in the era of the Gregorian church reforms, would have likely affected the customs of the Cassinese community as much or more than elsewhere. Secondly, Montecassino's tradition of keeping necrologies was ancient and fully developed, and its connections to other monasteries throughout Europe wide and deep. Lastly, the necrology of the abbey, now Archivio dell'Abbazia, MS 47, fos 275v-311v, is a record of more than four centuries.

What is the evidence of the necrology of Montecassino for the permanence and importance of the subdiaconate? This question is best answered by beginning with the state of affairs at the abbey in the middle of the twelfth century. Sometime between September 1164 and July 1166, the scriptorium finished work on a new chapter book containing a martyrology, Rule of St. Benedict, homiliary, and necrology.[4] The scribe copied names from older necrologies, so that the new work included names from the entire history of the community.

---

4   The necrology of the abbey was published in photographic plates by Mauro Inguanez, ed., *I necrologi cassinesi*, 1: *Il necrologio del Codice Cassinese 47*, Fonti per la Storia d'Italia, 83 (Rome, 1941); Dom Inguanez provided an index of the names in the necrology. Heinrich Dormeier, *Montecassino und die Laien im 11. und 12. Jahrhundert*, *MGH Schriften*, 27 (Stuttgart, 1979), 108-27, has published the most thorough study of the necrology thus far. Dormeier's arguments for the date of composition incorporate past studies, including Hartmut Hoffmann, 'Der Kalender des Leo Marsicanus', *Deutsches Archiv für Erforschung des Mittelalters*, 21 (1965), 126-7. Hoffman gave a *terminus post quem* of 1159 based upon the first-hand death notice of Pope Hadrian IV (1 Sept) and a *terminus ante quem* of 1166 based upon the addition of the death notice of Abbot Raynald (15 July). Dormeier ventured a *terminus post quem* of 1164 based upon the addition of the death year 1164 to a first-hand entry of the priest-monk Berardus (21 Sept.). See Mariano Dell'Omo, 'Liturgia della memoria a Montecassino: il "Libro dell'Ufficio del Capitolo" nel codice casinense 47', *Benedictina*, 48 (2001), 239-50, for an essential recent study by the sub-archivist of the abbey. The citations in the present paper are from my own working edition of the text.

Table 4.1   Subdeacons in the Necrology of Montecassino 47, fos 275v-311v (cited by name, day and month)

Subdeacons remembered, pre-1164/6	Subdeacons remembered, post-1164/6
Heinricus. 7.I	Placidus. 6.I
Iohannes. 12.I	Bartholomeus de Sancto angelo subd. domini pape. 15.I
Iohannes. 16.I	
Conradus. 18.I	**Benedictus. 22.I**
Rachisius. 22.I	Albertus. 22.I
Gummarius. 28.I	**Gentilis de scarpa. 24.I**
Iohannes. 28.I	Dodo. 25.I
Iohannes. 1.II	Frater Ambrosius. 28.I
Iohannes. 5.II	Landulfus. 29.I
Iohannes. 6.II	Rosellus. 1.II
Algardus. 6.II	Roggerius. 2.II
Iohannes. 12.II	Raynaldus. 2.II
Guido. 15.II	Bartholomeus. 7.II
Lando. 16.II	**Bartholomeus temmari. 10.II**
Guido. 18.II	Iohannes de cell… 23.II
Vitus. 18.II	Siluester. 4.III
Iacobus. 24.II	Dominicus. 7.III
Iohannes. 6.III	Nicolaus. 16.III
Roffridus. 8.III	Benedictus. 17.III
Petrus. 16.III	Ubaldus. 20.III
Octauianus. 20.III	Senebaldi RAINALDVS SVBD. domini pape. 20.III
Homodei. 25.III	
Carbo. 27.III	Landulfus. 23.III
Desiderius. 27.III	Rychardus. 2.IV
Petrus. 28.III (*bis*)	**Matheus subd. et mon. sancte marie de leto. 5.IV**
Timmarius. 1.IV	
Iohannes. 6.IV	Petrus. 6.IV
Petrus. 7.IV	Landulfus. 12.IV
Sanson. 8.IV	Iohannes. 14.IV
Benedictus. 12.IV	Robbertus. 17.IV
Iohannes. 26.IV	Raynaldus. 25.IV
Iohannes. 7.V	Lando. 2.V
Adenulfus. 9.V	Iohannes. 6.V
Sergius. 12.V	Oderisius. 9.V
Iaquintus sub. et abbas. 19.V	Adenulfus. 11.V
Petrus. 22.V	Leo. 19.V
Ingezzo. 31.V	**Bartholomeus subd. et cappellanus domini pape, et Archidiaconus Sancti Germani.** Anno M.CCXLVIII. 19.V
Gezzo. 2.VI	
Benedictus. 24.VI	
Gerardus. 26.VI	Theodinus. 20.V
Iohannes. 30.VI	Nycolaus. 23.V
Landulfus. 4.VII	**Lando subd.** nat… 24.V
Oldericus. 6.VII	Iohannes. 28.V
Teuzo. 12.VII	Guitholus. 29.V
Azzo. 13.VII	Petrus. 7.VI
Deodatus. 22.VII	Bonushomo. 10.VI

Subdeacons remembered, pre-1164/6

Iohannes. 23.VII
Ambrosius. 1.VIII
Otto. 5.VIII
Lando. 9.VIII
Bonus. 9.VIII
Benedictus. 13.VIII
Iohannes. 15.VIII
Pandulfus. 18.VIII
Benedictus. 19.VIII
Raynaldus. 19.VIII
Adelmodus. 23.VIII
Raynaldus. 24.VIII
Rodulfus. 26.VIII
Randisius. 31.VIII
Petrus. 5.IX
Iohannes. 5.IX
Dauferius. 7.IX
Leo. 10.IX
Bernardus. 10.IX
Guido. 14.IX
Landulfus. 15.IX
Ptolomeus. 21.IX
Adenulfus. 26.IX
Petrus. 27.IX
Petrus. 29.IX
Iohannes. 14.X
Spanus. 17.X
Iohannes. 18.X
Paldi. 27.X
Godericus. 29.X
Carolus. 2.XI
Lando. 4.XI
Moyses. 5.XI
Nycolaus. 5.XI
Lambertus. 7.XI
Adenulfusus. 9.XI
Iohannes. 18.XI
Vgo. 21.XI
Benedictus. 26.XI
Manso. 28.XI
Pontius. 1.XII
Mirandus. 3.XII
Benedictus. 3.XII
Guinardus. 7.XII
Richardus. 8.XII
Landulfus. 10.XII
Petrus. 13.XII
Gebizo. 19.XII
Sciphridus. 21.XII

Subdeacons remembered, post-1164/6

Gyradus. 13.VI
Lodoycus. 15.VI
Lando de fun… 16.VI
Theodinus ant… 21.VI
Petrutis de fracte. 23.VI
Petrutius. 25.VI
Guido. 2.VII
Donninus. 7.VII
Matheus. 7.VII
Landulfus. 12.VII
Nicolaus. 12.VII
Franciscus. 18.VII
Otto. 23.VII
Germanus. 24.VII
HENRICVS. 24.VII
Senebaldus. 25.VII
Nycolaus. 25.VII
Laurentius. 25.VII
Leo. 28.VII
Gregorius. 31.VII
Frater Antonius de napoli. 31.VII
Cataldus. 1.VIII
Raynaldus. 3.VIII
Guilielmus. 10.VIII
Arnaldus. 11.VIII
Guilielmus. 11.VIII
Romanus. 12.VIII
Iohannes. 16.VIII
Stephanus. 20.VIII
Rogerius. 24.VIII
Matheus de colle alto. 24.VIII
Iacobus. 25.VIII
Iohannes. 28.VIII
Anzelmus. 29.VIII
Theodinus. 31.VIII
Symon. 1.IX
Gregorius. 2.IX
Guillielmus. 4.IX
Petrus. 6.IX
Berardus. 8.IX
Roggerius. 12.IX
Bonushomo. 18.IX
Iohannes. 18.IX
Raynaldus. 19.IX
Bartholomeus. 20.IX (*bis*)
Guido. 21.IX
Gualterius. 22.IX
Beraldus. 22.IX
Bartholomeus. 23.IX
Leo. 23.IX

Subdeacons remembered, pre-1164/6	Subdeacons remembered, post-1164/6
	Gentilis. 23.IX
	Beraldus. 24.IX
	Nicolaus subd. mon. albanete. 27.IX
	Ptolomeus sublacu... 1.X
	Raynaldus. 3.X
	Guilielmus. 4.X
	Adenulfus. 4.X
	Germanus. 5.X
	Petrus. 7.X
	Raynerius. 8.X
	Roffridus subd. et Notarius *** pape. 9.X
	Berardus. 10.X
	Petrus. 15.X
	Mallerius. 17.X
	Herricus. 18.X
	Beraldus. 20.X
	Iacobus. 20.X
	Symon. 22.X
	Matheus. 27.X
	Gualterius. 7.XI
	Tomas diac. et mon. subd. 10.XI
	GVILIELMVS de ramphi SVBD. 11.XI
	Thomas marentinus(?). 21.XI
	anonymous. 23.XI
	Pandulfus. 30.XI
	Otto. 30.XI
	Manardus. 4.XII
	Iulianus medicus. 5.XII
	Baruson. 6.XII
	Tholomeus. 6.XII
	Amicus. 7.XII
	L***. 7.XII
	Ionathas. 7.XII
	Iohannes. 11.XII
	Raynaldus. 13.XII
	Iohannes. 17.XII
	Petrus. 20.XII
	Raynaldus. anno MCCXIIII. 26.XII

There are 226 subdeacons remembered in the necrology, ninety-six by the scriptorium that produced the book and 130 by later scribes.[5] Occasionally, in the

---

5   A later hand added the title 'subdiaconus' to the monk Iacobus, among the original list of names on 24 February. The addition may mean that a later scribe altered an original entry in order to remember a subdeacon of the same name. With the more than 6500 names, the number of subdeacons is about three and a quarter per cent of the total in the necrology. Given that the regular remembrance of the title of subdeacon seems to have been an eleventh-century development, there is no way to recover the total number of monk-subdeacons within the Cassinese confraternity, the records of which were kept from before the turn of the millennium.

later centuries, names were highlighted in capital letters or in red ink (bold-face above), which indicated special anniversary prayers; still others bear a cognomen or the year of death. The subdeacons whose death preceded the writing of the book, on the other hand, were remembered simply by name and the titles of 'subdiaconus et monachus'. The one among their rank who was recorded in red was an abbot, Iaquintus (19 May), probably the same Iaquintus who gave a personal account of the affairs in his monastery to the historian Leo Marsicanus, and who has been identified by Hartmut Hoffmann as the abbot of San Benedetto in Salerno and a former monk of Montecassino.[6] Two features of the necrology, simplicity and hierarchy, support analyzing the record of subdeacons in the text as evidence of their place within major orders in the middle of the twelfth century. More tentatively, one can read the substantial number of subdeacons that were transcribed into the new book as evidence of the promotion of the subdiaconate to the rank of a major order already at the end of the preceding century.

There is a stately simplicity about the necrology produced in 1164/6, a quality shared by other early monastic necrologies. Names are given without titles, such as 'domnus', or even 'frater'. There are no instances of family or geographic origins, what modern historians might recognize as last names. The *catena* of names reads like a parallel to the names of the saints as they are found in the martyrology. In the latter one finds for men, 'martyr' or 'confessor', coupled with 'episcopus', 'sacerdos', 'diaconus' or 'levita', and sometimes the minor orders; in monastic martyrologies 'heremita' (hermit) appears often.[7] For women in the martyrologies, 'virgo' often appears with 'martyr'. In monastic necrologies, however, 'monachus' is joined to 'abbas', 'episcopus', 'sacerdos', 'diaconus' or 'levita', and 'subdiaconus'. The community's aim seems to have been to create a simple and sober reading of the dead as would befit the divine liturgy. The key thus to the short list of titles is their liturgical or sacramental character. The inclusion of subdeacons in this short

---

6   Leo Marsicanus, *Chronica monasterii casinensis*, 3.13, ed. Hartmut Hoffmann, *MGH Scriptores*, 34 (Hanover, 1980), 376, ll. 26-30, and n. 13. Herbert Bloch, *Monte Cassino in the Middle Ages*, 3 vols (Cambridge, Mass., 1986), i, 224-5, dated the events involving Iaquintus to after 1085. Given the date of Leo's work on the chronicle in *c*. 1100, Abbot Iaquintus must have flourished at the end of the eleventh century and perhaps into the twelfth.

7   In the martyrology of Montecassino 47, one finds subdeacons named three times, all in notices of martyrs of the early church. See 1 May: 'In galliis, territorio uiuariensi sancti andeoli subdiaconi. Quem misit ab oriente sanctus policarpus, cum beato benigno et andochio presbiteris, et tyrso diacono ad predicandum uerbum dei in galliam ...'; 6 August: 'et quattuor subdiaconorum [Xysti papae], ianuarii, magni, uincentii, et stephani ...'; and 17 August: 'Apud africam natale sanctorum martiris liberati abbatis, bonifacii diaconi, seruii et rustici subdiaconorum rogati et septimini monachorum, et maximi pueri ...,' referring to a monastic community in Africa, martyred by the Vandals; see fos 62v, 90r, and 92v. The same memorials may be found within the same Beneventan cultural zone as Montecassino in the martyrology of a Benedictine monastery, Santa Maria de Gualdo Mazzocca, written *c*. 1200; see Vatican City, Biblioteca Apostolica Vaticana, MS Vat. lat. 5949, fos 39r, 71r, and 74r.

list argues for their place among the major orders. The exclusivity of this small
group of titles is all the more clear when one considers the rare instances of offices
that were so important to the daily life of a monastery. Among the major monastic
officers at Montecassino were the 'praepositus' or 'rector casinensis', 'decanus',
'camerarius', 'thesaurarius', 'cellararius', 'vestiarius', 'infirmarius', 'sacrista', and
'hospitalarius'; and, at a later date, a vicar general and an 'yconomus' or procurator
of the monastery.[8] In the necrology there are only thirty references in total to any of
the preceding offices, and all of these are later additions.[9]

A strict hierarchy of names is also evidence of Montecassino's inclusion of the
subdiaconate in major orders in the eleventh century. Monks precede seculars, and
among the monks, names are arranged in the following order. Monks who were
also bishop or abbot are listed first. Next comes priest-monks, followed by deacon-
monks, and in fourth place are subdeacon monks.[10] Following those who are in
Holy Orders are lay monks and, at the end of the list and before the secular names,
the collective title 'monachi'. So in the example above from 19 May, one reads,
'Benedictus, Iohannes, Berardus, Iohannes, Azzo, Petrus, et Iohannes, monachi'.
The clerical hierarchy observed among the names of the professed monks seems to
have been the invention of the makers of Montecassino 47, at least with respect to
the Cassinese community. The fragmentary necrology that survived from the
abbacy of Desiderius does not observe such a hierarchy, nor did the earlier
necrologies in close proximity to the Cassinese community.[11] Leo Marsicanus, the
first author of the abbey's *Chronicle,* was inconsistent, in his liturgical calendar of
the dead, at times naming ordained monks by orders but just as often not.[12] In the
oldest necrology at Montecassino, that of a nearby daughter-house of the abbey,
San Nicola della Cicogna, from the middle of the eleventh century, there is no
evidence of a clerical hierarchy.[13] All of this is to argue for the novelty of the

---

8   The best and most thorough study of the monastic offices at Montecassino is by Luigi Fabiani, *La
    Terra di San Benedetto: Studio storico-giuridico sull'Abbazia di Montecassino dall'VIII al XIII
    secolo,* 2 vols, Miscellanea Cassinese, 34 (Montecassino, 1968), ii, 97-162.

9   For 'praepositus' see 4 April, 23 May, 12 and 20 July, 2 and 27 Sept., and 27 Oct.; and 'prior' on 6
    Jan., 10 March, 6, 18, and 21 Aug. For 'decanus', see 10 Jan., 25 and 28 March, 13, 19, and 21
    April, 29 June, and 16 Dec. For 'camerarius', see 11 June. For 'thesaurarius', see 22 April and 11
    Sept. For 'cellararius', see 3 July and 5 Sept. For 'infirmarius', see 15 June and 8 Nov. For
    'sacrista', see 30 May. For 'hospitalarius', see 6 April.

10 There are no monks in minor orders remembered in the original work. Eighteen acolytes are
    recorded by adding hands. See 21 Feb.; 15 April; 2 and 29 May; 2 June; 21 and 28 Aug.; 2, 6, 16
    (bis), and 24 Sept.; 7, 21 and 22 Oct.; and 3, 27, and 30 Nov.

11 See Dormeier, *Montecassino und die Laien,* 122-5.

12 Note, for example, 25 July: 'Benedictus diaconus et monachus. Winizo monachus. Nantari
    sacerdos et monachus'; 28 July: 'Todinus monachus et diaconus. Iohannes (sar.) episcopus et
    monachus. Azzo monachus'; and 3 December: 'Mirandus subdiaconus et monachus. Benedictus
    sacerdos et (S. D.) abbas'. See Hoffmann, 'Der Kalender', 114 and 124.

13 See Charles Hilken, ed., *The Necrology of San Nicola della Cicogna,* Studies and Texts, 135,
    Monumenta Liturgica Beneventana, 2 (Toronto, 2000), 59-62.

hierarchical arrangement in Montecassino 47. This innovation is consistent with two points stressed by Roger Reynolds. First, the centrality of the eucharist for the theology of orders at this time led to a similar increase in respect for the ministers of the altar.[14] Secondly, this rising tide of liturgical and theological approbation lifted the subdiaconate into the major orders, that is, among those who preside at the altar.

It is difficult to determine how long the monks had been remembering the title of subdeacon in their death notices. In the Cicogna necrology, written sometime between 1031 and 1058/71, and supplemented thereafter, there are 1150 names, most of which are of men and women who died before the end of the twelfth century. Of these, there are twenty-one subdeacons. Furthermore, the title of sub-deacon seems to be absent from the earliest stratum of names, an observation that argues for the change that Reynolds has discerned in the progress of the subdiaconate to a major order in the eleventh and twelfth centuries. As one approaches the end of the eleventh century, there exists clear evidence of a liturgi-cal remembrance of the subdiaconate. Leo Marsicanus' calendar records thirteen subdeacons (of a total of 357 entries), ten of whom are part of the earliest stratum of names in the necrology. The new interest in recording the names of subdeacons cannot be taken as evidence for the lack of subdeacons before the end of the eleventh century. As Reynolds has shown there is ample evidence for the ordination of subdeacons in the liturgical and theological books, although it remains to be seen whether the number of subdeacons increased, and whether the office itself developed during the eleventh and twelfth centuries. These questions are related to the topic of the permanence of the subdiaconate, or its place as a terminal ministry within the hierarchy. What light can the necrologies shed on the office itself?

Apart from the indirect evidence of such a great number of subdeacons remem-bered, there is no way of determining from the necrology in what ways monastic life provided subdeacons a life-long ministry. The simplicity of the notices ob-scures the knowledge of what other monastic offices subdeacons might have held. In this regard, the record shows only that, in the early group of names, Iaquintus was also an abbot; and that, after 1164/6, four subdeacons were in service to the papal court, and yet a fifth was a physician at the abbey. The fact that one of the chaplain-subdeacons was also an archdeacon of San Germano shows that local clerics could receive additional ordinations in the Roman church. Enough is known

---

14 Roger E. Reynolds, *The Ordinals of Christ from their Origins to the Twelfth Century*, Beiträge zur Geschichte und Quellenkunde des Mittelalters, 7 (Berlin, 1978), 162: 'Throughout the early Middle Ages the theological presupposition underlying the chronological Ordinals was a type of recapitulation theory, but with the late eleventh and early twelfth centuries the theological pre-supposition changed to the eucharistic sacrifice of the true *sacerdos*. Just as the Last Supper was the determinative event in the institution of the ecclesiastical grades, so the hierarchical relation-ship of the grades was determined by their relationship to the Eucharist'.

from diplomatic and historical sources to give some understanding of the ministries of these few subdeacons whom the necrology highlights.

Whereas the election of subdeacons to the abbacy did not appear controversial in the eleventh century, it became so in the twelfth. Leo's account of Iaquintus made no mention of his clerical status. His identity as a subdeacon comes only from the necrology, where his anniversary enjoyed special rites. The election of subdeacons as abbots became problematic with the increased respect for the sacredness of the eucharist and its ministers. One can see this in the work of the continuator of Leo's *Chronicle*, Peter the Deacon, who recounted the removal of an abbot of Montecassino in 1137, partly on the grounds that his status as subdeacon jeopardized the dignity and right functioning of the office of abbot. The deposition of Abbot Raynald I (10 Feb.-8 Sept. 1137) was part of the larger struggle of the schism between Pope Innocent II (1130-43) and Pope Anacletus II (1130-38), and that struggle was most to blame for the abbatial crisis at Montecassino in 1137.[15] Emperor Lothar II (1125-38) and Pope Innocent II conspired to remove Abbot Raynald because of their doubt about his political loyalties, while military troops loyal to King Roger of Sicily, the supporter of Pope Anacletus, had supervised the election of the abbot, who was a subdeacon of Anacletus.[16] Emperor Lothar's successful military campaign against King Roger in the spring and summer of 1137 gave the imperial court, with the assistance of Pope Innocent II, the occasion to judge and depose Raynald. Once in July and again in September, the imperial court tried Raynald. In July, the prosecutor, who spoke for the Roman church, was Gerard, cardinal priest of Santa Croce in Gerusalemme, himself the future Pope Lucius II (1144-5). Raynald's defender was Peter the Deacon, librarian and the very narrator of these same events. After Peter defended the legitimacy of the election and therefore of the elect, Gerard countered with a canon from Pope Eugenius I (824-7) that would seem to have disallowed the election of anyone below the order of deacon.[17] Peter responded with the sage observation that papal

---

15 There are two accounts of the deposition, both by Peter the Deacon. One is in the *Chronica*, 4.102-22, *MGH Scriptores*, 34.564-96; and the other in *Petri diaconi altercatio pro cenobio Casinensi*, ed. Erich Caspar, *Petrus Diaconus und die Monte Cassineser Fälschungen* (Berlin, 1909), 248-80.

16 *Chronica*, 4.104, *MGH Scriptores*, 34.565, ll. 28-31: 'Quod dum Raynaldus certo certius agnovisset, clam cum Canzolino aliisque fidelibus regis paciscitur, eique fidelitatem faciens, abbatiam illi confirmant; sicque sacramentum a colonis monasterii accipiens a filio Petri Leonis, cuius subdiaconus erat, in Casinensi abbatia firmatur'. Here the author referred to Pope Anacletus as the son of Pietro Leone. Little or nothing is known about Raynald, except a vague reference to his origins. Peter called him 'Raynaldus Hetruriensis', or the Tuscan Raynald, in order to distinguish him from his rival and later successor, Raynald of Collimento.

17 *Chronica*, 4.113, *MGH Scriptores*, 34.584, ll. 36-7: 'Abbates per monasteria tales eligantur, qui levitico vel sacerdotali honore sint prediti'. Compare this with the original in *Concilium Romanum, 14-15 November 826*, c. 27, in *Concilia aevi Karolini*, ed. Albertus Werminghoff, *MGH Concilia*, 2/ii (Hanover and Leipzig, 1908), 578: 'XXVII. Quales abbates sint constituendi. Abbates etenim per coenobia vel, ut instanti tempore nuncupantur, monasteria tales constituantur, qui sui vocabuli

laws have been many times changed and that what was important was that a Cassinese abbot be elected by his congregation and 'according to the fear of God and Rule of blessed Benedict'.[18] Gerard appealed to the abbey's need to stay in communion with the catholic church and therefore the importance of the legal canon. But Gerard then went further and gave good reason for the canonical restrictions. His argument is a valuable witness to his generation's concern for hierarchy and the ordination to ministry.

> And if those who are elected do not enjoy the levitical or sacerdotal honor, how according to the precept of the Rule can they read the Gospel lesson or how sing the mass? How can they loose or bind anyone? How would priests and deacons fall down at the feet of a subdeacon? How could he place incense and bless priests and deacons? For lectors, exorcists, porters, acolytes, and subdeacons are subject to the offices of levites and priests, and, if subject to, how could they be set over? For indeed, as Saint Sylvester says, let not lector, exorcist, porter, acolyte, [or] subdeacon be placed over deacon or priest. Thus Father Benedict desiring to send an abbot into Gaul, sent not a subdeacon or any one else there but Maurus the most holy deacon. How therefore can the election said to be ratified of an excommunicated and schismatic subdeacon?[19]

The excommunication was *de facto* because Raynald was in communion with an anti-pope, and the schism was the conclusion that Gerard reached based upon his reading of the force of the canon of Pope Eugenius. It is important to note that the difficulties that Gerard saw derived mostly from monastic customs and partly from a concern for right worship. Gerard's understanding of ordination and the sacraments presented obstacles to the right functioning of an abbot who was a layman or in minor orders (and here he seems to have assigned the subdiaconate to the minor orders). He could cite an ancient canon and paint mental pictures of seemingly unacceptable situations in monastic ritual. Peter the Deacon conceded nothing to

---

ministerium Deo possint indubitanter supplere, ita docti, ut, quandoque fratrum neglegentia acciderit, omnino cognoscere possint et emendare. Sacerdotalem quoque sint honorem adepti, ut peccantium sibi subiectorum fratrum valeant omnimodis refrenare et amputare commissa, et ita observent, ut statuta regularum per omnia non inveniantur delinqui.—Forma minor. XXVII. Abbates per monasteria tales ordinentur, qui sibi subiectos bene regere possint. Sacerdotali quoque sint honore adepti'. It should be noted that Cardinal Gerard's citation differs from the ancient canon by the addition of the levitical, that is, diaconal order.

18 *Chronica*, 4.113, *MGH Scriptores*, 34.585, l. 12.

19 *Ibid.*, ll. 16-27: 'Et si levitico vel sacerdotali honore non funguntur hii, qui eligendi sunt, quomodo iuxta preceptum regule lecturi sunt lectionem evangelii, et missam cantare quomodo possunt? Quomodo aliquem possunt solvere vel ligare? Qualiter ad subdiaconi pedes presbiteri vel diaconi ruent? Qualiter incensum ponent et presbiteris vel diaconibus benedicent? Nam lectores, exorciste, hostiarii, acoliti et subdiaconi subiacent officiis levitarum et sacerdotum et, si subiacent, quomodo preficientur? Non enim, ut ait sanctus Silvester, lector, exorcista, hostiarius, acolitus, subdiaconus super diaconum vel presbiterum preponatur. Hinc pater Benedictus abbatem in Gallia dirigere cupiens non subdiaconum vel alium quemque, set Maurum ibi levitam direxit sanctissimum. Quomodo ergo electio de subdiacono excommunicato vel scismatico rata dici poterit?'

Gerard's argument; and the emperor, tiring of the debate, brought things to a close by allowing that the monks had the right to judge themselves as to the justice or injustice of their practices.[20]

The emperor then referred the entire case to the pope asking for a judgment within four days. The ensuing discussions between Peter and the papal representatives were confined to papal prerogatives in the affairs of Montecassino. On the fourth day, the pope restored Raynald to full communion and accepted his oath of loyalty. The emperor named Raynald an imperial chaplain and so honored and forgiven, Raynald returned to Montecassino.

Abbot Raynald's downfall happened in the following manner. He returned in the company of a cardinal to Montecassino and there with the monks rejected and broke communion with Pope Anacletus. Shortly thereafter, however, his rivals reported to the emperor that he had received the messengers of King Roger. This report was enough to make the emperor seek Raynald's removal, and the emperor presided over a second trial in the chapter room of Montecassino. Peter the Deacon, this time, was only a witness. Before the trial, Abbot Raynald assembled the monks to urge them to testify that they had indeed elected him, lest control of the abbey pass out of their hands. At this, an argument broke out between the monks and certain lay members present, in which the monks accused Raynald of wanting to remain abbot for the laymen and not for them. This division within the chapter room surfaced again in the trial before the emperor. After removing Raynald's supporters from the room, the emperor listened to the arguments against the abbot. Many monks stepped forward to accuse Raynald of making promises in order to gain the election. The 'vestiarius' Pandulf presented the final and definitive argument, which resembled Gerard's argument about the unsuitability of the subdiaconate for the ministry of an abbot:

> Though there are many things that we could bring forth about this election, there is one nevertheless, that seems to be intolerable, namely that he [Raynald] was ordained by Pietro son of Pietro Leone, and it is most unworthy that, in so great a church, which is head and mother of all monasteries, a subdeacon abbot be had, who can neither celebrate mass nor confer remission of sins.[21]

Pandulf managed to join the argument about Raynald's connections to the antipope to his major argument that an abbot should be able to preside at mass and

---

20 *Ibid.*, ll. 27-29: 'Ea, que vel inuste vel iuste usque modo Casinenses fecere monachi, eis per omnia dimittere dignum duximus'.

21 *Chronica*, 4.120, *MGH Scriptores*, 34.595, ll. 5-10: 'Cum multa sint, que in electo proferre possemus, unum tamen est, quod in eo intolerandum esse videtur, scilicet quod a Petro filio Petri Leonis ordinatus, et valde indignum est, ut in tanta ecclesia, que caput et mater est omnium monasteriorum, abbas subdiaconus habeatur, qui nec missarum sollempnia celebrare nec veniam possit conferre delictorum'.

confess sins. His intervention was persuasive. The emperor referred the judgment to Pope Innocent II who was below in San Germano. Two days later, a team of cardinals read the sentence of deposition, and Raynald then placed his pastoral staff, ring, and Rule of St. Benedict on the tomb of the founder.

The deposition of Abbot Raynald offers good evidence of the new theology of holy orders. At the same time, it shows that the subdiaconate still inhabited a middle ground between the major and minor orders. Ironically, the same theology that began to raise the order of subdeacon to the major orders in the minds of Gregorian reformers of the eleventh century is at work here in keeping the subdiaconate in its place, behind deacons and especially priests. In other words, the ministry of the altar has become the paradigm of sacred orders. Yet, as monastic life is sacred and a parallel to ordained ministry, so the abbot, at the pinnacle of the monastic community, must parallel the fullness of sacred orders.

According to the new reasoning, the late eleventh- or early twelfth-century abbacy of Iaquintus at San Benedetto in Salerno becomes an anomaly. As the case of Raynaldus shows, after Iaquintus there will be no more abbots who cannot preside at mass; thus it would be pointless to look for abbot-subdeacons among later necrological notices. Before the mid-eleventh century monks did not record the subdiaconate as a matter of custom; thus the number of abbots who were subdeacons or even laymen cannot be established. Cardinal Gerard's citation of the canon of Pope Eugenius is the work of a reformer, who had found an ancient proof-text in his bid to abolish a 'modern' custom. Peter the Deacon's reminder of the vagaries of papal decretals was certainly the more conservative view. Perhaps he had the last word. The entry of Iaquintus in the necrology for 19 May is in rubric letters that signal a special liturgical cult. The entry is part of the original work of 1164/6, perhaps half a century after Iaquintus' death. It is not impossible to imagine that the Cassinese community chose to highlight abbot and subdeacon Iaquintus as a nod to its own wholesome and ancient traditions.

Abbot Iaquintus is evidence that the subdiaconate could be a terminal or perma-nent order for an individual monk or churchman. Even greater is the evidence offered by the four papal subdeacons:

Bartholomeus de sancto angelo subdiaconus domini pape (15 January).
Senebaldi RAINALDVS SVBDIACONVS domini pape (20 March).
Anno M.CCXLVIII. **Bartholomeus subdiaconus et cappellanus domini pape. et Archidiaconus Sancti Germani** (19 May).
Roffridus subdiaconus et Notarius *** pape (9 October).

These subdeacons, all ordained to service in the Roman church, hold three different titles, 'subdiaconus domini pape', 'subdiaconus et cappellanus domini pape', and 'subdiaconus et Notarius [domini] pape', all of which can be found with some frequency in papal diplomas. The indispensable study for the history of the subdiaconate at Rome is Reinhold Elze's work on the papal chapel.[22] Elze's findings that make the appearance of papal subdeacons in a Cassinese necrology understandable are the following. Early in the development of a papal court that would resemble and in some ways emulate the imperial German court, that is, in the eleventh century, offices that had been primarily liturgical became governmental. So, for example, the papal chaplain expanded in number and duties, from one to nine, from private chaplain to scribe, notary, and judge. Eventually Innocent IV (1243-54) would develop the office into an honorary title bestowed widely throughout Europe. The papal subdiaconate underwent a parallel development. By the end of the eleventh century there were three kinds of subdeacons, grouped mostly according to their ancient liturgical functions. The subdeacons of the basilica attended at pontifical liturgies; the seven regional subdeacons served at stational liturgies; and the seven subdeacons who formed the papal 'schola cantorum' sang at pontifical liturgies. Throughout the twelfth century and into the thirteenth, the papal subdiaconate expanded to perhaps as many as a hundred individuals.[23] In addition to the works cited for the chaplains, its duties expanded as well to include papal legates and judges. By the end of the eleventh century, popes were ordaining canons of Italian and French cathedrals as papal subdeacons, thereby drawing closer the ties that bound Rome to the episcopal sees.[24] The death notice of archdeacon Bartholomew of San Germano (19 May), who was also a papal subdeacon and chaplain, is evidence of this last development.

There is ample evidence that the papal subdiaconate was a training ground for leadership in the church.[25] Elze cited examples of popes choosing subdeacons to be cardinals and even bishops![26] Nevertheless, given the great number of papal

---

22 Reinhold Elze, 'Die päpstliche Kapelle im 12. und 13. Jahrhundert', *ZRG KA*, 37 (1950), 145-204, especially §2. 'Päpstliche Kapelläne und Subdiakone im 12. Jahrhundert', 153-71.

23 See Elze, 'Die päpstliche Kapelle', 169, where the author cited a passage from the *Liber Censuum* of Cencius: 'Priori subdiaconorum unum melequinum. Omnibus aliis subdiaconibus simul, si etiam centum essent vel quinque vel plus aut minus, duodecim melequinos'. Here *melequinus* is a coin.

24 Elze, 'Die päpstliche Kapelle', 155-6: 'So ist anscheinend mit der wachsenden Macht des Papsttums auch die Zahl derer gestiegen, die sich vom Papst weihen ließen, in Rom, wo anscheinend die Subdiakonstitel vermehrt wurden, noch öfter aber an anderen Orten, wozu die vielen Reisen der Päpste Möglichkeiten genug geboten haben. Infolgedessen finden sich viele päpstliche Subdiakone—seit dem Auftreten dieser Bezeichnung—als Kanoniker italienischer und französischer Kirchen'.

25 At Montecassino one finds a relation of Abbot Raynald II (1137-66), the monk Simon, who became a subdeacon of Pope Eugenius III (1145-53) and later the abbot of Subiaco and cardinal deacon of Santa Maria in Domnica. See Bloch, *Monte Cassino*, ii, 995-6, and 1034-6.

26 Papal election of bishops—the examples that Elze gave are from the late eleventh century—from the ranks of subdeacon is surprising given the Roman argument in 1137 against the Cassinese practice of electing subdeacons as abbots. It may be noted, however, that Elze found that the practice happened seldom; see 'Die päpstliche Kapelle', 167-8.

subdeacons and the variety of ministries that they could fulfill, the subdiaconate must have been a lifelong office for many churchmen.

The diplomatic record at Montecassino gives some evidence of the diversity and importance of work assumed by subdeacons. The *Chronica* cites evidence for the liturgical ministry of the subdeacon in the will and testament of Abbot Desiderius (Pope Victor III, 1086/1087), who bequeathed three golden offertory cloths for subdeacons ('fanones aurei pro subdiaconibus tres').[27] Furthermore, the description of the papal party of Paschal II (1099-1118) that greeted Emperor Henry V to Rome in 1111, was arranged formally according to ancient Roman liturgical offices, the pope with many bishops, with cardinal priests and deacons, with subdeacons and other ministers of the *schola cantorum*. Regarding government service, one finds a papal subdeacon, Hermann, who was part of a papal legation of Callistus II (1119-24) to Capua. Soon after, Pope Callistus seems to have promoted this same subdeacon to cardinal deacon.[28] The earliest reference to a subdeacon in the Chronicle is from the abbacy of Angelarius (883-9) and is of a secular subdeacon, Hermefridus, a wealthy man who became an oblate in Ascoli Satriano in the province of Foggia. Subdeacons also appear as witnesses in the charters of the abbey. More often than not subdeacons in the charters from the Desiderian era onward may be found in the necrology. For example, Iulianus, one of three subdeacons in a charter of Abbot Roffredus (1188-1210) in 1195, is found in the necrology on 5 December, where an adding hand has written 'Iulianus medicus et subdiaconus', thereby revealing that the subdeacon was also a physician.[29] The monastic scriptorium preserved yet more information about the existence and work of subdeacons. Francis Newton, in his study of the Cassinese scribes of books written in Beneventan minuscule, found four subdeacons among twenty scribes.[30]

The range of dates for subdeacons remembered in the necrology begins, as has been argued here, in the eleventh century and extends through the entire history of

---

27 The Chronicle mentions subdeacons nine times, five of which are in relation to the Abbot Raynald controversy. For the four remaining references, see *Chronica*, 1.46, 3.74, 4.37, and 4.70; *MGH Scriptores*, 34.122 ll. 24-5, 456 l. 27, 503 l. 23, and 537 ll. 26-7.

28 Elze, 'Die päpstliche Kapelle', 165.

29 Among the charters edited by Luigi Fabiani, *La Terra di San Benedetto*, one may find the subdeacons Mirandus (ann. 1079; i, 424), who died on 2 December; Theodorus (ann. 1190; i, 430), with no record in the necrology; Iacobus (ann. 1190; i, 433), whose death may be any of the three recorded on 24 Feb. (see n. 5 above), 25 Aug., and 20 Oct.; Rogerius (ann. 1195; i, 434), whose death may be any of three recorded on 2 Feb., 24 Aug., and 12 Sept.; Gerardus (ann. 1195; i, 434), whose death may be recorded on 13 June; and Iulianus (ann. 1195; i, 434), who died on 5 Dec.

30 Francis Newton, 'Beneventan Scribes and Subscriptions with a List of Those Known at the Present Time', *The Bookmark*, 43 (1973), 1-35. The subdeacons are Ascarius (Ascarus?), subdeacon of Carminiano, fl. 1145; Iohannes, fl. end of the ninth century; Iohannes, subdeacon of Montecassino, fl. 1011-22; and Petrus, subdeacon of Naples, fl. beginning of the tenth century.

the book, that is, through the remainder of the Middle Ages. A formal study of the scripts of the additions is still to be done, but an initial consideration of the evidence does point to the ongoing remembrance of subdeacons. The entries added after the production of the book adhere to the hierarchical placement of names but not always with the liturgical simplicity of earlier days. Names begin to appear with historical and personal additions. Sometimes, especially after the second half of the thirteenth century, the scribe would write the year of death. Of the 130 subdeacons in the years 1164/6 to 1504, twelve have last names and two have the year of their death. Nine names are written in red ink, which would have denoted a heightened remembrance, perhaps an office of the dead.

Three conclusions can be made based upon the necrological record of subdeacons. First, the subdiaconate could be a terminal office. It was the last of the Holy Orders received by many clerics whose professional lives were occupied by ministries outside the 'cursus honorum'. The subdiaconate was a permanent office in yet another way. It continued to be a title conferred in the necrology throughout the remainder of the Middle Ages. Secondly, by the time of the composition of the necrology of Montecassino, in 1164/6, the church of Montecassino honored the subdiaconate as a major order. This honor it gave notwithstanding the recent controversy over the clerical status of Abbot Raynald I, and the indignation that some members of his community expressed at having a lowly subdeacon as abbot. Finally, the honoring of the subdiaconate as a major order was a recent development at Montecassino. The regular recording of the title in necrological notices seems to have begun after the middle of the eleventh century, but, it seems, the strict adherence to a hierarchy of names based upon the ecclesiastical hierarchy began only with the writing of Montecassino 47.

Chapter 5

Questions on Ordination, the Mass, and the Office in Guerric of Saint-Quentin's *Quaestiones de quolibet*

Jonathan Black

The most comprehensive lists of medieval liturgical commentaries include certain theological works such as Hugh of St Victor's *De sacramentis* and the fourth book of Peter Lombard's *Sentences*,[1] and the association of liturgical commentaries with theological writings on the sacraments is particularly evident when the same comments on church ritual appear in both contexts.[2] Nevertheless, differences between liturgical and theological writings in terms of their focus, form, and purpose limit the amount of shared material and generally result in quite distinct treatments of baptism, the mass, ecclesiastical orders, and other corresponding subject matter. It is therefore of some interest to find three properly liturgical questions among the hundred or so philosophical and theological questions in the Quodlibets of the early Dominican master Guerric of Saint-Quentin (d. 1245): why orders are conferred on Saturday of ember days; why the kiss of peace is omitted in the Mass for the dead; and why the readings from the prophets and the readings from the New Testament have different endings.[3] An examination of these

---

1 See, for example, the list (through the thirteenth century) in Roger Reynolds, 'Guillaume Durand parmi les théologiens médiévaux de la liturgie', in *Guillaume Durand, évêque de Mende (v. 1230-1296)*, Actes de la Table Ronde du C. N. R. S., Mende 24-27 mai 1990, ed. Pierre-Marie Gy (Paris, 1992), 155-68, at 164-8.

2 For examples of material on the orders included in liturgical commentaries and in theological tracts or collections, see Roger E. Reynolds, 'The "Isidorian" *Epistula ad Leudefredum*: an early medieval epitome of the clerical duties', *Mediaeval Studies*, 41 (1979), 252-330, at 312-22. There are also many instances in which liturgical commentaries and writings on the sacraments appear in a single manuscript.

3 Guerric of Saint-Quentin, *Quaestiones de quolibet*, ed. Walter H. Principe, with editorial revision and a preface by Jonathan Black and an introduction by Jean-Pierre Torrell, Studies and Texts, 143 (Toronto, 2002), 296-7 and 336-9 (Quodlibet 6, article 7, and Quodlibet 7, article 7a and 7b). Another question pertaining to the liturgy—why there is no prayer for excommunicates on Good Friday—is found in Quodlibet 5, article 7, but there the focus seems to be on the status of excommunicates (as in Quodlibet 8, article 7); other liturgical references in the Quodlibets (including an explanation of the water, ashes, salt, and wine at the consecration of a church in Quodlibet 5, article 6) are in the context of more general questions.

questions allows us to determine the extent to which quodlibetal questions and the responses to them by a thirteenth-century master of theology could be drawn from the tradition of liturgical commentaries.

Quodlibet 6, article 7: 'De ordinibus'

The question on orders is included in two of the manuscripts containing Guerric's quodlibetal questions: Vatican City, Biblioteca Apostolica Vaticana, MS Vat. lat. 4245 (= *V*), fo 69rb; and Paris, Bibliothèque Nationale de France, MS lat. 16417 (= *P*), fo 67rb. They present different versions or *reportationes* of the article, consisting of a compound question and response.[4] The question is why orders are conferred on a fast day (ember days) rather than on Sunday (in *V*) or a solemnity (in *P*), and why they are conferred on Saturday rather than Friday even though Friday is a more solemn fast day. The response begins with the assertion that the conferring of an order is a consummation of the spirit and a forsaking of the flesh, which is suited more to a time of fasting than to a Sunday or a solemnity;[5] then in *P* alone it is noted that through orders peace of mind (*quies mentis*) is conferred and we are ordered toward the peace or rest of eternity (*quies aeternitatis*), so orders are conferred on the seventh day; and both versions refer to Moses sanctifying the people 'today and tomorrow' so that they would be prepared on the third day (Ex. 19: 10-11), taking it to mean that the first two days of the ember-day fast (Wednesday and Friday) prepare the ordinands for the third day (Saturday). This is followed in *P* alone by a paragraph on the institution of the episcopate, stating that it has a twofold purpose—utility and honor (*decentia*)—and explaining that it was necessary for the conferring of other orders.

The day on which the clergy can be ordained is a subject of liturgical commentaries and canonistic sources (which will be discussed below), and Hugh of St Victor includes a brief chapter in *De sacramentis* indicating when ordination can take place,[6] but it is not a subject that is included in Lombard's questions on orders (*IV Sent.* d. 24) or, it seems, in the corresponding sections of the *Sentences* commentaries and theological *summae* of the thirteenth century. It is also not a matter that is regularly addressed in collections of questions on the sacraments. In fact, Guerric's own ten-part *Quaestio de sacramento ordinis* is quite distinct from the quodlibetal question; it pertains instead to the name of the sacrament, its status as single sacrament, the number and sequence of orders, the composition and nature of the sacrament, the power to ordain, the Old and New Testament priesthood, the

---

4   Other articles in Guerric's Quodlibets include formal arguments, but the articles discussed in this
      study contain only questions and responses.
5   *P* here refers to Sunday and solemnities (feasts), whereas *V* again refers only to Sunday.
6   See below at n. 14.

church's assimilation to the celestial hierarchy, and the prohibition against the ordination of women—and its treatment of some of these subjects is comparable to that of other authors.[7] The ten-part question appears in five known manuscripts from the thirteenth century: in *P*, fos 55vb-57ra, Assisi, Biblioteca Comunale, MS 138, fo 152ra-vb, and Prague, Národní knihovna (Universitní knihovna), MS IV. D. 13 (667), fo 194ra-va, it appears among numerous questions by Guerric and others on the sacraments;[8] in Paris, Bibliothèque Nationale de France, MS lat. 15610, fos 243va-244vb, it appears with Guerric's questions on extreme unction (244vb-246rb) but without the questions on the other sacraments;[9] and in Todi, Biblioteca Comunale, MS 71, the questions on orders and extreme unction appear on fos 68ra-vb and 69ra-vb, after the questions on the other sacraments but in a different hand.

The Todi text is substantially different from the versions in the other manuscripts and has supplementary material that is of particular interest here: the ten numbered parts of the question are followed immediately by a text that is closely related to Quodlibet 7, article 6. The supplementary text begins with the question why the conferring of orders is on a fast day instead of a solemnity and why it is not observed on Friday; the response corresponds to version *P* of the Quodlibet in particular. The remainder of the text is a question and response on the 'ordo dignitatis' and grace; it generally corresponds to the paragraph at the end of version *P* but is more extensive.

The part of the supplementary text that corresponds most closely to the Quodlibet also appears in the Prague manuscript but not as a continuation of the ten-part question on fo 194ra-va. It appears earlier, on fo 35va, embedded within an abridged and rearranged version of the same *Quaestio de sacramento ordinis*.[10] A textual comparison of the five copies of the complete ten-part question and the abridged version in the Prague manuscript shows that the latter shares many of the

---

7   For example, the third part and fourth parts of the question—on the number and sequence of orders with reference to the model of the *Celestial Hierarchies* of Pseudo-Dionysius ('purgatio, illuminatio, perfectio')—is comparable to Alexander of Hales, *Glossa in librum IV Sententiarum Petri Lombardi*, 24.3, ed. PP. Collegii S. Bonaventurae (Quaracchi, 1957), esp. 404-7.

8   The questions on fos 25r-65v of *P* were ascribed to Guerric by F. M. Henquinet and listed in 'Les écrits du Frère Guerric de Saint-Quentin, O.P.', *Recherches de théologie ancienne et médiévale*, 6 (1934), 184-214, 284-312, 394-409, at 292-9, with references to the corresponding questions in Assisi, Bibl. Com., 138; the questions in the Prague manuscript were listed (with references to all the other manuscripts) by Bertrand-G. Guyot, 'Quaestiones Guerrici, Alexandri et aliorum magistrorum Parisiensium (*Praha, Univ. IV. D. 13*)', *Archivum fratrum praedicatorum*, 32 (1962), 5-125, at 70-83.

9   A blank line on fo 243va separates the question on orders from the preceding text, Hugh of Saint-Cher's Postill on John (see Henquinet, 'Les écrits du Frère Guerric', 291), and fo 246v is blank.

10 For a precise summary of the manner in which the ten-part question has been abridged and rearranged in the version on fo 35rb-va and in the lower margin of fo 35ra, see Guyot, 'Quaestiones Guerrici', 19 (no. 21 II), where the correspondence of the embedded text and Guerric's Quodlibet 6, article 7 is noted.

Todi variants and therefore seems to be based on a model that closely resembled the Todi text with the supplementary material included; and although the abridgment preserves just half of the supplementary text found in the Todi manuscript, some of its readings are preferable to those in the Todi text and more consistent with the readings in the *P* version of the Quodlibet. An edition of the supplementary text on fo 35va of the Prague manuscript (= *G*) and fo 68vb of the Todi manuscript (= *T*) is presented below next to the *P* version of the Quodlibet.[11]

Quodlibet 6, A. 7: 'De ordinibus'	***Quaestio de sacramento ordinis* (additio)**
P	*GT*

56 Septimo quaesita sunt quaedam circa ordines. Cum habeant solemnitatem, quare non fiunt in diebus solemnibus? Item, cum fiant in diebus ieiuniorum, quare non fiunt in 5 sexta feria?

Postea quaeritur cum in collatione ordinis sit solemnitas, quare in diebus solemnibus non celebrantur ordines. Vel si tempore ieiunii debent celebrari, quare non in die Veneris.

57 Item, cum die Veneris sit solemnius ieiunium quam in die sabbati et cum magis sit deputatus ieiunio quam dies sabbati, quare non dantur die Veneris, sed die sabbati?

10 **58** Potest dici quod ordinis collatio est consummatio spiritus quantum est ex vi sacramenti: consummatio autem spiritus est defectio carnis, et ideo fiunt in tempore ieiunii, nec fiunt in dominico nec in solemni-15 tatibus quia maxime diversi sunt a ieiunio.

Responsio: In collatione ordinis est consummatio spiritus, et ideo defectus carnis et maceratio quae est maxime per ieiunium, et ideo tempore ieiunii congrue fit ordinis collatio,

59 Item, per ordines confertur quies mentis et ordinamur ad quietem aeternitatis. Ideo fiunt in sabbato.

et in ordine confertur quies mentis ordinata ad quietem aeternitatis quae designatur per sabbatum, et ideo magis fit in sabbato.

60 Item, dicit Ex 19 Moysi quod sancti-20 ficaret *populum hodie et cras*, ut *tertia die* essent *parati* suscipere legem. Ideo praecedit duplex ieiunium et in illis diebus in quibus maxime consuevit fieri ieiunium, scilicet in quarta et in sexta.
25

Item sicut dicitur Moysi in Ex 19, *Sanctifica populum hodie et cras* ante dationem legis, et dationem legis praecessit duorum dierum sanctificatio, sic collationem ordinum ministrorum legis praecedit duorum dierum per ieiunium sanctificatio. Vnde praecedit ieiunium quartae feriae et sextae, et conferuntur ordines in sabbato.

---

11 The text of the Quodlibet is taken from col. b of the edition, but the scribal slips noted in the apparatus of the edition are not reported here and the capitalization has been modified. For the text of the supplement to the *Quaestio de sacramento ordinis*, I have modified the orthography of the manuscripts so that it corresponds to the orthography used in the edition of the Quodlibet.

61 Item, institutio episcopatus duplicem ... institutio ordinis quae est dignitas, ut est
habet <rationem> scilicet utilitatem et episcopatus, duplicem habet intentionem,
decentiam: necesse enim fuit instituere unam necessitatis, et sic est ad conferendum
30 episcopatum ut conferret <alias ordines>. officium, alium decoris, sicut est ad gratiam
conferendam confirmando et consecrando....

---

1 postea queritur] item *T*   ordinis] ordinum *T* | 2 diebus solemnibus *inv. T*   3 celebrantur ordines]
celebratur ordinis collatio *T*   tempore *marg. T* | 4 debent] debet *T*   in] celebratur *T* |
10 ordinis] ordinum *T* | 11 consummatio] consumpatio *T* | 12 est *om. T* | 17 quae designatur]
quod significatur *T* | 18 ideo *om. G*   sabbato] *add.* ordinis collatio *T* | 19 dicitur Moysi] dicit
Moyses *G*   in Ex 19 *om. T* | 19-20 sanctifica] sacrifica *T* | 21 dationem legis] legis datio *T* |
22 sanctificatio] sacrificio *T* | 25-31 et sexte ... consecrando *om. G*

From a comparison of the two texts printed above (including the *V* version of
the Quodlibet, which is not shown here) it is clear that the texts are closely related,
but the exact nature of their relationship cannot be established with certainty. The
V and *P* versions of Quodlibet 6 are nearly identical in paragraph 57, which does
not appear in the supplement to the *Quaestio de sacramento ordinis,* and the
paragraphs of the *P* version of the Quodlibet that are found nearly verbatim in the
supplement (59 and 61) do not appear in the *V* version of the Quodlibet. If the *V*
and *P* versions are two *reportationes* of a quodlibetal dispute, the supplement of
the ten-part question may be viewed as a text derived from the *P* version or from
another nonextant report of the Quodlibet, but we cannot rule out the possibility
that the *P* version could be derived in part from a text like the supplement.[12] It
may, then, be impossible for us to determine the original form of the question that
appears in Quodlibet 6, article 7 and in the supplement to the *Quaestio de sacramento ordinis,* but its presence in either context is remarkable since it addresses a
subject that is more commonly found in liturgical commentaries.

In the various liturgical commentaries written between the early Middle Ages
and the end of the thirteenth century there were several general lines of explanation
for the day on which orders are conferred. One line of explanation, also found in
canon law collections, is simply the citation of papal decrees stating the time of
ordination, in particular those of Leo I and Gelasius I:[13] the latter—indicating the

---

12 It should be noted that paragraph 61 of the Quodlibet is not a response to a question announced at
the beginning of the article and may therefore not have been part of the original Quodlibet; the
corresponding text in the supplement is the beginning of a response to a distinct question on the
episcopate and its relationship to the sacrament of orders.

13 Leo, Ep. 9 (*PL* 54.625-6; see *Decretum,* D. 75 cc. 4-5); Gelasius, Ep. 14, c. 11. ed. Andreas Thiel,
Epistolae Romanorum pontificum genuinae, i (Braunsberg, 1868), 368-9 (= Ep. 9, c. 11 in *PL*
59.52; see *Decretum,* D. 75 c. 7). On the implementation of the practices set out in the letter of
Gelasius, see Bruno Kleinheyer, *Die Priesterweihe im römischen Ritus: eine liturgiehistorische
Studie,* Trierer theologische Studien, 12 (Trier, 1962), 35-47.

seasons, day (Saturday), and hour (vespers)—is used by Hrabanus Maurus and
Sigebert of Gembloux in their accounts of ember Saturdays, and it also serves as
the basis for Hugh of St Victor's chapter on the time of ordination;[14] the former—
noting that the Saturday vespers observance pertains to Sunday—is mentioned by
John of Avranches and quoted in full by Rupert of Deutz;[15] and both Leo and
Gelasius are cited by Bernold of Constance.[16]

Another general line of explanation was developed in the ninth century by
Amalar of Metz as part of his account of the ember-day fast and observance, which
draws on the authority of Augustine and Innocent I as well as Leo and others.[17] In
this account ordination is tied to fasting, with reference to the apostles, and the
ember-day terms in which ordination takes place are associated with the cardinal
figures in the generations leading to Christ.[18] After some comments on the
characteristics of the seasons in which the ember-day fasts occur (in respect to
warmth, moisture, and human temperament), and on the association of the three
days in each fast with the passion and death of Christ,[19] Augustine's remarks on the
sanctification of the seventh day in Genesis and its designation as a day of rest are
presented as an explanation for having ordination on Saturday.[20] Individual components of Amalar's account of the ember-day fast and observance appear in many of
the liturgical commentaries written in the subsequent centuries, either selectively
or in extended blocks. Amalar's account is quoted verbatim and rearranged in
various ways in the ember-day accounts of Ps.-Alcuin,[21] Berno of Reichenau,[22] the

---

14 Hrabanus Maurus, *De institutione clericorum libri tres*, 2.24, ed. Detlev Zimpel, Freiburger
    Beiträge zur mittelalterlichen Geschichte, 7 (Frankfurt am Main, 1996), 368; Sigebert of
    Gembloux, *De differentia quatuor temporum* (*PL* 160.821); Hugh of St Victor, *De sacramentis
    christianae fidei*, 3.20 (*PL* 176.431-2).

15 *Le 'De officiis ecclesiasticis' de Jean d'Avranches, archevêque de Rouen (1067-1079)*, ed. R.
    Delamare (Paris, 1923), 45; Rupert of Deutz, *Liber de divinis officiis*, 3.9, ed. Hrabanus Haacke,
    CCCM, 7 (1967), 73-4.

16 Bernold of Constance, *Micrologus de ecclesiasticis observantibus*, 24 and 29 (*PL* 151.996 and
    1002).

17 Amalar, *Liber officialis*, 2.1-3, ed. Ioannes Michaelis [Jean-Michel] Hanssens, in *Amalarii episcopi
    Opera liturgica omnia*, 3 vols, Studi e Testi, 138-40 (Vatican City, 1948-50), ii, 197-209.

18 *Ibid.*, 2.1.1-5 and 10-14 (ed. Hanssens, ii, 198 and 200-201).

19 See esp. *ibid.*, 2.2.3-5 and 12 (ed. Hanssens, ii, 202 and 204-5).

20 *Ibid.*, 2.2.13 (ed. Hanssens, ii, 205). For the source text, see Augustine, Ep. 55 ('Ad Ianuarium'),
    18-19, ed. Al. Goldbacher, *CSEL*, 34 (Vienna, 1895), 188-90. Cf. the account of the Saturday fast
    in Amalar's separate work on ember days, the *Epistula Amalarii ad Hilduinum* (ed. Hanssens, i,
    355), which uses Augustine's Ep. 36 ('Ad Casulanum'), noting Saturday as the day in which the
    body of Christ rested in the tomb.

21 Ps.-Alcuin, *De divinis officiis liber*, 28 (*PL* 101.1227-8); the chapter, a compilation drawn almost
    entirely from individual sentences in Amalar's *Liber officialis*, 2.1-3, also appears (in a slightly
    curtailed form) in Ps.-Bede, *De officiis libellus* (*PL* 94.538-9).

22 Berno of Reichenau, *Libellus de quibusdam rebus ad missae officium pertinentibus*, 7 (*PL*
    142.1073-80); and *Dialogus qualiter quatuor temporum ieiunia per sua sabbata sint observanda*,
    esp. 3 and 5 (*PL* 142.1292-4). Many of the excerpts from Amalar used by Berno appear in the same

Liber quare,[23] and others,[24] and a condensed version of Amalar's text, retaining the original sequence, appears in the chapters on orders and ember days in the *Sacramentarium* of Honorius Augustodunensis.[25]

Honorius uses other lines of explanation in his *Gemma animae*. In the chapter entitled 'De ordine ministrorum', Honorius explains that ordination takes place on Saturday, the day of rest, since the ministers are required to refrain from servile work and to make themselves available for divine service.[26] In the following chapter, 'De presbyteris', Honorius notes that the ordination of priests at vespers pertains to the Lord's day, explaining that presbyterial ordination represents embodiment in Christ; and the conferring of orders in ember days ('in quatuor temporibus') is explained in terms of the four grades of acolytes, subdeacons, deacons, and priests elected to service in the four parts of the world under the care of the four gospels.[27] Honorius repeats these lines of explanation in the chapter entitled 'Quare in quatuor temporibus ordines fiant' (and the following chapter on the Sunday after the Octave of Pentecost) but also includes others, identifying the spiritual or moral characteristics proper to the festal seasons in which ember days are observed and associating Saturday, the seventh day, with the gifts of the Holy Spirit and the orders.[28]

The explanations presented by Honorius in *Gemma animae* appear with Amalar's explanations in several later commentaries from the twelfth and thirteenth centuries. In John Beleth's chapter on ember days and orders, material from Honorius identifying the spiritual characteristics of the four seasons is followed by material from Amalar on the generations leading to Christ, with

---

order in book 2.40-42 of the liturgical commentary in Bamberg, Staatsbibliothek, MS Misc. Lit. 134 (fos 123r-126r), and Berno may therefore be added to Vincent L. Kennedy's list of apparent sources for this commentary, possibly written by Frutolphus of Michelsberg; see 'The "De officiis divinis" of Ms. Bamberg Lit. 134', *Ephemerides liturgicae*, 52 (1938), 312-26.

23 *Liber quare*, qq. 119-33, ed. Georgius Polycarpus Götz, *CCCM*, 60 (1983), 48-53.

24 Excerpts appear, e.g., in the commentary of John of Avranches (ed. Delamare, 46) and in the later commentaries discussed below.

25 Honorius Augustodunensis, *Sacramentarium seu de causis et significatu mystico rituum divini in ecclesia officii liber*, 21: 'De tempore sacros ordines conferendi', 22: 'De ieiuniis quatuor temporum', and 23: 'De ordinatione' (*PL* 172.757-9).

26 Honorius, *Gemma animae*, 1.190 (*PL* 172.602).

27 *Ibid.*, 1.191 (*PL* 172.602).

28 *Ibid.*, 3.155 (*PL* 172.686). Cf. the more general association of the seventh day and the sevenfold working of the Holy Spirit in Amalar, *Liber officialis*, 4.29.4: 'De octavis Pentecostes' (ed. Hanssens, ii, 497), drawn from Augustine's *De sermone Domini in monte*, 1.4.11 and 12. *Gemma animae*, 3.155 is the last of a set of chapters in which Honorius lists the characteristics of the four seasons; in 3.151 the seasons are described in terms of work in the fields, and in 3.152 they are described in terms of festal observances and fasting.

additional comments.[29] The same material from Honorius and Amalar was used by Sicard of Cremona but in two distinct explanations of ordination on ember days: the chapter on the third Sunday in Advent contains an explanation based on Honorius, and the chapter on the fourteenth Sunday after Pentecost contains an explanation based on Amalar.[30] In the chapter on the third Sunday in Advent, Sicard introduces another explanation as well, associating the ember days as 'dierum primitiae' (first-offerings of days) with the ordinands as 'primates ecclesiae',[31] and he draws from Honorius again to explain why ordination takes place on Saturday.

Another work that refers to 'primitiae' in an explanation of orders and ember days is the liturgical commentary written by Prepositinus of Cremona; noting that priests and other clergy correspond to the Levites offered to God in place of first-born (Num. 3: 13), and identifying first-born and first-offerings, Prepositinus explains that it is fitting that we should make first-offerings of men (holy orders) during the first-offerings of the seasons.[32] He then turns to the question why orders are conferred on Saturday—and at the ninth hour—rather than on the fourth or sixth feria. His explanation of the hour is similar to the explanation used by others authors in respect to vespers (namely, the observance pertains to Sunday), and he adds that the ordinands may be understood to have been resurrected.[33] But he

---

29 John Beleth, *Summa de ecclesiasticis officiis*, 134o, ed. Heribertus Douteil, 2 vols., *CCCM*, 41-41A (1976), ii, 256-7. This section of chapter 134 does not appear in all recensions of the *Summa*, and it repeats some of the material from Honorius that appears in the preceding chapter (133i, p. 253).

30 Sicard of Cremona, *Mitrale*, 5.3 and 5.14 (*PL* 213.212, 397). Although the explanations are in the context of December and September ember days respectively, each of these chapters refers to all four ember-day seasons and ordination. Another author who seems to have used material from Amalar's and Honorius's accounts of ordination and ember days in separate chapters is Robertus Paululus; Honorius's explanation of Saturday as a day of rest is used in *De caeremoniis, sacramentis, officiis et observationibus ecclesiasticis* 1.44: 'Quare episcopi die Dominica consecrentur' (*PL* 177.403), while excerpts from Amalar on ember-day fasting appear in 3.1: 'De officio in ieiuniis quatuor temporum' (*PL* 177.439).

31 Sicard, *Mitrale*, 5.3 (*PL* 213.212). On the ember days as first-offerings of days, see Peter Comestor, Sermon 13, Dom. II in Quadragesima (*PL* 198.1759).

32 Prepositinus of Cremona, *Tractatus de officiis*, 3.21, ed. James A. Corbett, Publications in Mediaeval Studies, 21 (Notre Dame, 1969), 210-1: 'Fiunt autem ordines in .IIII. temporibus quia sacerdotes et alii clerici obtinent locum quam obtinuerunt levite in populo Israel. Levitas vero ... *Dominus pro primogenitis recipit* ... . Primitie vero sunt primogenita, quomodo primitias hominum offerimus cum aliquos ad sacros ordines offerimus. Conveniens autem erat ut in primitiis temporum offerremus primitias hominum'.

33 *Ibid.* (ed. Corbett, 211): 'Sed quare potius in sabbato et hora nona plus quam in .IIII^a. feria vel .VI^a. fiunt ordines? Quia hora illius temporis iam intelligitur pertinere ad diem dominicum, ad diem scilicet Resurrectionis, ut nostri ordinandi ad similitudinem Christi resurrexisse intelligantur.' See the references to similar explanations in nn. 13, 15-16, and 27 above; see also Sicard, *Mitrale*, 5.3 (*PL* 213.212), and cf. the comments on the Easter vigil in Augustine's Sermon 221, ed. Suzanne Poque, *Sermons pour la Pâque*, SChr., 116 (Paris, 1966), 218 (quoted by Amalar in *Liber officialis*, 1.12.33, ed. Hanssens, ii, 78).

introduces a further explanation: orders are conferred on Saturday as a sign that the ordinands should have rest of the heart, so that they may pass at length to the rest of eternity.[34] This reference to *sabbatum pectoris* and *sabbatum aeternitatis* is in the same context as the reference to *quies mentis* and *quies aeternitatis* in the *P* version of Guerric's Quodlibet 6, article 7 and in the supplement to his *Quaestio de sacramento ordinis*.

Apart from this one instance, Prepositinus offers no parallels for the explanations in Guerric's Quodlibet and in the supplement. For the preceding chapters on the ember-day fasts, Prepositinus uses Amalar's explanations (although Prepositinus adds the association of spring, summer, autumn, and winter with lechery, avarice, pride, and infidelity or malice),[35] and neither these nor the explanations of the other authors presented above served as the basis for Guerric's explanations. While many of the commentaries associate the time of ordination with fasting or self-castigation, none of the accounts of ember days or ordination seems to present it in terms of 'consummatio spiritus' and 'defectio carnis'; and while many of the commentaries point to the sanctification of the seventh day in Genesis as an explanation for ordination on Saturday, none seems to provide an explanation based on the 'third day' of Ex. 19: 10 ff. But even if Guerric's explanations seem to have little basis in the tradition of liturgical commentaries, the question itself as posed by Guerric is unmistakably part of this tradition.

Most of the liturgical commentaries mentioned address both parts of the question—why orders are conferred on ember days and why specifically on Saturday—within a larger exposition or series of questions on the ember-day observance. Particular focus is given to the two parts of the question by Honorius, who devotes a short chapter of *Gemma animae* to them,[36] and Prepositinus, who also devotes a chapter to them and, like Guerric, explicitly asks why on Saturday rather than on Wednesday or Friday of ember days.[37] Another commentary that should be mentioned in this regard is the *Manuale* of Peter of Roissy, written in the early thirteenth century. As V. L. Kennedy has shown, the work survives in a short version found in several manuscripts and a much longer version that makes abundant use of the *De sacro altaris mysterio* of Lothar of Segni (Innocent III) and is

---

34 Prepositinus, *Tractatus de officiis*, 3.21 (ed. Corbett, 211): 'Fiunt etiam in sabbato in signum quod debent habere sabbatum pectoris, ut transeant tandem ad sabbatum eternitatis'. Cf. Peter Lombard, *In Ps* 91, titulus (*PL* 191.855), where *sabbatum pectoris/cordis/mentis* is distinguished from *sabbatum aeternitatis* and *sabbatum temporis*.

35 Prepositinus, *Tractatus de officiis*, 3.14-20 (ed. Corbett, 207-10); the excesses associated with the seasons are described in 3.16.

36 Honorius, *Gemma animae*, 3.155 (*PL* 172.686): 'Quare in Quatuor Temporibus ordines fiant ... . Ideo in Sabbato ordines fiunt, quia ...' (for Honorius's explanation, see above at n. 28).

37 The chapter is quoted in nn. 32-4 above.

found in Paris, Bibliothèque Nationale de France, MS nouv. acq. lat. 232.[38] Neither version introduces any new explanation to the tradition presented above; in the short version the section explaining when ordination takes place seems to be taken from the *Liber quare* (based on Amalar), and when this section was reworked in the long version, Peter used the corresponding section of Beleth's commentary (also based on Amalar).[39] But of interest here is the fact that Peter presents this source material in the form of two successive questions, 'Quare in ieiuniis quatuor temporum potius clerici ordinantur quam in aliis temporibus' and 'Quare clerici potius consecrantur in sabbato quam in aliis diebus'.

It has been seen that while Guerric's Quodlibet 6, article 7 and the supplement to his *Quaestio de sacramento ordinis* address a question rooted in the tradition of liturgical commentaries, the response sets Guerric apart from this tradition. It also sets him apart from the continuation of this tradition in the later thirteenth century: William Durand explains why ordination takes place on ember days and why on Saturday rather than on Wednesday or Friday in successive paragraphs of his liturgical commentary, but the explanation seems to be taken directly from Prepositinus, Sicard, and a source such as the *Liber quare* which included Amalar's explanation.[40] Thus liturgical commentaries continued to employ previously formulated explanations, while the Quodlibet served to provide something new.

---

38 V. L. Kennedy, 'The Handbook of Master Peter Chancellor of Chartres', *Mediaeval Studies*, 5 (1943), 1-38, at 5-6 for the two versions, and 21-38 for a list of the chapters in the long version. Additional manuscripts of the short version are listed in Marie-Thérèse d'Alverny, 'Les mystères de l'église, d'après Pierre de Roissy', in *Mélanges offerts à René Crozet*, ed. Pierre Gallais and Yves-Jean Riou, 2 vols (Poitiers, 1966), ii, 2085-1104, at 1091-3.

39 For the text of the short version, see, e.g., Paris, Bibliothèque Nationale de France, MS lat. 14500, fo 135va-vb, and for the text of the long version, see nouv. acq. lat. 232, fo 56ra-rb. Both versions are based on *Liber quare*, qq. 124, 126, and 128, but for the comments on the generations leading to Christ (from Amalar, *Liber officialis*, 2.1.10-13), the long version replaces the text from *Liber quare* 126 with one that agrees in part with Beleth, *Summa*, 134o (*CCCM*, 41A.256-7) and in part with the *additio*, 134hda (*CCCM*, 41.120).

40 William Durand, *Rationale divinorum officiorum*, 2.1.34-5, ed. A. Davril, T. M. Thibodeau, and B.-G. Guyot, 3 vols, *CCCM*, 140-140B (1995-2000), i, 134-5. The use of Prepositinus, *Tractatus de officiis*, 3.21 at ll. 462-70 and 487-94; Sicard, *Mitrale*, 5.3 at ll. 471-5; and the Augustinian explanation in Amalar, *Liber officialis*, 2.2.13, or *Liber quare*, 128 (with additional references inserted) at ll. 477-86 should be added to the *apparatus fontium*. On the extensive of use of these sources by Durand in other parts of the *Rationale*, see iii, 252-65 and the index, although at *Rationale*, 6.6.2-4 (ii, 154-5), in the separate account of the ember-day seasons, the reference to Prepositinus, *Tractatus de officiis*, 3.15-16 needs to be qualified; Durand seems to have drawn *luxuria*, *superbia*, and *auaritia* from Prepositinus but must have used at least one other source for the explanations—mostly from Amalar—in the rest of this passage, and the following paragraph—6.6.5—is from Beleth, *Summa*, 133i.

Quodlibet 7, Article 7a: 'Quare in Missa pro defunctis non datur osculum pacis?'

The most integral set of Guerric's Quodlibets—the set in *V*—breaks off at the beginning of Quodlibet 7, article 7, but the entire article is preserved in *P*, fo 67va, and in Assisi, Biblioteca Comunale, MS 186 (= *A*), fo 115vb. Both have a simple response to the question why there is no kiss of peace in the Mass for the dead: it is a mass for those who have no peace, so peace is not given.[41] As in the case of Quodlibet 6, article 7, the question is one that appears in a number of liturgical commentaries with various responses.

In Amalar's chapter on the Mass for the dead, repeated in part by Ps.-Alcuin, it is simply noted that the kiss of peace is omitted in imitation of the observances for the Lord's passion.[42] John Beleth offers three responses to the question why the *pax* is omitted in the Mass for the dead: first, in reference to Christ's passion and Judas's kiss; second, because we do not communicate with the dead, as they do not respond; and third, because among the faithful that constitute the Church there are good and bad members, and when one dies it is not known whether the person is in conformity with the church and has peace with God.[43] This triple response was repeated by Peter of Roissy and served as the basis of the responses given by Sicard of Cremona and later William Durand in their chapters on the Mass for the dead,[44] but Durand adds that there is a fourth reason and refers back to his account of the kiss of peace in the mass. There he notes that it is omitted in the Mass for the dead because the souls of the faithful are no longer in the turmoil of this world but are rather at peace in the Lord and therefore have no need of the kiss of peace, a

---

41 In *P* the response is as follows: 'Illa Missa fit tunc pro purgandis qui sunt in tribulatione, et quia petitur eis pax qui non habent, in signum huius non datur ibi pax' (ed. Principe, 336); *A* has a similar but slightly longer response, adding that 'Domine det nobis pacem et vitam aeternam' is said in place of the *pax* (ed. Principe, 337).

42 Amalar, *Liber officialis*, 3.44.2 (ed. Hanssens, ii, 381); Ps.-Alcuin, *De divinis officiis*, 50 (*PL* 101.1279).

43 Beleth, *Summa*, 161g (*CCCM*, 41A.315-17): 'Quare ad missam mortuorum pax non datur, triplex assignatur ratio. Primo est, quoniam hoc officium ... triduanam Christi sepulturam significat, ubi pax non datur propter osculum Iude. Secunda, quia non communicamus mortuis, quia non nobis respondent ... . Tertia est, quoniam ... ex multis fidelibus, quorum quidam boni, quidam mali, una ecclesia constituitur et coadunatur. Quia ergo mortuo homine nescitur, utrum ipse sit de conformitate ecclesie et pacem habeat cum Creatore suo, ideo pacem ad missam non damus'.

44 The chapter 'Quare in missa mortuorum pax non datur' is included in the long version of Peter of Roissy's *Manuale* (Paris, BNF, nouv. acq. lat. 232, fo 95vb); the chapter does not appear in the short version. Sicard uses Beleth's explanation in *Mitrale*, 4.50 (*PL* 213.426); and Durand presents Beleth's explanation in full in his *Rationale*, 7.35.30-32 (*CCCM*, 140B.96) but inserts a comment taken from Sicard's version.

sign of peace and concord.[45] This fourth reason provides a striking contrast with the response in Guerric's Quodlibet.

In the commentaries on the mass written before Durand,[46] reference is seldom made to the omission of the kiss of peace in the Mass for the dead, but Hugh of Saint-Cher provides one instance; in his chapter on the *pax* he notes that it is omitted in the Mass for the dead because they do not require temporal society necessary for the living.[47] Other explanations, somewhat closer to the one in the Quodlibet, are found among the questions that were added to the *Liber quare* in certain manuscripts: in one of the added questions found in several manuscripts from twelfth century and later, it is noted that the kiss of peace is not given in the Mass for the dead on account of the purgation of the deceased through the sacrifice of the priest;[48] and in one found in a single thirteenth-century manuscript there is a reference to purgatory in what seems to be a variation of Beleth's triple explanation.[49] By focusing strictly on the dead who have no peace, Guerric gives a response that is distinct from Beleth's response and its variation in the *Liber quare* addition, but in this instance he does not appear to be introducing an entirely new explanation. The response he gives is at least implicit within the tradition of liturgical commentaries.

---

45 Durand, *Rationale*, 4.53.8 (*CCCM*, 140.546): 'In missa uero pro defunctis, pax non datur quia fideles anime iam non sunt, nec ulterius erunt, in turbatione huius mundi sed quiescunt in Domino; unde non est eis necessarium pacis osculum, quod est pacis et concordie signum'. Cf. the explanation in the *Elucidationes variae in scripturam moraliter*, 6 (*PL* 177.482): '... quoniam hi, ... ab hac vita subtracti, humanae conversationis pacem vel concordiam tenere amplius aut exhibere non possunt'. A similar comment also appears after Beleth's explanation in Peter of Roissy's chapter noted above (n. 44): 'Cum autem duplex sit pax, temporis et pectoris, utraque indigemus nos qui sumus in hoc mundo, ut scilicet habeamus tranquilla temporalia et ne in mente ab inmundis spiritibus infestemur, quarum neutra indigent mortui; requiescunt enim a laboribus suis, et illa die peribunt omnes cogitationes eorum'.

46 See the list of commentaries (designated with the code M) in Reynolds, 'Guillaume Durand parmi les théologiens médiévaux de la liturgie', 165-8; see also the list in Gary Macy, 'Commentaries on the Mass during the Early Scholastic Period', in *Medieval Liturgy: a book of essays*, ed. Lizette Larson Miller (New York, 1997), 25-59, at 55-9.

47 Hugh of Saint-Cher, *Tractatus super missam seu speculum ecclesiae*, ed. Gisbertus Sölch, Opuscula et textus, series liturgica, fasc. 9 (Münster, 1940), 49: 'Diaconus autem dat pacem aliis et alii inter se in signum, quod omnes debent habere pacem et maxime filii ecclesiae. Et per hanc rationem potest haberi, quare pax non datur in missa pro defunctis. Defuncti enim non indigent temporalis societatis, quia solum necessaria vivis'.

48 *Liber quare*, Appendix II, *additio* 13 (*CCCM*, 60.139): 'Osculum non datur hic, quia ibi est purgatio mortui hominis per sacrificium sacerdotis'.

49 *Ibid.*, Appendix II, *additio* 33 (*CCCM*, 60.184): 'Et quare non datur *Pax Domini* clero et populo in illa [missa] sicut in aliis? Quia in illa quaedam speciales orationes et approprietates pro fidelibus defunctis dicuntur, et quia non communicamus id est non participamus cum illis, dimissum est. Quia plures in purgatoriis, plures in requie beatitudinis sunt'.

Quodlibet 7, Article 7b: 'De fine lectionum'

The remainder of Quodlibet 7, article 7 seems to pertain to the readings at nocturns in the divine office. The question is why the readings from the prophets (in *A* the Old Testament readings) end with 'Haec dicit Dominus: Convertimini' (in *A* 'Haec dicit Dominus Deus'), while the New Testament readings end with 'Tu autem, Domine, miserere nobis'. The response is that 'dicit Dominus' is an assertion of the promises made in the Old Testament, and since what was promised in the Old Testament was fulfilled in the New Testament, we say 'Tu autem, Domine' to acknowledge this and to ask for mercy.[50]

In this case, neither the question nor the response appears to have a model within the tradition of liturgical commentaries. Several commentaries have comments or a chapter on the meaning of 'Tu autem';[51] and Beleth—followed by Sicard and Durand—notes that there are four endings for the readings at nocturns: 'Tu autem ...' (Ps. 40: 11); 'Haec dicit Dominus: Convertimini ...' (Is. 45: 22) during Advent, Christmas, and Epiphany; 'Iherusalem, Iherusalem, convertere ad Dominum Deum tuum' when Lamentations is read on Holy Thursday; and 'Beati mortui, qui in Domino moriuntur' (or no ending) in the Office for the dead.[52] But Beleth and Sicard simply list the alternatives to 'Tu autem', and Durand merely supplies brief comments on their meaning; no liturgical commentary seems to address the question why the endings vary.

The question addressed in the Quodlibet not only appears to have no precedent in liturgical commentaries but also describes a liturgical practice that was contrary

---

50 The question in *P* is 'quare in lectionibus prophetarum dicitur in fine "Haec dicit Dominus: Convertimini" etc., in lectionibus Novi Testamenti "Tu autem"'; and in *A* 'quare in lectionibus Veteris Testamenti in fine subditur "Haec dicit Dominus Deus," in fine lectionum Novi "Tu autem, Domine, miserere nobis"' (ed. Principe, 336-7). Whereas the response in *P* (ed. Principe, 338) indicates the sense in which each expression should be taken, the more concise response in *A* is as follows: 'In Veteri Testamento factae sunt promissiones, et ideo in illis lectionibus ad maiorem assertionem et confirmationem subiungitur "Dicit Dominus omnipotens" vel "Haec dicit Dominus Deus". Sed iam cum in Novo factae sint et completae <promissiones>, non restat nisi quaerere misericordiam ne illis efficiamur indigni' (ed. Principe, 339).

51 The interpretations of Rupert of Deutz, *Liber de divinis officiis*, 1.13 (*CCCM*, 7.12) and Honorius, *Gemma animae*, 2.5 and 3.88 (*PL* 172.618 and 666) are repeated in Sicard, *Mitrale*, 4.2 (*PL* 213.156-7), Prepositinus, *Tractatus de officiis*, 1.221 (ed. Corbett, 119; cf. 4.14 on 222), and Durand, *Rationale*, 5.2.47 (*CCCM*, 140A.37); and part of the interpretation of Beleth in *Summa*, 25g-h (*CCCM*, 41A.52) is used by Prepositinus, *Tractatus de officiis*, 4.14 (ed. Corbett, 222) and Durand, *Rationale*, 5.2.46 (*CCCM*, 140A.36-7). Another part of Beleth's interpretation appears (in conjunction with Rupert's) in both versions of Peter of Roissy, *Manuale* (see fo 15va of the long version). The original form and function of 'Tu autem' has also been the subject of a debate among modern liturgists; see esp. C. Callewaert, '"Tu autem Domine miserere nobis"', printed in *idem*, *Sacris erudiri* (Bruges, 1940), 185-8.

52 Beleth, *Summa*, 62l and 161d (*CCCM*, 41A.114 and 315); Sicard, *Mitrale*, 4.2 and 50 (*PL* 213.157 and 425-6); and Durand, *Rationale*, 5.2.49 (*CCCM*, 140A.37-8).

to actual usage. Despite local differences in the arrangement of readings, books of the secular (Roman) and monastic office are generally consistent in using 'Haec dicit Dominus: Convertimini' at the end of readings from the prophets—usually in the first or first and second nocturns of Sundays and feasts and in the ferial nocturns—during Advent and certain other times of the year; 'Tu autem' was used at the end of most of the other readings, including those from the Pentateuch (beginning at first nocturns in Septuagesima) and the Old Testament histories (after Pentecost) as well as those from the New Testament.[53] The question in version *P* correctly refers to 'Haec dicit Dominus: Convertimini' as the ending for the readings from the prophets, but the reference to 'Tu autem' as the ending for New Testament readings presents a somewhat distorted picture of its usage, and the distortion is compounded in the response, where the phrases 'dicit Dominus' and 'Tu autem, Domine' are associated with the Old Testament and New Testament readings respectively.

Version *A* only seems to complicate the problem: the question refers to 'Haec dicit Dominus Deus' and 'Tu autem, Domine, miserere nobis' as the respective endings for Old and New Testament readings, and the response refers to 'Dicit Dominus omnipotens' and 'Haec dicit Dominus Deus' as endings for the Old Testament readings. The fact that these formulas are mentioned in place of 'Haec dicit Dominus: Convertimini' indicates that this version is referring to the mass, for instance in ember days, when Old Testament readings were used with 'dicit Dominus omnipotens' at the end ('Haec dicit Dominus Deus' was more common at the beginning of prophecies in the mass). This version, however, does not appear to be concerned only with the mass, since it mentions 'Tu autem', which is most likely a reference to the office, as it is in version *P*.[54]

The difference between the two versions attests to some confusion in the thirteenth century concerning the precise subject of the question, but regardless of whether *P* or *A* is considered as the more faithful report of the original question, it remains uncertain whether the question and response should be viewed as a reflection or a misrepresentation of actual liturgical usage. It is also uncertain whether

---

53 Various ordinals and customaries further restrict the use of 'Haec dicit dominus' by stating that 'Tu autem' should be used in its place if the reading does not actually conclude with the words of the Lord, or by stating that the readings from the prophets end in 'Haec dicit dominus' only in ferial nocturns. See, e.g., *Ordinarium canonicorum regularium s. Laudi Rotomagensis (PL* 147.157-8) and *Constitutiones Hirsaugienses,* 1.80 *(PL* 150.1007), and cf. the different instructions in *Antiquiores consuetudines Cluniacensis monasterii,* 2.29 *(PL* 149.714) and the *Disciplina Farfensis,* 1.39 *(PL* 150.1242); and for the distinction between Sunday and ferial nocturns, see, e.g., *Consuetudines Floriacenses saeculi tertii decimi,* ed. Anselmus Davril, Corpus Consuetudinum Monasticarum, 9 (Siegburg, 1976), 5.

54 See Joseph A. Jungmann, *The Mass of the Roman Rite: its orgins and development,* 2 vols (New York, 1951-5), i, 404-5, who notes that a closing formula was sometimes used for readings at mass but, apart from the formula 'dicit Dominus omnipotens' at the end of the readings of the prophecies, the closing formula did not become a rule in the mass as 'Tu autem' did in the office.

the question was prompted by the observation of a liturgical practice or was based on a question from an earlier source, but it seems unlikely that a liturgical commentary could have been the source for a question on a liturgical practice defined in such a problematic manner.

The three questions discussed above vary in terms of their apparent relationship to medieval liturgical commentaries. The questions regarding the time of ordination and the omission of the kiss of peace are formulated in the Quodlibets as they are in various liturgical commentaries, but the responses are more or less distinct from the standard explanations that circulated among the commentaries; and the question pertaining to the readings does not appear to be drawn from the tradition of commentaries on the liturgy.

What distinguishes Guerric's liturgical questions from the commentaries cannot be accounted for by the context in which they appear. There seems to be nothing comparable to Guerric's treatment of these liturgical questions in other quodlibetal disputes. In fact, the two articles in Guerric's Quodlibets are the only items that P. Glorieux listed under the general entry 'Liturgia' in the index to his repertory (although he included a cross-reference to 'Ritus missae et officii' where other items are listed).[55] It should be added that Guerric's liturgical questions are among a mere two dozen (out of several thousand listed by Glorieux in his two volumes) formulated with *quare,* as in liturgical commentaries, instead of *utrum,* the usual format in quodlibetal or disputed questions.

Guerric's Quodlibets are among the earliest examples of quodlibetal questions and do not necessarily conform to the procedures in use since the middle of the thirteenth century. The basis on which the individual questions were introduced in Guerric's Quodlibets is not entirely clear, and we cannot be sure whether the extant manuscripts are in fact reports of public disputes or compilations drawn from written sources. This makes it difficult to determine the exact relationship between Quodlibet 6, article 7 and the supplement to the *Quaestio de sacramento ordinis,* the only text noted above that provides a close parallel to any of the liturgical questions in the Quodlibets. Unless additional parallels are found which could place these questions within the tradition of liturgical commentaries, questions on the sacraments, or other genres, the liturgical questions must be viewed as isolated and notable examples of the medieval interpretation of the liturgy.

---

55 P. Glorieux, *La littérature quodlibétique II* (Paris, 1935), 358; the item listed as 'VII,8' should read 'VI,8', which is Quodlibet 6, article 7 in Principe's edition.

Chapter 6

From Durand of Mende to St Thomas More:
Lessons Learned from Medieval Liturgy

Timothy M. Thibodeau[1]

In May of 1990, I attended an international colloquium in the episcopal see of the famed medieval canonist and liturgist, William Durand the Elder, bishop of Mende (*c.* 1230-96).[2] When I first set foot in the picturesque little village of Mende, in the midst of the stunning scenery of the rugged Provençal terrain, I could scarcely contain my enthusiasm and emotion. 'Durand' and 'Mende' had become oft-repeated names in my household. For almost three years I had labored on a doctoral thesis in medieval history at the University of Notre Dame (USA), devoting nearly every waking moment to the study of Durand's mammoth liturgical exposition, the *Rationale divinorum officiorum*. By happy coincidence, I joined Professor Roger Reynolds at the formal opening of the colloquium, a scholar whom I much admired since I first met him when I was a graduate student. Later, as we sat in a little outdoor café in the shadow of the medieval cathedral of Mende, I was the beneficiary of Professor Reynolds' astonishing knowledge of medieval liturgy, his sharp wit, and his affable personality.

As Professor Reynolds knows, this conference was the birthplace of the modern critical edition of Durand's *Rationale*. Having presented a paper on the sources used by Durand to compile his liturgical commentary,[3] I was formally invited to collaborate with Fr. Anselme Davril, O.S.B., a monk at St Benoît-sur-Loire, and emeritus faculty member at the Insititut Catholique in Paris, in what we knew would be a gargantuan enterprise. A full decade (and 1,693 pages) later, we published

---

1   I wish to express my deep gratitude to my wife, Susan Corazza Thibodeau, for critiquing and editing early drafts of this essay.

2   To date, there is still no complete modern biography of Durand. Though antiquated, there are two well-known surveys of his life and career: Victor Leclerq, 'Guillaume Duranti, Évêque de Mende, surnommé le Spéculateur', in *Histoire Littéraire de la France* (Paris, 1895), xx, 411-80; and Louis Faletti, 'Guillaume Durand', in *Dictionnaire de droit canonique*, (1953), v, 1014-75.

3   Timothy M. Thibodeau, 'Les sources du *Rationale* de Guillaume Durand', in *Guillaume Durand, Évêque de Mende (v. 1230-1296): canoniste, liturgiste et homme politique*, ed. Pierre-Marie Gy (Paris, 1992), 143-53. My paper was followed by Professor Reynolds' own presentation, 'Guillaume Durand parmi les théologiens médiévaux de la liturgie', *ibid.*, 155-68.

the last volume of a three-volume edition in the series, *Corpus Christianorum, Continuatio Mediaeualis.*[4]

Divided into eight books, Durand's treatise provides an exhaustive treatment of a wide variety of topics that are of interest to art historians, liturgists, theologians and any serious students of medieval Christian culture: 1). the symbolism of church buildings and ecclesiastical art; 2). the clerical orders, their ordination rites, and respective ministries; 3). the symbolism of all liturgical vestments and liturgical colors; 4). a lengthy explication of the prayers, hymns and processions in the mass; 5). the divine office (its biblical lessons, hymns, prayers); 6). the Temporal cycle of the church year (with a treatment of its lessons, prayers and hymns); 7). the Sanctoral cycle; 8). the 'computus' and the arrangement of the solar calendar (the bewildering science, the mastery of which led Nicholas Copernicus to propose heliocentrism in 1543).

Published between 1294 and 1296, and disseminated in two distinct redactions from Paris, Bologna and Milan, Durand's text soon became the definitive medieval liturgical treatise. Reading a commentary such as the *Rationale* was often the only formal instruction a cleric might get in what we would today call liturgical theology, and this undoubtedly accounts for the many abridged Latin and vernacular versions of the text that appeared soon after its publication.[5] Because of its scope, magnitude and the author's own editorial practice of synthesizing the roughly four-hundred years of liturgical commentary that stood behind him, Durand's treatise rapidly became a 'best seller' by both medieval and modern standards. Even the thundering polemic of the father of the Protestant Reformation, Martin Luther, provides testimony to the enduring appeal of Durand's allegorical exposition of the liturgy. In his *Babylonian Captivity of the Church* (1520), in the midst of a broadside against medieval allegorical methods of biblical exegesis, Luther derides the *Rationale* by name, declaring that 'such allegorical studies are for idle men ... . [W]ho has so weak a mind as not to be able to launch into allegories?'[6]

Durand's treatise fared much better during the Catholic Restorationist liturgical revival that spread through France in the first half of the nineteenth century. In his classic study of the liturgy, the founder of the French monastic community of

---

4   *Guillelmi Duranti Rationale Divinorum Officiorum I-VIII*, ed. A. Davril et T. M. Thibodeau, 3 vols, *CCCM*, 140, 140A, 140B (Turnhout, 1995; 1998; 2000). The third volume contains all of our introductory material, including an analysis of the manuscript tradition and complete indices for the text of all three volumes.

5   Not long after Durand's death, a number of vernacular translations of portions of the *Rationale* began to appear, principally in Old French and Late Middle German. For an analysis of the French vernacular tradition, see Claudia Rabel, 'L'illustration du *Rational des divin offices* de Guillaume Durand', in *Guillaume Durand*, 171-81. For the German vernacular text, see G. H. Buijssen, *Durandus' Rationale in spätmittelhochdeutscher Übersetzung*, 4 vols (Assen, 1966-83).

6   Martin Luther, *Three Treatises*, ed. and trans. Charles M. Jacobs, A. T. W. Steinhaeuser, and W. A. Lambert (Philadelphia, 1984), 241. Luther's critique has little to do with liturgics, per se, but rather is rooted in his campaign to create a reformed method of scriptural exegesis.

Solesmes, Dom Prosper Guéranger, declared the *Rationale* to be 'the final word from the Middle Ages on the mystery of the Divine Services'.[7] The existence of over 300 complete medieval manuscripts and scores of textual fragments is indisputable confirmation of Guéranger's appraisal of the text. The *Rationale* has the distinction of being the second non-Biblical book printed at Gutenberg's press in 1459 (preceded only by Donatus' second-century A.D. grammar), and it saw another 104 printings by 1859, the year that the last modern diplomatic edition appeared in Naples.[8] Because of its length and the complexity of its sources, the *Rationale* had not been published in a modern critical form before the current edition appeared.

In the many years that have passed since I first began my research on Durand—as the tide of the academic culture wars has ebbed and flowed in North American colleges and universities—I have encountered many colleagues in the field of history who cannot fathom the merit of my research, nor can they begin to imagine the satisfaction I have derived from reconstructing a famous medieval liturgical encyclopedia. Modern scholars of liturgical theology often take an equally dim view of the study of medieval liturgics. Since the implementation of the liturgical reforms of the Roman Catholic Church (from the 1950s to the 1970s), medieval liturgists such as Durand have routinely been viewed with embarrassment by Catholic theologians and liturgists, and are often relegated to the dust heap of historical theology. One of the great pioneers of modern Catholic liturgical reform went so far as to criticize medieval allegorical liturgical treatises for their 'intrinsic absurdity'. In his *Liturgical Piety*, Louis Bouyer declared: 'the history of the Roman Mass in the Middle Ages is the history of how it came to be misunderstood by the clergy as well as by the faithful, and how it began to disintegrate through the fault of the medieval liturgists themselves'.[9]

In light of the cultural and ecclesial milieux within which a new generation of medievalists now works, I find it especially fitting to offer this essay in honor of Professor Reynolds' long and distinguished career. Inspired by his many scholarly contributions to our field, I am happy to count myself among the ranks of historians of the Middle Ages who have concentrated their scholarship on liturgical history in general, and clerical treatises on the liturgy in particular. While a good many historians might view my work as the mastery of an obscure genre that belongs to the periphery of the academic study of pre-modern European history,[10] I would

---

7   Prosper Guéranger, *Institutions liturgiques*, 3 vols (Paris, 1840-51), i, 355.

8   For the definitive analysis of the early printed editions of the *Rationale*, see Michel Albaric, 'Les Éditions imprimées du *Rationale divinorum officiorum* de Guillaume Durand de Mende', in *Guillaume Durand*, 183-200; and Bertrand Guyot, 'Essai de classement des editions du *Rationale*', in *Guillaume Durand*, 201-5.

9   *Liturgical Piety* (Notre Dame, IN, 1955), 16.

10 Two recent works make a brilliant case for the centrality of liturgical studies in any serious attempt at understanding the Reformation and its aftermath: Eamon Duffy, *The Stripping of the Altars:*

argue that a treatise such as the *Rationale* majestically towers like a gothic cathedral over the landscape of late medieval culture. This work of a canonist, bishop, and liturgist *par excellence* is the synthesis of a variety of disciplines that modern medievalists have often pursued in isolation from each other as specialized areas (viz., history, theology, law, and liturgy). What is more, the method of liturgical exegesis codified by Durand's treatise persisted virtually unchallenged into the age of the Christian humanism of the fourteenth and fifteenth centuries.

Professor Reynolds himself made an important contribution to the recovery of liturgical studies for historians of the Middle Ages twenty-five years ago, in his groundbreaking work on the relationship between the Investiture Controversy and the liturgical reforms of that era.[11] An ocean of ink had been spilled on the political dimensions of this controversy (e.g., the issue of Church-State relations), but Professor Reynolds argued that what the papal reformers and imperialists battled over was, properly speaking, a *liturgical ceremony*: the consecration and investiture of a bishop or abbot. While the eleventh century was a watershed era in medieval politics, he noted that few scholars were aware that many of the polemicists of the Investiture Controversy were 'avid observers of the liturgy', and that 'this same period was also a high plateau in the history of liturgical scholarship'.[12]

In that tumultuous age of monastic and papal reform, formal liturgical commentary, one of the oldest and most enduring genres of the entire medieval period (dating back to the patristic age), was revived and continued to flourish until the end of the Middle Ages.[13] What we now call 'expositiones missae' or 'mass expositions' continued to draw the attention of some of the greatest theologians and spiritual writers of the later medieval period:[14] Rupert of Deutz, Honorius Augustodunensis, Sicard of Cremona, Innocent III, and William Durand, to name a few. Beginning with Rupert's comprehensive treatise on the divine offices, all of these expositors worked within an allegorical system of liturgical exposition that came to its full flowering in Durand's *Rationale*.

---

traditional religion in England 1400-1580 (New Haven, CT, 1992); and David Cressy, *Birth, Marriage and Death: ritual, religion, and the life-cycle in Tudor and Stuart England* (Oxford/New York, 1997).

11 'Liturgical Scholarship at the Time of the Investiture Controversy: past research and future opportunities', *Harvard Theological Review*, 71 (1978), 109-24.

12 Reynolds, 'Liturgical Scholarship', 109.

13 I have treated the subject of monastic-papal reform and its relation to liturgical exposition in a forthcoming chapter titled, 'The Gothic Age', in *The Oxford History of Christian Worship*, ed. Geoffrey Wainwright and Karen B. Westerfield Tucker (Oxford/New York—in press).

14 Among the best known works on the subject of the medieval liturgy and 'expositiones missae' are: Joseph A. Jungmann, *The Mass of the Roman Rite: its origins and development*, trans. Francis A. Brunner, 2 vols (New York, 1951-5; repr. Westminster, MD: 1986); Roger E. Reynolds, 'Liturgy, Treatises on', in *Dictionary of the Middle Ages*, ed. Joseph R. Strayer (1986), vii, 624-33; and Cyrille Vogel, *Medieval Liturgy: an introduction to the sources*, rev. and trans. William G. Storey and Niels Krogh Rasmussen (Washington, D.C., 1986).

But the proper performance and interpretation of the liturgy should not be dismissed as solely the preoccupation of the medieval clerical elite. Medieval people, in whatever state of life—monks, clerics, lay men and women, both lords and peasants—were profoundly shaped by the official cultic practices of the medieval church. Whether they 'prayed, fought or worked', to use the taxonomy ascribed to King Alfred the Great, their lives were governed in myriad ways by the church's liturgical seasons and the daily rhythms of the liturgy. Time was 'sacred time' and was reckoned according to the church's liturgical calendar. What one could eat, what one could wear, when one could be married and to whom, when one could have sex, when one could fight for a just cause: these and more were strictly regulated by an elaborate code of liturgical and sacramental jurisprudence which reached its apogee in precisely the era that Durand's *Rationale* was written. The *Rationale* stands between the publication of two pillars of medieval canonical science: Gratian's *Decretum* (*c.* 1140), and the *Liber Sextus* (1298) of Durand's contemporary and confidant, Pope Boniface VIII (r. 1294-1303).[15]

One of the most eloquent and enduring presentations of the all-encompassing influence of the liturgy on late medieval culture was produced by a Dutch anthropologist, not a modern student of canon law or liturgy. In 1919, Johan Huizinga published his classic study of the last flowering of art and literature in late medieval Christendom. This tome, recently translated as *Autumn of the Middle Ages,* remains an elegant and provocative account of what Huizinga judged to be the 'overripe' literary and artistic forms of northern Europe in the waning years of the Middle Ages. Huizinga's work opens with a vivid passage that underscores the capaciousness of the 'liturgical mindset' of late medieval culture. From a cultural-anthropological perspective, liturgy is not simply defined as a set of 'texts that are read, sung or performed'. Rather, liturgy in this sense is fundamentally a series of solemn acts, comprising numerous public and private rituals that shaped the mental landscape of an entire civilization:

> When the world was half a thousand years younger all events had much sharper outlines than now. The distance between sadness and joy, between good and bad fortune, seemed to be much greater than for us; every experience had that degree of directness and absoluteness that joy and sadness still have in the mind of a child. Every event, every deed was defined in given and expressive forms and was in accord with the solemnity of a tight and invariable life style. The great events of human life—birth, marriage and death—by virtue of the sacraments, basked in the radiance of divine

---

15 I have discussed the relationship between canon law and Durand's work as a liturgist in two articles: 'The Influence of Canon Law on Liturgical Exposition c. 1100-1300', *Sacris Erudiri*, 37 (1997), 185-202; and 'Canon Law and Liturgical Exposition in Durand's *Rationale*', *BMCL*, NS 22 (1998), 41-52.

mystery. But even the lesser events—a journey, labor, a visit—were accompanied by a multitude of blessings, ceremonies, sayings and conventions.[16]

The opening words of William Durand's *Rationale*, provide a particularly poignant proof-text for Huizinga's characterization of the late-medieval *mentalité*:

Whatever belongs to the liturgical offices, objects, and furnishings of the Church is full of signs of the divine and the sacred mysteries, and each of them overflows with a celestial sweetness when it is encountered by a diligent observer who can extract 'honey from rock and oil from the stoniest ground' [Deut. 32: 13]. Who knows 'the order of the heavens and can apply its rules to the earth' [Job 38: 33]? Certainly, he who would attempt to investigate the majesty of heaven would be overwhelmed by its glory. It is, in fact, a deep well from which I cannot drink [cf. Joh. 4: 11], unless he who 'gives all things abundantly and does not reproach us' [Jas. 1: 5] provides me with a vessel 'so that I can drink with joy from the fountains of the Savior' [Is. 12: 3] 'which flow between the mountains' [Ps. 103: 10].[17]

Huizinga's perception of the symbolic contours of late medieval culture is also affirmed in a famous essay by the great Dominican theologian, Marie-Dominique Chenu. He coined the phrase 'symbolist mentality' when describing the medieval approach to the natural order. In his detailed study of twelfth- and thirteenth-century philosophy, theology, literature and the plastic arts, Chenu concluded that medieval people, both clerics and the illiterate multitudes to whom they provided pastoral care, eagerly searched for traces of the divine in almost every element of their daily lives. He declared that this 'symbolist mentality' was:

[A] permeating influence, of which men were more or less aware, upon their ways and turns of thought; a cast or coloration given to even the commonest notions; a body of assumptions rarely expressed yet accepted everywhere and by all and very difficult to uncover. Masters in the schools, mystics, exegetes, students of nature, seculars, religious, writers and artists—these men ... had the conviction that all natural or historical reality possessed a *signification* which transcended its crude reality and which a certain symbolic dimension of that reality would reveal to man's mind. This conviction, enforced by the context of their lives, dominated their judgment by supplying it with an intrinsic set of categories and values.[18]

When applied to the liturgical rites of the Church, this paradigm, so lucidly expressed by Durand in the opening paragraph of his *Rationale*, demonstrates one of the inherent strengths of medieval Christian piety. Liturgical expositors could and

---

16 Johan Huizinga, *The Autumn of the Middle Ages*, trans. Rodney J. Payton and Ulrich Mammitzsch (Chicago, 1996), 1.

17 *Rationale*, Pro. 1, *CCCM*, 140.3.

18 M.-D. Chenu, 'The Symbolist Mentality', in *Nature, Man and Society in the Twelfth Century*, trans. Jerome Taylor and Lester K. Little (Chicago, 1979), 102.

often did reach poetic heights in offering vivid allegorical interpretations of the church's rites. Durand and his contemporaries viewed the liturgy as a whole—the mass, the divine office and saints' feasts throughout the entire course of the year—as one harmonious, iconographic representation of the unfolding of the great events of salvation history, from the creation of the world to the final judgment. This theme of the reenactment of salvation history, prefigured typologically in the Old Testament and consummated in the death, resurrection, and future coming of Christ, is the thread that is woven throughout the complex fabric of medieval liturgical piety.[19]

One such example of this medieval hermeneutical approach to the liturgy is Durand's commentary on the office of vespers, or evening prayer in book 5 of the *Rationale*. This prayer service was mandated by canon law in all of the cathedrals of Europe in Durand's time. Along with morning prayer, it was one of the most solemn liturgies of the medieval church. Its psalmody, biblical lessons and hymns followed an ancient tradition, which was mostly invariable.[20]

We know from his numerous pastoral works that Durand was a conscientious bishop: he compiled synodal statutes for his diocese,[21] produced an Ordinal for his cathedral,[22] and his famous Pontifical[23] was unrivalled in the Latin Church until the reforms of the Second Vatican Council. Durand was also keenly aware that for clerics engaged in a wide range of activities (e.g., university study, administrative tasks or pastoral care), the many liturgical services that they were obligated to observe could be seen as a burden which they might perform halfheartedly, or worse still, that they would scarcely understand even as they performed them.

In the *Rationale*, Durand's treatment of evening prayer (which would take roughly forty to fifty minutes to complete, depending upon the solemnity of the day), therefore amounts to an inspirational sermon on the liturgy of vespers. He encourages his readers to be mindful that the prayers, hymns, processions and liturgical ornaments of this service embody a sacred reality far beyond its bare words or gestures, a reality perhaps comparable to the real presence of Christ in the eucharistic bread:

---

19 I have discussed the relation between allegorical biblical exegesis and liturgical commentary in my article: '*Enigmata Figurarum*: biblicial exegesis and liturgical exposition in Durand's *Rationale*', *Harvard Theological Review*, 86 (1993), 65-79.

20 For a thorough analysis of the historical development of the divine office, see Robert Taft, *The Liturgy of the Hours in East and West: the origins of the divine office and its meaning for today* (Collegeville, MN, 1986).

21 J. Berthelé and M. Valmary, 'Les Instructions et Constitutions de Guillaume Durand le Spécula-teur', *Memoires de l'Académie des sciences et lettres de Montpellier*, 2nd serie, 3 (1905), 1-148.

22 Pierre-Marie Gy, 'L'Ordinaire de Mende, une oeuvre inédite de Guillaume Durand l'Ancien', *Cahiers de Fanjeux*, 17 (1982), 239-49.

23 Michel Andrieu, ed., *Le Pontifical romain au Moyen Age*, vol. 3: *Le Pontifical de Guillaume Durand*, Studi e Testi, 88 (Vatican City, 1940).

At vespers, the church represents the first coming of the Lord, which was near the twilight of the world's [history], that is the final age of the world; for this reason She gives thanks to God by singing this office, as the Apostle says: 'Upon us the final age of the world has come' [cf. I Cor. 10:11]. Moreover, Christ was taken down from the cross at Vespers; at the same hour he instituted the sacrament of his body and blood at the Last Supper [and] he washed the feet of his disciples; and dressed as a pilgrim, he revealed himself to his disciples going to Emaus in the breaking of the bread. The Church, therefore, rightly gives thanks to Christ at this hour ... . The Church recites five psalms at this hour. First, on account of the five wounds of Christ, who offered himself as a sacrifice for us in the evening time of the world. Second, for our correction, so that we may weep and ask for forgiveness for the sins which we commit every day through the five corporeal senses, just as Jeremiah says: 'Death has entered through our windows' [cf. Jer. 9:21].[24]

This same sense of immediacy or transparency of time permeates Durand's understanding of the yearly liturgical cycle as a whole, and each of the daily liturgies in particular. As Durand notes in several instances, many of the Church's hymns begin with an emphatic 'hodie' ('today'); for example the Christmas chant, 'Hodie, Christus natus est' ('Today Christ is born').

When pushed to the extreme, the allegorical hermeneutics of a writer such as Durand could unwittingly lead, as Huizinga argued, to the profanation of the sacred. Medieval piety could rapidly move from allegory and metaphor to a crude realism which did not blush to depict, in the most graphic terms, some of the core mysteries of the Christian faith:

Symbolism, with its handmaid allegory, had become a mere mental game; the meaningful had become meaningless ... .There was an awareness of looking at an enigma yet here were attempts to distinguish the images in the mirror, to explain images through images, and to hold up mirrors to mirrors. The whole world was capsulated in independent figures; it was a time of overripeness and the falling of blossoms. Thought had become too dependent on figures; the visual tendency, so very characteristic of the waning Middle Ages, was now overpowering. *Everything that could be thought had become plastic and pictorial* [my emphasis].[25]

This 'fatuous familiarity with God in daily life',[26] to use Huizinga's memorable line, led to some rather bizarre and even crude (to us) depictions of the sacred. One startling example is the practice of creating ornate, jewel-encrusted statues of the Virgin Mary, which featured bellies that could be opened to reveal an anthropomorphic depiction of the Trinity.[27] Durand himself did not blush to discuss in a

---

24 *Rationale*, 5.9.1-3, *CCCM*, 140B.105-6.
25 Huizinga, *Autumn of the Middle Ages*, 247-8.
26 *Ibid.*, 178.
27 *Ibid.*, 179.

rather mundane fashion the relic of Christ's circumcised foreskin that was housed in the treasury of relics of the Lateran basilica since the time of Charlemagne.[28]

Crude realism in art was often accompanied, or so the religious reformers of the Renaissance and Reformation complained, by a crass and overconfident scholastic theology which they believed trivialized the sacred mysteries of the Christian faith. (Still, the humanists oftentimes seemed to be responding more to Erasmian caricatures of scholasticism than actual scholastic texts). As early as the turn of the thirteenth century, scholastic theologians were debating the doctrine of the real presence of Christ in the Eucharist in terms that would later be mocked by some Christian humanists and Protestant theologians. In his lengthy liturgical commentary, *De missarum mysteriis* (c. 1195), Pope Innocent III (then a cardinal) openly speculated on what happens to a consecrated host when a mouse nibbles it; miraculously, he concluded, the real presence of Christ ceases to exist.[29] Writing a century later, Durand viewed Innocent's words as authoritative, copied them verbatim, and enshrined them in his own discourse on the doctrine of transubstantiation in book 4 of the *Rationale*.[30]

Despite the many virtues of Huizinga's work, his vibrant portrait of late medieval piety is sometimes painted with too bold strokes, with an overemphasis on the inevitable 'decline' of Christian art forms in northern Europe in the fourteenth and fifteenth centuries. Many textbook accounts of the Renaissance and Reformation era unhesitatingly start with Huizinga's premise of the 'decline and fall' of the medieval church, and assume profound incongruities and conflicts between the degenerate state of the rituals and pious expressions of the late medieval Church and the basic tenets of reform movements such as the *Devotio moderna* or the enlightened Catholicism of the Christian humanists who were their heirs.

Yet when we examine the voluminous literature of these Christian reformers, as it relates to the liturgy and liturgical piety, this dichotomous view must be greatly modified and in some cases discarded altogether. The many texts of the *Devotio moderna*, for example, reveal the fundamental flaws associated with setting late medieval Christian reform against medieval liturgiology. It is true that Geert Grote (1340-84), the founder of the Brothers and Sisters of the Common Life, and other spiritual writers within his movement were harsh in their criticisms of the inanity and vanity of contemporary university theology. But Grote and his followers firmly rooted their spirituality in a medieval-monastic conception of the liturgy (in both a

---

28 The context of this odd report is a discourse on why Christ had to observe the requirements of the Old Law before establishing the New. Durand discuss this in two instances: *Rationale*, 4.52.8, *CCCM*, 140.467; and 6.15.16, *CCCM*, 140A.198. His source is Innocent III's *De missarum mysteriis*.

29 *De missarum mysteriis*, 4.9, *PL* 217.861D-862A.

30 *Rationale*, 4.41.31-32, *CCCM*, 140.450. See my article, 'The Doctrine of Transubstantiation in Durand's *Rationale*', *Traditio*, 51 (1996), 308-17.

broad and more technical sense).[31] Even the most famous and widely known devotional treatise of the movement, Thomas à Kempis' (1380-1471) *Imitation of Christ*, concludes with a tractate on reverence for the Eucharist.

It is equally facile to suggest that somehow early Christian humanism,[32] and late medieval spirituality were necessarily at odds with each other or were mutually exclusive.[33] In fact, the famous humanist-scholastic debate that pitted the spirited polemics of the humanist philologists against the logic of the scholastics did not find any parallel in liturgiology at the end of the Middle Ages.

In his last published work, one of the premiere Christian humanists, St Thomas More (1478-1535),[34] offered an allegorical reflection on the Passion of Christ that is strikingly 'medieval' in its rhetorical structure and content. Secretly composed in the lonely isolation of the Tower of London as he awaited his inevitable execution, More's *De Tristitia Christi*[35] offers many distinctly allegorical interpretations on the Passion narratives found in the Gospels. It is often difficult to distinguish the reflective homiletics of More, the great sixteenth-century lawyer-humanist, from the liturgical hermeneutics of Durand, the thirteenth-century Provençal canonist-bishop.

To give but one example, More ponders at length the multiple layers of meaning in the terse Gospel accounts of Christ's journey to the Mount of Olives before his arrest and trial. Beginning his treatise with a simple text, 'When Jesus had said these things, they recited the hymn and went out to the Mount of Olives', More then provides a moral exhortation chastising himself and others for the idleness of 'our conversation during meals'; how it is 'meaningless and inconsequential'.[36] He then goes well beyond the literal meaning of the biblical text to consider its hidden

---

31 John Van Engen, *Devotio Moderna: basic writings* (New York, 1989), has rejected such a dichotomy in refusing to equate the spirituality of the Brothers and Sisters of the Common Life with 'proto-Protestantism'.

32 Seminal treatment of the term can be found in Paul Oskar Kristeller, 'The Role of Humanism in Renaissance Religion and Platonism', in *The Pursuit of Holiness in Late Medieval and Renaissance Religion*, ed. Charles Trinkaus and Heiko A. Oberman (Leiden, 1974), 367-70. Kristeller argues against defining humanism as a 'philosophical school' or a particular 'theology'. Humanists are best understood, he says, as being concerned with a particular set of scholarly pursuits, chiefly grammar and rhetoric.

33 See Steven Ozment, *The Age of Reform 1250-1550* (New Haven, Conn., 1980), 73-117. The author exposes the subjectivity of the terms 'scholastic' and 'humanist' when he discusses the criticisms levelled against 'scholastic theology' by two trained scholastics, Jean Gerson (1363-1429) and Nicholas of Clémanges (c. 1363-1437). See also Erika Rummel, *The Humanist-Scholastic Debate in the Renaissance and Reformation* (Cambridge, MA, 1995).

34 The best known modern biographies are: Richard Marius, *Thomas More: a biography* (New York, 1984); and Peter Ackroyd, *The Life of Thomas More* (New York/London, 1998).

35 *De Tristitia Christi*, ed. and trans. Clarence H. Miller, in *The Yale Edition of the Complete Works of St. Thomas More*, 14/i-ii (New Haven, CT, 1976).

36 *Ibid.*, 3.

or interior sense by Christologizing Psalm 62 and linking it typologically to the literal text:

> 'They went out to the Mount of Olives', not bed. The prophet says, 'I arose in the middle of the night to pay homage to you', but Christ did not even lie down in bed. But as for us, I wish we could truly apply to ourselves even this text: 'I thought of you as I lay in my bed'.[37]

More seeks the meaning of the text that was 'hidden away' ('recondere') by the sacred author later to be ferreted out by the exegete with the aid of the Holy Spirit:

> Mount Olivet itself also has a mysterious significance, planted as it was with olive trees. For the olive branch was generally used as a symbol of peace, which Christ came to establish between God and man after their long alienation. Moreover, the oil which is produced from the olive represents the anointing by the Spirit, for Christ came and then returned to His Father in order to send the Holy Spirit upon the disciples so that His anointing might then teach them ... .[38]

The same exegetical principles are applied to the other place names associated with Christ's passion since More believes that the Holy Spirit has 'concealed' in them a 'store of sacred mysteries' to be uncovered by devout exegetes:

> The stream Cedron lies between the city of Jerusalem and the Mount of Olives, and the word 'Cedron' in Hebrew means 'sadness'. The name 'Gethsemani' in Hebrew means 'most fertile valley' or 'valley of olives'. And so there is no reason for us to attribute it merely to chance that the evangelists recorded these place names so carefully. For if that were the case, once they had reported that He went to the Mount of Olives, they would have considered that they had said quite enough, if it were not that God had veiled under these place-names some mysterious meanings which attentive men, with the help of the Holy Spirit, would try to uncover because the names were mentioned. And so not a single syllable can be thought inconsequential in a composition which was dictated by the Holy Spirit as the apostles wrote it ... .[39]

In the final days of his life, More instinctively found consolation not in academic discourse on papal sovereignty over the church, the humanist embrace of Greco-Roman texts, or the fine points of Roman or canon law, but rather in what Jean Leclercq called the 'poem of the liturgy'. Joining his own anguish to the sufferings of Christ in Gethsemane and finally on the cross, More discovered in the medieval allegorical understanding of the liturgy (both its biblical texts and its liturgical formulae) a refuge for coming to terms with his own fears and frailty. He could anchor his own seemingly insignificant life in the broader context of the

---

37 *Ibid.*, 7-9.
38 *Ibid.*, 11.
39 *Ibid.*, 14-15.

cosmic drama of salvation history, so poetically and palpably articulated in the seasonal rhythms of the liturgy (and most especially, in the sacred rituals of the Triduum).

In this sense Jean Leclercq's final assessment of the monastic liturgy—'that it is the mirror of a culture and its culmination'—finds a compelling witness in the last written work of St Thomas More. His variegated personality and his sometimes-discordant life's journey (from Carthusian novice, to lawyer, to politician, to humanist, to Catholic polemicist, to condemned criminal) found its reintegration and final solace in the liturgical piety of the late medieval Church:

> [I]t is in the atmosphere of the liturgy and amid the poems composed for it, *in hymnis et canticis*, that the synthesis of the *artes* was effected, of the literary techniques, religious reflection, and all the sources of information whether biblical, patristic or classical. In the liturgy, all these resources fully attained their final potentiality; they were restored to God in a homage which recognized that they had come from Him ... . In the liturgy, love of learning and desire for God find perfect reconciliation.[40]

---

40 Jean Leclercq, *The Love of Learning and the Desire for God: a study of monastic culture*, trans. Catharine Misrahi (New York, 1982), 250-51.

Chapter 7

Latin and Italian Prayers in a Sixteenth-Century Beneventan Manuscript from Naples[*]

Virginia Brown

Introduction

Evidence continues to accumulate for the prolonged use of Beneventan script at Naples into the first half of the sixteenth century. Nine witnesses representing eight codices have been analyzed and identified as Neapolitan products of the Cinquecento.[1] Quite remarkable is the fact that most of these manuscripts survive intact or

[*] I should like to thank warmly Dr Martin Schøyen for his extraordinary generosity and good will that have made possible my investigation of MS 1981 in his collection. The texts and plates published here are reproduced with his permission. I am also indebted to Dr Richard C. Linenthal for unstinting and cordial assistance when I consulted the codex in London. Prof. Annamaria Facchiano has freely shared with me her expertise in the field of Neapolitan religious history, and I gratefully acknowledge here and in the relevant instances below the valuable suggestions she has made.—Research for this article was conducted for the 'Monumenta Liturgica Beneventana' program under the auspices of a Research Grant from the Social Sciences and Humanities Research Council of Canada.

1   For the nine previously identified examples of sixteenth-century Beneventan, see the following studies by the present writer:

'The Survival of Beneventan Script: Sixteenth-Century Liturgical Codices from Benedictine Monasteries in Naples', in *Monastica. Scritti raccolti in memoria del IV centenario della nascita di S. Benedetto (480-1980)*, 7 vols (Montecassino, 1981-92), i, 237-355 and 8 plates—Naples, Biblioteca della Società Napoletana di Storia Patria, MSS Cuomo 2-4-10 (necrology of the monastery of Santa Patrizia) + Cuomo 2-4-12 (martyrology of the monastery of Santa Patrizia) (both manuscripts originally formed part of the same chapter book); New York, Columbia University, Butler Library, MS X264.02.C28 (book of hours for the use of Giulia Caracciolo, a nun at the monastery of Santa Patrizia); Vatican City, Biblioteca Apostolica Vaticana, MSS Barb. lat. 517 (enchiridion monasticum for use at the monastery of San Gregorio Armeno), Borgia lat. 356 (book of hours for the use of Cizola Minutulo, a nun at the monastery of Santa Patrizia and later abbess of the monastery of Santa Maria ad Agnone), and Chigi C. IV. 113 ('book of hours' formerly belonging to Beatrice Galeota, a nun at the monastery of San Gregorio Armeno).

'The Montevergine 6 Codex and Sixteenth-Century Beneventan Script in Naples', in *Per la storia del Mezzogiorno medievale e moderno. Studi in memoria di Jole Mazzoleni*, ed. Giulio Raimondi and Stefano Palmieri, 2 vols, Pubblicazioni degli Archivi di Stato, Saggi 48 (Rome, 1998), i, 407-18, including 2 plates—Montevergine, Biblioteca dell'Abbazia, MS 6 (breviary).

'A New List of Beneventan Manuscripts (IV)', *Mediaeval Studies*, 61 (1999), 340—Cosenza, Biblioteca Civica, Cinq. C 350 (4), binding fragments (Psalter of the Virgin Mary); 351—Lecce, Biblioteca Provinciale, Cinq. XXI B 81, binding fragments (breviary).

in a substantial number of folios; exceptions are the items at Cosenza (four scraps joining to form two complete leaves) and Lecce (four strips joining to form two pieces). In 'New List (IV)', 340, I suggested on the basis of format, script, and contents that the Cosenza fragments may contain some of the opening text now missing from MS Borgia lat. 356. While this may well be the case, I would like to note here that the much cleaner and whiter parchment in the Cosenza leaves is so strikingly different as to raise another possibility, i.e., these fragments may be the remnants of a third book of hours copied at Santa Patrizia from the same codicological and liturgical template. If so, this would yield nine (instead of eight) Beneventan manuscripts copied in the first half of the sixteenth century. A recent addition to this group is a complete prayerbook, as yet unstudied, with the shelf mark Oslo-London, The Schøyen Collection, MS 1981.[2]

MS 1981, however, has another and equally distinctive claim to fame. With two prayers in Italian (fos 13r-17v shown on our Pls 7.2-7), it is the first manuscript presently known to preserve a substantial amount of vernacular text written in Beneventan.[3] Naturally this does not overturn in the least the undeniable fact that Latin was the preferred language of Beneventan scribes. But the appearance of the vernacular in MS 1981 is a striking palaeographical and linguistic phenomenon. Interesting as well is the mix of prayers, both early and late, seen in the remaining contents. These features, then, provide the justification for the following study and edition of MS 1981 (hereafter S).[4] It should be noted that the edition includes a transcription of the Italian prayers, but there is no detailed discussion of the linguistic features; this has been left to those scholars whose competence in this regard is far greater than that of the present writer.[5]

Description of S

Codicology i (paper) + 76 fos (parchment). 135 x 98 (90 x 60) mm., 14 long lines, with text beginning above top line. The parchment is smooth, of average thickness, yellowed on the hair side, and somewhat whiter on the flesh side. Brown stains are visible at the bottom of fos 1-5 and intermittently thereafter; black stains at the top,

---

2 Notice of the Schøyen volume first emerged in 1994; see the Sotheby's sale catalogue *Western Manuscripts and Miniatures. Sale LN4725 ... Day of Sale Monday, 5th December, 1994*, 114-17, lot 88 and plate on 115 (fo 1r). The codex was acquired by its current owner at that time. Here the date and origin are given as 'Southern Italy, perhaps Naples, fifteenth century'.

3 Previously the single example known of the use of Beneventan for the vernacular was the *nota possessoris* in MS Chigi C. IV. 113, fo 114r: 'Quisto offitio ei de la signora beatrice galiota' (Brown, 'Survival of Beneventan Script', 253-4 and Pl. IV. a).

4 S was described briefly in Virginia Brown, 'A Second New List of Beneventan Manuscripts (III)', *Mediaeval Studies*, 56 (1994), 349 (under London); and the current shelf mark was noted in Brown, 'New List (IV)', 386-7 with mention of a forthcoming study (= the present article).

5 Prof. Lucia Gualdo Rosa and Prof. Maria Elisabetta Romano have confirmed the Neapolitan cast of language.

towards the gutter, of fos 72-76 and on the inside back cover. Foliated lightly in pencil, mostly by tens, at the bottom in the outer corner (1, 2, 10, 20, 30, 40, 50, 60, 70, 74, 75, 76). Collation scheme: $i + 1^8-9^8 + 10^4$, with flesh side on the outside of every quire. Quires are numbered 1-10 in red crayon on the first recto (lower, outer corner) of each gathering; a '+' sign in red crayon appears on the recto of the fifth folio (= one half of the central bifolium) in each quaternion. Ruling in fine brown ink (?) on both sides of every leaf; single vertical bounding lines. Catchwords on fos 8v, 16v, 24v, 32v, 40v, 48v, 56v, 64v, and 72v consist of three to five letters written perpendicular to the text along the inner vertical bounding line.

Text ink is black, with some fading on the flesh side (e.g., fos 45r, 46v-47r, 60v-61r, 62v-63r, 73r). Rubrics are in red ink. The most lavish decoration is on fo 1r (Pl. 7.1) where the text is surrounded on three sides by a border consisting of a vertical blue bar in the inner margin to whose extremities are attached in the upper and lower margins horizontal sprays of colored and burnished gold flowers, leaves, and rayed discs; the sprays terminate in larger flowers. Leafy majuscule *O*, five-lines high, is burnished gold outlined in red. Infilling the center of this letter is a stylized floral pattern in varying shades of green heightened with yellow that is placed on a blue ground embellished with white tracery. Majuscules beginning other prayers occupy two or three lines in height and normally alternate in color between burnished gold with full-page purple penwork or dark blue with full-length red penwork. An identical color scheme is reflected on fos 33v-47r in some majuscules beginning sentences; one-line high, blue with penwork in red alternates with burnished gold with penwork in purple. Elsewhere other majuscules beginning sentences are embellished only with *Cadellen* in the same ink used for the text.

The binding is sixteenth-century limp vellum, stained and discolored on the outside. The inside of the front cover is lined with old paper on which various hands have written, in descending order, '8661dz', '87', '76 ff.', 'Legato con un portolano / dell'Italia meridion\<ale\>'. The inside back cover displays a truncated map of the lower part of Apulia, beginning with the coastline between Brindisi and Lecce at Torre Rinalda south as far as Porto Badisco, then inland and west to San Pietro Galatina and continuing northwards past Lecce to Trepuzzi.[6] On the spine of the volume is a title in black ink: 'Orationes S^{ti} Thomae de Aquino'.

The provenance is 'a private collection in Connecticut where it has remained for many years'.[7]

---

6   See Pl. 7.9. The fold at the bottom and sides obscures the names of some localities: (south of the Capo d'Otranto) La palasia, S. Meliano, P. Badisco; (westward) Bosardo, Muro (to the north), Scorano, S. p.° galatina; (northwards) Salato, Sternate (visible), Lecule, Campi, Lece, Treposo.

7   According to the description in the Sotheby's sale catalogue, 116 (cited in n. 2 above).

Palaeography S was copied by a single scribe. The letter-forms in both the Latin and vernacular texts exhibit all the features already noted[8] as characteristic of sixteenth-century Neapolitan manuscripts, namely:

– despite the evident attempt at regularity and evenness, a frequent lack of connecting hairstrokes and touching of bows results in letters that stand in isolation;

– the shaft of initial and medial *r* does not descend below the base-line, and the shoulder of *r* is straight except when used in the *ri* ligature;

– the shaft of *f* and *s* usually rests on the base-line;

– in the *fi* ligature, *i* has no organic link with *f* but rather takes the shape of a comma placed beneath a curve;

– the upper loop of *e* may be left open;

– *-ct-* is preferred, in Latin words, to *-tt-*;[9]

– capitals beginning a sentence are often embellished with *Cadellen*;

– for more ambitious majuscules, Gothic-style decoration has replaced the familiar Beneventan motifs of panels, cablework, pearls, heads and bodies of fantastic dogs and birds, etc.

As for abbreviations and punctuation, naturally there would not be the same opportunities for copyists of devotional material to employ the same wide range available for secular texts. Clearly the scribe of S operated within these limitations in a manner identical with that of other Beneventan scribes in Cinquecento Naples.

First let us consider abbreviations in the Latin prayers of S.

There are many examples, of course, of the shortening of the Nomina Sacra. S employs the ancient forms for the various cases of *deus* and *dominus*: *d(eu)s d(e)i d(e)o d(eu)m* and *d(omi)n(u)s d(omi)ni d(omi)no d(omi)n(u)m*. However, instead of *ie(su)s*, *ie(su)m* and *chr(istu)s*, *chr(istu)m*, Gothic practice prevails and this explains the appearance of *ie(s)us* (5v13, 33r13, 72v8), *ie(s)um* (63v8, 70r10) and *chr(ist)us* (4v7, 33r13, 72v8).[10] In abbreviating *spiritus*, the scribe uses only the Gothic *sp(irit)us* (27v3, 39r5, 40r10 and elsewhere for a total of thirteen instances); for *spiritum*, *sp(irit)um* occurs seven times (29r11, 39v13, 40v4, 48v10, 50r6, 61v8 and 10) as opposed to one instance of *sp(iritu)m* (40v6 line-end). More variety is noticeable in the treatment of *sanctus*: the nominative form occurs twice and is not abbreviated (1r2, 66v1); *s(an)c(t)i* (genitive singular and nominative plural) and *s(an)c(t)o* (dative and ablative singular) follow the ancient model; however, for

---

8   Brown, 'Survival of Beneventan Script', 256-7; and 'The Montevergine 6 Codex', 410.

9   I have noted fourteen instances of *-ct-* as opposed to five instances of *-tt-*. Compare 'dimic*t*at' (61r3), 'dimi*c*te' (8r4), 'dimi*c*tere' (67r2), 'emi*c*tentem' (29r11), 'immi*c*te' (46r6), 'permi*c*tas' (6r11, 6v2 and 7, 8v6, 13r5), 'promi*c*tis' (24v7, 25r3), 'promi*c*tit' (25v7), 'remi*c*tat' (21v4) with 'gu*tt*e' (4v13), 'a*tt*endite' (6r4), 'a*tt*endo' (57v2), 'a*tt*ollat' (36r4), 'a|*tt*rita' (57v13-14).

10 Note also *chr(ist)um* (70r10) in mid-line and two instances of *chr(istu)m* at line-end (63v8, 74r9).

sanctum, only the later abbreviation *s(an)c(t)um* (30v12 line-end, 48v10, 52r13 line-end [*sacros(an)c(t)um*], 52v13, 61v8 and 10, 70r11) appears in S.

With respect to the abbreviation of other words with devotional connotations, we may observe the unequivocal preference on the scribe's part for the shortened forms of *anima* that are in favor during the twelfth and thirteenth centuries: *a(n)i(m)a* (27v6, 28v11, 68r8, 69r7); *a(n)i(m)e* (54r11 [line-end]); *a(n)i(m)am* (2v7, 3v11, 24r5 [line-end], 28v14, 54r8, 56v8, 61r10); *a(n)i(m)arum* (4r7 [line-end], 24v10); *a(n)i(m)as* (4r10). The abbreviation of *homo* is much less frequent, but the forms *ho(m)i(n)e* (20r1) and *ho(m)i(n)um* (26v4, 54v14) reflect a method of treatment beginning in the late eleventh century.

Some abbreviations widely used in copying both religious and secular texts in Beneventan also point to a date for S that is, generally speaking, later rather than earlier. For example, omitted *m* is normally indicated in the customary Beneventan fashion, i.e., by a suprascript symbol resembling *3*. However, the angularity of this *3*-sign and its frequent horizontal rather than slanting placement above the vowel are symptomatic of manuscripts copied in the late twelfth century and afterwards. It is interesting to note as well that at least eighteen times a large *3*-sign for omitted *m* is placed on the base-line at line-end.[11] The numerous occasions when the suprascript *3*-sign instead of the macron signifies omitted *n* at line-end is a weakening of the longstanding Beneventan tradition.[12]

In similar keeping with a later date is S's abbreviation of *ipse -a -um*. Beneventan scribes begin to shorten this word with some regularity in the thirteenth century, and there are frequent occurrences in S of the normal *ip(s)e* (53r7 [bis]), *ip(s)a* (25v5, fem. sing.), *ip(su)m* (51v1, 55r4, 9, 14), *ip(s)o* (56v7) as well as instances of the Gothic *ip(si)us* (74r6) and *ip(s)um* (65r3, 70r11 [line-end]). The abbreviation for *autem* and *non* are invariably the Gothic *aut(em)* (4v7, 20v3, 29v9, 42r8, 43v9) and *no(n)* (e.g., 2r14, 4r13, 8v12, 22r12, 38v3, 49r8, 65r12, 71v11).

Sharply contrasting, however, with these new abbreviations is S's consistent use of the older method of abbreviating *omnis -e* by retaining the *m*.[13] The newer method of shortening the above words is generally used at line-end, presumably to save space: *o(mn)i* (53v1); *o(mn)ia* (47v6, 58r10); *o(mn)ibus* (73r12). Exceptions

---

11 See 18v1 *bonu3*; 20v2 *mea3*; 23r8 *regnu3*; 24r14 *mundu3*; 26r1 *du3*; 33v7 *meu3*, 8 *mea3*; 38r11 *larga3*; 40r12 *miseria3*; 41r6 *portu3*; 45r7 *humiliatu3*, 8 *probatu3*; 46r5 *duru3*; 46v8 *ualea3*; 52r6 *cu3*; 52v4-5 *su3|me*; 70r1 *scutu3*; 71v14 *misericordia3* (*mia3*).

12 By my count there are at least thirty-one instances; e.g., 10v14-11r1 *oste³|do*; 13r9-10 *a³|gelis*; 20r8-9 *co³|spectu*; 21v5-6 *insipie³|ter*; 23r1-2 *se³|tiam*; 23v13-14 *pende³|tis*; 28v4-5 *mere³|tur*; 34v5-6 *consta³|ter*; 39r3-4 *elo³|gor*; 48v7-8 *precede³|tibus*; 49r12-13 *profu³|da*; 50v13-14 *Qua³|ta*; 52v9-10 *sa³|guinem*; 53v11-12 *ma³|ducat*; 55r7-8 *a³|tique*; 57r1-2 *uenie³|te*; 59r10-11 *desce³|dat*; 63v7-8 *po³|tificem*; 64r11-12 *fle³|tem*; 65r3-4 *condesce³|de*; 71v5-6 *me³|tis*.

13 Some representative examples in S are: *om(n)is* (61r14, 66r5); *om(n)em* (19v14, 24r7, 41v14, 68r11); *om(n)e* (26v14 [line-end], 53v5); *om(n)i* (25r11, 27r4, 41v7, 54r6, 61r6 [line-end], 62r9); *om(n)es* (6r3, 22v12, 39r1, 50v7, 52v6, 61v6, 67r3, 70r3, 72v4); *om(n)ia* (9r6, 54v8 [line-end], 58r11, 63r4, 70v4); *om(n)ibus* (9r3 [line-end], 29v1, 32r9, 40v14, 42v10, 54v9, 68v4, 71r7, 72r4).

are the occurrences of *om(ne)s* on 60v6 and 11 in initial and medial position respectively. This word is often seen in liturgical/devotional texts, and the appearance of the older method (saec. VIII med.-XI med.) in S reflects a certain conservatism on the part of the scribe.[14] An exception is the genitive plural, with twelve occurrences of the newer *o(mn)ium* as opposed to a single *om(n)ium*.[15]

The noticeably fewer abbreviations in the vernacular prayers (fos 13r-17v) generally demonstrate, like their Latin counterparts, accepted Beneventan practice or, where there is an anomaly as in the case of omitted *n*, at least the practice of the scribe of S. In the single instance of the shortening of a Nomen Sacrum, the customary *ie(s)u* (15r1) is used. For *anima*, there is a continuing preference for *a(n)i(m)a* (13v12, 17v4 and 11) over *ani(m)a* (13v6); the latter, which occurs at line-end, is slightly longer and so may have been written to help fill up space. Forms of *sanctus* are restricted to the vocative *s(an)c(t)issime* (13r12). Here it should be noted that the one occurrence of *sp(irit)u* (14v6) is used in the context of the person reciting the prayer. The abbreviation used most frequently, relatively speaking, is *p* with a line through the shaft to signal '*per*' either as a preposition (13v11; 14r3, 7; 14v10; 15r2; 15v9, 12; 16r8, 10; 17r2, 7-9, 11 [bis], 12-14; 17v1) or as part of a word (14v10 *p[er]donati*; 15v7 *sup[er]ba*; 17v1 *ap[er]te*). Another type of -*er*- abbreviation is signalled by *t* with a macron (14r9 *et[er]no* and 15v14 *t[er]ra*). An -*re*- sequence is shortened in *p(re)go* (13v3, 14r10, 14v3, 17v8), *p(re)sencia* (13v11, 14v10), and *p(re)sen|tia* (14r12-13). Instances of other abbreviations involve *an|g(e)li* (16r9-10); *ip(s)o* (16r14); *no(n)* (13v12, 16v14); suprascript 3-sign for omitted *m* (15r4 'infla³mato') and at line-end omitted *n* (14r3-4 'mu³|do', 16v4-5 'colo³|na', 17v3-4 'che³|ce'); macron for omitted *m* (13vb 'ani*m*a') and *n* (17v6 'passione'); and suprascript 2-sign at line-end for omitted *r* (14v2-3 'cor|po').

Turning now to the issue of punctuation, we find many similarities in the way the scribes of S and other sixteenth-century Neapolitan manuscripts in Beneventan functioned in this regard. Certainly the symbols in S for both Latin and vernacular texts are illustrative of restrictions imposed by liturgical content: these punctuation signs are few in number and do double or triple duty. The simple point closes a sentence or designates a major pause. An angular point intersected by a diagonal can also fulfill these functions and at times seems to be a line-filler as well. In many instances a thin diagonal serves as comma or hyphen or occasionally even as a final stop (e.g., 3r9, 26r2). The same thin diagonal is frequently used to produce dotted *i*.

---

14 Francis Newton, *The Scriptorium and Library at Monte Cassino, 1058-1105*, Cambridge Studies in Palaeography and Codicology, 7 (Cambridge, 1999), 171 observes that Cassinese copyists of liturgical manuscripts also preferred the older system of *om(n)is om(n)e*.

15 See 26v9 and 14, 50r1, 62v4, 64v5, 67r14, 68v6 (line-end), 69v14, 71r3, 72r2, 72v11, 73r11 for *o(mn)ium*; *om(n)ium* is found on 72v2.

With respect to Latin orthographical practice, the normal Cinquecento preference for -*ct*- over -*tt*- has been noted on p. 98 above. Other interesting variations involving *t* are the substitutions of *t* for *d* (2r7-8 'obtura|tis') and assibilated -*ti*- for *g* (36r7-8 'con|ta*tione*'), -*ci*- (22r4 'fidu*ti*am', 22r9-10 'fa*ti*|unt') and -*ct*- (8r11 'satisfa*ti*onem'). Further modifications of the normal Latin spelling will be evident below in the edition of the prayers, and some notable examples are 3v7 'e*ci*am' (for 'e*ici*am') and 67r10 'aug*u*mentum'.

Origin and Date   The codicological and palaeographical features just described coincide perfectly with the same kind of data accumulated for the six Beneventan manuscripts copied in the first half of the sixteenth century in the Neapolitan Benedictine monasteries of Santa Patrizia and San Gregorio Armeno.[16] Hence S was also copied at Naples during the first half of the Cinquecento. In terms of its size, layout, script, abbreviations, and punctuation, S closely resembles the books of hours produced for Giulia Caracciolo (New York, Columbia University, Butler Library, MS X264.02.C28 = **Co**) and Cizola Minutolo (Vatican City, Biblioteca Apostolica Vaticana, MS Borgia lat. 356 = **Bo**), both nuns of Santa Patrizia. The former seems to have flourished in both halves of the sixteenth century; and the latter died on 21 November 1552 as abbess of Santa Maria ad Agnone, Naples.[17] As one example of the striking similarity, it is helpful to compare the measurements of these codices:

S: 139 x 99 (93 x 60) mm., 14 long lines
Co: 140 x 100 (93 x 62) mm., 14 long lines
Bo: 125 x 98 (91 x 66) mm., 14 long lines.

Moreover, the same scribe who copied **Bo** may also be responsible for **S**, to judge from the general aspect and the treatment of individual letters (*d, g,* medial and final *r,* majuscule *A* with *Cadellen,* etc.) and ligatures (especially *fi* and assibilated *ti*). The artist who provided **Bo** with penwork decoration that runs the full height of the leaf seems to have done the same for **S**, and in the same colors.

Like **Co** and **Bo**, **S** was intended for a feminine user, more specifically for a nun. This is evident from the mention of *religiosa* in the title on fo 1r ('Iste sunt deuotissime orationes quas conposuit sanctus tomas de aquino et debent dici a religiosa quando accedit ad communicandum') and from many occurrences of feminine nouns like *ancilla, famula, peccatrix,* and *simulatrix* together with the feminine forms of various adjectives.[18] Originally the model(s) used by the scribe

---

16 See n. 1 above.

17 Brown, 'Survival of Beneventan Script', 249-51; Annamaria Facchiano, *Monasteri femminili e nobiltà a Napoli tra medioevo ed età moderna. Il Necrologio di S. Patrizia (secc. XII-XVI),* Fonti per la Storia del Mezzogiorno Medievale (Altavilla Silentina, 1992), 179-80, 158-9.

18 In S see, e.g., 60r11 *ancillam tuam;* 61r12 *ancilla tua;* 48v1-3 *doce me famulam tuam miseram et indignam;* 51v4-5 *inter tuas famulas;* 52r7-8 *me indignam famulam tuam;* 52v6 *nos omnes tue*

of S may have had masculine forms that were changed, for the most part, to the feminine during the copying process. Those masculine adjectives and pronouns still remaining in S are 39r6 *accensus*; 41v2-3 *transgressus sum* (but this is followed by a string of feminine adjectives); 46v7-8 *subditus ... ualeam* (preceded on l. 7 by the ungrammatical *subiectum*); 60r12 *pro quo tradere dignatus* (instead of *pro qua tradere dignatus*).[19] However, unlike Co and Bo, the name of an individual nun does not appear in any of the texts in S. See, however, pp. 105-7 below for the suggestion that the user of the volume may have been named Dorotea.

Contents of S

Descriptions given in the following list are based on the Latin titles; when these are lacking in S, angle brackets enclose headings that have been supplied. Boldface numbers in parentheses refer to the serial numbers of texts in the edition on pp. 109-20 below.

Of the fifty-six texts in Beneventan, fifty-four are in Latin (**1-3**, **6-56**) and two (**4-5**) are in Italian. Almost all of these are prayers; the exceptions are **38** (capitula, designated in S as versicles and responsories), **47** (antiphons), and **55** (verses). **1-35** prepare the recipient to receive Communion by evoking feelings of penitence

---

famule; 33v11-12, 35v4, 41r13, 71v2 *peccatrix*; 40r13, 45v11, 68r5, 69v3-4 *peccatricem*; 55r11-13 *me ... miserrimam ... peccatricem*; 57v14-58r1 *michi ... peccatrici* and 72r13 *michi peccatrici*; 60v12-13 *pro me misera peccatrice*; 41v6 *simulatrix* (and accompanying adjectives 5 *superba*, 5-6 *auara*, 6-7 *inuidiosa*, 7 *iracunda*, 8 *plena*); 57r3-5 *ego hoc stigmate signata inuenior*, 11-12 *ego ... mole depressa*; 60v2 *ego miserrima*; 62r2 *serue tue* (corr. ex *seruo tuo*); 64v11-12, 69r4 *non sum digna*; 71v3 *non fui digna*; 72r7-8 *faciant me ... esse deuotam*.

19 The presence of masculine forms in manuscripts destined for the use of nuns has also been observed by Jean Mallet and André Thibaut, *Les manuscrits en écriture bénéventaine de la Bibliothèque Capitulaire de Bénévent*, 3 vols (Paris-Turnhout, 1984-97), i (1984), 78 n. 4.

and devotion; **36-52** are concerned with the procedure for reception of the Host and subsequent prayers of thanksgiving. Subsequently there is a shift of direction since **53-56** contain petitions on behalf of the dead and to a specific saint.

S's version of the *ordo ad communicandum* (**36-52**) is the fifth Beneventan copy now located. This text has definite medieval and Cassinese roots since it resembles fairly closely the versions in Beneventan copied at Montecassino: Paris, Bibliothèque Mazarine, MS 364 (saec. XI/XII); and Los Angeles, J. Paul Getty Museum, MS Ludwig IX 1 (olim Montecassino, Archivio dell'Abbazia, 199; saec. XII[2]; signed in 1153 by the scribe Sigenulfus). There are also a certain number of similarities with an *ordo ad communicandum* in Vatican City, Biblioteca Apostolica Vaticana, MS Vat. lat. 4928 that was written in Beneventan *c.* 1100 at the monastery of Santa Sofia, Benevento. Decidedly less close to S, however, is the version found in Montecassino, Archivio dell'Abbazia, MS 246, copied in Beneventan at Montecassino (*ut vid.*) in the last third of the twelfth century.

Ugo Facchini's recent edition and comparative study of the four witnesses just named make it unnecessary to go into great detail regarding texts common to these manuscripts and to S.[20] It will be sufficient to observe the following differences between S's version of the *ordo* and that in the Paris and Los Angeles texts:

– the introductory psalms, Kyrie, Pater noster, and Credo (Facchini, 584, no. 1*) are omitted in S;

– S reverses the order of the two prayers (**39-40** = Facchini, 585-6, nos. 6*, 5*) following the capitula;

– before the moment of actual reception of the Eucharist, S omits another prayer (Facchini, 587, no. 8*) but compensates by inserting four more prayers (**42-45**);

– prayers after reception of the Eucharist appear also in S but there are changes; i.e., **49** = Facchini, 588, no. 13*; **50** is substituted for Facchini, 588, no. 12*; and **52** has been added as the concluding prayer.

Obviously much of the variation exhibited by S involves rearrangement and addition. This feature is true of the prayers before the cross that are traditionally joined to the *ordo ad communicandum*. The other four Beneventan witnesses preface the *ordo* with three prayers of Peter Damian *ante crucem*.[21] S does the same

---

20 Ugo Facchini, *San Pier Damiani: l'eucologia e le preghiere. Contributo alla storia dell'eucologia medievale. Studio critico e liturgico-teologico*, Bibliotheca 'Ephemerides liturgicae', 'Subsidia' 109 (Rome, 2000), 548-51 and 584-602 for the edition of the relevant texts, and 358-9, 363-75 for a helpful comparative table of texts. The parallels cited in our edition on pp. 116-19 below will also illustrate the texts shared by S and the four other Beneventan witnesses. For an earlier edition of the *ordo ad communicandum* in Mazarine 364 and Vat. lat. 4928, see André Wilmart, 'Prières pour la communion en deux psautiers du Mont-Cassin', *Ephemerides liturgicae*, 43 (1929), 320-28.

21 On these prayers, see André Wilmart, 'Prières médiévales pour l'adoration de la Croix', *Ephemerides liturgicae*, 46 (1932), 58-61 (for the authorship); and Facchini, *San Pier Damiani*, 548-51 (for an edition). They are unattributed in S.

(33-35) but adds many other prayers (1-32). Moreover, S enriches, as it were, the Eucharistic ritual by inserting prayers (53-56) to be recited once the *ordo* concludes.

As shown by the list of contents on p. 102 above, the prayers preceding the *ordo* can be divided into four groups. Taking them in order, we observe the following:

(fos 1r-17v) despite the attribution to Thomas Aquinas in the rubric, none of the first five prayers is the work of the saint.[22] In fact, 1, 4, and 5 are presently unidentified, while 2 and 3 are anonymous compositions found in French books of hours. No vernacular parallels have been found for 4 and 5, both in Italian (and not out of place from the viewpoint of their subject matter: both refer to Christ present in the Eucharist and plead for mercy and forgiveness of sins committed). 4 is a translation of the Latin prayer 'Aue sanctissimum corpus dominicum in hoc sacramento contentum'.[23] A Latin source for 5 has yet to be located.

(fos 17v-33v) the next group (6-11) begins with a prayer (6) of ps.-Anselm of Canterbury.[24] Parallels have yet to be found for 7. 8-10 are the well-known prayers wrongly attributed to Peter Damian.[25] 11 is found in both earlier Beneventan and non-Beneventan sources.

(fos 33v-47v) 12-31 constitute a series of prayers or *meditationes* on Ps 50, the fourth of the seven Penitential Psalms. The two other Beneventan witnesses now known (Montecassino, Archivio dell'Abbazia, MS 442, pp. 286-301 and Vatican City, Biblioteca Apostolica Vaticana, MS Archivio S. Pietro G 49, fos 41r-35v) attest respectively to the circulation of these texts at Montecassino in the third quarter of the eleventh century and in the region of Campania in the late twelfth century. The Vatican codex is still the only Beneventan witness to contain *meditationes* on all seven Penitential Psalms; however, it is missing the leaf containing the conclusion of the prayer for Ps 50: 17 and the entire prayer for Ps 50: 18, and S, along with Montecassino 442, helps to fill the lacuna.

(fos 47v-60r) 33-35 appear in a different order in the other four Beneventan witnesses, and 32 does not figure in these manuscripts.

Of the Beneventan texts (53-56) in S that follow the *ordo*, a convincing parallel has been found only for 55. No other instances have yet been located for the vernacular invocations in 57-63 written in humanist cursive.

---

22 They are not included in the *piae preces* attributed to Thomas Aquinas by Stanislaus Edouard Fretté, ed., *Doctoris Angelici divi Thomae Aquinatis sacri Ordinis F. F. Praedicatorum Opera omnia*, 34 vols (Paris, 1871-80), xxxii, 819-23; and Raimondo M. Spiazzi, ed., *Opus theologica*, 2 vols (Turin-Rome, 1954), ii, 283-9.

23 The Latin text of this prayer is easily accessible in Pius Künzle's edition of Henry Suso's *Horologium sapientiae* (cited in the parallels on p. 111 below). At the conclusion of 4, the Latin *exitus beatus* is rendered as 'beato uestimento et bono recapito'; this is perhaps the most noticeable addition in the vernacular version.

24 6 = *Oratio* 43 (*PL* 158.939-41, ascribed to 'Anselmus archiepiscopus Cantuariensis').

25 André Wilmart, 'Les prières de saint Pierre Damien pour l'adoration de la Croix', *Revue des sciences religieuses*, 9 (1929), 513-23 (reprinted in Wilmart, *Auteurs spirituels et textes dévots du Moyen Age latin. Études d'histoire littéraire* [Paris, 1932; rpt. 1971], 138-46).

Possible Owner of S

Codicological and palaeographical data show that the odds are strong indeed that **S** is a product of the scriptorium of the Benedictine monastery of Santa Patrizia at Naples. This is reinforced by the presence in **S** of the *ordo ad communicandum* which also appears in monastic manuscripts copied at other Benedictine centers, namely, Montecassino and Benevento. Hence the logical place to begin is the Benedictine world of sixteenth-century Naples. While any conclusions drawn in this regard must necessarily be speculative simply because the contents of **S** do not name a specific user, it is helpful to examine whatever evidence might be telling.

I would propose, then, that **56**, the final text in Beneventan, merits attention. Shown on Pl. 7.8, this is a seemingly hitherto unattested prayer addressed to St Dorothea. Perhaps irrelevant to our purpose is the exact identification of Dorothea, i.e., whether she is the saint martyred under Nero at Aquileia along with Euphemia, Thecla, and Erasma (feast day 3 September) or the saint martyred with Theophilus at Caesarea during the reign of Diocletian (feast day 6 February) or rather Dorothea of Alexandria (saec. IV in., feast day 6 February).[26] The important point is the mention of a saint such as Dorothea who does not loom large, if at all, in Neapolitan religious life since there is no church or monastery in that city dedicated to Santa Dorotea.[27] Nor do we currently have any documentation for a 'Dorotea' who was once a nun at Santa Patrizia.[28] Similarly, there is no evidence that the monastery possessed any relics of this saint.[29] **56**, however, is not an addition; it was written by the same scribe who copied in similar ink the other Beneventan texts in **S**, and there is space after **56** (it ends on fo 74r4) for the original scribe to have continued writing. Some significance, then, presumably attaches to the prayer to St Dorothea especially since the name was not in common use at Naples at any time during the Cinquecento.

Prof. Annamaria Facchiano has suggested two possible avenues of exploration for the first half of the century (when **S** was copied):[30]

(a) the church of Santa Maria del Popolo serving the Ospedale degli Incurabili (founded in the early sixteenth century by Francesca Maria Longo and located

---

26 On these saints who bore the name of Dorothea, see, besides the information given for the relevant day in the *Acta sanctorum*, also *Bibliotheca sanctorum*, 14 vols including indices and appendix (Rome, *c.* 1961-*c.* 1969), iv, 816-26.

27 See, e.g., Cesare D'Engenio Caracciolo, *Napoli sacra* (Naples, 1623), 'Indice Di tutte le Chiese contenute in questo libro per ordine de Alfabeto'; Stanislao d'Aloe, 'Catalogo di tutti gli edifizi sacri della città di Napoli e suoi sobborghi tratto da un Ms. autografo della chiesa di s. Giorgio *ad forum*', *Archivio storico per le province napoletane*, 8 (1883), 111-52, 287-315, 499-546, 670-737.

28 'Dorotea' does not appear in the necrology of Santa Patrizia (Cuomo 2-4-10); see the 'Indice dei nomi' in Facchiano, *Monasteri femminili*, 325-73.

29 Dorothea is absent from D'Engenio Caracciolo's list of relics found in Santa Patrizia (*Napoli sacra*, 181-2).

30 This information, together with many bibliographical references cited in the following notes, was generously communicated to me in Prof. Facchiano's letter of 25 September 2002.

opposite Santa Patrizia) is reported to have possessed the head of St Dorothea. Franciscan nuns were in charge of the hospital.[31]

(b) a likely bearer of the name in the first half of the century is Dorotea Malatesta (1478-1527), illegitimate daughter of Roberto Malatesta, who in 1504 married the famous Neapolitan *condottiere* Giovanni Battista Caracciolo (*c.* saec. XV med.- 1508), son of Oliviero Caracciolo and Viola di Rostaino della Leonessa. Dorotea had four children (Viola, Isabella, Battista, Marco Oliviero) and lived near the church of Sant'Aniello a Caponapoli. In 1527, stricken with malaria, she made a handsome bequest to the canons of this church. They, in turn, commissioned the sculptor Giovanni Merliano to erect an altar to St Dorothea. Merliano's efforts, completed in 1534, also included a statue of the saint.[32] The church of Sant'Aniello a Caponapoli, severely damaged in the bombardment of 1943 and by subsequent vandalism, was restored in the 1990s. What remains of the altar and statue of St Dorothea was preserved for a time in the *depositi* of the Soprintendenza per i Beni Artistici e Storici.[33]

Whether S belonged to either of these two candidates cannot, of course, be proven beyond doubt.

In favor of (a) is the fact that there was a monastery of nuns attached to the Ospedale degli Incurabili, and this would explain feminine use of the manuscript.

A stronger argument might be made for (b) in view of the Caracciolo connection that Dorotea Malatesta would have had through her husband with the monastery of Santa Patrizia where her nieces Paola and Vittoria were nuns and where their sisters Luchina and Angela were reared.[34] This is the Paola Caracciolo whose presence at Santa Patrizia can be attested from 1520 to 14 January 1555, and who on 16 January 1555 is recorded as abbess of the monastery of Santa Maria ad Agnone, Naples. The book of hours that she owned (Co) is copied in sixteenth-century Beneventan and bears her name ('PAULA .CARA.') on the front cover.[35] Practically speaking, then, Paola or indeed any of Dorotea Malatesta's other nieces at Santa Patrizia would have

31 Carlo Celano, *Notizie del bello, dell'antico e del curioso della città di Napoli*, enlarged by Giovanni Battista Chiarini, 1 vol. in 3 (Naples, 1970), i, 245.

32 D'Engenio Caracciolo, *Napoli sacra*, 213; A. Caracciolo, *Un ratto di Cesare Borgia* (Naples, 1921), 135-8 (with the will of Dorotea Malatesta); F. Fabris, *La genealogia della famiglia Caracciolo*, revised and enlarged by A. Caracciolo (Naples, 1966), Pl. 38, with additions and corrections; 'Caracciolo, Giovanni Battista', in *Dizionario biografico degli italiani* (Rome, 1976), xix, 384-6 (F. Petrucci); Gennaro Aspreno Galante, *Guida sacra della città di Napoli*, ed. Nicola Spinosa (Naples, 1985), 55-6 and 68-9 (additions and corrections).

33 See Soprintendenza per i Beni Artistici e Storici, *Napoli sacra. Guida alle chiese della Città. 3o Itinerario* (Naples, 1993),168-70 and figs 140-42, 145 on pp. 162-4.

34 Paola, Vittoria, Luchina, and Angela Caracciolo were daughters of Francesco (brother of Dorotea Malatesta's husband Giovanni Battista Caracciolo) and Dianora Caracciolo; see Facchiano, *Monasteri femminili*, 158-9 ('Caracciolo d. Paola') and 183 ('Caracciolo d. Vittoria').

35 Co was not actually written for Paola Caracciolo since the name 'Iulia' appears in many of the prayers; see Brown, 'Survival of Beneventan Script', 249-50 for the evidence that the nun in question was Giulia Caracciolo. The precise identity of this Giulia Caracciolo and her relationship to Paola Caracciolo was not established by Brown (*ibid.*) or by Facchiano, *ibid.*, 179-80 ('Caracciolo, Giulia, 9/9').

been well placed to help her obtain a book produced there. Here it is helpful to recall the identical decoration displayed by S and **Bo**; Cizola Minutolo, owner of the latter, was at Santa Patrizia from 1506 to at least 1538.[36] Hence these dates also accord.

Finally, perhaps significant is the focus of S's many prayers on Christ's suffering and death. Naturally this could be nothing more than an indication of general Franciscan influence on the piety of the time and so would be suitable for either (a) or (b). While this may not be enough to tip the balance in favor of Dorotea Malatesta, it should be pointed out that Sant'Aniello a Caponapoli had a famous crucifix in a side chapel that was an object of much devotion[37] and could have inspired the vernacular invocations added in a non-Beneventan hand (**57-63**).

Of course there are almost surely other plausible alternatives that have not yet come to light.

Edition of S

Considerations of space require that only those texts for which unpublished parallels have not yet been located can be reproduced in full; otherwise incipits and explicits are given.[38] It is helpful to note again that, for purpose of convenient reference, texts are numbered serially by arabic numbers in boldface.

The presentation of every text observes these practices:

–manuscript orthography has been preserved, but punctuation follows modern usage, with the period, semi-colon, and comma used in place of the Beneventan symbols described on p. 100 above;

–letters added suprascript by the scribe are placed between the diagonals \ /;

–abbreviations in Latin texts have been silently expanded in accord with standard convention, while parentheses enclose any letter(s) supplied in expanding abbreviations in the vernacular prayers (**4-5**);

–angle brackets enclose editorial interventions (kept to a minimum);

–rubrics are reproduced in small capitals, as are the lemmata from Ps. 50 in **12-31**;

–sources and parallels cited by sigla or short titles in the notes are drawn from the following Beneventan and non-Beneventan material.

---

36 Facchiano, *ibid.*, 158-9.

37 Galante, *Guida sacra*, 55 and 68 n. 217.

38 It is regrettable that my complete transcription of S could not be published here since the numerous variants might eventually be useful vis-à-vis textual transmission as well as for linguistic purposes (in view of the late date of S and the presence of both Latin and Italian in the manuscript). Some typical or interesting instances of variants are: **2** (11v8) 'ut miserearis michi plena (for *plene*) miseriis'; **6** (18v13-14) 'Ardor quidem gratia uite' (for *Arctor quoque grauiter*), (20v4) 'pendis (for *pendens*) in cruce', (24v14) 'ubi tuus' (for *ubi tu uis*); **29** (45v4) 'nisi uix' (for *quamuis*); **48** (70r13) 'pro nostra in te' (for *pro nostra salute*).

Sources and Parallels

Beneventan material from Benevento

Mallet-Thibaut = Jean Mallet and André Thibaut, *Les manuscrits en écriture bénéventaine de la Bibliothèque Capitulaire de Bénévent*, 3 vols (Paris-Turnhout, 1984-97), iii, 1347-1439 ('Index euchologique').

Vl4928 = Vatican City, Biblioteca Apostolica Vaticana, MS Vat. lat. 4928, fos 89r-95r. Copied at the monastery of Santa Sofia, Benevento saec. XI/XII. Ed. Ugo Facchini, *San Pier Damiani: l'eucologia e le preghiere. Contributo alla storia dell'eucologia medievale. Studio critico e liturgico-teologico*, Bibliotheca 'Ephemerides liturgicae', 'Subsidia' 109 (Rome, 2000), 548-51 (nos. 132-134), 589-94 (nos. 15*-30*).

Beneventan material from Montecassino

Maz = Paris, Bibliothèque Mazarine, MS 364, fos 23r-28v. Copied at Montecassino saec. XI/XII (a. 1099-1105). Ed. Facchini, 548-51 (nos. 132-34), 584-9 (nos. 1*-10*).

Mc199 = Los Angeles, J. Paul Getty Museum, MS Ludwig IX 1 (olim Montecassino, Archivio dell'Abbazia, 199), fos 128r-130v, 135r-137v. Copied at Montecassino by Sigenulfus saec. XII² ('a. 1153'). Ed. Facchini, 548-51 (nos. 132-134), 598-602 (nos. 41*-54*).

Mc246 = Montecassino, Archivio dell'Abbazia, MS 246, pp. 145-148. Copied at Montecassino saec. XII ex. Ed. Facchini, 548-51 (nos. 132-134), 595-7 (nos. 32*-40*).

Mc442 = Montecassino, Archivio dell'Abbazia, MS 442, pp. 171-368. Copied by Leo Marsicanus at Montecassino saec. XI¾ (unsigned). Ed. Mariano Dell'Omo, 'Cultura liturgica e preghiera a Montecassino negli anni dell'abate Desiderio (1058-87) (con una giunta sulla raccolta di preghiere del cod. Casin. 442)', in *L'età dell'abate Desiderio*, 3 vols, Miscellanea cassinese 59, 60, 67 (Montecassino, 1987-92), iii.1: *Storia arte e cultura. Atti del IV Convegno di studi sul Medioevo meridionale (Montecassino-Cassino, 4-8 ottobre 1987)*, ed. Faustino Avagliano and Oronzo Pecere (1992), 279-361 (edition of the prayers on 317-57); ed. Facchini, 548-51 (nos. 132-134).

Urb585 = Vatican City, Biblioteca Apostolica Vaticana, MS Urb. lat. 585, fos 255r-257r. The body of the manuscript was copied at Montecassino saec. XI/XII (a. 1099-1105), but fos 186v-235v, 255r-257r were written 'no earlier than saec. XII med.' (Newton, *Scriptorium and Library at Monte Cassino*, 343). Ed. Facchini, 548-51 (nos. 132-134).

Beneventan material from other origins

AsP49 = Vatican City, Biblioteca Apostolica Vaticana, MS Archivio S. Pietro G 49, fos 2r-61v. Copied saec. XII ex. in Campania. Ed. Virginia Brown, '*Flores psalmorum* and *Orationes psalmodicae* in Beneventan Script', *Mediaeval Studies*, 51 (1989), 424-66 and 4 plates.

Non-Beneventan Sources and Parallels

CO = *Corpus orationum*, ed. Eugenius Moeller et al., *CCSL*, 160, 160A-K (Turnhout, 1992-2001).

Deschamps-Mulder = Jan Deschamps-Herman Mulder, *Inventaris van de Middelnederlandse handschriften van de Koninklijke Bibliotheek van België (voorlopige uitgave)*, fasc. 4 (Brussels, 2001).

Leroquais i, ii = V. Leroquais, *Les livres d'heures manuscrits de la Bibliothèque Nationale*, 3 vols (Paris, 1927).

Salmon = Pierre Salmon, *Analecta liturgica. Extraits des manuscrits liturgiques de la Bibliothèque Vaticane. Contribution à l'histoire de la prière chrétienne*, Studi e Testi, 273 (Vatican City, 1974), 174-75 (nos. 488-506).

Wilmart, 'Prières médiévales' = André Wilmart, 'Prières médiévales pour l'adoration de la Croix', *Ephemerides liturgicae*, 46 (1932), 22-65.

Text

ISTE SUNT DEUOTISSIME ORATIONES QUAS CONPOSUIT SANCTUS TOMAS DE AQUINO ET DEBENT DICI A RELIGIOSA QUANDO ACCEDIT AD COMMUNICANDUM INCIPIT PRIMA.

1 (fos 1r-9r) O iesu creator, o iesu redemptor, o iesu saluator humani generis, parce michi inobedienti de tuis preceptis et falsaria de tuis donis quod michi donasti. O benedicte iesu, o benigne iesu, parce cordi meo uacuo de tuis deuotionibus et plena de multis et illicitis sollicitudinibus huius fallaciis seculi. O dulcissime iesu et suauissime iesu, parce menti mee quia de te meditare neglexi et contra te sollicita nimis. O iesu desiderabilis, o iesu inenarrabilis, parce lingue mee et labiis meis ligatis ad laudandum nomen tuum et sollicitis ac incorruptis et iniquis uerbis. O iesu bone et gaudium cordis mei, parce oculis meis clausis ad uidendum iusticiam, apertis ad uidendum iniquitates uanitates et multa mala. O uenerabilis iesu et incorruptibilis iesu et incomprehensibilis iesu, parce auribus meis obturatis ad audiendum uerba salutis, apertis ad audiendum fabulas et iniquitates. O altissime iesu et potentissime iesu, tuam incomprehensibilem misericordiam sine qua lauari non potest magnitudo peccatorum meorum. O domine iubilator cordis mei, quando respicio magnitudinem beneficiorum tuorum quam pro me operatus es et similiter multitudinem peccatorum meorum que contra me sunt et animam meam, quasi desperacio quedam accidit michi de uenia. Unde ego sic orphana sine patre et matre derelicta, tamen non desperata, habens aliquod argumentum, deinde (?) cogito sentio et uideo quod illud misterium et immensam misericordiam quod deus pater operatus est per unige<ni>tum filium tuum iesum benedictum, hoc est, carnem de carne mea assumere et quam fecisset contra naturam quoniam ipse est immortalis et fecit mortalem. Ubi? in ligno crucis. Qua causa? certe pro salute nostra. Gloria in altissimis deo pro qua spes et fiducia magna accidit michi. Propter hanc dulcedinem, saluator noster iesus benedictus qui operatus est in nobis. Domine iesu gloriose et benigne, cum corde aperto a te peto et uolo quia tu es adiutor meus fortis et pius pater. Sicut tu dixisti in euangelio: Omnis enim qui uenit ad me, non eciam foras. Peccaui nimis; recipe me ad penitentiam. Domine iesu saluator, salua me, munda me, et salua a malis animam meam quia sine te saluari non potest. Heu me quia peccaui quoniam per me non ualeo lauari. Domine, prospexisti de sede sancta tua et cogitasti de nobis ut lauares nos. O domine iesu, inmensa dulcedo et benignitas tua iesu, nonne aperuit nobis sufficientem fontem in latere ad lauandum animarum maculas? Quas fecisti quoniam secundum quod nos inquinauimus animas nostras cum quinque sensibus corporis nostri, macule immobiles ad lauandum uidisti quia aqua non erat sufficiens. Heu me misera, quid fecisti? Dirupisti de saxo m<a>gno et altissimo quinque fontes largissimas et currentes. Heu michi, que fueriunt (*sic*) iste fontes in

---

Apparatus locorum parallelorum

1   ?

quibus illa petra? Certe illa de qua dicit petrus. Petra autem erat christus; quinque fontes fuerunt quinque uulnera christi de quibus emanauit nobis sanguis et aqua largissime currens, sicut scriptum est. Erat autem sudor eius quasi gutte sanguinis decurrentis in terram propter magnitudines peccatorum nostrorum et ablutione macularum nostrarum. He me misera, quomodo audeo preterire unum de minimis preceptis domini mei iesu christi qui tantum se humiliauit pro me? Heu me, quomodo potest substinere cor meum durum quod tu non diuides per medium, considerans te tuum conditorem, confixum propter te? Heu me, quomodo propter carnem tu, mea mens, non alienaris uidente tuum redemptorem perforatum, in suo sanctissimo latere lanceam? Heu me, oculi mei quomodo possunt prospicere coronam spineam in capite, Iesu benedicte, et sanguinem currentem super faciem suam desiderabilem et cooperiens oculos suos preclaros quod tenebre non occecant nos statim? Heu me, lingua mea et labia quomodo non sunt confixi in uos, dentes mei, propter grauissimum dolorem quem saluator noster iesus in cruce positus fuit felle et aceto? Unde bene conqueritur scriptura sancta per yheremiam prophetam dicentem: *o uos omnes qui transitis per uiam, attendite et uidete si est dolor sicut dolor meus* [Lm 1: 12]. O ponderosus dolor qui pondus peccatorum nostrorum portauit. Domine iesu christe fili dei uiui, miserere mei per sancta beneficia que pro me operatus es, non permictas me facere uel fieri inutilem ad tam magna beneficia tua domine promerenda. Domine iesu christe qui me creasti ad societatem angelorum, non me permictas sociari maledictis infernorum. Domine iesu christe qui gratiam sanctissimi tui baptismatis michi donasti et sancte crucis signum triumphale in fronte, non permictas me descendere in manus inimici cum hiis sanctissimis tuis signis unde ualeat me delere. Domine iesu christe, *manus tue domine fecerunt me et plasmauerunt* (dicit iob [10: 8]): da michi intellectum ut discam mandata tua et ne perdas me. Miserere michi domine quia in te peccaui quoniam sine adiuuari non ualeo; sicut tu dixisti: *sine nichil potestis facere* [Jo 15: 5]. Domine iesu christe, tu me creasti ad uitam; quoniam sine te me facere dignum ad uitam nequeo, quid faciam si iniquitates obseruaueris domine? Domine, quis substinebit quo uadam aut ubi reuertar et ubi queram consilium et auxilium? Dulcissime iesu, ne desereas creaturam tuam. Certis<si>me uideo quod preter te auxilium habere non ualeo. Domine iesu christe bone qui tantum fecisti pro me, modo te dignemini hoc residuum adimplere, quod me plenum facias in plenitudine sanctorum. Domine iesu christe, da michi operari hac fine ut ualeam gaudere ibi ubi non est finis. Domine iesu christe, multa sunt peccata mea sed multissima est misericordia tua; laua et munda me domine et memoriale nomen tuum memorare illam peccatricem ad quam dixisti: *uade et noli amplius peccare* [Jo 8: 11]. Sanctissime iesu, ita dic michi et dimicte animam meam. Similiter memorare iesu latronem in cruce ad quem dixisti: *hodie mecum eris in paradiso* [Lc 23: 43]. Munda me, domine iesu christe, ab occultis meis, et de peccatis perfectam contrictionem, confessionem et satisfationem michi tribuas ut in die mortis mee ualeam audire gloriosam illam et dulcissimam vocem: hodie mecum eris in paradiso. Amen. Habe me in tua custodia. Offero me tibi, domine iesu, in sanctissima uulnera tua et inde admouere non me permictas per hoc sanctissimum misterium quod in celo et in terris et in inferno operatus es in nobis. Domine iesu christe, si ego sine te nichil possum facere, quoniam paratus sum et non sum turbatus ut custodiam mandata tua, christe unice uince in me uitia et peccata. Christe, regna in me per fidem et caritatem. Christe, impetra in me ut in omnibus tibi obediam omnibus diebus uite mee. Qui uiuis et regnas deus per omnia secula.

2 (fos 9r-12v) ORATIO. In mensam dulcissimi conui<ui>i, domine iesu christe rex angelorum ... per te qui nos creasti cum non essemus. Qui uiuis et regnas cum deo patre et spiritu sancto per infinita secula seculorum. Amen.

3 (fos 12v-13r) O anima christi sanctissima, sanctifica me ... ut cum angelis tuis laudem in secula seculorum. Amen.

4 (fos 13r-15r) Aue s(an)c(t)issime corpo del signore mio in quisto sacramento tenuto. Te confesso con le labra et con tucto el core te amo (*corr. ex* amor); te desidero con tucte le cose mei intime. P(re)go te che te digne ogi et uisitare si piatosamente et gratiosamente la infirma ani(m)a mia desiderosa receuere te, salutifero sacrificio et fonte de tucte le gracie, che io me reallegra auere trouata p(er) la p(re)sencia toa medecina innell'a(n)i(m)a et nel corpo. No(n) resguardare signore alle multe iniquitate mei et negligencie; resguarda alla infinita mis(er)icordia toa. Che si collui, p(er) el quale ei creato lo mu(n)do et sanato et cui tucte le uirtute so date. Tu si quillo immaculato agnello che ogi p(er) redemptione de tucto el mundo si sacrificato al patre et(er)no. O dulcissima manna, o suauissimo odore, da p(re)go te alla bocca mia melato gusto de tua saluteuele p(re)sentia. Accende in me la toa caritate, spingi li uitii, infunde le uirtute, accrisce le gracie et da salute de mente et de co(r)po. *Inclina* p(re)go te *li toi celi et descendi* [Ps 143: 5] ad me azoche coniunto teco et mute (*sic*) deuente uno sp(irit)u teco. O uenerabile sacramento, io te prego che per te tucti li inimici mei siano scacciati et li peccati mei siano p(er)donati, et p(er) la p(re)sencia toa tucti mali siano exclusi. Damme bona uolunta, corregi le costume et despuni tucti li acti mei in la uolunta toa. Et qua, ie(s)u dulcissimo, p(er) te lo intellecto illuminato sia de uno nouo lume et lo effecto sia infla(m)mato; la speranza sia per te fortificata azoche la uita mia emendata melgliore sempre, poy alla fine me sia conceduto beato uestimento et bono recapito in uita eterna. Amen.

5 (fos 15r-17v) Eccome auante ad te signore, uile peccatrice et scanoscente, uengo te ad pilgliare con poco amore, supplice redemptore ad me negligente. De niente nobile me ay creata et de tanti beni me ay ornata. Aime, ad penitentia

---

2   Leroquais ii, 372 (Index, *s.v.* 'Ad mensam dulcissimi convivii tui').

3   Leroquais ii, 340, no. 27 (text from Paris, Bibliothèque Nationale de France, lat. 10561, saec. XV, fo 80r); Deschamps-Mulder, 79-80, G56.

4   (Latin version) Leroquais i, 155; Deschamps-Mulder, 83, G72; *Heinrich Seuses Horologium sapientiae*, ed. Pius Künzle, Spicilegium friburgense, 23 (Fribourg, 1977), 571-2.

5   ?

expectata et in tucta uita mia te so stata ingrata. Sup(er)ba e stata la mia uita, degna de lo inferno p(er) mei peccati et ad te signore sempre inimica. Recolgli sta peccatrice in toa pietate. P(er) mio amore signore te incarnasti. Dalli celi fi alla t(er)ra humiliato, fame sete frido et caldo patiste et tante uolte da iudei iniuriato. Tu si quillo che de sangue fuste sudato, como ad latro con fune ligato, buctato et crodelemente tirato, con gangate (*corr. ex* tang-) pungne (*corr. ex* iung-) et canna battuto. Fo la toa testa p(er) capilli tirata et la facce alli ang(e)li grata p(er) li multi colpi stecte tormentata liuida lacrimosa sputata. Fuste como ad pazo da herode reputato (*corr. ex* -te), da ip(s)o et suo populo desprezato, la toa ueste con uituperio spolgliata, con uergongna et con ueste bianca remandato. Fuste alla colo(n)na duramente flagellato et tuo capo de spine coronato, con la canna in mano et de purpura uestito, allo populo como ad re in desprezo monstrato. Gridando lo populo 'sia crucifigato', alla morte iniusta fuste sententiato; che portasse la croce te fo comandato. No(n) la potiste cha eri debilitato. In t(er)ra alla croce p(er) me te extendiste et le mano et li piedi te foro chiauati, et quelle crodele piache patiste et po in alto fuste con la croce leuato. Scorrea lo sangue p(er) le spalle flagellate, scorrea p(er) la facce lo sangue delle spine. Scorrea p(er) lo corpo lo sangue delle braccia, scorrea p(er) li piedi lo sangue p(er) la croce. P(er) me fuste de fele abeuerato, p(er) me moriste innamorato, signore, p(er) me te foro ap(er)te le costate p(er) me monstrare lo cordiale amore. Pero lo tuo corpo ce uoliste lassare che(n)ce fosse de l'a(n)i(m)a cibo sp<irit>uale. Chi de tanto amore se debia descordare, et la toa passio(n)e abia ad significare. Pero te p(re)go, o alto signore, che te, o pilgliata ingrata et indigna mente, dona ad questa a(n)i(m)a forteze et amore che faccia toa uoluntate continuamente. Amen.

DEVOTE ORATIONES AD CRUCEM

6 (fos 18r-26v) Salue sancta crux, salus et uita mea. Salue crux quam adorat ... permaneam in tua fide et dilectione, redemptor meus, mediator dei et hominum. Qui cum.

7 (fos 26v-30r) ORATIO. Salue sancta et uenerabilis crux a qua ego saluari desidero et expecto. Tu es enim uerba et unica salus omnium in te credentium. Tu es fortitudo uiuentium et uita morientium. Tu es consolatio lugentium et refrigerium penitentium. Denique tu es omnium bonum et omne gaudium his qui te diligunt et qui ad te fugiunt. Propterea ego peccatrix et misera et orphana et ab omni adiutore destituta et soli tibi derelicta fugio ad te et maneo coram te ut pro sensu meo te adorem et indulgeas de peccatis meis a te implorem. Fugio quidem et uenio ante te tam necessitate conpellentem quam uoluntate persoluentem Voluntas enim bona quodamodo aducit me sed maior est necessitas que compellit me. Preualuit quippe nimis aduersus me spiritus meus; multiplicata est super munera iniquitas mea et facta est quasi crudelis anima mea; prolongata est sine fructu uita mea et ingrauata est

---

6   'Oratio s. Augustini' (*PL* 158.939-41).

7   ?

supra modum miseria mea. Videtur michi plaga mea insanabile ut ita facta sim tamquam desiderabilem. Et super hunc modum qui me adiuuet non est, qui consoletur non est, qui redimat neque qui me saluam faciat. Tu bone iesu redemptor et protector meus, hac necessitate compulsa uenio et maneo ante te gemens et dolens pro peccatis meis. Sed cum ego diligenter intueor fixuram clauorum in manibus et pedibus tuis, apponitur dolor super dolorem meum ita ut quodammodo dolorem meum non sentiam cum morte domini mei lugeam et doleam. Sed o reuerendissime domine quam pena non merentur impie manus mee cum clauis affiguntur innocentes manus tue, et quos cruciatus non merentur inutiles infelices pedes mei cum sic cruciantur recti et beati pedes tui. Heu misera, heu me dolentem, quomodo non est anima mea tristis plusquam ad mortem? Non audio te dicententen (*sic*): *tristis est anima mea usque ad mortem* [Mt 26:38]? Et quomodo non clauidius suppremi doloris permansit animam meam, uir lancea militis perforat latus tuum? Heu me peccatrix, quomodo possum hec cogitare et quibus auribus possum hec audire de domino meo? Ve michi, quibus oculis possum intuere deum meum crucifigi et manus que me fecerunt clauis affigi? Cum quanta angustia spiritus considero te, desiderabilis domine, spiritum emictentem et cum quanto dolore anime inspicio te exanime in cruce pendentem. Verumtamen de his omnibus, misericordissime et omnipotentissime domine, grandem inuenio consolationem cum tuam respicio uenerabilem resurrectionem et ad celos admirabilem ascensionem, et pariter ancillarum mearum desiderant redemptionem. De peccatis autem et negligentiis meis, de perdictione et mortis anime que est consolatio mea et que est redemptio mea nisi tu, spes mea et expectatio mea? Suppliciter itaque oro et deprecor te, pie exaudibilis iesu anima mea et exaltatio mea, ut tu consoleris me et ut tu sis adiutor meus in tribulationibus que inuenerunt me nimis quatenus per te liberata ab aduersitatibus uniuersis, secura tibi liberate deseruiam. Salua.

8 (fos 30r-31v) IN DIE PARASCEUEN ORATIO ADORANDAM SANCTAM CRUCEM +. Domine iesu christe, deus uerus de deo uero, qui pro redemptione generis humani … insigniti ab hostis perfidi sunt incursione securi. Per te iesu christe qui cum patre et spiritu sancto.

9 (fos 31v-32v) IN SECUNDA GENUFLEXA DICIT HANC ORATIONEM. Deus qui moysi famulo tuo in uia … uincamus et eterne uite participes esse mereamur. Per.

10 (fos 32v-33r) ORATIO. Domine iesu christe qui nos per passionem crucis … ab inflictis euacuari uulneribus et ad uitam eternam ualeamus (*sic*) peruenire per te iesu christe qui cum patre et spiritu sancto uiuit et regnat in secula seculorum. Amen.

---

8   Maz 23r ('In prima genuflexione'); Mc246 145 ('In prima genuflexione'); Urb585 256v ('Item alie or. ad crucem'); Vl4928 89r; Wilmart, 'Prières médiévales', 34-5.

9   Maz 23r-v ('In secunda genuflexione'); Mc246 147 ('in secunda genuflexione'); Urb585 256v-257r; Vl4928 89r-v ('in secunda genuflexione'); Wilmart, 'Prières médiévales', 35.

10 Mallet-Thibaut 703; Maz 23v ('In tertia genuflexione'); Mc246 147-148 ('in tertia genuflexione'); Urb585 257r; Vl4928 89v ('in tertia genuflexione'); Wilmart, 'Prières médiévales', 35.

11 (fo 33r-v) ORATIO. Deus a quo et iudas proditor reatus sui penam ... ablato uetustatis errore resurrectionis sue gratiam largiatur. Per.

<MEDITATIONES SUPER MISERERE>

12 (fos 33v-34r) MISERERE MEI DEUS SECUNDUM MAGNAM MISERICORDIAM TUAM (Ps. 50: 3). Non peto secundum meritum meum ... mea mala agere deposco sed secundum pietatem tuam.

13 (fo 34r-v) ET SECUNDUM MULTITUDINEM MISERATIONUM TUARUM DELE INIQUITATEM MEAM (Ps. 50: 3). Peri<i> enim in peccatis, lapsa sum mirabiliter ... firmiter atque constanter imperpetuum perseuerare.

14 (fos 34v-35r) AMPLIUS LAUA ME AB INIUSTICIA MEA ET A PECCATO MEO MUNDA ME (Ps. 50: 4). Noui peccata mea maxima. Tamen tu pie ... pre multitudine numerari non possunt.

15 (fo 35r-v) QUONIAM INIQUITATEM MEAM EGO AGNOSCO, ET DELICTUM MEUM CORAM ME EST SEMPER (Ps. 50: 5). O benigniss<im>e medice, adhibe michi ... quia tu pius es, miserere mei.

16 (fos 35v-36r) TIBI SOLI PECCCAUI ET MALUM CORAM TE FECI UT IUSTIFICERIS IN SERMONIBUS TUIS ET UINCAS DUM IUDICARIS (Ps. 50: 6). Considera ergo misericors deus substantiam infirmitatis ... parentibus meis concede gaudia sine mensura.

17 (fos 36r-37r) ECCE ENIM IN INIQUITATIBUS CONCEPTUS SUM ET IN DELICTIS PEPERIT ME MATER MEA (Ps. 50: 7). Ne reminiscaris domine delicta mea uel parentum ... qui omnia potes, solus potes me mundare.

18 (fo 37r-v) ECCE ENIM UERITATEM DILEXISTI INCERTA ET OCCULTA SAPIENTIE TUE MANIFESTASTI MICHI (Ps. 50: 8). Memoriam peccatorum meorum domine ignem (*sic*) ... partem te largiente sine fine inuenire merear. Amen.

19 (fos 37v-38r) ASPERGES ME DOMINE ISOPO ET MUNDABOR; LAUABIS ME ET SUPER NIUEM DEALBABOR (Ps. 50: 9). Doce me domine recordari semper peccatorum meorum ... uenite benedicti patris mei, percipite regnum.

20 (fo 38r-v) AUDITUI MEO DABIS GAUDIUM ET LETITIAM, ET EXULTABUNT OSSA HUMILIATA (Ps. 50: 10). Dico enim iniquitatem meam aut (*sic*) largam clementiam ... merear feliciter sine fine laudare te. Amen.

---

11 Mallet-Thibaut 357; CO 1086a.
12 AsP49 41r (no. 33); Mc442 286 (no. 51b); Salmon, no. 488; cf. 'Anselmus ep. Cantuariensis', *Meditatio super Miserere* 5 (*PL* 158.823C).
13 AsP49 41r-v (no. 34); Mc442 286-287 (no. 51c); Salmon, no. 489.
14 AsP49 41v-42r (no. 35); Mc442 287 (no. 51d); Salmon, no. 490.
15 AsP49 42r-v (no. 36); Mc442 287-288 (no. 51e); Salmon, no. 491.
16 AsP49 42v-43r (no. 37); Mc442 288 (no. 51f); Salmon, no. 492.
17 AsP49 43r-v (no. 38); Mc442 289 (no. 51g, *expl.* potes si uis uales me mundare); Salmon, no. 493.
18 AsP49 43v (no. 39); Mc442 289-290 (no. 51h); Salmon, no. 494.
19 AsP49 43v-44r (no. 40); Mc442 290 (no. 51i *expl.* regnum quod uobis paratum est a constitutione mundi); Salmon, no. 495.
20 AsP49 44r-v (no. 41); Mc442 291 (no. 51j); Salmon, no. 496.

21 (fos 38v-39v) AUERTE FACIEM TUAM A PECCATIS MEIS ET OMNES INIQUITATES MEAS DELE (Ps. 50: 11). Emunda pollu<tu>m cor meum deus, et per quod ... sorte tuo merear auxilio sine fine gaudere. Amen.

22 (fos 39v-40v) COR MUNDUM CREA IN ME DEUS, ET SPIRITUM RECTUM INNOUA IN UISCERIBUS MEIS (Ps. 50: 12). Domine iesu christe qui et filius hominis es propter humilitatem ... per tuam clementiam participes fieri mereamur. Amen.

23 (fos 40v-41r) NE PROITIAS ME A FACIE TUA, ET SPIRITUM SANCTUM TUUM NE AUFERAS A ME (Ps. 50: 13). Consolatorem nostrum spiritum tuum fac ... clementer me defendat in isto seculo atque in futuro. Amen.

24 (fos 41r-42r) REDDE MICHI LETICIAM SALUTARIS TUIS, ET SPIRITU PRINCIPALI CONFIRMA ME (Ps. 50: 14). Curro ergo ad communionem peccantium portum ... glorificent nomen tuum sanctum quod est benedictum in secula. Amen.

25 (fo 42r-v) DOCEBO INIQUOS UIAS TUAS, ET IMPII AD TE CONUERTENTUR (Ps. 50: 15). Abieci enim domine suaue iugum tuum ... furiosam per me exercere preualeant potestatem.

26 (fos 42v-43r) LIBERA ME DE SANGUINIBUS DEUS DEUS SALUTIS MEE, ET EXULTAUIT LINGUA MEA IUSTICIAM TUAM (Ps. 50: 16). Solue me de uinculis peccatorum ... cum ueneris in regnum tuum.

27 (fos 43r-44r) DOMINE LABIA MEA APERIES, ET OS MEUM ANNUNTIABIT LAUDEM TUAM (Ps. 50: 17). Recordare misericors deus fragilitatis ... sacrifitium aptare dignare.

28 (fos 44r-45r) QUONIAM SI UOLUISSES SACRIFITIUM, DEDISSEM UTIQUE; HOLOCAUSTIS NON DELECTABERIS (Ps. 50: 18). Deprecor inmensam pietatem tuam domine deus ... ualeat sacrifitium sicut scriptum est.

29 (fo 45r-v) SACRIFITIUM DEO SPIRITUS CONTRIBULATUS; COR CONTRITUM ET HUMILIATUM DEUS NON SPERNIT (Ps. 50: 19). Magna fiducia et magna spes est ... a te piissime domine deus meus.

30 (fos 45v-46v) BENIGNE FAC DOMINE IN BONA UOLUNTATE TUA SYON, UT HEDIFICENTUR MURI IERUSALEM (Ps. 50: 20). Ostende domine super me fragilem benignitatem ... famulatu sine fine merear permanere.

21 AsP49 44v-45v (no. 42); Mc442 291-292 (no. 51k); Salmon, no. 497.
22 AsP49 45v-46r (no. 43); Mc442 292-293 (no. 51l); Salmon, no. 498.
23 AsP49 46r-v (no. 44); Mc442 293 (no. 51m *inc.* Consolatorem spiritum sanctum tuum domine fac); Wilmart, 'Prières médiévales', 35; Salmon, no. 499.
24 AsP49 46v-47v (no. 45); Mc442 294-295 (no. 51n); Salmon, no. 500.
25 AsP49 47v-48r (no. 46); Mc442 295-296 (no. 51o); Salmon, no. 501.
26 AsP49 48r-v (no. 47); Mc442 296 (no. 51p); Salmon, no. 502.
27 AsP49 48v (no. 48, *des. mutil.* in tua me deinceps cu-); Mc442 296-297 (no. 51q); Salmon, no. 503.
28 Mc442 297-298 (no. 51r); Salmon, no. 504.
29 AsP49 34r (no. 49); Mc442 298-299 (no. 51s); Salmon, no. 505.
30 AsP49 34r-35r (no. 50); Mc442 299-300 (no. 51t); Salmon, no. 506.

31 (fos 46v-47v) TUNC ACCEPTABIS SACRIFITIUM IUSTICIE OBLATIONES ET HOLOCAUSTA; TUNC IMPONES SUPER ALTARE TUUM UITULOS (Ps. 50: 21). Gloria patri ingenito qui proprio filio ... ante omnia secula et nunc et imperpetuum. Amen.

<ORATIONES ANTE CRUCEM>

32 (fos 47v-54v) DEUOTA ORATIO. Summe sacerdos et uere pontifex qui te optulisti deo patri hostiam puram et sacrifitium ... societate mirifica ita ut neque exuriam neque siciam in eternum. Amen.

33 (fos 54v-57r) ORATIO. Mediator dei et hominum, domine iesu christe, qui ueram carnem ex intemeratis beate marie uisceribus ... ut crucifixo configurata in pena, consors fieri merear resurgentis in gloria.

34 (fos 57r-59r) Si pietatem tuam mitissime deus humanam mensuram habere congnoscerem, ego de immanissimo scelerum mole ... quam proprio mercatus es sanguine per continuam digneris gratiam possidere. Qui.

35 (fos 59r-60r) Dum crucem dilectissimi filii tui omnipotens pater adoro, pateat michi obsecro ut et oracio mea ... nec abicias ancillam tuam pro quo tradere dignatus es filium. Qui tecum uiuit et regnat in unitate.

36 (fo 60v) INCIPIT ORDO AD COMMUNICANDUM. Ego miserrima et infelix confiteor coram deo et tibi sancta et gloriosa uirgo maria ... ut orare dignemini pro me misera peccatrice.

37 (fos 60v-61r) ORATIO. Intercedentibus omnibus nobis (*sic*) pro me ad dominum, misereatur michi omnipotens deus ... et perducat me ad uitam eternam. Amen.

38 (fos 61r-62r) VERS. Ego dixi domine miserere mei ... RESP. Et clamor.

31　AsP49 35r-v (no. 52, s.v. 50: 21 GLORIA PATRI ET FILIO); Salmon, no. 507.

32　Jean de Fécamp (ps.-Ambrosius). Leroquais i, 51, ii, 227, 286; cf. Anselmus Cantuariensis, *Oratio* 19 (*PL* 158.921 ff.); A. Wilmart, 'L'*Oratio sancti Ambrosii* du Missel Romain', in *Auteurs spirituels*, 114-24; Deschamps-Mulder, 72, G16.

33　Maz 25v-26r ('In secunda genuflexione') (no. 132); Mc199 136r-137r ('In secunda genuflexione') (no. 132); Mc246 147 (no. 132); Urb585 255r-v ('In tertia [*sic*] genuflexione') (no. 132); Vl4928 90r-91r ('In secunda genuflexione') (no. 132); *PL* 145.927A-C (*Oratio* 26); Wilmart, 'Prières médiévales', 59.

34　Maz 26r-v ('In tertia genuflexione') (no. 133); Mc199 137r-v ('In tertia genuflexione') (no. 133); Mc246 148; Urb585 255v-256r ('In tertia genuflexione') (no. 133); Vl4928 91r-v ('In tertia genuflexione') (no. 133); *PL* 145.927C-928B (*Oratio* 27); Wilmart, 'Prières médiévales', 59.

35　Maz 25v ('Orationes domni petri hostiensis episcopi. In prima genuflexione') (no. 134); Mc199 136r ('Orationes uenerabilis petri hostiensis episcopi') (no. 134); Mc246 145-146 ('In secunda genuflexione') (no. 134); Urb585 255r ('In prima genuflexione') (no. 134); Vl4928 90r ('In prima genuflexione') (no. 134); *PL* 145.926C-D (*Oratio* 25); Wilmart, 'Prières médiévales', 59.

36　Maz 26v (no. 2*); Mc199 128r (no. 42*).

37　Maz 26v-27r (no. 3*); Mc199 128r ('Item absolutionis') (no. 43*).

38　Maz 27r (no. 4*); Mc199 128r-v (no. 44*); Mc246 146 (no. 33*); Vl4928 92r (no. 16*).

39 (fo 62r-v) ORATIO. Domine deus benignissime et clementissime pater, da michi facinorose et omni scelere ... et preter me non est alius, cuius gloriosum nomen permanet in secula seculorum. Amen.

40 (fos 62v-63v) ORATIO. Deus dilecti et benedicti filii tui iesu christi pater, per quem tui agnitionem suscepimus ... Propterea in omnibus laudo benedico et glorifico te per eternum dominum et pontificem uerum iesum christum filium tuum dominum nostrum. Per quem et cum tibi et spiritu sancto gloria et nunc et semper et in futuro seculo. Amen.

41 (fos 63v-64v) ORATIO. Domine yesu christe fili dei unigenite qui es et qui eras cum patre et spiritu sancto unus in essencia deus ... sed ad remedium anime mee proueniat et gratiam sempiterne salutis. Qui uiuis.

42 (fos 64v-66v) Domine non sum digna ut intres sub tectum anime mee quoniam tota deserta est atque prostrata, nec habes apud me ubi capud reclinet. Sed sicut ex alto propter nos (*corr. ex* uos) humiliasti te ipsum, condescende et iam nunc humiliatus me, sicut suscepisti in speluncha et presepio reclinare, eciam in presepe inrationabilis anime mee et meum quamuis uiaticum corpus ingredi. Et sicut non est (*sic*) <de>dignatus intrare et cenare in domo symonis leprosi, ita benigne domine non dedigneris ingredi domum contaminate anime mee. Quia suscepisti similem michi meretricem accedentem et tangentem te, longanimis esto michi queque (*sic*) indigne accedenti et accipienti uiuificam hanc et incontaminatam communionem sanctissimi tui corporis atque sanguinis. Et sicut non fastidi<s> os eius sordi\d/um et fetidum deosculantis te, nec scelestam eciam et inmundam, labia contaminata oris mei fastidias et peccatricem linguam meam, sed fiat michi ignem sanctissimi tui corporis atque sanguinis, alleuiatio grauitatis multarum mearum offensionum in abrenuntiatione omnis diabolice actionis et inmutationem malam peruersque (*sic*) mee consuetudinis. Non enim quasi temptens accedo ad te christe sed confitens ineffabili tua benignitate et pietate. Et ne diutius remota communione ab intemerata tua captiua uisibili lupo fiam, ideo queso te, sicut qui solus es sanctus domine, sanctifica mentem cor renes et uiscera mea; totam tamque me renoua et irradiata (*sic*) timorem tuum in membris meis et sanctificationem inseparabilem, estoque michi adiutor et susceptor, dignans me a dextris tuis assistere, orationibus et interuentibus intemeratissime uirginis et matris tue et omnium sanctorum tuorum complacuerunt (*sic*).

43 (fos 66v-67v) ORACIO. Domine iesu christe deus noster qui solus habes potestatem peccata dimicere, <dimicte> meas omnes offensas quas uel conscientia uel ingnorantia perpetraui, et dignam me fac sine dampnatione recipere diuina et gloriosa et intemerata misteria tua, non in pondus nec penam nec augumentum

---

39   Maz 27r-v (no. 6*); Mc199 128v-129r (no. 46*); Mc246 146 (no. 34*); Vl4928 93r (no. 18*).
40   Maz 27r (no. 5*); Mc199 128v ('Oratio Sancti policarpi') (no. 45*).
41   AsP 32v-33v (no. 84); Maz 27v (no. 7*); Mc199 129r (no. 47*).
42   ?
43   ?

peccati sed in purificationem et sanctificationem et adiutorium in effugationem aduersarii et absolutionem omnium mearum offensionum. Tu enim es deus misericordie et pietatis et miserationum et tibi gloria redimet patri et filio et spiritui sancto nunc et semper et in secula seculorum. Amen.

44 (fos 67v-68v) ORATIO. Gracias ago tibi benigne domine quia per multam benignitatem tuam et longaminitatem concessisti participem me fieri et contaminati (*sic*) tui corporis et preciosi sanguinis. Et non es abominatus quasi pollutam nec quasi susceptionem sanctificationis tue indignam inuisibili digna uirtute tua repulisti, sed uoluisti me quoque peccatricem immortali tua mensa reficere. Cuius gratiam imminutam in humili anima mea conserua, et accipiente in me lumen inextinguibile illuminans, me, omnem intellectum, omnem sensum sine offensa me custodiens et inconcussum uentilante peccato ut glorificent et gratias agant tibi secundum tuam sanctam uoluntatem omnibus diebus uite mee intercessionibus intemerate domine nostre dei genitricis et omnium sanctorum qui a seculo tibi placuerunt. Qui uiuis et.

45 (fos 68v-69r) Incontaminati corporis et preciosi sanguinis dignas effectas fieri particeps gratias ago; laudo glorifico adoro magnificans domine salutes tuas sine cessacione nunc et semper et in secula seculorum. Amen.

46 (fo 69r) ANTEQUAM ACCIPIAT CORPUS DOMINI DICAT. Domine non sum digna ut intres sub tectum meum sed tanctum dic uerbum et sanabitur anima mea. TRIBUS UICIBUS.

47 (fo 69r) POST ACCEPTUM CORPUS DOMINI DICAT HAS ANTIPHONAS TRIBUS UICIBUS. Verbum caro factum est ... Tibi laus tibi gloria ... .

48 (fos 69v-70v) Gracias tibi ago domine sancte pater omnipotens eterne deus qui me peccatricem et indignam saciare dignatus es sacrosancto corpore ... optulit et nos suo precioso sanguine redemit et tecum uiuit et regnat in unitate eiusdem spiritus sancti deus per omnia secula seculorum. Amen.

49 (fo 70v) ORATIO. Corpus tuum domine quod sumpsi et calix quem potaui adhereat ... quem pura et sancta refecerunt sacramenta.

50 (fos 70v-71r) ORATIO. Post communionem sacramentorum tuorum percepta fiat in me domine remissionem (*sic*) ... ab illorum deinceps contagione immaculata conseruet in secula seculorum. Amen.

51 (fos 71r-72r) ORATIO. Scio domine iesu christe et confiteor clementie ... et faciant me semper tibi toto corde esse deuotam. Saluator mundi qui uiuis.

---

44 ?

45 ?

46 Maz 28r (no. 9*); Mc199 129v (no. 49*); Vl4928 94r (no. 22*).

47 Maz 28r (no. 10*); Mc199 129v (no. 50*); Vl4928 94r (nos. 24*-25*).

48 Mallet-Thibaut 824; Maz 28r (no. 11*); Mc199 129v-130r (no. 51*); Mc246 146 (38*); Vl4928 94r-v (no. 26*).

49 Mallet-Thibaut 277; Maz 28r-v (no. 13*); Mc199 130r (no. 53*); Mc246 146 (no. 40*).

50 Vl4928 95r (no. 29*); cf. CO 850a, 850b.

51 Maz 28v (no. 14*); Mc199 130r-v (no. 54*); Vl4928 (no. 27*).

52 (fo 72r-v) Misericors et miserator domine qui parcendo sustentas et ignoscendo ... purificationem mentis et corporis et mearum omnium absolucionem culparum.

<ORATIONES PRO DEFUNCTIS>

53 (fos 72v-73r) ORATIO. Auete omnes christi fideles anime quarum corpora hic et ubique requiescunt. Det uobis requiem ille qui est uera requies, iesus christus filius dei uiui, qui natus est de maria immaculata uirgine pro nostra omniumque salute et nos redemit suo precioso sanguine. Benedicat nos et a penis liberet et angelorum choris associet faciatque resurgere in die resurrectionis et secum sine fine gaudere ibique nostri memores dignemini suppliciter exorare ut uobiscum coronemur et gaudiis perfruamur eternis. Amen. Pater noster. Aue maria gratia plena.

54 (fo 73r-v) ORATIO. Domine sancte pater omnipotens eterne deus, te deprecor pro animabus patris et matris mee et omnium benefactorum meorum, et rogo te pro omnibus illis qui et que in penis purgatorii sunt ut tua mediante pietate et misericordia liberentur ut cum sanctis et electis tuis uita et requie possint perfrui sempiterna, et ego cum migrauero, quia tu es deus meus et ductor meus, cum illis habeam partem in regno tuo. Qui uiuis et regnas in secula seculorum. Amen.

<VERSUS>

55 (fo 73v) Spine, crux, claui, mors, pena quam tolleraui | ostendunt qua in miserorum crimina laui.

<ORATIO AD S. DOROTHEAM>

56 (fos 73v-74r) ORATIO. Deus qui gloriosam dorotheam uirginem et martirem tuam ad agnitionem sancte trinitatis peruenire fecisti, da cunctis deuotis tuis eius passionis memoriam uenerantibus ut te solum deum ipsius intercessione et toto corde semper diligant et ab inuocatione tui sanctissimi nominis numquam desistant. Per christum.

<INVOCATIONES AD CHRISTUM>

57 (fo 74r-v) O sacrosantissimo ochino de pieta, o uirtute santissima de carita, o signore sagratissimo da li iudei venduto et accactato.

---

52 VI4928 95r (no. 30*); CO 3382.
53 Cf. Leroquais ii, 341, no. 29: 'Transeundo per aliquod cimiterium'(text from Paris, Bibliothèque Nationale de France, lat. 1363, saec. XV, fo 124v; only the incipit resembles our prayer).
54 ?
55 Hans Walther, *Initia carminum ac versuum Medii Aevi posterioris latinorum* (Göttingen, 1959), no. 10100 ('Lancea, crux, clavi, spine, mors').
56 ?
57 ?

58 (fo 74v) O carne preciossima a la colon(n)a bactuto et legato.

59 (fo 74v) O facze dolcessema ch(e) multe ore timido liuida lacrimosa et bactuta et sputata.

60 (fo 75r) O capo santissimo de spine incoronato.

61 (fo 75r) O carne sacratissima in la croce chiauata.

62 (fo 75r) O bocca perfectissima de fele et acito et calze abeuerato.

63 (fo 75r) O lato sacratissimo con la lanza lanzato.

Index of Liturgical Formulae

Note: an asterisk (*) precedes texts in Italian

Abieci enim domine suaue iugum tuum...furiosam per me exercere praeualeant potestatem: 25 (Or.)

Amplius laua me ab iniustitia mea: 14 (Ps. 50: 4)

Asperges me domine hysopo et mundabor: 19 (Ps. 50: 9)

Auditui meo dabis gaudium et laetitiam: 20 (Ps. 50: 10)

Aue Maria gratia plena: 53 (Or.)

*Aue sanctissime corpo del signore mio in quisto sacramento...sia conceduto beato uestimento et bono recapito in uita eterna: 4 (Or.)

Auerte faciem tuam a peccatis: 21 (Ps. 50: 11)

Auete omnes Christi fideles animae quarum corpora hic et ubique requiescunt det uobis requiem...dignemini suppliciter exorare ut uobiscum coronemur et gaudiis perfruamur aeternis: 53 (Or.)

Benigne fac domine in bona uoluntate: 30 (Ps. 50: 20)

Considera ergo misericors deus substantiam infirmitatis...parentibus meis concede gaudia sine mensura: 16 (Or.)

Consolatorem nostrum spiritum tuum fac... clementer me defendat in isto saeculo atque in futuro: 23 (Or.)

Cor mundum crea in me deus: 22 (Ps. 50: 12)

Corpus tuum domine quod sumpsi et calix quem potaui adhaereat...quem pura et sancta refecerunt sacramenta: 49 (Or.)

Curro ergo ad communionem peccantium portum...glorificent nomen tuum sanctum quod est benedictum in saecula: 24 (Or.)

Deprecor immensam pietatem tuam domine deus...ualeat sacrificium sicut scriptum est: 28 (Or.)

Deus a quo et Iudas proditor reatus sui poenam... ablato uetustatis errore resurrectionis suae gratiam largiatur: 11 (Or.)

Deus dilecti et benedicti filii tui Iesu Christi pater per quem tui agnitionem suscepimus... Propterea in omnibus laudo benedico et glorifico te per aeternum dominum et pontificem uerum Iesum Christum filium tuum dominum nostrum. Per quem et cum tibi et spiritu sancto gloria et nunc et semper et in futuro saeculo: 40 (Or.)

Deus qui gloriosam Dorotheam uirginem et martyrem tuam ad agnitionem sanctae trinitatis peruenire...et ab inuocatione tui sanctissimi nominis numquam desistant: 56 (Or.)

Deus qui Moysi famulo tuo in uia...uincamus et aeternae uitae participes esse mereamur: 9 (Or.)

Dico enim iniquitatem meam aut largam clementiam...merear feliciter sine fine laudare te: 20 (Or.)

Doce me domine recordari semper peccatorum meorum...uenite benedicti patris mei percipite regnum: 19 (Or.)

Docebo iniquos uias tuas et impii: 25 (Ps. 50: 15)

Domine deus benignissime et clementissime pater da mihi facinorosae et omni scelere...et praeter

---

58 ?

59 ?

60 ?

61 ?

62 ?

63 ?

me non est alius cuius gloriosum nomen permanet in saecula saeculorum: 39 (Or.)

Domine Iesu Christe deus noster qui solus habes
potestatem peccata dimittere meas omnes offensas...et tibi gloria redimet patri et filio et spiritui
sancto nunc et semper et in saecula saeculorum:
43 (Or.)

Domine Iesu Christe deus uerus de deo uero qui
pro redemptione generis humani...insigniti ab
hostis perfidi sunt incursione securi: 8 (Or.)

Domine Iesu Christe fili dei unigenite qui es et qui
eras cum patre et spiritu sancto unus in essentia
deus...sed ad remedium animae meae proueniat
et gratiam sempiternae salutis: 41 (Or.)

Domine Iesu Christe qui et filius hominis es propter humilitatem...per tuam clementiam participes fieri mereamur: 22 (Or.)

Domine Iesu Christe qui nos per passionem crucis...ab inflictis euacuari uulneribus et ad uitam
aeternam ualeamus peruenire per te Iesu Christe
qui: 10 (Or.)

Domine labia mea aperies: 27 (Ps. 50: 17)

Domine non sum digna ut intres sub tectum animae meae quoniam tota deserta...et interuentibus intemeratissimae uirginis et matris tuae et
omnium sanctorum tuorum complacuerunt: 42
(Or.)

Domine non sum digna ut intres sub tectum meum
sed tantum dic uerbum et sanabitur anima mea:
46 (Or.)

Domine sancte pater omnipotens aeterne deus te
deprecor pro animabus patris et matris meae et
omnium benefactorum...quia tu es deus meus et
ductor meus cum illis habeam partem in regno
tuo: 54 (Or.)

Dum crucem dilectissimi filii tui omnipotens pater
adoro pateat mihi obsecro ut et oratio mea...nec
abicias ancillam tuam pro quo tradere dignatus
es filium: 35 (Or.)

Ecce enim in iniquitatibus conceptus sum: 17 (Ps.
50: 7)

Ecce enim ueritatem dilexisti: 18 (Ps. 50: 8)

*Eccome auante ad te signore uile peccatrice...che
faccia toa uoluntate continuamente: 5 (Or.)

Ego dixi domine miserere mei: 38 (Vers.)

Ego miserrima et infelix confiteor coram deo et
tibi sancta et gloriosa uirgo Maria...ut orare
dignemini pro me misera peccatrice: 36 (Or.)

Emunda pollutum cor meum deus et per
quod...sorte tuo merear auxilio sine fine gaudere: 21 (Or.)

Et clamor: 38 (Resp.)

Et secundum multitudinem miserationum tuarum:
13 (Ps. 50: 3)

Gloria patri ingenito qui proprio filio...ante omnia
saecula et nunc et in perpetuum: 31 (Or.)

Gratias ago tibi benigne domine quia per multam
benignitatem tuam et longanimitatem... intercessionibus intemeratae dominae nostrae dei
genitricis et omnium sanctorum qui a saeculo
tibi placuerunt: 44 (Or.)

Gratias tibi ago domine sancte pater omnipotens
aeterne deus qui me peccatricem et indignam
satiare dignatus es sacrosancto corpore... optulit
et nos suo pretioso sanguine redemit et tecum
uiuit et regnat in unitate eiusdem spiritus sancti
deus per omnia saecula saeculorum: 48 (Or.)

In mensam dulcissimi conuiuii domine Iesu
Christe rex angelorum...per te qui nos creasti
cum non essemus: 2 (Or.)

Incontaminati corporis et pretiosi sanguinis dignas
effectas fieri...salutes tuas sine cessatione nunc
et semper et in saecula saeculorum: 45 (Or.)

Intercedentibus omnibus nobis pro me ad dominum misereatur mihi omnipotens deus...et perducat me ad uitam aeternam: 37 (Or.)

Libera me de sanguinibus deus: 26 (Ps. 50: 16)

Magna fiducia et magna spes est...a te piissime
domine deus meus: 29 (Or.)

Mediator dei et hominum domine Iesu Christe qui
ueram carnem ex intemeratis beatae Mariae uisceribus...ut crucifixo configurata in poena
consors fieri merear resurgentis in gloria: 33
(Or.)

Memoriam peccatorum meorum domine
ignem...partem te largiente sine fine inuenire
merear: 18 (Or.)

Miserere mei deus secundum magnam misericordiam tuam: 12 (Ps. 50: 3)

Misericors et miserator domine qui parcendo sustentas et ignoscendo...purificationem mentis et
corporis et mearum omnium absolutionem
culparum: 52 (Or.)

Ne proicias me a facie tua: 23 (Ps. 50: 13)

Ne reminiscaris domine delicta mea uel parentum...qui omnia potes solus potes me mundare:
17 (Or.)

Non peto secundum meritum meum...mea mala
agere deposco sed secundum pietatem tuam: 12
(Or.)

Noui peccata mea maxima tamen tu pie...prae
multitudine numerari non possunt: 14 (Or.)

O anima Christi sanctissima sanctifica me...ut
cum angelis tuis laudem in saecula saeculorum:
3 (Or.)

O benignissime medice adhibe mihi...quia tu pius
es miserere mei: 15 (Or.)

*O bocca perfectissima...abeuerato: 62 (Invoc.)

*O capo santissimo...incoronato: 60 (Invoc.)

*O carne preciossima...et legato: 58 (Invoc.)

*O carne sacratissima...chiauata: 61 (Invoc.)

*O facze dolcessema...bactuta et sputata: 59 (Invoc.)

O Iesu creator o Iesu redemptor o Iesu saluator humani generis parce mihi inoboedienti...ut in omnibus tibi oboediam omnibus diebus uitae meae: 1 (Or.)

*O lato sacratissimo...lanzato: 63 (Invoc.)

*O sacrosantissimo ochino...venduto et accactato: 57 (Invoc.)

Ostende domine super me fragilem benignitatem...famulatu sine fine merear permanere: 30 (Or.)

Pater noster: 53 (Or.)

Perii enim in peccatis lapsa sum mirabiliter...firmiter atque constanter imperpetuum perseuerare: 13 (Or.)

Post communionem sacramentorum tuorum percepta fiat in me domine remissionem...ab illorum deinceps contagione immaculata conseruet in saecula saeculorum: 50 (Or.)

Quoniam iniquitatem meam ego agnosco: 15 (Ps. 50: 5)

Quoniam si uoluisses sacrificium: 28 (Ps. 50: 18)

Recordare misericors deus fragilitatis...sacrificium aptare dignare: 27 (Or.)

Redde mihi laetitiam salutaris: 24 (Ps. 50: 14)

Sacrificium deo spiritus contribulatus: 29 (Ps. 50: 19)

Salue sancta crux salus et uita mea salue crux quam adorat...permaneam in tua fide et dilectione redemptor meus mediator dei et hominum: 6 (Or.)

Salue sancta et uenerabilis crux a qua ego saluari desidero et expecto...liberata ab aduersitatibus uniuersis secura tibi liberate deseruiam: 7 (Or.)

Scio domine Iesu Christe et confiteor clementiae...et faciant me semper tibi toto corde esse deuotam: 51 (Or.)

Si pietatem tuam mitissime deus humanam mensuram habere cognoscerem ego de immanissimo scelerum mole...quam proprio mercatus es sanguine per continuam digneris gratiam possidere: 34 (Or.)

Solue me de uinculis peccatorum...cum ueneris in regnum tuum: 26 (Or.)

Spinae crux claui...miserorum crimina laui: 55 (Versus)

Summe sacerdos et uere pontifex qui te optulisti deo patri hostiam puram et sacrificium... societate mirifica ita ut neque esuriam neque sitiam in aeternum: 32 (Or.)

Tibi laus tibi gloria tibi gratiarum actio honor uirtus et fortitudo in saecula saeculorum: 47 (Ant.)

Tibi soli peccaui et malum: 16 (Ps. 50: 6)

Tunc acceptabis sacrificium iustitiae: 31 (Ps. 50: 21)

Verbum caro factum est et habitauit: 47 (Ant.)

Plate 7.1 Oslo/London, The Schøyen Collection, MS 1981, fo 1r.
All facsimiles are life-size.

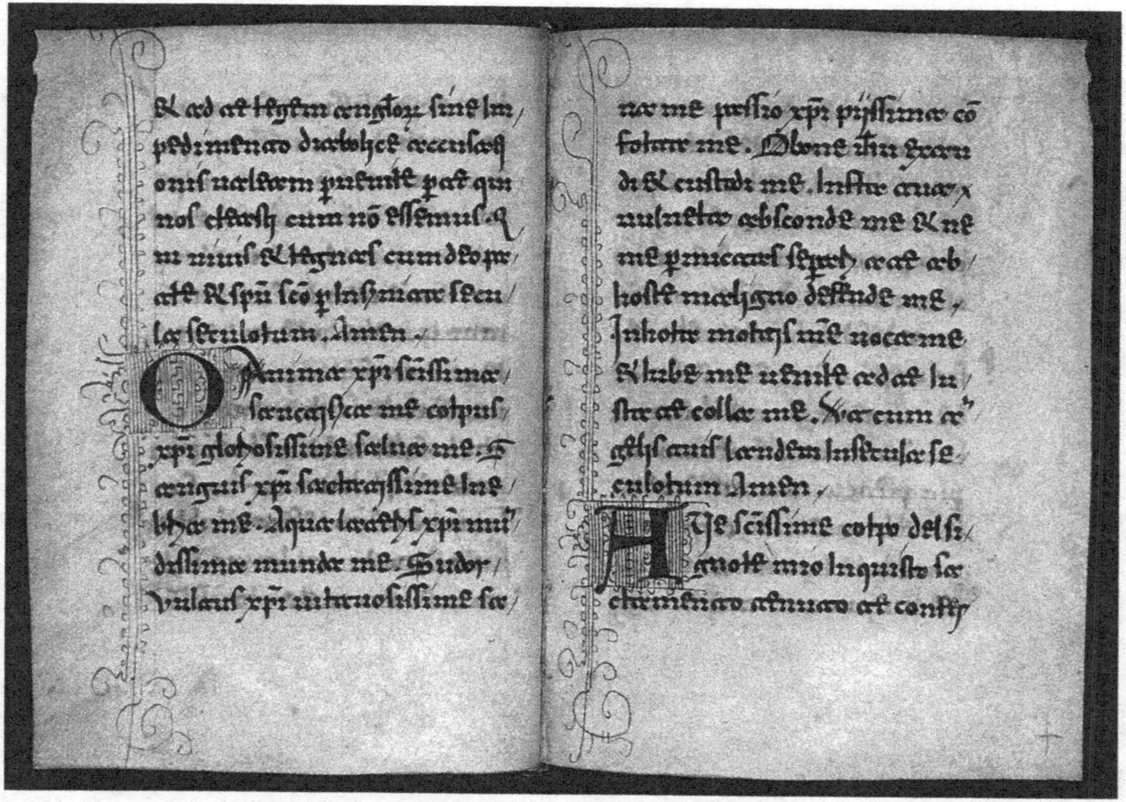

Plate 7.2 Oslo/London, The Schøyen Collection, MS 1981, fos 12v-13r

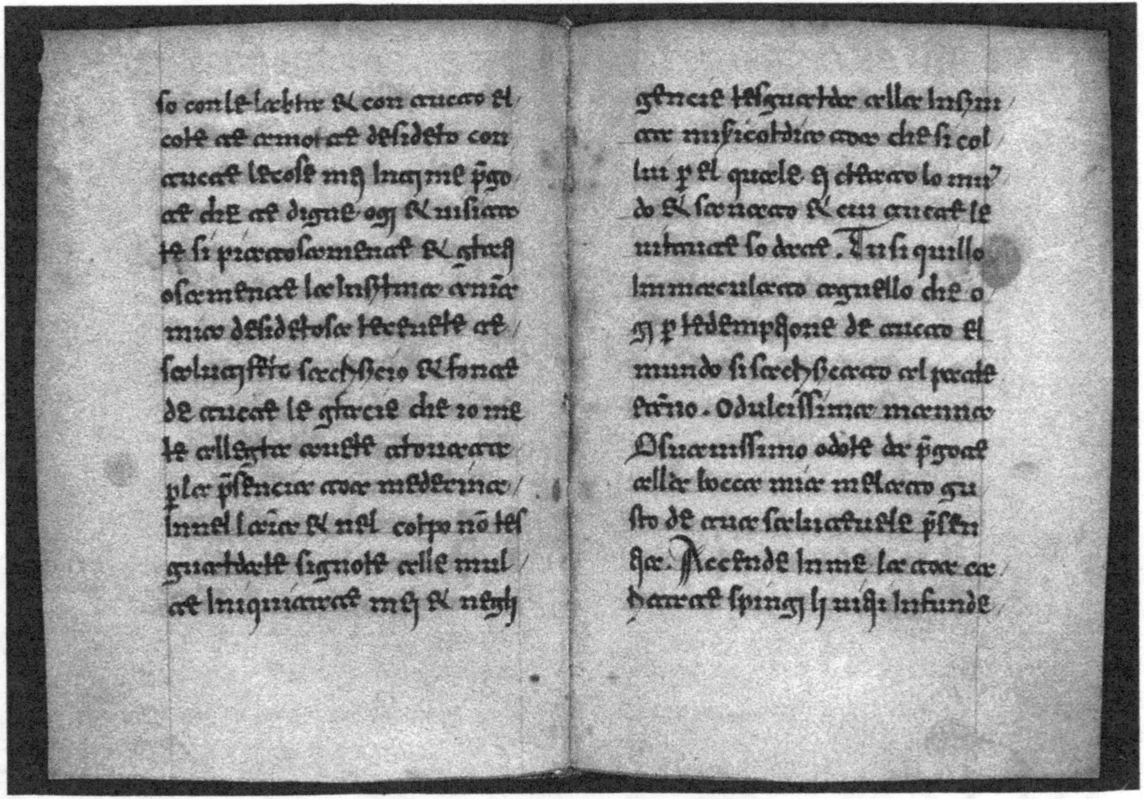

Plate 7.3 Oslo/London, The Schøyen Collection, MS 1981, fos 13v–14r

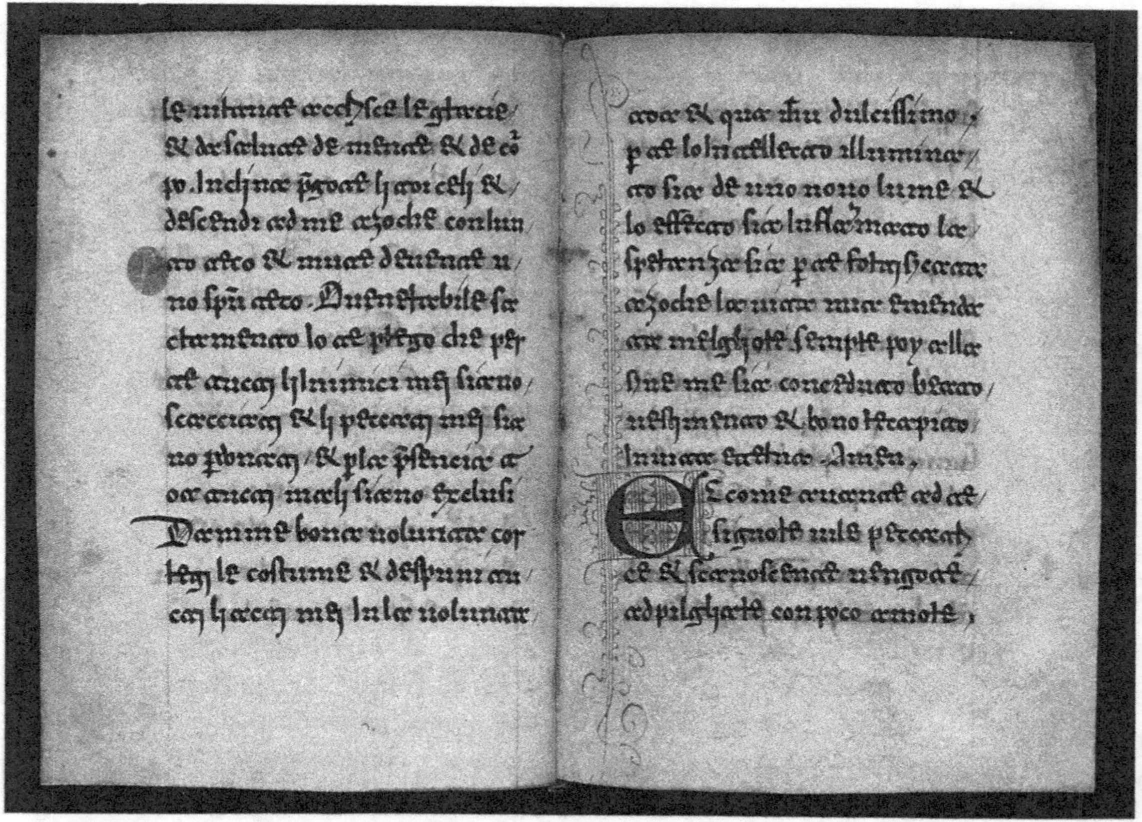

Plate 7.4 Oslo/London, The Schøyen Collection, MS 1981, fos 14v–15r

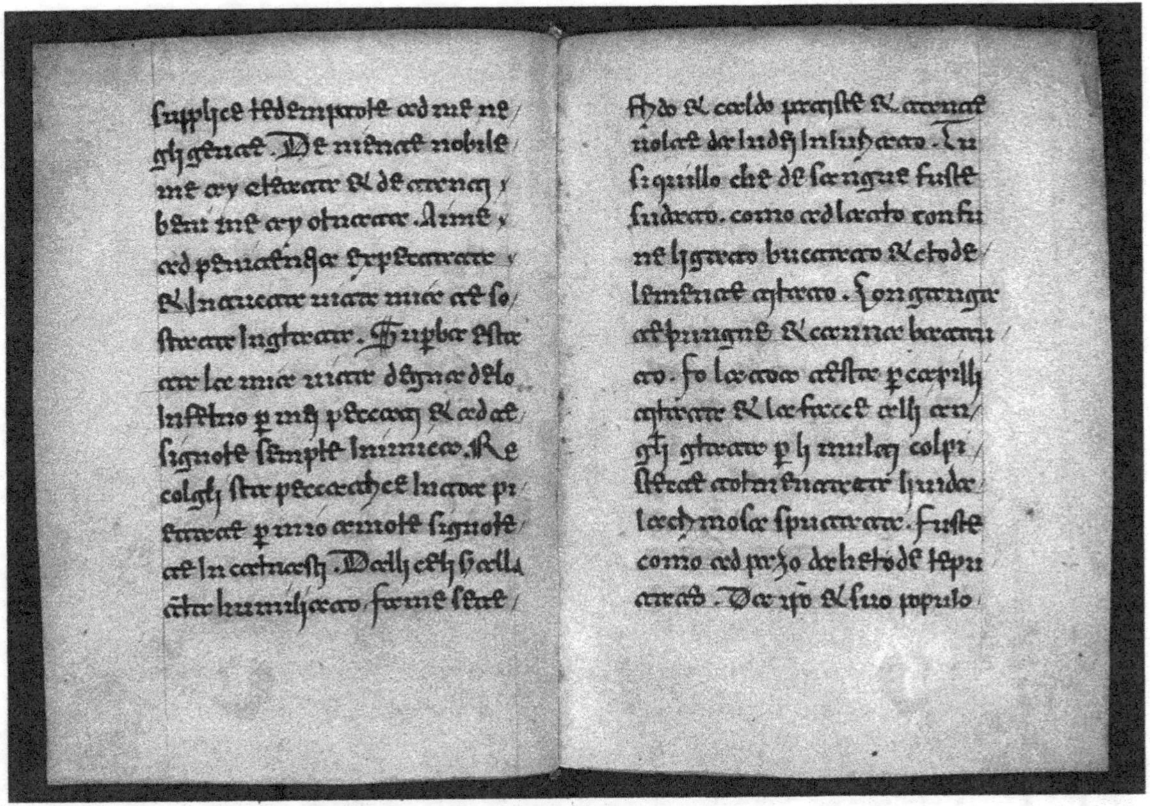

Plate 7.5 Oslo/London, The Schøyen Collection, MS 1981, fos 15v-16r

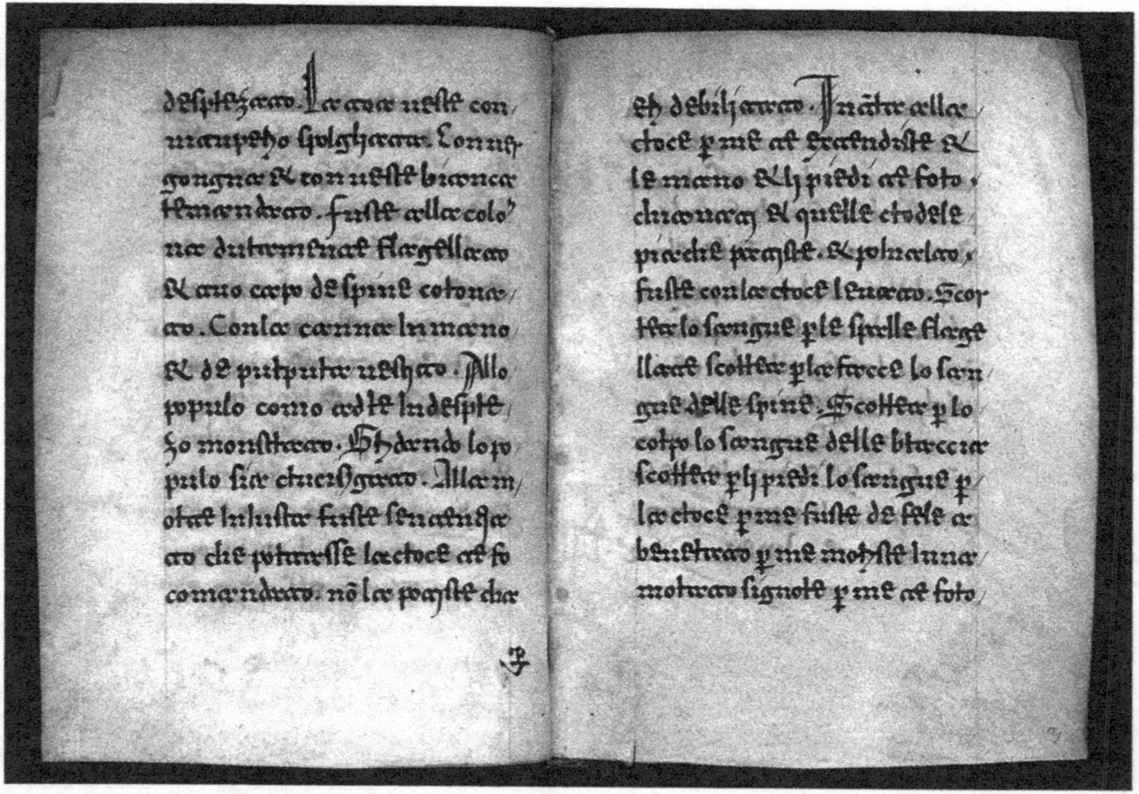

Plate 7.6 Oslo/London, The Schøyen Collection, MS 1981, fos 16v–17r

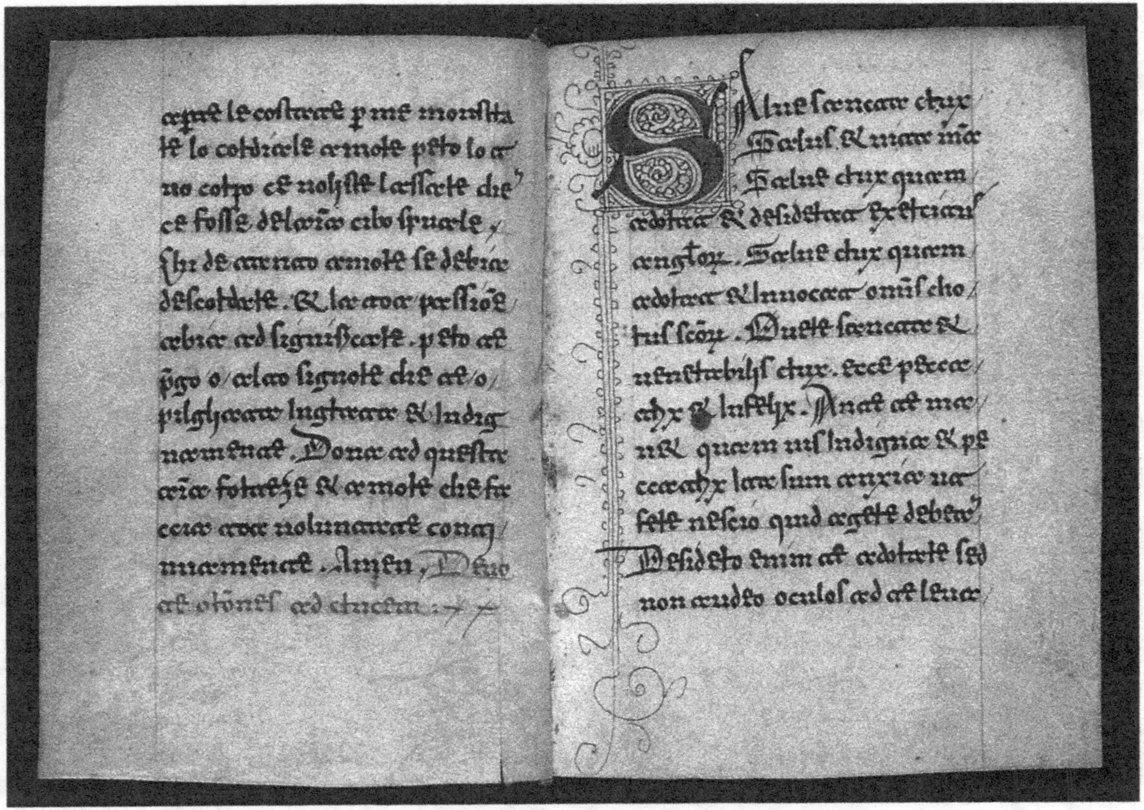

Plate 7.7 Oslo/London, The Schøyen Collection, MS 1981, fos 17v–18r

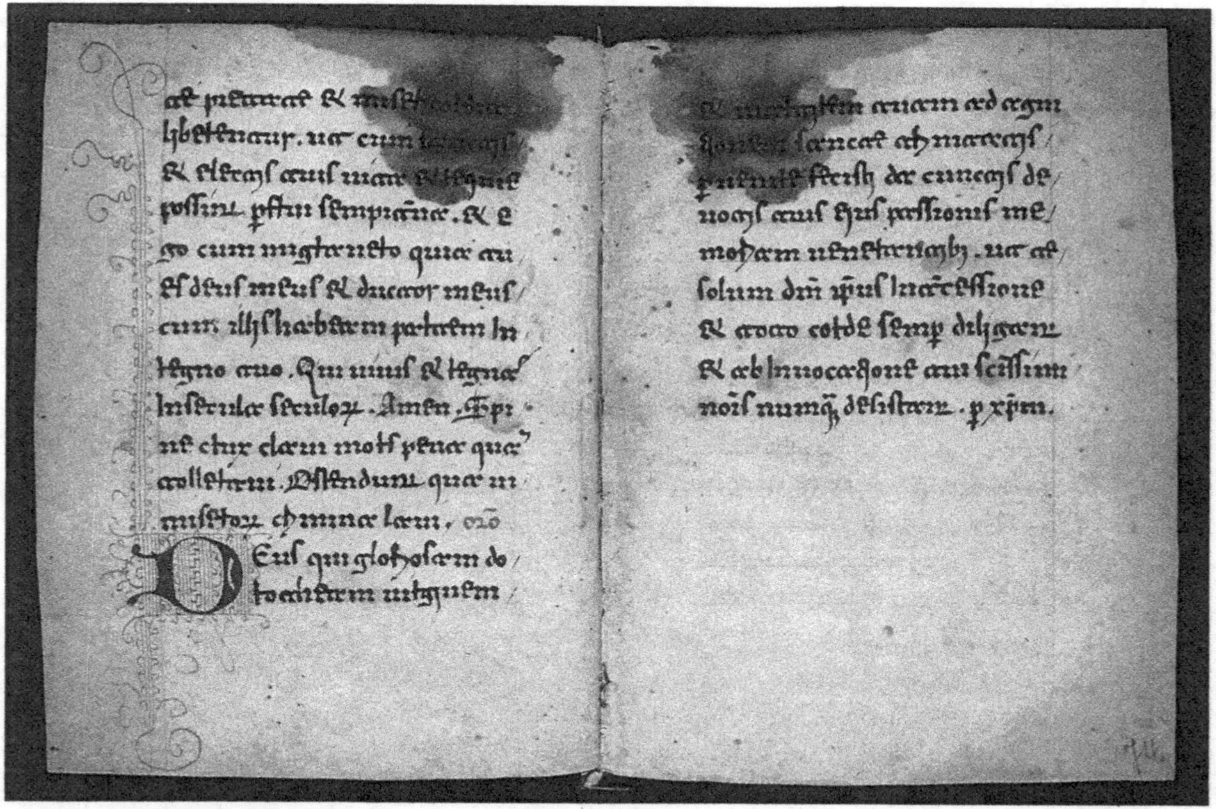

Plate 7.8 Oslo/London, The Schøyen Collection, MS 1981, fos 73v-74r

Plate 7.9 Oslo/London, The Schøyen Collection, MS 1981, inside back cover

PART II
Text and Law

Introduction

Text and Law

Kathleen G. Cushing

From the time of his dissertation at Harvard in 1968, Roger Reynold's work on liturgy and canon law has been characterized by a rigorous but nuanced understanding of the intellectual activity which transformed thought about the Church, its nature, its rituals, and its regulation, as well as the world in which it operated during the middle ages.[1] As is to be expected of a scholar of his caliber, Reynolds' comprehension of varied medieval texts—whose many intricacies he has brought to light—has always been informed by a keen awareness of the different cultural and even linguistic assumptions of medieval writers, as well as the distance of that world from our own. Medievalists, of course, have long recognized the necessity of approaching different types of sources carefully. Even the supposedly more reliable sources of legislation, pontificals and charters as against the 'constructions' of chronicles and *vitae*—although ostensibly documenting specific exchanges, giving instruction and establishing normative practice—may often conceal lengthy processes of dispute resolution; they may have symbolic rather than normative value; or they may even have been 'forgeries'. None of these factors in any way diminishes a source's value to scholars interested in understanding and explicating texts.[2]

Yet, in many ways, Reynolds has provided an excellent example of the importance for historians working on medieval topics, especially those dealing with the Church, to understand—as Dominique Iogna-Prat has recently cautioned—that the task is not 'religious history' but rather 'social history'.[3] Inasmuch as it is vital, where possible, to try to gauge medieval society's attachment to religious values, Reynolds has amply shown that often we can do little more than assess how these intersected with the enactment of belief in accordance with the prescriptive rules and rituals of an institution, in other words, with the Church. Reynolds has also implicitly recognized that studying the Latin west during the earlier middle ages offers an additional challenge. This, after all, was a time when the production and dissemination

---

1 See the List of Principal Publications in this volume for details and for the phenomenal range of Roger E. Reynolds' scholarship.

2 See esp. *Fälschungen im Mittelalter: Internationaler Kongreß der Monumenta Germaniae Historica München, 16.-19. September 1986*, 6 vols, *MGH Schriften*, 33/i-vi (Hanover, 1988).

3 Dominique Iogna-Prat, *Order and Exclusion: Cluny and Christendom face heresy, Judaism and Islam (1000-1150)* , trans. Graham Robert Edwards (Ithaca, NY, 2002), 4.

of ideas was the exclusive province of a very small elite: educated clerics and monks, whose writings and accounts inevitably leave us with one side of a very complicated story. Even more important, he has frequently drawn attention to the fact that the changes and improvements in religious life described in such accounts may often be evidence of aspirations to *effect* change rather than real change itself. The issue is even more problematic with collections of canon law and other texts containing canonical requirements. However much these may have been promulgated as proscriptive or normative measures, that is, as establishing uniformly binding and enforceable law, in reality they were ostensibly prescriptive measures, advocating certain standards of practice. As Reynolds has shown, these in the end perhaps tell us more about what ecclesiastical writers aspired to achieve for the Church and by extension for Christian society rather than providing evidence of the status quo at any given time.

It is therefore scarcely surprising that texts and their significance have been central to Roger Reynolds' scholarship, whether he has been concerned with the liturgy, clerical orders, canon law or the Beneventan script. Although all historians implicitly concede the importance of written documents as sources, for medievalists such as Reynolds, as well as for the contributors to this volume among others, medieval texts are not merely sources of historical knowledge but also fundamental objects of study in themselves. Moreover for medievalists, 'texts' extend beyond the written record of chronicles, *vitae*, necrologies, pontificals, homilies, liturgical works, canon law collections and letters to include among other things reliquaries, liturgical objects, vestments, architecture and the evidence of archaeology.[4] At the present time, in a post-structuralist and post-modernist intellectual climate, preoccupations with text and textual analysis have widely challenged historians in general to bring to their analysis and explication of texts linguistic theories as well as insights from social and cultural anthropology. For post-modernists, such approaches are used to de-stabilize efforts to 'discover what happened' by focusing on how texts were/are (re)created, (re)shaped and especially understood by differing audiences. While approaches such as these are valid and useful in understanding how texts may have been read and recreated in different social contexts and at different times, they can perhaps minimize what Reynolds and the contributors to this volume have long recognized as the imperative to understand texts in terms of genre, textual production and in the context of the other texts with which a given text was (or may have been) bound in manuscript, read and disseminated. Even here, moreover, genre may not always be the most helpful conceptual tool; the artificiality of distinguishing liturgical from canonical or even theological sources—long recognized by Reynolds—is explicitly discussed in this volume by Keefe, Mordek, Brett and Blumenthal, and is implicit in almost every other article.

---

4   See the List of Principal Publications, 309-18 in this volume for works on vestments and other 'texts'.

Central, however, to Reynolds' work and implicit in all the contributions in this volume (though especially to those in this section) is the awareness of the imperative need to establish texts themselves before moving on to the issues of their interpretation and context. The prerequisite of such work is of course rigorous attention to codicology, paleography, and the study of Latin and other languages, in addition to familiarity with wide-ranging canonical, liturgical and theological writings. This is no easy task. Editing texts, identifying formal and material sources, being aware of the multifaceted traditions that may underlie a given text, establishing the often hairsplitting connections between variants and different recensions requires not just wide-ranging knowledge but also meticulous attention to detail. These have been the cornerstones of Reynolds' work, not least of all within the Monumenta Liturgica Beneventana project.

In the field of medieval canon law, with which most of the articles in this section are concerned, the work of identifying material and formal sources and especially the connections between recensions has long been a fundamental issue. Here attention to detail is especially imperative as even the most minor variant could be critical in establishing a link between different canonical works, especially when an intermediate source is posited but not extant. Ever since the time of the Ballerini brothers, though especially throughout the later nineteenth and early twentieth centuries, phenomenal research on pre-Gratian canonical collections (with which Reynolds and the contributors are preoccupied), their formal and material sources, their manuscript traditions and transmissions by scholars such as Friedrich Maassen, Friedrich Wasserschleben, Herman Schmitz, Victor Wolf von Glanvell, Friedrich Thaner and especially Paul Fournier, among others, have set impressively high standards, even if their editions, like those in Migne, are no longer deemed as reliable as could be desired. Many of their modern day successors, including Reynolds and some of the contributors, began their own invaluable research in a pre-computer age. Canon law, like liturgical and theological studies, has been revolutionized by computer databases such as the *Patrologia Latina* database, the *Acta Sanctorum* database, Timothy Reuter's word concordance for Gratian, Linda Fowler-Magerl's tremendous *KanonesJ*, and also by the placing of working editions on the web such as the *Panormia* by Martin Brett and Bruce Brasington. It is only to be hoped that continued work in this direction will enable further understanding of the relationships between canonical collections.

The articles in this section cover issues of canon law and textual transmission from the fourth to the fourteenth centuries and reflect many of the topics with which Roger Reynolds has been occupied throughout his career. In the first paper, John Gibaut examines the transmission of the Council of Sardica's canon 13 on the 'cursus honorum', the canonical requirement of promotion through a sequence or series of ordinations, over the *longue durée*, from the fourth to the thirteenth centuries. He argues in particular that, although theologians, liturgists and canon lawyers often insisted on sequential ordination from priest to bishop, these requirements were in practice not always followed and that an alternative tradition (from deacon to bishop) was widely known, especially in Roman practice before the eleventh century. As Gibaut remarks in his opening paragraphs, the assessment of such historical changes in the treatment of orders has been a central concern in Reynolds' work, one with implications for contemporary churches.

The next three papers address topics in the transmission of texts and ecclesiastical culture of the Carolingian period. Giles Constable focuses on an interesting late ninth-century *Homilia sacra* (in Copenhagen, Kongelike Bibliotek, MS GKS 143), and provides here the first modern critical edition of the text. The Homily treats the Christian life from baptism to death and describes the behaviour expected of a Christian. While demonstrating that the homily draws heavily on previous writers, especially Caesarius of Arles, Constable notes that it is compiled in an original way and probably exerted influence on later works including perhaps *Scarapsus* and later ecclesiastical legislation. Constable comments in particular on the baptismal scrutiny, in which the priest poses questions on belief to those about to be baptized, who answer 'credo'. In the next paper dealing with a Carolingian text, Hubert Mordek explores, with some striking examples of how texts were quite spectacularly corrupted through scribal error or ignorance, the transmission of a new excerpt from Charlemagne's *Capitulare generale* (802), the influence of which was rather minimal apart from the Collection in Five Books and its derivatives. In his comparison of the text in Paris, Bibliothèque, MS lat 4613 and Vatican City, Biblioteca Apostolica Vaticana, MS Vat. lat. 7790, which has a radically different ending, Mordek first questions whether the latter is an exceptional or a muddled copy, and then makes a compelling case for the continuing use of canonical sources with 'new readings' long beyond their original contexts. Susan Keefe's contribution, with its extensive catalogue of creed commentary collections in Carolingian manuscripts derived from her large catalogue project, takes to heart Roger Reynolds' oft-repeated assertion that florilegial collections were rational compositions ordered to an end. By exploring such seeming miscellanies, Keefe identifies eighty creed commentary collections formed from the selection and arrangement of individual works. In this group, Keefe finds a tremendous diversity in opinions of how to interpret the faith under the Carolingians, an observation which stands in contrast to the received opinion of the Carolingian quest for uniformity and *correctio*, and shows that compilers were individualistic, selective and drew on a wide variety of liturgical, theological and canonical material.

The remaining articles all consider canonical collections of the eleventh to fourteenth centuries. In an article which includes discussion of the problems of editing canon law collections and manuscript traditions, Martin Brett challenges scholarship that would consider early medieval canonical collections only from the perspective of Gratian. This vertical approach, as he calls it, has led to false standards, whereas in fact a well-known collection such as the *Panormia* cannot be read as representative of medieval canonical thought because its variants reveal very different understandings of the canons. In additional telling examples, Brett shows how readers even after Gratian inhabited a far from monolithic world of canonical experience, and continued to read and annotate earlier medieval collections. With such examples in mind, Brett calls for a horizontal approach, in which the study of collections would be based on careful study of individual manuscripts, their users and their connections with contemporaries.

It is the consideration of the context, purpose and limits of authors and collections, as determined through the close examination of manuscripts, that guides the next contributions. This is the approach advocated by Brett, and is typical of much of Roger Reynolds' work, especially on individual schools or institutions, whether Salzburg, Toledo or Montecassino. In examining the relationship between a collection of the reform period and its predecessors, Kathleen Cushing considers the less than straightforward ties between the *Liber decretorum* of Burchard of Worms and book 11, *de penitentia*, of Anselm of Lucca, recension A. By examining the use of Burchard as a formal source in the context of other sources used, especially the late eighth- or early ninth-century *Capitula Iudiciorum*, Cushing shows that Anselm A was seemingly aware of the merits and deficiencies of his sources, and was willing to use material, such as the *Capitula Iudiciorum*, not considered by his more prominent sources, including Burchard or even his contemporaries. Richard Gyug focuses on the relationship between the illustrations of canonical authorities and the text of the Collection in Five Books in Vatican City, Biblioteca Apostolica Vaticana, MS Vat. lat. 1339, showing that the illustrations are very precise in their representation of the collection's sources, and more appropriate for the collection than for other contemporary collections. The correspondence between illustration and text indicates the degree to which readers, in this instance the illustrator, were familiar in quite detailed ways with the contents of early collections.

The last four articles offer fresh insights into the formal sources employed by compilers and also underline the continuing validity and use of earlier material. Peter Landau looks to clarify the sources of the Collection in Seven Books (Vatican City, Biblioteca Apostolica Vaticana, MS Vat. lat. 1346) with reference to other collections compiled earlier and during the first half of the twelfth century, by reviewing various opinions from scholars from Theiner onwards. He reveals that a much more complicated series of sources than previously thought was available to the compiler, which he argues must challenge us to rethink our acceptance of what we mean by pre-Gratian canonical knowledge. Linda Fowler-Magerl examines the different versions of the *Collectio Caesaraugustana* which, although compiled *c.* 1120 in southeastern France and relying on collections from northern and central Italy such as Anselm of Lucca, also used canonical sources available only in northeastern France. Underlining the connections of the various versions of the *Caesaraugustana* with canons regular, especially those at St Ruf, she focuses on the version in Barcelona, Archivo de la Corona de Aragón, MS San Cugat 63, which historians have seen as an abbreviated version of the text. Fowler-Magerl compellingly shows that the compiler in fact rigorously reordered, and even corrected, the collection by taking into account many canonical traditions and sources. Turning to a late fourteenth-century manuscript from Benevento (albeit not one in the Beneventan script whose use Roger Reynolds has done so much to elucidate), Robert Somerville, with an extensive range of sources, examines a text with close links to the later eleventh-century *Collectio canonum* of Deusdedit. Although surviving complete in only one medieval manuscript, Deusdedit has long been known to have exerted wider influence on collections such as the *Collectio Britannica* and the *Caesaraugustana* as well as polemical literature associated with the Investiture Contest. Somerville thus provides another tantalizing example of the continuing use and influence of earlier canonical material. Finally, Uta-Renate Blumenthal addresses the twelfth-century canonical collection from St Victor in Paris (Bibliothèque de l'Arsenal, MS 721), and reveals the selective even individualistic methodology of the compiler, who had close links with Burchard but who frequently interrupted this with texts from the *Collectio Lanfranci* and the *Tripartita*. Also noting parallels with texts in the *Codex Udalrici* and the compiler's partisan veneration of Gregory VII, Blumenthal reminds us of the importance of being aware of the multifaceted traditions underlying a compilation. The compiler's partisan interest also brings this survey to the Gregorian period, which is central to Reynolds' work and the scholarship of many of the contributors, and which is where this tribute began in the opening of the first introduction.

Although the articles in this section address different texts across several different centuries, in the end they all have in common an attempt to understand, by means of the explication of texts, the complicated thought world of ecclesiastical writers grappling to come to terms with the nature of the Church, its regulation and rituals. At the centre of their work, thus, is a fundamental preoccupation with identifying and interpreting connections, and trying to understand textual transmission. Their contributions in the end testify to comments made by Martin Brett in his paper for the Tenth International Congress of Medieval Canon law in Syracuse in 1996, that 'establishing texts is the laborious ... precondition of asking more interesting questions'.[5] In his long and distinguished career, Roger Reynolds has succeeded in both providing us with authoritative texts and asking fundamental questions, often prompted by the problems associated with establishing the texts. It is therefore fitting that in a volume in his honour, the contributors have done likewise.

---

5   Martin Brett, 'The Manuscripts of the *Collectio Tripartita*', to appear in *Proceedings of the Tenth International Congress of Medieval Canon Law*, MIC, Series C, Subsidia (Vatican City, forthcoming).

Chapter 8

The Peregrinations of Canon 13 of the Council of Sardica

John St H. Gibaut

Roger Reynolds' magisterial contributions to the study of medieval canon law and the theology of orders galvanized my own interest years ago in the canonical requirement of promotion through a sequence or series of ordinations through the grades, known as the 'cursus honorum'. The earliest instance of canonical legislation prescribing sequential ordination is c. 13 of the Council of Sardica, A. D. 343. This article seeks to trace the appearance and use of Sardica 13 in canonistic collections from the late patristic period to the twelfth-century *Decretum Gratiani*. As there is 'no text without context', the circumstances in which the canon arose will be examined, and the subsequent contexts in which it was used and modified will be considered. The context of this present investigation is the serious (albeit limited) re-examination of the inherited pattern of sequential ordination in some quarters of the contemporary Roman Catholic and Anglican churches.[1] In this current reconsideration, the history of sequential ordination—and with it the history of Sardica 13—is a weighty piece of evidence.

The Emergence of Sequential Ordination

The earliest canonical prescriptions for sequential ordination appear in the mid-fourth century. Until the mid-third century there is no explicit evidence of sequen-

---

1 Of note is a Roman Catholic study by Patrick McCaslin and Michael G. Lawler, *Sacrament of Service: a vision of the permanent diaconate* (New York, 1986); esp. 14 and 124. The more extensive debate within Anglicanism, again in relationship to the restored diaconate, is reflected in the 2001 International Anglican Liturgical Consultation's statement on ordination: 'Because the three orders are viewed as distinct ministries, direct ordination to the presbyterate, and even the possibility of direct ordination to the episcopate, are being advocated by some in the Anglican Communion. There is historical precedent for both sequential and direct ordination. In the pre-Nicene church, direct ordination was commonly practised, and sequential ordination did not become universal until the eleventh century. Provinces may therefore wish to consider the possibility of direct ordination to the episcopate and to the presbyterate'; ed. Paul Gibson, *Anglican Ordination Rites, The Berkeley Statement: 'To Equip the Saints', findings of the Sixth International Anglican Liturgical Consultation, Berkeley, California, 2001* (Cambridge, 2002), 9.

tial ordination, although biographical information suggests that it may have happened from time to time. The pre-Nicene pattern seems to have been direct
ordination to all of the ecclesiastical offices, with the sole sacramental prerequisite
being the rites of Christian initiation.[2] The earliest unequivocal evidence of sequential appointment from one ministry to another appears in the letters of Cyprian of
Carthage (d. 258). In *Epistle* 38 (*c*. 250), Cyprian explains that a certain confessor,
although worthy of the 'higher grades', will 'begin' at the lectorate; here one ministry is being used as a preparatory stage before promotion to another. A more
significant text is *Epistle* 55.8, where Cyprian describes the ecclesiastical career of
Cornelius, bishop of Rome (251-3):

> Venio iam nunc, frater carissime, ad personam Corneli collegae nostri... nam quod Cor-
> nelium carissimum nostrum Deo et Christo et ecclesiae eius, item consacerdotibus
> cunctis laudabili praedicatione commendat, non iste ad episcopatum subito pervenit, sed
> per omnia ecclesiastica officia promotus et in divinis administrationibus Dominum
> saepe promeritus ad sacerdotii sublime fastigium cunctis religionis gradibus ascendit.[3]

Apparently, Cornelius did not become a bishop suddenly, but 'was promoted
through all the ecclesiastical offices'; he 'ascended through all the grades of
religion to the exalted pinnacle of the priesthood', that is, the episcopate. Commentators regard this text as evidence of the 'cursus honorum' in the third century.[4]
Certainly in the case of Cornelius, who had 'advanced through all the ecclesiastical
offices', what emerges later as the clerical 'cursus' is clearly embryonic. By the
mid-third century, particular ministries were no longer exclusively life-long
vocations; individuals could and did 'advance' from one grade to another. Yet, at
this time, it was probably Cornelius' career that was the exception. There is no
suggestion that Cyprian understands the example of Cornelius as normative or
prescriptive. His own ecclesiastical career corresponds neither to that of Cornelius
nor to the later clerical 'cursus'. The most one can say is that here Cyprian merely
describes the career of one bishop.

Together, Cyprian's *Epistles* 38 and 55.8 indicate that by the mid-third century,
at least in Rome and North Africa, one ministry could be, and was, used as a preparatory stage prior to promotion to another. Moreover, an individual might well
serve sequentially in 'all the ecclesiastical offices'. While sequential ordination

---

2 See John Gibaut, *The Cursus Honorum: a study of the origins and evolution of sequential
   ordination* (New York, 2000), 11-58.

3 Cyprian, *ep.* 55.8, *S. Thascli Caecli Cypriani Opera omnia*, ed. Guilelmus [Wilhelm] Hartel, *CSEL*,
   3/i-ii (Vienna, 1871), ii, 629.

4 E.g., Clarke states that *Epistle* 55.8 is testimony to the extent to which the clerical 'cursus' was
   established in the mid-third century; *The Letters of St. Cyprian of Carthage*, trans. and comm.
   G. W. Clarke, 4 vols, Ancient Christian Writers, 43, 44, 46, 48 (New York, 1984-8), iii, 173. See
   also J. Robert Wright, 'Sequential or Cumulative Orders vs. Direct Ordination', *Anglican
   Theological Review*, 75/ii (Spring, 1993), 248.

was neither a sacramental priority nor a canonical necessity, it did without doubt occur regularly in the pre-Nicene church, concurrent with the practice of direct ordination. As Dom Gregory Dix has summarized:

> If a man were chosen to be bishop, then he was ordained bishop, regardless if he were already an acolyte or a presbyter or a simple layman; if a deacon were elected then he was ordained bishop without first being ordained presbyter, and so on.[5]

After the Peace of the Church, however, the earlier more flexible and diverse means of appointing the higher clergy was frequently abused by the unscrupulous, the ambitious or the unworthy. As patristic ecclesiastical histories report, unsuitable candidates for the episcopate were frequently motivated by greed and ambition. Civil appointment, ambition, and simony—referred to by Gregory the Great as 'that terrible disease'—were all too often accompanied by, and associated with, *per saltum* or direct ordination.

The seriousness of the problem of ordaining the 'unworthy' to the episcopate is reflected in numerous patristic papal writings. For example, Pope Celestine (422-32) complained that known criminals were made bishops.[6] Leo the Great (440-61) protested that those ignorant of the church's lawful institutions, lacking in all humility, inexperienced and unskilled, were likewise made bishops.[7] Gregory the Great (590-604) commented that the 'illicit promotion of the few' was becoming the ruin of many through the lack of respect for the governance of the church.[8]

Hence, patristic conciliar and papal texts frequently speak of the need for 'probatio', the testing of orthodox faith and morals. The need for probation became met by sequential ordination through the grades in prescribed intervals. Known as the 'cursus honorum' and accompanied by designated times or interstices to be spent in each grade, this process had a long tradition in the imperial Roman military and civil services. One of the original functions of the ecclesiastical 'cursus' was to test the holiness and worthiness of clergy for periods of years in the lower offices. This procedure was an attempt to ensure that those unworthy of the 'dignity' of the episcopate or the presbyterate would not find themselves in these offices.

Episcopal candidates without adequate preparation also proved to be a serious problem for the church. Not surprisingly, the patristic texts also speak of progression through the grades in terms of 'praeparatio'; i.e., training and education, or

---

5 Gregory Dix, 'The Ministry of the Early Church, c. A.D. 90–410', in *The Apostolic Ministry*, ed. Kenneth E. Kirk (London, 1957), 284.

6 Celestine, *ep.* 4.4, *PL* 56.578.

7 Leo I, *ep.* 12.4, *PL* 54.649-51.

8 *Gregorii I papae Registrum epistolarum*, 9.213, ed. Paulus Ewald and Ludovicus M. Hartmann, *MGH Epistolae*, 1-2 (Berlin, 1887-99), ii, 198-9.

becoming a disciple before becoming the teacher. Bishops who were unprepared for the tasks of episcopal leadership—theology, liturgy, diplomacy, canon law, and administration—were almost as undesirable and unsuitable as candidates who had never been tested. Since there were no seminaries or schools of theology in the early church, this need for preparation became met by sequential ordination and the interstices: the 'cursus honorum'.

The abundant condemnations of the ordination of the unworthy and of those untrained in conciliar statements, papal letters and decretals, and patristic ecclesiastical histories indicate that in the new situation of the fourth and fifth centuries, the church needed an effective means to select, prepare, and test its leaders. Sequential ordination was the method that emerged as the practical and pastoral solution to the problem of appointing the unworthy or the incapable to ecclesiastical leadership in the recently christianised Roman Empire. Not only was it a practical means, but a proven one as well within the socio-political culture of the Roman Empire, which had successfully applied the 'cursus honorum' for centuries. From the mid-fourth century, the practice of sequential ordination emerged as the preferred and canonical way of training and selecting members of the clergy. The earliest canonical requirement of sequential ordination extant is Sardica 13.

The Council of Sardica

A decisive step towards establishing the clerical 'cursus' was taken by the Council of Sardica. The council was convened by the emperors Constans and Constantine II in the autumn of 342 or 343.[9] Sardica, the present-day Sofia, is on the western side of the boundary between the eastern and western halves of the Empire. Unlike the Council of Nicaea, the western bishops outnumbered the eastern bishops (ninety-six to seventy). In many ways the council was a failure because the eastern bishops left *en masse* for Philippolis before the conclusion of the council, where they condemned Athanasius, as well as Julius, the bishop of Rome.

The purpose of the council was primarily theological; it was anti-Arian and had as its goal the vindication of Athanasius and the re-affirmation of the creed promulgated by the Council of Nicaea. The council also dealt with matters of discipline. The twenty-one canons of the Council of Sardica deal with issues such as the translation of bishops, the reception of excommunicate clergy, rights of appeal, and episcopal journeys to the imperial court. Sardica 13[10] (from the *versio*

---

9   On the date of the Council of Sardica, see Hamilton Hess, *The Canons of the Council of Sardica, A.D. 343* (Oxford, 1958), Appendix I, 140.

10 C. 8 according to the enumeration in Cuthbert Hamilton Turner; *Ecclesiae occidentalis monumenta iuris antiquissima*, 2 vols (Oxford, 1899-1939), i, 472-4. It is generally referred to as c. 13 in the

Caeciliani) of the council deals with the testing of candidates for the episcopate. It is the fundamental patristic conciliar text on the 'cursus honorum':

Canon XIII [VIII]

Ossius episcopus dixit: Et hoc necessarium arbitror ut diligentissime tractetis: si forte aut dives, aut scolasticus de foro, aut ex administratore, episcopus postulatus fuerit, non prius ordinetur nisi ante et lectoris munere et officio diaconii et ministerio praesbyterii fuerit perfunctus; ut per singulos gradus (si dignus fuerit) ascendat ad culmen episcopatus. Potest enim per has promotiones, quae habebunt utique prolixum tempus, probari qua fide sit, qua modestia, qua gravitate et verecundia: et si dignus fuerit probatus, divino sacerdotio inlustretur. Nec conveniens est nec rationis disciplina patitur ut temere aut leviter ordinetur aut episcopus aut praesbyter aut diaconus—maxime qui sit neofitus, cum beatissimus apostolus magister gentium ne hoc fieret denuntiasse et prohibuisse videatur; quia longi temporis examinatio merita eius probabit. Universi dixerunt placere sibi haec.[11]

The express purpose of the canon is to assure that worthy candidates be chosen for office. The emphasis is upon testing or probation: 'ut per singulos gradus (si dignus fuerit) ascendat ad culmen episcopatus'. It is the intent of the canon that by means of service in successive offices, candidates will have been proved worthy in terms of faith, modesty, seriousness, and reverence. Moreover, although the time to be spent in the various offices is not mentioned, the process will be lengthy ('prolixum tempus'). One notes the use of the word 'gradus' ('grade' or 'step') in the text of the canon. This term has a particular connection with the 'cursus honorum' in the civil and military services of the empire.[12]

From the first line of the canon, it is clear that one of the problems faced by the fourth-century church was the election of unsuitable candidates for the episcopate. Evidently, worthiness for office was not the only operative criterion for promotion; too many candidates were appointed to the episcopate because they were rich, public advocates, or civil servants. The wealthy, who were also well-connected in secular and political life, were often sought after in the hopes that they would provide strength and leadership for the church, and that they would attract the favour of the state in the construction of new cathedrals, or even pay for them themselves.[13] The bishops of the Council of Sardica were eager to move away from this sort of thing.

It is interesting to note the sequence of offices listed in Sardica 13: lector, deacon, presbyter, and bishop. There is no mention of the subdeacon, acolyte, exorcist,

---

western church according to the enumeration of the Council of Sardica in the *Dionysiana* and *Prisca* canonical collections; see Hess, *Canons of the Council of Sardica*, Table A, 136.

11 Turner, *Ecclesiae occidentalis monumenta*, i, 472-4.
12 David Power, *Ministers of Christ and his Church* (London, 1963), 63.
13 Ramsay MacMullen, *Christianizing the Roman Empire AD 100-400* (New Haven, 1984), 53.

or doorkeeper, though these offices were clearly in existence in some parts of the church.[14] The canons of the Council of Sardica appeared in many versions in the western church. As we shall see, Sardica 13 was of great significance in the development of the 'cursus honorum': its themes are repeated in later conciliar legislation, in papal writings, and in the emerging canonical tradition of the western church.

Sardica 13 in the Patristic Canonistic Collections

While conciliar and papal legislation enjoining the 'cursus honorum' was essential to the introduction and promotion of the clerical 'cursus' and the interstices, equally important were the canonistic collections, the intermediate sources by which the canons of popes and councils were transmitted to the church.[15] Of the many patristic collections, this section will examine four: the *Breviatio canonum* of Fulgentius, the Roman *Collectio Dionysiana*, the *Concordia canonum* of Cresconius, and the *Collectio vetus gallica*.

Some of the earliest canonistic collections are North African. For example, the *Breviatio canonum*,[16] compiled *c.* 546/7 by Fulgentius Ferrandus, a deacon of the church at Carthage, contains 232 capitula from eastern and African councils, arranged systematically on an assortment of topics, including holy orders. It is one of the earliest to use, although not reproduce, Sardica 13, and is significant because it had such a widespread circulation in Europe in the early medieval period.[17] The *Breviatio canonum* contains five canons dealing with the 'cursus honorum' and the interstices. Canon 1 of the collection is based on the Council of Nicaea, c. 2, Sardica 13, and the Council of Laodicea, c. 3; and it states that neophytes are not to be ordained.[18] Although several legislative sources of the 'cursus' and the interstices are included in the *Breviatio canonum*, what is perhaps more significant are the sources that are explicitly not included, especially Sardica 13, which is merely used with two other canons as the basis for canon 1.

---

14 E.g., the list of offices provided by Cornelius from the Roman church in the third century, as preserved by Eusebius: bishop, presbyter, deacon, subdeacon, acolyte, exorcist, lector, doorkeeper; see Eusebius, *Historia ecclesiastica*, 6.43. ed. Eduard Schwartz and Theodor Mommsen, *Eusebius' Werke*, 2; *GCS*, 9/i-iii (Leipzig, 1903-9), ii, 618.

15 Roger E. Reynolds, 'Law, Canon: to Gratian', in *The Dictionary of the Middle Ages*, ed. Joseph R. Strayer, 13 vols (New York, 1982-9), vii (1986), 395-413 at 395.

16 See the edition in *Concilia Africae A. 345-A. 525*, ed. C. Munier, *CCSL* 149 (Turnhout, 1974), 287-306. For bibliography, see Lotte Kéry, *Canonical Collections of the Early Middle Ages (ca. 400-1140)*, History of Medieval Canon Law, 1, ed. Wilfried Hartmann and Kenneth Pennington (Washington, D.C., 1999), 23-4.

17 Reynolds, 'Law, Canon', 400. In the *Brevatio canonum*, the full texts are not provided, but only the introductions (rather than simply the incipits) to the canons.

18 *Concilia Africae*, *CCSL*, 149.287.

A second important canonistic source is the fifth- or sixth-century Roman collection, the *Dionysiana*, compiled by the monk known as Dionysius Exiguus. It is particularly noteworthy for correcting the mistaken attribution of the canons of Sardica to the Council of Nicaea, an attribution that was current in the Roman church from the fourth century to the sixth. For instance, as Hess notes, the Roman synod of 485 assumed that the Sardican canons were Nicene; Pope Zosimus quotes them as Nicene canons in a letter sent to the Council of Carthage in 418; and Leo the Great likewise identifies them as Nicene. It was only with the *Dionysiana* that the canons of the Council of Sardica were recognised as such in Rome.[19]

The *Dionysiana* includes Sardica 13, but the Dionysian recension differs from the original in one significant respect. The text of the Sardican canon had been subtly modified from '... et officii diaconii *et* ministerio presbyterii' to '... et officii diaconii *aut* ministerio presbyterii'.[20] The *Dionysiana*, a product of the so-called Gelasian Renaissance, came to have an almost official status in the Roman church, becoming the basis for later Italian canonistic collections, such as the *Collectio Dionysio-Hadriana*, which would in turn affect many of the Frankish and later medieval collections. Its modification of Sardica 13, which would be reproduced again and again in later collections, represents the typical western revision of the Sardican canon and survives as late as the *Decretum Gratiani*.

The source of the change to Sardica 13 in the *Dionysiana* was undoubtedly the contemporary Roman practice of electing and ordaining either deacons or presbyters as bishops. As Andrieu asks: 'Pourquoi donc Denys a-t-il modifié son modèle?—L'explication la plus simple serait qu'il a voulu éviter de le mettre en contradiction avec les usages qu'il voyait régner à Rome'.[21] In Rome, the practice of electing and ordaining deacons directly to the episcopate continued well into the tenth century. The long-standing practice of ordaining bishops from among either the deacons or presbyters of Rome is reflected in the papal biographies in the *Liber pontificalis*,[22] and in liturgical rites. An important witness to Roman practice is *Ordo romanus* 34, an ordination rite from the mid-eighth century,[23] which contains the oldest extant description of Roman ordination practice since the *Apostolic Tradition*. Germane to this discussion on sequential ordination is the provision in the episcopal ordination rite for candidates who may be *either* deacons *or* presbyters. At the presentation of the candidate, the pope asks what office the candidate

---

19 Hess, *Sardica*, 49-55.

20 *Die Canonessammlung des Dionysius Exiguus in der Ersten Redaktion*, ed. Adolf Strewe, Arbeiten zur Kirchengeschichte, 16 (Berlin, 1931), 67 [emphasis added]; on the collection, see Kéry, *Canonical Collections*, 9-13.

21 Michel Andrieu, *Les Ordines Romani du haut Moyen Age*, 5 vols (Louvain, 1931-51), iii, 564.

22 E.g., Gregory II (715-31), Zacharias (741-52), Stephen II (752-7), Paul I (757-67), Constantine II (antipope, 767-9), Hadrian I (772-95), Stephen IV (816-7), Valentine (827), Nicholas I (858-67), Benedict V (964-6), Benedict VI (973-4), and Boniface VIII (antipope, 974, 984-5).

23 Ed. Andrieu, *Ordines Romani*, iii, 603-13.

fulfils, deacon or presbyter, and for how long.[24] The pope asks the same question of the candidate in the examination.[25] Later, when the pope invites the assembly to pray for the one to be consecrated bishop, he refers to him by name as a deacon *or* presbyter.[26] Furthermore, the rite itself is identical for both diaconal and presbyteral candidates for the episcopate.

An important tenth-century ordination rite is found in *Ordo romanus* 35.[27] The text is largely based on *Ordo romanus* 34, but contains many more Frankish elements. Andrieu notes that its archetype must have been redacted in Rome during the first quarter of the tenth century.[28] Vogel concurs with Andrieu, since the archetype was used by the mid-tenth-century compilers of the Romano-Germanic Pontifical.[29] Like *Ordo romanus* 34, *Ordo romanus* 35 assumes that candidates for the episcopate will be either deacons or presbyters. At the presentation, the pope asks what office the candidate currently fulfils, deacon or presbyter, and for how long.[30] The same questions are again asked of the candidate at the examination.[31]

There is one major development in the way that deacons and presbyters are consecrated bishops from *Ordo romanus* 34 to *Ordo romanus* 35. The presbyteral ordination rite in the latter contains an anointing of the hands; the rite also enjoins anointing the hands of the new bishop, if the bishop has not previously had his hands consecrated.[32] Although a formula is not provided, it must have resembled the formula used in the ordination of a presbyter, and would have conferred sacerdotal and liturgical graces on the new bishop. Presumably, if a presbyter was ordained to the episcopate according to the rite of *Ordo romanus* 35, his hands would not have been anointed, since such an anointing would have taken place at his ordination to the presbyterate. On the other hand, if the episcopal candidate was a deacon, then his hands would have been anointed for the first and only time.[33]

In short, the Roman practice of ordaining deacons or ('aut') presbyters to the episcopate survived well into the medieval period. This convention is reflected in

---

24 *Ordo romanus*, 34.22, ed. Andrieu, *Ordines Romani*, iii, 608.

25 *Ibid.*, 34.27, iii, 610.

26 *Ibid.*, 34.38, iii, 612.

27 *Ordo romanus*, 35, ed. Andrieu, *Ordines Romani*, iv, 33-46.

28 Andrieu, *Ordines Romani*, iv, 3.

29 Cyrille Vogel, *Medieval Liturgy: an introduction to the sources*, rev. and trans. William G. Storey and Niels Krogh Rasmussen (Washington, D.C., 1986), 176.

30 Ed. Andrieu, *Ordines Romani*, iv, 41.

31 *Ibid.*, iv, 42.

32 *Ibid.*, iv, 45.

33 Michel Andrieu, 'La carrière ecclésiastique des papes et les documents liturgiques du moyen âge', *Révue des sciences religieuses*, 21 (1947), 103, asserted that the anointing rubric applies only to deacons; there is no mention of presbyters who had not been anointed. Andrieu later speculated, however, that this direction could also apply to presbyters ordained under a rite such as *Ordo romanus* 34, because they, like deacons, would not have had their hands anointed; see *Ordines Romani*, iv, 20. Given the certainty that deacons were still envisaged as candidates for episcopal consecration in *Ordo romanus* 35, they were likely the primary object of this rubric.

both papal biographies and Roman liturgical rites, in addition to the Roman canonical tradition, with its particular version of Sardica 13 found the *Collectio Dionysiana* and its later medieval successors, such as the *Collectio Dionysio-Hadriana*.

To return to the patristic period, a third important canonistic collection is the *Concordia canonum*, compiled in the middle of the sixth century.[34] Attributed to Cresconius, the collection is said to have been drawn up by an African bishop as a supplement to the *Breviatio canonum* of Ferrandus. The *Concordia canonum* appears to be based on the Roman *Collectio Dionysiana*: Reynolds refers to the *Concordia canonum* as the 'systematized version' of the *Collectio Dionysiana*, and notes speculation that it could have been drawn up by Dionysius Exiguus himself.[35] The *Concordia canonum* includes not only conciliar statements, but papal letters and decretals as well. The *Concordia canonum* of Cresconius is an important collection for two reasons. First, all the major papal and conciliar texts dealing with the 'cursus' and the interstices are represented in it, including Sardica 13 in its *Dionysiana* form.[36] Second, since the *Concordia canonum* was so widely distributed, like the *Breviatio canonum* of Ferrandus, it became an important vehicle for the transmission of papal and conciliar texts concerning the 'cursus honorum' and the interstices throughout the medieval church.

The last canonical collection in this period to be examined is the *Collectio vetus gallica*, the most important of the many early Gallican canon law collections, and an important vehicle for the transmission of conciliar and papal statements on the 'cursus' and interstices.[37] The collection was compiled between 585 and 626/627, somewhere in Burgundy (probably Lyons); its most likely author is Etherius of Lyons.[38] There was a wide distribution of the *Vetus gallica*, which underwent many recensions and redactions, and became an important source for many later canonistic collections. The author of the collection was a reformer concerned with the structure and administration of the church and its properties. One of his concerns was ordination. *Vetus gallica* IV.13 includes Sardica 13 in its *Dionysiana* version, albeit in a much truncated form:

---

34 Klaus Zechiel-Eckes, *Die Concordia canonum des Cresconius: Studien und Edition*, Freiburger Beiträge zur mittelalterlichen Geschichte, 5 (Freiburg am Main and New York, 1992); also in *PL* 88.829-942; see Kéry, *Canonical Collections*, 33-7.

35 Reynolds, 'Law, Canon', 400.

36 *Concordia canonum*, *PL* 88.839.

37 Hubert Mordek, *Kirchenrecht und Reform im Frankenreich: Die Collectio Vetus Gallica, dei Älteste systematische Kanonessammlung des fränkischen Gallien: Studien und Edition*, Beiträge zur Geschichte und Quellenkunde des Mittelaters, 1 (Berlin, 1975); see Kéry, *Canonical Collections*, 50-53.

38 Reynolds, 'Law, Canon', 402.

Si forte aut dives aut scolasticus de foro aut aministracione episcopus fuerit postulatus, ut non prius ordinetur nisi et lectores munere et officio diaconi aut presbyteri perfunctus, ut per singulos gradus, si dignus fuerit, ascendat ad culmen episcopatus.[39]

Despite the abbreviated form, all the ingredients of the 'cursus honorum' are present in this recension of Sardica 13; what is omitted is the rationale for the 'cursus'. The *Vetus gallica* follows the Dionysian version of the original.

Early Medieval Collections

Canon law collections from the eighth to the tenth century are important witnesses to the transmission of Sardica 13, even when this canon is overlooked entirely. Of the many collections composed in this period, this section will examine the Irish *Collectio canonum hibernensis*, the Roman *Collectio Dionysio-Hadriana*, the Carolingian *Collectio Dacheriana*, the Pseudo-Isidorian *Decretals*, the Italian *Collectio Anselmo dedicata*, and the tenth-century Frankish *Libri duo* of Regino of Prüm.

The early eighth-century Irish *Collectio canonum hibernensis* contains nearly 1600 canons.[40] Of the many dealing with ordination, only a few consider sequential ordination; Sardica 13 is not mentioned. Perhaps its editor was more interested in the interstices and a more typically medieval sequence of grades than that found in Sardica 13.

An extremely important early medieval collection is the *Collectio Dionysio-Hadriana*, an eighth-century Roman collection based on the earlier *Collectio Dionysiana*. It was this collection that was given to Charlemagne, at his request, by Pope Hadrian I in 774. It represents another instance of imposing Roman usages on the Frankish church, and reproduces Sardica 13 in its *Dionysiana* version.[41]

A subsequent Frankish canonistic collection is the *Collectio Dacheriana*. Its compiler was probably Florus of Lyons, although it is sometimes ascribed to Bishop Agobard of Lyons.[42] The compilation of the *Dacheriana* belongs to the process of Carolingian ecclesiastical reform. It includes material from two Hispanic collections, the *Collectio hispana gallicana* and the *Collectio hispana systematica*, as well as the *Collectio Dionysio-Hadriana*. Although there are relatively few canons dealing with the 'cursus honorum' and the interstices in the *Collectio Dacheriana*, several standard conciliar and papal texts on the topics are present and were transmitted by the collection, especially through a section of

---

39   Ed. Mordek, *Kirchenrecht und Reform*, 373-4.
40   Reynolds, 'Law, Canon', 403; see Kéry, *Canonical Collections*, 73-80.
41   *PL* 67.135-229 at 180; see Kéry, *Canonical Collections*, 13-20.
42   See Reynolds, 'Law, Canon', 404; and Kéry, *Canonical Collections*, 87-92. The collection is named after its seventeenth-century editor, Jean Luc d'Achéry.

book 3 entitled the 'Collectio antiqua canonum poenitentiarum'. It contains many conciliar texts of the patristic period dealing with sequential ordination and related issues, including Sardica 13 according to the version from the *Dionysiana*.[43]

One of the largest and most influential of the medieval canonistic collections is the Pseudo-Isidorian *Decretales*.[44] The Decretals are a large series of forgeries compiled in the archdiocese of Rheims in the mid-ninth century (*c.* 847-52). Although it was known already in the ninth century to be a forgery, the Pseudo-Isidorian collection became immensely popular and influential. The Pseudo-Isidorian Decretals contain about 10,000 fragments of earlier canons, including both genuine and false conciliar and papal texts. Because of its size, it is not surprising that the collection contains a vast array of texts dealing with the 'cursus honorum' and the interstices, including Sardica 13, although not in the *Dionysiana* version. Unlike the *Dionysiana* version transmitted in the *Collectio Dacheriana* and other contemporary collections, the text does not allow bishops to have served in either the diaconate or the presbyterate, but requires both: '... non prius ordinetur, nisi ante lectoris munere, et officio diaconi *et* presbyteri fuerit perfunctis'.[45]

The return to the original requirement of Sardica 13 reflects a change in ordination practice in the Frankish church, which now insisted on presbyteral ordination prior to episcopal consecration. The practice of ordaining deacons directly to the episcopate in the Frankish church seems to have ended by the late ninth century, certainly by the time of Hincmar, archbishop of Rheims (845-82). Hincmar states, for instance, in *Epistle* 29 to Adventius of Metz that bishops may be chosen from among the deacons, but such candidates must first be ordained presbyters.[46] While insistence that bishops first be presbyters conforms to the original Sardica 13, at the same time it marks a shift away from the inherited western pattern in which the presbyterate was often omitted. The change seems to have arisen out of theological and liturgical considerations. Amalarius of Metz (*c.* 780-*c.* 850) writes, for instance, in the *Liber officialis* that a bishop received the power to offer the eucharistic sacrifice when his hands were anointed at his

---

43 *Collectio Dacheriana*, 3.142, ed. Lucas D'Achery, *Spicilegium sive Collectio Veterum Aliquot Scriptorum*, 3 vols (Paris, 1793), i, 561.

44 See Reynolds, 'Law, Canon', 404 (Rheims origin); and Kéry, *Canonical Collections*, 100-14 (at 100, 'probably western part of the Frankish empire'). Some scholars have argued for a Le Mans provenance for the decretals; e.g., Walter Goffart, *The Le Mans Forgeries* (Cambridge, MA, 1966) 90-94.

45 Paulus Hinschius, *Decretales Pseudo-Isidorianae et Capitula Angilramni* (Leipzig, 1863; repr. Aalen, 1963), 268; also *PL* 13-.276 [emphasis added]. The source for the transmission of this version to the False Decretals is most probably the *Collectio hispana*, ed. *PL* 84.119 (Sardica 13 in the original version), through the *Collectio hispana gallica Augustodunensis*; for which see Reynolds, 'Law, Canon', 405; and Kéry, *Canonical Collections*, 61-7, 67-9.

46 *PL* 126.186.

ordination to the presbyterate.[47] Once again, Sardica 13 has been subtly, albeit significantly, altered to reflect and corroborate current regional practice.

The *Collectio Anselmo dedicata* is a collection of northern Italian provenance, compiled in the late ninth century, *c.* 885, and dedicated to a bishop Anselm, probably Anselm II of Milan (882-96).[48] The collection was popular in the Frankish church as well as in Italy. The *Collectio Anselmo dedicata*, which incorporates much of the Pseudo-Isidorian material, includes many patristic texts dealing with the 'cursus honorum' and the interstices. It, too, contains Sardica 13.[49]

The last canonistic collection to be surveyed from this period is the *Libri duo de synodalibus causis et disciplinis ecclesiasticis* of Regino of Prüm (840-915), compiled *c.* 906 at Trier. Regino relied on the *Dacheriana*, the Pseudo-Isidorian corpus and other sources.[50] What is astonishing about Regino's collection is the dearth of texts relating to the 'cursus honorum' and the interstices, including Sardica 13. There are, however, a few texts that deal with issues of probation and the ages of clerics. Given the many canons relating to the clergy and issues surrounding their ordinations, such as continence, and the relation between clerics and their feudal masters, Regino is clearly interested in the state of the clergy, but the 'cursus honorum' was an issue he either did not need to deal with or was not prepared to handle.

Eleventh-century pre-Gregorian Reform Collections

The eleventh century was a period of economic and social change in the west as well as a period of upheaval and reform for the medieval church. Reform was seen as needed on account of several factors: clerical standards and morality were low; clerical celibacy, especially among the rural clergy, had fallen into virtual desuetude; and simony and lay investiture were increasingly viewed as serious problems. Although often associated with the pontificate of Gregory VII in the second half of the eleventh century, reforms were initiated as early as the later tenth century, perhaps with the monastic movement associated with Cluny. In the early eleventh century, lay rulers such as the emperors Henry II and III encouraged ecclesiastical reform, and nominated several German popes. The medieval 'cursus honorum' received its final shape in the midst of these major reforms.

---

47 *Liber officialis,* c. 14: 'De pontifice'; *Amalarii episcopi Opera liturgica omnia,* ed. Ioannes Michaelis [Jean Michel] Hanssens, 3 vols, Studi e Testi, 138-40 (Vatican City, 1948-50), ii, 233.

48 Reynolds, 'Law, Canon', 406; Kéry, *Canonical Collections,* 124-8.

49 *Collectio Anselmo dedicata,* 2.40; ed. Jean-Claude Besse, *Histoire des Textes du Droit de l'Église au Moyen-Age de Denys à Gratien: Collectio Anselmo dedicata: étude et texte,* (Paris, 1957), 10. Since Besse's edition provides only the incipits of the canons, it is impossible to say from the edition whether it follows the Dionysian version or not.

50 Reynolds, 'Law, Canon', 407; Kéry, *Canonical Collections,* 128-33.

It was once maintained that the period from the tenth to the mid-eleventh century was one of decline in the history of canon law.[51] Yet a number of reform collections pre-date the Gregorian reforms of the mid-eleventh century, and include canons dealing with many areas of church life, including the clerical grades. This section will examine the treatment of the 'cursus honorum' and related issues in two collections from the period: the transalpine *Liber decretorum* of Burchard of Worms, and the Italian *Collectio canonum in V libris*.

One of the most important early eleventh-century collections is the *Liber decretorum*, compiled between 1008 and 1012 by Burchard, bishop of Worms (1000-25), in collaboration with Bruncicho, 'praepositus' of the cathedral at Worms; Walter, bishop of Speyer; and Olbert, later abbot of Gembloux.[52] The *Liber decretorum* sets out the principles that were to guide imperial reform; it was widely used by the early eleventh-century reformers, and was copied well into the thirteenth century. The *Liber decretorum* contains over 1700 capitula on a variety of ecclesiastical topics, including holy orders. Three canonistic collections already surveyed in this study were among the sources used by Burchard in the compilation of the *Liber decretorum*: Regino of Prüm's *Libri duo*, the *Collectio Anselmo dedicata*, and the *Collectio hibernensis*. Burchard is noted for altering his sources and rearranging material in response to contemporary needs.[53] Although there are only thirteen capitula in the *Liber decretorum* that touch upon the clerical 'cursus', the interstices, and the ages of clerics; book 1, c. 17: 'De primato ecclesiae' repeats Sardica 13 in its *Dionysiana* version,[54] in contrast to contemporary Frankish ordination practice.

Another important early eleventh-century collection is the Italian *Collectio canonum in V libris*.[55] The *Collectio hibernensis*, the Pseudo-Isidorian Decretals, the *Dacheriana*, and the *Concordia Cresconii* were all sources for the collection, which contains almost 1300 capitula on a variety of topics, including holy orders. The compiler has gathered various texts dealing with the 'cursus honorum', the interstices, ages of clerics, and *per saltum* ordination. The major patristic texts are all present. While some have been altered, most appear in their original forms. The

---

51 E.g., Charles Munier, 'False Decretals to Gratian: Canon Law, History of', in *New Catholic Encyclopedia* (New York, 1967), iii, 39.

52 Reynolds, 'Law, Canon', 407; Kéry, *Canonical Collections*, 133-55

53 Reynolds, 'Law, Canon', 408; Kéry, *Canonical Collections*, 128-33.

54 *PL* 140.554. The canons relating to the 'cursus' and the interstices are found in books 1-3 of the *Liber decretorum*.

55 For the *Collectio in V libris*, see the partial edition in *Collection canonum in V libris (lib. I-III)*, ed. M. Fornasari, *CCCM*, 6 (Turnhout, 1970). For bibliography and references, see Roger E. Reynolds, 'The South Italian *Collection in Five Books* and its Derivatives: a south Italian appendix to the *Collection in Seventy-Four Titles*', *Mediaeval Studies*, 63 (2001), 353-65; idem, *The 'Collectio canonum Casinensis duodecimi seculi (Codex terscriptus)': a derivative of the south-Italian Collection in Five Books*, Studies and Texts, 137, Monumenta Liturgica Beneventana, 3 (Toronto, 2001); and Kéry, *Canonical Collections*, 157-60.

fact that twenty-two capitula dealing with the ecclesiastical 'cursus' appear more or less together is significant, and indicates how important this area had become in the reforms of the early eleventh century. Moreover, since most of the patristic texts are (often) accurately reproduced, it demonstrates that the early eleventh-century reformers were well aware of the historic reasons behind the 'cursus'; that is, probation and preparation. Book 1 of the collection contains canons dealing with holy orders, many of which deal with the clerical 'cursus', including related questions such as the ages for ordination and the interstices. References to the needs for testing and preparation abound. Book 1, c. 99.1 is Sardica 13, in the *Dionysiana* version.[56]

Collections of the Gregorian Reform

The reform movement of the eleventh century, underway by the middle of the century, is identified with the pontificates of Leo IX (1049-54), Nicholas II (1058-61), and especially Gregory VII (1073-85). Associated with the reforms was increased attention to canon law, resulting in the compilation of a great number of canonistic collections. The primary objectives of the eleventh-century reformers were the abuses of simony and lay investiture, although these were not the only targets. The reformers paid particular attention to the standards and morality of the clergy. Roger Reynolds has observed, for instance, 'Conciliar and papal strictures against the sexual liaisons of the clergy are almost as numerous as those against simony and lay investiture'.[57]

One of the abuses that probably confronted the reformers of the eleventh century was a certain laxity with respect to the 'cursus honorum'. It would appear that in certain places, reception of the minor orders, in particular the subdiaconate, had fallen into desuetude. Reformers responded by legislating at synods such as Rouen (1072), c. 10, against the omission of grades from the 'cursus', particularly the subdiaconate.[58] From the pontificate of Alexander II (1061-73), papal letters such as his *Epistle* 32 confirmed the indispensable place of the subdiaconate within the 'cursus';[59] without it, deacons and presbyters were inhibited from the exercise of their offices.

Conciliar legislation prohibiting members of the laity from being elected to the episcopate, such as that of Rome (1059), c. 13, Benevento (1091), c. 1, and

---

56 Ed. Fornasari, *CCCM*, 6.74-5.

57 Roger Reynolds, 'Sacred Orders in the Early Middle Ages: shifts in the theology of the lower and higher ecclesiastical orders from late patristic antiquity through the early middle ages as reflected in the Ordinals of Christ and related literature' (Ph.D. Diss. Harvard University, 1968), 252.

58 Mansi, xx, 37.

59 JL 4510; see Mansi, xix, 963, and *PL* 146.1349.

Clermont-Ferrand (1095), c. 5, was no doubt directed against the abuse of sim-ony.[60] The same rationale probably accounts for the large number of patristic texts in the canonistic collections, culminating in the selection in Gratian's *Decretum*, which were directed against the election of members of the laity to the episcopate. Insistence on sequential ordination with a proper observance of the interstices was part of the arsenal used against the practice of simony. The purchasing of a high ecclesiastical office by the unscrupulous and ambitious would have been rendered senseless by the canonical observance of a long period of probation and prepara-tion in the lower offices.

This section will investigate the use (or not) of Sardica 13 in the most promi-nent canonistic collections of the Gregorian Reform: the *Diversorum patrum sententiae*, the *Collectio canonum* of Anselm of Lucca, and the *Collectio canonum* of Deusdedit. It will examine collections of the post-Gregorian period: the *Liber de vita christiana* of Bonizo of Sutri, and Ivo of Chartres' *Panormia* and *Decretum*. Lastly, the mid-twelfth-century *Concordantia discordantium canonum* of Gratian will be examined for its treatment of Sardica 13.

One of the earliest collections from this period is the Italian *Diversorum patrum sententiae* or the *Collection in Seventy-Four Titles* (= 74T).[61] The collection contains 315 capitula arranged under seventy-four titles. Although the date and authorship of 74T are disputed, it was probably compiled sometime before 1067, and was known during the pontificate of Gregory VII. One of the primary sources for 74T is the Pseudo-Isidorian Decretals.[62] However, since the relevant canons on holy orders, including those on the clerical 'cursus', are all drawn from papal letters and decretals, there is no mention or use of Sardica 13.

One of the canonistic collections influenced by the 74T was the *Collectio canonum* of Anselm II of Lucca, c. 1083.[63] In addition to the papal sources found in the 74T, Anselm also used conciliar material. The *Collectio canonum* is a

---

60 Mansi, xix, 899 (Rome); Mansi, xx, 738-9 (Benevento; cf. Letter to Urban II, JL p. 667); Mansi, xx, 817 (Clermont-Ferrand).

61 Reynolds, 'Law, Canon', 409 (compiled by 1067); John Gilchrist, trans., *The Collection in Seventy-Four Titles: a canon law manual of the Gregorian Reform* (Toronto, 1980), ix (for a date of c. 1076); Kéry, *Canonical Collections*, 204-10. Edition in *Diuersorum patrum sententie siue Collectio in LXXIV titulos digesta*, ed. Joannes T. Gilchrist, MIC Series B, Corpus collectionum, 1 (Vatican City, 1973).

62 Gilchrist, *Collection in Seventy-four Titles*, 15, estimating that out of the 315 *capitula* in 74T, 252 were from Pseudo-Isidore.

63 For references, see Kathleen G. Cushing, *Papacy and Law in the Gregorian Revolution: the canonistic work of Anselm of Lucca*, Oxford Historical Monographs (Oxford, 1998); and Kéry, *Canonical Collections*, 218-26. See the partial edition in *Anselmi episcopi Lucensis Collectio canonum una cum collectione minore*, ed. Fridericus [Friedrich] Thaner (Innsbruck, 1906-15), covering to book 11.15, although the edition is flawed by its idiosyncratic use of different recensions; see Martin Brett, 'Editions, Manuscripts and Readers in some Pre-Gratian Collections', in the present volume, 205-24 at 205 n. 1.

systematic collection. The material on bishops and their appointments, including the 'cursus honorum' and related issues, is found in book 6 of the collection. Like 74T, Anselm includes a heavy dose of papal letters and decretals, in addition to some canons from patristic councils as well as the *Statuta ecclesiae antiqua*. A curious omission is Sardica 13.

Similarly, another major Italian collection, the *Collectio canonum* of Cardinal Deusdedit, which appeared *c.* 1087, making it concurrent with the collection of Anselm of Lucca, also omits the Sardican canon.[64] The *Collectio canonum* of Deusdedit is likewise a systematic collection, divided into four books. Book 2 contains most of the material relating to the 'cursus' and related issues. Like Anselm, Deusdedit relied on 74T, and other sources. Nevertheless, he included considerably less material on the 'cursus honorum' than either Anselm or the compiler of 74T, although the texts selected by Deusdedit for his *Collectio canonum* summarize the basic issues concerning the clerical 'cursus'.

A third example of an Italian collection of the reform period is the *Liber de vita christiana* of Bonizo of Sutri written during the pontificate of Urban II (1088-99).[65] The *Liber de vita christiana* is a systematic collection, dealing with a broad spectrum of topics from baptism to penance. As in the *Collectio canonum* of Deusdedit, one is again struck by the dearth of material on the clerical 'cursus' and related issues. This dearth may be partly explained by the fact that Bonizo compiled his collection principally to deal with much broader issues of the Christian life.

Two of the most important transalpine collections of the period just after the Gregorian reform are the *Panormia* and the *Decretum* attributed to Ivo (*c.* 1040-1115), bishop of Chartres. The shorter, and more popular, of Ivo's canonistic collections is the *Panormia*, a collection in eight books. Apart from a selection of canons primarily concerned with the ages of clerics, the *Panormia* does not demonstrate much concern for the 'cursus honorum' and the interstices. Not surprisingly, Sardica 13 does not appear. The much larger of Ivo's canonistic collections is the *Decretum*. The *Decretum* is a collection consisting of almost 3,800 canons in seventeen books, and reflected both canonical and theological concerns. Material on the 'cursus' is contained in part 5, dealing with bishops, and part 6, dealing with the orders below the episcopate. Part 5, c. 71, copies Sardica 13 according to the *Dionysiana* version.[66]

It is striking to note that in a period when simony was being condemned by popes and councils, and various councils inhibited the election of laymen to the

64 *Die Kanonessammlung des Kardinals Deusdedit*, ed. Victor Wolf van Glanvell (Paderborn, 1905; repr. Aalen, 1967); see Kéry, *Canonical Collections*, 228-33.

65 Bonizo of Sutri, *Liber de vita christiana*, ed. Ernst Perels, Texte zur Geschichte des römischen und kanonischen Rechts im Mittelalter, 1 (Berlin, 1930); see Kéry, *Canonical Collections*, 234-7.

66 Ivo, *Decretum*, 4.71, PL 161.350. For references, see Kéry, *Canonical Collections*, 250-53 (*Decretum*), 253-60 (*Panormia*).

higher ecclesiastical offices, the canonists of the Gregorian reform, unlike their earlier eleventh-century predecessors, seem to have had little interest in the foremost legislation enjoining sequential ordination, Sardica 13. Of the six collections surveyed, only Ivo's *Decretum* reproduces it. Possibly the issues of the interstices and the ages of clerics were deemed essential by the reformers, and their lack in Sardica 13 rendered it unserviceable to contemporary canonists. Moreover, the sequence of grades in the fourth century canon is hardly that of the late eleventh century. In particular, of the minor orders Sardica 13 mentions only the lector; at a time when the subdiaconate was becoming a major order and its omission was consistently condemned, the earlier canon cannot have been too helpful.

Gratian and the Scholastics

Although referred to as the 'father of canon law', little is known about the life of Gratian, and little about the composition of the *Concordantia discordantia canonum* or *Decretum* can be asserted with confidence.[67] Perhaps compiled in some form *c.* 1140, the *Decretum* came to form the first part of the *Corpus Iuris Canonici* of the Roman church. The compilation of the *Decretum* has long been regarded as the inauguration of the classical period in the history of western canon law.

The *Decretum Gratiani* is a systematic collection containing nearly 4,000 patristic texts, conciliar statements, and papal decrees on all aspects of the church's life. Given the sheer size of the *Decretum*, and Gratian's practice of comparing conflicting canons, it is not surprising that it contains all the major patristic and medieval texts relating to the 'cursus honorum', the interstices, and the ages of clerics. In *Distinctio* 61, pars 1, Gratian argues that members of the laity not be ordained directly to the episcopate, but must proceed through each of the grades: 'Item laici non sunt in episcopum elegendi, sed per singulos ordines prius sunt probati'. In support of this assertion, a variety of patristic papal texts are marshaled. Gratian concludes: 'his omnibus auctoritatis laici prohibentur in episcopum eligi'.

On the other hand, in *Distinctio* 61, pars 2, Gratian cites three instances in which members of the laity have been elected bishops: a bishop Nicholas, an archbishop Severus, and Ambrose of Milan. Gratian posits that the reason such elections are prohibited is the fact that a layperson who has not been instructed through the ecclesiastical grades cannot by experience demonstrate an example of reverence. Nonetheless, when a layperson by merit of his perfection ascends to the

---

67 For recent questions about the composition of the Decretum, see Anders Winroth, *The Making of Gratian's Decretum*, Cambridge Studies in Medieval Life and Thought, 4th series, 49 (Cambridge, 2000). For an earlier survey, see Munier, 'False Decretals to Gratian', 40.

clerical life, his election may be approved by the example of Nicholas, Severus, and Ambrose. (Gratian does not discuss whether Ambrose or the others were ordained sequentially through the orders or not after their election.)

By way of reply, in D. 61, c. 10, Gratian cites the first section of Sardica 13, in the Dionysian form, namely, that no one be put forward and ordained as a bishop except those who have served as lectors, deacons or presbyters. The use of the Dionysian form may bear testimony to Gratian's desire to be faithful to the inherited canonical tradition, that is, the Roman tradition. But this use of the Dionysian version of the canon, as opposed to the Frankish version (not to mention the original), is odd, since the earlier Roman practice of consecrating either deacons or presbyters as bishops did not continue after the tenth century.

In the tenth and eleventh centuries, bishops of Rome tended to be elected from among presbyters or the bishops of other sees. In the tenth century, however, three deacons were elected: Benedict V (964-6), Benedict VI (973-4), and the antipope Boniface VIII (974, 984-5). It is likely that Benedict VI and Boniface VIII were the last deacons to be elected and ordained directly to the episcopate in Rome.[68] In the later eleventh and twelfth centuries, several deacons were elected to become bishops of Rome, but all were ordained to the presbyterate prior to their episcopal consecration. Gregory VII is the first in the eleventh-century series, and the first for whom the ordination as priest before the episcopal consecration is recorded. Concerning Gregory's ordination and consecration in 1073, Bonizo of Sutri writes: 'nam in ieiunio pentecostes sacerdos ordinatur, et in natale apostolorum ad altare eorundem a cardinalibus secundum antiquum morem episcopus consecratur'.[69] Hildebrand was archdeacon of Rome when he was elected pope on 22 April 1073. Bonizo says that he was ordained a presbyter ('sacerdos') on the Pentecost ember days (22 May) and ordained a bishop on 29 or 30 June.[70] This event marks the acceptance by the church of Rome, and ultimately the western church, of the complete sequence of the 'cursus honorum' from doorkeeper to bishop.[71]

---

68 For the consecration of deacons as popes in the tenth century, see Andrieu, 'La carrière ecclésiastique' (see n. 33 above), 109; adding, 'mais nous ignorons s'ils demeurent diacres jusqu'à leur sacré'.

69 Bonizo of Sutri, *Liber ad amicum*, 7, ed. E. Dümmler, *MGH Libelli de lite*, 3 vols (Leipzig, 1891-7), i, 598-620, at 601; also in Philippus Jaffé, *Monumenta Gregoriana*, Monumenta Rerum Germanicarum, 2 (Berlin, 1865), 657.

70 *MGH Libelli de lite*, i, 601; Jaffé, *Monumenta Gregoriana*, 599.

71 Michel Andrieu, 'Le sacre épiscopal d'après Hincmar de Reims', *RHE*, 48 (1953), 29, noting that 'quand le diacre Hildebrand, élu au souverain pontificat depuis le 22 avril, se fit ordonner prêtre, le 22 mai 1073, aux Quatre-Temps de la Pentecôte, il ne se doutait vraisemblablement pas qu'il renouait avec l'ancienne discipline officielle du Siège apostolique par l'intermédiaire de la liturgie franque'. One must add, however, that an interval of thirty-nine days between the reception of the presbyterate and ordination to the episcopate was hardly part of the 'ancienne discipline officielle' of the see of Rome.

The eleventh century is noted for the resurgence of what Roger Reynolds has termed 'patristic presbyterian' theories of episcopacy.[72] Medieval commentators on sacred orders argued that in the celebration of the eucharist there was a basic equality between bishops and presbyters. Moreover, it was the presbyter who was primarily the 'sacerdos', episcopal office being only derivatively sacerdotal. Scholastic theologians also commented on the question of sequential ordination, particularly from the presbyterate to the episcopate. In the Supplement to the *Summa Theologiae* (*c.* 1272), Thomas Aquinas asked, for instance, 'whether the character of one order necessarily presupposes the character of another order'; and answered that it was not necessary for the major orders to receive the minor, since their respective powers are distinct.[73] Noting that in the early church there were some who were ordained priests without having received the lower orders, he adds: 'it was decided by the legislation of the church' that candidates for the higher orders must first have humbled themselves in the lower. And so those who are ordained without the lower orders are not re-ordained, but receive what was lacking through subsequent ordination to the lower orders. Thus, according to Aquinas one could validly, though illicitly, be ordained a presbyter without having been ordained a deacon.

On the other hand, Aquinas teaches that there is a theological imperative regarding sequential ordination from the presbyterate to the episcopate. For Aquinas, there are only three sacred orders: the 'priesthood', the diaconate, and the subdiaconate.[74] In Question 40 of the Supplement, where he asks whether the episcopate is an order, Aquinas restates the conviction that one order does not depend on a preceding order in terms of validity. With regard to the episcopate, however, he states that 'episcopal power depends on the priestly power since no one can be a bishop who has not received priestly power'.[75] For Aquinas, the sacrament of order is related primarily to the eucharist.[76] The presbyterate is the summit of the orders since it is directed to the consecration of the eucharist.[77] Because the episcopate is not directed to the eucharist, he argued, it is not an order. Consequently, episcopal consecration depends on ordination to the presbyterate; without prior ordination as a presbyter, a bishop would have jurisdiction, but not order.

---

72 Roger E. Reynolds, 'Patristic "Presbyterianism" in the Early Medieval Theology of Sacred Orders', *Mediaeval Studies*, 45 (1983), 311-42, at 328.

73 Thomas Aquinas, *Summa Theologiae*, Suppl. Q. 35, art. 5; Pars IIIa et Supplementum, ed. [Bernardo Maria] De Rubeis, [Charles Réné] Billuart, and [Xavier] Faucher (Rome, 1953), 758.

74 *Ibid.*, Suppl. Q. 37, art. 3, 766.

75 *Ibid.*, Suppl. Q. 40, art. 5, 780.

76 *Ibid.*, Suppl. Q. 37, art. 2, 765.

77 *Ibid.*, Suppl. Q. 37, art. 5, 769-70.

Other scholastic theologians held similar views.[78] For example, Richard Fishacre in the *Commentarium in libros sententiarum* (*c.* 1241-5) admits that one may be validly ordained to the priesthood without prior ordination to the diaconate, but one must be ordained a priest prior to ordination to the episcopate. Without prior ordination as a priest, a bishop is not a bishop. A new order is not conferred in episcopal consecration, but a new office with new power.[79]

Even though from the eleventh century deacons continue to be elected to the episcopate throughout the western church, they were required to be ordained presbyters prior to episcopal ordination, often within a matter of days.[80] Sequential ordination from the presbyterate to the episcopate had become a theological and sacramental concern, as well as a matter of canon law.

Conclusion

Although modified, and at times overlooked, through the mediation of the canonists Sardica 13 exercised a considerable influence on the practice of sequential ordination in the medieval church. The Roman recension of Sardica 13 in the *Dionysiana* reflects a particularly western understanding of sequential ordination, one reflected and enshrined in the Roman practice of electing and ordaining either deacons or presbyters to the episcopate. This practice continued in the Frankish church until at least the late ninth century, and in Rome well into the tenth century. Dionysius Exiguus may have altered the canon to match the practice of his time, and Pseudo-Isidore may well have done in the same in his context. However, the insistence on the Dionysian version of Sardica 13 by western canonists such as Ivo and Gratian demonstrates that although theologians, liturgists, and canon lawyers required sequential ordination from the presbyterate to the episcopate, the medieval church was aware of an alternative pattern. The canonists, at least, knew that bishops were once ordained from either the diaconate *or* the presbyterate. Such perspective may offer some insights to theologians and canonists today, who wish either to reconsider the inherited pattern or to maintain it as some immutable pearl of great price.

---

78 Cf. Augustine McDevitt, 'The Episcopate as an Order and Sacrament on the Eve of the High Scholastic Period', *Franciscan Studies*, 20 (1960), 96-127.

79 Richard Fishacre, *Commentarium*, in McDevitt, 'The Episcopate as an Order', 124, n. 95.

80 E.g., in Rome: Gregory VII, 1073; Gelasius II, 1118; Innocent II, 1130; Celestine III, 1191; and Innocent III, 1198. Elsewhere: Peter of Anicium, 1053; Alfanus of Salerno, 1058; and Thomas Becket, 1162.

Chapter 9

The Anonymous Early Medieval Homily in MS Copenhagen GKS 143[*]

Giles Constable

Introduction

The only known manuscript of the *Homilia sacra* is Copenhagen, Kongelike Bibliotek, GKS 143, which was written probably in southern France in the late ninth century,[1] and the only printed edition is in a volume edited by Geverhard Elmenhorst at Hamburg in 1614, together with the *De ecclesiasticis dogmatibus* of Gennadius of Marseilles and the letters attributed to Martial of Limoges.[2] Elmenhorst said in his notes to the *Homilia* that he found it in 'a very ancient ('perveteris') codex of Friedrich Lindenbrog', which is almost certainly the manuscript

---

[*]   In addition to the abbreviations listed above, the following abbreviations will be used:
   Homilia: *Homilia sacra* (as cited n. 2)
   RegB: *Regula Benedicti*
   Scarapsus: Gall Jecker, *Die Heimat des hl. Pirmin des Apostels der Alamannen*, Beiträge zur Geschichte des alten Mönchtums und des Benediktinerordens, 13 (Münster in W., 1927)
[1]   See Hubert Mordek, *Bibliotheca capitularium regum Francorum manuscripta*, MGH Hilfsmittel, 15 (Munich, 1995), 192-5, with further references. I am indebted to Professor Mordek for bringing the manuscript to my attention and to Dr Erik Petersen of the Royal Library of Copenhagen for sending me a photocopy of the text, which is found on fos 64r-67v, between the *Lex Alamannorum* and a small collection of formulary letters. See also Michael Glatthaar, 'Rätisches Recht des 8. Jahrhunderts in der Predigt *De signum Christi*', in *Quellen, Kritik, Interpretation. Festgabe zum 60. Geburtstag von Hubert Mordek*, ed. Thomas Martin Buck (Frankfurt a. M., 1999), 72.
[2]   *Gennadii Massiliensis presbyteri Liber de ecclesiasticis dogmatibus, veteris cuiusdam theologi Homilia Sacra, Marcialis episcopi Lemovicensis epistolae*, ed. Geverhard Elmenhorst (Hamburg, 1614). According to Professor Josef Semmler there are copies of this work in only six German university libraries: see Ursmar Engelmann, *Der heilige Pirmin und sein Missionsbüchlein* (Constance, 1958), 20. On Elmenhorst (*c.* 1580-1621), see *Allgemeine Deutsche Biographie*, 56 vols (Leipzig, 1875-1912; repr. 1967-71), vi, 59. On the so-called letters of Martial of Limoges, which Elmenhorst said were found in the sacristy of the church of St Peter at Limoges, see Henri Leclercq in the *Dictionnaire d'archéologie chrétienne et de liturgie*, 15 vols in 30 (Paris, 1907-53), ix, 1100, who described them as 'composées vraisemblement au IXe siècle' and listed several printings, of which the latest is in the *Maxima bibliotheca veterum patrum*, 27 vols (Lyons, 1677), 2/i, 106-14, citing the views of Robert Bellarmine, who listed many points 'quae his Epistolis fidem detrahere videntur' and Philippe Labbe, who said that they were first found *c.* 1060. Karen Corsaro of the Channing Laboratory, Boston, is working on a new edition.

now in Copenhagen, and that 'Since it is not recorded as published elsewhere, and is germane to the matters Gennadius treats, I wished to add it to the Gennadian material'.[3] It is impossible to discuss all the questions concerning its date, authorship, sources, and influence within the scope of this article, of which the primary purpose is to make available an accurate version of the text based on the manuscript.

Elmenhorst provided a series of notes, which are still of value and have been helpful for the notes to the present edition.[4] He described the author on the title page as 'a certain old theologian' and said in the notes that 'The author of this is believed to have lived 800 years ago', that is, in the early 800s. He may have been a monk, in view of the reminiscences of the Rule of Benedict, and was certainly a preacher. The homily was addressed to married laymen and has a strongly pastoral character. The relatively few modern scholars who have studied the homily have not gone much beyond this. Germain Morin in his edition of the works of Caesarius of Arles refuted the attribution of the homily to Caesarius proposed by Casimir Oudin and Ferdinand Kattenbusch.[5] Gall Jecker in his edition of the *Scarapsus* attributed to St Pirmin, the founder of Reichenau, said that though not by Caesarius the homily drew on him and that it was probably a 'product of the south Gallic-west Gothic cultural sphere'.[6] Claude Barlow in his edition of the

---

3 On Lindenbrog or Lindenbruch (1573-1648), see *Nouvelle biographie générale*, ed. Jean C. F. Hoefer, 46 vols (Paris, 1854-66), xxxi, 260; and *Deutsche biographische Enzyklopädie*, 12 vols (Munich, 1995-2000), vi, 404. I have not seen the dissertation by Eva Horváth, *Friedrich Lindenbruch. Späthumanist und Handschriftensammler des 17. Jahrhundert* (Hamburg, 1988) cited by Mordek, *Bibliotheca* (cited n. 1), 195. Lindenbrog edited several historical and legal texts and left his books and manuscripts to the town of Hamburg, but Dr Tilo Brandis (letter dated 21 September 1967) kindly informed me that the manuscript of the *Homilia* was not in the library there.

4 *Homilia*, 189-201.

5 *Sancti Caesarii Arelatensis sermones*, ed. Germain Morin, *CCSL*, 103, 104 (Turnhout, 1953), xviii, xxii, and 1031, where Morin said in the entry for Elmenhorst in the index that the *Homilia* 'ab eo an. 1614 edita, et a nonnullis eruditis viris Caesario, sed immerito, adscripta'.

6 *Scarapsus*, 103, 125, and 158. Jecker's text of the *Scarapsus* was reprinted by Engelmann, *Der heilige Pirmin* (cited n. 2), who called it a 'Missionsbüchlein'. A new edition is in preparation by Eckhard Hauswald of the University of Konstanz. There is a large literature on Pirmin (or Primin, as he is called in some sources) but relatively little on his origin, which is of interest here in view of the similarities between *Homilia* and the *Scarapsus*. Jecker's conclusion concerning the homily reflected his view of Pirmin's Spanish origins, which has been followed by some scholars, including Engelmann, who said that Pirmin came to France from Visigothic Aquitaine or Spain (7) and the *Homilia* 'wohl in Spanien entstand' (19). He is listed as 'certe Hispanus' in M. C. Díaz y Díaz, *Index Scriptorum Latinorum Medii Aevi Hispanorum*, Acta Salmanticensia: Filosofia y Letras, 13/i-ii (Salamanca, 1958-9), i, 106, no. 394, with a reference to J. Pérez de Urbel. See on the other hand Theodor Mayer, 'Bonifatius und Pirmin', in *Sankt Bonifatius: Gedenkgabe zum zwölfhundertsten Todestag* (Fulda, 1954), 452-3; Friedrich Prinz, *Frühes Mönchtum im Frankenreich* (Munich and Vienna, 1965), 213-17; Heinz Löwe, 'Pirmin, Willibrord und Bonifatius. Ihre Bedeutung für die Missionsgeschichte ihrer Zeit' (1967), repr. in his *Religiosität und Bildung im frühen Mittelalter*, ed. Tilman Struve (Weimar, 1994), 133-77, esp. 135-7; and especially Arnold Angenendt, *Monachi Peregrini. Studien zu Pirmin und den monastischen Vorstellungen des frühen*

works of Martin of Braga suggested that the homily was 'most likely ... written more than a hundred years later [than Caesarius], borrowing material from both Caesarius and Martin of Braga'.[7] For the time being, the question of the precise date and localization of the homily remains open.

It would take too much space to demonstrate here the many textual resemblances and relationships between the homily, the works of Caesarius and Martin, and the *Scarapsus*,[8] which are confirmed by the variants in biblical citations. Both the homily and the *Scarapsus*, for instance, have 'ab origine mundi' in place of 'a constitutione mundi' (Matt. 25: 34) and 'orate sine intermissione et in omnibus deo gratias agite' (1 Thess. 5: 17-18).[9] These resemblances do not indicate that one work was dependent on the other but that the authors used similar versions of the bible. Other variants, such as 'ex minimis meis' in place of 'ex fratribus meis minimis' (Matt. 25: 40), were common in the liturgy and the works of the fathers. They show that the author used versions of the bible that were current at the time and are of little use in dating and localizing the work.[10] A more interesting comparison can be made between the passages on first-fruits and tithes in the homily, the *Scarapsus*, and a diocesan statute found (in somewhat different versions) in Benedictus Levita and a collection in a manuscript from Vesoul published by De Clercq, who dated it before 813.

Homily
Primicias frugum uestrarum ad benedicendum ad ecclesiam adferte, cum benediccione postea manducate ... Decimas ex omnibus uiris [uestris?] uel de pecoribus uestris annis singulis ad ecclesias reddite. De nouem partibus helimosinas facite.

Scarapsus[11]
Primitias omnium frugum uestrarum ad benedicendum ad sacerdotes adferte et sic

---

Mittelalters, Münstersche Mittelalter-Schriften, 6 (Munich, 1972), 61-74, who argued that Pirmin came not from Spain but from an Iro-Frankish monastic background and who doubted the attribution to him of the *Scarapsus*, which he dated in the second half of the eighth century rather than the traditional 710/24. Josef Semmler, 'Pirminius', *Mitteilungen des historischen Vereins der Pfalz*, 87 (1989), 91-113, called Pirmin 'ein herausragender Vertreter der fränkischen Kirche der endenden Merowingerzeit und des gallofränkischen Mönchtums' and questioned the attribution to him of the *Scarapsus* (112-13).

7   Martin of Braga, *Opera omnia*, ed. Claude W. Barlow, Papers and Monographs of the American Academy in Rome, 12 (New Haven, 1950), 165. Cf. Giles Constable, *Monastic Tithes from their Origins to the Twelfth Century*, Cambridge Studies in Medieval Life and Thought, NS 10 (Cambridge, 1964), 23, n. 2; and Angenendt, *Monachi* (cited n. 6), 62-3, who mentioned the *Homilia* only once in his discussion of the *Scarapsus*.

8   See the texts in parallel columns and notes in *Scarapsus*, 105-31, and Martin of Braga, *Opera* (cited n. 7), 166-7. On the influence of Caesarius in the early Middle Ages, see Prinz, *Mönchtum* (cited n. 6), 82, 216, and 475-9.

9   *Scarapsus*, 62.18, 65.21, and 67.25.

10 I am indebted to Paul Meyvaert for help on these points.

11 *Scarapsus*, c. 29 (p. 68.18-21). See Angenendt, *Monachi* (cited n. 6), 66-7.

postea inde manducate. Decimas ex omnibus fructibus uel de pecoribus uestris annis singulis ecclesiis reddite. De noue partes, que uobis remanserint, elimosinas facite.

Vesoul Statute[12]

Et adnuntient etiam presbiteri plebem ut primitias omnium frugum terrae ad dicendum adferant ad domos illorum et sic postea inde manducent; et decimas ex fructibus et pecoribus terrae annis singulis ad ecclesias reddant, et de nouem partibus quae remanserint elemosinas faciant.

Here again there is no evidence of direct dependence between those passages, except perhaps between the homily and the *Scarapsus*, but they are clearly related. Most scholars (including those cited above) have assumed that the author of the *Scarapsus* made use of the *Homilia*, but the dependence may have been the other way around.[13]

The text of the homily treats briefly of the conduct of Christian life, from baptism to death, showing that those who are called and call themselves Christians should behave in a Christian manner. At baptism Christians renounce the devil and his ways, which are listed at length, and dedicate themselves to God and His laws. Any breach must be atoned for by confession and penance. This is followed by sections on religious observances, including prayer, attendance at mass, and another list of sins to be avoided, on the giving of first-fruits, tithes, and alms, and on the performance of good works, which should be inspired by fear of the Last Judgment and desire for eternal life. It ends with a plea for the listeners to improve their lives, to act justly, and to merit salvation.

Nothing in the homily is very original. Indeed, it draws heavily on the works of previous writers, especially Caesarius of Arles, but it is put together in an original way and may have exercised some influence on later works, including the *Scarapsus* and ecclesiastical legislation. The section on baptism and the creed is particularly interesting. The tripartite *credo* in the *Homilia* (from 'Credo in Deum' to 'unusquisque nostrum, credo') was included in Hahn's *Bibliothek der Symbole und Glaubensregeln* with six other early Christian *interrogationes de fide*, which it

---

12 Carlo de Clercq, *La législation religieuse franque de Clovis à Charlemagne*, Université de Louvain: Recueil de travaux publiés par les membres des conférences d'histoire et de philologie, 2 S., 38 (Louvain and Paris, 1936), 371, cf. 284-8. See the similar text in Stephanus Baluzius [Etienne Baluze], *Capitularia regum Francorum*, curante Petro [Pierre] de Chiniac, 2 vols (Paris, 1780), i, 956; and *MGH Leges* in fol., 2/ii, 83 (*Capitularia spuria*, ii, 192). Emil Seckel, 'Studien zu Benedictus Levita, VII', *NA*, 35 (1909-10), 146-9, suggested that this statute derived from a Burgundian synod after 800 and, ultimately, from Caesarius and the *Scarapsus*, without mentioning the *Homilia*.

13 See Honoratus Millemann, 'Caesarius von Arles und die frühmittelalterliche Missionspredigt', *Zeitschrift für Missionswissenschaft und Religionswissenschaft*, 23 (1933), 22, who argued that the *Homilia* depended on the *Scarapsus*. If so, and if (following Angenendt) the *Scarapsus* was written in the second half of the eighth century, the *Homilia* dates from about 800.

resembles but with none of which is identical.[14] The history of the questions or scrutinies associated with baptism in the early church is obscure.[15] They tended to disappear as time went on and infant baptism increasingly replaced adult baptism,[16] but they were apparently revived north of the Alps in the eighth century perhaps owing to the growing number of adult converts and also to the influence of the Roman baptismal rite,[17] which had seven questions. One of the creeds of the Bobbio missal, which is now commonly dated to the eighth century, is broken down into three questions, as in the homily.[18] Charlemagne in his letter concerning baptism to archbishop Odilbert of Milan specifically asked 'Concerning the scrutiny, what is the scrutiny?'[19]

The text is printed here from the Copenhagen manuscript, with emendations and a few corrections from the Elmenhorst edition (E) but not including many small differences in orthography, tenses, and word-forms (especially word-endings). When in doubt, preference has been given to the manuscript, including variant spellings, such as 'ecclesia/ecclaesia/aecclesia', 'diabolus/diabulus', 'eli-mosina/helimosina/aelimosina', the alternative uses of 'c/t' and 'd/t', and the occasional use of an adjectival form for an imperative, including 'inpendere', 'consolare', 'uisitare', and 'sepelire', for 'inpendite', 'consulate', 'uisitate', and 'sepelite'. The punctuation is based for the most part on that of the manuscript, which uses ·, ´ and ·´ with the addition of question marks and the introduction of colons and periods before capital letters, which often mark the beginning of

14 August Hahn, *Bibliothek der Symbole und Glaubensregeln der alten Kirche*, 3rd edn G. Ludwig Hahn (Breslau, 1897), 36, no. 1g; see 96-7 (and n. 247) on Pirmin and 103-4, no. VI.10, for an abbreviated version of a Reichenau symbol resembling that in the *Scarapsus*, 41, on which see Angenendt, *Monachi* (cited n. 6), 69-70; and generally, J. N. D. Kelly, *Early Christian Creeds* (London, New York, and Toronto, 1950), 398-420, on the creed in the *Scarapsus* (but not the *Homilia*).

15 Arnold Angenendt, 'Der Taufritus im frühen Mittelalter', in *Segni e riti nella chiesa altomedievale occidentale, 11-17 aprile 1985*, 2 vols, Settimane di studio del Centro italiano di studi sull'alto medioevo, 33 (Spoleto, 1987), i, 175-82 (bibliography on 182, n. 13).

16 Andrew Hughes, *Medieval Manuscripts for Mass and Office: A Guide to their Organization and Terminology* (Toronto, Buffalo, and London, 1982), 255. George H. Williams, *Anselm: Communion and Atonement* (St Louis, 1960) discussed the progressive 'depression and routinization' (20) of baptism in the early Middle Ages and its replacement by the eucharist as the principal means of Christian redemption.

17 Christopher A. Jones, *A Lost Work by Amalarius of Metz*, Henry Bradshaw Society, Subsidia 2 (London, 2001), 138-9.

18 *The Bobbio Missal: A Gallican Mass-Book (MS. Paris, Lat. 13246)*, ed. E. A. Lowe, 3 vols, Henry Bradshaw Society Publications, 53, 58, and 61 (London, 1917-24), i, 74-5, nos. 245-7. See the notes in *ibid.*, ii, 130 (and 98-9 on the date); Kelly, *Creeds* (cited n. 14), 401 and 417; and Angenendt, *Monachi* (cited n. 6), 70.

19 *MGH Capitularia*, i, 247, no. 125. See Burkhard Neunheuser, *Baptism and Confirmation*, tr. John Jay Hughes (New York, 1964), 166, and Peter Cramer, *Baptism and Change in the Early Middle Ages, c. 200-c. 1150*, Cambridge Studies in Medieval Life and Thought, 4 S. 29 (Cambridge, 1993), 140-41.

quotations, phrases, and sentences. The lacuna marked by '...' on p. 51 of the 1614 edition (variant t after the words 'Decimas ex omnibus') is not in the manuscript, where a word (such as 'fructibus') may have been omitted or the following word 'uiris' may be a misreading for 'uestris'. Quotations from the bible and other sources, even when they differ from the published sources, are indicated by italics.

Text

Fratres karissimi, intellegimus quia per bonam uoluntatem et dei amorem ad aecclaesiam uenitis, et audire uerba dei, et eius precepta cupitis. Pensate, quia labor uester utilis sit. Et ut nobis proderit, et uobis quia *debitores sumus*[20] deo auxiliante uobis ex diuinis inpendere necessaria presentis uitae siue futurae. Ammonet ergo nos dominus, et[a] terribiliter per prophetam dicens: *Si non adnunciaueris populo meo iniquitates illius, sanguinem eius de manu tua requiram.*[21] Inde fratres rogamus uos ut diligentius cogitemus: Quare dicti sumus christiani, *si christiana opera non facimus?*[22] *A Christo enim christiani sumus uocati,*[23] primum quae illut nomen in babtismo suscepimus et in illo babtismo diabolo renunciauimus et operibus eius. Post istam abrenunciacionem, nos interrogati a sacerdote: Credis in deum patrem omnipotentem creatorem caeli et terre? Vnusquisque respondit, credo. Credis et in Ihesum[b] Christum filium eius unicum, dominum natum ex Maria uirgine, passum et sepultum? Et respondit, credo. Tertia interrogatio: Credis et in spiritum sanctum, sanctam ecclesiam catholicam, sanctorum communionem, remissionem peccatorum, carnis resurreccionem, et uitam aeternam? Et respondit unusquisque nostrum, credo. Ecce fratres qualem renunciacionem diabolo fecimus, et qualem confessionem, et pactum deo patri, et Ihesu Christo filio eius, simul et spiritu sancto promissimus[24] et si[c] creduli babtizati fuimus in nomine patris et filii et spiritus sancti in remissionem omnium peccatorum.[25] Oportet ergo nos fratres qui babtizati sumus, et diabolo[d] negauimus, et credulitatem deo promissimus ut mandata dei, et eius precepta seruemus, et opera diaboli derelinquamus. Sicut spiritus

---

[a] et *om.* E | [b] dominum E | [c] sic E | [d] diabolum E

---

20 Rom. 8: 12.
21 Ezech. 3: 18.
22 Ps-Ambrose, *Serm.* 24.3 (*PL* 17.674A); see *Clavis patrum latinorum*, ed. Eligius Dekkers, 3rd edn (Turnhout, 1995), 180 and 368, no. 251. Cf. Caesarius, *Serm.*, 13.1 and 16.2 (*CCSL*, 103.64 and 77).
23 Isidore, *Etym.*, VII, 14.1 (ed. W. M. Lindsay [Oxford, 1911]); and *Scarapsus*, c. 12 (pp. 44.6-7 and 106).
24 Cf. Martin of Braga, *De correctione rusticorum*, 15.11-16.1 (ed. Barlow [cited n. 7], 196-7); and *Scarapsus*, c. 12 (pp. 43.12-25 and 105) on 'Post istam ... promisimus'.
25 Cf. *Scarapsus*, c. 12 (pp. 43.25-7 and 106) on 'et sic creduli ... peccatorum'.

sanctus per propheta nos ammonet: *Deuerte a malo et fac bonum.*[26] Quid est *deuerte a malo*, nisi diabulum derelinquere cum omnibus operibus suis, et facere opera Christi? Haec sunt opera diaboli, quibus renunciauimus: cupiditas, gula, fornicacio, ira, tristitia, pigricia, uana gloria, superbia. Haec sunt octo uicia principalia, et ex ipsis oriuntur ista: furtum, falsum testimonium, periurium, rapacitas, saturitas, ebrietas,[27] stultiloquium id est uerba luxoriosa et inhonesta et cantaciones uanas et luxoriosas, homicidium, obprobrium, iurgium haec^e est iniuria, inuidia, odium, murmoracio, detraccio, contenciones.[28] Vnde possumus fratres, deo ueraces esse, qui in babtismo renunciauimus et operibus eius, si hec opera facimus et in consuetudine illa habemus? Et quid^f proderit christianum nomen habere, si christiana opera non facimus?[29] Renunciauimus opera diaboli, et illa sequamur quae promissimus deo. Inde rogamus et obsecramus, de peccatis quae supra memorauimus, si in aliquo se culpabilem cognoscat unusquisque, faciet confessionem puram et agat penitentiam[30] quod male fecit. Et deuertat se a uia mala et conuertat se ad deum omnipotentem et misericordem, qui ait: Nolo mortem peccatoris,^g sed ut conuertatur et uiuat in aeternum.[31] Penitentiam agite, adpropinquauit enim regnum caelorum.[32] Item per prophetam: In quacumque die conuersus fuerit peccator, *uita uiuet et non morietur.*[33] Fratres magna necessitas est nobis quod nos conuertamur ad dominum qui pius et misericors et patiens est in peccatis nostris et non solum ille nos ammonet et nobis parcet ut nos delinquamur opera mala sed ut magis opera bona facimus. Id est primum omnium de bonis operibus fides nostra seruanda est, sicut in babtismo recepimus. Hoc est credimus in deum patrem et in filium et in spiritum sanctum, unum deum in trinitate et unitatem in trinitate, ut diligamus eum ex toto corde, et timeamus illum et diligamus[34] nosmetipsos, propter timorem dei, et sic diligamus nos, sicut ipse dominus precepit nobis: *Quemcumque uultis ut faciant uobis homines facite illis.*[35] Quare^h debet christianus homo, altere facere malum,^i quod non uult ut alter illi faciat? Ammonemus et ortamur uos ut

---

^e hoc E | ^f qui MS | ^g peccatores MS | ^h non *add.* E | ^i malo MS

---

26 Ps. 33: 15.
27 Cf. *Scarapsus*, c. 13 (pp. 44.14-22 and 108) on 'Oportet ergo ... ebrietas'.
28 Cf. Cassian, *Conf.*, V, 2 and 16 (*SChr.*, 42.190 and 208); and *Scarapsus*, c. 13 (pp. 44 and 107, n. 14). See Angenendt, *Monachi* (cited n. 6), 63.
29 See n. 22 above.
30 Cf. ps-Aug., *Serm.*, 250.2 (*PL* 39.2209; see Morin in *CCSL*, 104.985, calling this sermon a farrago of excerpts from Caesarius and others); and *Scarapsus*, c. 25 (pp. 59.8-11 and 120) on 'Inde rogamus ... poenitentiam'.
31 Ezech. 33: 11.
32 Matt. 3: 2 and 4: 17.
33 Ezech. 18: 28.
34 See *RegB*, c. 4; and *Scarapsus*, c. 28b (pp. 66.10-13 and 124) on 'Credimus in deum ... diligamus'.
35 Matt. 7: 12.

post actam confessionem frequenter ad ecclesiam ueniatis et[j] orare pro peccatis propriis cum bona uoluntate et fide recta. Quia domus dei, *domus orationis uocabitur*.[36] Et apostolus nos ammonet: *Orate sine intermissione, et in omnibus deo gratias agite*.[37] Et iterum: *Oratio et deprecatio assidua multum ualet*.[38] Unusquisque homo sciat orationem dominicam et credulitatem, sicut christianus cognoscere debet. Omnibus dominicis[k] diebus et cunctis festiuitatibus preclaris tam uespertinis et uigiliis uel[l] matutinis quam[m] ad missas caelebrandas ad ecclesias frequenter uenite ibi dei[n] uerba audiatis orantes cum puro corde et silencio. *Cantica luxoriosa* uel *diabolica*[39] neque *quando ad ecclesiam uenitis*[40] neque in domibus nostris[o] non coletis. Viri et femine diabolicas culturas non colent. Aguria[p] et inpuris[q] diuinaciones, et ligaturas femine, incantaciones, pociones unde partum auortiuum faciunt non erubescit fornicacionem perpetrare postea homicidium. Vota uestra bona deo ad ecclesiam reddite. Primicias frugum uestrarum ad benedicendum ad ecclesiam adferte, cum benediccione postea manducate, sicut Salomon ait: *Honora dominum de tua substantia et de primiciis frugum tuarum ut impleantur[r] orrea tua saturitate*,[s] *et uino torcolaria redundant*.[41] *Decimas ex omnibus*[42t] uiris,[u] uel de pecoribus uestris, annis singulis ad ecclesias reddite. De nouem partibus, helimosinas facite et qui plus habet plus donet in helimosina. Quia sicut *aqua extinguit ignem, ita elimosina extinguet peccatum*.[43] Elimosina interpretatur misericordiam.[44v] Multiplex est in pauperes qui pauperiori[w] de quo paruum habet donet, tamen et qui non habet unde faciat misericordiam, habeat bonam uoluntatem[45] ad faciendum.[46] Pauperibus secundum possibilitatem argentum aut in cibo aut in potu aliquod donate. Quando ad ecclaesiam uenitis incensum aut[x] cereolus,[y] oleum in luminaribus ecclesiae,[z] iuxta quod preualetis ibidem date, quia dominus ait: *Non*

---

[j] *et om.* E | [k] domicis MS | [l] et E | [m] quam *om.* E | [n] ibidem *pro* ibi dei E | [o] uestris E
[p] Auguria E[q] in pueris E | [r] impleatur MS | [s] saturitatem MS | [t] ... *add.* E | [u] *pro* uestris?
[v] misericordia E | [w] pauperiorem MS | [x] ad E | [y] cereolos E | [z] ecclesiam MS

---

36 Cf. Is. 56: 7, and Matt. 21: 13.
37 1 Thess 5: 17-18.
38 Iac. 5: 16.
39 Caesarius, *Serm.*, 13.4 and 19.3 (*CCSL*, 103.67 and 89). Cf. *Scarapsus*, c. 28 (pp. 67.24-68.6 and 124) on 'apostolus nos admonet ... diabolica'.
40 Caesarius, *Serm.*, 19.3 (*CCSL*, 103.89).
41 Prov. 3: 9-10.
42 Gen. 14: 20.
43 Eccli. 3: 33.
44 Augustine, *Enchir.*, c. 76 (*CCSL*, 46.90). Cf. Rabanus Maurus, *De institutione clericorum*, II, 28 (ed. Aloisius Knoepfler [Munich, 1910], 110).
45 Caesarius, *Serm.*, 31.1 and 182.2 (*CCSL*, 103.134, and 104.741).
46 See intro. on 'primitias frugum ... faciendum'.

apparebitis in conspectu meo uacui.[47] *Oblaciones* quoque *quae in altario consecrentur offerte,*[48] et de ipsis secundum consilium sacerdotis communicate. Et ante plures dies, a[aa] propriis uxoribus abstinete, ut puro corde sacrificium accipere possitis.[49] Sacerdotibus nostris[bb] honorem inpendite, et propter dominum obedite,[50] filius et filia honoret patrem et matrem, hospites, pauperes et *peregrinos recipite in domibus uestris.* Secundum possibilitatem illis honorem inpendere, *pedes illorum lauate.*[51] Nudos uestite, sicut dominus in euuangelio ait: *Quod uni ex minimis meis fecistis, mihi fecistis.*[52] In tribulacione positos[cc] adiuuate. Dolentes consolare,[dd] infirmos uisitare, mortuos sepelire, in carcere positos requirite, et de bonis uestris ministrate.[53] Viduas et orfanos in tribulacionibus eorum adiuuate. Pauperes et omnes oppressos a prauis hominibus uel de iniquo iudicio illis in[ee] quantum potestis, adiutorium prestate. Iudicium rectum semper seruate, quia per prophetam dicitur:[ff] *Vae*[gg] *qui iustificastis impium pro muneribus et iustitiam iustis auertistis.*[54] Et in euuangelio: *In quo enim iudicio iudicaueritis, iudicabimini.*[55] Misericordiam diligite, et[hh] discordes ad concordia reuocate.[56] *Simbolum et oracionem dominicam ipse*[ii] *tenete,*[jj] filios et filias uestras docetis.[57][kk] Qualis christianus[ll] est qui fidem suam nescit, neque orare scit? *Filios quos in babtismo excepistis fidemiussores uos scitis pro his aput deum*[mm] *extetisse*[58] ueritatem[nn] ex corde et ore dicite, ieiunium amate, castitatem seruate, seniores honorate, iuniores diligite, caritatem habete, patienter[oo] estote,[pp] et super omnia castitatis dilectio sit in cordibus uestris, id est in cogitatione, in uerbo, in operibus bonis.[59] Spes uestra in deo semper maneat. Cum aliquit in uos[qq] bonum uideritis non ad uestra laude sed ad dei conputatis. Mala cum uideritis neglegenciam uestram[rr] uel culpe deputetis. Timete fratres diem iudicii et penam futuram et desiderate uitam aeternam, transitum uestrum de hoc

---

[aa] ad MS | [bb] uestris E | [cc] positus MS | [dd] consolamini E | [ee] in *om.* E | [ff] dicit E
[gg] uel MS | [hh] de MS | [ii] ipsi E | [jj] et *add.* E | [kk] docete E | [ll] christianis MS
[mm] dominum E | [nn] seueritate E | [oo] patientes E | [pp] stote MS | [qq] uobis E | [rr] negligentiae uestrae E

---

47 Exod. 23: 15.
48 Caesarius, *Serm.*, 13.2 and 16.2 (*CCSL*, 103.65 and 77).
49 Caesarius, *Serm.*, 16.2 (*CCSL*, 103.78).
50 Cf. *Scarapsus*, c. 30 (pp. 69.19-22 and 126) on 'pauperibus secundum ... obedite'.
51 Ps-Aug., *Serm.*, 250.3 (*PL* 39.2209). See n. 30 above.
52 Matt. 25: 40.
53 See *RegB*, cc. 4 and 53.
54 Is. 5: 22-3.
55 Matt. 7: 2.
56 Cf. *Scarapsus*, c. 31 (pp. 70.1-14 and 126-7) on 'Filius et filia ... reuocate'.
57 Caesarius, *Serm.*, 13.2, 16.2, and 19.3 (*CCSL*, 103.65, 78, and 89).
58 Caesarius, *Serm.*, 13.2 (*CCSL*, 103.65), cf. 204.3 (*ibid.*, 104.821).
59 Cf. *RegB*, c. 4.

seculo, qui omni homini incertum est omni die sperate, precepta dei cottidie adimplete et de dei misericordia numquam disperate. Haec sunt opera fratres karissimi et precepta dei quibus fidem nostram firmare debemus et uitam aeternam merere⁶⁰ si illa custodiamus. Idcirco nullus se conueniat^ss fratres quia omnis homo qui post babtismum mortalia crimina commisit, de quibus supra memorauimus si penitentiam ueram non egerit et aelimosinas iustas non fecerit, et in bonis operibus non perseuerauerit numquam intrabit in regno^tt dei nec possedebit gloria aeterna. Sed cum diabolo descendit in infernum sicut apostolus ait: Qui talia agunt *regnum dei non possedebunt*.⁶¹ Et in euuangelio ait: *Discedite a me maledicti in ignem aeternum, qui preparati estis^uu diabolo et angelis eius*.⁶² Ideo fratres festinemus iam emendare uitam nostram et certissime credite, quia omnis homo quamuis peccator, quamuis criminosus fuisset et multa mala perpetrasset si uera penitentia ageret^vv et aelimosinas iustas fecerit et in bona uoluntate cum operibus iustis de quibus supra diximus, quando mors illum inuenerit, et ultimus dies numquam descendit in infernum, sed ab angelis eleuatur^ww in caelo et gloriam possidebit in aeternum. Vnde scriptum est: *Si nos ipse^xx iudicaremur^yy utique a domino, non re^zz iudicaremur*.⁶³ᵃᵃᵃ Ergo multo magis fratres quod quic^bbb contra dei precepta fecimus, defleamus et emendemus et ulterius peccare cessemus. Et conseruemus nos in bona uoluntate, et cogitatione recta, cum uerbis et operibus sanctis ut mereamur audire sententia desiderabile: *Venite benedicti patris mei, percipite regnum quod uobis paratum est ab origine mundi*.⁶⁴ Ipso auxiliante et gubernante domino nostro Ihesu Christo qui cum patre et spiritu sancto uiuit et regnat deus per omnia secula seculorum. Amen.⁶⁵

---

^ss circumueniat E | ^tt regnum E | ^uu praeparatus est E | ^vv ueram penitentiam egerit E
^ww eleuabitur E | ^xx ipsos E | ^yy iudicaremus E | ^zz re *om.* E | ^aaa iudicauemur MS
^bbb quic *om.* E

---

60 Cf. *Scarapsus*, c. 32 (pp. 70.15-71.17 and 127-8) on 'Symbolum et orationem … mereri'. On the obligations of godparents, see Joseph Lynch, *Godparents and Kinship in Early Medieval Europe* (Princeton, 1986), 189, citing Caesarius and the *Scarapsus*; and Bernhard Jussen, *Spiritual Kinship as Social Practice: Godparenthood and Adoption in the Early Middle Ages*, ed. and trans. Pamela Selwyn (Newark and London, 2000), 232-8.

61 1 Cor. 6: 9.

62 Matt. 25: 41.

63 1 Cor. 11: 31.

64 Matt. 25: 34.

65 Cf. *Scarapsus*, c. 34 (pp. 72.23-73.3 and 129) on 'Ideo fratres … Amen'.

Chapter 10

'Quod si se non emendent, excommunicentur': Rund um ein neues Exzerpt des Capitulare generale Kaiser Karls des Großen (802)

Hubert Mordek

Roger E. Reynolds—sein Name steht für die Sache: stets quellenfundierte Forschung, oft Vorstöße in unbekanntes Neuland als Folge sensationell vieler Handschriftenfunde. Es war diese gemeinsame Liebe zum 'Original' vor allem kirchenrechtlichen Inhalts, die uns vor Jahrzehnten schon über Länder und Grenzen hinweg zusammenführte,[1] und so schien es mir beim Aufruf zur Festschrift nur ganz natürlich, den Jubilar mit dem zu ehren, was wir beide besonders schätzen: seltene Texte, neue Tradenten. Die folgenden Lesefrüchte resultieren aus meiner langjährigen Beschäftigung mit dem fränkischen Herrscherrecht der Kapitularien und sollen Roger E. Reynolds bei der Lektüre Vergnügen bereiten, auch wenn ihre Überlieferungen nicht in Beneventana gehalten sind—sie kommen immerhin aus Italien.[2]

Das Aachener Capitulare generale von 802, nach der bekannten Admonitio generalis von 789 das zweite programmatische Kapitular jetzt des Kaisers Karl,[3]

---

1 Allgemein sichtbarer Ausdruck unserer Kooperation war der gemeinsame Aufsatz 'Bischof Leodegar und das Konzil von Autun', in *Aus Archiven und Bibliotheken: Festschrift für Raymund Kottje zum 65. Geburtstag*, ed. Hubert Mordek, Freiburger Beiträge zur mittelalterlichen Geschichte, 3 (Frankfurt am Main, Bern, New York, Paris, 1992), 71-92.

2 Dieser kleine Festschriftbeitrag ist als textkritische Studie konzipiert. Demgegenüber mussten andere Gesichtspunkte wie ins einzelne gehende Inhaltsangaben, Strukturanalysen u. ä. zurücktreten. Quellen- und Literaturangaben beschränken sich auf Titel speziell zum Thema. Für eine breitere Information verweise ich auf die erst vor wenigen Jahren erschienene Monographie *Studien zur fränkischen Herrschergesetzgebung* (Frankfurt am Main, Berlin, Bern u. a., 2000); sie stellt den Stand der Forschung dar und handelt speziell von Kapitularien und Kapitulariensammlungen.

3 *Capitulare missorum generale*, ed. Alfred Boretius, *MGH Capitularia*, i (Hannover, 1883), 91-9, Nr. 33. Analog zur *Admonitio generalis*, deren Name sich trotz manchen Widerspruchs etabliert hat, wird unser Stück hier *Capitulare generale* genannt, denn es ist kein spezifisches Capitulare missorum. Boretius' Nomenklatur bemängelte schon Gerhard Seeliger, *Die Kapitularien der Karolinger* (München, 1893), 69, und in dieser Ablehnung sind sich seitdem viele Forscher einig. Ein weiteres Capitulare generale erließ Karl der Große kurz vor seinem Tod, ed. Hubert Mordek-Gerhard Schmitz, 'Neue Kapitularien und Kapitulariensammlungen', *Deutsches Archiv*, 43 (1987), 361-439, hier 414-23; wiederabgedruckt in Mordek, *Studien zur fränkischen Herrschergesetzgebung*, 81-159, hier 134-43; der Text inklusive Kurzkommentar findet sich auch in Hubert

ist—anders als der königliche Erlass dreizehn Jahre zuvor—vollständig nur in einer einzigen Handschrift erhalten: Paris, Bibliothèque Nationale, MS lat. 4613, entstanden im 10. Jahrhundert in Oberitalien[4] und inhaltlich gefüllt mit langobardischen Gesetzen und fränkischen Kapitularien (Collectio Thuana).[5]

Der dünne Strang der Überlieferung hätte für die Textqualität des Aachener Gesetzes an sich wenig zu bedeuten, wenn er von solider Tragfähigkeit wäre. Dem ist aber nicht so. Wie der Vergleich mit noch anderweitig erhaltenen Kapitularien des Parisinus ergab, haben wir es hier mit einem ungewöhnlich stark korrumpierten Tradenten zu tun.[6] Das Resultat dieser ruinösen Reproduktion geht entweder auf das Konto eines völlig unbedarften Kopisten,[7] oder die Verantwortung

---

Mordek, *Bibliotheca capitularium regum Francorum manuscripta: Überlieferung und Traditionszusammenhang der fränkischen Herrschererlasse*, MGH Hilfsmittel, 15 (München, 1995), 990-94. Um Verwechslungen zu vermeiden, wäre es wohl angebracht, das Stück von 813 genauer zu bezeichnen, z. B. als Capitulare generale ultimum.

4   Eingehende Beschreibung des MS Paris BN lat. 4613 in Mordek, *Bibliotheca capitularium*, 469-76. Marie-Noël Colette. 'Un graduel-antiphonaire-responsorial noté sauvé de l'oubli (Palimpseste Paris, B.N.F., Grec 2631) Région de Turin, Xe siècle', *Revue de musicologie*, 83 (1997), 65-79, hier 70 Anm. 20 erwähnt eine Mitteilung von Marie Thérèse Gousset, wonach bei Schmuckinitialen im Leges Langobardorum-Teil des MS Paris BN lat. 4613 die gleiche Art von Zierelementen vorkomme wie in der von Colette behandelten palimpsestierten Pariser Musikhandschrift, die sie (in Absprache mit François Avril, Marie Thérèse Gousset und Jean Vezin) im 10. Jahrhundert in der Gegend von Turin entstanden sieht. Unser oberitalienischer Parisinus lat. 4613 dürfte bei Colette mit 'Xe-XIe s.' allerdings etwas spät datiert sein. Die Schrift ist keine besonders schöne, aber durchaus gefällige karolingische Minuskel, unter die sich vorkarolingische, teilweise der Raetica oder Beneventana eigene Buchstabenformen und Signa mischen wie unziales 'd', langes 'i' am Wortanfang, langer Schaft des 'r', häufig 'ri'- und 'st'-, selten 'ti'-Ligaturen, verschiedene Formen des Kürzungszeichens (glatter oder gewellter waagrechter Strich oder Häkchen). Erwähnenswert scheint zudem das leicht nach links gebogene Schaftende des 'q' und anderer Buchstaben mit Unterlänge. Einer solchen Schrift könnte man wohl schon in den letzten Jahrzehnten des 9. Jahrhunderts begegnen, das Manuskript wird aber, wenn wir das Urteil der Kunsthistoriker mit ins Kalkül ziehen, meines Erachtens zu Recht in das 10. Jahrhundert gesetzt. Zur Anzahl der Hände siehe unten Anm. 43.

5   Im 16./17. Jahrhundert befand sich die Handschrift im Besitz von Jacques-Auguste de Thou, daher der Name Collectio Thuana. Den Vorbesitzer de Thou kennen wird durch Étienne Baluze, der das Capitulare generale erstmals edierte mit der Provenienzangabe '... ex veteri Codice Longobardico manuscripto Bibliothecae Thuanae': *Capitulare primum anni DCCCII sive Capitula data missis dominicis, anno secundo imperii*, ed. Stephanus Baluzius [Étienne Baluze], *Capitularia regum Francorum*, i (Paris, 1677), 361-2. Schon Baluze war also bei der Herausgabe unseres Stückes allein auf den jetzigen Parisinus lat. 4613 angewiesen.—Die Sammlung selbst wird im folgenden nicht erneut untersucht, siehe dazu unten S. 174.

6   Diese traurige Tatsache konstatierte bereits Alfred Boretius, *Die Capitularien im Langobardenreich: Eine rechtsgeschichtliche Abhandlung* (Halle, 1864), 45.

7   Wenn vom Kopisten oder Schreiber gesprochen wird, so soll damit keineswegs behauptet werden, er sei auch der Urheber der pejorativen Redaktion gewesen. Dieser kann sein Werk schon früher an irgendeiner Stelle des Vorlagenstranges von MS Paris BN lat. 4613 verrichtet haben. Im nächstliegenden Fall hat er es selbst (mit) abgeschrieben oder von Personen seines 'Vertrauens' abschreiben lassen; denn vieles spricht dagegen, dass sich im Parisinus sein Arbeitsexemplar erhalten hat, siehe auch unten S. 178 f. mit Anm. 43 und 44.

liegt bei einem eigenwilligen, raffiniert agierenden Überarbeiter, der den unschuldigen Text für seine eigenen Ziele missbrauchte, vielleicht aber auch nur seinen Schabernack mit ihm treiben wollte (oder richtiger: seinem Auftraggeber? Heute dem Editor!).[8] Singuläre, in erstaunlicher Fülle auftretende Abweichungen von der Vorlage führen jedenfalls nicht selten zu grotesken Sinnentstellungen. Im folgenden seien einige wenige—so hoffe ich—'erhellende' Kostproben geboten.

Karls Vorschrift gegen heidnische Praktiken war in der Admonitio generalis unmissverständlich formuliert: '... ubi aliqui stulti luminaria vel alias observationes faciunt, omnino mandamus, ut iste pessimus usus et Deo execrabilis, ubicumque inveniatur, tollatur et distruatur'.[9] Und was macht der Parisinus daraus? '... ubi aliquis instulti luminaria vel alia subservatione omnino damnamus ut isto proximo usus et deo etsecrabilis ubicumque inveniat ac tollatur et dextruatur'.[10] Man beachte das fehlende 'faciunt' und die Sinnwendungen 'stulti' zu 'instulti', 'alias observationes' zu 'alia subservatione', 'mandamus' zu 'damnamus' und 'pessimus' zu 'proximo'.[11] Durch solche und ähnliche Manipulationen entstehen neue, mehr oder weniger bekannte Wörter, die aber, im Zusammenhang gelesen, nichts oder zumindest etwas anderes bedeuten, als vom Gesetzgeber intendiert. Sie erfüllen demnach die merkwürdige Funktion, die Aussage des ursprünglichen Textes aufzuheben, statt sie in einzelnen Punkten zu verbessern oder zu modifizieren.

Manchmal hat man den Eindruck, der Redaktor spiele mit dem Leser. Dem mit 'sunt' beginnenden und mit 'sunt' endenden Schlusssatz des Binnenprooems der Admonitio[12] (der Parisinus nennt sie in unserem Satz 'omnititio') werden willkürlich andere Rahmenworte verpasst: 'Una' bzw. 'sum',[13] während sich kurz zuvor noch umgekehrt 'scit' durch 'sunt' ersetzt sah.[14]

---

8   Weitere Gründe für Textveränderungen im Laufe der Tradition sind etwa angeführt bei Leonard E. Boyle, 'Optimist and Recensionist: "Common Errors" or "Common Variations"?', in *Latin Script and Letters A. D. 400-900: Festschrift presented to Ludwig Bieler on the occasion of his 70th birthday*, ed. John J. O'Meara-Bernd Neumann (Leiden, 1976), 264-74, hier 268-9. Auf manch ungewohnten Gedanken kommt Sebastiano Timpanaro, *The Freudian Slip: psychoanalysis and textual criticism* (London, 1976), 19 ff. (Übersetzung der italienischen Erstausgabe *Il Lapsus Freudiano*, 1974, von Kate Soper).

9   *Admonitio generalis*, c. 65, 2. Teil, *MGH Capitularia*, i, 52-62, Nr. 22, hier 59.

10 MS Paris BN lat. 4613, fo 78r-v.

11 Lektürefehler sind praktisch ausgeschlossen, denn die Schrift ist klar und deutlich lesbar; siehe auch oben Anm. 4.

12 *Admonitio generalis*, c. 60, Schluss, *MGH Capitularia*, i, 57: 'Sunt quoque aliqua (alia) capitula quae nobis utilia huic praecedenti ammonitione subiungere visa sunt'.

13 MS Paris BN lat. 4613, fo 77r: 'Una quoque alia capitula que nobis subtilia huic predicentia omnititione subiungere visa sum'. Die auch im Satzinnern erkennbaren Veränderungen ('utilia' zu 'subtilia', 'praecedenti' zu 'predicentia', 'ammonitione' zu 'omnititione') sind weitere Beispiele dafür, wie dem Redaktor permanent sinnverwandte Wörter aus der Feder flossen. Ein solcher Wortsalat muss aber selbst schon für die damals Lateinkundigen ungenießbar gewesen sein.

14 Wie Anm. 12 und 13.

Gold hatte es dem Korruptor offenbar besonders angetan. Wer seinen Wert mindern wollte—und sei es Christus selbst, der den Altar über das Gold erhob[15]—, dem leistete er vom Schreibpult aus erbitterten Widerstand: In einer einzigen Phrase[16] ließ er 'aurum' gleich dreimal verschwinden; 'plus aurum' verwandelte er in 'pulsarum', 'aurum' in 'a nostris' und 'sanctificat aurum' in 'sanctificaturus', dann noch ein kleiner Buchstabendreh, 'altare' wird zu 'altera' und das Ganze zu einem Buch mit sieben Siegeln.[17]

Aus dem Kuriositätenkabinett der Sprachver(w)irrungen könnte noch seitenlang schier Unglaubliches berichtet werden,[18] doch, um das Thema nicht zu verfehlen, breche ich hier ab und werde an anderem Ort näher auf die wichtige, nur durch Paris BN lat. 4613 vertretene Rechtssammlung eingehen mit ihrem in Leges Langobardorum und (vielen italienischen) Kapitularien geteilten Inhalt, auf ihre Entstehungszeit und ihre Heimat. Dass der Urheber der uns vorliegenden redigierten Version der Collectio capitularium Thuana kein naiver Stümper gewesen sein kann, lässt sich schon heute mit Fug und Recht behaupten. Nach einer vollständigen Kontrolle der überlieferten Texte dürfte auch die zweite eingangs gestellte Alternative reif sein zur Entscheidung, ob er vornehmlich aus intellektuellem Vergnügen ständig in die Rechtstexte eingegriffen oder ob er—zugespitzt formuliert—nichts Geringeres im Schilde geführt hat als einen lautlosen Angriff auf die fränkische Gesetzgebung und damit auf die fränkische Herrschaft in Italien.

Nicht nur die Verbreitung—womit hat solch ein bedeutender Text einen derart skrupellosen Transmitter verdient?—, auch die Rezeption des programmatischen Kapitulars von 802 war im Mittelalter minimal. Nachgewiesen ist sie für die im frühen 11. Jahrhundert in Zentral- oder Süditalien entstandene Collectio canonum V librorum, der unser Jubilar wiederholt weiterführende Studien gewidmet hat.[19]

---

15 Matth. 23: 17 und 19, von der *Admonitio generalis*, c. 64, in leicht abgewandelter Form zitiert, *MGH Capitularia*, i, 58.

16 *Admonitio generalis*, c. 64, *MGH Capitularia*, i, 58: 'Item cavendum est, ne farisiaca superstitione aliquis plus aurum honoret quam altare; ne dicat ei Dominus: Stulte et caece, quid est maius: aurum vel altare, quod sanctificat aurum?'

17 MS Paris BN lat. 4613, fo 78r. Der Satz ist insgesamt verunstaltet: 'Item cavendum est nec fara sicca subscriptione aliquid pulsarum honorem quam altera nec dicant ei dominus: Stulte et ecce quod est malus a nostris vel altare quod sanctificaturus'.

18 Von anderen Schreibern und Überarbeitern, ihren Stärken und Schwächen, ihren Fehlern und Korrekturen, handelt generell wie detailliert mit vielen zeitgenössischen Quellenzitaten Wilhelm Wattenbach in seinem immer noch lesenswerten Buch *Das Schriftwesen im Mittelalter*, 3. Auflage (Leipzig, 1896), 317 ff. Vgl. neuerdings die ebenso vorbildlich quellennahe Studie von Paul Gerhard Schmidt, *Probleme der Schreiber—der Schreiber als Problem*, Sitzungsberichte der Wissenschaftlichen Gesellschaft an der Johann Wolfgang Goethe-Universität Frankfurt am Main, 31, 5 (Stuttgart, 1994), 169-86, hier S. 176 ff. (auch separat erschienen, dort S. 8 ff.).

19 Als Glieder einer Kette von Publikationen sind bislang erschienen: 'The South-Italian Canon Law *Collection in Five Books* and its Derivatives: new evidence on its origins, diffusion, and use', *Mediaeval Studies*, 52 (1990), 278-95; und 'The South-Italian *Collection in Five Books* and its

Wie Mario Fornasari[20] und jetzt—bezüglich der Kapitularienrezeption in Kanones-sammlungen umfassender und präziser—Valeska Koal[21] zeigen konnten, schöpfte der unbekannte Autor der 5-Bücher-Sammlung mehrere Kapitel aus seiner illustren Vorlage:[22]

Capitulare generale (802) (ed. Boretius, Nr. 33)	Collectio V librorum[23] (ed. Fornasari)	(Vallicelliana, MS B 11)
c. 10	2.13	2.14 (fo 60v)
c. 19	3.251	3.207 (fo 136v)
cc. 22-23	2.15.1	2.16.1 (fos 60v-61r)
c. 24	2.15.2	2.16.2 (fo 61r)
c. 27	4.396	4.433 (fo 234v)

Derivatives: the *Collection of Vallicelliana Tome XXI*, in *Proceedings of the Eighth International Congress of Medieval Canon Law*, ed. Stanley Chodorow, MIC Series C, Subsidia, 9 (Vatikan, 1991), 77-91; beide Artikel sind wiederabgedruckt in ders., *Law and Liturgy in the Latin Church, 5th-12th Centuries* (Aldershot, 1994), Nr. XIV und XVI; danach 'The South-Italian *Collection in Five Books* and its Derivatives: Maastricht Excerpta', *Mediaeval Studies*, 58 (1996), 273-84; 'The South Italian *Collection in Five Books* and its Derivatives: a south Italian appendix to the *Collection in Seventy-Four Titles'*, *Mediaeval Studies*, 63 (2001), 353-65; und *The* Collectio cano-num Casinensis duodecimi seculi (Codex terscriptus): *a derivative of the south-Italian Collection in Five Books*, Studies and Texts, 137, Monumenta Liturgica Beneventana, 3 (Toronto, 2001).

20 *Collectio canonum in V libris (lib. I-III)*, ed. M. Fornasari, *CCCM*, 6 (Turnhout, 1970).

21 Valeska Koal, *Studien zur Nachwirkung der Kapitularien in den Kanonessammlungen des Frühmittelalters*, Freiburger Beiträge zur mittelalterlichen Geschichte, 13 (Frankfurt am Main, Berlin, Bern u. a., 2001), 249: Stellenindex.

22 Über die 5-Bücher-Sammlung lief z. B. später die Nachwirkung des Capitulare generale in der *Collectio canonum Reatina* des Rieti, Archivio Capitolare, MS V, fo 31 (c. 27), nach Boretius, *MGH Capitularia*, i, 96, Anm. l. Das Gleiche gilt für die *Collectio canonum Regesto Farfensi inserta*, 4.20 (c. 19), ed. Theo Kölzer, MIC Series B, Corpus collectionum, 5 (Vatikan, 1982), 252 und die zweite Sammlung des MS Vat. lat. 4977 (c. 10), Paul Fournier, 'Un groupe de recueils canoniques italiens des Xe et XIe siècles', *Mémoires de l'Institut national de France. Académie des inscriptions et belles-lettres*, 40 (1916), 95-213, hier 207 mit Anm. 1, wiederabgedruckt in Paul Fournier, *Mélanges de droit canonique*, ed. Theo Kölzer, mit einem Vorwort von Jean Gaudemet, 2 Bde (Aalen, 1983), 2: *Études sur diverses collections canoniques*, 213-331, hier 325 mit Anm. 1. Alles weitere in den oben Anm. 19 zitierten Studien von Reynolds. Die Edition der Sammlung des Toledo, Biblioteca Capitular, MS 22-32, von John Douglas Adamson, 'The *Collectio Toletana*: an eleventh-century Italian collection of canon law' (Lic. Thesis, Pontifical Institute of Mediaeval Studies, Toronto, 1987) war mir bislang nicht zugänglich.

23 Die aus dem Capitulare generale stammenden Kapitel der ersten drei Bücher sind gedruckt bei Fornasari, *Collectio canonum, CCCM*, 6.188-9, 437; der Text von 4.396 findet sich bei Koal, *Studien zur Nachwirkung der Kapitularien*, 223. Beide Editionen bevorzugen MS Vat. lat. 1339, nicht die wohl älteste Überlieferung in Montecassino, Archivio dell'Abbazia, MS 125. Die in Rom, Biblioteca Vallicelliana, MS B 11 erhaltene Version weicht in Kapitelzählung und Text zum Teil erheblich von der gedruckten Form ab.

Auch wenn die Textzeugen eng miteinander verwandt sind—aus dem Vergleich ergibt sich mancher Hinweis auf die Irrungen des Parisinus und wie sie geheilt werden könnten—, nicht immer werden wir damit den Ersttext zweifelsfrei wiedergewinnen. Um nur zwei unterschiedliche Beispiele anzusprechen:

Im Parisinus ist Karls des Großen Vorschrift zur Gastfreundschaft kaum verständlich (c. 27): 'Precipimusque ut in omni regno nostro neque dives neque pauper neque per nemini inspicia denegare audeant'.[24] Baluze präsentierte als Ersteditor eine elegante Lösung: '... neque dives neque pauper, peregrinis hospitia denegare audeant ...'[25]—'weder ein Reicher noch ein Armer darf Fremden (Pilgern) die Gastrechte verweigern'. Auf diese Weise bleibt der Anfang mit den beiden Nominativen 'dives' und 'pauper' erhalten, die unvermeidlichen Konjekturen beschränken sich auf 'peregrinis' und 'hospitia'. Weniger zufrieden stellen kann der Wegfall des dritten 'neque' und von 'nemini' (bei letzterem wäre noch an ein Aufgehen in 'peregrinis' zu denken). Pertz hielt sich weitgehend an Baluze: '... neque dives neque pauper, peregrino nemini hospitia denegare audeant ...'.[26] Wie Baluze ließ er den ersten Teil unverändert und verzichtete auf das dritte 'neque', führte aber, um möglichst wenig einzugreifen, 'nemini' in den Text zurück und glich 'peregrino' im Singular daran an.

Frischen Wind in die Editionsgeschichte der Stelle brachte erst die 5-Bücher-Sammlung. Ihrer Version folgte Boretius wortwörtlich: '... neque divitibus neque pauperibus neque peregrinis nemo hospitium denegare audeat ...'[27]—'weder Reichen noch Armen oder Fremden (Pilgern), niemand darf ihnen das Gastrecht verweigern'. Auf den ersten Blick wirkt es befremdlich, dass Reiche eigens als zu versorgende Gäste hervorgehoben sind, wo man sie doch eher als Gastgeber erwartete, so wie es der Parisinus vorsieht, und es hat sich bislang auch im ganzen Bereich der Herrscherkapitularien und der Capitula episcoporum kein zweiter derartiger Beleg gefunden.[28] Andererseits betonte Karl der Große mehrfach, das

---

24 MS Paris BN lat. 4613, fo 88v.

25 *Capitulare generale*, c. 27, ed. Étienne Baluze, *Capitularia*, i, 370.

26 *Capitulare Aquisgranense a. 802*, c. 27, ed. Georg Heinrich Pertz, *MGH LL*, i (Hannover, 1835), 94.

27 *Collectio canonum V librorum*, 4.396, in Koal, *Studien zur Nachwirkung der Kapitularien*, 223; *Capitulare generale*, c. 27, ed. Boretius, *MGH Capitularia*, i, 96.

28 Das Wortpaar 'dives' und 'pauper' taucht dort selten auf, und wenn, dann in anderem Zusammenhang (verpachtetes Land, Zehnten). Es begegnet auch in der zeitgenössischen Geschichtsschreibung, in den Lorscher Annalen zum Jahre 802, wo von Karls sorgsam bedachten Maßnahmen zur Revision der Gesetzgebung berichtet wird, vom öffentlichen Verlesen und Erläutern bis hin zum Emendieren auch der weltlichen Rechte ('leges') und ihrer schriftlichen Fixierung mit dem Ziel: '... ut iudices per scriptum iudicassent et munera non accepissent, sed omnes homines, pauperes et divites, in regno suo iustitiam habuissent'; zitiert nach Wien, Österreichische Nationalbibliothek, MS 515, fo 5r: *Das Wiener Fragment der Lorscher Annalen ... Facsimileausgabe*, ed. Franz Unterkircher, Codices selecti, 15 (Graz, 1967), 41; ältere Ausgabe ed. Georg Heinrich Pertz, *MGH SS*, 1 (Hannover, 1826), 39. Die wohl vom Capitulare generale

Gastrecht sei jedem ohne Ansehen der Person zu gewähren: 'Ut infra regna Christo propitio nostra omnibus iterantibus nullus hospitium deneget ...',[29] oder mit eigener Nennung wieder der Armen: 'Ut hospites et peregrini omnesque iterantes et pauperes benignam susceptionem habeant et nemo iteranti hospitium denegare presumat'.[30] Solche zum Teil wörtlich sich gleichende Bestimmungen stützen wiederum die mittelalterliche, von Boretius akzeptierte Interpretation. Trotzdem bleibt eine gewisse Unsicherheit darüber, wie der Satz einst wirklich ausgesehen haben mag.

War die 5-Bücher-Sammlung für das Verständnis von c. 27 des Capitulare generale schon hilfreich genug, so entscheidet sie das Problem definitiv in c. 22, wo vom vorschriftsmäßigen Leben der Kanoniker die Rede ist: 'Canonici autem pleniter vitam obserbent canonicam ... non per vicos neque per villas ad ecclesiam vini vel terminantes sine magisterio vel disciplina, qui sarabaiti dicuntur ...', heißt es im Parisinus.[31] Die bisherigen Herausgeber rätselten, was mit 'vini vel terminantes' gemeint sein könne. Sie dachten an 'vicini vel terminantes' (so Baluze[32] und Pertz[33]) bzw. 'vicinas vel terminantes' (so Boretius[34]), kamen damit dem Redaktor aber nicht auf die Schliche. Auch die Konjektur blieb für den Übersetzer schwer verständlich: 'Kanoniker ... sollen nicht ohne Aufsicht durch Dörfer und Gutshöfe zu den nahen und entfernteren Kirchen gehen wie die sogenannten Wandermönche ...'.[35] Wie das? Antwort gibt der Autor der 5-Bücher-Sammlung mit der Lesung: 'singuli vel bini vel terni manentes'[36] statt 'vini vel terminantes'. Der Parisinus-Text entledigte sich also der ersten zwei Worte und vereinte die letzten zwei zu einem neuen ganz anderer Bedeutung. Kein Wunder, dass sich

---

angeregte Einteilung der Menschen in Arme und Reiche—der Annalist kannte das Kapitular und nannte die Armen doch an erster Stelle—wäre für unser Problem von Interesse, wenn der Beleg nicht in einem andersartigen Ambiente und in einer zum Vergleich ungeeigneten Satzkonstruktion auftreten würde. Zumindest aber bestätigt er, dass das problematischere 'dives/divitibus' nicht erst durch die Umbildung eines unbekannten anderen Wortes 'entstanden', sondern schon vor der Generalredaktion fester Bestandteil des Textes gewesen ist.

29 *Capitula omnibus cognita facienda (802/813)*, c. 1, *MGH Capitularia*, i, 144.

30 Der Text stammt aus einem der letzten Kapitularien Karls des Großen, entstanden 813 im Zusammenhang einer erneuten Reformoffensive des Kaisers, c. 27, ed. Mordek-Schmitz, 'Neue Kapitularien und Kapitulariensammlungen', 420; wiederabgedruckt in Mordek, *Studien zur fränkischen Herrschergesetzgebung*, 140, mit Hinweis auf weitere Parallelstellen, und in Mordek, *Bibliotheca capitularium*, 993. Als Vorbild diente *Admonitio generalis*, c. 75, *MGH Capitularia*, i, 60: '... ut hospites, peregrini et pauperes susceptiones regulares et canonicas per loca diversa habeant ...'.

31 MS Paris BN lat. 4613, fo 88r.

32 *Capitulare generale*, c. 22, ed. Baluze, *Capitularia*, i, 370.

33 *Capitulare generale*, c. 22, ed. Pertz, *MGH LL*, i, 94.

34 *Capitulare generale*, c. 22, ed. Boretius, *MGH Capitularia*, i, 96.

35 Alfred Baumgartner (Übersetzer), in Jacques Delperrié de Bayac, *Karl der Große*, Heyne-Buch, 5598 (München, 1979), 298-9 (Anhang Text V).

36 *Collectio canonum V librorum*, 2.15.1, *CCCM*, 6.188.

niemand einen Reim aus der Sache machen konnte; genau dies aber hat der 'Täter' gewollt. Mit dem Ersatz des Buchstabens 'b' durch 'v', einer im Romanischen häufig anzutreffenden Erscheinung,[37] war zudem aus 'bini' verständniser-schwerend 'vini' geworden: Unser 'vini' hat also weder etwas mit Nachbarn zu tun, noch sollte man es gedanklich mit einem guten Tropfen Wein in Verbindung bringen[38]. Es galt vielmehr, den als Singles oder in Zweier- und Dreiergruppen hausenden Kanonikern scharf entgegenzutreten. Der Vergleich mit den verrufenen Sarabaiten, die der Ordensgründer Benedikt gleich in Kapitel 1 seiner Regel als Abschaum des Mönchtums auf den vorletzten Rang verwiesen hatte,[39] aber immerhin noch vor den Gyrovagen, sollte wohl weiterer Anstoß für sie sein, mit einem solch unwürdigen Leben zu brechen.

Für den kritischen Herausgeber des Kapitulars bedeutet die vorgetragene, aus der Rezeptionsgeschichte gewonnene Klärung der Korruptel in c. 27 zweifellos, dass ihm ein Festhalten am Parisinus nicht mehr 'als klügliches Bewahren des gerade noch Verständlichen'[40] ausgelegt werden kann. Hier muss er das für Unikate gern tolerierte Prinzip der 'Handschriftenanbetung'[41] verlassen und der korrekten, wenn auch nur von zweiter Hand gesicherten Form den Vorzug geben. Zugleich ist jetzt bewiesen: Vor der erhaltenen existierte eine andere Fassung der Collectio Thuana, die noch mehr oder weniger frei war von fatalen Verunstal-tungen. Der gleichmäßig geschriebene, mit Schmuckinitialen versehene und äußer-lich wenig korrigierte Text der Handschrift[42] lässt eher an eine ordentliche Ab- oder Reinschrift denken,[43] als dass er uns einen Einblick eröffnete in ein Stadium

---

37 Auch umgekehrt kann 'v' zu 'b' werden, siehe z. B. gleich am Anfang unseres c. 22: 'obserbent' statt 'observent'. Zu den Phonemen 'b' und 'v' etwa Mario A. Pei, *The Language of the Eighth-Century Texts in Northern France: a study of the original documents in the Collection of Tardif and other sources* (New York, 1932), 94-6; Veikko Väänänen, *Introduction au latin vulgaire*, Bibliothèque française et romane, Sér. A: Manuels et études linguistiques, 6, 3. Auflage (Paris, 1981), 50-51.

38 Ob es der Redaktor tat, bleibe dahingestellt. In c. 17 unseres Kapitulars assoziierte er 'alium' jedenfalls gleich mit 'olium' (= 'oleum'?): MS Paris BN lat. 4613, fo 86v und *MGH Capitularia*, i, 94. Wein und Öl gehören nun einmal zu jeder guten italienischen Küche.

39 *Benedicti Regula*, c. 1, ed. Rudolphus [Rudolf] Hanslik, *CSEL*, 75 (Wien 1960), 18, mit wörtlichen Anklängen: 'Tertium uero monachorum teterrimum genus est sarabaitarum, qui ... bini aut terni aut certe singuli sine pastore, non dominicis, sed suis inclusi obilibus pro lege eis est desideriorum uoluptas ...'. Auf c. 1 der Benediktregel bezog sich schon das *Duplex capitulare missorum*, c. 1, *MGH Capitularia*, i, 63, Nr. 23.

40 Karl Stackmann, 'Grundsätzliches über die Methode der altgermanistischen Edition', in *Texte und Varianten: Probleme ihrer Edition und Interpretation*, ed. Gunter Martens-Hans Zeller (München 1971), 293-9, hier 296.

41 *Ibid.*

42 Zum Codex siehe auch oben Anm. 4 und 5.

43 Der laufende Text ist offensichtlich von einer kräftigen Hand geschrieben, deren oben Anm. 4 notierte Eigenheiten sich mehr oder weniger auf allen Seiten des Manuskripts zeigen. Ob einige Seiten, die bei unterschiedlicher Größe unserer Kopien einen anderen Gesamteindruck vermitteln, nicht doch von einer zweiten, sehr ähnlichen Hand stammen, wäre noch am Original zu

der Revision.[44] Wie die Vorlage, so wäre demnach auch das anzunehmende Werksexemplar des Überarbeiters als verloren zu betrachten.

Wir haben es schon angedeutet: Das Weiterleben des Aachener Capitulare generale von 802 vollzog sich im Mittelalter vor allem über die 5-Bücher-Sammlung und deren mannigfache Derivate.[45] Damit aber verengte sich die Kenntnis des Stückes—abgesehen von der mager verbreiteten Vollform—auf wenige der insgesamt 39 (40) Kapitel.[46]

Es gibt nun ein weiteres, bislang unbekanntes Exzerpt unseres Kapitulars, das sich als Addendum in der mittelitalienischen Burchard-Handschrift Vatikan, Biblioteca Apostolica Vaticana, Vat. lat. 7790 wohl aus dem ersten Viertel des zwölften Jahrhunderts[47] gefunden hat. Dort sind in einer Lücke zwischen Dekret 8.38 und 8.49[48] die Kapitel 14 und 15 des Capitulare generale[49] von einer etwas jüngeren, gleichfalls italienischen Hand des 12. Jahrhunderts kopiert. Die Kapitel fehlen in

---

verifizieren. Des weiteren bleibt unklar, in welchem italienischen Skriptorium der Codex entstanden ist.

44 Deutliche Merkmale einer Redaktion wie zahlreiche Korrekturen, Rasuren und Zusätze zeigt etwa noch der nach 855 gleichfalls in Oberitalien verfertigte Wolfenbüttel, Herzog August Bibliothek, MS Blankenb. 130, der eine der größten italienischen Leges- und Kapulariensammlungen der späten Karolingerzeit bewahrt hat, vgl. Mordek, *Bibliotheca capitularium*, 920-43.

45 Reynolds in den Anm. 19 zitierten Arbeiten, passim.

46 Die Kapitelzahl hängt davon ab, ob die Schlussermahnung des Herrschers mitnummeriert wird oder nicht. Im Parisinus bleiben außer dem letzten weitere sechs Kapitel ohne Zählung, so dass der gesamte Text nur in 33 Kapitel eingeteilt ist.

47 Vgl. Hubert Mordek, 'Handschriftenforschungen in Italien: I. Zur Überlieferung des Dekrets Bischof Burchards von Worms', *QF*, 51 (1972), 626-51, hier 640-41, 648, wo der Codex 'saec. XII¹' datiert ist. Für die paläographisch verwandte Burchard-Handschrift Rom, Biblioteca Vallicelliana, A 20 hat E. B. Garrison, *Studies in the History of Mediaeval Italian Painting*, iii/3-4 (Florenz, 1958), 287 und iv/2 (Florenz, 1961), 199 umbrisch-römische Entstehung im ersten Viertel des 12. Jahrhunderts angenommen.

48 Der Text von 8.38 bricht fo 85ra nach 9 Zeilen mit 'cohabitare tecto' ab und beginnt wieder fo 85rb oben in 8.49 mit 'valeat custodiri'; den fehlenden Text ed. Gérard Fransen-Theo Kölzer, *Burchard von Worms, Decretorum libri XX*, (Aalen, 1992; ergänzter Neudruck der Editio princeps Köln 1548,), fos 118ra-119vb; auch *PL* 140.799C-802D. Der wohl von der Vorlage übernommene Leerraum hätte auf keinen Fall für den Nachtrag der fehlenden Burchard-Kapitel gereicht, das Kapitularienexzerpt ließ dagegen immer noch ca. 16-17 Zeilen der linken Spalte frei. Wer die Kapitel hinzufügte, hat sich demnach bewusst auf diese beiden beschränkt.—Die Auslassung zwischen Burchard 8.38 und 49 ist Merkmal eines bestimmten Zweiges der Dekret-Überlieferung, dessen Vertreter meist aus Italien stammen, vgl. Gérard Fransen, 'Le Décret de Burchard', in Fransen-Köhler, *Burchard von Worms*, 25-42, hier 34-6. Der Autor hatte seine Forschungsergebnisse schon früher ausführlicher publiziert: G. Fransen, 'Le Décret de Burchard de Worms: Valeur du texte de l'édition. Essai de classement des manuscrits', *ZRG KA*, 63 (1977), 1-19.

49 *MGH Capitularia*, i, 94. Auch in anderen Burchard-Codices, welche die Lücke zeigen, sind Texte nachgetragen, vgl. etwa zu Modena, Biblioteca Capitolare, MS O. II. 15; Jörg W. Busch, *Der Liber de Honore Ecclesiae des Placidus von Nonantola: Eine kanonistische Problemerörterung aus dem Jahre 1111. Die Arbeitsweise ihres Autors und seine Vorlagen*, Quellen und Forschungen zum Recht im Mittelalter, 5 (Sigmaringen 1990), 80 mit Anm. 20.

der 5-Bücher-Sammlung, sie müssen ihren Text also aus einer anderen Quelle bezogen haben.

Dass sie gerade an dieser freien Stelle des Vaticanus nachgetragen sind, dürfte kaum Zufall sein. Offenbar interessierte sich der Dekret-Benutzer besonders für das Thema von Buch 8 'De viris ac feminis Deo dicatis',[50] auch unser Füllsel hat einen Schwerpunkt im monastischen Bereich. Die Texte in Parallele:[51]

Paris BN lat. 4613, fos 85v-86r	Vatikan, BAV, Vat. lat. 7790, fo 85ra
XIIII	
Ut episcopi, abbates adque abbatisse comite	Ut episcopi, abbates adque abbatisse comite
que unanim invicem sint consentientes	que **unianimiter** invicem sint consentientes
legem ad iudicium iustum terminandum	legem ad iudicium iustum terminandum
cum omni caritate et concordia pacis et ut	cum omni caritate et concordia pacis et ut
fideliter vivant secundum voluntate dei ut	fideliter vivant secundum **voluntatem** dei ut
semper ubique et propter illos et inter illos	semper ubique et propter illos et inter illos
iustum iudicium **ibique** perficiantur.	iustum iudicium **ubique** perficiantur (ci
pauperes, vidue, **orphani** et	über der Zeile). pauperes, vidue, **orfani** et
peregrini consolationem adque	peregrini consolationem adque
de**confessionem** hab eis habent ut et nos per	de**fensionem** hab eis habent ut et nos per
eorum bona voluntatem magis **premium**	eorum bona voluntatem magis **premiunt**
vite ęterne quam supplicium mereamur.	vitę eternę quam supplicium mereamur.
Abbates autem et monachis omnis **modis**	abbates autem et monachis **omnimodis**
volumus et precipimus ut episcopis suis	volumus et precipimus ut episcopis suis
omni humilitate et **hobhedientia** sint	omni humilitate et **obedientia** sint
subiecti, sicut canonica constitutione	subiecti, sicut canonica **constitutionem**
mandat. et omnis eclesie adque basilice	mandat. Et **omnes ecclesię** adque basilice
in eclesiastica defensione et potestatem	in **ecclesiastica defensionem** et potestatem
permaneat. et de rebus ipse basilice nemo	permaneat. et de rebus ipse basilice nemo
ausus sit in divisione aut in **sorte** mittere.	ausus sit in divisione aut in **sortes** mittere.
et quod semel offeritur, non revolvatur et	et quod semel offeritur, non revolvatur et
sanctificat et vindicet. et si autem aliter	sanctificat et vindicet. et si autem aliter
presumpserit, presolvatur et bannum	presumpserit, presolvatur et bannum
nostrum **conponat**.	(nostrum **radiert) ab episcopo** componat.
et monachi ab episcopo provincie ipsius	et monachi ab episcopo provincie ipsius
corripiantur. quod si se non emendent,	corripiantur. quod si se non emendent,
tunc archiepiscopis eos ad sinodum	**excommunicentur.**
convocet. et si neque sic consurrexerint,	
tunc ad nostra presentiam simul cum	
episcopo suo veniant.	

---

50 Ed. Fransen-Kölzer, *Burchard von Worms*, fos 113r-124r; auch *PL* 140.787-812.
51 Beide Texte werden ohne Konjekturen so wiedergegeben, wie sie in den Manuskripten stehen. Unterschiede sind durch Fettdruck kenntlich gemacht.

Der auf der rechten Spalte wiedergegebene Auszug bietet das Paradigma einer weiteren Nutzungsvariante der Vorlage: Sie wird nicht, wie vielfach im Parisinus nachgewiesen, bis zur Sinnlosigkeit verunstaltet, sie wird vielmehr bewusst modifiziert und erhält so zum Teil eine neue, gegenwartsaktuelle Bedeutung. Doch paraphrasieren wir vorab den Gesamtinhalt.

Zu Beginn ergeht an Bischöfe, Äbte, Äbtissinnen und Grafen der Appell, einmütig in Liebe und Eintracht gemäß dem Gesetz und nach dem Willen Gottes miteinander zu leben, damit unter ihnen 'immer und überall' Gerechtigkeit herrsche. Sie sollten sich besonders um Arme, Witwen, Waisen und Fremde kümmern, das heißt, um die Schwachen und Wehrlosen in der Gesellschaft—keine billige Floskel, sah doch der Gesetzgeber im Vollzug der Vorschriften sein eigenes Seelenheil mit eingeschlossen. Die Verquickung von allgemeinem und persönlichem Wohl musste für alle Angesprochenen ein dauernder Ansporn sein, auch im Sinne der Anweisungen zu handeln.

Die beiden Überlieferungen unterscheiden sich im ersten Teil nur geringfügig, ja sie gleichen sich zuweilen bis ins Detail: 'adque' statt 'atque', 'comite que' statt 'comitesque', 'hab eis' statt 'ab eis' und weitere Wendungen im zweiten Teil (vor allem 'presolvatur' statt des zu erwartenden 'persolvatur') verdeutlichen ihre enge Verwandtschaft und könnten im Parisinus sogar die unmittelbare Vorlage für das Vaticanus-Exzerpt vermuten lassen. Kleinere Zurechtrückungen wie 'unianimiter' statt 'unanim' und 'ubique' statt 'ibique' drängen sich dem Benutzer geradezu auf. Und wieder einmal findet eine Konjektur von Baluze ihre glänzende Bestätigung:[52] 'consolationem adque defensionem' ist korrekt, nicht 'consolationem adque deconfessionem', wie der Parisinus will.

Der von Boretius als c. 15 gedruckte, in beiden Texten aber nicht eigens nummerierte zweite Teil des Kapitels[53] spricht gleich drei große Themen an. Äbte und Mönche haben sich ihren Bischöfen gemäß den Kanones in aller Demut und in bedingungslosem Gehorsam zu unterwerfen. Sämtliche Kirchen und Basiliken sollten in kirchlicher Hand bleiben. Und schließlich geht es um das Kirchengut; es dürfe weder geteilt noch vereinnahmt, auch nicht zurückgefordert oder sonst irgendwie geschädigt werden. Wer das Verbot übertritt, müsse dafür zahlen und 'unseren Bann' entrichten. 'nos', '-mur', '-mus', 'nostrum'—die durchgängige wir-Form mochte den mittelalterlichen Leser nach dem Autor der nachgetragenen Sätze fragen lassen, dessen Name an keiner Stelle genannt wird. Dass im 12. Jahrhundert außer vielleicht dem Exzerptor noch viele andere auf Karl den Großen getippt hätten, wage ich zu bezweifeln. Die Macht, über hohe kirchliche Amtsträger ebenso wie über staatliche zu gebieten, und nun die Banngewalt verrieten aber fraglos einen weltlichen Herrscher als Urheber, den König. Unser

---

52 Ed. Baluze, *Capitularia*, i, 366.
53 *MGH Capitularia*, i, 94.

Kopist scheint dies gespürt zu haben: Das Wort 'nostrum' bei 'bannum' störte ihn offenbar noch während des Schreibens, denn die folgende Einfügung 'ab episcopo' ist im laufenden Text platziert und als solche gar nicht mehr zu erkennen. Dann (wann?) wurde 'nostrum' radiert. Nicht ganz ausschließen möchte ich die Möglichkeit, der Schreiber habe das drei Worte später folgende 'ab episcopo' (irrigerweise) nochmals in den Text gezogen. Sollte dies nicht zutreffen, wäre die Tendenz der Änderung eindeutig: weg von der königlichen, hin zur bischöflichen Gewalt als zuständiger Instanz in Kirchengutsfragen.

Und in die gleiche Richtung zielen die Schlusssätze, deren Thematik zum Anfang des zweiten Teils zurücklenkt. Erneut werden die Mönche der Aufsicht ihres Bischofs unterstellt. Wenn sie sich nicht besserten, so Karl der Große, dann solle sie der Erzbischof zur Synode zusammenrufen. Und sollte auch dies nicht helfen, (erst) dann gestattet ihnen das Gesetz den Gang zum König, und zwar zusammen mit dem Bischof. Der hier vorgeschriebene Rechtsweg ist keine Neuerung. In Anlehnung an Pippins des Jüngeren Kapitular von Ver (755)[54] hatte Karl schon in Frankfurt 794 einen ähnlichen Beschluss gefasst[55]—ob seine Novellierung die Folgerung erlaubt, er sei nicht so eingehalten worden, wie vom Herrscher erwartet?

Das Exzerpt jedenfalls trennt sich am Ende des Textes entschieden von seiner Vorlage. Es verzichtet radikal auf den gesamten Instanzenzug. Mönche, die den Vorhaltungen des Bischofs nicht folgten, seien zu exkommunizieren—so der lakonische Bescheid: 'Quod si se non emendent, excommunicentur'.

Das ist nicht mehr der alte Geist prosperierender Zusammenarbeit zwischen Herrscher und hohem Klerus, wie er die Politik der Karolinger und insbesondere Karls des Großen bestimmte. Der Investiturstreit des 11. und 12. Jahrhunderts, in dessen auslaufende Phase unser Text fallen dürfte, machte viele Kirchenführer selbstbewusst. Als Ausdruck dieser neugewonnenen Stärke erscheint uns die Redaktion des Kapitularienauszugs wohl von bischöflicher oder bischofsfreundlicher Hand in dem Dekret-Codex Vat. lat. 7790 Burchards von Worms.

Ende des Kaleidoskops der Textvarianten, Ende unserer Hommage an Roger E. Reynolds—Was fehlt, ist noch das Resümee.

Wir sahen, wie jede Art von brauchbarer Zweitüberlieferung besonders für Unikate verständnisfördernd, ja problemklärend sein kann, ob es sich nun um eine vollständige Handschrift handelt oder um ein Fragment, um eine Teilrezeption wie jene des Capitulare generale von 802 durch die 5-Bücher-Sammlung oder um ein einzelnes Exzerpt. Auch der zuletzt vorgestellte Kapitulariennachtrag in Burchards Dekret bezeugt den hohen Wert der Tradition. Er ist zwar nicht inskribiert, seine

---

54 *Concilium Vernense*, c. 5, *MGH Capitularia*, i, 34, Nr. 14.
55 *Synodus Franconofurtensis*, c. 6, *MGH Capitularia*, i, 74-5, Nr. 28.

Provenienz dürfte dem damals weniger kundigen Leser, ich sagte es schon,[56] verborgen geblieben sein, zumal in einer Kirchenrechtssammlung des frühen 11. Jahrhunderts als Nachtrag des 12. Jahrhunderts nicht unbedingt ein Text aus der weltlichen Gesetzgebung der Karolingerzeit zu erwarten war. Aber er hilft uns Heutigen trotzdem, durch Bestätigung der singulären Vorlage oder durch indirekte Aufforderung zur Korrektur. Freilich, zwischen der Entstehung des Kapitulars und seiner hochmittelalterlichen Nutzung waren über drei Jahrhunderte vergangen, die Welt hatte sich gründlich verändert. Und dieser Wandel des Makrokosmos, so gewahrten wir, fand seinen drastischen Niederschlag auch im Mikrokosmos des veralteten Gesetzes Kaiser Karls des Großen.

Nicht (nur) freudiger Jagd- und Spürsinn lässt Gelehrte immer wieder auf die Suche nach verlorenen Handschriften gehen. Jeder noch so bescheiden scheinende neue Traditionszeuge kann uns ein kleines Stück weiterführen in der rechten Erkenntnis einer lange vergangenen Zeit.

---

56 Siehe oben S. 181.

Chapter 11

Creed Commentary Collections
in Carolingian Manuscripts

Susan Ann Keefe

Some years ago I began a project to identify and catalogue creed commentaries and explanations of the faith in Carolingian manuscripts.[1] Although the catalogue is far from exhaustive, it does permit a picture of the tradition of interpretation of the faith under the Carolingians that contradicts any idea of a uniform catechesis or a generally agreed upon corpus of texts to explain the creed.[2] This may seem surprising, considering that instruction on the creed to the people was a primary mandate of clerical reform legislation, and the leaders of the reform sought to create unity in other fundamental guides for the lives of the faithful by establishing model texts.[3]

Most often, instruction on the creed consists of a selection of works of various authors strung together in one section of a manuscript. These 'creed commentary collections', as I have termed them, are the focus of this article. Little attention has been paid to the creed commentary collection as an expression of Carolingian creativity in passing on the *fides recta*. One feature of the collections as a whole is the wide range of works employed by their compilers. Beyond obvious creed commentaries (phrase-by-phrase expositions on a creed text and etymological or historical explanations of the word 'symbolum'), they assembled snippets of, or entire, patristic and Carolingian

---

1   The catalogue is forthcoming as *Inuentarium symbolorum, expositionum et explanationum fidei in codicibus Karolini aeui* (Turnhout). I wish to express my deepest thanks to Roger Reynolds for the inspiration of this project and his continued assistance in alerting me to texts and MSS.

2   By 'the creed' I refer to any of the four explicated, the Apostles', original Nicene, Nicene-Constantino-politan, and Athanasian, including variations of the *textus receptus* form of them. By 'the faith' I refer to the articles of belief contained in the creeds.

3   For legislation on the creed, see *MGH Capitularia*, ed. Alfredus Boretius and Victor Kraus, 2 vols (Hanover, 1883-97), i, 59, 61-2: *Admonitio generalis*, 789, cc. 70, 82; i, 77: *Synodus Franconofurtensis*, 794, c. 33; i, 103: *Capitulare missorum item speciale*, 802?, cc. 28-30; i, 106: *Capitula a sacerdotibus proposita*, 802, c. 5; i, 110: *Capitula de examinandis ecclesiasticis*, 802, cc. 8-9; also Susan A. Keefe, *Water and the Word: baptism and the education of the clergy in the Carolingian empire*, 2 vols (Notre Dame, 2002), i, 14. On model texts to promote uniformity in intellectual and religious matters, see Roger Reynolds, 'Unity and Diversity in Carolingian Canon Law Collections: the case of the *Collectio Hibernensis* and its derivatives', in *Carolingian Essays: Andrew W. Mellon lectures in early Christian studies*, ed. Uta-Renate Blumenthal (Washington, D. C., 1983), 99-100. On a corpus of texts given to guide clergy in their teaching, see Rosamond McKitterick, *The Frankish Church and the Carolingian Reforms, 789-895* (London, 1977), 14.

works of many literary genres. A second feature is the great variety of combinations of these works in individual collections. Rarely is any creed commentary collection completely replicated in a second manuscript, although it may be partially replicated and supplemented with other works.

I give here, first, a list of the works used in Carolingian creed commentary collections identified to date; following it, a list of the creed commentary collections themselves, with the manuscript(s) in which each collection is found. To show the extent of the individuality of the collections, any partially-identical collections are grouped together. To save space and repetition in the second list, the works comprising each creed commentary collection are identified by their number (in bold) from the first list.[4] In the second part of this article the possible role that canon law collections played in supplying texts for the compilers of the creed commentary collections will be considered. Thus, an asterisk following the work indicates that the work also exists in a canon law collection.

---

4   This number is the number of the work in *Inuentarium*; the present list does not include all the items in the inventory. There the MSS are described in full. Generally one can recognize a creed commentary collection, understood as a deliberate combination of sometimes quite diverse works, by one or more of the following characteristics: the presence in the collection of a creed exposition in the strict sense of a phrase-by-phrase explanation of a creed text; the collection's position in the MS immediately before or after, or in between, commentaries on baptism, the Lord's Prayer, the mass, or other liturgical commentaries; the MS book as a whole, which was intended as a clerical-education reader, containing instruction on the items listed in Carolingian capitularies that every priest must be able to explain, including the creed (see my *Water and the Word*, i, 23-6); a title, such as 'De symbolo', preceding the collection. The largest creed commentary collection, in Karlsruhe, Badische Landesbibliothek, MS Aug. XVIII, written by Reginbert of Reichenau *c*. 806, was described by him in his catalogue of books at Reichenau in 821: 'Deinde super symbolum apostolorum quamplurimorum orthodoxorum tractationes cum caeteris de fide tractantibus diverso modo explanationibus'; see Paul Lehmann, ed., *Mittelalterliche Bibliothekskataloge Deutschlands und der Schweiz*, 2 vols (Munich, 1918-28; repr. 1969), i: *Die Bistümer Konstanz und Chur*, 258.

List of Works in Creed Commentary Collections[5]

1	Augustinus, *Sermo de symbolo ad catechumenos*; *CPL* 309; CAP-typum.
2	Ignotus, *De caelesti generatione*; breuis EF.
3b	Ps.-Vigilius, Ps.-Athanasius, *De Trinitate libri XII*, 11; cf. *CPL* 105; DF.
4	Valerianus episcopus Calagoritanus, *Fides S. Valeriani*; *CPL* 558a; breuis PF.
6	Ignotus, *Sermo de symbolo et uirtutibus*; EF.
7	Rufinus, *Apologia ad Anastasium*; *CPL* 198; PF.
8	Ignotus, *Sententiae sanctorum Patrum*; *CPL* 1754; EF.
9	Dubie Hilarius episcopus Arelatensis, *Expositio de fide catholica*; *CPL* 505; CAP-typum.
10	Isidorus, *Origines*, 7.1-4; EF.
10b*	Benedictus abbas Anianensis, *Opuscula, I*; cf. *CSLMA* i, 224 sq., BENA 20; prolixa DF/EF.
11	Ignotus, *Damnatio blasphemiae Arii et expositio integrae et catholicae fidei*; DF.
12	Ps.-Fulgentius, Ps.-Augustinus, *Testimonia de fide catholica* (siue *Aduersus Pintam Arianum*), duo excerpta; cf. *CPL* 843; DF/EF.
13	Ambrosius, *Explanatio symboli ad initiandos*; *CPL* 153; CAP.
14	Theodulfus episcopus Aurelianensis, *De ordine baptismi ad Magnum Senonensem liber*, 7; CAP-typum.
16	Boethius, *De fide catholica*; *CPL* 893; EF.
17	Ps.-Augustinus, *Symbolum 'Clemens Trinitas'*; *CPL* 1748; PF.
20*	Concilium Toletanum XI (an. 675), *Symbolum*; cf. sub *CPL* 111e; PF.
22*	Ps.-Vigilius, Ps.-Athanasius, *De Trinitate libri XII*, 10; cf. sub *CPL* 105; EF.
25	Augustinus, *De Ciuitate Dei*, 11.24; cf. *CPL* 313; PF.

---

5   In this list, the title is the title given the work in the following repertories, or, if the work is not in these, the title given it by its editor. If the work is unedited, I give its title in the codex, or, that lacking, my own descriptive title for **2, 6, 44, 46, 58, 95, 96, 132, 141, 143aa, 147a, 154, 195, 204b, 221aa, 242**.

   CPL = *Clauis patrum Latinorum,* ed. Eligius Dekkers, 3rd edn (Steenbrugge, 1995);

   CPPM = *Clavis patristica pseudepigraphorum medii aeui,* ed. Iohannes Machielsen, 2 vols (Turnhout, 1990, 1994);

   CSLMA = *Clauis scriptorum Latinorum medii aeui,* ed. Marie-Hélène Jullien and Françoise Perelman, 2 vols (Turnhout, 1994, 1999).

   Abbreviations for the genre or types of each work are as follows:

   CAP = Commentary on the Apostles' Creed in a phrase by phrase manner.

   CAP-typum = Commentary on a variation of the Apostles' Creed (not precisely the *textus receptus*) in a phrase-by-phrase manner.

   CNIC = Commentary on the Nicene Creed (original) in a phrase-by-phrase manner;

   CN-typum = Commentary on a variation of the *textus receptus* form of the Nicene-Constantino-politan Creed in a phrase-by-phrase manner;

   CAT = Commentary on the Athanasian Creed in a phrase-by-phrase manner;

   EF = Explanation of the Faith (for example, a definition of the word 'symbolum', a sermon, letter, treatise or extract explaining some aspect of the creedal faith);

   PF = Profession of Faith (a creed of a council or a personal confession of faith);

   DF = Defense of the Faith (for example, a polemical tract, synodal decree, list of anathemas, dialogue with a heretic);

   interr./respon. = questions and responses.

26   Pelagius, *Libellus fidei ad Innocentium papam*; CPL 731; PF.
30   Ps.-Hieronymus, *'Fides S. Hieronymi'*; CPL 638; PF.
31   Ps.-Hieronymus, Ps.-Damasus, Ps.-Gregorius Illiberitanus, *Fides Catholica* siue *Fides Damasi*; CPL 554; PF.
32*   Ps.-Phoebadius Agennensis, Ps.-Gregorius Illiberitanus, Ps.-Gregorius Nazianzenus, Ps.-Damasus, *Fides Romanorum*; CPL 552; PF.
33   Ps.-Augustinus, *Sermo 235 (De fide catholica. III)*; CPPM i, A 1020; PF.
34a   Carolus Magnus, *Epistola ad Elipandum et episcopos Hispaniae*, excerptum; PF contra Adoptianos.
35   Ps.-Hieronymus, *Epistola 17 seu Explanatio fidei ad Cyrillum*, siue *Commentarius alter in Symbolum Nicaenum siue potius in Tomum Damasi papae*; CPL 1746; prolixus CNIC.
36*   Concilium Toletanum I (an. 400), *Symbolum*; cf. CPPM ii, A 1325; PF/DF.
38   Alcuinus, *Confessio de Trinitate*; cf. sub *CSLMA* ii, Alc 28; EF.
39*   Gennadius, presbyter Massiliensis, *Liber siue diffinitio ecclesiasticorum dogmatum*; CPL 958; EF.
40a   Ignotus, *Definitio dogmatum ecclesiasticorum eiusdem concilii* (= **39**, cc. 1-32 cum multis uarietatibus).
41   Gennadius, *Liber ecclesiasticorum dogmatum*, 1-5 (uide **39**); EF.
43   Dubie Isaac Iudaeus (fl. *c*. 384), *Expositio fidei catholicae*; CPL 190; PF/EF.
44   Ignotus, *De resurrectione carnis et iudicio nouissimo*; breuissima EF per interr./respon.
46   Ignotus, *Florilegium in symbolum apostolorum*; prolixus CAP.
48a   Ignotus, (sine titulo); CAP(-typum?).
50   Ignotus, *Sermo de symbolo*; CPL 1758; CAP.
52   Ignotus, *Incipit symbolum*; CAP.
55(*) Ps.-Gregorius I papa, *Fides Sancti Gregorii papae* (= Gregorius episcopus Turonensis, *Historiarum libri decem*, 1.Prologus, excerptum); PF.
58   Ignotus, *Florilegium in symbolum apostolorum*; prolixus CAP.
61   Ignotus, *Catholica fides*; CPL 1752a; CN-typum.
62   Ps.-Damasus, Ps.-Gregorius Illiberitanus, Dubius-Hieronymus, *Fides S. Hieronymi*; CPL 553; breuis PF.
63   Ignotus, *Symbolum*; CPL 1752; CN-typum.
64   Ignotus, *Incipit expositio de credulitate*; breuis PF et EF per interr./respon.
64b   Ps.-Vigilius, Ps.-Athanasius, *Contra Arianos dialogus*; CPPM ii, A 1692; DF.
65   Ps.-Maximus Taurinensis, *Homilia 83 in traditione symboli*; CPL 220/hom. 83; CAP-typum.
66   Incertus (Leidradus episcopus Lugdunensis?), *Symboli apostolici explanatio*; CAP.
66aa Cerealis episcopus Castelli Ripensis, *Libellus contra Maximinum Arianum*; CPL 813; EF.
66a   Vigilius episcopus Thapsensis, *Contra Arianos, Sabellianos, Photinianos dialogus libri tres*; CPL 807; DF.
67   Ps.-Augustinus, *De unitate s. Trinitatis dialogus*; CPL 379; EF per interr./respon.
69a   Quoduultdeus episcopus Carthaginensis, *Aduersus quinque haereses*; CPL 410; DF.
73   Alcuinus, *De Trinitate ad Fredegisum quaestiones 28*; CSLMA ii, ALC 36; EF.
73a   Fausti Reiensis discipulus anonymus, *De mysterio s. Trinitatis*; CPL 980; EF.
75   Ps.-Alcuinus, *Disputatio puerorum*, 11, pars prima; CSLMA ii, ALC 42; CAP-typum.
76   Ignotus, *Interrogatio de fide catholica*; CPL 1755; EF per interr./respon.

78 Ps.-Alcuinus, *Disputatio puerorum*, 11, pars altera; *CSLMA* ii, ALC 42; EF et CAP.

80* Athanasius, *Epistola ad Epictetum Corinthiorum episcopum, contra eos qui de domini incarnatione spiritu blasphemiae diuersa sensuerunt*; DF.

84 Fulgentius episcopus Ruspensis, *Epistola (8)* siue *Liber ad Donatum de fide orthodoxa et diuersis erroribus haereticorum*; *CPPM* ii, A 189; EF.

85* Cyrillus episcopus Alexandrinus, *Epistola ad Iohannem Antiochenum episcopum*; DF/PF.

85b* Cyrillus episcopus Alexandrinus, *Epistola tertia synodica directa Nestorio Constantinopolitanae urbis episcopo, duodecim continens anathematum capitula*; DF.

88 Ignotus, *Sermo de symbolo*; *CPL* 1759; EF et CAP-typum.

89 Quoduultdeus, *Sermo 3 de symbolo ad catechumenos*; *CPL* 403; CAP-typum.

91* Ps.-Nestorius, *Exemplar expositionis falsitatis fidei Nestorii*, siue *Symbolum Nestorianum*; EF.

92 Fulgentius, *De fide ad Petrum*; *CPL* 826; EF.

95 Ignotus, *Interrogationes in fidem*; EF per interr./resp.

96 Ignotus, *Interrogationes de Trinitate et duabus in Christo natiuitatibus, operationibus, uoluntatibus, et formis*; EF per interr./resp.

96a Dubie Vigilius Thapsensis, *Contra Felicianum Arianum de unitate Trinitatis liber I*; *CPL* 808; DF.

97 Isidorus, *Sententiarum libri tres*, 1.21; EF.

99 Ignotus, *Professio fidei*; PF episcopi priusquam consecratur.

102 Ps.-Eusebius Emesenus ('Gallicanus'), *Homilia 2, de symbolo (2)*; cf. *CPL* 966; CAP.

102a Ps.-Eusebius Vercellensis, Ps.-Augustinus, Ps.-Athanasius, *Expositio fidei S. Augustini episcopi*; *CPPM* ii, A 196; (= PF concilii Cordubensis an. 839).

105 Fulgentius Ruspensis, *Epistola ad Faustinum*, excerptum; cf. *CPL* 817a; EF.

105b Agnellus episcopus Rauennatensis, *Epistola de ratione fidei ad Arminium*; *CPL* 949; EF contra Arianos.

108 Ps.-Ambrosius, *Exhortatio ad neophytos de symbolo*; CAP-typum.

109 Isidorus, *De ecclesiasticis officiis*, 2.24 (De regula fidei); EF.

111* Dionysius Exiguus?, *Annotatio symbolo Nicaeno*; breuis EF.

113* Ps.-Augustinus, *Sermo 238*; *CPL* 368/serm. 238; commentarius in uerbos symboli, 'Et in Iesum Christum filium eius, qui natus est de Spiritu Sancto ex Maria uirgine'.

115 Gregorius episcopus Turonensis, *Historiarum libri decem*, excerpta (5.43-4 et 6.5, 40); DF contra Arianum, Sabellianos, et Iudaeum.

115a Paschasius Radbertus (Ps.-Hieronymus), *Epistola 9 ad Paulam et Eustochium de assumptione Mariae uirginis*, excerpta; cf. *CPPM* ii, A 858; EF.

115b Felix episcopus Orgellitanae, *Confessio fidei*; PF.

115c Ps.-Augustinus, *Testimonia de Patre et Filio et Spiritu Sancto*, siue *Florilegium Fuldense*; *CPL* 386; DF.

116 Alcuinus, *De fide sanctae et indiuiduae Trinitatis libri tres*; *CSLMA* ii, ALC 28; prolixa EF.

117a Ps.-Augustinus, *Sermo 242*, excerptum; CAP.

118 Gennadius, *Liber ecclesiasticorum dogmatum*, 43-5; breuis EF de sexu corporum in resurrectione et praemio animarum.

120 Ps.-Priscillianus episcopus Abilensis, *De Trinitate fidei catholicae*; *CPL* 788; prolixa EF.

122   Ignotus, *Diligentia Armonii et Honorii de libris canonicis*; *CPL* 1757; EF de nominibus
        Christi in sanctis scripturis.
122a   Isidorus, *Differentiarum libri duo*, 2.1-6; EF.
124   Quoduultdeus, *Sermo 4, contra Iudaeos, paganos et Arianos*; *CPL* 404; quasi CAP.
127   Boethius, *Quomodo Trinitas unus Deus ac non tres dii*; *CPL* 890; EF.
131a   Isidorus, *De fide catholica ex uetere et nouo Testamento contra Iudaeos libri duo*; *CPL*
        1198; EF/DF.
132   Ignotus, *Sermo in traditione symboli ad competentes*; EF.
132aaa Ps.-Vigilius, Ps.-Augustinus, *Altercatio cum Pascentio Ariano*; *CPL* 366; DF.
132a*   Leo I papa, *Epistola 28 ad Flauianum ('Tomus Leonis')*; *CPL* 1656/ep. 28; DF.
132c   Ps.-Augustinus, *Dialogus quaestionum 65 Orosii percontantis et Augustini
        respondentis*; *CPL* 373a; EF.
133   Rufinus presbyter Aquileiensis, *Commentarius in symbolum apostolorum*; *CPL* 196;
        CAP-typum.
134   Fulgentius episcopus Ruspensis, *Contra Fabianum* (fragmenta 39 de opere deperdito);
        cf. sub *CPPM* ii, A 752a; EF et CAP-typum.
136   Gregorius episcopus Illiberitanus, Ps.-Ambrosius, Ps.-Phoebadius, Ps.-Vigilius, Ps.-
        Gregorius Nazianzenus, *De fide orthodoxa contra Arianos*; *CPL* 551; prolixus CNIC.
136a   Isidorus, *Origines*, 7.2-4; EF.
136b   Benedictus abbas Anianensis (ob. 821), *Forma fidei*; *CSLMA* i, BENA 14; EF et PF.
137   Ignotus, *Sermo*; CAP-typum.
139aa* Nestorius?, *Nestorii blasphemiarum capitula 12*; DF.
139a   Ps.-Augustinus, *Dialogus quaestionum 65 Orosii percontantis et Augustini
        respondentis*, 1-11; (uide **132c**); EF.
140a   Ps.-Ambrosius, *Fides S. Ambrosii*; *CPPM* ii, A 48; EF.
141   Ignotus, *Professio fidei in Trinitate*; breuis PF.
142   Dubie Lucifer episcopus Calaritanus, *Fides S. Luciferi*; *CPL* 118; breuis PF.
143*   Ps.-Ambrosius, Ps.-Priscillianus, *Fides S. Ambrosii*; *CPL* 789; breuis PF.
143aa   Ignotus, *Sententiae de fide catholica; symbolum apostolorum cum nominibus
        apostolorum; anathema contra Adoptianos*; EF.
143b   Syagrius episcopus Hispanus, *Regulae definitionum contra haereticos prolatae*; *CPL*
        560; prolixa EF.
144   Ignotus, *Cerase opus est* (explanatio philosophica de uerbis symboli, 'ingenitum',
        'genitum', et 'factum'); breuis EF.
144a   Bachiarius Peregrinus, *De fide*; *CPL* 568; PF.
146   Ps.-Ambrosius, Ps.-Hieronymus, Ps.-Augustinus, *De essentia diuinitatis*; *CPPM* ii, A
        35, 172, 205, 863; EF.
147a*   Concilium Toletanum III (an. 589), *Primae 17 anathematae intra confessionem fidei*;
        DF contra Arianos.
150*   Ps.-Augustinus, *Sermo 239*; *CPL* 368/serm. 239; commentarius in uerbos symboli, 'in
        Spiritum Sanctum'.
151*   Ps.-Augustinus, *Sermo 237*; *CPL* 368/serm. 237; commentarius in uerbum symboli,
        'omnipotentem'.
153   Ps.-Hieronymus, *Libellus de Trinitate*; *CPL* 1749; EF.
154   Ignotus, *De duabus in Christo natiuitatibus*; breuis EF.
156*   Ignotus, *Symbolum uel Fides apostolorum* (symbolum cum singulis uersibus attributis
        singulis apostolis); EF.

157   Ignotus, *Expositio symboli* (similis **156**).

160   Leidradus episcopus Lugdunensis, *Liber de sacramento baptismi*, c. 'De credulitate'; EF et CAP-typum.

160a*   Damasus I papa, *Epistola 4*, siue *Confessio fidei*; *CPL* 1633/ep. 4; DF (24 anathematae).

160dd   Ps.-Vigilius Thapsensis, *Solutiones obiectionum Arianorum*; *CPL* 812; DF.

162   Ps.-Faustus Reiensis, Ps.-Eusebius Emesenus ('Gallicanus'), *De symbolo*; *CPL* 977; CAP-typum.

163   Augustinus, *Sermo 214*; *CPL* 284/serm. 214; CAP-typum.

165(*) Mansuetus episcopus Mediolanensis seu Damianus episcopus Ticinensis, *Expositio fidei*; *CPL* 1171; PF synodi Mediolanensis an. 679 contra Monothelitas.

166   Ps.-Maximus Taurinensis, Ps.-Augustinus, *Tractatus [2] de baptismo*; cf. *CPL* 222; *CPPM* i, A 1118. Maxima pars de symbolo ad catechumenos; CAP-typum, ex parte.

167   Boethius, *Vtrum Pater et Filius et Spiritus Sanctus de diuinitate substantialiter praedicentur*; *CPL* 891; EF.

168(*) Ps.-Augustinus, *Sermo 242*; *CPL* 368/serm. 242; CAP-typum.

169   Ignotus, *Sermo antequam symbolum traditur*; EF.

173a*   Ignotus, *Statuta ecclesiae antiqua*, Prologus; cf. *CPL* 1776; PF.

176   Ignotus, '*Commentarius Parisiensis*'; CAT.

176a   Ignotus, *Commentarius in symbolum Athanasianum*; CAT.

177   Fortasse Venantius Fortunatus, *Commentarius Fortunati in symbolum Athanasianum*; *CPL* 1747; CAT.

178   Ignotus, '*Commentarius Trecensis*'; CAT.

183   Ignotus, '*Commentarius Oratorianus*'; CAT.

192   Ignotus, *Interrogatio sacerdotalis*, pars; EF et CAP-typum.

192a   Faustus Reiensis?, *De ratione fidei*; *CPL* 964; EF.

194   Theodulfus episcopus Aurelianensis, *De ordine baptismi ad Magnum Senonensem liber*, c. 6; EF.

195   Ignotus, *Interrogationes de Patre, Filio, Spiritu Sancto, Christo et iudicio nouissimo*; breuis EF.

197   Ignotus, *Item de sancta Trinitate qualiter quisque credat*; breuis PF.

200   Ignotus, *Interrogatio sacerdotalis de fide*. EF de Trinitate et Christo.

201   Augustinus, *De fide et symbolo liber*; *CPL* 293; CAP-typum.

202*   Hieronymus, *Epistola 15 ad Damasum papam*; cf. *CPL* 620; DF.

203   Iunilius (Iunillus) Africanus, *Instituta regularia diuinae legis libri duo*, excerptum; cf. *CPL* 872; EF.

203c   Eugenius episcopus Carthaginensis, *Fides*; *CPL* 799; PF.

204   Ambrosius, *De fide ad Gratianum libri quinque*; *CPL* 150; prolixa PF/EF contra Arianos.

204a   Faustinus presbyter Luciferianus, *De Trinitate, siue de fide contra Arianos*; *CPL* 120; EF.

204b   Augustinus, *Excerpta duo de sancta Trinitate ex Augustino*; EF.

204c*   Cyrillus episcopus Alexandrinus, *Epistola secunda ad Nestorium*; DF.

206   Ignotus, *Expositio fidei*; *CPL* 1763; CAP-typum.

208   Quoduultdeus, *Sermo 1, de symbolo 1*; *CPL* 401; CAP-typum.

209   Quoduultdeus, *Sermo 2, de symbolo 2*; *CPL* 402; CAP-typum.

210   Augustinus, *Sermo 215, in redditione symboli*; *CPL* 368/serm. 215; CAP-typum.

210a   Alcuinus, *Epistola 204*; *CSLMA* ii, ALC 45.204; EF contra Adoptianos per interr./resp.

213   Augustinus, *In Iohannis Euangelium*, Tractatus 29, 6; cf. *CPL* 278; breuis EF de 'credatis in eum' et 'credatis ei'.

218   Augustinus, *De Trinitate*, excerpta; cf. *CPL* 329; EF.

220   Ignotus, *Ordo qualiter symbolum tradere debeant*; CAP-typum.

221   Ps.-Chrysostomus, *Sermo 38* siue *Fides S. Iohannis Chrysostomi*; *CPL* 1750; EF.

221aa* Concilium Bracarense I (an. 561), *Anathematae 17 contra Priscillianos*; cf. sub *CPL* 1786a; DF.

224   Ps.-Eusebius Emesena ('Gallicanus'), *Homilia 9, de symbolo (1)*; cf. *CPL* 966; CAP-typum.

224a   Caesarius Arelatensis, *De mysterio s. Trinitatis*; *CPL* 1014; prolixa DF/EF ponens quaestiones ad quemdam Arianum.

225*   Faustinus presbyter Luciferianus, *Confessio fidei Theodosio Imperatori oblata*; *CPL* 119; breuis PF.

227   Athanasius, *Epistola contra Arianos ad honoratissimos in Africa episcopos*; prolixa EF.

234   Ignotus, *Incipit apertio symboli*; EF et CAP per interr./ respon.

234a*   Ignotus, *De symbolo* (= *Collectio duorum librorum*, 1.52-3 [ex Isidoro]); EF, interr./resp. in parte.

235   Ignotus, *Apertio symboli*. EF et CAP.

235a   Ignotus, *Expositio symboli* (= **235** in forma extensa).

236a   Ignotus, *Expositio symboli*; symbolum apostolorum-typum cum singulis uersibus attributis singulis apostolis; EF.

238   Ignotus, *Item expositio symboli*; CAP-typum.

240   Ignotus, *De symbolo* (ultima pars traditionis symboli in *Sacramentario Gelasiano*); EF et CAP.

242   Ignotus, *Explanatio uerbi symbolum adhibens Isidorum*; EF.

247a   Leidradus episcopus Lugdunensis, *Liber de sacramento baptismi*, c. 4: 'De symbolo'; EF.

248   Ps.-Hieronymus, *Est etiam super hoc alia Hieronymi explanatio*; EF (definitio symboli et symbolum apostolorum-typum cum singulis uersibus attributis singulis apostolis).

249   Ignotus, *Sermo de symbolo*; *CPL* 1760; EF et CAP-typum.

250   Ignotus, *Incipit expositio in symbolo*; breuis EF.

251   Ignotus, *Item alia expositio symboli*; CAP.

252   Ignotus, *De symbolo*, fragmentum; EF.

257   Ignotus, *De symbolo apostolorum Isidorus*; EF.

259   Augustinus, *Sermo 212*; *CPL* 284/serm. 212; CAP-typum.

261a   Isidorus, *Origines*, 7.4.1-12; EF de Trinitate.

262*   Eusebius episcopus Vercellensis, *De Trinitate, I-VII*; cf. *CPL* 105; prolixa EF per interr./resp.

262a*   Ps.-Vigilius Thapsensis, *Sermo de duplici in Christo natura*; *CPL* 810; EF.

263a   Ps.-Isidorus, *Liber de ordine creaturarum*, 1: 'De fide Trinitatis'; EF.

263b   Ignotus, *Professio fidei*; PF.

263c*   Leo I papa, *Testimonia de fide*, siue *Exemplaria testimoniorum diuersorum sanctorumque patrum*, in Epist. 165; *CPL* 1656/epist. 165; EF.

264   Ignotus, *Similitudines per quas potest Christianus firmiter fidem catholicam credere et cognoscere*; *CPL* 1756; EF.

266   Gregorius Thaumaturgus episcopus Neocaesariensis, *Confessio fidei*; breuis PF.

266 (alt. forma)* (forma Hispana).

267 Ps.-Ambrosius, *Libellus fidei*; *CPL* 174; PF.

268 Ps.-Iohannes Maxentius, Ps.-Petrus Diaconus, Ps.-Augustinus, *Epistola Petri diaconi et sociorum scripta ad Africanos in Sardinia exsules, siue De incarnatione et gratia Domini nostri Iesu Christi ad Fulgentium et alios episcopos Africae*; *CPL* 663; PF.

270 Ps.-Augustinus, *Incipit praedicatio Augustini episcopi de fide catholica*; EF.

symb. Ap.   symbolum apostolorum

symb. N.*   symbolum Nicaenum (originalem)

symb. N.-C.*   symbolum Nicaeno-Constantinopolitanum

symb. Ath.*   symbolum Athanasianum

List of Creed Commentary Collections

The numbers (in bold print) identifying the texts, separated by commas, show the order in which the texts appear adjacent to one another in their manuscripts. The reference 'MS' has been omitted from shelfmarks.

1. **194, 14** (in eight Carolingian MSS, within the treatise of Theodulf, bishop of Orléans, *c.* 798-*c.* 818, *De ordine baptismi*)

2. **247a, 160** (in three Carolingian MSS, within the treatise of Leidrad, archbishop of Lyons, 789-*c.* 814, *De sacramento baptismi*)

3. **44, 95, 2** (within the same *Interrogatio sacerdotalis*, in Paris, Bibliothèque Nationale de France [= BNF], lat. 1603, s. VIII-IX, north-eastern France, in region of palace, and Albi, Bibliothèque municipale [= BM], 40, s. IX$^{1/2}$, southern France)

4. **44, 95** (in partially the same *Interrogatio sacerdotalis* as no. 3, in El Escorial, Real Biblioteca de San Lorenzo [= RBSL], L. III. 8, *c.* 860-70, Senlis)

5. **139a, 95, 2** (in partially the same *Interrogatio sacerdotalis* as no. 3, in Paris, BNF lat. 2718, perhaps *c.* 830, Tours)

6. **66aa, 105b, 192a, 140a, 115c, 32*, symb. N.*, 36*** (in Fulda, Dommuseum, Bonif. 2, s. VIII$^{1/2}$, Luxeuil?; and formerly in Rome, Biblioteca Nazionale, Sessor. 77, s. VIII, perhaps Novara)

7. **symb. N.*, 143*, 55(*), 266, 26** (in Vienna, Österreichisches Nationalbibliotek [=ÖNB], 1861, the 'Dagulf Psalter', *c.* 794, Aachen; and in Rome, Casa Madre dei Padri Maristi, A. II. 1, *c.* 800, Aachen or Lyons)

8. **symb. Ath.*, symb. N.*, 143*, 55(*), 26, 266, 39*** (in Brussels, Bibliothèque royale Albert 1er, 8654-72, s. IX$^{in.}$, St Bertin in Flanders)

9. **26, 143*, 55(*), 266** (in Paris, BNF lat. 14085, fos 91-232 = different hands, s. IX?)

10. **136b, 116, 38, 73** (followed by other works of Alcuin traditionally associated with **73**), **10b*, 39*, 143*, 26, 55(*)** (in Paris, BNF lat. 2390, s. XI, but the collection is by Benedict of Aniane, *c.* 800)

11. **39*, 168(*), 206, 263c*, 132a*, 204c*, 85*, 263a, 261a, 122a, symb. Ath.*, 55(*)** (in Paris, BNF lat. 3848B, s. VIII-IX, Flavigny, immediately before the *Collectio Heroualliana*)

12. **39*, 168(*), 206, 263c*** (in Paris, BNF lat. 2123, an. 814-6, Flavigny, an extracted form of Paris, BNF lat. 3848B, also immediately before the *Collectio Heroualliana*)

13.   **69a, 66a (only L. I), 64b, 111*, 11, symb. Ath.*, 31, 266, 32*, 4, 266 (alt. form)*, 143*, 39*** (in Paris, BNF lat. 2341, s. $IX^{2/4}$, Orléans)

14.   **symb. N.*, 31, 266, 32*, symb. Ath.*, 143*, 17, 132c** (in Leiden, Bibliotheek der Rijksuniversiteit [= BR], BPL 67.F, s. VIII, IX or s. IX)

15.   **39*, 111*, symb. N.*** (in Albi, BM 2 = *Collectio Albigensis*, s. $IX^{2/2}$, southern France, perhaps Albi)

16.   **39*, 92, 84** (in Bamberg, Staatsbibliothek, Patr. 20, s. IX)

17.   **84, 92, 31, 266** (in Vienna, ÖNB 2223, s. $IX^{in.}$, region of the Main River)

18.   **84, 92** (in Laon, BM 265, s. $IX^{1/2}$, St-Amand; came to Laon before 875)

19.   **39*, 92** (in Paris, BNF lat. 2718, perhaps *c.* 830, Tours)

20.   **151*, 113*, 150*** (in Montpellier, Bibliothèque Interuniversitaire [= BI], Sec. Méd. 308, s. $IX^{med.}$, St-Claude in Jura; and within nos. 21 and 22 below)

21.   **266 (alt. form)*, 30, 225*, 80*, 227, 22*, 3b, 262*, 143b, 262a*, 36*, 92, 96a, 132aaa...151*, 113*, 150*, ... 166, ... 263c (frag., cc. 21-24)*, ... 69a, 143*, 85b*, 139aa*, 91*** (in Berlin, Staatsbibliothek Preussischer Kulturbesitz, Phillips 1671 [= Phillips 1671], s. $IX^{2/2}$, perhaps Fleury)[6]

22.   **156*, symb. N.*, 160a*, symb. N.-C.*, 36 (1st part)*, 20*, symb. Ath.*, 143*, 31, 26, 35, 202*, 17, 25, 266, 225*, 109, 218, 127, 167, Boethius, 16, 221, 201, 168(*), 151*, 113*, 150*, 108, 84, 105, 124, 92, 143b, 66a (L. III), Basilius, 7, Hieronymus, 65, 9, 39*, 8, 38, 73, 203, 264, 76, 10, 122, 36 (last part)*, 147a*, 221aa*** (in Karlsruhe, Badische Landesbibliothek, Aug. XVIII [= Karlsruhe XVIII], *c.* 806, Reichenau)

23.   **76, 264, 143*** (in Vatican City, Biblioteca Apostolica Vaticana [= BAV], Reg. lat. 191, s. $IX^{ex.}$, perhaps also partly s. $X^{in.}$, Reims)

24.   **264, 143*** (in El Escorial, RBSL L. III. 8, *c.* 860-70, Senlis)

25.   **55(*), 249** (in El Escorial, RBSL L. III. 8, *c.* 860-70, Senlis)

26.   **249, 75** (in St Gallen, Stiftsbibliothek, 732, *c.* 815-7, region of Freising)

27.   **249, 176** (in Paris, BNF lat. 1012, s. $IX^{1/3}$)

28.   **249, 177** (in Laon, BM 288, s. $IX^{1/3}$, eastern France; Laon uncertain)

29.   **6, 97, 88, 26, 9, 177** (in Wolfenbüttel, Herzog-August-Bibliothek [= HAB], Weiss. 91, s. $IX^{1/2}$, Wissembourg)

30.   **88, 9, 177** (in Munich, Bayerische Staatsbibliothek [= BSB], Clm 14508, s. $IX^{3/4}$, north-eastern France)

31.   **177, 64b, 66a(L. I, excerpts), 176a** (in Fulda, Hessische Landesbibliothek, LB Aa 2, an. 865 and s. $IX^{2/3}$, Bodensee area)

32.   **131a, 111(1st part)*, symb. N.*, 143*, 177** (in Vienna, ÖNB 1032, s. $IX^{in.}$, upper Rhine region)

33.   **symb. Ap., 50, symb. Ath.*, 177** (in St Gallen, Stiftsbibliothek, 27, s. IX)

34.   **213, 58, 177** (in Bamberg, Staatsbibliothek, Lit. 131, s. $IX^{4/4}$ or s. IX/X, southern Germany)

35.   **177, 63** (in Munich, BSB Clm 19417, s. $IX^{1/3}$, southern Germany or perhaps Switzerland)

---

6   Phillips 1671 may be considered in its entirety a creed commentary collection, with the addition of a few pieces that entered the collection due to the MS's model but are not on the creed, indicated by elipses. For example **151, 113, 150** are followed by three tracts on baptism, only the second of which is on the creed handed over to the catechumens (**166**).

36. **177, 26** (in Oxford, Bodleian Library, Junius 25, s. IX$^{in.}$, Murbach)
37. **146, 177** (in Paris, BNF lat. 1008, s. IX-X, France)
38. **61, 177** (in Merseburg, Dombibliothek, 103, s. IX$^{1/2}$, northern Italy)
39. **48a, 177** (Paris, BNF lat. 18104 I, s. IX)
40. **234 (containing 192 and 234a*, frags.), 73, 177, 99, 200, 165(*)** (in Verdun, BM 27, s. IX$^{2/3}$, eastern France)
41. **195, 73, 99, 200, 2, 144, 122a** (in Einsiedeln, Stiftsbibliothek, 27, s. VIII or IX)
42. **2, 195** (in Verdun, BM 27, s. IX $^{2/3}$, eastern France)
43. **240, 99, 200, 2** (in Montpellier, BI Sec. Méd. 387, s. IX$^{2/3}$, France)
44. **240 (containing 249), 235 (containing 235a, frag.), 99, 200** (in Monza, Biblioteca Capitolare [= BC], e-14/127, s. IX-X or IX$^{3/4}$, northern Italy)
45. **1, 208, 209, 89** (in Laon, BM 136, s. IX, perhaps Laon)
46. **33, 96a, 12** (in Laon, BM 136, s. IX, perhaps Laon)
47. **96a, 12** (in Laon, BM 135, s. IX$^{2/2}$, Laon)
48. **96a, 132aaa, 224a** (in Montecassino, Archivio dell'Abbazia [= Montecassino], 19, s. VII or VIII or IX$^{in.}$, Spain; Córdoba?)
49. **131a, 220** (in Arras, BM 731, s. IX$^{1/4}$, north-eastern France)
50. **162, 252, 270, 31, 197** (in Albi, BM 38bis, s. IX$^{c. med.}$, perhaps southern France; Albi uncertain)
51. **132, 117a** (in Karlsruhe, Badische Landesbibliothek, Aug. CCXXIX [= Karlsruhe CCXXIX], an. 806-22, Abruzzi)
52. **symb. Ath.*, 143aa** (in Karlsruhe CCXXIX, an. 806-22, Abruzzi)
53. **132c, 67, 31** (in Lyons, BM 611, s. IX)
54. **225*, 36*, 153,** letter of Gratian to Ambrose, 'Cupio ualde', **204, 267** (in Milan, Biblioteca Ambrosiana [= BA], D. 268 inf., s. VIII or IX, Bobbio)
55. **143*, 142, symb. N.*, 102a, 43** (in Milan, BA I. 101. sup., s. VIII, Bobbio)
56. **39*, 144a, symb. Ath.*** (in Milan, BA O. 212. sup., s. VIII$^{in.?}$, Bobbio)
57. **73a, 31** (in Milan, BA O. 212. sup., s. VIII$^{in.?}$, Bobbio)
58. **204, 32*** (in Montecassino 4, s. VIII, Córdoba or s. IX$^{in.}$, Spain)
59. **263b, 266** (in Montecassino 4, s. VIII. Córdoba or s. IX$^{in.}$, Spain)
60. **169, 46, 116, 38** (in Montpellier, BI Sec. Méd. 141, s. VIII-IX)
61. **symb. Ath.*, 32*, symb. N.-C.*, 39*, 137** (in Munich, BSB Clm 6330, c. an. 800, Germany; Lorsch uncertain)
62. **250, 52, 154, 96** (in Paris, BNF lat. 1008, s. IX-X, France)
63. **250, 52, 154** (in Merseburg, Dombibliothek, 103, s. IX$^{1/2}$, northern Italy)
64. **39*, 36*, 124** (in Munich, BSB Clm 15818, an. 824-855, Würzburg)
65. **symb. Ath.*, 76, 26, 39(excerpt)*, 118, 173a*, 115** (in Paris, BNF lat. 1451, an. 800-16, region of Tours; came to St Maur-des-Fossés, region of Paris)
66. **75, 58** (in Paris, BNF lat. 1535, s. IX-X)
67. **141, 64** (in Paris, BNF lat. 2796, an. 813-5, France)
68. **69a, 201** (in Paris, BNF lat. 12218, s. IX$^{1/2}$, Corbie)
69. **242, 248** (in Paris, BNF lat. 14085, fos 91-232 = different hands, s. IX?)
70. **66, 183** (in Vatican City, BAV Reg. lat. 231, an. 820-30, north-eastern France, and in Paris, BNF lat. 2832 [*membrum disiectum* of Troyes, BM lat. 1165, s. IX$^{2/2}$, Lyons], much of which is the same as Vatican City, BAV Reg. lat. 231; BNF 2832 contains only fragments of **66** and **183** due to the loss of folios.)
71. **160dd, 62, 31** (in St Mihiel, BM 28, s. IX)

72.   **259, 251, 66, 178, 183, 257, 238, 157** (in Troyes, BM 804, s. IX$^{2/4 \text{ or } 2/3}$, Loire)
73.   **259, 251** (in Paris, BNF lat. 2373, s. IX-X)
74.   **168(*), 26** (in Vatican City, BAV Reg. lat. 191, s. IX$^{ex.}$, perhaps also partly s. X$^{in.}$, Reims)
75.   **136a, 41** (in Wolfenbüttel, HAB Weiss. 68, s. IX^{med}, Wissembourg)
76.   **73, 204b, 115a, 10, 122a** (in Zurich, Zentralbibliothek [= ZB], Rh. 102, s. IX)
77.   **73(part), 40a** (in Zurich, ZB Rh. 102, s. IX)
78.   **235a, symb. N.-C.*** (in Zurich, ZB C 64, s. VIII/IX, perhaps St Gallen)
79.   (questionably a creed commentary collection) **133, 204, 204a (containing 68a)** (in Cologne, Dombibliothek, 33, s. IX)
80.   (questionably a creed commentary collection) **120, 203c** (in Laon, BM 113, s. IX; came to Laon in s. IX)

Of the creed commentary collections, only one group, nos. 7-10, deserves comment in regard to the idea of a programmatic set of texts that achieved general recognition. No. 7 is the set of professions of faith in the Dagulf Psalter of Vienna, ÖNB 1861, exactly replicated in Rome, Casa Madre dei Padre Maristi, A. II. 1, and partially replicated in nos. 8, 9, and 10.[7] The Dagulf Psalter is probably the earliest manuscript of the four collections, and it may be the manuscript of origin of the combination **symb. N., 143, 55, 266, 26**. Written at the court of Charlemagne *c.* 794 by the scribe Dagulf, the manuscript is entirely in gold letters, and was intended as a gift from Charlemagne to Pope Hadrian (d. 795). The creed commentary collection comes at the beginning, followed by other prefatory material (the Lord's Prayer in a poetic paraphrase, the Gloria, and a series of texts explaining the origin and interpretation of the Psalms attributed to Jerome, Damasus, Isidore, and Augustine) prior to the Psalter proper. The Nicene Creed followed by four professions of faith might not be considered a 'creed commentary collection', except for its association with this other prefatory material, partly didactic, and its replication, or partial replication, in four schoolbooks, including the second manuscript of no. 7, Rome, Casa Madre dei Padri Maristi, A. II. 1, which is a schoolbook given by Leidrad, archbishop of Lyons, to the church of St Stephen's of Lyons, *c.* 800.[8]

---

7   I will refer to the creed commentary collections by the number (not in bold) given them in the second list.
8   Rudolf Beer, ed., *Monumenta Palaeographica Vindobonensia. Denkmäler der Schreibkunst aus der Handschriftensammlung des Habsburg-Lothringischen Erzhauses* (Leipzig, 1910), 48. There is some opinion that it may have been written at Aachen, and not in Lyons; see Kurt Holter, *Der Goldene Psalter 'Dagulf-Psalter'. Vollständige Faksimile-Ausgabe im Originalformat von Codex 1861 der Öster-reichischen Nationalbibliothek*, Codices Selecti Phototypice Impressi, Facsimile Vol. 69, Commentarium Vol. 69* (Graz, 1980), ii, 45. The Dagulf creed collection comes near the end, accompanied by the same other prefatory material as in the Dagulf Psalter. Leidrad was an intimate of the court, where he had been Alcuin's favorite pupil. In 798 Charlemagne sent him as a *missus dominicus* with Theoldulf of Orléans to Narbonnaise Gaul. He was in Spain in 789-99 to fight the Spanish Adoptionism of Felix of Urgel. Brussels, Bibliothèque royale Albert 1er, 8654-72 (no. 8) (questions on the Gospel, excerpts from Bede, Isidore, canon law, Carolingian legislation, the liturgy and the computus, dicta of the fathers), except for the creed material, has no other texts in common with the Dagulf Psalter or Leidrad's codex; nor does Paris, BNF lat. 14085 (no. 9) (almost entirely excerpts from Isidore's *Origines)*. Paris, BNF lat. 2390

Although Leidrad's codex and the manuscripts of nos. 8, 9, and 10 are related, directly or indirectly, to the Dagulf Psalter, Lawrence Nees dismisses the idea that the creedal collection in the Psalter was intended as a model catechesis for Charlemagne's realm.[9] Probably only because Leidrad, an intimate of the court, incorporated it into a schoolbook, through his codex it won appearance in three other schoolbooks, although not without additions and omissions.

Nees acknowledges that the Dagulf creedal collection could have served, by codifying 'the sources upon which all could (presumably) agree', as 'the *basis* for doctrinal instruction or explanation';[10] however, there is little evidence that it did so. It is true that individual texts of the Dagulf creed collection appear in other creed commentary collections.[11] I hope to provide elsewhere a critical edition of each of the five texts using all their known manuscripts, but to summarize briefly, the Dagulf Psalter and its related manuscripts (the MSS of nos. 7-10) have distinct forms of texts **143**, **266**, and **26** that are not found in any of the other creed commentary collections.[12]

(no. 10) contains Benedict of Aniane's *Munimenta fidei*, which he compiled shortly after 800 as 'a program of theological studies' he wished to see pursued in his monastery at Aniane; see J. Leclercq, 'Les "Munimenta Fidei" de saint Benoit d'Aniane', *Analecta monastica, ser. 1*, Studia Anselmiana 20 (Rome, 1948), 67-8. Near the end of the *Munimenta* are texts **39, 143, 26, 55**, which Benedict seems to have lifted from a MS with a creed commentary collection similar to the Dagulf collection, if not the Dagulf Psalter itself (to which he added text **39**). Although text **266** is missing, he uses a large excerpt of **266** at two places earlier in the *Munimenta*. Benedict was a close friend of Leidrad of Lyons, and even if he did not know the Dagulf Psalter directly, a copy of its creed commentary collection is in Leidrad's schoolbook (Rome, Casa Madre dei Padri Maristi A. II. 1); see D. A. Bullough, 'The Continental Background of the Tenth-Century English Reform', in *idem, Carolingian Renewal: sources and heritage* (Manchester, 1991), 292, n. 30; and *idem*, 'Alcuin and the Kingdom of Heaven', in *Carolingian Renewal*, 176, 178-9.

9   Lawrence Nees, in a review of Kurt Holter, *Der goldene Psalter*, in *The Art Bulletin*, 67 (1985), 687. Nees sees the purpose of the creed collection in relation to the court's stand against Pope Hadrian on images; see also D. A. Bullough, '*Imagines regum* and Their Significance in the Early Medieval West', in *Carolingian Renewal*, 58-9, and '*Aula renovata*: The Carolingian Court Before the Aachen Palace', in *ibid.*, 146.

10   Nees, in his review of Holter, *Der goldene Psalter*, 687 (his emphasis).

11   The **Symb. N.** is also in the following creed commentary collections: nos. 6, 14, 15, 22, 32, and 55. **143** is also in nos. 13, 14, 21, 22, 23, 24, 32, and 55; **55** is also in nos. 11 and 25; **266** is also in nos. 13, 14, 17, 22, and 59; and **26** is also in nos. 22, 29, 36, 65, and 74.

12   For example, text **143** in the Dagulf Psalter group (nos. 7-10) begins, 'Patrem et filium et spiritum sanctum ...', whereas in all our other collections **143** begins, '*Nos* patrem et filium et spiritum sanctum ...'. Also, in nos. 7-10, text **143** lacks the phrase, 'Nam tres deos dicit qui divinitatem separat trinitatis', present in all the other collections. (The *Collectio Quesnelliana* also has these differences against nos. 7-10.) Text **266** ends with the word 'manet' in the Dagulf Psalter group (nos. 7-10), yet the word is lacking in all the other creed commentary collections (nos. 13, 14, 17, 22, and 59). Text **26** is especially interesting, because it was included in the corrected version of the *Libri Carolini*, finalized at the court just before, or possibly at the same time, as the creation of the Dagulf Psalter; see Bullough, '*Imagines regum* and Their Significance', 58. The form of **26** in the Dagulf Psalter has thirty-eight small differences (such as inverted word order, omission of words, 'est' for 'enim', 'sed' for 'ita', etc.) from the form of **26** in the *Libri Carolini*, ed. Ann Freeman, *MGH Concilia, 2, Supplementum 1: Opus Caroli Regis Contra Synodum (Libri Carolini)* (Hanover, 1998), 336-40. The differences might not be important,

Even the form of the **symb. N.** in the Dagulf group (nos. 7-10) is different than in other creed commentary collections.[13] Only text **55** is the same in the Dagulf group as in our other collections (nos. 11 and 25).[14] The manuscript of no. 11 may have been written before the Dagulf Psalter.[15] In sum, it is certain, or in the case of text **55** possible, that the Dagulf Psalter played no exemplary role in these creedal collections.[16] The creed commentary collections offer no evidence of any court-promulgated catechesis on the creed.

From the first list given above, one can see the diversity of works used to help interpret the creed and explain the faith. Furthermore, it is likely that the list represents only a fraction of the different works used as creed commentaries, because even our far from exhaustive catalogue of creed commentary collections indicates the independent way the compilers put together these collections. (Of the 193 works listed, 120 appear only once, in one creed commentary collection.) One question, then, for the tradition of interpretation of the faith under the Carolingians concerns the sources of these texts for the creed commentary compilers. From where were they gathering them?

Given the variety of the works used as creed commentaries, probably the answer is a large number of different sources. Almost no literary genre is out of bounds, and any combination of literary genres may be found in a single creed commentary collection (for example, a sermon, a clerical interrogation, a list of anathemas, a letter, a personal confession of faith, and a conciliar decree). Only one source among many that seems to have contributed to the compilation of creed commentary collections, but to which I

---

except that at least one of our collections (no. 22 of Karlsruhe XVIII) almost always follows the *Libri Carolini* instead of the Dagulf Psalter in these differences. While there are only a few very minor differences in text **26** among the Dagulf Psalter group (nos. 7-10), the differences between this group and other collections containing text **26** (nos. 36, 65, 74, 29) are numerous. No. 74 contains a substantially different form of text **26** found in Ps.-Augustine, Sermon 236. Although I was not able to compare the entire text in no. 29, it has more or less the same additional sentence at the end as it does in no. 36, suggesting that these two collections followed a similar model for text **26**, different from the Dagulf.

13 There are several different readings from the MS of no. 22, and substantial differences from the MSS of nos. 6, 32, and 55. None of these collections agree among themselves, either, for the entire text of the **symb. N.** I was not able to compare the **symb. N.** in Leiden, BR BPL 67. F (no. 14), or in Albi, BM 2 (no. 15); the latter belongs to a canonical tradition of this creed in a canon law collection.

14 In no. 11 (of Paris, BNF lat. 3848B), text **55** is in almost perfect agreement with the Dagulf Psalter, including orthographical details, and in no. 25 (of El Escorial, RBSL L. III. 8), it has twelve minor differences against the Dagulf Psalter and no. 11, which could be a copyist's errors.

15 This MS (Paris, BNF lat. 3848B) is also the earliest known MS of the *Collectio Heroualliana*, which immediately follows the creed commentary collection. The *Heroualliana* cannot have been written before the mid-eighth century, according to Friedrich Maassen, *Geschichte der Quellen und der Literatur des canonischen Rechts im Abendlande*, 1: *Die Rechtssammlungen bis zur Mitte des 9. Jahrhunderts* (Graz, 1870; repr. Graz, 1956), 833.

16 Even nos. 8, 9, and 10 were probably influenced by Leidrad's codex, rather than directly by the Dagulf Psalter. Holter, *Der goldene Psalter*, ii, 56, also concludes that the Dagulf Psalter, while containing texts that are important witnesses of the Carolingian liturgical reform movement, was not itself an instrument of the reform.

would like to draw attention, is canon law collections. Canon law collections often contain teaching on the faith in the form of letters, decrees, *symbola*, anathemas, and excerpts from Scripture and patristic works that had addressed the heresies dealt with at the great ecumenical councils and at local councils. We have identified (with an asterisk) the texts that are canonical pieces; that is, can be found in at least one canon law collection circulating in the Carolingian period. There are thirty-six of them, although perhaps more of the 193 will still be found in canon law collections.[17]

Some of these canonical pieces are well attested outside of canon law collections (for example, the **symb. Ath.**, the **symb. N.**, the **symb. N.-C.**, **32, 39**, and **132a**) and it is not necessary that our compilers derived these pieces from canon law collections. Closer examination of some of the canonical pieces in creed commentary collections, however, strongly suggests that their compilers turned to canon law collections for them, even if it is not possible to assert the specific canon law manuscript used by the creed commentary compiler. The evidence is important to show, because the deposit of the faith in canon law collections is rich in diversity and heterodoxy, preserving adversaries' points of view. Transferred from canon law collections to creed commentary collections, canonical pieces were no longer simply historical documents of the past, but pastoral guides for a living community. The creed commentary compilers' use of canon law collections might help to explain the diversity of theological ideas that persisted in the Carolingian period.

The compiler of the collection in Karlsruhe XVIII (no. 22) almost undoubtedly drew on a Spanish collection for **20**,[18] **147a**,[19] **36**,[20] and perhaps for **221aa**,[21] **160a**,[22]

---

17   I have not examined the contents of every known canonical collection in search of our texts. Roger Reynolds has listed some ninety-one canonical collections in Carolingian MSS (of which fifty-six have received no edition, and two others only partial editions) in a still unpublished inventory, which he graciously shared with me some years ago. I relied essentially on Maassen, *Geschichte der Quellen*, in order to locate each of the thirty-six texts in at least one and sometimes many canon law collections. The number thirty-six includes three texts (**55, 165, 168**) that Maassen lists as *addenda* to a canon law collection.

18   In the edition of **20** by Joseph Madoz, *Le Symbole du XIe Concile de Tolède*, Spicilegium sacrum Lovaniense, fasc. 19 (Louvain, 1938), 16-26, Karlsruhe XVIII agrees with the *Collectio Hispana Gallica* of Vatican City, BAV Pal. lat. 575 against all the other MSS thirty-eight times.

19   Compared to the edition of **147a** in *La Colección canónica Hispana*, ed. Gonzalo Martínez-Díez and Félix Rodríguez, Monumenta Hispaniae Sacra, Serie canónica, 1-5 (Madrid, 1966-92), v, 78-83, Karlsruhe XVIII comes closest in its variations to the *Collectio Hispana Gallica* of Vatican City, BAV Pal. lat. 575, as it does for text **20**.

20   J. A. de Aldama states that Karlsruhe XVIII follows a Hispanic canonical collection in his critical edition of text **36**: *El Simbolo Toledano I*, Analecta Gregoriana, 7 (Rome, 1934), 21.

21   According to Maassen, *Geschichte*, 218, no. 229, and 710-11, text **221aa** is only in the *Collectio Hispana* and derivative collections (*Collectio Hispana Gallica, Collectio Epitome Hispana, Collectio Sancti Amandi*). Since **221aa** has no known MS tradition outside of canonical collections, it suggests the Karlsruhe compiler turned to a Hispanic collection.

22   In Karlsruhe XVIII, **160a** follows directly after the **symb. N.** This is how **160a** appears, and with exactly the same canonical title, in the different forms of the *Collectio Hadriana*, one of which is the *Hadriana-Hispanica*, that is, the *Hadriana* supplemented with a Gallican form of the *Hispana*; see Maassen, *Geschichte*, 233, 238, and 454, no. 597.

symb. N.,[23] and the **symb. N.-C.**[24] There are ten further canonical pieces in Karlsruhe XVIII (**156, 202, 225, 39, 151, 113, 150, 168, 143, symb. Ath.**), which are not in the *Hispana* or its derivatives, but may have been taken from other canonical collections.[25]

The compiler of Phillips 1671 (no. 21) seems to have taken from a canonical collection (now lost?), similar to the *Collectio Veronensis incompleta*, seven of its fifteen canonical pieces (**22, 262, 262a, 151, 113, 150, 263c**, all found in the *Veronensis*).[26] He also very probably turned to a codex of the *Collectio Quesnelliana* for one (**80**)[27] and perhaps three other of the pieces (**36,**[28] **143,**[29] **225**[30]), and possibly to

---

23 See Karl Künstle, *Eine Bibliothek der Symbole und theologischer Tractate zur Bekämpfung des Priscillianismus und westgothischen Arianismus aus dem VI. Jahrhundert*, Forschungen zur Christlichen Litteratur- und Dogmengeschichte, 1 (Mainz, 1900), 29.

24 See Künstle, *ibid.*, 31. Künstle says that many signs of the **symb. N.-C.** in Karlsruhe XVIII speak for its coming from the Acts of Toledo III (589), although it does lack the *filioque*. This, however, is thought to be a later MS addition to the original form of the Nicene-Constantinopolitan Creed included in Toledo III.

25 **156** in Karlsruhe XVIII is very close to the form in two MSS of the *Collectio Vetus Gallica*, one written perhaps in Chur, the other in the Bodensee area; but this form is also in the *Scarapsus* of Ps.-Pirminius; on the MSS of text **156** see Hubert Mordek, *Kirchenrecht und Reform im Frankenreich: die Collectio Vetus Gallica, die älteste systematische Kanonessammlung des Fränkischen Gallien: Studien und Edition*, Beiträge zur Geschichte und Quellenkunde des Mittelalters, 1 (Berlin/New York, 1975), 359. Text **202** is in five canon law collections (see Maassen, *Geschichte*, 354, no. 373.1), but it is also in MSS of Jerome's letters. It can only be said that Karlsruhe XVIII does agree quite closely with the edition of **202** in *PL* 22.355-6, one of whose MSS is the *Collectio Dionysio-Bobbiensis* (= Milan, BA S. 33. sup.). **225** is in the *Collectio Quesnelliana* (this is the only canonical collection Maassen lists, *Geschichte*, 348, no. 353). Karlsruhe XVIII has a number of small differences from the *Quesnelliana*, most of which, but not all, can be explained by a copyist's omissions. **151, 113, 150** are a series of Ps.-Augustine sermons on the creed that appear together earliest in the *Collectio Veronensis incompleta* of Verona, Biblioteca Capitolare [= BC], LIX (s. VI-VII). It, or a collection similar to Verona, BC LIX, may be the ultimate source for the tradition of these three sermons together in Karlsruhe XVIII and three other ninth-century MSS (not canon law collections), but Pierre-Patrick Verbraken states that it is difficult to establish a relation between all these MSS; see Verbraken, 'Le sermon CCXIV de saint Augustin pour la tradition du symbole', *RB*, 72 (1962), 10-11. There appear to be at least three independent traditions of **151, 113, 150**, one represented by Karlsruhe XVIII, another by Phillips 1671 (no. 21), and a third by a lost Reims MS and Verona, BC LIX. **168**, known only in canonical sources as an addendum to the *Collectio Heroualliana* (nos. 11 and 12), has a completely different form in Karlsruhe XVIII (in its entirety much briefer) than in the *Heroualliana* MSS. **168** is also known in no. 74, but with yet a different form. For **143**, see n. 12 above. **143** is in at least four canon law collections; Karlsruhe XVIII agrees with the *Quesnelliana* form, which is different than the form of **143** in the other three canon law collections.

26 On Phillips 1671's relationship to the *Collectio Veronensis incompleta* of Verona, BC LIX, see Eduardus Schwartz, ed., *Acta conciliorum oecumenicorum*, 1/v (Berlin/Leipzig, 1924-6), i-iiii; C. Lambot, 'Le florilège Augustinien de Vérone', *RB*, 79 (1969), 80; and Verbraken, 'Le sermon CCXIV', 10-11.

27 Schwartz, *Acta*, 1/v, xiiii, says Phillips 1671 [Berolin. 78] transcribed **80** 'rather carelessly [satis neglegenter] from some codex of the *Quesnelliana*'.

28 De Aldama, *El Simbolo*, 24-5, shows that Phillips 1671 was influenced by the *Collectio Quesnelliana* (in both, **36** is attributed to Augustine).

29 See n. 12 above. Phillips 1671 follows the *Quesnelliana* form against the form of **143** in three other canon law collections.

30 See n. 25 above. Phillips 1671 also has a number of small differences from the *Quesnelliana* form of **225**. For the most part, Phillips 1671 does not agree with Karlsruhe XVIII (no. 22) in these differences.

other canonical collections for the pieces not in the *Veronensis* or *Quesnelliana* (**85b**,[31] **91**,[32] **139aa**,[33] **266 [alt. form]**).[34]

The compiler of the Paris, BNF lat 3848B collection (no. 11) almost unquestionably turned to a canon law collection for **85** and **204c**.[35] Its version of **263c** is similar to a canonical form in the *Collectio Veronensis incompleta*.[36]

Paris, BNF lat. 2341 (no. 13) has **111** in a quite different form than in nos. 15 or 32 or any canon law collection. Because **111** is a canonical text in origin (perhaps

---

31   **85b** I know elsewhere only in canonical collections. There exist at least three forms of the text according to the editions of Schwartz, *Acta*, 1/ii (Berlin/Leipzig, 1925-6), 45-51; *Acta*, 1/iii, 26-35; and *Acta*, 1/v, 236-44. He edits Phillips 1671 in *Acta*, 1/v, 236-44 with the form in the *Collectio Palatina* (Vatican City, BAV, Vat. Pal. lat.234), *Collectio Hispana* of Vienna, ÖNB 411, *Collectio Hadriana* (only specific MSS), and the *Collectio* of Oxford, Bodleian Library, e Mus. 102. Phillips 1671's readings agree sometimes with one, or sometimes with another of these MSS, and numerous times it has small spelling differences from any of them.

32   **91** is in many different recensions in different canon law collections. I have found none in which it is identical to Phillips 1671, but a version very close to Phillips 1671's is edited by Mansi, vi, 889-92, 'in actibus synodi Chalcedonensis, an. 451' from a 'cod. Paris.' and a 'cod. Diuion.', which is the *Collectio Rustici canonum concilii Chalcedonensis*; see Maassen, *Geschichte*, 745. The earliest MS of this Collection is Vatican City, BAV Vat. lat. 1322, s. VI^{ex}, probably Verona. The 'Dijon' MS of Mansi is Montpellier, BI, Sec. Méd. 58, s. VIII-IX.

33   **139aa** consists of only the counter-anathemas of Nestorius, which in the *Collectio Vaticana* and the *Collectio Hadriana aucta* are intercalculated with Cyril's twelve anathemas. Phillips 1671 may represent a canonical collection that abbreviated the *Vaticana* or *Hadriana aucta*. It has small differences from these two canonical collections, edited by Schwartz, *Acta*, 1/v, 71-9.

34   **266 (alt. form)** is a distinct form of **266** that is found only in the *Collectio Hispana* and derivative Spanish collections. The text is not known outside canon law collections, except in our creed commentary collections nos. 21 and 13.

35   These two letters against Nestorius belong to the canonical material surrounding the Council of Ephesus and are only known in canon law collections, apart from this creed commentary collection. **85** has two different forms, one beginning 'Laetentur caeli' in the *Collectio Quesnelliana*; the other beginning 'Exsultent caeli' in the Collections of Tours, Verona, Salzburg, Notre-Dame, and Rusticus; for these collections, see Maassen, *Geschichte*, 359, no. 3. Our MS begins 'Exsultent caeli', thus using some source other than the *Quesnelliana*. **204c** has at least four different versions in canon law collections, one represented by the *Quesnelliana*; another by the Collection of Tours of the Council of Ephesus; another by the Collections of Salzburg, Verona BC LVII, Notre-Dame, Rusticus, and the Acts of the Fifth Ecumenical Council; and a fourth by the *Collectio Palatina*; Schwartz, *Acta*, 1/v, 49-57; 337-340; 1/ii, 37-9; 1/iii, 20-2. Maassen says that **204c** in Paris, BNF lat. 3848B (no. 11) agrees with the version in the collections of Salzburg, Verona BC LVII, Notre-Dame, Rusticus, and the Acts of the Fifth Ecumenical Council (*Geschichte*, 358-9, no. 381.2). Although the Collection of Salzburg is made up of the Collections of Tours and Verona, it did not receive **204c** from the Collection of Tours (c. 6), but from the Collection of Verona (c. 14); see Maassen, *Geschichte*, 732.

36   **263c** is in six canon law collections in different forms, varying in the number of the church fathers cited, and also in the order of the 'testimonia'. According to the edition of Schwartz, only the *Collectio Quesnelliana*, the *Collectio Veronensis incompleta* of Verona BC LIX, and a MS of a collection of Leo's letters (Munich, BSB Clm 14540) begin at the same point as Paris, BNF lat. 3848B and come close to having the same number and order of 'testimonia'; see Schwartz, *Acta*, 2/iv (Berlin/Leipzig, 1932), 119-31. Paris, BNF lat. 3848B seems to follow the *Veronensis* most closely, in that they both lack a long excerpt from Cyril beginning, 'Ait igitur'.

composed by Dionysius Exiguus), the Paris compiler may have taken this text from a canonical collection now lost.[37] The creed commentary collection in Paris 2341 has both **266** and **266 (alt. form)**, which could indicate that its compiler was aware of the two forms of **266** because of a Hispanic collection under his eyes.[38]

Paris, BNF lat 2390 (no. 10) has **10b**, Benedict of Aniane's reiteration, with his own prologue, of Caesarius of Arles' *Breuiarium aduersus haereticos*. According to the editor of the *Breuiarium*, Germain Morin, Benedict took the text from the *Collectio Corbiensis* (Paris, BNF lat. 12097, s. VI-VII, southern France) or the *Collectio Pithoeana* (Paris, BNF lat. 1564, between an. 785-810, northern France, which derived the *Breuiarum* and other pieces from the *Collectio Corbiensis)*, but, Morin says, Benedict knew a better exemplar of the *Collectio* than these manuscripts represent.[39]

Verdun, BM 27 (no. 40) has **165**. Its version of **165** agrees very closely with the version appended to the *Collectio canonum Cresconii* of Vatican, BAV, Vat. lat. 1347.[40]

The above cases show close connections between creed commentary collection manuscripts and canon law collections. Also it is possible that the unique forms of some of the canonical pieces in the creed commentary collections indicate the existence of now lost canon law collections to which the creed commentary compilers had access. Still, it may be asked whether these connections represent a true exploitation of canon law collections, or whether most of our compilers acquired their canonical pieces indirectly, by copying them out of a few large creed commentary collections. Indication that this is not the case (although our evidence is limited) is that the vast collection of Karlsruhe XVIII (no. 22) accounts for only seventeen of the thirty-six canonical pieces. Furthermore, seven of the seventeen are found only in Karlsruhe XVIII. The second largest collection, no. 21, contains fifteen of the thirty-six canonical pieces, seven of which are found only in this collection. In all, twenty of the thirty-six canonical pieces appear only once, in one creed commentary collection. The other sixteen are in more than one creed commentary collection, but often in different forms. For example, Karlsruhe XVIII (no. 22) and Phillips 1671 (no. 21)

---

37 Also nos. 15 and 32 both have different forms of 111 than the two forms of 111 in canon law collections, represented by the *Quesnelliana* and the *Hispana*; see Maassen, *Geschichte*, 39-40, no. 43. Paris, BNF lat. 2341 is closer to the *Hispana* form than to the *Quesnelliana* form.

38 See n. 34 above.

39 See Germanus [Germain] Morin, ed., *Sancti Caesarii episcopi Arelatensis opera omnia*, 2 vols (Maredsous, 1937-42), ii, 180-1. One can see in the apparatus criticus to the text (182-208) some places where Benedict gives a better reading against *Corbiensis* and *Pithoeana*; e.g., 190, l. 6, and 196, l. 27, where Benedict has a word that fell out in *Corb./Pith.*, which belongs to the original text according to a parallel passage in another work of Caesarius. There are two other MSS of the *Breuiarium*, unidentified by their editors, which Morin uses in his edition. Morin says that one of these MSS almost never disagrees with Sirmond's edition of the *Breuiarium* using *Corb.* and *Pith.*, that the other MS seems to be of a later date, and that its variant readings with respect to the other MSS are of small importance.

40 I have not ascertained all the canon law MSS of **165**.

both have **36**, but they acquired it from different sources with different forms. **111** appears in three creed commentary collections (nos. 13, 15, and 32), but in a different form in each. **168** is in three commentary collections (nos. 11 [and its copy, no. 12], 22, and 74), yet in a different form in each.[41] We are left with the impression that the creed commentary compilers went to the canonical collections themselves to acquire their canonical pieces, and did not depend for them on a few large creed commentary collections. The implications are important, because our list of creed commentary collections is only a tiny number of those that once existed. We must imagine literally hundreds of such collections, making free use of a vast and variegated canonical literature, in parishes and missionary provinces across Carolingian Europe.

Speaking in general of the creed commentary collections that contain several canonical pieces, there is little evidence that the compilers simply lifted material *en bloc* from a single canonical collection.[42] In fact, if our compilers turned to the *Collectio Quesnelliana*, as it seems they did, their selectivity is almost astonishing. This collection contains together, in sequence (cc. 37-41), texts **143, 225, 32, 36,** and **263c**, and a little later on (cc. 52-3) texts **80** and **85**; yet neither of these blocks of material is ever repeated as a whole in any creed commentary collection, or even partially repeated.[43] One gets the sense that the creed commentary compilers sought specific texts in the canon law collections that allowed them to interpret the faith more meaningfully for a particular audience and in sympathy with their own views.[44]

While I have focused on canon law collections as a source for the compilers of creed commentary collections, the contribution of creed commentary collections to canon law collections is yet to be explored. Some of the thirty-six 'canonical pieces' include,

---

41 Text **55** in no. 25, we saw above, could have derived from nos. 7-10. I have not yet compared all of the MSS of **32**, or of **225, 151, 113, 150, 143**, or **39** to ascertain whether these texts have different forms in different creed commentary collections.

42 The exception is Phillips 1671 (no. 21), which took seven pieces from a MS related to the *Collectio Veronensis incompleta*; but its compiler also turned to other canon law collections for further material.

43 Neither '**143, 225**' (contiguously), nor '**225, 32**' nor '**32, 36**' nor '**36, 263c**' is found in any creed commentary collection. There are three other cases where a canon law collection has a group of our texts in a block, but the block as a whole is not found repeated in a creed commentary collection. These are: '**39, 111**', in the *Collectio Albigensis* of Albi, BM 2; '**32, 143**', in the *Collectio Sanblasiana* and *Collectio Colbertina*; and '**263c, 32**', in the *Collectio Vaticana* of Vatican City, BAV, Barb. lat. 679 and Vat. lat. 1342.

44 One wonders whether an explanation for the persistence of canon law collections of a chronological order side by side with systematic collections through at least the first half of the ninth century, despite the advantage of the newer systematic collections for disciplinary use, is that the chronological collections preserve so much doctrine from the councils, material that is almost totally lacking in the systematic collections. Of the forty-nine different canon law collections containing our texts reported by Maassen, thirty-eight are chronological, eleven systematic. But of the eleven systematic, five contain only **173a** (the Prologue to the *Statuta ecclesiae antiqua*); one contains only the widely copied 'Tome' of Leo (**132a**). In three others the creed material was appended to the collection, perhaps in an effort to supplement these systematic collections with material that would help the clergy know and teach the faith.

for example, Gennadius' *Liber ecclesiasticorum dogmatum* (**39**); Ps.-Vigilius' *De Trinitate libri XII*, 10 (**22**); and 'Ignotus', *De symbolo* (**234a**). While it is well known, through Roger Reynolds and others, that canon law collections were padded with useful explanatory texts when these collections were copied for clergy in training centers such as Salzburg,[45] it has not been shown if these 'para-canonical' texts include works on the explanation of the faith that were taken from creed commentary collections, a phenomenon that would extend the influence of creed commentary collections much further than we have imagined in manuscripts of pastoral instruction.

This article simply brings attention to creed commentary collections as a resource for scholars. A number of illuminating works have come out recently dealing with the Carolingians' faith.[46] They have shown that to assess how the Carolingians responded to the second council of Nicea on images, or to Spanish adoptionism, or debated about the *filioque*, predestination, and the bodily presence of Christ in the Eucharist, it is necessary to know the tradition of the faith available to them. The creed commentary collections, in their wide range of different works and the great variety of ways these works were combined, are evidence of the richness of the tradition of interpretation of the faith put to creative use not only among a few high-brow theologians in court and monastic circles, but much more broadly among teachers and pastors, anonymous individuals whose compilations touched the lives and shaped the thought of the common people.

---

45 See Reynolds, 'Canon Law Collections in Early Ninth-century Salzburg', in *Proceedings of the Fifth International Congress of Medieval Canon Law, Salamanca, 21-25 September 1976*, ed. Stephan Kuttner and Kenneth Pennington, MIC, Series C, Subsidia 6 (Vatican City, 1980), 23-4.

46 For example, John Cavadini, *The Last Christology of the West: Adoptionism in Spain and Gaul, 785-820* (Philadelphia, 1993); Susan Rabe, *Faith, Art, and Politics at Saint-Riquier: the symbolic vision of Angilbert* (Philadephia, 1995); and Celia Chazelle, *The Crucified God in the Carolingian Era: theology and art of Christ's Passion* (Cambridge, 2001).

Chapter 12

Editions, Manuscripts and Readers in Some Pre-Gratian Collections*

Martin Brett

The subject of this paper is in many ways peculiarly appropriate to a volume in honour of Roger Reynolds. All his work has been marked by two qualities whose importance I hope to underline here: a thorough mastery of the variety of forms in which material of a broadly legal character has survived in the manuscripts, and equally an acute sense of the artificiality of those sub-disciplinary categories into which too easily we divide law, theology, liturgy or homiletics. No-one has been more alert to the distortions of understanding which such anachronistic divisions must generate. He has also been a major contributor to our understanding of the complex world in which the pre-Gratian canon-law collections find their place.

The history of the publication of collections compiled between Burchard and Gratian has been in general a lamentable one since 1900. It resembles indeed a crowded and dangerous waterway littered with such highly visible wrecks as the aborted publication of Anselm of Lucca by Thaner or Fornasari's partial text of the Five Books.[1] A multitude of less visible but equally discouraging enterprises did not even get so far. Though there have been valuable and substantial analyses of relatively uninfluential collections, such as Motta's account of the Collection in 183 Titles, or Reynolds' own very recent *Collectio canonum Casinensis*,[2] only four complete editions of extended texts have made it to port: von Glanvell's problematic Deusdedit in 1905, Perels' *Liber de vita Christiana* of Bonizo of Sutri in 1930,

* I am grateful to the editors for accepting this paper at a very late stage in their preparations, to Professor Somerville for encouraging me to submit it and to Professor Flint for reading an earlier version.

1 *Anselmi episcopi Lucensis Collectio canonum una cum collectione minore*, ed. Fridericus [Friedrich] Thaner (Innsbruck 1906-15), to XI.15, based on an incoherent selection of the manuscripts; *Collectio canonum in V libris: (lib. I-III)*, ed. M. Fornasari, *CCCM*, 6 (1970), devastatingly handled by Gérard Fransen, 'Principes d'édition des collections canoniques', *Revue d'histoire ecclésiastique*, 66 (1971), 125-36, and by others later.

2 *Liber canonum diversorum sanctorum patrum sive Collectio in CLXXXIII titulos digesta*, ed. Joseph Motta, MIC Series B, Corpus collectionum, 7 (Vatican City, 1988)—in three manuscripts, one largely re-organised; Roger E. Reynolds, *The* Collectio canonum Casinensis duodecimi seculi (Codex terscriptus): *a derivative of the south-Italian 'Collection in Five Books'*, Studies and Texts, 137, Monumenta Liturgica Beneventana, 3 (Toronto, 2001), from a single manuscript.

Gilchrist's admirable edition of the *Diversorum patrum sententiae* or *Collection in Seventy-Four Titles* in 1973 and Kretzschmar's *De misericordia et iustitia* of Alger of Liège in 1985.[3] Of these, Deusdedit, surviving in only one complete medieval copy, is a special case to which I will return; Bonizo's work, complete in four early copies, had only the most limited influence on later works which are predominantly canonical; and Alger too had a limited circulation, if significant influence. The *Seventy-Four Titles* stands alone for the breadth of its diffusion and the deep imprint it left on later collections.

In fact most of the collections which were most widely copied and read are still only available either in no edition at all or in ancient, uncritical and often profoundly idiosyncratic versions. Too often it remains true that the more widespread a work was, the less likely it is that we can form an accurate idea of its content. There are, of course, good reasons why this should be so. Even the twenty-five odd copies of a reasonably stable collection, such as the *Tripartita* associated with Ivo of Chartres, represent a serious challenge to the industry of a potential editor. Since the collections largely rehearse material which is in some sense familiar, even painfully so, to many readers, the return on this labour often seems quite disproportionate to the effort, both to editors and publishers. Further, the more widely a collection is found in time and space, the more complex and bewildering the transformations to which it has been subjected by readers and copyists. To produce a usable text which adequately represents the jungle of shifting rubrics, variants, omissions, insertions, reversals and revisions through which the greater collections were known and understood, or misunderstood, is a daunting task. Perhaps even more urgently, the enormous volume of modern work on the transmission of individual canons encourages a sense that any adequate edition should bear such a burden of commentary as to sink the vessel before it even leaves harbour.[4]

Anyone who seeks to understand the evolution of something like a culture of legal learning in the Church between 1000 and 1200 still needs some trustworthy guide to the forms in which the texts circulated, and the variety of ways in which they were represented; a solution to the dilemma remains as urgent, therefore, as it

---

3   *Die Kanonessammlung des Kardinals Deusdedit*, ed. Victor Wolf von Glanvell (Paderborn, 1905; repr. Aalen, 1967)—an intended second volume of commentary did not appear; *Bonizonis Liber de vita Christiana*, ed. Ernst Perels, Texte zur Geschichte des römischen und kanonischen Rechts im Mittelalter, 1 (Berlin, 1930); *Diuersorum patrum sententie siue Collectio in LXXIV titulos digesta*, ed. Joannes T. Gilchrist, MIC Series B, Corpus collectionum, 1 (Vatican City, 1973); Robert Kretzschmar, *Alger von Lüttichs Traktat 'De misericordia et iustitia'*, Quellen und Forschungen zum Recht im Mittelalter, 2 (Sigmaringen, 1985).

4   The late Leonard Boyle offered a characteristically penetrating but daunting set of instructions to any would-be editor of such texts in his contribution to a round-table discussion at Berkeley in 1980, *Proceedings of the Sixth International Congress of Medieval Canon Law*, ed. Stephan Kuttner and Kenneth Pennington, MIC Series C, Subsidia, 7 (Vatican City, 1985), xxii. Though it is a pity the text was never published, the shortage of subsequent editions by those who heard him will not surprise any of the participants.

is elusive. The publication of Dr Fowler-Magerl's magnificent indices to the collections in her evolving *Kanones* is one pointer to a longer-term answer.[5] My concern here, however, is not to wave a magic wand over these intractable problems, but rather to consider a few aspects of the manuscript transmission which will be, at best, visible only to the closest reader of any edition we do get, and, at worst, wholly concealed.

The first of these aspects is in principle extremely obvious—the number and date of the surviving copies. Simple though the point is, its implications are easy to miss. Speaking in general terms, and ignoring many useful and prudent reservations, the history of canonical studies up to the time of Gratian has been dominated from the time of the *Correctores Romani* by a method which one might describe as vertical, or evolutionary. To borrow a term of abuse from another field it might even be called a 'Whig' version of canonistic learning. The dominant objective has been to map the multiple streams which eventually flowed together into the broad river of Gratian, or now perhaps the Gratians.[6] Such a method privileges those sources which shaped Gratian's collection, however slight their resonance if measured by the breadth of their diffusion. This is most easily shown with the Italian *Collection in Three Books*, surviving in its first form in only two manuscripts and in an augmented form in two more, one of the early thirteenth century.[7] Had it not fallen into the hands of the Master, it is hard to believe the collection would have attracted more than the most passing attention. Similarly, the *Collectio Britannica*, now surviving in only one copy, if at least two more may be inferred, continues to exercise the minds of modern scholars, for all its baffling character, partly for the texts of which it is the unique source, but at least as much because it supplied critical materials to the Ivonian circle, through which a mass of Roman Law texts, and a curious selection from the letters of Alexander II and Urban II, passed into Gratian.[8]

---

5   For analysis of collections, see the CD-Rom, Linda Fowler-Magerl, *KanonesJ*, and the descriptions of the collections in the book which accompanies the CD: *A Selection of Canon Law Collections compiled between 1000 and 1140: access with data processing* (Piesenkofen in der Oberpfalz, 2003).

6   The intense debate which surrounds the relation between the earlier and later forms of Gratian as first defined by Anders Winroth, most fully in *The Making of Gratian's* Decretum, Cambridge Studies in Medieval Life and Thought, 4th series, 49 (Cambridge, 2000), has no direct bearing on the issues raised below.

7   The impending edition for MIC by G. Motta is keenly anticipated. Almost all the relevant literature for this (as for most of the collections discussed here) is collected in Lotte Kéry, *Canonical Collections of the Early Middle Ages (ca. 400-1140)*, History of Medieval Canon Law, 1, ed. Wilfried Hartmann and Kenneth Pennington (Washington, 1999), 269-71.

8   Kéry, *Canonical Collections*, 237-8; Robert Somerville's fundamental studies on the book are largely brought together in Robert Somerville with Stephan Kuttner, *Pope Urban II, the* Collectio Britannica *and the Council of Melfi* (Oxford, 1996); see also his 'Papal excerpts in Arsenal MS 713B: Alexander II and Urban II'; and Martin Brett, 'The Sources and Influence of Paris, Bibliothèque de l'Arsenal MS 713', in *Proceedings of the Ninth International Congress of*

To consider the distribution and evidence of use in the manuscripts of pre-Gratian collections as a whole is to find a way into what one might call the horizontal axis of canonical experience—what was being read, where and how it was being read—on its own terms, rather than as mere mileposts on the road to the *Concordia discordantium canonum*. Thus, the world of reflection on God's law in the twelfth century is represented at least as much by the multitude of copies of Burchard, Pseudo-Isidore, or even the *Dionysio-Hadriana* being made, studied and annotated in the period as it is by the collections which directly fuelled or anticipated the novel techniques of Gratian.[9] To enunciate such a claim is easy; to vindicate it in practice, however, is much more difficult.

Precisely because all scribes, or their employers, who copied a text were free to adapt, enlarge, shorten or even pervert their source, there are no indisputable units upon which to build systematic maps of frequency and distribution. The point may be conveniently illustrated by the late John Gilchrist's celebrated demonstration of the restricted circulation of canons attributed to Gregory VII. For his purposes what was to be counted was the number of judgements by individual compilers; in his tables, therefore, the *Panormia* in its hundred and thirty odd manuscripts represents one unit, as do any number of collections surviving in a solitary copy.[10] The point is reasonable, but not irresistible. To the degree that any copyists felt free to abbreviate or expand the exemplar, each may be making a choice, canon by canon.

Medieval Canon Law, ed. Peter Landau and Joerg Mueller, MIC Series C, Subsidia, 10 (Vatican City, 1997), 169-84, 149-67. The existence of two further copies may be assumed since it is common ground that Ivo's *Decretum* depends on a better, and possibly fuller, text than that of the surviving manuscript, and since it is highly probable that the source for the 'Ivonian' *Tripartita* lacked some of the material found in the one used in the *Decretum*. The texts in Arsenal 713 from a *Britannica*-type source clearly contained Urban II material presumed absent in the version used for the *Tripartita*, but it has not yet been determined whether the Arsenal texts could have been taken directly from the form (or copy) used for the *Decretum*. Klaus Herbers, *Leo IV. und das Papsttum in der Mitte des 9. Jahrhunderts: Möglichkeiten und Grenzen päpstlicher Herrschaft in der späten Karolingerzeit*, Päpste und Papsttum, 27 (Stuttgart, 1996), 49-91 is also valuable. The suggestion of Prof. Schilling, reported there at 63, that the surviving MS of the *Britannica* was written in northern Italy is striking, though against the trend of other recent opinion.

9 The fourteen manuscripts of the Dionysio-Hadriana written between *c.* 1100 and *c.* 1500 are listed in Kéry, *Canonical Collections*, 14-7; the sixty copies of Pseudo-Isidore from the same period at *ibid.* 100-5, with more detailed accounts of most of them in Schafer Williams, *Codices Pseudo-Isidorianae: a palaeographico-historical study*, MIC Series C, Subsidia, 3 (Vatican City, 1971): the thirty-three complete copies of Burchard of *c.* 1100 or after are listed by R. Pokorny in Kéry, *Canonical Collections*, 134-42. It is striking that while the two historically ordered collections continued to be copied throughout the middle ages, there are very few copies indeed of the topical (complete) Burchard currently dated after 1200. Such raw figures take no account of evidence of later study in earlier copies.

10 John Gilchrist, 'The Reception of Pope Gregory VII into the Canon Law', *ZRG KA*, 59 (1973), 35-82; *ZRG KA*, 66 (1980), 192-229 (repr. *Canon Law in the Age of Reform, 11th-12th Centuries* [Aldershot, 1993], nos VIII-IX).

Certainly any copy modified in this way may be treated with equal force as an independent witness to the circulation of particular texts.

To take up this point in a rather different way, the boundaries between collections are thoroughly uncertain. At what point, for instance, do the various forms of the *Collection in Seventy-Four Titles*, with or without the 'Swabian appendix', become something else? The *Collection in Two Books*, or *Eight Parts*, the *Collection in Four Books* or the first version of the *Collectio Tarraconensis* are all so heavily dependent on it as to represent almost a sub-group of its circulation, however significant their additions.[11] On the most restrictive view, the *Seventy-Four Titles* is a fascinating but obsolescent collection of relatively limited circulation; on the most liberal, it was one of the central means for the dissemination of a particular and partly novel view of papal authority well into the twelfth century, and even beyond. At a more modest level one could equally ask oneself whether the two versions of the *Polycarpus* or the three forms of the *Caesaraugustana* are one unit of calculation or two, or three?[12] Nor can one be confident that manuscripts of pre-Gratian collections survive in anything like a constant proportion to those that once existed. The classic demonstration here is the case of Deusdedit, with its solitary surviving complete medieval copy. The other collections which seem to depend on independent knowledge of his work are, however, surprising both for their number and their geographical distribution.[13]

---

11 Kéry, *Canonical Collections*, 204-7, 214-15, 227-8; John Gilchrist, 'The Manuscripts of the Canonical Collection in Four Books', *ZRG KA*, 69 (1983), 64-120; Linda Fowler-Magerl, 'Fine Distinctions and the Transmission of Texts', *ZRG KA*, 83 (1997), 146-86 at 152-66; and 'The Restoration of the Canon Law Collection in the MSS Vat. lat. 3832 and Assisi BC 227', in *Grundlagen des Rechts. Festschrift für Peter Landau zum 65. Geburtstag*, ed. Richard H. Helmholz, Paul Mikat, Jörg Müller and Michael Stolleis, Rechts- und Staatswissenschaftliche Veröffentlichungen der Görres-Gesellschaft, NF 91 (Paderborn-München-Wien-Zürich, 2000), 179-203; Fowler-Magerl, *Selection*, 53-61, 74-6, 90-93, 105-6.

12 See particularly Uwe Horst, *Die Kanonessammlung Polycarpus des Gregor von S. Grisogono. Quellen und Tendenzen, MGH Hilfsmittel*, 5 (München,1980), esp. 11-13; the second version is now represented only by Paris, Bibliothèque Nationale, MS lat. 3882, for which see esp. Paul Fournier, 'Les deux recensions de la collection canonique romaine dite le *Polycarpus*', *Mélanges d'archéologie et d'histoire de l'École française de Rome*, 37 (1918/19), 55-101, at 80-101; repr. in Paul Fournier, *Mélanges de droit canonique*, ed. Theo Kölzer, 2 vols (Aalen, 1983), ii, 703-49; Paul Fournier and Gabriel Le Bras, *Histoire des collections canoniques en Occident depuis les Fausses Décrétales jusqu'au Décret de Gratien*, 2 vols (Paris, 1931-2; repr. Aalen, 1972), ii, 180-85; for the multiple forms of the *Caesaraugustana*, esp. Paul Fournier, 'La collection canonique dite *Caesaraugustana*', *Nouvelle revue historique de droit français et étranger*, 45 (1921), 53-79 (repr. in *Mélanges de droit canonique*, ii, 815-41), esp. 71-4; largely summarised in Fournier-Le Bras, *Histoire*, ii, 269-84; Linda Fowler-Magerl, 'Vier französische und spanische vorgratianische Kanonensammlungen', in *Aspekte europäischer Rechtsgeschichte. Festgabe für Helmut Coing*, Ius Commune, Sonderhefte 21 (1982), 123-46 at 144-6; Kéry, *Canonical Collections*, 260-62, 266-9; Fowler-Magerl, *Selection*, 169-71,179-83.

13 The only complete ms is Vatican City, Biblioteca Apostolica Vaticana, MS lat. 3833; Kéry, *Canonical Collections*, 229 lists seven medieval mss containing extracts, but none are substantial.

Nevertheless, the evidence of surviving manuscripts, and the number of cases in which they were written apparently after the diffusion of copies of Gratian and its dominance in the schools, are a precious reminder that the world as seen from Bologna in 1170 was not the one in which all, or even most, readers lived and thought. Even where the manuscript may have been written before 1150, the multiple traces of subsequent use are abundant proof of the process of active reflection which they generated long after their copying. I have chosen two cases to demonstrate such readers at work. It is worth stressing from the outset that these cases could be multiplied more or less indefinitely; there is nothing freakish or unusual about these two examples.

The first is the copy of the *Collection in Four Books* now in the Cathedral Library at Canterbury, Litt. ms B 7. This is an important if incomplete witness to the text, written in not very expert hands perhaps in northern or eastern France around 1100, which certainly seems to have reached Canterbury well before the Reformation (Pl. 12.1).[14] It reveals two levels of thought and annotation which

---

Fournier-Le Bras, *Histoire*, ii, 52-3 listed some of the derivatives of Deusdedit; a fuller list would include at least:

The Varia II of the *Collectio Britannica* (and thence the whole Ivonian complex of *Tripartita*, *Decretum* and *Panormia*). There is a useful statement of the position with the modern literature by Jasper in Detlev Jasper and Horst Fuhrmann, *Papal Letters in the Early Middle Ages*, History of Medieval Canon Law, 2, ed. Wilfried Hartmann and Kenneth Pennington (Washington, 2001), 122-3.

The *Collectio Caesaraugustana*, for which see n. 12 above, esp. Fournier, 'La collection *Caesaraugustana*', 63-4; this represents the most systematic exploitation of the whole text to survive from a later compiler.

The second recension of the *Polycarpus*, for which see n. 12 above.

The collection in Vatican City, Biblioteca Apostolica Vaticana, MS Vat. lat. 3829: Fournier-Le Bras, *Histoire*, ii, 210; Kéry, *Canonical Collections*, 288.

The third part of the collection in Roma, Biblioteca Vallicelliana, MS F 54 , described by Uta-Renate Blumenthal: 'An Episcopal Handbook from Twelfth-Century Southern Italy', in *Studia in honorem eminentissimi cardinalis Alphonsi M. Stickler*, ed. Rosalius Iosephus Cardinal Castillo Lara, Studia et Textus Historiae Iuris Canonici, 7 (Roma, 1992), 13-24, esp. 20-21, (repr. *Papal Reform and Canon Law in the 11th and 12th Centuries* [Aldershot, 1998], no. XVIII).

A second collection from the Vallicelliana: Wilfried Hartmann, 'Die Kanonessammlung der Handschrift Rom, Biblioteca Vallicelliana, B. 89', *BMCL*, NS 17 (1987), 45-64, esp. 47, 58-9.

The Collection of Torino, Biblioteca Nazionale Universitaria, MS E.V.44 (903): Fournier-Le Bras, *Histoire*, ii, 218-22; Kéry, *Canonical Collections*, 284; Fowler-Magerl, *Selection*, 100-101, 112.

The *Collection in Seven Books* in Torino, Biblioteca Nazionale Universitaria, MS D.IV.33 (239): Fournier-Le Bras, *Histoire*, ii, 165-6; Kéry, *Canonical Collections*, 265-6; Fowler-Magerl, *Selection*, 102-3.

Placidus of Nonantula: *Liber de honore ecclesie*, cc. 121-9, ed. Lothar de Heinemann and Ernst Sackur, *MGH Libelli de Lite*, 3 vols (1891-7), ii, 627-8, incorporating Deusdedit, IV. 68, 56, 58-9, 61, 64-6.

The interpolated version of Ivo's *Panormia* in Vatican City, Archivio San Pietro, MS G 19bis.

14 Z. N. Brooke, *The English Church and the Papacy* (Cambridge, 1931; repr. 1989), 239-41; Gilchrist, 'The Manuscripts', 65-6; Fowler-Magerl, *Selection*, 59. N. R. Ker, *Medieval Manuscripts in British libraries*, 4 vols (Oxford, 1969-92), ii, 270 identified the hand of two added texts

deserve attention in this context. The first is the less visible; the marginal rubrics separating the sub-divisions of each book are apparently significantly later than the main hand, perhaps even as late as *c.* 1300. On any view, it is striking that a later reader was ready to spend such effort on a collection which was in the conventional sense obsolete and had always been awkward to use for lack of clear thematic organisation. However, there is more to it than that, for the subdivisions are not the invention of the anonymous annotator; they reflect pretty faithfully the rubrics found in other copies of the Collection, usually inserted at the time of their writing, and in turn largely derived from the *Collection in Seventy-Four Titles.*[15] A serious if belated exercise in the comparison of exemplars lies behind these rubrics. The second level of annotation is represented by a positive barrage of comments inserted by Matthew Parker (archbishop of Canterbury 1559-75), and his principal Latin secretary, apparently John Joscelyn. Some are traditional in form,—for example, on fo 5v, 'Clerici in monasteriis non degant' against I. 4. 4.[16] Many are much more obviously polemical; for example's sake only, 'Papa Caesari minitatur', or 'Si ab ipso Domino Caeremoniae institutae populum sanctificabant, Quanto magis a sanctissimo papa. Argumentum a fortiori papisticum' appear in the distinctive large italic hand of the archbishop on fos 3v and 40r.[17] It is a curious experience to follow the impassioned arguments of the Reformation down the margins of a copy of a relatively obscure collection of the reform period.

The second case is rather a whole class of similar examples, the surprisingly large number of copies of pre-Gratian collections through which later annotators have worked carefully to identify and insert the cross-references to Gratian. The simplest form may be illustrated from Paris, Bibliothèque Nationale, MS latin 3858, a copy of the first version of the Ivonian *Tripartita* (Pl. 12.2). This first

---

on fo 91 (92) as English and early s. xii; this has been called into question by Richard Gameson, *The Manuscripts of Early Norman England* (Oxford, 1999), 77.

15 For example's sake only, the early rubrics are: 'De primatu Romane ecclesie' (fo 1r), 'De auctoritate privilegiorum' (fo 3v), 'De libertate monasteriorum et monachorum' (fo 4v), 'De ordine accusationis et personis accusantium' (fo 6r), 'Ut causa accusatoris in sua provincia terminetur, et quid sit provincia' (fo 7v), 'Quod inferiores non debent accusare superiores' (fo 7v). These represent the rubrics to Titles 1, 3-7 of the *Diversorum patrum sententie,* ed. Gilchrist, 19, 33, 39, 44, 52, 54, also used by the *Collection in Four Books,* lightly modified; cf. Gilchrist, 'The Manuscripts', 80-2. Title 2 ('Quod Petrus et Paulus passi sunt una die', before 1.2.1) is missing, though at fo 3v (Pl. 12.1) John Joscelyn (see below), Parker's secretary, inserted 'Petrus et Paulus ambo simul Roma extincti sunt, ut antea' against 1.2.2, according to the numbering scheme of Fowler-Magerl, *KanonesJ*; the canon is 1. 22 in Gilchrist's analysis, 'The Manuscripts', 80. The Canterbury text of the Four Books ends with 4.5 (Gilchrist's 4.138) on fo 54r, with the rubric 'Ne Iudeis Christiana mancipia deserviant', but the same rubricator continues to supply headings for the remaining material, which is idiosyncratic.

16 The canon is 1.42 in Gilchrist's analysis, 'The Manuscripts', 82.

17 I owe a great debt to Dr de Hamel, Librarian of Corpus Christi College, Cambridge, now custodian of Parker's own collection of manuscripts, and to Tim Bolton of that College, who devoted much time and thought to these annotations on my behalf.

version, particularly in the historically organised Part A, is notable for its absence of rubrics and capitulations, which makes the book hard to use for conventional legal purposes, and the citations of Gratian are virtually the only indication that this copy was studied at all. Cambridge, University Library, MS Ff. 4. 41 (Pl. 12.3) is altogether more elaborate: there are plenty of later added cross-references to Gratian, and to other authorities, but the text has also been glossed at quite remarkable length, and by appeal to historical and scriptural as much as legal sources.[18] These cross-references, often in tiny hands and heavily abbreviated, are easy to neglect and hard to interpret. They illustrate, however, the continued study of collections for some purposes long after one would suppose they had ceased to play any serious role in the practice of the law, but by readers perfectly familiar with the changed world.

There is almost as much to be learned from the physical characteristics of the surviving manuscripts as from their numbers and their evidence of later study. The way the text is presented in script and format can offer an important indication of what it was conceived to be, and how it was to be used. Among the Ivonian collections the *Decretum* is by far the longest, and such surviving copies of the complete text as the magnificent Canterbury copy in Cambridge, Corpus Christi College, MS 19 reflect its monumental character—written in double columns in a grand and stately script, on carefully prepared leaves some 330 x 240. It is emphatically a work to remain in a library. Though there are a few very interesting early additions, there are no other indications that it was ever subjected to later close analysis.[19] The other complete copies in Paris, Bibliothèque Nationale, MS lat. 14315; Vatican City, Biblioteca Apostolica Vaticana, MS Vat. lat. 1357; and London, British Library, Royal MS 11 D vii are comparably massive, as is the fragmentary Sigüenza, Archivo de la Catedral, MS 61; the Paris copy has been systematically corrected, apparently from another exemplar, but only the Vatican copy shows any significant history of subsequent additions.[20]

---

18 Bruce Brasington has made a special study of this manuscript, the first report of which appears in his 'Glossing Strategies in Pre-Gratian Canonical Collections', in *Grundlagen des Rechts*, 155-62. I have benefited, as ever, from many discussions with him on the whole transmission of the *Panormia*.

19 The indispensable guide to the content of these manuscripts is Peter Landau, 'Das Dekret des Ivo von Chartres: die handschriftliche Überlieferung im Vergleich zum Text in den Editionen des 16. und 17. Jahrhunderts', *ZRG KA*, 70 (1984), 1-44. For the additions to Cambridge, Corpus Christi, MS 19 see Robert Somerville, 'A Textual Link between Canterbury and Lucca in the Early Twelfth Century', in *Cristianità ed Europa: miscellanea di studi in onore di Luigi Prosdocimi*, ed. Cesare Alzati, 2 vols in 3 (Roma-Freiburg-Wien, 1994), i/2, 405-15. For the Corpus copy see also Gameson, *The Manuscripts*, 77, who treats the Royal copy (by omission) as later.

20 The additions to the later-twelfth-century Vat. lat. 1357 are listed in Stephan Kuttner and Reinhard Elze, *A Catalogue of Canon and Roman Law Manuscripts in the Vatican Library*, 1, Studi e Testi, 322 (1986), 123-4. Paris, BN lat. 14315 is, however, another of the manuscripts to include cross-references in several hands to Gratian.

The *Panormia* is much shorter, and in some ways far better suited to practical or private use, particularly when supplied with the capitulations and rubrics characteristic of many of the later copies. By no means every copy, however, is comparably utilitarian in physical structure. The most extreme example of a 'reference' text seems to be Pennsylvania, University of Philadelphia Library, MS lat. 58 (723), which contrives to spread the text over 256 folia measuring 260 x 200, with wide margins, roughly double the number of leaves needed by more conventional copies.[21] At the opposite extreme, the copy from Weissenau now in the Hermitage collection is of unremarkable format, but manages to squeeze the whole text into 56 leaves.[22] Three other copies present a very different aspect.

Edinburgh, National Library of Scotland, Advocates' MS 18. 8. 6 (Pl. 12.4) is a copy from the late twelfth century which presents many points of interest. Puzzlingly, from the beginning of Book I to mid-Book III it has many brief rubrics, but few inscriptions, while from the end of Book III there are virtually no rubrics but many abbreviated inscriptions; one could imagine how some readers might prize one sort of information above the other, but it is harder to see why they should change their mind in mid-text. The simplest explanation is that the exemplar resembled many other early copies in lacking rubrics from Book IV on, though that does not account for the omission of so many inscriptions earlier. It also has a number of additions at the foot of the leaves, on inserted slips and at the end. The appearance of some decretals of Alexander III shows that more recent legislation was of continuing interest to its owner,[23] while a few other additions of a moral or

---

21 Martin Brett, 'Creeping up on the Panormia', in *Grundlagen des Rechts*, 205-70, at 260-70 provides an interim list of *Panormia* manuscripts, with no pretence to palaeographical rigour. A draft text of the collection, with a rather fuller version of the manuscript list, can be seen at http:-//wtfaculty.wtamu.edu/~bbrasington/panormia.html. The Philadelphia copy is briefly described in Norman P. Zacour and Rudolf Hirsch, *Catalogue of the Manuscripts in the Libraries of the University of Pennsylvania to 1800* (Philadelphia, 1965), 13. It was formerly Phillipps MS 7408. I am grateful to Dr Greta Austin and Michael Gullick for providing a more detailed account of the book. By common consent it is French, and Gullick identifies the script as of the first half of the twelfth century.

22 St Petersburg, Publiknaia Biblioteka im. M.E. Saltykova Shchedrina, MS Ermit. lat. 25, ex-Weissenau—though not of course necessarily or even probably written there; the main text is in a very compressed hand with 51 lines to the page, though there are important additions, including a fuller version of Lateran II than Brant included in the *editio princeps*: Brett, 'Creeping up', 215. For the Weissenau MSS at St Petersburg see Paul Lehmann, 'Verschollene und wiedergefundene Reste der Klosterbibliothek von Weissenau', *Zentralblatt für Bibliothekswesen*, 49 (1932), 1-11 (the book is possibly the 'Excerpta decretorum' in the later twelfth-century catalogue printed *ibid.*, 10); Sigrid Krämer, *Handschriftenerbe des deutschen Mittelalters*, Mittelalterliche Bibliothekskataloge Deutschlands und der Schweiz, Erg. Bd 1, 3 vols (München, 1989-90), ii, 819.

23 I owe my knowledge of this manuscript to Robert Somerville, who has been characteristically generous with further information. It has not yet proved possible to identify its former home, or origin. For the inserted decretals see fo 40v: 'A. III Winton' episcopo. Innotescat sollicitudini tue—committere potest' (from JL 14156); fos 55v-56r: 'Alexander III Rectrodo Rothomagensi archiepiscopo. Quoniam quesitum est a nobis—debet remitti. Dat' Tuscl' v id. Octob'' (JL 13583);

ethical character point to the various levels at which the text could be read. In Plate
12.3 the additions are a paraphrase of a passage of Gregory the Great, *Moralia in
Iob* and a hexameter from the dismal Maximianus the Etruscan.[24] The most striking
feature of the manuscript, however, is its diminutive size, roughly 160 x 112 mm.
This is emphatically a book for private use.

Two other English copies of the *Panormia* with a distinctive appendix illustrate
the same point by rather different means. Oxford, Jesus College, MS 26 eventually
reached Cirencester as the gift of Mr Alured; beautifully written in a minute script
with inscriptions and rubrics entered in red in the margin, it is a small, dense slab of
a book, some 170 x 130 mm, still in its twelfth-century boards.[25] The copy formerly
in the Lumley collection (perhaps from Waltham abbey), which is now Firenze,
Biblioteca Nazionale Centrale, MS Magliabechiano xxxiv 73 (Pl. 12.5), seems to
have been copied directly from the Jesus book, but suggests its function as a
working copy less by its size than by its rapid and informal script, and by the
deplorable quality of the parchment on which it is written. The leaves are often
strikingly irregular in shape, many contain gaping holes, and the skins seem to have
been so thin that the hair side could only be used by leaving a rough and pitted
surface to work on. It is an occasion for surprise and gratitude that it has survived
at all.[26]

In principle, the text of manuscripts should be clear enough from any well-
constructed edition, and certainly so if the number of manuscripts is reasonably
restricted. In practice, however, any widely circulated text presents so many variants from copy to copy that it will be difficult to convey to the reader the
extraordinary variety of readings, and meanings which are now buried behind the

---

fo 86 (addition at end): 'Bartholomeo episcopo Exoniensi. Super eo vero quod—clericum ledat'
(JL 12180, 13771). For these decretals see Charles Duggan, *Twelfth-century Decretal Collections
and their Importance in English History* (London, 1963), 125, 164, 174 noting their occurrence in
some early English collections; and C. R. Cheney and Mary G. Cheney, *Studies in the Collections
of Twelfth-Century Decretals from the Papers of the late Walther Holtzmann*, MIC Series B,
Corpus collectionum, 3 (Vatican City, 1979). The small inserted slips have notes on procedure.

24 *S. Gregorii Magni Moralia in Job*, ed. Marcus Adriaen, *CCSL*, 143B (1985), 1227; *Maximiani
elegiae ad fidem codicis Etonensis*, 1 line 5, ed. M. Petschenig, Studien für classische Philologie
und Archaeologie, 11(ii) (Berlin, 1890; repr. Nedeln, 1975), 1. I am grateful to Professor Michael
Reeve for this identification.

25 Brooke, *English Church*, 94n, 245; N. R. Ker, *Catalogue of Manuscripts containing Anglo-Saxon*
(Oxford, 1957), 433, no. 355; *Councils and Synods*, ii, 720 (where the Florentine MS was
unknown to the editor). Michael Gullick is preparing a study of this group of Cirencester
manuscripts.

26 The characteristic ownership mark of Lord Lumley (d. 1609), is found at the foot of fo 1; it is
presumably to be identified with the octavo manuscript listed as no. 1350 in *The Lumley Library.
The Catalogue of 1609*, ed. Sears Jayne and Francis R. Johnson (London, 1956), 167. Michael
Gullick and Dr Tessa Webber have both advised me on this book, and I owe the suggestion of its
possible home at Waltham to them.

apparent consensus of the inadequate editions we have to use. Two examples drawn from the *Panormia* provide a powerful illustration of the uncertainties in the manuscript transmission. The first is in a passage from the *Institutes* reproduced as *Panormia* II. 160:

> *[Quis usus, qui mores debeant teneri]*[a]. *Constitutionum libro I, titulo i*
> Non scripto[b] in ius venit quod usus probavit. Nam diuturni mores consensu utentium approbati legem imitantur. Item. Ea que ipsa sibi queque civitas constituit sepe mutari solent vel tacito consensu principis vel alia postea lege lata.[27]
>
> [a] *in mg.* AdCaMgPf, *in text* Ea*(no inscr.)*Vm; *om.* BdFbPkPwTbTc; De eodem *in mg.* Sg
> [b] Non scripto Bd²MgPfPwSgTbTc *Coll. Brit.*; Conscripto AdBdEaPkSeVm; Cum scripto Be; Ex non scripto CaFb; Ex scripto Cc

The variants here show a random selection of manuscripts which divide roughly half and half over the central doctrine of the canon. 'Non scripto' is the reading of the *Britannica* and of the manuscripts (but not the *editio princeps*) of the *Decretum* of Ivo, and so probably stood at the origin of the *Panormia* transmission.[28] The origin of the variant 'Conscripto' and its relatives is not particularly difficult to discern, for confusion is always likely where the key word of a canon is the first. The indication to the rubricator of the coloured letter to be inserted may be either missing, wrong, obscure or misunderstood. Brussels, Bibliothèque Royale Albert 1er, MS 1817-2501, fo 42r (Bd in the apparatus above) illustrates the point with gratifying clarity, for 'Con-' seems to have been altered to 'Non-' almost at once, although it could possibly have been the other way round. The shared reading of CaFb is altogether more interesting, for it cannot be explained mechanically, but is

---

27 *PL* 161.1120, Migne's revised reprint of Vosmedian's 1557 re-edition of the *editio princeps* by Sebastian Brant of 1499. The growing distance between the printed text and the manuscript which Brant used each time the text was reprinted is described with magisterial authority by Peter Landau, 'Die Rubriken und Inskriptionen von Ivos Panormie: Die Ausgabe Sebastian Brants im Vergleich zur Löwener Edition des Melchior de Vosmédian und der Ausgabe von Migne', *BMCL*, NS 12 (1982), 31-49; Brant's source, and the copies supposedly collated by Vosmedian, remain unidentified. The source of the canon is *Institutes*, 1.2.9. For the transmission of the texts of the *Institutes* and *Digest* in the *Collectio Britannica* see most recently Antonia Fiore, 'La "Collectio Britannica" e la riemersione del Digesto', *Rivista internazionale di diritto comune*, 9 (1998), 81-121, esp. 88.

28 *Collectio Britannica* (London, British Library, Add. MS 8873), fo 56v; Ivo, *Decretum*, 4.194, repr. from Fronteau's 1647 re-edition of Ioannes Molinaeus [Jan van der Meulen], *Decretum D. Ivonis episcopi Carnutensis, septem ac decem tomis sive partibus constans* (Louvain 1561), 136 in *PL* 161.308. Molinaeus used two manuscripts now lost, and for some purposes his edition has the status of a manuscript itself (Landau, 'Das Dekret'). Fronteau occasionally adapted the text of Molinaeus by reference to Paris, BN lat. 14315, but did not do so here. The manuscripts have 'Non scripto in', the edition 'Ex non scripto'. Gratian only incorporated the second half of the canon as D. 12, c. 6; it is tempting to suppose he was confronted by a *Panormia* with one of the more distracting variants in the first part. For the manuscripts and most of the sigla used here see Brett, 'Creeping up', 260-70.

in fact the reading of the ultimate source, the *Institutes*; it also apparently stood in the manuscript behind the editions. Ca is the Cambridge University Library MS described earlier, probably written in France though later at Durham. Fb is Firenze, Biblioteca Nazionale Centrale, MS Conventi Soppressi G. I. 836, from Vallombrosa.[29] Textually these copies are some distance apart, and they certainly cannot have a single exemplar. In both cases, and independently, the scribes of the two books appear to have amended their text from the source, or copied from exemplars where this had already happened. It seems likely that the ancestor of Cambridge, Pembroke College, MS 103 (Cc), which is unrelated to either Ca or Fb, had undergone a similar process, though the scribe of Cc then undid the good work by omitting the 'non'.[30]

A second case is rather less easy to explain. *Panormia* III. 101 is canon 12 of Urban II's council at Melfi, recently given an admirable edition. The manuscripts divide over two significant variants:

Urbanus II, in sinodo apud Melfiam: Eos qui post subdiaconatum[a] uxoribus vacare noluerint[b] ab omni sacro ordine removemus, officioque atque beneficio ecclesie carere decernimus. Quod si ab episcopo commoniti non correxerint, principibus licentiam indulgemus, ut eorum feminas mancipent servituti. Si vero episcopi consenserint eorum pravitatibus, ipsi officii interdictione multentur.[31]

[a] subdiac. PkSgTbVmVoA*Grat*; diaconatum BdBeCaEaFbMgPfPw; diaconatum ab Tc
[b] nol- MgPfPkPwSgTcVmVo; vol- BdBeCaFbTbA*Grat*

Of these the first is of profound practical importance and there is no obvious mechanical explanation for its origin. While the second appears to reverse the sense, this may not have been what the scribes intended. It seems at least as likely that the copyists were uncertain what 'vacare' meant. Those who rightly thought it meant 'give up' followed it with 'noluerint'; others may well have supposed it meant 'devote themselves to', and so thought the sense required 'voluerint'. There

---

29 For Ca see above, n. 18; for Fb see Detlev Jasper, *Das Papstwahldekret von 1059. Überlieferung und Textgestalt*, Beiträge zur Geschichte und Quellenkunde des Mittelalters, 12 (Sigmaringen, 1986), 92.

30 The Pembroke manuscript is written in a curious and rather heavy hand, perhaps an archaising one. It ends at IV. 104, and its most striking distinctive features are:
    a) two additional canons after II. 42, Brett, 'Creeping up', 229 nn. 84-5.
    b) c. 15 of the Council of Piacenza (1095) after II. 45 (Brett, 'Creeping up', 229 n. 86), which it shares with Paris, Bibliothèque Nationale, MS lat. 10742, another enlarged copy apparently once at S. Giustina, Padua.
    None of these are found in Ca or Fb.

31 *PL* 161.1152; Somerville and Kuttner, *Pope Urban II*, 256, cap. 12; Arsenal 713, fo 149v; D. 32, c. 10. Roger E. Reynolds, 'The Subdiaconate as a Sacred and Superior Order', in *Clerics in the Early Middle Ages* (Aldershot, 1999), no. IV, 1-39.

is of course no way of determining how any subsequent reader would understand the second reading in either form.

Both canons illustrate two simple points. Firstly, any proposition of the kind 'According to the *Panormia*' is thoroughly insecure. Even the most cautious scholar who verifies the text of the edition against three or four manuscripts may still miss the extent of the uncertainty. Secondly, the reactions of some copyists to ambiguities of this kind provide striking examples of the thinking scribe, the copyist as editor.

A final example from the manuscripts of the *Tripartita* illustrates the same process in a way that also raises different issues. The text of canon 12 of the Second Council of Seville as it is preserved in Part A 2 depends directly upon Pseudo-Isidore, and runs:

> *De desertoribus clericis ut episcopis suis restituantur. cp. iii:* Placuit ut si quis clericus ministris[a] ecclesie proprie destitutis ad aliam transitum fecerit, compellente ad quem fugerit sacerdote ad ecclesiam quam prius incoluerat remittatur. Qui uero eum susceperit, nec statim sine ullo nisu exceptionis ad propriam ecclesiam remittendum elegerit, quamdiu eum restituat communione se priuatum agnoscat. Desertorem autem clericum cingulo honoris atque ordinis sui exutum aliquo tempore monasterio religari conuenit, sicque postea in ministerio ecclesiastici ordinis reuocari. Nam non poterit in talibus propagationis[b] aboleri[c] licentia, nisi fuerit in eis propter correptionem[d] discipline subsecuta[e].[32]

> [a] ministris B; ministeriis A(misteriis **h**) | [b] -ionis X (-ionibus **z**; -ionum **oa**); pervagationibus *Hispana* | [c] obiliri X (aboleri *over erasure* **c**l^2*Grat.*; abiliri **l**; *om. with erasure* **w**; oboleri **r**^{2}) | [d] correptionem X (corruptionem **ha**) | [e] censura *add.* **c**^{2}**l**^{2}**r**^{2}*Hispana*, correctio *add. Grat., om.* X

In the apparatus X represents the consensus of both versions, A the reading of the manuscripts of the first version, B the readings of the second, while lower case sigla in brackets represent aberrant readings within the consensus. Whilst almost every variant reveals some level of uncertainty on the meaning, it is the last that is the most striking and puzzling. The original version in both the first and second states lacked a subject for 'subsecuta', and this form seems to have been used by Gratian.[33] Presumably by the light of nature he supplied the very reasonable 'correctio'. The three manuscripts of the most developed form of the second version (**c**, **l** and **r** in the apparatus above) are closely related. Paris, Bibliothèque Nationale MS lat. 3858B (**c**), is a Colbertine book from le Mans, the basis of

---

32   C. of Seville II c. 3b as printed in *Isidori mercatoris decretalium collectio*, repr. from the edition by Merlin, *PL* 130.597, from a late ms; *Decretales Pseudo-Isidorianae*, ed. Paulus Hinschius (Leipzig, 1863; repr. Aalen, 1963), reproducing the earlier *Hispana* edition, at 438a; C. 21, qu. 2, c. 2.

33   Winroth, *The Making*, 217.

Fournier's detailed account of the whole collection;[34] Vatican City, Biblioteca Apostolica Vaticana, MS Reg. lat. 973 (r), is from another French scriptorium, while Olomouc, Státní vedecká knihovna, Kapitulni knihovna, MS C.O. 205 (I) was one of the manuscripts written for the cathedral there for Bishop Henry Zdík around 1130-40.[35] The detailed evidence of the readings throughout the three copies shows that none can be a copy of either of the others, though all to a varying degree have been altered by erasure or insertion to restore the readings of the first version, and all three must share an ultimate archetype. As evidence for the dissemination of such texts these connections are striking enough, but it is perhaps even more surprising that in this case all three have also been corrected later in the same way—by the insertion of 'censura', rightly by reference to Pseudo-Isidore's *Hispana* text. This agreement contrasts with the very different ways in which all three tried to solve the problem offered by the archaic and unusual spelling 'obiliri'. The 'censura' emendation is clearly not a mere conjecture, and the source for it was reasonably accessible. The special feature here is rather that the same emendation should be made in the same way in three distinct centres and at about the same time. The process of comparison of text and source which can be inferred in the *Panormia* case above can here be seen as it occurred.

Both this case of a comparison of the *Tripartita* against its Pseudo-Isidorean source and that of the *Panormia* extract from the *Institutes* discussed above are illustrations on a small scale of a larger issue. The more widely circulated collections were naturally subject to all the ills that scribes are heir to, and their errors are as valuable to editors of canonistic materials as they are in any other branch of medieval thought. Because in principle the law had a direct importance for action, one may suspect that horizontal contamination, the early collation of one form of the text with another, is even commoner in the canons than elsewhere. Evidence that this occurred very widely can be found wherever one looks, though one can scarcely quantify its relative frequency in canonical texts and elsewhere. For the same reasons, however, the collections are peculiarly liable to 'decontamination' by the copyists, the restoration of the text from an earlier form of the source. When, under Gregory XIII, the *Correctores Romani* completed their task of 'purging' the transmitted text of Gratian from its errors by reference to his sources, they were

---

34 Paul Fournier, 'Les collections canoniques attribuées à Yves de Chartres', *Bibliothèque de l'École des chartes*, 57 (1896), 645-98, 58 (1897), 26-77, 293-326, 410-44, 624-76; repr. in *Mélanges de droit canonique*, i, 451-678; largely summarised in Fournier-Le Bras, *Histoire*, ii, 58-66.

35 The fullest account of the scriptorium, and the MS, is offered by Miroslav Flodr, *Skriptorium Olomoucké*, Opera Universitatis Brunensis, Facultas Philosophica, 65 [67, wrongly, on title page] (Praha, 1960), esp. 66-73, 251-4, 293-4. Jan Bistřicky, 'Studien zum Urkunden-, Brief- und Handschriftenwesen des Bischofs Heinrich Zdík von Olmütz', *Archiv für Diplomatik*, 26 (1980), 135-258, at 198-204 proposes a yet more precise date of 1138 x 1142. For the early additions see Timothy Reuter, 'Zur Anerkennung Papst Innocenz' II.', *Deutsches Archiv für Erforschung des Mittelalters*, 39/ii (1983), 395-416.

following the halting footsteps of many humbler predecessors. While all such decontamination is a tribute to the learning and energy of those who undertook it, the consequences for the modern editor, and the modern reader, are often severe.

The broader lesson I draw from all the exhibits paraded in this paper is that it is not sufficient for a broad understanding of the intellectual ferment which transformed twelfth-century thought about the Church, its nature, its regulation and the world in which it operated, to study the various collections simply as units in an evolutionary sequence. The manuscripts in which they survive are the work of a living community of scribes, readers and editors. Too easily an edition may become a dead and static representation of its text, as little true to its lively originals as the most inept of stuffed animals in a glass case in an old-fashioned museum. Outside its confines the texts are in a clamorous ferment. The canonist must work, so to speak, in the field to capture the full variety and vitality of the material.

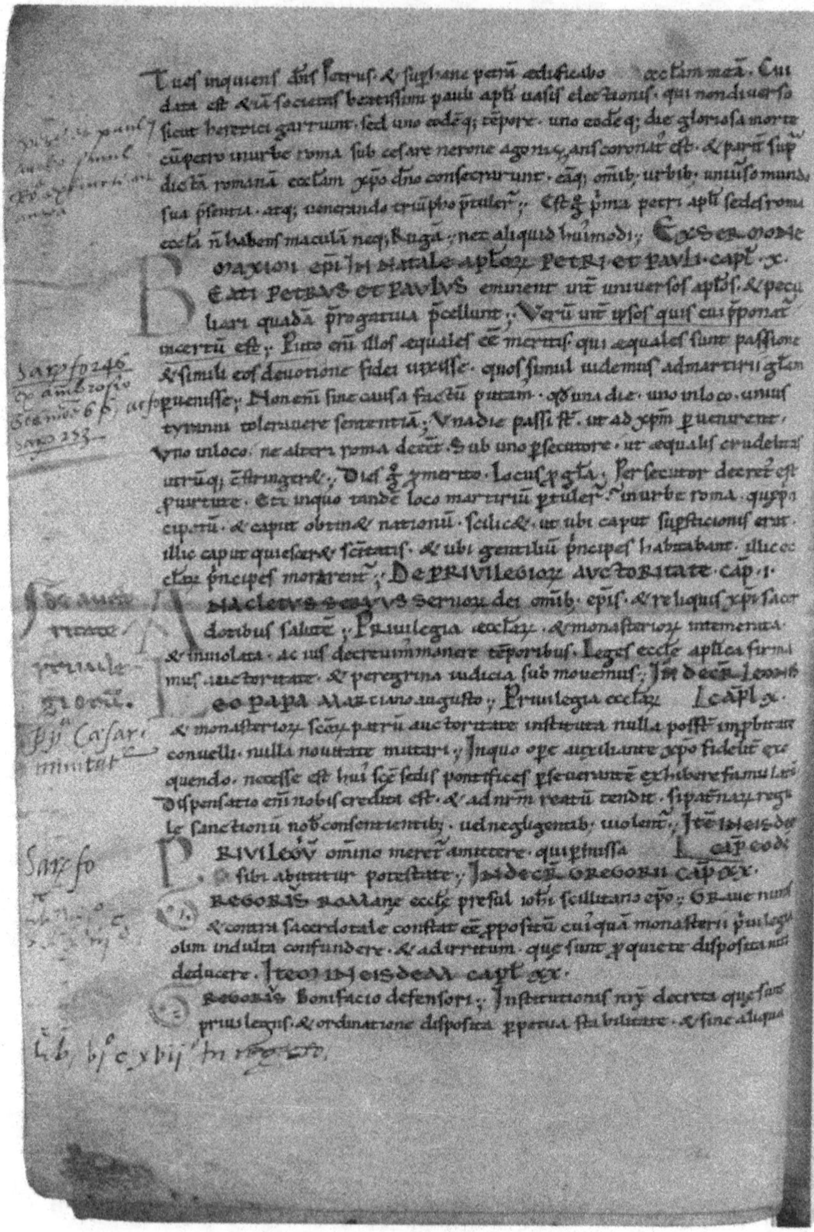

Plate 12.1 Canterbury, Cathedral Library, Litt. ms B 7, fo 3v. By permission of the Dean and Chapter of Canterbury Cathedral.

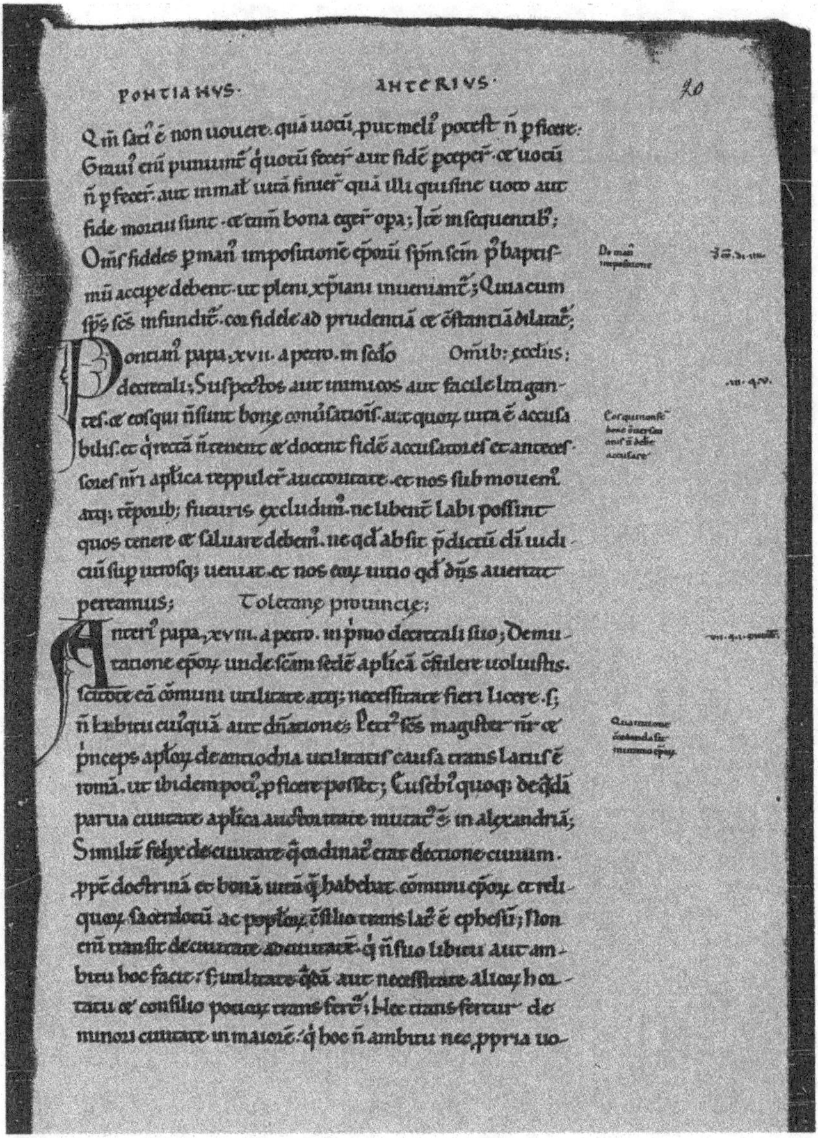

Plate 12.2 Paris, Bibliothèque Nationale, MS latin 3858, fo 20. By permission of the Director of the Bibliothèque Nationale de France.

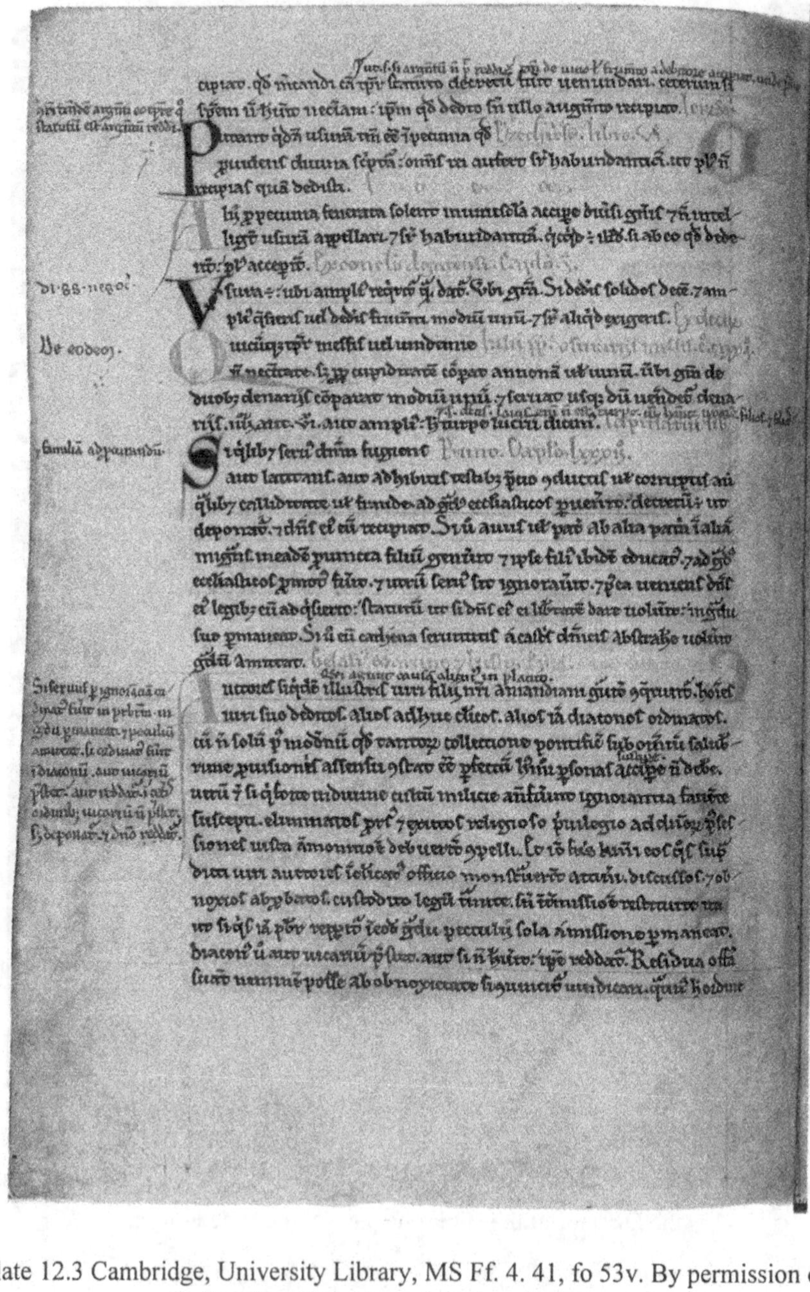

Plate 12.3 Cambridge, University Library, MS Ff. 4. 41, fo 53v. By permission of
the Syndics of Cambridge University Library.

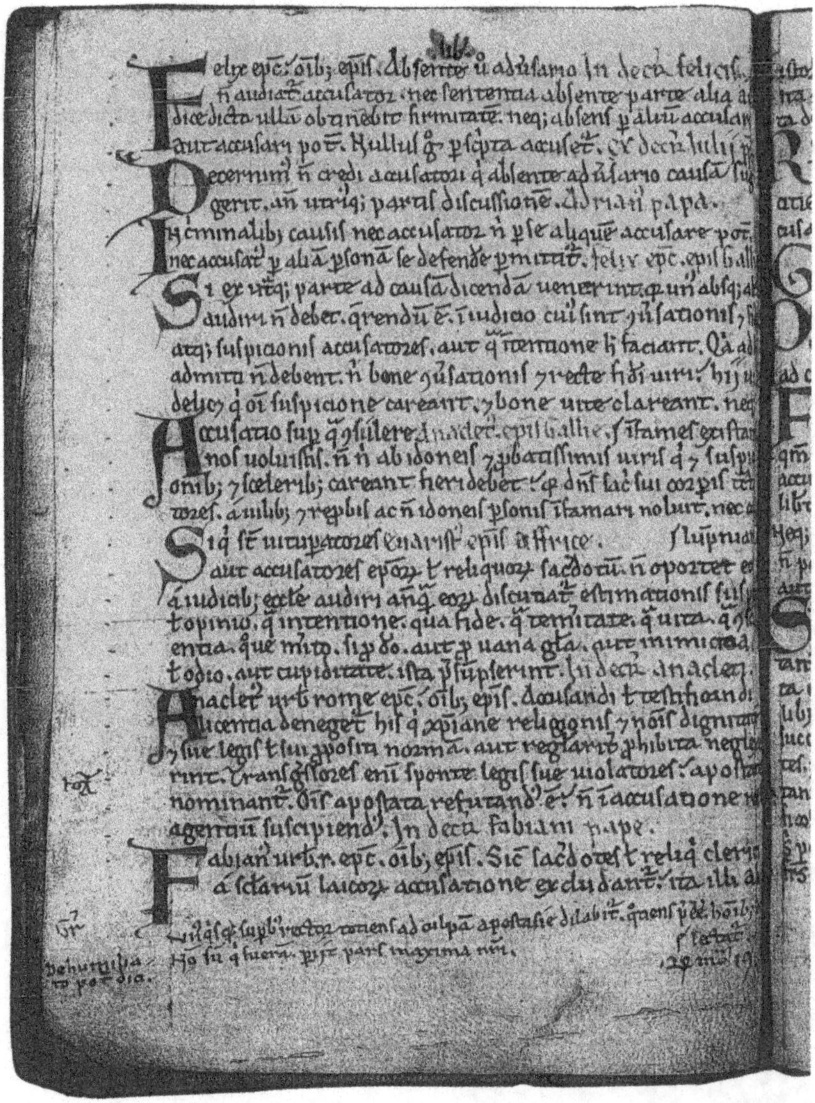

Plate 12.4 Edinburgh, National Library of Scotland, Advocates' MS 18. 8. 6, fo 39v. By permission of the Trustees of the National Library of Scotland.

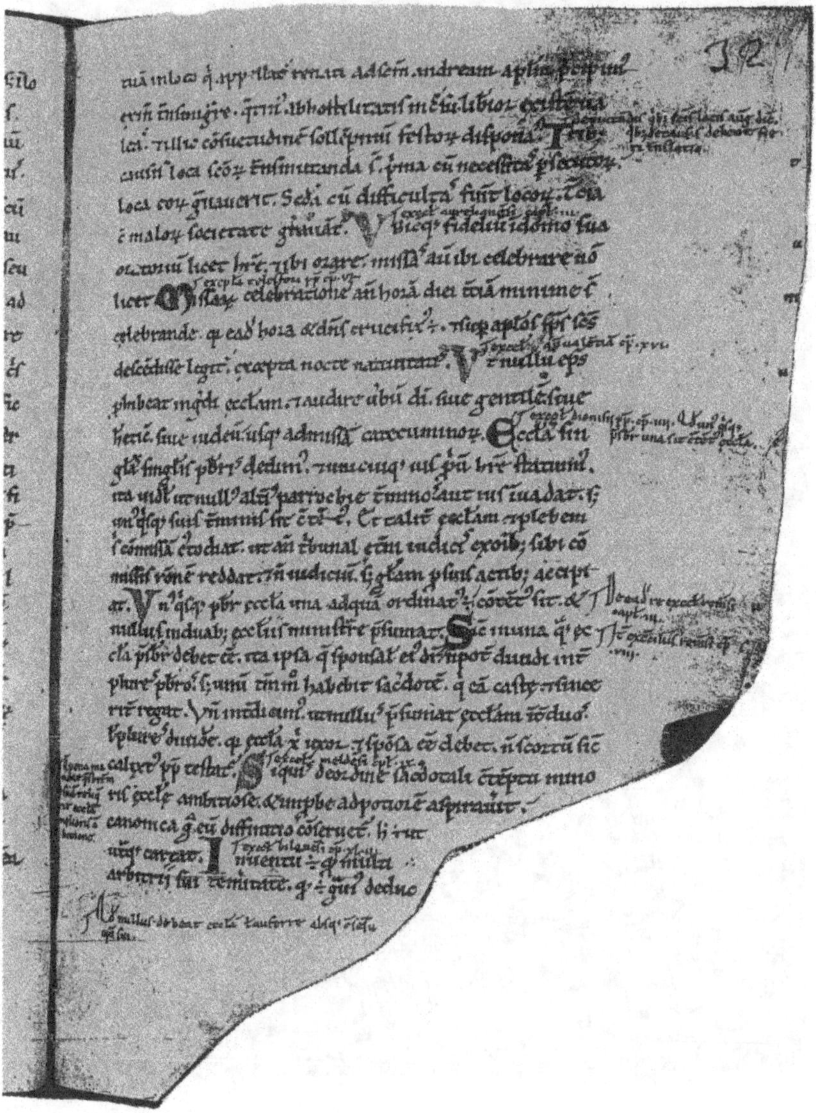

Plate 12.5 Firenze, Biblioteca Nazionale Centrale, MS Magliabechiano xxxiv 73, fo 32v. By permission of the Director of the Biblioteca nazionale centrale at Firenze.

Chapter 13

Anselm of Lucca and Burchard of Worms: Re-Thinking the Sources of Anselm 11, *De Penitentia*

Kathleen G. Cushing

It has long been established that the *Liber decretorum* of Bishop Burchard of Worms, compiled between 1008 and 1012 according to Paul Fournier and Gabriel Le Bras but before 1023 according to Rudolf Pokorny, was a chief formal source for the important 'Gregorian' *Collectio canonum* of Bishop Anselm II of Lucca, compiled between 1081 and 1086.[1] The precise nature of this relationship, however, particularly with regard to Anselm's Book 11, *De penitentia* (= Ans. 11) needs clarification in light of its implications for the transmission of canonical texts during the second half of the eleventh century. The topic of this paper thus is particularly appropriate for a volume in honour of Roger Reynolds, whose work has made invaluable contributions to our understanding of how collections were created and disseminated. Anselm was the only 'reform' canonist, at least in recension A, with a separate book of some 151 chapters on penance, apart, that is, from Gregory of San Grisogono, whose *Polycarpus* was heavily dependent on Anselm.[2] It should be conceded here at once, though, that Anselm's collection was also reasonably well circulated in recension B, that is, without the penitential, a fact that has prompted several historians to speculate that the simultaneous dissemination of

---

1 *Decretorum libri XX.*, PL 140.537-1043. *Anselmi episcopi Lucensis Collectio canonum una cum collectione minore*, ed. F. Thaner (Innsbruck, 1906, 1915), covers only to book 11.15. For this paper I have used the A recension of the collection: Vatican City, Biblioteca Apostolica Vaticana, MS Vat. lat. 1363; Paris, Bibliothèque Nationale, MS lat. 12519; and Cambridge, Corpus Christi College, MS 269. For Burchard's dates, see Paul Fournier and Gabriel Le Bras, *Histoire des collections canoniques depuis les Fausses Décrétales jusqu'au Décret de Gratien*, 2 vols (Paris, 1931-2), i, 366; and Hartmut Hoffmann and Rudolf Pokorny, *Das Dekret des Bischofs Burchard von Worms: Textstufen—Frühe Verbreitung—Vorlagen*, MGH Hilfsmittel, 12 (Munich, 1991), 11-15, 19-20, 110-13, 160. For bibliography, see Lotte Kéry, *Canonical Collections of the Early Middle Ages (ca. 400-1140)*, History of Medieval Canon Law 1, ed. Wilfried Hartmann and Kenneth Pennington (Washington, D.C., 1999), 149-55.

2 For *Polycarpus*, see Uwe Horst, *Die Kanonessammlung Polycarpus des Gregor von S. Grisogno: Quellen und Tendenzen*, MGH Hilfsmittel, 5 (Munich, 1980); and Kéry, *Canonical Collections*, 266-89.

two versions resulted from a general lack of interest in penance among the reformers associated with Pope Gregory VII.[3]

In some ways, Ans. 11 is a miscellany of penance with no topic especially privileged over others, apart from strong emphasis on homicide, false testimony and general definitions. The canons are sometimes repetitive. They also sometimes conflict with little attempt to reconcile different amounts of penance. Topics run the gamut of tariffed penances with all their various, often hairsplitting, permutations depending on status and age for sins such as homicide, adultery, theft, divination, false testimony, and sexual activity, although it should be noted here that, unlike Burchard, there is relatively limited treatment of sexual behavior in Ans. 11. Other topics include moral exhortations, priestly discretion, and the importance of the secrecy of confession.

The purpose of this article, however, is not a discussion of the thematic content of Ans. 11 but rather a consideration of its canonical sources, particularly its most securely identifiable *fontes formales*: Burchard's *Liber decretorum* and the late eighth- or early ninth-century tripartite penitential known as the *Capitula Iudiciorum* (= *CI*).[4] Although the following discussion remains formative rather than summative, it looks to clarify further the relationship of Burchard and Anselm of Lucca by examining the blocks or sequences of sources which in part, but not in whole, characterize Anselm's reliance on Burchard in book 11. The aim is thereby to draw attention to the unusual, quite selective, use of Burchard by showing its position within the context of other sources employed, particularly *CI*. At the same time, by drawing attention to parallels with other contemporary collections such as the *Liber canonum sanctorum patrum* (= 183T) and the collection that now needs to be known as the *Collection in Two Books/Eight Parts* (= 2L/8P), and by pointing to the presence of analogous, even identical texts in first part of the extremely interesting Kynzvart (Königswart b. Marienbad) MS 75, it is hoped that it may become increasingly possible to go beyond simply 're-thinking the sources', and to begin to speculate about the transmission of canonical texts in northern and central Italy in the second half of the eleventh century, even 're-constructing' the bookshelves of a compiler such as Anselm.[5] It is important to emphasize here, though, as

---

3 See Paul Fournier, 'Observations sur les diverses récensions de la collection canonique d'Anselme de Lucques', *Annales de l'université de Grenoble*, 13 (1901), 427-58; and Peter Landau, 'Erweiterte Fassungen der Kanonessammlung des Anselm von Lucca aus 12. Jahrhundert', in *Sant'Anselmo, Mantova e la lotta per le investiture*, ed. Paolo Golinelli (Bologna, 1987), 323-37. Pierre J. Payer, *Sex and the Penitentials: the development of a sexual code, 550-1150* (Toronto, 1984), suggests that the two recensions may have originated for this reason.

4 Ed. Herm. Jos. [Herrmann Joseph] Schmitz, *Die Bussbücher und das kanonische Bussverfahren* (Dusseldorf, 1898), ii, 204-51; see n. 9 below.

5 For 183T, see *Liber canonum diversorum sanctorum patrum sive Collectio in CLXXXIII titulos digesta*, ed. Joseph Motta, MIC Series B, Corpus Collectionum, 7 (Vatican City, 1988); and n. 15 below. For 2L/8P, see Jean Bernhard, ed., *La Collection en deux livres (Cod. Vat. Lat. 3832), I: La forme primitive de la Collection en deux livres, sources de la Collection en 74 titres et de la*

Roger Reynolds and others have shown, that most compilers in the later eleventh century for various reasons probably did not have access to multiple sources. Indeed, as Peter Landau has shown, even Gratian used only a limited number. To put it another way, therefore, we are looking for fewer but better books of canonical texts.

As can be seen in Table 13.1, Burchard was a very important formal source for Ans. 11, accounting for as many as forty-seven of the 151 texts, although in some cases (as indicated), while there are similarities, these are not enough to prove conclusively that it was the formal source. For instance, in the case of Ans. 11.11, 11.14, 11.22, and 11.43, Burchard has only a partial text. Similar hesitation arises at Ans. 11.51, which offers as its inscription 'Ex poenitentiali Theodori' whereas Burchard 12.4 reads 'ex decretis Pii pape', although the text is closer to Burchard's transmission. In other cases, such as Ans. 11.12, 11.36, 11.52, 11.53, and 11.85, there are enough variants to suggest an alternative formal source such as Pseudo-Isidore, or, at the least, that comparative readings and supplements were perhaps being made. Some of these ambiguities could probably be resolved if it could be established more precisely which copy of the *Liber decretorum* Anselm used. It was clearly what is known as an Italian 'Order of Worms, Type B' version, but whether it was an exemplar of Lucca, Biblioteca Capitolare Feliniana, MS 124; Pistoia, Archivio Capitolare del Duomo, MS C.125 or C.140; or possibly an exemplar from Polirone, like Padua, Biblioteca del Seminario Vescovile, MS 529, at this point remains unclear.[6]

It is interesting to note, however, that Burchard does in some sense act as a comprehensive formal source for Ans. 11, providing decretals, numerous conciliar canons, penitential texts, patristics, and all of the capitulary material. These last include some of Burchard's legendary falsifications, both via and independently of Regino of Prüm's *Libri duo de synodalibus causis et disciplinis ecclesiasticis*, such as in Ans. 11.8, 11.41. 11.57, and 11.76.[7] Also of interest is what Ans. 11 actually does use. There are, perhaps surprisingly, few texts from the *Liber decretorum* 19, the *Corrector sive medicus*, the famous penitential that so often obscures the fact that other books in the *Liber decretorum* have many canons on penance. The lack of texts from book 20, the *Speculator*, is also probably noteworthy. As can be seen in Table 13.1, Ans. 11 principally exploits book 6 on homicide, book 11 on excommunication and theft (though chiefly for theft), book 12 on perjury, along with some texts from book 7 on incest, book 10 on divination, book 17 on false testimony and book 18 on visitation and pastoral care. What needs to be emphasized,

---

Collection d'Anselme de Lucques, 1-2, Revue de Droit Canonique, 12 (Strasbourg, 1962); Kéry, *Canonical Collections*, 227-8; and the references at n. 18 below. For Kynzvart 75, see n. 20 below and Table 13.2 at the end of this article.

6   See Kéry, *Canonical Collections*, 133-55.

7   For Regino's *Libri duo*, see Kéry, *Canonical Collections*, 128-33; and the text in *PL* 132.185-370.

however, is the fact that blocks of texts taken from Burchard do not always, or even most often, follow their original sequence. This is especially apparent in the early chapters of Ans. 11 where texts seem to be selected randomly. Yet, this continues, even when Burchard appears to be a more consistent formal source. Consider for example, Ans. 11.15-18, where the order is not straightforward; in this instance, the fact that 11.16 has the correct inscription ('in eodem') probably accounts for the lack of sequential order. Ans. 11.39 onwards offers a clearer example of straight-forward progressive appropriation from Burchard on the issue of homicide. This 'series', however, is interrupted at 11.45 by a text from Ambrose, and at 11.44 by the very interesting presence from an undetermined source of the (apocryphal?) decretal of Gregory III (JE 2239), but which is probably closer to a variant of the Penitential of Ps.-Gregory, c. 3; the text appears also only in the *Collection in Nine Books* (= 9L), the *Collection in Five Books* (= 5L), 183T, and the 2L/8P.[8] After a break at 11.50 with a text on penance for self-castration, another Burchardian 'series' begins with material on perjury, although some of these penitential texts (e.g., 11.52-53) could derive from one of several versions and thus perhaps not directly from Burchard. The order here, though, is quite consistently followed, broken only by Augustinian texts of unclear origin. After this, texts from Burchard occur in quite small sequences; e.g., 11.70-71 (false testimony); 11.75-76 (incest), 11.79-80 (violation of vowesses), and 11.112-13 (divination). Thereafter the direct use of Burchard becomes increasingly sporadic and tenuous. The impression, however, even from this brief discussion, is that this is not blind or automatic copying of Burchard on Ans. 11's part, but rather deliberate selection—on grounds about which we can only speculate—reflecting a need for supplementary formal sources.

It is here, I would suggest, that *Capitula Iudiciorum* (= *CI*) may have had its role to play.[9] Along with the *Sangallense Tripartitum*, *CI* represents one of the early tripartite penitentials, compiled in the late eighth or early ninth century before the Carolingian reforms, probably in Francia, but spreading quickly into Italy. According to Fournier, the structure of such tripartite penitentials reflected their compilers' desire to reunite all known penitential sources.[10] Like *Sangallense Tripartitum*, *CI* contained a series of canonical judgments (*iudicium canonicum*), a Theodorean series (*iudicium Theodori*), and a series derived from the Latin Irish

---

8 *Penitential of Ps.-Gregory*, c. 3; ed. F. W. H. Wasserschleben. *Die Bussordnungen der abendländischen Kirche* (Halle, 1851), 538. Motta, *Liber canonum*, gives 183T 125.1 as Gregory III; Bernhard, *La Collection en deux livres*, does not identify 2.285. The text also appears in *Polycarpus*, vi.9, 4, where it is also not identified; see Horst, *Die Kanonessammlung Polycarpus*, 178, 226. For 9L and 5L, see Kéry, *Canonical Collections*, 271-2, and 157-60 respectively.

9 *CI* (as n. 4). See Letha Mahadevan, 'Überlieferung und Verbreitung des Bussbuchs *Capitula Iudiciorum*', *ZRG KA*, 103 (1986), 17-75; and Ludger Körntgen, *Studien zu den Quellen der frühmittelalterlichen Bussbücher*, Quellen und Forschungen zum Recht im Mittelalter, 7 (Sigmaringen, 1993), 125-9.

10 Fournier-Le Bras, *Histoire*, i, 99 ff.

Cummean penitential (*iudicium Cummeani*). Yet unlike *Sangallense Tripartitum* with its three separate series, *CI* was systematically arranged into thirty-five chapters, the rubrics of which were supported by the relevant *iudicium canonicum*, *Theodori* and *Cummeani*. This systematic method clearly gave *CI* far greater influence, despite attempts by the Carolingian reformers to purge penitentials. This is reflected by the eight extant manuscripts of varying completeness (one is a palimpsest), dating from the early ninth to the late twelfth or early thirteenth centuries.[11]

What is striking, however, is that despite its reasonable diffusion, *CI* seems to have made little direct impression on canonical compilers. There is no evidence whatsoever of it being used by prominent earlier canonical collections; e.g., Regino's *Libri duo*, the *Collectio Anselmo dedicata* and Burchard. It is also lacking among Anselm's contemporaries: 183T, the *Collection in 74 Titles* (= 74T), Atto, Deusdedit, Bonizo, and even the 2L/8P (the *Polycarpus* of course is a special case because of its dependency on Anselm).[12] Indeed apart from Anselm, the only other eleventh-century collections of any significance that utilized *CI* were earlier: the 9L, 5L; and the *Summa de iudicis omnium peccatorum*—a collection that was also heavily dependent on Burchard.[13] It is this rather conspicuous avoidance during a time in which, as manuscript evidence shows, it clearly was both circulating and being copied in Italy and in reform circles that makes its direct exploitation by Ans. 11 so very important.

Leaving to one side the issue of Anselm's access for a moment, as can be seen in Table 13.1, *CI* was not an insignificant source, accounting for some twenty-four, even twenty-five texts (if 11.23 is included), though some of these are not entirely secure. At the same time, it is important to look at precisely what Ans. 11 did use. As with Burchard, *CI* texts are usually but not always incorporated into small sequences; e.g., Ans. 11.30-31 (clerics committing homicide); 11.33-5 (attacks and infanticide); 11.83-4, 86-8 (adultery, sodomy and incest) intermingled with Ancyra, c. 15 on homosexuality); 11.100-103 (sacrilege); and 11.105 onwards (various sexual acts). The actual authorities used are equally revealing. For Ans. 11 above all exploited the canonical series, which account for some fifteen texts. Although having recourse to Theodorean material for some eight texts, Ans. 11 scrupulously avoided the Irish, non-Roman material of the *iudicium Cummeani*, apart from one occasion: c. 72, which is attributed to Theodore. When this is put in the context of the material from penitentials appropriated from Burchard as well as the others of

---

11 Mahadevan, 'Überlieferung und Verbreitung', 21-45.

12 For Deusdedit: *Die Kanonessammlung des Kardinals Deusdedit*, ed. Victor Wolf von Glanvell (Paderborn, 1905; repr. Aalen, 1967); Bonizo: *Bonizonis Liber de vita Christiana*, ed. Ernst Perels, Texte zur Geschichte des römischen und kanonischen Rechts im Mittelalter, 1 (Berlin, 1930); and 74T: *Diuersorum patrum sententie siue Collectio in LXXIV titulos digesta*, ed. Joannes T. Gilchrist, MIC Series B, Corpus collectionum, 1 (Vatican City, 1973).

13 Mahadevan, 'Überlieferung und Verbreitung', 45-8.

undetermined origin (e.g., Halitgar 6, some of which are found in Kynzvart 75), the picture is intriguing. The texts from actual penitentials taken from Burchard only account for maybe eleven texts: Ans. 11.46-7, (possibly) 51-6, 113, 117, 127, and there are questions about many of these. According to the tabulations of Hoffmann and Pokorny, the *Liber decretorum* has some 138 texts from penitentials as well as considerable material from Hrabanus's *Paenitentiale ad Heribaldum* and Halitgar.[14] In the midst of such vast penitential resources, Ans. 11 still went elsewhere.

It is useful here to turn, very briefly, to other contemporary collections seemingly related to Anselm. As can be seen from Table 13.1, both 183T and 2L/8P contain many analogous, even identical texts to those in Ans. 11. The two cases, however, are different. 183T was probably compiled in Tuscany in a monastic ambience and has been dated by Motta to between 1063 and 1083/85, but probably at the beginning of Gregory VII's pontificate, though this dating has not been universally accepted.[15] Heavily dependent on Burchard's *Liber decretorum*, 183T also relied on Pseudo-Isidore, Regino, and perhaps the *Collectio Anselmo dedicata*. It also appears to have had independent access to the *Hispana Gallica* as well as patristic *florilegia*, among which Augustine was prominent. Our chief concern here, however, is the relationship of 183T and Anselm. As can be seen from Table 13.1, there is a large amount of correspondence (echoed elsewhere, especially in books 12 and 13), though it must be conceded that much of this is due to 183T's dependence on Burchard. The problem, however, becomes particularly acute in the center sections of 183T, where, according to Motta, it is difficult to specify the formal source.[16] Here, one finds texts with significant coincidence both in inscriptions and rubrics, especially with the Augustinian material. Yet while the order is often similar to Anselm, there is much that is missing as well as independent additions of Augustine. Motta concluded (as had Fournier) that despite such overlap, this indicated a shared common source rather than a strict dependency.[17] I would suggest, however, that the small sequences need more rigorous examination, as they may reveal a more complicated relationship.

2L/8P is a different case altogether. Once described by Jean Bernhard as the source both of 74T and Anselm (though this contention is now wholly rejected), our understanding of the nature and complexities of 2L, itself part of a larger collection in eight parts, has been aided by Linda Fowler-Magerl's restoration,

---

14 Hoffmann-Pokorny, *Das Dekret des Bischofs Burchard von Worms*, 245-74.

15 Motta, *Liber canonum*, xxvi-xxx. Also, see his, 'I rapporti tra la Collezione canonica di S. Maria Novella e quella in Cinque libri', *BMCL*, NS 7 (1977), 89-94. Cf. Uta-Renate Blumenthal, 'Decrees and Decretals of Pope Paschal II in Twelfth-Century Canonical Collections', *BMCL*, NS 10 (1980), 15-30, who argues that the Paschal material is integral to the collection and hence for a later dating.

16 Motta, *Liber canonum*, xxxiv-xxxvi.

17 *Ibid.*, xxxvi. Cf. Fournier-Le Bras, *Histoire*, ii, 151-5.

which allows us to see that its relationship to Anselm is much more complicated.[18] While it is impossible here to address this in any detail, 2L/8P is a particularly valuable collection because it is so intensely moulded by the compilations that were its formal sources (e.g., 74T, Ans., Pseudo-Isidore, the *Collectio Anselmo dedicata*, Burchard) rather than by any historically arranged or programmatic principle. It is, however, only with Anselm's collection that the blocks or sequences of sources do not follow their original order, though as I have shown elsewhere, there are small groupings that suggest comparative formal source selection.[19] Of particular interest here is book '2' after c. 106 (where the use of 74T ends). The material is largely patristic but includes numerous decretals from Gelasius and Pelagius dealing with sin, penance, excommunication, marriage, etc. There is no apparent system or method to these blocks, apart from 'authorial' sequences that might indicate the use of patristic florilegia. They include many analogous texts in Anselm, with some in Burchard and 183T, a more exacting comparison of which remains to be done. There is, however, much that is not in Anselm, and even those that are do not necessarily entail that it was the formal source. Indeed, in some cases, 2L/8P seems to transmit patristic texts more faithfully than Anselm. It is, I would suggest, an important piece of this wider puzzle.

This brings me finally to Kynzvart MS 75, the first part of which, fos 1-78, dates from the first half of the twelfth century.[20] It was copied most likely at St Blasien for their priory at Ochsenhausen, founded before 1100, where the manuscript remained until 1803 when it came into the possession of Metternich who transported it to Königswart bei Marienbad in western Bohemia—after the second world war, Czechoslovakian territory. As can be seen from the description in Table 13.2 at the end of the article, it is a 'collection' of canonical texts and penitential material including Halitgar 6 in two parts, Hrabanus' *Paenitentiale ad*

---

18 Bernhard, *La Collection en deux livres* (as n. 5). On the 2L, see John Gilchrist, 'The Collection of Cod. Vat. Lat. 3832, a source of the Collection in Seventy-Four Titles?', in *Études d'histoire du droit canonique dediées à Gabriel Le Bras*, 2 vols (Paris, 1965), i, 141–56, and especially, Linda Fowler-Magerl, 'The Restoration of the Canon Law Collection in the MSS Vat. Lat. 3832 and Assisi BC 227', in *Grundlagen des Rechts: Festschrift für Peter Landau zum 65. Geburtstag*, ed. Richard H. Helmholz, Paul Mikat, Jörg Müller, Michael Stolleis, Rechts- und Staatswissenschaftliche Veröffentlichungen der Görres-Gesellschaft, NF 91 (Paderborn-Munich-Vienna-Zurich, 2000), 179-203.

19 Kathleen G. Cushing, 'Anselm of Lucca and the Collection in Two Books (BAV Lat. 3832): a missed opportunity? Some New Thoughts', preliminary version presented at the International Congress of Medieval Studies, Kalamazoo, 2001, and forthcoming.

20 For descriptions, see: František Cada, *Rukopisy knihovny statniho zamku v Kynzvarte* (Prague, 1965), 118-20; Raymund Kottje, *Die Bussbücher Halitgars von Cambria und des Hrabanus Maurus*, Beiträge zur Geschichte und Quellenkunde des Mittelalters, 8 (Berlin, 1980), 32-3; Mahadevan, 'Überlieferung und Verbreitung', 21-4; Hubert Mordek, 'Papst Urban II., St Blasien und die Anfänge des Basler Klosters St Alban', in *Festgabe Gerd Tellenbach zum 80. Geburtstag* (=*Zeitschrift für die Geschichte des Oberrheins*, 131 [1983]), 199-224, esp. 212-14; Hubert Houben, *St Blasianer Handschriften des 11. und 12. Jahrhunderts* (Munich, 1979), 125-31.

Heribaldum, excerpts from Burchard and the *Iudicia Theodori*, a significant excerpt of *CI*, and a collection of fifty-eight canons of penitential material including conciliar canons, decretals, Augustine as well as a fragment from Urban II (c. 37). What is most significant about these canons is the fact that many of them are found not only in Ans. 11, but also elsewhere in his collection. Kottje and Authenrieth have noted the strong resemblance of fos 1-47 to a group of manuscripts from the area around Constance, details of which are indicated in Table 13.2.[21] It is unclear at this stage whether the series of fifty-eight canons also figures in these manuscripts.

It is with the *CI* excerpt and this series of canons that I am, predictably, interested. According to Kottje, this *CI* excerpt represents an obscure, unusual tradition.[22] As can be seen from the description in Table 13.2, it is excerpted internally, but done so systematically, preserving both the outline and shape of the work. Moreover, it retains the *iudicium canonicum* and *Theodori*, but dispenses with some of the Cummean material, which as already indicated above, Ans. 11 had all but ignored. Furthermore, all save one of Ans. 11's *CI* texts (Ans. 11.84) are to be found in the Kynzvart *CI*.

The overlap of the Kynzvart collection of canons may also be relevant. According to Mordek, the characteristic mixture of canonical and theological material betrays echoes of Burchard and Regino, to which the Kynzvart compiler (or its exemplar) was indebted, but still more so to Anselm and esp. Ans. 11.[23] While there are variations, deviations and differences, there are also similar rubrics and variants that strongly point to an important direct connection. There remain too many questions at this stage to suggest that Kynzvart 75 (or even its unknown immediate exemplar at St Blasien) accounts for Anselm's *CI* texts. At this point, there is no compelling reason not to accept Mordek's contention that Kynzvart is likely descended from an Italian intermediate collection that was or may have been Anselm's source. The site of its origin, St Blasien, makes this all the more likely. Mordek, however, did not take into account the parallels of Anselm with 183T. These along with the undeniable connection of Anselm and 2L/8P, to say nothing of the predilection of both 183T and 2L/8P for monastic issues, probably strengthen this connection. Although a single text cannot explain everything, Ans. 11.23, *Caveat ante omnia*, a text like 11.44, that is found only in 9L, 5L, 2L/8P, and here also in the Kynzvart collection presents a tantalizing possibility.[24]

---

21 Kottje, *Die Bussbücher Halitgars*, 32-3.
22 *Ibid.*, 33.
23 Mordek, 'Papst Urban II.', 214-23.
24 As indicated on Table 13.1, 11.44 is also found in the 183T. See Roger E. Reynolds, ed., *The Collectio canonum Casinensis duodecimi seculi: a derivative of the south Italian Collection in Five Books*, Studies and Texts, 137, Monumenta Liturgica Beneventana, 3 (Toronto, 2001), c. 7, 34.

In the end, what is to be made of all of this? Is this deliberate sifting and collecting on the part of Ans. 11, or rather fortuitous chance? It has increasingly become my opinion that the latter may very well better explain formal source selection in pre-Gratian canonical collections than deliberate canonistic erudition. Regrettably, this is a very difficult thing to prove. It is, of course, always more difficult with a systematic collection where texts do not tend so uniformly to follow the sequence of the original to be positive about formal sources, and especially, the reasons for their selection. We know that Burchard and *CI* were on Ans. 11's bookshelves. Although the book itself continues to elude us, there is a sense that between 183T, 2L/8P and Kynzvart 75, we may be getting closer to Ans. 11's supplement to Burchard.

Table 13.1   Fontes Capitulorum—Anselm 11, *De penitentia*

Abbreviations

Ans   Anselm of Lucca, *Collectio canonum*; see n. 1 above for bibliography
Aug.   Augustinus
Burch. Burchard of Worms, *Liber decretorum*; see n. 1.
CI   *Capitula Iudiciorum*; see nn. 4 and 9.
Greg.   Gregorius
Kynz   Kynzvart (Königswart b. Marienbad) 75 (K.20.K); see n. 20 above and Table 13.2 below (nos. refer to Mordek's *incipit* edition).
Ps-Is *Decretales Pseudo-Isidorianae*, ed. Paulus Hinschius (Leipzig, 1863; repr. Aalen, 1963).
RP   Regino of Prüm, *Libri duo de synodalibus causis*; see n. 7.
183T   *Liber canonum diversorum sanctorum patrum*; see n. 5.
2L/8P *Collection in Two Books (Eight Parts)*; see nn. 5 and 18.
74T   *Diversorum patrum sententie*; see n. 12

ANS	TEXT	BURCH.	183T	2L/8P	KYNZ	PROVENANCE
11.1	Aug., ep. 265.7,8					
11.2	Greg. I, Hom. in evang., 2.34.15, 16					
11.3	Ibid., 1.20.8					
11.4	Aug., Sermo 351.12		178.4	2.327	14	
11.5	Gelasius, ep. 10.3 (JK 622)		92.1			Ps-Is?
11.6	Ps-Pius, ep. 1.6					Ps-Is
11.7	Ps-Evaristus, ep. 2.9					Ps-Is
11.8	Herard of Tours, Capitula, c. 69	18.16				Burch.
11.9	Elvira (306-14), c. 32		166.5			
11.10	Carthage, II (419), c. 7					
11.11	Leo, ep. 108.4-5 (JK 485)	Cf. 18.4 (part)	92.6	2.55	22a-e	

ANS	TEXT	BURCH.	183T	2L/8P	KYNZ	PROVENANCE
11.12	Leo, ep. 167.8 (JK 544)	11.52	88.19		24	Burch.?
11.13	Unknown	18.11		2.270	4	Burch.
11.14	Innocent I, ep. 25.8	Cf. 18.2 (part)		2.268		Ps-Is?
11.15	Carthage, IV (c. 436), c. 78	18.23		2.272	5	Burch.
11.16	Ibid., c. 76	18.10		2.269	3	Burch.?
11.17	Vaison, I (442), c. 2	18.24				Burch. (via RP 1.115)
11.18	Celestinus, ep. 2.2	18.22	92.4	2.271		Burch.?
11.19	Carthage, II (419), c. 10	19.40				Burch.?
11.20	Unknown					
11.21	Nicaea (325), c. 13	18.6		2.79		Burch.
11.22	Leo, ep. 168.2 (JK 545)	Cf. 19.159 (part)	92.7	2.275		
11.23	Unknown; cf. CI, c. 35, post 3			2.365	1	
11.24	Aug., Sermo 82.7, 8, n. 10, 11			2.192		
11.25	Innocent, ep. 25.7 (JK 311)	18.18		2.53		74T c. 251
11.26	Leo, ep. 90 (87), c. 2 (JK 544)	19.71	68.3		23	Burch.?
11.27	Apostolic Canons, c. 25		66.4			
11.28	Aug., Enchiridion, 19.70					
11.29	Ps-Fabianus, ep. 2.18					Ps-Is
11.30	CI, 1.1				fos 48v-49r	CI
11.31	CI, 1.1				fo 49r	CI
11.32	Elvira (436), c. 5	6.19				Burch.
11.33	CI, 2.1				fo 49r/v	CI
11.34	CI, 3.1				fo 49v	CI (cf. Ancyra, 21)
11.35	CI, 4				fo 49v	CI
11.36	Ps-Clement, ep. 1.40	6.28	122.1		8	Burch.?
11.37	Ps-Alexander, ep. 3.17				10	Ps-Is
11.38	Unknown	6.31	122.2	2.267		Burch. (via RP 2.49)
11.39	Ancyra (314), c. 21	6.13	122.5	2.276		Burch.
11.40	Ibid., c. 22	6.15	122.3	2.277		Burch.
11.41	Theodulf, Capit., 2.4.2	6.16	122.4	2.278	7	Burch.
11.42	Unknown	6.20	122.6	2.279	9	Burch.
11.43	Nicholas I, ep. 133 (JE 2850)	Cf. 6.46	125.3	2.280	11	?

ANS	TEXT	BURCH.	183T	2L/8P	KYNZ	PROVENANCE
11.44	Greg. III, JE 2239; cf. Penit. Ps-Greg., c. 3		125.2	2.285		
11.45	Ambrose, De Cain et Abel, 2.4.15		121.15			
11.46	Bedae-Egberti, 13.1; cf. Ps-Theodore., 6.22	6.32	122.9			Burch.
11.47	Bedae-Egberti, 13.1	6.17				Burch.
11.48	Adge (506), c. 62	6.18				Burch.
11.49	Lerida (546), c. 2					
11.50	CI, 5	Cf. 11.30		2.258 (diff.)	fo 49v	CI
11.51	Cf. Ps-Theodore, 9.3/Bedae Egberti, 18.1	12.4 (diff. inscript.)	164.19	1.119		
11.52	Unclear: CI, 15.2; Penit. Theodore U 6.4 / Bedae-Egberti, 18.2	12.5	164.22	1.120		Burch.?
11.53	Unclear: Ps-Theodore; CI, 15.1,2; Bedae-Egberti, 18.1	12.6		1.121		Burch.?
11.54	Unknown: cf. CI, 15.3; Pelagius (JK 967)	12.9	164.21	1.122		Burch.
11.55	Unknown: cf. Halitgar 4.28	12.8	164.20	1.123		Burch. (via RP 2.330)
11.56	Excarpsus Cummeani, 5.8 w/modifs; CI 15.3	12.11	164.25	1.124		Burch. (via RP 2.332)
11.57	Ansegis, Capit., 1.61	12.12	164.9	2.262		Burch.(via RP 2.316)
11.58	Theodulf, Capit., 1.26	12.14	164.11	2.263		Burch.
11.59	Julian, Epit. Nov Iustiniani, 71.1; Stat. Eccles. Ant., c. 74 (61); Julian, 71.1.2	12.15	164.16	2.264		Burch.
11.60	Bede, Hom., 2.20	12.18	164.5	2.265		Burch. (via RP 2.339)
11.61	Hohenaltheim (916), c. 23	12.21	164.28	2.266		Burch.
11.62	Aug., ep. 47.2		164.17	2.319		
11.63	Isidore, Sententiae, 2.31.8-9	12.10	164.2			Burch.?
11.64	Aug., De ser. Domini in monte, 1.17.51			2.137		
11.65	CI, 15.1				fo 54r	CI
11.66	Aug., Ennarationes in Psalmos, 5.7		163.6			
11.67	CI, 15.4				fo 54r	CI
11.68	Arles I (314), c. 14					
11.69	Ps-Fabianus, ep. 3.28					Ps-Is

Ans	Text	Burch.	183T	2L/8P	Kynz	Provenance
11.70	Unknown	16.16				Burch. (via RP 2.350)
11.71	Agde, c. 37	16.17				Burch.
11.72	CI, 15.5, 6				fo 54v	CI
11.73	Aug., Sermo 392, 3.3			2.159	12	
11.74	Ancyra, c. 19					
11.75	Agde, c. 61	7.4				Burch.
11.76	Benedictus Levita, Capit. Spuria, 3.433	7.5.5	156.3			Burch.
11.77	Ps-Calixtus, ep. 2.16	7.1	147.3			Ps-Is/Burch.?
11.78	Pelagius, ep. 64 (JK 1022)					
11.79	Innocent I, ep. 2.12 (JK 286)	8.13	142.3	2.54		74T c. 252
11.80	Gelasius, ep. 14.20 (JK 636)	8.32	142.7	2.56		74T c. 254
11.81	Elvira, c. 9	9.63				Burch.?
11.82	Ansegis, Capit., 1.99	9.37	148.5			Burch. (via RP 2.155)
11.83	CI, 7.10				fo 51v	CI
11.84	CI, 8.3	Cf. 17.1				CI
11.85	Ancyra, c. 15	17.30	160.1			Burch.?
11.86	CI, 7.1				fo 50r	CI
11.87	CI, 8.1				fo 51v	CI
11.88	CI, 8.9				fos 51v-52r	CI
11.89	Leo, ep. 90 (87).11 (JK 544)		147.76		27	
11.90	Aug., Quaest. in Heptat., 2.9	Cf. 11.53	166.3	2.154		
11.91	Jerome, Com. in ep. ad Titum, 2.9,10	11.55		2.261		Burch.
11.92	Greg. I, Reg. 11.56a		47.1		35 (1st part)	Ps-Is?
11.93	Aug., ep. 153.20, 21, 23-24		167.1	2.225		
11.94	Aug., In Ioh. Evang., 50.10		98.6	2.140		
11.95	Meaux-Paris (845/6), c. 60	11.22		2.256	fo 53r/v[25]	Burch.(via RP 2.289); CI?
11.96	CI, 12.2	Cf. 11.56			fo 53v	CI?
11.97	Halitgar, 6.47				fo 17r	
11.98	Ps-Theodore, 8.2-3					
11.99	Halitgar, 6.29				fo 16r	
11.100	CI, 11.2				fo 53r	CI

---

25   Where it is cited (in the midst of CI) 'ex decreto Leonis papae', as Ans. 11's inscription.

ANS	TEXT	BURCH.	183T	2L/8P	KYNZ	PROVENANCE
11.101	CI., 13				fo 53v	CI
11.102	No rubric, inscription or text					
11.103	CI 6	Cf. 19.103			fo 50r	CI
11.104	Elvira, c. 69					
11.105	CI, 7.9				fo 51r	CI
11.106	CI., 7.10	Cf.17.12			fo 51v	CI
11.107	CI., 9.1				fo 52r	CI
11.108	CI, 10.1	Cf. 17.56			fo 52r/v	CI
11.109	CI., 7.8				fo 51r	CI
11.110	Halitgar, 6.31-33				fo 16r	
11.111	Ibid., 6.34-44				fos 16r-17r	
11.112	Toledo IV (633), c. 28	10.48	59.7	2.254		Burch.
11.113	Penit. Theodore U, 2.10.5	10.50		2.255		Burch.
11.114	Greg. I, Reg. 9.204 (JE 1731)	Cf. 10.3	175.2			
11.115	Greg. I, Reg. 8.19 (JE 1507)	Cf. 10.2	175.1			
11.116	Nicaea, c. 11 (with diffs)			2.98		
11.117	Excarpsus Cummeani, 11.25-32	19.105		2.274		Burch.?
11.118	Elvira, c. 22					
11.119	Aug., Sermo 393, excerpts					
11.120	Aug., Sermo 18.5	178.1	2.138	15		
11.121	Leo I, ep. 90 (87).9					
11.122	Greg. I, Hom. in ev., 2.24.1					
11.123	Leo I, ep. 90 (87).8					
11.124	Aug., Liber de continentia, 6.15			2.155	16	
11.125	Greg. I, Reg. Past., 3.30					
11.126	Aug., Enchiridion, 17.65		178.2	2.145	6	
11.127	Halitgar, pref.	19.31		2.273		Burch.?
11.128	Greg. I, Dialogues, 4.44					
11.129	Leo I, ep. 90 (87).10	19.66	11.4			Burch.?
11.130	Unknown					
11.131	Nicaea, c. 12 (ex Dion)		60.10	2.78		
11.132	Toledo IV (633), c. 54	8.27				Burch.?

ANS	TEXT	BURCH.	183T	2L/8P	KYNZ	PROVENANCE
11.133	Siricius, ep. ad Himerium (ex Dion, c. 5)					
11.134	Greg. I, Dialogues, 4.60			2.235		
11.135	Ibid., 4.44			2.236		
11.136	CI, 11.1				fos 52v-53r	CI
11.137	Aug., Quaest. In Heptat., 4.24		173.8	2.153		
11.138	Jerome, Comm. in Prophetas minores, 1.3.5		178.3	2.176		
11.139	Greg. I, Moralia, 9.27			2.148		
11.140	Aug., De pecc. mer. et remiss., 2.34.55-56			2.149		
11.141	Greg. I, Dialogues, 4.39			2.340		
11.142	Aug., De trinitate, 14.17			2.341		
11.143	Greg. I, Dialogues, 4.25			2.338		
11.144	Aug., De genesi ad litteram, 12.14-15					
11.145	Aug., De bono coniugali, 20.23			2.158		
11.146	Aug., Ennarationes in Psalmos, 37.3			2.146		
11.147	Aug., De civitate Dei, 21.26			2.144		
11.148	Aug., ep. 93.53			2.293		
11.149	Aug., Retract. libri duo, 1.19.4			2.369		
11.150	Pelagius, ep. 34 (JK 993)		11.2	2.123		
11.151	Unknown; cf. Constantinople 4, c. 25					
11.152	Ambrose, De penitentia (excerpts); Silvester II, ep. 13 (JE 3930)		178.5-9	2.368		

Table 13.2   Kynzvart (Königswart b. Marienbad) 75 (K.20.K),[26] Part 1—fos 1v-78r, Canonical Texts and Penitential Material

1v-4r   Liturgical part of Penitential of Halitgar 6, Ordo: *Quotienscumque* (*Incipit liber penitentialis...aeternam.*)

4r-14r   Penitential and eschatological material excerpted from Burchard, *Liber decretorum* (same as in 3 MSS from Lake Constance region: Munich Clm 3909; Stuttgart HB VI 107; St Gallen 676[27])

14r-21r   Penitential of Halitgar 6 (*Qualiter iudicandi sint...potestatem habet.*)

21r-47r   Hrabanus Maurus, Penitential *ad Heribaldum* (*Incipit liber penitentialis...non graveris. Explicit.*)

47v-48v   Iudicia Theodori, Can Greg., 1-8; 12-16, 21-25, 29-31 (*Ex penitentiali Theodori. In ordinatione...emendaverit.*)

48v-57r   Capitula Iudiciorum (excerpted texts on homicide, fornication, and diverse themes)[28]

   48v-50r: Capitulatio I-VI, Cap.1.1-2; 2, Rubric, 1; Cap.3-6

   50r-53r: Capitulatio VII-XI (here numbered 1-5), Cap.7.1-10; Cap.8, rubric, 1; Cap.9, rubric, 1; Cap.10, rubric, 1-2; Cap.11

   53r-57r: Capitulatio XII-XVII, XIX-XXIV (here 1-12), Cap.12.1-2; 13; 14, rubric,1; 15, rubric,1-3, 5-6; 16, rubric,1,4,2 (parts); 17, rubric and interp.;17-18 (texts); 19; 20, rubric, 1-2; 21; 22, rubric,1-2; 23.1, 2 (parts); 24.

57r-71v   58 canons, penitential and eschatological material[29]

72r-78r   excerpts from Regino, *Libri duo de synodalibus causis*

---

26 For descriptions, see: Cada, *Rukopisy*, 118-20; Kottje, *Die Bussbücher Halitgars*, 32-3; L. Mahadevan, 'Überlieferung and Verbreitung', 17-75, esp. 21-4; H. Mordek, 'Papst Urban II.', 199-224, esp. 212 ff.

27 See Kottje, *Die Bussbücher Halitsgars*, 32-3.

28 Kottje, *Die Bussbücher Halitsgars*, 33; Mahadevan, 'Überlieferung and Verbreitung', 23-24; Mordek, 'Papst Urban II.', 213 and n. 72.

29 Mordek, 'Papst Urban II.', 215-23, for incipit-explicit edition.

Chapter 14

The List of Authorities in the Illustrations of the Collection in Five Books (MS Vat. lat. 1339)[*]

Richard F. Gyug

Among the many fields to which Professor Roger E. Reynolds has contributed insights, the study of illuminated liturgical and canonical manuscripts looms large; it is an area typical of Reynolds' interdisciplinary interests, and of his expertise in both early medieval law and liturgy. A second field in which Reynolds' contribution has been noteworthy has been the study of the south-Italian *Collectio canonum in V libris* or Collection in Five Books (= 5L), a canonical collection compiled in the third decade of the eleventh century. It is preserved complete in three manuscripts, and has long been recognized as an important and influential regional collection.[1] The two concerns, manuscript illustrations and 5L, meet in the

[*] Research for this article has been generously supported by the Social Sciences and Humanities Research Council of Canada as part of the Monumenta Liturgica Beneventana program.—The question of the relationship between illustrations and text in Vat. lat. 1339 was the topic of my B.A. Honors thesis at Carleton University, Ottawa, written under the direction of Roger Reynolds and defended in the spring 1977. At that time, the issue was to demonstrate a close unity between the illustrations and the text of 5L in the same codex because Horst Fuhrmann had raised doubts about whether the gathering with the illustrations belonged with the gatherings containing 5L; Horst Fuhrmann, 'Eine Propagandaschrift des Erzbischofs Gunthar von Köln', *Archiv für Diplomatik*, 4 (1958), 1-51 at 32 n. 94, noting that the gathering with the illustrations, the second in the MS, was not numbered as part of the original collation, which begins with 'I' after the third gathering (fo. 22v for gathering 15r-22v). In commenting on Fuhrmann's observation, Roger E. Reynolds, 'Rites and Signs of Conciliar Decisions in the Early Middle Ages', in *Segni e riti nella chiesa altomedievale occidentale, 11-17 aprile 1985*, Settimane di Studio del Centro Italiano di Studi sull'Alto Medioevo, 33/i-ii (Spoleto, 1987; repr. in *idem, Clerics in the early Middle Ages: hierarchy and image* [Aldershot, 1999], no. VIII), i, 207-49 at 219-20, with characteristic generosity and thoroughness in giving credit to his students, cited my Honors thesis as proving that the illustration 'could only have "fit" the text of the Collection in Five Books and none of the other known collections circulating in Italy in the eleventh century'. The current question is more the illustrator's knowledge of the collection, and less the MS's unity, which is no longer challenged.

consideration of the authorities illustrated in a series of coloured illustrations of councils, popes, doctors and others in the copy of 5L preserved in Vatican City, Biblioteca Apostolica Vaticana, MS Vat. lat. 1339 (= Vat. lat. 1339). As will be demonstrated, the illustrations reflect more closely the contents of 5L than the contents of any other contemporary collection. This close relationship is remarkable testimony to how one illustrator assessed the contents of a canonical collection, and how familiar medieval illustrators and canonists must have been with the specific range of authorities that legitimated the canons within the collection.

Collectio canonum in V libris (= 5L)[2]

5L is a systematic collection compiled early in the eleventh century, after Henry II and Benedict VIII's synod of 1014, which was the source for several canons in the collection, but before 1022.[3] Owing to possible connections between Montecassino and two of Henry II's canons in 5L, it is likely that the collection was composed at the abbey of Montecassino, or perhaps at San Liberatore, a Cassinese dependency

---

Archaeological Reports, International Series, 101 (Hampshire, 1990; 1st edn, 1981), 241-60; 'The portrait of the ecclesiastical officers in the Raganaldus Sacramentary and its liturgico-canonical significance', *Speculum*, 46 (1971), 432-42; 'Image and text: the liturgy of clerical ordination in early medieval art', *Gesta*, 22 (1983), 27-38; and 'Rites and Signs' (see the previous note); the last three are reprinted in *idem*, *Clerics in the early Middle Ages: hierarchy and image* (Aldershot, 1999), nos. VI-VIII. Reynolds' studies of 5L and its derivatives begin with articles such as 'The *De officiis vii graduum*: its origins and early medieval development', *Mediaeval Studies*, 34 (1972), 113-51 at 130 n. 71; and continue to the present day with studies such as *idem*, 'The South Italian *Collection in Five Books* and its Derivatives: the south Italian appendix to the *Collection in Seventy-Four Titles*', *Mediaeval Studies*, 63 (2001), 351-63; and *The 'Collectio canonum Casinensis duodecimi seculi (Codex terscriptus)': a derivative of the south-Italian Collection in Five Books*, Studies and Texts, 137, Monumenta Liturgica Beneventana, 3 (Toronto, 2001), from Montecassino, Archivio dell'Abbazia, MS 216.

2   Edition of the first three books of the collection: *Collectio canonum in V libris (lib. I-III)*, ed. M. Fornasari, *CCCM*, 6 (Turnhout, 1970). For recent bibliography on 5L, see the works by Roger Reynolds cited in n. 1; and Lotte Kéry, *Canonical Collections of the Early Middle Ages (ca. 400-1140)*, History of Medieval Canon Law, 1, ed. Wilfried Hartmann and Kenneth Pennington (Washington, D. C., 1999), 157-60; also Bruce Brasington 'Selected Glosses to the Collection of Five Books: Vat. lat. 1339', *BMCL*, NS (forthcoming); and among earlier studies, esp. Paul Fournier, 'Un groupe de recueils canoniques italiens des Xe et XIe siècles', *Memoires de l'Académie des Inscriptions et Belles-Lettres*, 40 (1915), 95-213 at 159-89; reprinted in Paul Fournier, *Mélanges de droit canonique*, ed. Theo Kölzer, 2 vols (Aalen, 1983), ii, 213-331 at 277-307. Other works will be cited below as they are discussed.

3   Canons from the synod of 1014 are cited in 5L 1.72, 90, 178; ed. Fornasari, 63, 69-70, 115. The argument for pre-dating 1022 is more tenuous: the collection does not use Henry II and Benedict VIII's synod of Pavia (1022); and the Chronicle of Montecassino refers to a 'liber canonum', perhaps 5L, made in 1023 at the order of Abbot Theobald; see Leo Marsicanus, *Chronica monasterii casinensis*, 2.53, ed. Hartmut Hoffmann, *MGH Scriptores*, 34 (Hanover, 1980), 266.

in the Abruzzi.[4] Through either the collection in Rome, Biblioteca Vallicelliana, MS T. XVIII, or the *Collectio canonum in IX libris* (= 9L),[5] or perhaps through collections resembling them, the compiler of 5L had access to material from the *Collectio hibernensis*, Irish and insular penitentials, the *Collectio herovalliana*, and the *Concordia canonum* of Cresconius. Yet many of the patristic texts and elements of Roman, Lombard and Carolingian law in 5L are not found in Vallicelliana T. XVIII or 9L, and were adopted from other sources.[6]

In 5L, each of the five books treats a different major area of ecclesiastical law: book 1, offices of the clergy and ecclesiastical hierarchy; book 2, councils and the regulation of clerics and monks; book 3, the cult and sacraments other than penance; book 4, penance and its administration; and book 5, marriage and moral conduct. Its overall emphasis resembles the reforming interests of the *Liber decretorum* (1008-12) of Burchard, bishop of Worms, but with different texts and sources. Despite the dominance elsewhere of more up-to-date collections such as the Collection in Seventy-Four Titles, the *Collectio canonum* of Anselm II of Lucca or the collections of Ivo of Chartres, all of which were more current with the interests of the Gregorian reformers, 5L's regional influence was substantial and lasted well into the twelfth century.[7] The reason may be that 5L provided something that more recent collections did not, namely, copies of patristic texts and penitential literature noticeably absent from many collections of the reformers.[8]

---

4   To support a Cassinese origin, Roger Reynolds, *Collectio canonum*, 4-5, refers to 5L 3.211, ed. Fornasari, 412-13, which is a canon of Henry II anathematizing the plunderers of ship wrecks, and could have been occasioned by the loss at sea of Abbot Atenulf and nine precious bulls with gold seals; and 5L 4, c. 'De eo qui pignus vel donum de ornamentis ecclesiae acceperit' (Montecassino, Archivio dell'Abbazia, MS 125, p. 247), attributed to Henry II and prohibiting the pawning of ecclesiastical property, which may have been prompted by Henry's gift in 1022 to Montecassino of items that had been previously pawned and needed to be redeemed at the time of the gift.

5   Vallicelliana T. XVIII: Kéry, *Canonical Collections*, 34, 56, 74, 176-7 (with bibliography), 177-8 ('De episcoporum transmigratione'). For 9L: Kéry, *Canonical Collections*, 196-7; the chapter headings are edited in *PL* 138.397-442; 9L is contained only in Vatican City, Biblioteca Apostolica Vaticana, MS Vat. lat. 1349, s. xi med., although the collection was composed *c*. 920, probably in southern Italy (Naples or Benevento). On both collections, see esp. Fournier,'Un groupe', 96-158; repr. Fournier, *Mélanges*, ii, 214-76.

6   Fournier, 'Un groupe', 185; Fornasari, *Collectio canonum*, xvi.

7   Montecassino, Archivio dell'Abbazia, 216 (ed. Reynolds, *Collectio canonum*) is a derivative of 5L copied in the late twelfth century, well after the composition of Gratian's *Decretum*.

8   On the popularity of 5L and its possible role as a canonistic 'vademecum', see Carlo Guido Mor, 'La relazione al *Decretum Burchardi* in Italia avanti la riforma gregoriana', *Studi Gregoriani*, 1 (1947), 201; for the literature on its derivatives and reasons for its continued use, see Reynolds, *Collectio canonum*, 2-3; and Kéry, *Canonical Collections*, 158, for lists of derivatives, excerpts and combinations of 5L with Burchard and the Collection in 74 Titles.

MS Vat. lat. 1339[9]

5L is extant in three complete copies and a fragment.[10] None of the surviving manuscripts are the original, because all date to the middle of the century or later. Vat. lat. 1339 was long considered the most complete of the surviving copies of 5L, and formed the basis for Mario Fornasari's edition of the first three books of the collection,[11] but Roger Reynolds has argued that Montecassino, Archivio dell'Abbazia, MS 125, copied in the mid-eleventh century at Montecassino, is probably 'the earliest and best surviving' copy of 5L.[12] The third complete manuscript, Rome, Biblioteca Vallicelliana, MS B 11, is a 'romanesca' copy by the scribe Ubertus for S. Eutizio in Val Castoriana near Norcia, and dates to the mid-eleventh century, before 1087.[13]

Although it is no longer considered the closest copy to the original 5L, Vat. lat. 1339 remains an important and imposing volume, a witness not only to the diffusion of 5L in central Italy, but also to the persistence of the collection decades after it was composed, well into a period of more papally-oriented reform movements. The manuscript is a large codex, 400 x 278 mm, with a written area 240 x 207 mm in two columns; it was copied in a 'romanesca' script typical of central Italian manuscripts, and from its script has been dated to the middle of the eleventh century and located at the abbey of S. Maria in Narni.[14] Annotations

9   For recent study on Vat. lat. 1339, see the works on 5L above, esp. Reynolds, *Collectio canonum*; in addition see Reynolds, 'Rites and Signs', 215-21; and Stephan Kuttner and Reinhard Elze, *A Catalogue of Canon and Roman Law Manuscripts in the Vatican Library*, 2 vols, Studi e Testi, 322, 328 (Vatican City, 1986-7), i, 71-4.

10 The fragment is Rome, Biblioteca Vallicelliana, MS R 32, fo 50, s. xi$^{3/4}$; Reynolds, *Collectio canonum*, 2 n. 6; and Kéry, *Canonical Collections*, 158.

11 Fornasari, *Collectio canonum*, x, identifies Vat. lat. 1339 as the base text.

12 Reynolds, *Collectio canonum*, 4.

13 *Ibid.*, 2 n. 6, for the location and date; although Paola Supino Martini, *Roma e l'area grafica romanesca (secoli X-XII)*, Biblioteca di Scrittura e Civiltà, 1 (Alessandria, 1982), 202-6, n. 14 (pl. 47), suggests a date 's. xi ex.'

14 Reynolds, *Collectio canonum*, 2 n. 6 ('saec. xi med.'); Kuttner-Elze, *Catalogue*, 71 ('saec. XI'); and, with the greatest authority, Supino Martini, *Roma e l'area grafica*, 226-31 ('s. XI med.'), arguing that the hands of Vat. lat. 1339 are found also in Vatican City, Biblioteca Apostolica Vaticana, MS Vat. lat. 7172, a hymnary located by its sanctoral to Narni, and Paris, Bibliothèque Nationale de France, MS lat. 1092; Supino Martini agreed with the earlier conclusions of E. B. Garrison, *Studies in the History of Mediaeval Italian Painting*, 4 vols (Florence, 1953-62), iv, 235-41 at 235 and 238. Mario Fornasari, 'Un manoscritto e una collezione dei secolo XI provenienti da Farfa', *Benedictina*, 10 (1956), 199-210; and *Collectio canonum*, *CCCM*, 6 (1970), vi, xvii-xix, argued that Vat. lat. 1339 was written at Farfa, and, because it was the original copy of the collection, must pre-date the production in 1023 of Theobald's 'liber canonum' (see n. 3 above), which Fornasari identified with Montecassino 125. Although Fornasari's points are not generally accepted, Kölzer has noted the dependence of the *Collectio farfensis* on 5L, and thus the presence of a copy at Farfa; see *Collectio canonum Regesto Farfensi inserta*, ed. Theo Kölzer, MIC, Series B, Corpus collectionum, 5 (Vatican City, 1982), 48-55.

referring to the church of Narni and an ex libris of the Dominicans of Narni show that it remained there well into the thirteenth century.[15]

The manuscript contains, besides a complete copy of 5L (fols 15-310), opening and closing gatherings of related but distinct canonical and liturgical excerpts (fols 1-6, 311-17), and a second gathering (fols 7-14) with depictions of the Ascension, six ecumenical councils (Nicaea, Constantinople I, Ephesus, Chalcedon, Constantinople II, and Constantinople III), and forty-five individual portraits of figures involved in the making of ecclesiastical law.[16] It is the relationship between these images and the texts of 5L that is of concern here. When this relationship has been remarked in the literature, it has usually been noted that the figures are canonical authorities, but without great concern for the precise ways in which the figures and text are related; the entry in Kuttner and Elze's *Catalogue of Canon and Roman Law manuscripts in the Biblioteca Vaticana* (1986) states, for instance, that the illustrations on fos 10v-14v portray 'the principal authors quoted in the collection'.[17] This view, which is reasonable as far as it goes, leaves open what the correspondence reveals about the precise relations between text and illustrations and between the illustrators and the law.

The illustrations of the ecumenical councils in Vat. lat. 1339 have been considered by Roger Reynolds in his study of the illustrations of early medieval councils presented in 1985 at the Spoleto Settimane. In the subsequent article, Reynolds noted that several early medieval manuscripts depict individual councils,[18] but Vat. lat. 1339 and the Vercelli Codex from the second quarter of the

---

15 Supino Martini, *Roma e l'area grafica*, 226-7; Garrison, *Studies*, iv, 236; and Fornasari, *Collectio canonum*, viii.

16 For the contents, see Kuttner-Elze, *Catalogue*, 71-3. On the illustrations, Reynolds, 'Rites and Signs', 215-21; Kuttner-Elze, *Catalogue*, 74; Christopher Walter, *L'Iconographie des conciles dans la tradition byzantine* (Paris, 1970), 61-7 and figs on 64 (fos 8v, 9v); Carlo Ludovico Ragghianti, *L'Arte in Italia dal secolo V al secolo XI* (Rome, 1968), cols 857-8, for colour reproduction of fo 7r (Ascension); Garrison, *Studies*, iv, 235-241, and figs 186-90 (fos 7r, 8v supra and infra, 13v infra, and 14v supra) on 239-43; Fornasari, 'Un manoscritto', 201-3; and Fournier, 'Un groupe', 160 (repr. *idem*, *Mélanges*, 278). The illustrations have been discussed recently by Alessia Trivellone, 'Immagine ed eresia: la rappresentazione degli eretici nel manoscritto Vat. Lat. 1339', in a paper presented at a conference, 'Medioevo immagini e ideologie', in Parma, 23-7 September 2002. The MS also contains two full-page figural diagrams in the last gathering of 5L on fo 303r-v, an 'arbor consanguinitatis' and 'arbor affinitatis'; Kuttner-Elze, *Catalogue*, 72-3.

17 Kuttner-Elze, *Catalogue*, 74; see also Garrison, *Studies*, iv, 238: the figures are those 'implicated, or thought to have been implicated, in the establishment of Canon Law and its authority' (without specific reference to 5L); and Walter, *Iconographie*, 63: the figures 'représentent les docteurs de l'Église et autres personages cités dans les canons'.

18 Reynolds, 'Rites and Signs', 209-12, on council illustrations in Hrabanus Maurus' *De universo* (Montecassino, Biblioteca dell'Abbazia, MS 132, s. xi in. [ante a. 1023]) and two Burchard MSS; Lucca, Biblioteca Capitolare 124 (s. xi ex.), and Florence, Biblioteca Laurenziana, Plut. 16.21 (s. xi ex.); 221-5, on the Utrecht psalter (Utrecht, Universiteitsbibliotheek, MS 32/484, *c.* 820); and 225-44, for the many conciliar illustrations in the Visigothic Codex Vigilanus (El Escorial, Real Biblioteca de San Lorenzo, MS d. I. 2, written 976, Albelda) and Codex Aemilianensis (El

ninth century are unusual in portraying a series of councils, the first six ecumenical councils in Vat. lat. 1339, and the first three in the Vercelli Codex as it now stands.[19] Although it was possible that the six-council series in Vat. lat. 1339 had been influenced by southern Italian fresco cycles or their southern Italian or Greek antecedents, the illustrations of single authors on fos 11r-14v portrayed many western authorities, including Bede, Smaragdus and Cummean.[20] In consideration of an earlier question about whether the illustrations were intended for the collection in Vat. lat. 1339, Reynolds pointed out that Vat. lat. 1339 has images of the fifth and sixth ecumenical councils, and only Vat. lat. 1339 among 5L manuscripts mentions these two councils in one of its prefaces, that taken from Pseudo-Isidore.[21] With this reference, Reynolds showed that the conciliar illustrations precisely matched the codex to which they were attached. Although much remains to be said about the iconographic or stylistic elements of the figural illustrations that follow the councils, the rest of the present paper will address the relation between these figures and the text of 5L.

The following table lists all the figures illustrated in the opening of Vat. lat. 1339, and the number of occasions on which each is cited in 5L according to the collection's attribution of canons, not the modern identifications, where those exist. In the table, the councils have been identified from the extensive labels attached to each. For the individual figures, the unemended manuscript label has been used without further identification, except in a few instances. For many, the identifications are obvious, but others are ambiguous (e.g., which [Pope] Eugenius is being portrayed?). Because the same ambiguities exist in the attributions within the 5L itself, the tabulation of citations has followed the simplest of name correspondences, as it would have for medieval readers.

Escorial, d. I. 1, written 992, San Millán de la Cogolla).

19 Reynolds, 'Rites and Signs', 212-15, on Vercelli, Biblioteca Capitolare, MS CLXV 215-9 (s. ix²/⁴), arguing that the Vercelli Codex had at least four councils in its original state before the loss of a bifolium, and may have had all six ecumenical councils if in fact two bifolia have been lost; and 215-21, on Vat. lat. 1339.

20 Reynolds, 'Rites and Signs', 219.

21 See the first note (*) above for Fuhrmann's question about the relationship of the gathering with the images to the collection. On the Ps-Isidorian preface, Reynolds, 'Rites and Signs', 220-21, notes also that the preface is written before book 2, not book 1 where it would seemingly be more appropriate; in Montecassino 125 and Vallicelliana B. 11, the same preface is copied before book 1, but in a form lacking references to the fifth and sixth councils. Reynolds suggests that this textual history may indicate that the original 5L or an earlier copy had the preface both entire and placed before book 1. For the Ps-Isidorian preface, see the text in 5L, ed. Fornasari, 159-62; and a translation in Robert Somerville and Bruce C. Brasington, *Prefaces to Canon Law Books in Latin Christianity: selected translations, 500-1245* (New Haven and London, 1998), 82-91.

Table 14.1   Figures illustrated in Vat. lat. 1339, fos 7r-14v, with the number of citations in the *Collectio canonum in V libris* (= 5L)

Folio	Illustration	5L	Folio	Illustration	5L
7r	[Ascension]	36[a]		'Paterius'[e]	25
7v	[Council of Nicaea, 325]	27		'Anastasius'	4
8r	[Constantinople I, 381]	1	12v	'Petrus'	11
8v	[Ephesus, 431]	1		'Paulus'	61
9r	[Chalcedon, 451]	21		'Iohannes'	11
9v	[Constantinople II, 553]	1[b]		'Jacobus'	8
10r	[Council of Constantinople III, 680/1]	1		'Beda'	5
			13r	'Zacharias'	12
10v	'Ysidorus eps'[c]	133		'Hylarii'	3
	'Hieronimus pbrm'	151		'Gaudentii'	1
	'G[re]g[orius] pp'	216		'Celestini'	6
	'G[re]g[orius] Nanzanzenus'	7		'Clementis'	10
11r	'Silv[este]r pp'	19		'Hormisde'	6
	'Aug[ustinus] eps'	188	13v	'Prosper'	2
	'Syricus eps'	21		'Zosimi'	3
	'Leoni pp'	36		'Cesarii'	2
	'Innocentii pp'	23		'Xysti'[f]	3
11v	'Gelasii pp'	20		'Symachi'	1
	'Osii'	4	14r	'Felicius'	2
	'Theodorus eps'	36		'Faustinus'[g]	8
	'Ioh[anne]s Chrisostomus'	3		'Ioh[anne]s'[h]	9
	'Ambrosius'	1		*sine nomine*	0
12r	'Smaragdus'	17		*sine nomine*	0
	'Commeanus'	37		*sine nomine*	0
	'Pynifius'[d]	3	14v	'Hiesus filius Syrac'[i]	6
	'Eugenius'	14		*sine nomine*	0

a The number is a count of references to the *Canones apostolorum*.

b No canons in 5L are ascribed to Constantinople II or III, but the councils are cited in the Ps-Isidorian preface to book 2 (ed. Fornasari, 161-2).

c In the MS, the abbreviations 'eps' ('episcopus'), 'prbm' (*sic* for 'presbyter'), and 'pp' ('papa') are marked with a stroke over the abbreviated point; the abbreviations of such titles are not expanded in the table.

d I.e., 'Pinufius', the Egyptian monk quoted in Collation 20 of *Iohannis Cassiani Conlationes XXIIII*, ed. Michael Petschenig, *CSEL*, 13 (Vienna, 1886; repr. New York, 1966).

e The canons in 5L attributed to 'Paterius' are those in the *Collectio hibernensis* otherwise attributed to 'Patricius'.

f I.e., Pope Sixtus, perhaps Sixtus III (sedit 432-40).

g Perhaps 'Faustinus/Faustus', who is cited in 5L from the Hibernensis.

h Perhaps this is Iohannes Constantinopolitanus, who is cited nine times in book 5; Fournier, 'Un groupe', 180, was unable to identify this source, except to say it was not John Chrysostom, John the Scholastic, or John the Lesser; at 160, Fournier labelled this figure as John the Evangelist, but it is more likely that the figure 'Iohannes' on fo 12v is the Evangelist.

i Author of Ecclesiasticus.

The illustrations include many authorities common in the canonical tradition, such as councils, doctors, popes, biblical authors, and penitential authors. Burchard's lists of sources in the preface to the *Liber decretorum* reveals similar categories, and indeed many of the same sources:

> Ex ipso enim nucleo canonum, quod a quibusdam Corpus canonum uocatur, queque nostro tempore necessaria excerpsi: ex canone apostolorum quędam, ex transmarinis conciliis quędam, ex Germanicis et Gallicis et Hispanis quędam, ex decretis Romanorum pontificum quędam, ex doctrina ipsius ueritatis quędam, ex Veteri Testamento quędam, ex apostolis quędam, ex dictis sancti Gregorii quędam, ex dictis sancti Ieronimi quędam, ex dictis sancti Augustini quędam, ex dictis sancti Ambrosii quędam, ex dictis sancti Benedicti quędam, ex dictis sancti Ysidori quędam, ex dictis sancti Basilii quędam, ex Poenitentiali Romano quędam, ex Pęnitentiali Theodori quędam, ex Poenitentiali Bedę quędam.[22]

One would expect prefaces and introductory remarks to encapsulate what canonical compilers thought most significant about the law, including which authorities they ranked most highly. The immediate question is whether greater precision should be expected in an early medieval collection. Reynolds' assumption in considering the program of the councils in Vat. lat. 1339 was that illustrators would indeed be aware of a collection's contents in great detail.[23] Nonetheless, despite the particular correspondence between the Pseudo-Isidorian preface to book 2 of 5L and the illustrations of the six councils, no preface in 5L exactly matches the sources portrayed in the rest of the illustrations. The second preface to book 2, attributed to Pope Gregory [III], lists, for instance, the sentences of 'Ysidori, Augustini, Bede, Gelasii, Gregorii, Innocentii, Theodori, Cassiani, Keberti [Egbert], uel ceterorum'.[24] Such a list is too short to qualify as a program for the figures in Vat. lat. 1339; moreover, Cassian and Egbert are not among the illustrated figures, and Egbert is not cited elsewhere in 5L. The Pseudo-Isidorian preface to book 2 provides a more complete list, including the canons of the apostles, the decrees of early popes, the council of Nicaea, Greek and Latin councils in chronological order, especially the first four ecumenical councils, the decretals of the remaining popes up to and including Gregory, and several other figures, but several of the patristic doctors and penitential authors figuring in the illustrations are not in the preface's list.[25] Indeed,

---

22 *Burchard von Worms, Decretorum libri XX*, ed. Gérard Fransen and Theo Kölzer, (Aalen, 1992; repr. of the editio princeps, Cologne, 1548), 49; trans. Somerville-Brasington, *Prefaces*, 104; see also *PL* 140.537-1043 at 540, with variants For Burchard, see Hartmut Hoffmann and Rudolf Pokorny, *Das Dekret des Bischofs Burchard von Worms: Textstufen—Frühe Verbreitung—Vorlagen*, MGH Hilfsmittel, 12 (Munich, 1991); and Kéry, *Canonical Collections*, 133-55.

23 See 246 and n. 21 above.

24 Ed. Fornasari, 14.

25 Ed. Fornasari, 159-62; trans. Somerville-Brasington, *Prefaces*, 82-91. See also the fourth preface to book 2, attributed to Dionysius, for a similar ranking of authorities; ed. Fornasari, 167 ll. 23-37; or the

none of the texts in 5L appear to be as close as Burchard's list of sources is to the program in the illustrations of Vat. lat. 1339. The complete list of illustrated figures shows, however, that the manuscript's illustrator knew quite specifically who was cited in 5L.

Several general considerations point to the illustrator's knowledge of the collection. First, every figure among those illustrated is cited at least once in the collection. Second, as the table above shows, the ranking among the individual figures corresponds approximately to the number of citations, and not necessarily to chronological or hierarchical standing. Thus, Isidore, Jerome, Gregory the Great, and Augustine are among the first six figures, and each is cited over 100 times in 5L, whereas the final fifteen figures are cited no more than twelve times each.[26] The correspondence is far from absolute (e.g., the fourth figure, Gregory of Nazianzus, is cited only seven times), because medieval illustrators were presumably not counting references in collections. Nonetheless, it is likely not coincidental that every figure cited more than about thirty times in the collection is illustrated in the series.[27] In terms of citations, the first prominent figure to lack an illustration is Origen; thirty canons are attributed to him in 5L, but his controversial reputation may have counted against his depiction as an authority, especially since he is already depicted among the heretics at the foot of the fathers attending the council of Constantinople II![28]

---

listing of early authorities in the *Decretum Gelasianum de recipiendis libris* (CPL 1676) copied in book 4 of 5L.

26 It is noteworthy that doctors and popes are reversed from the positions in Burchard's preface or in the 5L's own Pseudo-Isidorian preface. Instead of councils, popes, doctors, etc., the illustrator has councils (fos 7v-10r), doctors (10v), and popes (11r), not all of whom are labelled as popes (e.g., instead of 'pp', the figures are labelled 'Silv[este]r eps', 'Syricus eps'; many of the popes on fos 12r-14r are not identified except by name). In addition, the illustrator grouped the figures only in very general terms; popes are scattered among the remaining individual figures without any apparent hierarchical priority. A principle of ranking figures by frequency of citation could account for this order.

27 Authorities cited in 5L, but not illustrated in Vat. lat. 1339, fos 7r-14v, include: Councils of Ankara (Ancyra), Vasion, Ireland (Hibernia), Carthage, Laodicea, Narbonne, Africa, Eliberis, Neocaesarea, Toledo, Arles, Braga, Agde, Urbica, Syracuse, Orléans, Vercelli, Servia, Soissons, Tarragona, Sardica, Lérida, Gangra, Antioch, Seville, Orange, Rome; Mark, Matthew, Visio Wettini, Pelagius, Origen, Boniface, Rufinus, Basil, Theonus, Alipius, Dionysius, Cassian, Aurelius, Paphnutius, Eusebius, Eucherius, Becanus, Meldanus, Pope Calixtus, Pope Simplicius, Vita Macarii, Ianuarius, Pope Virgilius, Exodus, Ezekiel, Liber regum, Annales hebrorum, 'Lex' (Num., Ex., Deut.), Isaiah, Abraham, Job, Deuteronomy, Prophets, Salomon, Moses, Tobias, Ieremias, Psalms, David, Jonah, Anna, Ioshua, Martin, Luke, Acts of the Apostles, Acta s. Bartholomei, Vitae patrum, Vitae monachorum, Vitae sanctorum, Chronica greca (Theophanis), Iudicium synodale, Iudicium canonum, Exempla canonum, Decretum patrum, Justinian, Charlemagne (Karolus), Louis the Pious (Lodovicus), Lothar, Pippin, Henry II, Roelus, Desiderius, Rothari, Achilepertus, Liutprand, Grimoald, Guy of Spoleto (Guido).

28 The labels of the councils (fos 7v-10r) list the heretics condemned by each council; for Constantinople II (fo 9v) the label lists Origen: 'Quinta synodus sub iustiniano maiore imperatore .clx. patrum contra originem et euagrium et dydimum impiissimos. Dicebant enim: non resurget caro nostra et quia non est paradysus factus a deo et finem habent poene impiorum et demones ut prius angeli exsistant'.

The fact that every illustrated figure is cited at least once in 5L is significant, because there is no contemporary collection, including Burchard, for which the same could be said. For instance, five biblical authors are illustrated in Vat. lat. 1339 (not including the apostles in the first image): Peter, Paul, John, James, and 'Hiesus filius Syrac', author of Ecclesiasticus. The five figures are cited ninety-seven times as authors in the collection, and the illustrator appears to have recognized this emphasis. Apart from the Hibernensis and collections dependent on it, such as 9L and Vallicelliana T. XVIII, few collections cite all six as authors of canons, and none have as many individual citations.[29] An earlier collection, Regino of Prüm's *Libri duo de synodalibus causis et disciplinis ecclesiasticis* (*c.* 906), does not cite any biblical authors as sources of canons.[30] Burchard's influential *Liber decretorum*, a close contemporary to 5L, attributes only seven canons to biblical authors.[31] Among the collections of the reformers, the Collection in 183 Titles (= 183T; written 1063-83/5) has three direct attributions to the Bible;[32] the Collection in Seventy-Four Titles (= 74T; written 1073-5) has one;[33] Bonizo of Sutri's *Liber de vita Christiana* (written 1089-95) has three scriptural attributions;[34] and Gregory of San Grisogono's *Polycarpus* (written by 1113 at the latest) has two.[35]

The illustrations of eastern authorities and figures associated with penitentials or insular sources are other areas in which the correspondence between illustrations and

---

29 Fornasari, *Collectio canonum*, xii, noting 5L's frequent citation of Scripture. In addition to the figures illustrated in Vat. lat. 1339, see n. 27 above for scriptural attributions not illustrated in the MS. Over ten percent of the canons in 5L are attributed to biblical sources; in the Hibernensis, the proportion is closer to thirty percent; see in general Rob Meens, 'The Use of the Old Testament in Early Medieval Canon Law: the *Collectio Vetus Gallica* and the *Collectio Hibernensis*', in *The Uses of the Past in the Early Middle Ages*, ed. Yitshak Hen and Matthew Innes (Cambridge, 2000), 67-77. For the Hibernensis: *Die Irische* Kanonensammlung, 2nd edn, ed. Hermann Wasserschleben (Leipzig, 1885; repr. Aalen, 1966); and Kéry, *Canonical Collections*, 73-80.

30 *Reginonis abbatis Primiensis Libri duo de synodalibus causis et disciplinis ecclesiasticis*, ed. F. G A. Wasserschleben (Leipzig, 1840), 517 (index). See Kéry, *Canonical Collections*, 128-33.

31 Hoffmann-Pokorny, *Das Dekret*, 248 for biblical authors (1 citation each from Exod and Iob; 2 from Matt; 3 from Paul); in addition, Burchard, 19.8, quotes 'Jesus filius Sirach' within the text (*PL* 140.980B).

32 *Liber canonum diversorum sanctorum patrum sive Collectio in CLXXXIII titulos digesta*, ed. Joseph [Giuseppe] Motta, MIC Series B, Corpus Collectionum, 7 (Vatican City, 1988), 331 (Lev 5: 1, 1 Tim 3: 1-13; and 1 Tim 5: 7, 9-11); the abridged form of the collection in Vatican City, Biblioteca Apostolica Vaticana, MS Vat. lat. 1348, has a fourth reference (Ezech 18: 26). See Kéry, *Canonical Collections*, 216-17 (183T) and 217-18 (Vat. lat. 1348).

33 *Diuersorum patrum sententie siue Collectio in LXXIV titulos digesta*, ed. Joannes [John] T. Gilchrist, MIC Series B, Corpus collectionum, 1 (Vatican City, 1973), 199 (Deut 17: 8-13). See Kéry, *Canonical Collections*, 204-10.

34 *Bonizonis Liber de vita Christiana*, ed. Ernst Perels, Texte zur Geschichte des römischen und kanonischen Rechts im Mittelalter, 1 (Berlin, 1930), 361 (from Lev 5: 1, 1 Cor 7: 12-14, and Hebr 5: 4-6). For Bonizo, see Kéry, *Canonical Collections*, 234-7.

35 Uwe Horst, *Die Kanonessammlung Polycarpus des Gregor von S. Grisogno: Quellen und Tendenzen*, MGH Hilfsmittel, 5 (Munich, 1980), 203 (1 Tim, Hebr). For *Polycarpus*, see Kéry, *Canonical Collections*, 266-9.

figures in the collection is significant. In the illustrations, the eastern fathers are Gregory of Nazianzus, John Chrysostom, the Egyptian monk Pinufius ('Pynifius'), who was known from Cassian's Collationes, and the figure 'Iohannes' on fo 14r, who may be John of Constantinople.[36] Together the four figures are cited over twenty times in 5L. Few western collections have as many citations from eastern fathers, and none have all four figures. Regino has, for instance, several references to Basil, Cassian (with his Egyptian sources), and Pachomius, but none to Gregory of Nazianzus, John Chrysostom, or Pinufius.[37] Burchard attributes several canons to eastern fathers, but does not quote Pinufius and does not assign canons to Gregory of Nazianzus or John Chrysostom.[38] None of the four representative Gregorian collections considered here—183T, 74T, Bonizo, and *Polycarpus*—have attributions to either Gregory of Nazianzus or John Chrysostom.

The case for associating the illustrations with 5L is similar for penitential and insular figures. Vat. lat. 1339 has illustrations of Theodore, Cummean, Bede, Patrick ('Paterius'), and Faustinus. In 5L, the penitentials of the first three are cited a total of seventy-eight times, with Theodore and Cummean cited most frequently; an additional thirty-four canons are attributed to Patrick or Faustinus.[39] Illustrations of these figures would have been out of place in collections that lacked penitential canons, a group that includes several collections of the Gregorian reformers, such as 74T. As Kathleen Cushing has demonstrated, at least one reform collection that used pentitential sources, the collection of Anselm II of Lucca, is conspicuous in its avoidance of Irish penitential canons.[40] 183T and Bonizo are equally cautious in their

---

36 Pinufius is cited in 5L as the source for three canons (4.5, 4.48-9). Although from Cassian originally, the Hibernensis and its copies were probably the means of transmission of these texts to 5L; see for instance, 5L 4.5 'De penitentia Deo soli confitenda proficiente', which is from the Hibernensis 47.5.a, ed. Wasserschleben, 197. See Table 14.1 on 247 above and n. 'h' for the identification of John of Constantinople.

37 Regino, ed. Wasserschleben, 524 (index).

38 Hoffmann-Pokorny, *Das Dekret*, 248, 258, for nine eastern references. Although Burchard does not attribute canons to Gregory of Nazianzus or John Chrysostom, searches through the *Patrologia Latina Database*, published on-line by Chadwyck-Healey (http://pld.chadwyck.co.uk), show several references to Gregory of Nazianzus (Burchard, 1.233, *PL* 140.617A; 19.8, *PL* 140.979B) and John Chrysostom (Burchard, 1.233, *PL* 140.616B), including references to both in Burchard's copy of the *Decretum Gelasianum* (3.220, *PL* 140.717D). Several canons are attributed to 'Johannes Constantinopolitanus', who is not to be associated with John Chrysostom; see Burchard, 7.19-20, *PL* 140.782-3; 19.44, *PL* 140.993-4. These are not, however, the same canons attributed to Johannes Constantinopolitanus in 5L 5.149, 151, 155-6, 158, 160-63.

39 Texts attributed to Patrick and Faustinus/Faustus are usually drawn ultimately from the Hibernensis. Fornasari, *Collectio canonum*, xii, estimated that about a quarter of the canons in book 1 of 5L were from the Hibernensis.

40 Kathleen G. Cushing, 'Anselm of Lucca and Burchard of Worms: re-thinking the sources of Anselm 11 *De penitentia*', in the present volume, 225-39, at 228 and 232, noting that one Cummean text is cited in Anselm 11, but attributed to Theodore; see also *eadem*, *Papacy and Law in the Gregorian Revolution: the canonistic work of Anselm of Lucca*, Oxford Historical Monographs (Oxford, 1998), 70. On the collection of Anselm II of Lucca, see Kéry, *Canonical Collections*, 218-26.

use of Irish canons.[41] Even Burchard's use of several penitential and insular sources, including over sixty canons from the Hibernensis, does not mean unequivocal acceptance of such sources.[42] Burchard lists three penitentials among his sources, but warns users of Bede's penitential that it may have been interpolated with unauthorized material;[43] and when presenting texts from Cummean Burchard's attributions do not refer to Cummean.[44] Although compilers taking material from the Hibernensis refer to the source of the text, not the collection itself, Burchard's references to some of the most prominently Irish components of the Hibernensis are scarce; there are, for instance, only two canons in the *PL* copy of Burchard said to be drawn 'ex conc. Hibern.' and none from 'Patricius'.[45] An illustrator seeking suitable images for Burchard's collection would have been unlikely to turn to Irish figures, whereas the notable place given to Irish sources in the illustrations of Vat. lat. 1339 is an appropriate response to their prominence in 5L.

Even collections such as 9L, which has many texts in common with 5L, are not as well suited to the illustrations as 5L is.[46] 9L has references to Greek sources, as does 5L, but does not have canons from Pope Anastasius, Caesarius, Pinufius or Pope Sixtus, all of whom are illustrated in Vat. lat.1339 and cited in 5L.

There is, however, a second means of discounting relations between the illustrations and other collections; i.e., through consideration of sources not depicted in the series. The illustrations in Vat. lat. 1339 do not themselves match perfectly the sources cited in 5L, but there are plausible explanations. As noted above, Origen is not illustrated among the authorities, despite frequent attributions in 5L, but the reason is probably Origen's controversial reputation.[47] Vat. lat. 1339 also lacks

---

41 183T, ed. Motta, 345, lists several penitential sources, but only two canons (123.4 and 124.2) are from Cummean; the collection cites the first as 'ex concilio Rotomagensi' and the second 'ex concilio Elibertano'; similarly a canon from the *Excarpsus Bedae* in 183T 123.5 is said to come 'ex penitentiali Romano'. Bonizo, *Liber de vita Christiana*, cites several penitentials and draws its canons 9.48 and 10.68 from Cummean, but without direct attribution.

42 Hoffmann-Pokorny, *Das Dekret*, 250-51, for Burchard's canons from the Hibernensis, and 269-71 for penitential sources.

43 Burchard, preface, quoted at 248 above; and 19.8, *PL* 140.979B: 'in Poenitentiali Bedae plura inveniuntur utilia: plura autem inveniuntur ab aliis inserta, quae nec canonibus, nec aliis Poenitentialibus conveniunt'.

44 About twenty-five canons in Burchard are from the *Excarpsus Cummeani*; see Hoffmann-Pokorny, *Das Dekret*, 270. Attributions to Cummean do not appear, however, in Burchard, at least not in the copy in *PL* 140. This lack of reference may have been due to borrowing from intermediate sources or misattribution in Burchard's *fontes formales*; e.g., Regino has three items from Cummean, but without specific attributions: 1.138 (no reference), 2.51 ('ex poenitentiali'), and 2.54 ('ex eodem'). See, however, Roger E. Reynolds, 'Law, Canon: to Gratian', in *Dictionary of the Middle Ages*, ed. Joseph R. Strayer (1986), vii, 395-413 at 407-8 noting Burchard's willingness to change attributions of canons from insular and penitential sources.

45 Burchard, 12.25-6, *PL* 140.881B. In comparison, 5L attributes twenty-four canons to Irish synods and councils.

46 For 9L, see n. 5 above, and the headings in *PL* 138.397-442.

47 See 249 above. And n. 27 for a list of all the sources in 5L not depicted on fos 10v-14v.

illustrations of regional and lesser councils, although almost twenty percent of the canons in 5L are attributed to them. Perhaps the prominent placement of the ecumenical councils suffices to show the authority of ecclesiastical gatherings, or it could be that lesser councils are represented by proxy. Thus, the council of Sardica (342) with ten citations in 5L could have been represented by the portraits of Osius and Gaudentius, both present at the council and both cited in its canons. Similarly, the council of Agde cited twenty-five times in 5L may have been associated with Caesarius, who is otherwise cited only twice; the councils of Carthage with over sixty references may have been linked, somewhat more tenuously, to Augustine; Irish councils with twenty-four references to the image of Patricius; and the forty-four references to Roman synods with several papal figures.[48] A second noteworthy gap is the absence of secular figures among the individual portraits, although emperors are illustrated in the council illustrations, and Justinian (illustrated on fo 9v at Constantinople II) could be considered to authorize the Roman law cited in 5L.[49] The remainder of the secular sources, in particular the ninth-century Franks, may be too recent for the illustrator: among the illustrated ecclesiastical figures, only Smaragdus dates from as late as the ninth century, although some of the unnumbered popes could be considered ninth century.[50] Apart from these few areas, none of which contain individuals cited more than thirty times, the illustrator of Vat. lat. 1339 has covered all the figures cited frequently in 5L.

Although there are plausible explanations for discrepancies between the sources in 5L and the illustrations in Vat. lat. 1339, similar discrepancies with other collections tend to highlight how well the illustrator understood the program and sources behind 5L. In addition to Burchard's lack of appropriate Greek and Irish references, Burchard has more Frankish councils and references to Frankish ecclesiastics than 5L does. While the illustrator of a collection like 5L could safely ignore ninth-century synods and ecclesiastical authorities, and by extension recent secular authorities, such a lack would have left a noticeable gap in a series intended to illustrate a Burchard manuscript. Similarly, a Gregorian collection would have been mis-read by its illustrator if its (imaginary) illustrations did not include some of the

---

48 Consideration of the Roman synods and popes presents a problem of interpretation. Does, for instance, the portrait of 'Leoni [sic] pp' (fo 11r) refer to Leo I, with many canonical references, or Leo IV, who convened the important Roman synod of 853? The same problem arises when references are made to canons from different popes of the same name; e.g., Gregory I and Gregory III. Although one individual in such a pair may indeed be more prominent, when it comes to depicting authority, a single un-numbered image can do double duty.

49 The emperors depicted in the councils are Constantine (fo 7v), Theodosius I (8r), Theodosius II (9r), Marcianus (9v), Justinian (10r), and Constantine IV (10v). Approximately five percent of the canons in 5L are attributed to secular sources; see Fornasari, *Collectio canonum*, xiv-xvii, noting that Roman law has thirty-eight references, Lombard law nine references, Frankish rulers fifty-six (Charlemagne 29; Louis 12; Lothar 10; Pepin 4, Childebert 1), Guy of Spoleto (889-95) one, and Henry II five.

50 I.e., if 'Eugenius' (fo 12r) is taken as Eugenius II (824-7). It is less likely that Leo (fo 11r) represents Leo III (795-816) or Leo IV (847-55), or that Gregory (10v) is Gregory IV (827-44).

eleventh-century reformers. Closer to home, Vallicelliana T. XVIII and 9L are very similar in their references to 5L, but both are noteworthy for using the False Decretals to defend the ordinations of Pope Formosus (891-6). There are, however, no images in Vat. lat. 1339 of Calixtus, Anterus, Marcellus, Jules, Alexander or Theophanis, author of the *Chronica greca*, whose works figure prominently in the defense of Formosus. If the principle of illustrating the significant figures in a collection were applied to the relationship between the images in Vat. lat. 1339 and the texts in Burchard, 9L or the collection of Vallicelliana T. XVIII, it would fail.[51]

The specificity of the correspondence between illustrations and text in Vat. lat. 1339 needs explanation. That an illustrator depicted Cummean instead of Hrabanus Maurus, or Caesarius—not to mention Patrick or Faustinus—instead of Hincmar, could be a sign of how comprehensively clerics assimilated their local ecclesiastical culture. In other words, when the illustrator of Vat. lat. 1339 thought of legal authorities, they were the figures cited in a collection like 5L, and not those that the near-contemporary Gregorian reformers would have considered. Or, alternatively, the correspondence between text and illustration may be an indication of how the illustrator sought to distinguish the collection from other collections, which requires a wide knowledge of what they also contain. In an age before canonical collections were issued by superiors who could compel obedience, canonical compilers used their prefaces to emphasize a collection's usefulness, and comment on the authenticity and authority of its contents. By illustrating so precisely the authorities in 5L, the illustrator of Vat. lat. 1339 was making a statement about the collection's contents, and promoting its selection of authorities, perhaps over the range of authorities in other collections. Whether the choice to illustrate certain figures out of the vast range of authorities within the canonical tradition was based on assumptions of who the chief authories were, or was a deliberate attempt to emphasize the collection's distinctive features, the illustrations are a sign that contemporaries would have been able to distinguish collections on such grounds and indicate a sophisticated and precise contemporary understanding of what early medieval collections contained.

---

51 Collections derived from 5L, of which there are many, should also provide close comparisons between their sources and the illustrations, except that many have modified the emphases of 5L by adding materials from Burchard; e.g., the collection in Florence, Biblioteca Medicea Laurenziana, MS Plut. 4, sin. 4; see Kéry, *Canonical Collections*, 276 (s. xi, Italy?). Others refer to decrees of the eleventh-century reformers; e.g., the collection of Vatican City, Biblioteca Apostolica Vaticana, MS Vat. lat. 4977; see Kéry, *Canonical Collections*, 280. Such changes may be reflected in what would be appropriate to illustrate each collection.

Chapter 15

Die Quellen der mittelitalienischen Kanonessammlung in sieben Büchern (MS Vat. lat. 1346)

Peter Landau

Zu den Kanonessammlungen aus der ersten Hälfte des 12. Jahrhunderts gehört eine in sieben Büchern eingeteilte Kompilation, die zuerst durch einen vatikanischen Codex (Città del Vaticano, Biblioteca Apostolica Vaticana, Vat. lat. 1346; Sigle: V) bekannt wurde.[1] Diese Sammlung darf nicht mit einer anderen ebenfalls in sieben Bücher aufgeteilten Collectio verwechselt werden, die ausschliesslich in der Handschrift Turin D.IV.33 überliefert ist und aus Poitiers oder Norditalien stammt.[2] Die Turiner Sammlung, die Anfang des 12. Jahrhunderts entstand, bietet eine Kombination von Burchard von Worms mit der 74-Titel-Sammlung und hatte wohl nur lokale Bedeutung.[3] Die Sieben-Bücher-Sammlung der vatikanischen Handschrift, für die ich die Sigle 7L verwende, muss hingegen zu den verbreiteteren Kanonessammlungen aus der ersten Hälfte des 12. Jahrhunderts gerechnet werden. Auf die vatikanische Handschrift wiesen als erste die Brüder Ballerini in einer kurzen Notiz ihres Werkes 'De antiquis collectionibus' 1757 hin.[4] Sie stellten bereits fest, dass die Sammlung mit einem Päpstekatalog verbunden ist, der mit Paschalis II. ohne Angabe eines Todesjahrs endet und folglich wohl kurz vor 1120 entstanden sein müsse; die jüngsten Texte dieser Sammlung sind zwei vor 1115 zu datierende Briefe Paschalis II. (JL 6426 und 6436).[5] Eine genauere Beschreibung der vatikanischen Handschrift gab 1836 August Theiner in seinen *Disquisitiones*

---

1   Allgemein orientierend zu dieser Sammlung Lotte Kéry, *Canonical Collections of the Early Middle Ages (ca. 400-1140)*, History of Medieval Canon Law, 1, ed. Wilfried Hartmann and Kenneth Pennington (Washington, D.C., 1999), 269.

2   Hierzu cf. Kéry, *Canonical Collections*, 265-6.

3   Cf. Roger E. Reynolds, 'The Turin Collection in Seven Books: a Poitevin canonical collection', *Traditio*, 25 (1969), 508-14; auch in *idem, Law and Liturgy in the Latin Church* (Aldershot, 1994), no. XVII.

4   Petrus [Pietro] et Hieronymus [Girolamo] Ballerini, *Disquisitiones de antiquis collectionibus et collectoribus canonum*, P. IV, cap. XVIII, n. 5 (*PL* 57.350).

5   Cf. Uta-Renate Blumenthal, 'Decrees and Decretals of Pope Paschal II in Twelfth-Century Canonical Collections', *BMCL*, NS 10 (1980), 15-30, hier 20-21.

criticae.[6] Er wies darauf hin, dass die Sammlung innerhalb der Bücher noch eine detaillierte Untergliederung in einzelne mit Sachrubriken versehene Abschnitte bringt, die der Sammler als 'Capitula' bezeichnet, so dass es sich um ein systematisches, überaus detailliert gegliedertes Werk handelt, dessen Gliederungsschema Parallelen zur Collectio Polycarpus aufweist. Theiner edierte die zahlreichen Rubriken der Sammlung[7] und machte Ausführungen zu den Quellen, aus denen der Autor geschöpft habe.[8] 1878 stellte Friedrich Thaner fest, dass 7L auch in einer Handschrift der Wiener Nationalbibliothek in einer erweiterten Fassung enthalten sei.[9] Eine umfangreichere Untersuchung wurde der Sammlung nur von Paul Fournier gewidmet, der im zweiten Band der *Histoire des collections canoniques* (1932) auf eine dritte Handschrift in der Bibliothek von Cortona hinwies (MS Cortona 43, Sigle: C), die Entstehung von 7L in der Region von Mittelitalien lokalisieren konnte, die Entstehungszeit zwischen 1112 und 1120 eingrenzte und Angaben über die Quellen der Sammlung machte.[10] Fournier hielt überdies eine genauere Untersuchung von 7L für wünschenswert, da er in ihr eine interessante Quelle zum Investiturstreit sah[11] und einen Einfluss von 7L auf das gratianische Dekret vermutete: 'Nous avons lieu de croire qu'elle ne serait pas sans intérêt pour qui voulait éclaircir les origines du Décret de Gratien'.[12] Die drei Handschriften spiegeln verschiedene Entwicklungsstufen der Sammlung, da Vat. lat. 1346 Zusätze bringt, die in den Manuskripten von Cortona und Wien in den Haupttext eingearbeitet sind, wobei Wien gegenüber Cortona eine dritte Redaktionsstufe darstellt.[13] Hartmut Zapp ist es vor kurzem gelungen, eine vierte Redaktionsstufe der Sammlung in der Handschrift Helmstedt 308 der Herzog-August-Bibliothek in Wolfenbüttel zu entdecken.[14] In dieser Handschrift wurde bisher eine selbständige Sammlung in acht Büchern gesehen,[15] während Robert Somerville und Hartmut

---

6 Augustin Theiner, *Disquisitiones criticae in praecipuas canonum et decretalium collectionibus* (Roma, 1836), 345-55.

7 Theiner, *Disquisitiones*, 347-55. Die Liste der Rubriken ist nicht ohne Fehler.

8 Theiner, *Disquisitiones*, 346-7.

9 Friedrich Thaner, 'Untersuchungen und Mittheilungen zur Quellenkunde des canonischen Rechts', *Sitzungsberichte der Kaiserlichen Akademie der Wissenschaften <Wien>*. *Philosophisch-Historische Klasse*, 89 (1878), 601-32, hier 603, Anm. 3. Es handelt sich um Wien, ÖNB, MS 2186 (Sigle: W).

10 Paul Fournier, Gabriel Le Bras, *Histoire des collections canoniques en Occident depuis les Fausses Décrétales jusqu'au Décret de Gratien*, 2 vols (Paris, 1931-2), ii, 185-92.

11 *Ibid.*, ii, 191.

12 *Ibid.*, ii, 192.

13 *Ibid.*, ii, 187.

14 Robert Somerville, Hartmut Zapp, 'An "Eighth Book" of the Collection in Seven Books', in *Grundlagen des Rechts: Festschrift für Peter Landau zum 65. Geburtstag*, ed. Richard H. Helmholz, Paul Mikat, Jörg Müller, Michael Stolleis, Rechts- und Staatswissenschaftliche Veröffentlichungen der Görres-Gesellschaft, NF 91 (Paderborn-München-Wien-Zürich, 2000), 163-77, hier 164.

15 *Ibid.*, 169-70.

Zapp nunmehr in einer minutiösen Studie zeigen konnten, dass das achte Buch der Sammlung von Wolfenbüttel nichts anderes als ein Supplement zu 7L ist. In ihm tauchen auch Texte aus Hugo von St. Viktor und dem gratianischen Dekret auf,[16] so dass die Redaktion von 7L im MS Wolfenbüttel (Sigle: Wo) wohl nach 1150 zu datieren ist. Die Handschrift scheint in Frankreich geschrieben zu sein, so dass sich daraus ergibt, dass 7L im 12. Jahrhundert über Mittelitalien hinaus Verbreitung fand. Eine genauere Untersuchung des Verhältnisses der vier Handschriften von 7L zueinander ist von Somerville und Zapp zu erwarten. In meinem Beitrag möchte ich ausschliesslich auf die seit Theiner mehrfach erörterte Frage der Quellen von 7L eingehen.

Theiner ging davon aus, dass 7L ein Derivat der Kanonessammlung des Anselm von Lucca gewesen sei—'ex Anselmi collectione orta est'.[17] Zusätzlich habe der Kompilator von 7L zahlreiche Fragmente der Collectio Anselmo dedicata und der Collectio Tripartita entnommen.[18] Fournier erstellte hingegen eine von Theiners Quellenangaben weitgehend abweichende Liste der Quellen von 7L. Nach ihm stand 7L vor allem unter dem Einfluss der Sammlung Polycarpus, aus der ganze Serien in 7L reproduziert seien.[19] Ferner seien zahlreiche Texte aus Pseudo-Isidor und Burchard von Worms entnommen worden.[20] Ausserdem könne man eine Benutzung der Sammlungen Anselms von Lucca, Bonizos von Sutri, der irischen Kanonessammlung, der Briefe Gregors des Grossen, patristischer Florilegien mit besonderer Berücksichtigung Augustins und schliesslich auch von Texten des römischen Rechts einschliesslich der Digesten feststellen.[21] Somerville-Zapp gehen kurz auf die Quellenfrage ein und stellen fest, dass in 7L Pseudo-Isidor, Burchard von Worms, eine Version des Anselm von Lucca, Bonizo und Polycarpus verwendet seien.[22] Man sieht, dass die Angaben über die Quellen von 7L in der bisherigen Forschung keineswegs übereinstimmen. Sollten alle seit Theiner genannten Quellen dem Kompilator von 7L zur Verfügung gestanden

---

16 *Ibid.*, 164.

17 Theiner, *Disquisitiones*, 345.

18 *Ibid.*, 346.

19 Fournier-Le Bras, *Histoire*, ii, 189.

20 *Ibid.*, ii, 188-9.

21 *Ibid.*, ii, 188-9.

22 Somerville-Zapp, 'Eighth Book', 163. In der Einleitung zum Programm Kanones J weist Linda Fowler-Magerl auch auf die Quellen von 7L hin; die Sammlung wurde von ihr aufgrund der Handschrift W in die Datenbank aufgenommen. Nach Linda Fowler-Magerl, *A Selection of Canon Law Collections compiled between 1000 and 1140* (Piesenkofen in der Oberpfalz, 2003), 172 ist auch zu erwägen, dass zu den Quellen von 7L die Sammlung der Handschrift von Assisi BC 227 gehören könnte, der nach neuen Forschungsergebnissen Fowler-Magerls als Teilstück auch die Sammlung in zwei Büchern (MS Vat. lat. 3832) zuzuordnen ist—cf. Linda Fowler-Magerl, 'The Restoration of the Canon Law Collection in the Mss. Vat. lat. 3832 and Assisi BC 227', in: *Grundlagen des Rechts: Festschrift für Peter Landau*, 179-203. Die Frage, ob diese bisher kaum analysierte Sammlung neben Anselm eine weitere Quelle von 7L war, bedürfte einer besonderen Untersuchung.

haben, so müssten für ihn mehr kanonistische Hilfsmittel als selbst für Gratian erreichbar gewesen sein.[23] Es kann daher aufschlussreich sein, die Angaben zu den Quellen von 7L im einzelnen zu überprüfen, zumal auch im Vergleich zu dem zeitgenössischen und in regionaler Nachbarschaft entstandenen gratianischen Dekret.

Dabei sei zunächst 7L mit Polycarp verglichen, da die Sammlung des Kardinals Gregor von S. Grisogono nur wenige Jahre vor 7L verfasst und auch in derselben Region verbreitet wurde.[24] Ein Vergleich lässt eindeutig erkennen, dass Fournier mit seiner Behauptung von der Übernahme ganzer Serien aus Polycarp recht behält. Der Autor von 7L hat sich darüber hinaus auch bei der Formulierung seiner Titelrubriken oft an Polycarp angelehnt.[25] Man vergleiche etwa in Buch 1 folgende Beispiele:

1. Pol. 1.4: De electione et ordinatione Romani pontificis.
   7L 1.6: De Romani pontificis electione.
   7L besteht aus vier Kapiteln, die Pol. 1.1-4 entsprechen.
2. Pol. 4.42: De inobedientibus et canonum violatoribus.
   7L 1.25: De contemptoribus canonum.
   7L 1.25 bringt fünf Kapitel = Pol. 4.42.4-8.
3. Pol. 4.2: Qualiter sit legenda lex dei.
   7L 1.26: Qualiter lex dei sit legenda vel docenda.
   Jeweils übereinstimmend vier Kapitel.
4. Pol. 4.3 und 7L 1.27: Quod nihil addendum est divino mandato.
   Jeweils übereinstimmend ein Kapitel.
5. Pol. 5.8 und 7L 1.28: Quod pro uno adversus plures non sit facile ferenda sententia.
   Jeweils übereinstimmend ein Kapitel.
6. Pol. 5.9 und 7L 1.29: Quando adversariis respondendum sit (et) quando minime.
   Jeweils übereinstimmend zwei Kapitel.
7. Pol. 1.26 und 7L 1.30: De praecepto, admonitione et consilio.
   Jeweils übereinstimmend drei Kapitel.
8. Pol. 1.27 und 7L 1.31: De auctoritate et ratione.
   Jeweils übereinstimmend elf Kapitel.

---

23 Zu den Quellen Gratians cf. meine Arbeiten in *Kanones und Dekretalen* (Goldbach, 1997), passim.
24 Zur Sammlung Polycarp zusammenfassend Kéry, *Canonical Collections*, 266-9. Aus der umfang-reichen Literatur zu der leider noch immer ungedruckten Sammlung grundlegend Uwe Horst, *Die Kanonessammlung Polycarpus des Gregor von S. Grisogono*, MGH Hilfsmittel, 5 (München, 1980).
25 Für den Vergleich der Rubriken habe ich auf die Angaben bei Theiner, *Disquisitiones*, 342-55, zurückgegriffen und die von ihm verzeichneten Texte mit den Handschriften Biblioteca Apostolica Vaticana, Reg. lat. 1026 (Polycarp) und Vat. lat. 1346 verglichen.

9. Pol. 2.20 und 7L 1.38: De usu et auctoritate pallii.
   7L 1.38, 1-7 = Pol. 2.10.1, 2.20.1-3, 2.24.7, 2.20.4-5.
10. Pol. 2.4 und 7L 1.46: Ut ecclesia saeculari potentia vel pretio vel laicali investitura minime pervadatur.
   Jeweils übereinstimmend fünf Kapitel.

Diese Beispiele dürften genügen, um die Benutzung und das Vorbild des Polycarp für 7L zu belegen.

An zweiter Stelle sei das Verhältnis von 7L zu Anselm von Lucca geprüft. Auch hier sind Übernahmen unverkennbar, obwohl nicht wie im Fall des Polycarp ganze Serien übernommen wurden und gelegentlich auch eine Rezeption aus anderen Sammlungen möglich bleibt.

Gleich zu Beginn scheint Anselm von Lucca für den Kompilator von 7L als Vorbild gedient zu haben, da das erste Buch, das wie bei Anselm zunächst dem päpstlichen Primat gewidmet ist, mit dem pseudo-isidorischen Text des Anacletus 'In novo testamento' einsetzt, in dem die Stelle 'Tu es Petrus' des Matthäusevangeliums zitiert wird.[26] Dieses erste Kapitel ist aber bei Anselm kürzer als in 7L, da Anselm bereits mit 'adduxit' endet,[27] während 7L wie Ivos Panormie und Gratian den Anaclet-Text bis 'constituti in ecclesia' bringt.[28] Anselm von Lucca hat hier also allenfalls die Anregung für den Auftakt der Sammlung geliefert. Als unmittelbare Quelle für 7L kommt hier vielmehr die in der Toskana um 1080 kompilierte Sammlung in 183 Titeln in Frage, die ebenso wie 7L mit 'constituti in ecclesia' endet.[29] Es folgen sodann in diesem ersten Abschnitt von 7L (c. 1) unter der Rubrik 'De primatu et auctoritate apostolicae sedis' noch fünf weitere Kapitel, die alle auch bei Anselm im ersten Buch zu finden sind, wobei c. 2 von 7L allerdings unvollständiger als die Parallelstelle bei Anselm ist.[30] Das c. 6 von 7L entspricht im Umfang nicht den Rezensionen A und B von Anselm, sondern der Lucca-Rezension Bb, die hier in Thaners unbefriedigender Edition ausnahmsweise im Kleindruck wiedergegeben wird; es ist im selben Umfang wie in 7L aber auch

---

26 Anselm II. Bischof von Lucca, *Collectio Canonum*, ed. Friedrich Thaner (Innsbruck, 1906-15; ND Aalen, 1965), 7.

27 Cf. *Decretales Pseudo-Isidorianae*, ed. Paulus Hinschius (Leipzig, 1863; ND Aalen, 1963), 79, Z. 7.

28 Hinschius, *Decretales Pseudo-Isidorianae*, 79, Z. 16.

29 Cf. *Liber canonum diversorum sanctorum patrum sive Collectio in CLXXXIII titulos digesta*, ed. Joseph Motta, MIC Series B, Corpus collectionum, 7 (Città del Vaticano, 1988), 16-17.

30 7L 1.1.2 entspricht zum Teil Ans. 1.66, ed. Thaner, 34. 7L om. 'Adhibita est etiam societas—in orationibus meis' und 'Inter beatos apostolos—tenendum tradiderunt'. Ansonsten: 7L 1.1.3 = Ans. 1.2, 2. Teil: "Haec apostolica sedes', ed. Thaner, 7-8, und Ans. 1.66, ed. Thaner, 34-5. Hier setzt MS Vat. lat. 1346 über das Kapitel in anderer Schrift: 'hoc est in *prima* pagina in primo quaternione de eadem re'—was auf eine Herkunft aus Anselm hindeuten könnte. In margine ist vermerkt: 'cap. XXXIIII'—was auf umittelbare Benutzung Pseudosisidors (A2) hinweist. Die Handschriften C und W von 7L haben nur: 'cap. XXXIIII'. 7L 1.1.4 = Ans. 1.14 bis 'emendare'; 7L 1.1.5 = Ans. 1.15: 7L 1.1.6 = Ans. 1.9; 7L 1.1.7 = Ans. 1.63 (JL 4424).

in der Collectio 183 Titulorum zu finden.[31] In den folgenden Abschnitten des ersten Buchs von 7L sind die Übereinstimmungen mit Anselm relativ selten—man findet sie in 7L 1.2,[32] 1.3,[33] 1.11[34] und 1.12.[35] Bei den Kapiteln von 7L 1.12 bringt 7L übereinstimmend mit Anselms Rezension Bb (Ans. Bb) einen erweiterten Text.[36] Man findet auch sonst Anleihen bei Anselm von Lucca, u.a. aus den Briefen Nikolaus I., deren Texte im allgemeinen erst in der Zeit der gregorianischen Reform von der Kanonistik rezipiert wurden.[37] Mit den immer wiederkehrenden Übernahmen aus Polycarp lässt sich die isolierte Rezeption einiger Anselmtexte nicht vergleichen. Nur im vierten Buch scheint ein grösserer Block von Kapiteln in 7L von Anselm zu stammen.[38] Allerdings hat dann 7L in Buch 7 häufiger beim Thema der Buße auf Anselms elftes Buch 'De poenitentia' zurückgegriffen[39]—Vorlage kann hier nicht die Rezension B des Anselm gewesen sein, in der bekanntlich Buch 11 fehlt.[40] Der Kompilator von 7L könnte ein Exemplar der Sammlung Anselms vor sich gehabt haben, das der Rezension Bb entsprach, aber nicht wie die Ans. Bb überliefernde Handschrift aus Lucca mit Anselms Buch 7 endete, sondern alle Bücher enthielt. Jedenfalls kann nicht mit Theiner gesagt werden, dass 7L 'ex Anselmi collectione orta est'.[41] Fournier hat das Richtige getroffen, als er Polycarp als Hauptquelle für 7L nannte und nur von 'emprunts' aus Anselm von Lucca sprach.

Als nächstes sei auf die Benutzung der Sammlung des Burchard von Worms in 7L eingegangen. Wegen der starken Verbreitung von Burchards Sammlung in

---

31 7L 1.1.6 = Ans. 1.9, ed. Thaner, 10. Dort auch in Petitdruck die Erweiterung in Ans. Bb: 'Ad quam tam summa—noverit redditurum'. Der Text ist in demselben Umfang auch in 183T 1.12—cf. Motta, *Liber canonum*, 18.

32 7L 1.2.3 = Ans. 1.64, ed. Thaner, 32-3; 7L 1.2.4 = Ans. 2.78, ed. Thaner, 12; 7L 1.2.6 = Ans. 1.31, ed. Thaner, 19-20 bis 'principatum'.

33 7L 1.3.2 = Ans. 2.68, ed Thaner, 108 bis 'contempnat'.

34 7L 1.11.4 = Ans. 2.67, ed. Thaner, 106-8. Zum sonstigen Vorkommen dieses Textes in Kanones-sammlungen cf. Ernst Perels, 'Die Briefe Papst Nikolaus' I., Teil II', *NA*, 39 (1914), 43-153, hier 146 (n. 129). Pol 1.22.1 kann hier nicht Quelle von 7L sein, da der Text in Pol. teilweise andere Fragmente umfasst—cf. auch Friedberg, Anm. 142 zu D. 21, c. 7: 'Pol. om. § 1 Gratiani'.

35 7L 1.12.1 = Ans. 1.48, ed. Thaner, 25-6; 7L 1.12.4 = Ans. 2.56, ed. Thaner, 101-2.

36 7L enthält folgende Zusätze: bei Ans. 1.48: 'In quo ergo sola—cognoscitur'—cf. ed. Thaner, Anm. u; bei Ans. 2.56 am Anfang: 'Nobis opponunt canones—refugiunt'—cf. ed. Thaner, Anm. a.

37 7L 6.71.un. = Ans. 10.21. 7L hat Rubrik von Ans. 10.20. Zur kanonistischen Verbreitung der Briefe Nikolaus' I. cf. die aufschlussreiche Tabelle bei Perels, 'Briefe Nikolaus' I.', 141-53.

38 7L 4.52.1 = Ans. 5.36; 7L 4.55.4 = Ans. 5.45; 7L 4.55.5 = Ans. 5.31; 7L 4.56.1 = Ans. 5.62, Teil I; 7L 4.56.2 = Ans. 5.64; 7L 4.57.un. = Ans. 5.29.

39 Vor allem ist Anselm Buch XI Quelle von 7L 7.61 'De penitentia et penitentibus'. Es entsprechen sich hier: 7L c. 3 = Ans. c. 148; c. 21 = Ans. c. 25; c. 27 =Ans. c. 22; c. 28 = Ans. c. 23. Auch bei anderen Kapiteln dieses Titels von 7L sind Übernahmen aus Anselm Buch XI wahrscheinlich.

40 Zur Rezension B des Anselm jetzt grundlegend Klaus Zechiel-Eckes, 'Eine Mailänder Redaktion der Kirchenrechtssammlung Bischof Anselms II. von Lucca', *ZRG KA*, 81 (1995), 130-47.

41 Cf. oben Anm. 17.

Mittelitalien seit dem 11. Jahrhundert[42] ist von vornherein zu vermuten, dass der Sammler von 7L häufig auf Burchard zurückgegriffen hat. Jedoch ist dies in den ersten drei Büchern von 7L keineswegs der Fall. Man findet hier nur am Ende von Buch 2 in der vatikanischen Handschrift eine Serie von Burchardkapiteln, die jedoch in den Manuskripten C und W fehlt, also ein später Zusatz von Vat. lat. 1346 zu sein scheint.[43] Erst im vierten Buch von 7L werden Übernahmen aus Burchard häufiger;[44] in den letzten drei Büchern ist Burchard dann zeitweilig die Hauptquelle,[45] so dass diese Bücher weitgehend aus Burchard, dem Register Gregors I. und Serien patristischer Texte zusammengesetzt sind.[46] Als Belege für die einzelnen 'Capitula' (Titel) von 7L werden teilweise ausschliesslich Texte aus Burchards Dekret verwandt. Dabei kann in einigen Fällen auch die Sammlung in 183 Titeln eine Zwischenquelle gewesen sein, über welche die Burchardtexte 7L erreicht haben. Der Einfluss Burchards ergibt sich aus dem Umfang und der Sequenz der Kapitel, teilweise aber auch daraus, dass 7L Rubriken übernimmt. Ich gebe ein Beispiel aus Buch 5: 7L 5.13.1-2 = Burch. 4.24-25.

Fälle fast übereinstimmender Rubriken sind etwa:

1. 'De uno patrino' (7L 5.13)
   'Ut unus patrinus vel patrina ad suscipiendum infantem accedat' (Burch. 4.25)
2. 'De viduis que professam continentiam prevaricantur' (7L 5.61)
   'De viduis que professam continentiam prevaricatae sunt' (Burch. 8.39)

Die Übernahmen aus Burchards Dekret sind übrigens auch in Buch 6 sehr zahlreich: so sind die Abschnitte (Capitula) 6.38-44 ausschliesslich aus Burchard-kapiteln übernommen.[47] Paul Fournier nahm an, dass ferner der 'Liber de vita christiana' des Bonizo von Sutri eine Quelle von 7L gewesen sei,[48] brachte aber dafür nur Belege aus den Zusätzen in den Handschriften C und W bei, so dass er schliesslich die Frage offen liess, ob nur der Verfasser der Additionen zu 7L auf einige Kapitel bei Bonizo zurückgegriffen haben könnte.[49] In der Tat trifft diese Vermutung Fourniers zu—in V findet man keine Spuren einer Benutzung Bonizos. Dagegen steht in den

---

42 Hierzu cf. Hubert Mordek, 'Handschriftenforschungen in Italien: I. Zur Überlieferung des Dekrets Bischof Burchards von Worms', *QF*, 51 (1971), 626-51.

43 Nach 7L 2.41.4 bringt MS Vat. lat. 1346 folgende Burchardtexte: Burch. 1.198, 19.151, 2.181, 2.236.

44 Die Übernahme von Kapiteln aus Burchard setzt mit 7L 4.34 'De ecclesiis hereticorum' ein: 7L 4.34.1 = Burch. 3.32; 7L 4.35.2 = Burch. 3.36; 7L 4.36.1 = Burch. 3.216; 7L 4.36.2 = Burch. 3.215.

45 Hierzu die Angaben unten im Text und in Anm. 47.

46 Zum Register Gregors I. und der Patristik als Quellen der Sammlung ebenfalls unten im Text.

47 7L 6.38.un. = Burch. 9.79; 7L 6.39.un. = Burch. 9.80;7L 6.40.1-3 = Burch. 9.81-82; 7L 6.41.un. = Burch 7.25; 7L 6.42.un. = Burch. 7.26; 7L 6.43.un = Burch. 7.27; 7L 6.44.1-7 = Burch. 7.28.

48 Fournier-Le Bras, *Histoire*, ii, 189.

49 *Ibid.*, ii, 149-50.

Handschriften C und W jeweils ein Fragment aus Bonizos Buch 4 (4.1-46) am Anfang der Handschrift vor 7L,[50] so dass man die Wiener Handschrift in der Forschung des 18. und 19. Jahrhunderts lange irrtümlich für ein Bonizo-Manuskript hielt.[51] Die Handschriften C und W bringen am Anfang zunächst die Papstchronik aus Bonizo 4.1-46[52] und schieben dann in Buch 1 von 7L folgende Titel ein:

1. 'De prelatorum differentia et episcoporum electione. Cap. LII' (= Bonizo 2.3-7)
2. 'Qualiter episcopus consecrari debeat. Cap. LV' (= Bonizo 2.27)
3. 'Quod non oporteat episcopos secularibus curis involvi. Cap. LVI' (= Bonizo 2.28)
4. 'De mensa episcopi. Cap. LVII' (= Bonizo 2.29.)
5. 'Quales vestes debeant esse episcopi. Cap. LVIII' (= Bonizo 2.30)
6. 'Quod sacratae vestes sint speciose. Cap. LIX' (= Bonizo 2.31)
7. 'De ornatu ecclesie. Cap. LX' (= Bonizo 2.32)
8. 'De choro. Cap. LXI' (= Bonizo 2.33)
9. 'Quod episcopus seculum de turpibus lucris non impleat. Cap. LXII' (= Bonizo 2.34)
10. 'Quod episcopo assidue sit orandum et legendum. Cap. LXIII' (= Bonizo 2.35)
11. 'De hospitalitate. Cap. LXIIII' (= Bonizo 2.36-37; 7L om. Inscriptionem Bon. 2.37)
12. 'De helemosina. Cap. LXV' (= Bonizo 2.38)
13. 'De assidua predicacione. Cap. LXVI' (= Bonizo 2.39)
14. 'De vitando malo ypocrisis et de cavendis ypocrisis. Cap. LXVII' (= Bonizo 2.40)
15. 'De castitate ab episcopis observanda. Cap. LXIII' (= Bonizo 2.41)
16. 'Quod episcopus non habeat familiares infames. Cap. LXVIIII' (= Bonizo 2.42)
17. 'Ut bellorum tumultibus se non immisceat episcopus. Cap. LXX' (= Bonizo 2.43)
18. 'De adulatione et detractione vitanda. Cap. LXXI' (= Bonizo 2.44)
19. 'De bene morigerato eius sermone et incessu. Cap. LXXII' (= Bonizo 2.45)[53]

50　*Ibid.*, ii, 186.

51　Cf. hierzu Ernst Perels, Einleitung zur Edition von: Bonizo, *Liber de vita christiana* (Berlin, 1930), XXX-XL. Der Irrtum geht auf ein Werk des Petrus Lambecius von 1669 zurück. Wilhelm Giesebrecht erkannte, dass die Handschrift Wien, ÖNB, 2186 eine andere Kanonessammlung als den 'Liber de vita christiana' Bonizos enthält—cf. Wilhelm Giesebrecht, 'Die Gesetzgebung der römischen Kirche zur Zeit Gregors VII.', *Münchener Historisches Jahrbuch* (1866), 93-193, hier 154, Anm. 65.

52　Bonizo, *Liber de vita christiana*, 111-33. Zum Vorkommen dieses Stücks in W cf. Perels: Bonizo, *Liber de vita christiana*, LVIII. In C steht dieselbe Papstchronik auf fos 26r-35v.

53　Man vergleiche diese Angaben mit den kürzeren bei Perels: Bonizo, *Liber de vita christiana*, LVIII zu W. Das Vorkommen aller aufgeführten Kapitel in C wurde von mir überprüft.

Die hier verzeichneten Kapitel stammen sämtlich aus selbständig formulierten Texten Bonizos im 'Liber de vita christiana': Jedoch hat die zweite Redaktion von 7L in den Handschriften C und W die Sammlung in Buch 6 und am Ende von Buch 7 noch um einige aus Bonizo geschöpfte Kapitel erweitert, die bereits von Perels in der Einleitung seiner Edition des 'Liber de vita christiana' verzeichnet wurden.[54] Perels gibt an derselben Stelle an, dass die Handschrift W am Ende unvollständig mitten im Text von Bonizo 2.52 abbricht. Er fügt hinzu: 'Der fragmentarische Schluss lässt durchaus die Möglichkeit noch weiteren Bonizo-Inhaltes im ursprünglichen Bestande des Vindob. offen'.[55] Diese Vermutung wird durch die Handschrift C von 7L bestätigt, die anders als W vollständig ist, am Ende dieselben Zusätze wie W bringt, nach Bonizo 2.52 jedoch noch eine ganze Serie von Bonizo-Kapiteln enthält, teilweise verkürzt.[56] Es wurden offenbar nur folgende der von Bonizo selbst formulierten Kapitel in die Appendices von 7L (C) nicht übernommen: Bonizo 2.1-2, 2.56-57, 5.4, 5.6a, 6.47, 8.65, 10.28. Dabei mag eine Rolle gespielt haben, dass einige dieser Texte eher als Ermahnungen denn als

---

54 Perels: Bonizo, *Liber de vita christiana*, LIX. Im einzelnen sind es folgende Kapitel: 7L (C et W) 6.21: 'De inhibitis nuptiis propter carnalem affinitatem' (= V 6.16), cc. 17-18 = Bonizo 9.28. Am Ende von Buch VII folgen nach dem letzten numerierten Titel in 7L (C et W) 7.112: 'De penitentia pro diversis criminibus agentibus' folgende aus Bonizo übernommene Kapitel unter nicht numerierten Titeln: 'De penitentia illius qui propriam coniugem interfecerit': Bonizo 10.8; 'De diversis homicidiis voluntarie sive nolenter. Sinodo CL patribus sub Theodosio seniore Constantinopoli congregata': Bonizo 10.9; 'Iudicium homicidii': Bonizo 10.12; 'De calumniis episcoporum ceterorumque ordinum': Bonizo 10.16 (2. Teil), 10.17; 'Formula christianorum dogmatum. De baptismate et ordinatione': Bonizo 1.43-44; 'De diversitate missarum sollemnium': Bonizo 2.51; 'De reconciliatione penitentum': Bonizo 2.52.

55 Perels: Bonizo, *Liber de vita christiana*, XLIX.

56 'Qualiter conficiendum sit crisma': Bonizo 2.55; 'Qui arceantur a sacerdotio': Bonizo 2.63; 'Unde sacerdotium sumpsit exordium': Bonizo 3.105; 'De sandaliis': Bonizo 3.106 bis 'debebatur' (ed. Perels, p. 107, Z. 2); 'De amictu': Bonizo 3.106 bis 'fine' (ed. Perels, p. 107, Z.9); 'De cingulo': Bonizo 3.106 bis 'spiritu' (ed. Perels, p. 107, Z. 18); 'De stola': Bonizo 3.106 bis 'possidebunt' (ed. Perels, p. 107, Z. 26); 'De tunica': Bonizo 3.106 bis 'populorum' (ed. Perels, p. 107, Z. 34); 'De casula': Bonizo 3.106 bis 'virtus omnis'; 'De fanone': Bonizo 3.107; 'De rationali': Bonizo 3.108; 'De anulo': Bonizo 3.109; 'Exortatio ad episcopos': Bonizo 3.110; 'De consecratione ecclesiarum et altarium': Bonizo 4.98; 'Quando ordinationes fieri debeant': Bonizo 5.5-6; 'De concordia diversarum sententiarum pro lapsis prolatarum': Bonizo 5.48; 'De regula canonica, unde sumpsit exordium': Bonizo 5.77; 'De vita sacerdotum Christi': Bonizo 5.80; 'De quatuor generibus monachorum': Bonizo 6.1, 6.30; 'De regali potestate': Bonizo 7.1; 'De iudicum diversitate eorumque officium': Bonizo 7.16; 'De militibus et qua etiam militare debeant': Bonizo 7.28; 'Interdictum de mulieribus': Bonizo 7.29; 'De artificibus, negotiatoribus et agricolis': Bonizo 8.1; 'De matrimonio': Bonizo 8.11; 'De penitentia secundum more medicorum': Bonizo 9.1-3; 'Qualiter excommunicati debeant reconciliari': Bonizo 9.4; 'Quod nemo sine communione moriatur': Bonizo 9.5; 'De septem criminalibus': Bonizo 9.8; 'De periurio': Bonizo 9.45; 'De falso testimonio': Bonizo 9.61; 'De furto': Bonizo 9.62; 'Epistola Ysidori spalensis urbis episcopi ad Laudefredum cordubensem episcopum de omnibus ecclesiasticis gradibus cap. XCIII': Bonizo 5.71.

Rechtsvorschriften formuliert sind.[57] Man gewinnt den Eindruck, dass der Verfasser des Appendix in 7L (C) sehr überlegt gearbeitet hat, indem er einmal im 'Liber de vita christiana' die Originaltexte Bonizos heraussuchte und ferner seine Exzerpte auch mit Blick auf den Inhalt auswählte. Als Ergebnis des Vergleichs bleibt jedenfalls festzuhalten, dass Bonizo nur für die Appendices in der zweiten Redaktion von 7L berücksichtigt wurde.

Paul Fournier nennt bei seiner Aufzählung der Quellen von 7L auch die irische Kanonessammlung (Collectio Hibernensis).[58] Er weist auf eine Serie eherechtlicher Kapitel im sechsten Buch von 7L hin, die aus der Hibernensis entnommen sei.[59] Diese Serie von sieben Kapiteln[60] ist jedoch nur in der zweiten Redaktion der Sammlung in den Handschriften C und W enthalten, so dass man ähnlich wie bei Bonizo feststellen kann, dass der Sammler zur Ergänzung auf ursprünglich nicht verwendete Quellen zurückgreifen konnte.

Bereits Theiner wies in seiner Abhandlung über 7L im Jahre 1836 darauf hin, dass der Sammler auch die Collectio Anselmo dedicata benutzt habe.[61] Die von Theiner angeführten bezifferten Beispiele blieben allerdings für mich unverständlich, so dass ich nochmals Vergleiche angestellt habe. Dabei ergab sich, dass in den ersten vier Büchern von 7L in der Tat offenbar die Anselmo dedicata (Ans. ded.) häufig als Quelle herangezogen wurde, da 7L und Ans. ded. im Umfang der Fragmente singulär übereinstimmen und auch blockartig Kapitel aus Ans. ded. übernommen wurden. Ich schätze, dass etwa 80 Kapitel in 7L aus Ans. ded. stammen. Es seien nur einzelne Beispiele gegeben:[62]

1. 7L 1.2.1 = Ans. ded. 1.18 (F. n. 132), 7L 1.2.2 = Ans. ded. 8.67 (F. n. 187)
2. 7L 1.4.1 = Ans. ded. 1.27 (F. n. 21), 7L 1.4.2 = Ans. ded. 1.29 (F. n. 27)
3. 7L 2.11.1 = Ans. ded. 3.36 (F. n. 24), 7L 2.11.4 = Ans. ded. 3.49 bzw. 3.94 (F. n. 285), 7L 2.11.5 = Ans. ded. 3.52 (F. n. 2), 7L 2.11.7 = Ans. ded. 3.95 (F. n. 122), 7L 2.11.8 = Ans. ded. 3.62 (F. n. 7), 7L 2.11.9 = Ans. ded. 3.66 (F. n. 407—7L kürzer als Ans. ded., bis 'admittatur')
4. 7L 2.17.1 = Ans. ded. 3.164 (F. n. 250), 7L 2.17.3 = Ans. ded. 3.22 bzw. 3.112 (F. n. 396), 7L 2.17.4 = Ans. ded. 3.114 (F. n. 308, 7L om. 'Deinde'), 7L 2.17.6

---

57 So z. B. Bonizo 2.2: 'Prima ac principalis Christianorum virtus est obedientia'. Oder Bonizo 2.56 und 2.57: 'Videant episcopi ...'.
58 Fournier-Le Bras, *Histoire*, ii, 188-9.
59 *Ibid.*, ii, 189, Anm. 2.
60 Es sind: Hib. 46.3, 46.2, 46.16 (bis 'elongabitur ab eo'), 46.4, 46.6, 46.5 und 46.11—cf. Hermann Wasserschleben, ed., *Die irische Kanonensammlung* (²Leipzig, 1885; ND Aalen, 1966), 185-8.
61 Theiner, *Disquisitiones*, 346.
62 Die Sigle F. bezieht sich jeweils auf die Nummer im Verzeichnis der Pseudoisidorstellen bei Horst Fuhrmann, *Einfluss und Verbreitung der pseudoisidorischen Fälschungen*, MGH Schriften, 24/i-iii (Stuttgart, 1974), iii, 784-1005.

= Ans. ded. 1.64 (F. n. 330, 7L om. 'Quas providentes'), 7L 2.17.7 = Ans. ded. 3.77 (F. n. 385)

5. 7L 3.69.1 = Ans. ded. 4.27 (F. n. 16), 7L 3.69.2 = Ans. ded. 4.41 (F. n. 246), 7L 3.69.3 = Ans. ded. 4.45 bzw. 2.57 (F. n. 271), 7L 3.69.3a (V in marg., W Haupttext) = Ans. ded. 4.46 (F. n. 326)

6. 7L 4.13.5 = Ans. ded. 3.51 (F. n. 267), 7L 4.13.8 = Ans. ded. 3.57 (F. n. 184), 7L 4.13.9 = Ans. ded. 3.63 (F. n. 114), 7L 4.13.10 = Ans. ded. 3.64, Teilstück (F. n. 133), 7L 4.13.11 = Ans. ded. 3.67 (F. n. 435)

Diese Beispiele liessen sich unschwer vermehren; jedoch dürfte die Auswahl für die Feststellung eines Einflusses von Ans. ded. auf 7L genügen. Angesichts der geringen handschriftlichen Verbreitung der Anselmo dedicata in Italien ist es jedenfalls bemerkenswert, dass 7L auf Ans. ded. zurückgreifen konnte.

Theiner behauptete ferner, dass 7L auch aus der Collectio Tripartita (Trip.) geschöpft haben müsse,[63] deren Kenntnis in Italien in der ersten Hälfte des 12. Jahrhunderts durch die umfangreiche Benutzung im gratianischen Dekret gesichert ist.[64] Insbesondere nahm Theiner an, dass 7L fast alle Konzilskanones aus Trip. entnommen habe,[65] ohne dabei zu erwägen, dass eventuell Pseudoisidor auch unmittelbar als Quelle von 7L gedient haben könnte. Eine umfassende Untersuchung dieses Fragenkomplexes—Tripartita oder Pseudoisidor direkt—würde den Rahmen eines Aufsatzes sprengen und ist überdies angesichts des Fehlens einer brauchbaren Edition des Konzilsteils von Pseudoisidor zur Zeit ohnehin kaum zu leisten. Theiner selbst führt für seine These nur ein einziges Beispiel an: eine Sequenz von Konzilstexten der Titel 3.40-46 in 7L.[66] Eine Nachprüfung ergab hier folgendes: 7L 3.40.un.: Cartag. IIII cap. LVII' = Trip. 2.18.56: 'LVII'; 7L 3.41.un.: 'Ex eod. cap. LVIIII' = Trip. 2.18.58: 'LVIIII'; 7L 3.42 un.: 'Ex eod. cap. LX' = Trip. 2.18.59: 'LX'; 7L 3.43.un.: 'Ex eod. concilio cap. LXI = Trip. 2.18.60: 'LXI'; 7L 3.44.1: 'Ex eod. concilio cap. LVI' = Trip. 2.18.55: 'LVI'; 7L 3.44.2: 'Ex Conc. Arelatensi I, cap. XIII—om. Trip.; 7L 3.44.3: 'Ex Conc. Agathensi cap. XXVI' = Trip. 2.31.24: 'XXVI'; 7L 3.45.1: 'Ex Conc. Cart. IIII cap. XLVIII' = Trip. 2.18.46: 'XLVII'; 7L 3.45.2: 'Ex eodem conc. cap. XLVIIII' = Trip. 2.18.47: 'XLVIII'. Es folgt darauf 7L 3.46.un.: 'Ex Conc. Laodicensi cap. XXIII'. Das Kapitel steht mit anderem Incipit und unterschiedlicher Numerierung ('cap. X') in Trip. 2.7.10. Theiners Angabe, dass in 7L auf c.49 von Carth. IV die c.11, 12 und

---

63 Theiner, *Disquisitiones*, 346.

64 Als erste Orientierung zu dieser Frage cf. Peter Landau, 'Neue Forschungen zu vorgratianischen Kanonessammlungen und den Quellen des gratianischen Dekrets', *Ius commune*, 11 (1984), 1-29, hier 25-7; auch in Peter Landau, *Kanones und Dekretalen* (Goldbach, 1997), 201-3.

65 Theiner, *Disquisitiones*, 346: 'Canones enim omnes, quos ex conciliis praecipue ex conciliis graecis, gallicanis, hispanis atque africanis auctor noster magno numere affert, ex sola collectione tripartita hausit'.

66 *Ibid.*

14 von Conc. Carth. III folgten,[67] ist unzutreffend. Das von ihm gegebene Beispiel ist demnach keineswegs beweiskräftig für die These, dass 7L die Konzilstexte überwiegend oder gar ausschliesslich aus Trip. bezogen habe; zumindest der Kanon des Konzils von Laodicea kann nicht aus Trip. stammen.

Allerdings habe auch ich bei Vergleichen häufig Parallelen der Kapitel in 7L zum Textbestand in Trip. festgestellt, so dass ich annehmen möchte, dass der Sammler von 7L ebenso wie Gratian Trip. gekannt haben muss. Ich gebe einige relativ willkürlich ausgewählte Beispiele:

1. 7L 4.6.1 = Trip. 1.18.4 (F. n. 52)—dasselbe Fragment auch C. 1, qu. 1, c. 85.
2. 7L 4.18.7 = Trip. 1.28.1 (F. n. 318, Anm. 929).
3. 7L 4.53.1 = Trip. 1.1.17 (F. n. 378, Anm. 1102).

Aufgrund dieser und anderer Übereinstimmungen im Umfang der Fragmente halte ich es für wahrscheinlich, das bei der Kompilation von 7L die Collectio Tripartita eine Rolle gespielt hat.

Ausser der Tripartita hat der Sammler von 7L jedoch mit Sicherheit auch die pseudoisidorische Sammlung selbst zur Hand gehabt, und zwar nicht nur für den Quellenbereich der Dekretalen, sondern auch für den der Konzilien. Aufgrund von Fuhrmanns Register lassen sich relativ leicht Dekretalenfragmente feststellen, die in gleichem Umfang in keiner anderen Kanonessammlung begegnen. Ich gebe folgende Beispiele mit Hinweis auf die Hinschius-Edition (H.):

1. 7L 2.7.2 = H. 166.10-20: 'Si enim a fide—eius (!) sanctifica'
2. 7L 4.12.1 = H. 68.33-69.4
3. 7L 4.12.2 = H. 111.27-29
4. 7L 4.12.3 = H. 114.27-28
5. 7L 4.12.4 =H. 114.28-115.1
6. 7L 4.12.5 = H. 169.2-6
7. 7L 5.2.un. = H. 160.23-161.4
8. 7L 5.24.1 = H. 711.22-31
9. 7L 5.24.2 = H. 242.19-28
10. 7L 6.68.un. = H. 86.20-26

Auch hier mögen die angeführten Beispiele genügen. Es bleibt festzuhalten, dass die Kapitelzählung bei den Papstdekretalen in 7L darauf schliessen lässt, dass der Kompilator von 7L eine A2-Handschrift des Pseudoisidor benutzt haben muss.[68] Ich vermute allerdings, dass ihm ausserdem noch eine weitere Pseudoisidorhandschrift

---

67 *Ibid.*
68 Zur Handschriftenklasse A2 der pseudoisidorischen Dekretalen allgemein orientierend Emil Seckel, Art. *Pseudoisidor*, RE³ 16 (1905), 265-307, hier 268-70.

(A1?) zur Verfügung stand, in der auch der Konzilienteil enthalten war. Jedenfalls wird die Schlussfolgerung Fourniers bestätigt, 7L habe 'nombreux éléments empruntés aux Fausses Décrétales'.[69]

Neben den genannten Kanonessammlungen wurden bei der Kompilation von 7L besonders die Briefe Gregors I. aus dessen Register und ferner patristische Quellen exzerpiert. Auf beides hat bereits Fournier nachdrücklich hingewiesen.[70] Der Sammler von 7L gibt jeweils das Buch des Gregorregisters und die Ziffer des Briefes an. Offenbar wurde wie auch sonst in italienischen Sammlungen das Register in der Form des Registrum Hadrianum benutzt.[71] Auffallend ist jedenfalls die große Zahl der Exzerpte aus Gregors Register, auch im Vergleich zu Gratian.[72]

Sehr erheblich ist dann der Anteil patristischer Exzerpte in 7L. Man findet die Namen der lateinischen Kirchenväter mit genauen Angaben über die Herkunft der Texte. Vermutlich konnte der Sammler patristische Florilegien benutzen. Ausserdem hat der Sammler von 7L jedoch gerade bei patristischen Texten in erheblichem Umfang auf die toskanische Sammlung in 183 Titeln (183T) zurückgegriffen.[73] So stammen in 7L 6.6 'De vindicta' bei insgesamt 9 Kapiteln 4 aus 183T,[74] in 7L 6.19 'Propter alterius desponsationem' sind sämtliche Texte schon in 183T zu finden;[75] ebenso bei 7L 6.65 'Quando minora peccata sunt eligenda'.[76] Im siebenten Buch gilt dasselbe für 7L 7.38 'Quando mali tolerandi sunt et quando separandi a bonis'[77] und für 7L 7.39: 'Quando fugiendum sit, quando minime'.[78] Das Material ist vielfach im Decretum Gratiani nicht zu finden, so dass ich diesen Umstand als ein Indiz dafür nehme, dass Gratian die Sammlung 7L ebenso wie 183T offenbar nicht gekannt hat. Das letzte siebente Buch von 7L mit weitgehend moraltheologischem Inhalt ist überwiegend aus patristischen Texten zusammengesetzt, wobei Augustinus den grössten Anteil hat.

Schliesslich sei noch auf die Frage der Rezeption römischen Rechts in unserer Sammlung eingegangen. Die von Fournier angeführten Digestenstellen im Anhang

---

69 Fournier-Le Bras, *Histoire*, ii, 188.

70 *Ibid.*, ii, 189-90.

71 So bereits Fournier-Le Bras, *Histoire*, ii, 189-90.

72 Zur Benutzung des Registers Gregors I. bei Gratian cf. Peter Landau, 'Das Register Papst Gregors I. im Decretum Gratiani', in *Mittelalterliche Texte. Überlieferungen—Befunde—Deutungen*, ed. Rudolf Schieffer, *MGH Schriften*, 42 (Hannover, 1996), 125-40.

73 Auf die Sammlung in 183 Titeln als Quelle von 7L weist neuestens Fowler-Magerl (wie Anm. 22) hin.

74 7L 6.6.3 = 183T 121.152; 7L 6.6.6 = 183T 121.11; 7L 6.6.7 = 183T 121.12; 7L 6.6.9 = 183T 121.14.

75 7L 6.19.1 = 183T 148.1; 7L 6.19.2 = 183T 147.84; 7L 6.19.3 = 183T 150.4.

76 7L 6.65.1 = 183T 164.8; 7L 6.65.2 = 183T 164.6.

77 7L 7.38.1 = 183T 98.1; 7L 7.38.2 = 183T 98.8.

78 7L 7.39.un. =183T 98.7.

hat 7L aus dem Polycarp übernommen.[79] In die Sammlung sind aus dem Corpus Iuris Civilis unmittelbar nur zwei Codexkonstitutionen Kaiser Leos I. aufgenommen: Cod.1.3.33 mit der präzisen Inskription: 'Ex codice Iustiniani in titulo tertio libri primi Imperator Leo a. Erithio (!) pp.' und Cod. 1.3.34: 'Idem a Dioscoro pp.'[80] Es sind die einzigen Texte des Titels 'De peculio et privilegiis clericorum' (7L 3.39). Der Kompilator von 7L verfügte demnach über einige Kennntnisse im römischen Recht.

Zusammenfassend lässt sich sagen, dass 7L vor allem als zeitgenössisches Parallelunternehmen zu Gratian aufschlussreich ist—gewissermassen ein Gratian ohne Dicta. Die Benutzung kanonistischer Quellen ist teilweise noch umfassender als bei Gratian, insbesondere in bezug auf die Anselmo dedicata, Burchard von Worms und die Sammlung in 183T. Im Vergleich zu Gratian fehlt allerdings Ivos Panormie unter den verwerteten Quellen. Die in West- und Mitteleuropa weitverbreitete Panormie wurde vielleicht erst kurz vor Gratian in Italien bekannt; sie diente hier zunächst oft als Ergänzung der Sammlung des Anselm von Lucca.[81] Die hier versuchte Bestimmung der unmittelbaren Quellen von 7L ist nur ein erster Schritt zur Analyse eines interessanten Werks aus der Endphase der vorgratianischen Kanonistik, das bei Berücksichtigung der Differenzen zu dem von Gratian verwendeten Quellencorpus wohl in einiger Entfernung von der Werkstatt des Vaters der Kanonistik entstanden sein muss.

---

79 Fournier-Le Bras, *Histoire*, ii, 190, Anm. 1, nennt Dig. 43.16.1.24 und Dig. 1.3.12.1. In MS Vat. lat. 1346 steht in einem Zusatztitel 'De iure ecclesiarum et possessione' (fo 167 v) mit der Inskription 'Ex libro digestorum' Dig. 43.16.1.24-29 + 43.16.3.9. Das Stück ist aus Pol. 3.12.36 übernommen. Es folgt in 7L auf zwei weitere Übernahmen aus Pol. 3.12.33 (= Ep. Juliani 8.1.44) und Pol. 3.12.34 (= Ep. Juliani 119.6.511). Den zweiten Text Dig. 1.3.12.1 gibt es nicht—gemeint ist wohl Dig. 1.3.32.1. Letzterer ist in Vat. lat. 1346 (fo 168r) enthalten und dort aus Pol 3.23.6 aufgenommen—er folgt in V auf Cod. 8.52.2 (= Pol. 3.23.5). Die Kapitel aus dem römischen Recht fehlen in den Handschriften C und W von 7L.

80 In MS Vat. lat. 1346 auf fos 73v-74r. Der Titel 'De peculio et privilegiis clericorum' mit den beiden Codextexten ist auch in den Handschriften C und W von 7L enthalten.

81 Das gilt besonders für die wohl kurz nach 1123 (*c.* 1130) entstandene Rezension A' der Sammlung des Anselm von Lucca—cf. Peter Landau, 'Erweiterte Fassungen der Kanonessammlung des Anselm von Lucca aus dem 12.Jahrhundert', in *Sant'Anselmo, Mantova e la lotta per le investiture*, ed. Paolo Golinelli (Bologna, 1987), 323-38, hier 327-8; auch in Landau, *Kanones und Dekretalen*, 81-96. Hierzu jetzt auch Szabolcs Anzelm Szuromi, 'Some Observations on the Developing of the Different Versions of the Collectio canonum Anselmi Lucensis', *Ius Ecclesiae*, 14 (2002), 425-49.

Chapter 16

The Version of the *Collectio Caesaraugustana* in Barcelona, Archivo de la Corona de Aragón, MS San Cugat 63

Linda Fowler-Magerl

The early twelfth-century canon law collection *Caesaraugustana* remains to date unedited despite a series of aborted attempts. This is a fate it does not deserve. The first version was compiled circa 1120, probably in the vicinity of Valence. This makes it the first systematic collection to combine the results of the earliest canonistic activity at Chartres with that of the activity in northern and central Italy. It is also evidence of the revival of interest in law in southeastern France which would be responsible in the 1130s for the first treatises by civilians on the nature and variety of actions and, somewhat later, for a number of the first judicial *ordines*. The *Caesaraugustana* shares its fate—that of being worthy but unedited—with many of the collections that Roger Reynolds has studied throughout his academic life, and the present study is a tribute to the success he has had in bringing attention to these collections.

The *Caesaraugustana* is transmitted in five medieval manuscripts: 1.) Salamanca, Biblioteca de la Universidad Civil, MS 2644; 2.) Paris, Bibliothèque Nationale, MS lat. 3875; 3.) Paris, BN, MS lat. 3876 (= P3876); 4.) Vatican City, Biblioteca Apostolica Vaticana, MS Vat. lat. 5715; and 5.) Barcelona, Archivo de la Corona de Aragón, MS 63 (= Barc63). Since P3876 was almost certainly used by the copyist responsible for the manuscript Vat. lat. 5715, only P3876 will be mentioned in the text below when reference is made to the version common to both. With the exception of P3876 and its double, each of the medieval manuscripts represents a unique recension.

The earliest complete version of the collection (if not the earliest copy) is found in the Salamanca manuscript. The transcription of that manuscript made for Antonio Agustín (d. 1586) is now in the Vatican library with the shelfnumber Barberini lat. 897.[1] Agustín named the collection *Caesaraugustana* after the

---

1   Stephan Kuttner, 'Some Roman manuscripts of canonical collections', *BMCL*, NS 1 (1971), 23.
     For bibliography see Lotte Kéry, *Canonical collections of the early Middle Ages (ca. 400-1140):*

charterhouse at Saragossa (Zaragoza) in northeastern Spain where the original had been found. F. Marcos Rodríguez rediscovered the Saragossa copy at Salamanca[2] and also identified a fragment of the first version (containing canons 1.1-54 and 2.11-12, 14-16) in a fourteenth-century manuscript: Salamanca, Biblioteca Universitaria, MS 81, fos 288r-297r.[3]

The copy in the Salamanca manuscript is divided into fifteen books, each with its own capitulation. The only other copy to be divided into books and supplied with capitulations is Barc63. For the convenience of the reader, the canons of the other copies will be numbered below as if they, too, were divided into fifteen books.[4] The copy in Paris BN MS lat. 3875 has approximately the same content as the Salamanca copy. It was once preserved at the monastery of Ripoll, to the northeast of Barcelona. It contains a better version of the text,[5] and the sequence of the canons is closer to that in one of the principal sources, the *Decretum* attributed to Ivo of Chartres.[6] It lacks the two last books, however, and the canons of book eleven are found at the end of the collection. This is the result of an attempt to reorganize the collection more rationally. The canons of book eleven deal with the Eucharist as do those of book thirteen.

The most complete description of the sources of the *Caesaraugustana* is still that of Paul Fournier.[7] The major Italian formal sources of the first version of the

---

a bibliographical guide to the manuscripts and literature, History of Medieval Canon Law, 1, ed. Wilfried Hartmann and Kenneth Pennington (Washington, D.C., 1999), 260-62.

2   It had long been kept in the royal library at Madrid. There it was found by J. Tarré, 'Les sources de la législation ecclésiastique dans la province tarraconnaise ...', Positions des thèses de l'Ecole des Chartes (1927), 134. Then it disappeared again until 1959.

3   F. Marcos Rodríguez, 'Tres manuscritos del s. XII con colecciones canónicas', *Analecta Sacra Tarraconensia*, 32 (1959), 35-44. See also Antonio García y García, *Historia del Derecho Canónico* (Salamanca 1967), 321; and 'Canonistica Hispanica (III)', *Traditio*, 26 (1970), 457.

4   The *Caesaraugustana* is analysed on my CD-Rom *KanonesJ*, as are the *Decretum*, *Tripartita* and *Panormia* of Ivo of Chartres, the collections of Anselm of Lucca and Deusdedit and the *Polycarpus*, the collections in Paris, Bibliothèque de l'Arsenal, MS 713, and Paris Bibliothèque Nationale, MS nouv. acq. lat. 326, the *Tarraconensis*, the collection in Turin, Biblioteca Nazionale e Universitaria, MS D.IV.33, the *Atrebatensis*, the *Collectio X partium* and the *Catalaunensis I*. The collections are described in the book which accompanies the CD: *A Selection of Canon Law Collections compiled between 1000 and 1140. Access with data processing* (Piesenkofen, 2003). An augmented final version of the text and CD will appear in the autumn of 2004 in the Hilfsmittel series of the Monumenta Germaniae Historica.

5   This was noted in regard to the transmission of letters of pope Pelagius I by Pius M. Gassó and Columba M. Batlle, *Pelagii I papae epistulae quae supersunt*, Scripta et documenta, 8 (Montserrat, 1956), xxxv-xxxix.

6   The text agrees often with that of the fragment in the manuscript Salamanca 81. See Martin Brett, 'The sources and influence of the Ms Paris Bibliothèque d'Arsenal Ms 713,' in *Proceedings of the Ninth International Congress of Medieval Canon Law*, ed. Peter Landau and Joerg Mueller, MIC Series C, Subsidia, 10 (Vatican City, 1997), 161 n. 29.

7   Paul Fournier, 'La collection canonique dite *Caesaraugustana*', *Revue historique de droit français et étranger*, 45 (1921), 53-79.

Caesaraugustana are the collection of Anselm of Lucca, the collection of Deusdedit, completed by 1087,[8] and the *Polycarpus*, completed during the first two decades of the twelfth century.[9] The first version of the collection of Anselm was compiled between 1083 and 1086.[10] It has been suggested that a later form was used for the *Caesaraugustana* and it may have been, but it has not been proven conclusively.[11] Some of the texts common to late versions of the collection of Anselm and the *Caesaraugustana* were used prior to 1120 in other central and northern Italian collections. Most of these collections were dependent on Anselm without being mere late versions of his collection,[12] and, of course, the texts may have circulated separately.

Among the sources from northeastern France are the *Decretum*[13] and *Tripartita*[14] attributed to Ivo of Chartres. Martin Brett has shown that the compiler of the *Caesaraugustana* also made direct use of the contents of the material collection in Paris, Bibliothèque de l'Arsenal, MS 713, which was also used by the compiler of the *Decretum*. The contents of this collection, he maintains, may come from Italy, but the manuscript was copied in northern France.[15]

The dating of the *Decretum* is controversial. Brett warns against dating it too early. I would argue that the *Decretum* was finished before 1110 because it was used by Ivo of Chartres for his *Panormia*,[16] and the *Panormia* was used in turn by

8   The most recent edition: *Die Kanonessammlung des Kardinals Deusdedit*, ed. Victor Wolf von Glanvell (Paderborn, 1905; repr. Aalen, 1967). See also Fowler-Magerl, *Selection*, 99-101. For bibliography: Kéry, *Canonical Collections*, 228-33.

9   For the *Polycarpus* and the *Caesaraugustana*, see Uwe Horst, *Die Kanonessammlung Polycarpus des Gregor von S. Grisogono: Quellen und Tendenzen*, MGH Hilfsmittel, 5 (Munich, 1980). See also Fowler-Magerl, *Selection*, 169-71, and Kéry, *Canonical Collections*, 266-91.

10 The collection was edited to canon 11.15 by Fridericus [Friedrich] Thaner, *Anselmi episcopi Lucensis collectio canonum, una cum collectione minore* (Innsbruck, 1906-15; repr. Aalen, 1965). For the most recent treatment of Anselm see Kathleen G. Cushing, *Papacy and Law in the Gregorian Revolutio: the canonistic work of Anselm of Lucca* (Oxford, 1998). See also Fowler-Magerl, *Selection*, 80-87, 96-7, 109-10, 157-61, 166, and Kéry, *Canonical Collections*, 218-26.

11 For the canons which have been proposed as proof for the use of the B and C forms of the collection of Anselm, see Brett, ' Sources and Influence', 165 n. 42.

12 Examples of such collections are the *Polycarpus*, the incomplete Luccan copy of a version of Anselm in Vatican City, Biblioteca Apostolica Vaticana, MS Barb. lat. 535, the *Collectio XIII librorum* in Vat. lat. MS 1361, the Pistoian *Collectio III librorum* and the *Collectio VII librorum*.

13 Edited by Jean Dumoulin in 1541. The most accessible edition is that of Jean Fronteau, which was reprinted in *PL* 161.59-1022. For the canons peculiar to each version of the *Decretum* see Peter Landau, 'Das Dekret des Ivo von Chartres, Die handschriftliche Überlieferung im Vergleich zum Text in den Editionen des 16. und 17. Jahrhunderts', *ZRG KA*, 70 (1985), 1-44. See also Fowler-Magerl, *Selection*, 133-6, and Kéry, *Canonical collections*, 250-53.

14 Martin Brett, together with colleagues, is preparing an edition of the still unedited *Tripartita*. See Fowler-Magerl, *Selection*, 126-29, and Kéry, *Canonical Collections*, 244-50.

15 Brett, 'Sources and influence', 160-67. See also Fowler-Magerl, *Selection*, 132.

16 Martin Brett and Bruce Brasington have made available on the Web a working edition of the *Panormia*. The work is far advanced and should be used rather than the *PL* edition.

the compiler of the *Collectio X partium*. This collection, as I have argued elsewhere, was conceived and begun in or shortly before 1110 at Thérouanne. Evidence for such an early dating of the *Collectio X partium* is found in the copy of that collection in the manuscript Paris, Bibliothèque Nationale, lat. 14145. This copy was never completed. The text of the canons stop at canon 1.5.1, but although the capitulation of the first part is otherwise complete, it does not contain references to the decrees of the councils of Poitiers (1100) and Toulouse (1119). All other copies have the texts of the decrees and the references to them in the capitulation.[17]

The most recent datable text in the first version of the *Caesaraugustana* is 3.69, a decree of the council of Benevento in 1108. Canon 7.112, *Ex divine legis preceptis* (JL 6613), could date from the beginning (1099) or the end (1118) of the papacy of pope Paschalis II. More precision is not possible.

The compiler of the *Caesaraugustana* must have spent time in northeastern France, in the vicinity of Paris. The material collection in Arsenal 713 survives in only that one manuscript. It was used only for the Ivonian collections and the *Caesaraugustana*, and the copy gives the impression of a private accumulation of material not intended for circulation.

A further indication of acquaintance with sources only available in northeastern France is the presence of a version of the *Visio Eucherii* which is found elsewhere, to my knowledge, only in the *Collectio Atrebatensis* (on fos 14v-15r of Arras, Bibliothèque municipale, MS 425) and at the beginning of the ninth book of the *Collectio Catalaunensis I* (on fo 34r-v of Châlons-sur-Marne, Bibliothèque municipale, MS 47). The *Atrebatensis* was probably compiled at Arras in the mid 1090s,[18] the *Catalaunensis I* perhaps at Châlons-sur-Marne in the second decade of the twelfth century.[19] In the *Collectio Atrebatensis* and in the *Collectio Catalaunensis I* the text has the inscription: 'Hoc est excerptum ex pontificali beati Eucherii episcopi'. The text is added to the end of the *Caesaraugustana* in the Salamanca manuscript and there it has the rubric: 'De eo qui primus decimas laicis dedit'. In P3876 it is integrated into the collection as canon 7.39. Thematically it belongs in the seventh book among other canons forbidding the transfer of ecclesiastical *predia* to laymen. There it has the rubric: 'Quis regum primus decimas laicis contulerit'. The text is found in Barc63 in the same context (2.152).

The text recounts that saint Eucherius had a vision of Charles Martel in hell. To confirm the truth of that vision the tomb at Saint-Denis was opened and a dragon escaped, leaving the empty grave blackened as if by fire. Pippin was called to the

---

17 See Fowler-Magerl, 'Fine Distinctions and the Transmission of Texts', *ZRG KA*, 83 (1997), 184-5; and *Selection*, 149-52; and Kéry, *Canonical Collections*, 263-4.

18 Fowler-Magerl, *Selection*, 144-145, and Kéry, *Canonical Collections*, 279.

19 Fowler-Magerl, *Selection*, 178, and Kéry, *Canonical Collections*, 290.

grave of his father and, shaken by what he saw, determined to return as much of the alienated church property as possible:

> Karolus princeps, Pipini regis pater, primus decimas ab altaribus divisit et militibus tradidit unde eternam dampnationem incurrit. Quod enim sanctus Eucherius aurelianensium episcopus qui in monasterio sancti Trudonis requiescit in contemplatione positus vidit Karolum Martellum in inferno inferiori torqueri propter hoc maxime scelus quod decimas Deo sacratas contra ius usibus laicorum concedere presumpsit. Ipse namque sanctus Eucherius ilico beatum Bonifacium et Fulradum abbatem monasterii sancti Dionisii archicapellanumque Pipini regis sibi arcersiri iussit eisque talia vidisse se dixit et ut sepulcrum illius aperirent probantes utrum que dicebat vera essent indixit. Qui ilico sepulcrum illius aperientes drachonem exinde exire viderunt et totum sepulcrum interius denigratum acsi fuisset exustum sed corporis eius vestigium nullum repererunt. Quod cognoscens filius eius Pipinus aput Liptinias sinodum congregavit cui prefuit cum sancto Bonefatio legatus apostolice sedis Georgius nomine. In qua denique sinodo res aecclesie quas pater male abstulit quantum valuit aecclesiis reddere procuravit. Sed integre non potuit ob Walferii Aquitaniensis debellationem. Unde idem rex edictum fecit et manu propria corroboravit ne huiusmodi scelus aliquis successorum ipsius aggredi possit. Huius namque plenitudinem edicti in libro capitulorum eius quicumque voluerit invenire valebit.

This legend is found in a slightly different form as chapter seven of an account of the council of Quierzy (858) composed probably by Hincmar, archbishop of Reims.[20] This version of the legend begins: 'Carolus princeps, Pippini regis pater, qui primus inter omnes Francorum reges ac principes res ecclesiarum ab eis separavit atque divisit'.[21] This second version circulated, separate from the other chapters, in several manuscripts, almost all traceable to northeastern France. One copy dates to the middle of the ninth century, that in Paris, Bibliothèque Nationale, MS lat. 4628A. Two other twelfth-century manuscripts also come from Saint-Denis: Paris, Bibliothèque Nationale, MS nouv. acq. lat. 326; and Paris, Bibliothèque Mazarine, MS 2013.

Although the compiler of the first version of the *Caesaraugustana* apparently had direct knowledge of sources available only in the northeast, he completed the collection in and for southeastern France. Evidence of this is the presence of a forgery attributed to pope Leo I, *Quali pertinentia* (JL †446), which rejects claims of the church of Arles to primacy in France.[22] This canon (2.50 in Salamanca,

---

20 Ulrich Nonn, 'Das Bild Karl Martells in den lateinischen Quellen vornehmlich des 8. und 9. Jahrhunderts', *Frühmittelalterliche Studien*, 4 (1970), 106-23.

21 This form is edited by Wilfried Hartmann, *Die Konzilien der Karolingischen Teilreiche 843-859, MGH, Concilia aevi Karolini* (Hanover, 1984), 414 l. 21-417 l. 3. For the manuscripts containing the form of Quierzy see 404-5.

22 'De Arelatensis episcopi amisso pro contumatia privilegio. Dilectissimis fratribus per Gallias et Viennensem provinciam episcopis constitutis. Leo episcopus salutem. Quali pertinacia Ylarius

2.16.2 in P3876, 1.84 in Barc63) appears in contemporary collections only once, in the eleventh-century Madrid, Biblioteca Nacional, MS lat. 11548, which was for a time in the library of the Jesuit college at Auch near Toulouse.[23]

The *Caesaraugustana* contains, moreover, a forgery attributed to pope Nicholas I and addressed to Radulfus, archbishop of Bourges (843-66): 'Conquestus est apostolatui nostro' (JE †2765).[24] It is found at the end of book two with a rubric referring explicitly to the bishoprics of Narbonne and Bourges: 'Quid Narbonensis Bituricensi debeat ecclesia'. The text appears for the first time in the first part of the *Collectio Tripartita*. In a rubric found in an articulated copy of the *Tripartita* no specific bishoprics are named: 'Ne clerici alicuius episcopi eo invito ad iudicium primatum ire compellantur'. The same text is found in the *Decretum* of Ivo (5.56) with the rubric: 'De iure primatum'. The rubric in the *Caesaraugustana* implies a contest between Narbonne and Bourges, and no such conflict is documented before the early twelfth century. The archbishop of Bourges began to call himself the primate of Aquitaine in 1120.[25] This would coincide with other indications that the first version of the *Caesaraugustana* was compiled circa 1120.

Another reason for suggesting that the first version of the *Caesaraugustana* was completed in southeastern France is that the text of the decree of pope Iohannes VIII on sacrilege found at the beginning of book seven is identical to that in the *Exceptiones legum Romanorum* (the *Exceptiones Petri*),[26] a collection of excerpts from Roman law compiled at Valence in the mid-twelfth century.[27] If the compiler of the *Exceptiones* did not made use of the first version of the *Caesaraugustana* at least he used the same source.

The fact that the collection of Deusdedit, one of the major sources, was compiled at Rome and is often called a 'Roman' collection, should not obscure the fact that several of the surviving fragmentary copies were made in France. The fragment in Paris, Bibliothèque Nationale, MS lat. 1458, for example, as Victor Wolf von Glanvell notes in the prologue to his edition, was present for a time at Valence. The *Polycarpus*, also called a 'Roman' collection, depends on Roman sources, but was dedicated to the archbishop of Compostela, Diego Gelmírez, and circulated in France and Spain as well as in Italy.

Arelatensis episcopus iudicium nostrum ...'. For the full text see the edition of Wilhelm Gundlach, *MGH Epistolarum*, 3, *Epistolae Merowingici et Karolini Aevi*, 1 (Berlin, 1902), 91.

23 Gérard Fransen, 'Une collection canonique de la fin du XIe siècle', *Revue de droit canonique*, 10-11 (1960-61), 136-56. See also Fowler-Magerl, *Selection*, 107.

24 The text is edited in full by Ernst Perels, *Nicolai I Papae Epistolae*, *MGH Epistolarum*, 6, *Epistolae Carolini aevi*, 4 (Berlin, 1925), 633.

25 Fedor Schneider, 'Ein interpolierter Brief Papst Nikolaus I. und der Primat von Bourges', *NA*, 32 (1907), 492.

26 Stephan Kuttner and Wilfried Hartmann, 'A new version of Pope John VIII's decree on sacrilege (Council of Troyes, 878)', *BMCL*, NS 17 (1987), 28.

27 The *Exceptiones Petri* were edited in Straßburg in 1500 and again by Carlo Guido Mor, *Orbis Romanus*, 10 (Milan, 1938).

A reference to what may have been a copy of the *Caesaraugustana* is found in a twelfth-century library catalogue listing the possessions of the canonry of Saint-Victor in Marseille. In this catalogue there is mention of two *volumina* which begin with 'De ra...'. This could be a reference to the rubric of the first canon in the *Caesaraugustana*: 'De ratione et auctoritate et que cui sit preponenda'. The monastery at Ripoll, in the library of which the copy of the first version of the *Caesaraugustana* in the Ms Paris BN lat. 3875 was found, was dependent in the early twelfth century on the canonry Saint-Victor of Marseille and the libraries of both profited from the relationship.[28]

P3876 and Barc63 contain closely related revisions of the *Caesaraugustana*. Both were completed shortly after 1143/1144 in southeastern France or Catalonia. Both contain a list of popes ending in the fourteenth year of pope Innocent II and the seventh year of the French king Louis VII (in Barc63 on fo 231r-232v). The revision in P3876 has been called a second version of the *Caesaraugustana* and the revision in Barc63 a third version. It is not that simple, however. The compiler of Barc63 certainly did not use the manuscript P3876. P3876 contains the canons of the council held at Reims by pope Eugene III in 1148 and these texts are missing in Barc63. The marginal note on fo 56v of P3876 which refers to the 'decreta' of Gratian[29] is also missing. P3876 and Barc63 add the same texts from the *Panormia* of Ivo of Chartres and *Exceptiones Petri* to the first version of the collection but they deal with them differently.

Both P3876 and Barc63 are closely associated with canons regular, specifically with the order of Saint-Ruf (which has seldom been the subject of study in England, Canada and America).[30] The order of Saint-Ruf originated in the early eleventh century in Avignon and was particularly active in Catalonia and southern France. Both P3876 and Barc63 contain the same expanded form of a well known text often associated with that order: *In die resurrectionis* (13.13 in P3876 and 4.12 in

28 For the library catalogue of Saint-Victor see Louis de Maslatrie, 'Collection de Documents inédits sur l'histoire de France', in *Mélanges historiques*, 1 (Paris, 1841), 663.

29 See Stephan Kuttner, 'Research on Gratian: Acta and Agenda', in *Proceedings of the Sixth International Congress of Medieval Canon Law*, ed. Stephan Kuttner and Kenneth Pennington, MIC Series C, Subsidia 7 (Vatican City, 1985), 19 n. 46.

30 Most recently and most thoroughly: Ursula Vones-Liebenstein, *Saint-Ruf und Spanien. Studien zur Verbreitung und zum Wirken der Regularkanoniker von Saint-Ruf in Avignon auf der Iberischen Halbinsel (11. und 12. Jahrhundert)*, 2 vols (Paris-Turnhout, 1996), i, 49-231. Also Pedro R. Rocha, 'Le rayonnement de l'Ordre de Saint-Ruf dans la péninsule ibérique, d'après sa liturgie', in *Les mondes des chanoines XIe-XIVe siècles*, Cahiers de Fanjeaux, 24 (Toulouse, 1989), 195-7. André Gouron, *La Science iuridique française aux XIe et XIIe siècles: Diffusion du droit de Justinien et influences canoniques jusqu'a Gratien*, Ius Romanum Medii Aevi, II.5 (Milan 1978), 76-8. Also Jean-Pierre Poly, 'Les maitres de Saint-Ruf. Pratique et enseignement du droit dans la France méridionale au XIIe siècles', *Annales de la Faculté de droit de l'Université de Bordeaux*, 2 (1978), 183-203. See also Charles Dereine, 'Saint-Ruf et ses coutumes au XIe et XIIe siècles,' *RB*, 59 (1949), 174.

Barc63).[31] The inscription of the canon in the *Caesaraugustana* is: 'Gregorius in generali sinodo residens dixit'. In most Italian collections (the Bb version of the collection of Anselm of Lucca, the Pistoian *Collectio III librorum* and the related *Collectio IX librorum*, the *Collectio Ashburnhamensis* as well as the *Polycarpus* and the related *Collectio VII librorum*) the text is attributed specifically to pope Gregory VII. The version in P3876 and Barc63 is the same as that in the Poitevin *Collectio Tarraconensis*, one copy of which is now preserved at Tarragona, south of Barcelona.[32] Uta-Renate Blumenthal has shown that Tarragona, Biblioteca Provincial, MS 26, which contains this copy of the *Tarraconensis*, was made in the diocese of Roda, in northeastern Spain.[33] It is therefore not surprising that the compiler of the *Caesaraugustana* took notice of the *Tarraconensis*, and there are other indications as well of the use of this and other Poitevin material.[34]

The author of *In die resurrectionis* criticizes the contemporary practice at Rome of reciting only three psalms and three readings at matins. The text requires an increase in the psalms and readings except at Easter and Pentecost. The version in the *Caesaraugustana* belongs to that category of transmission which traces the beginning of the contemporary laxity to the period in which 'teutonicis concessum est regimen nostre ecclesie'. Most transmissions of this text end with 'antiquos imitantes patres'. In the *Caesaraugustana*, however, the text goes on without a break. The continuation of the text in the *Caesaraugustana* explains the requirement of only three psalms and responses at Easter and Pentecost. This must be done, the author says, in consideration of those who are about to be baptized and who have had to fast. The rubric of the text reads: 'De officio paschali'. The continuation after 'antiquos imitantes patres' reads as follows:

Habita enim consideratione baptismi quod sibi uniformiter generale iuxta beatum Siricium papam sanctum pascha cum suo pentecosten privilegio sibi vendicat propter neophitos per vii. utriusque festivitatis dies in ecclesia presentandos et mane ad officium et ad missarum sollempnia quia et eorum infra actionem specialiter memoria agitur et ad

---

31 For the edition and transmission of the text see Arturo Bernal Palacios, 'La redacción breve del c. "In die resurrectionis" en las colecciones canónicas pregracianas', in *Proceedings of the Ninth International Congress of Medieval Canon Law*, 923-52.

32 For the *Tarraconensis* see Fowler-Magerl, *Selection*, 74-6; and 'Vier Kanonessammlungen', 139 and 142. See also Kéry, *Canonical Collections*, 214-5.

33 Her arguments will appear in full in the proceedings of the Congress of Medieval Canon Law held at Catania in 2000.

34 The collection of Turin, BN, D.IV.33, as Roger Reynolds was the first to realize, contains considerable Poitiers material. See Roger E. Reynolds, 'The Turin Collection: a Poitevin canonical collection', *Traditio*, 25 (1969), 508-14. It is also related to the *Caesaraugustana*, perhaps by way of the order of Saint-Ruf. For similarities in the transmission of canons of the council of Melfi in the *Caesaraugustana* and in the Turin collection see Robert Somerville with Stephan Kuttner, *Pope Urban II, The* Collectio Britannica *and the Council of Melfi (1089)* (Oxford, 1996), 197 n. 37. Furthermore, the canons of the council of Piacenza (1095) are found not only in the *Polycarpus* and in the *Caesaraugustana* but also in the Turin collection.

vesperas ad fontis processionem deducendos. Hac quidem ratione beatus Gregorius doctor pasche et pentecosten utriusque et per vii. subsequentes dies ad trium psalmorum totidemque responsoriorum brevitatem matutinum redegit officium at vero sabbato in albis nuper baptizati albas deponunt unde et congruum tamen nomen accepunt. In officii autem diurno pene mutantur omnia. Nam ad horas capitula et responsoria et ad vesperum capitula et versiculi reperantur.

A number of other transmissions of the text *In die resurrectionis* have continuations, but none of them is found in a canon law collection. These continuations deal with rules of fasting and refer specifically to canons regular.[35] Although the transmission in P3876 and Barc63 does not, both they and the Salamanca copy of the first version of the *Caesaraugustana* contain texts associated with the order. All versions of the *Caesaraugustana* (Salamanca 8.38, Barc63 2.203) contain a letter of pope Urban II to the abbot of Saint-Ruf, *Statuimus ne professionis canonice ...* (JL 5763), taken from the *Decretum* of Ivo (6.411). The decretal puts canons regular on the same level as monks and prohibits them from leaving their monasteries without the permission of their abbots even 'districtionis religionis obtentu'. In the *Decretum* and in all other transmissions the letter is adressed to the abbot of Saint-Ruf. The same text was sent to the canonry of Saint-Paul of Narbonne (JL 5482), to Saint-Quentin of Beauvais (JL 5496), to Maguellone (JL 5550) between Narbonne and Arles.[36]

The order of Saint-Ruf was particularly influential at Saint-Victor of Marseille and at Barcelona. Barc63 was present at an early date at the monastery Sant Cugat del Valles near Barcelona.[37] Oleguer, who had been abbot of Saint-Ruf between 1111 and 1116, served as bishop of Barcelona until 1137. In this period canons of Saint-Ruf were elected bishops at Tortosa, Vich, Tarragona, Lerida, Gerona and Urgel.

The first version of the *Caesaraugustana* in Salamanca 2644, it will be recalled, was divided into fifteen books, each with its own title and its own capitulation. The version in P3876 is not divided into books, but its use is facilitated by the description published by Paul Fournier. The version Barc63 is not much different from that in P3876 in content and in sequence and is divided neatly into six books with

---

35 Ch. Dereine, 'La prétendue règle de Gregoire VII pour chanoines réguliers', *RB*, 71 (1961), 108-18. Dereine edits the continuation of the text from Milan, Ambrosiana MS H.5 inf. See also D. G. Morin, 'Règlements inédits du Pape Saint Grégoire VII pour les Chanoines Réguliers', *RB*, 18 (1901), 177-83. Morin edits the continuation of the text from Vatican City, Biblioteca Apostolica Vaticana, MS Vat. lat. 629.

36 Charles Dereine, 'L'Élaboration du statut canonique des chanoines réguliers spécialement sous Urbain II', *RHE*, 46 (1951), 534-65, here 545-6.

37 See Francesc X. Miquel Rosell, 'Católeg dels llibres manuscrits de la Biblioteca del Monestir de Sant Cugat del Vallès existents a l'Arxiu de la Corona d'Aragó', *Butlletí de la Biblioteca de Catalunya*, 8 (Barcelona, 1937), 108-10. See also Ferran Valls y Taberner, *Estudis d'historia juridica catalona* (Barcelona, 1929), 82-8. See Fowler-Magerl, 'Vier Kanonessammlungen', 144-6.

capitulations. It is therefore easy to use and the rubrics make clear why the compiler chose the particular canons he did. But Barc63 is seldom used and is almost always misjudged. In an attempt to remedy this situation, the following listing shows the correspondence between the books of the Barc63 version and those of the Salamanca version:

Book 1 of Barc63 = books 1-4 of the Salamanca version, book 2 = books 5-9 nine, book 3 = books 10-12, book 4 = books 13-14, book 6 = book 15. The contents of book 5 will be described below. It is not the equivalent of book 14 as P. M. Gassó thought.[38]

Book 2 of the Salamanca version begins at Barc63 1.44 in Barc63, book 3 at 1.110, book 4 at 1.172, book 5 at 2.1, book 6 at 2.96, book 7 at 2.119, book 8 at 2.216, book 9 at 2.315, book 10 at 3.1, book 11 at 3.127, book 12 at 3.144, book 13 at 4.1, book 14 at 4.82, book 15 at 6.1.

Paul Fournier was of the opinion that the collection was poorly organized. In comparison with most other collections of the period this is not true, however, and none of the first ten books would ever be rearranged. In the later books, however, there is repetition and the titles are nothing more than the rubrics of the first canons of the books. Only book 8 is put together of truly disparate parts. It deals with the discipline of clerics, with Jews and with just war. This is reminiscent of the final books of the collection of Anselm of Lucca, also a source of the *Caesaraugustana*.

1.) De ratione et auctoritate et que cui sit preponende;[39] 2.) De Romane ecclesie privilegiis; 3.) De metropolitanis et episcopis; 4.) De variis delictis et officiis episcoporum et clericorum; 5.) De iudiciis ecclesiasticis; 6.) De iuriurando et periurio; 7.) De sacrilegiis et de privilegiis ecclesiarum; 8.) De vita clericorum et nominis interpretatione; 9.) De vita et officio monachorum; 10.) De nuptiis et virginibus;[40] 11.) Quod sacrificium altaris verum corpus Christi sit; 12.) Qualiter rudes predicari debeant; 13.) Quod in unica catholica ecclesia vera Christi hostia immolatur; 14.) De hereticis et schismaticis et quid distet heresis a schismate; 15.) De damnatione Constantini et reordinatione eorum qui ab eo fuerunt ordinati.

The reorganization of the original version began with the version in Paris BN MS lat. 3875, which moves the canons of book 11 to the end of book 13. In P3876

---

38 Gassò and Batlle, *Pelagii I papae epistulae* (see n. 5 above), 25-6.

39 For *ratio* and *auctoritas* in the collection see Eloy Tejero, '"Ratio" y Jerarquia de Fuentes Canonicas en las *Caesaraugustana*', in: *Hispania Christiana: estudios en honor del Prof. Dr. José Orlandis Rovira en sua septuagésimo aniversario*, ed. Josep-Ignasi Saranyana and Eloy Tejero (Pamplona, 1988), 303-22. See also R. Losada Cosmes, 'La teoría de las fuentes del derecho en la renascencia jurídica del s. XII', *Revista Espanola de Derecho Canónico*, 15 (1960), 328-68.

40 Eloy Tejero, 'El matrimonio en la Collectio Caesaraugustana', in *Proceedings of the Seventh International Congress of Medieval Canon Law*, ed. Peter Linehan, MIC Series C, Subsidia, 8 (Vatican City, 1988), 115-34.

and Barc63 the original core of texts is not rearranged, but the canons added to the version in Salamanca 2644 are inserted at different places. Since modern canonists know P3876 better than Barc63 they have come away with the false impression that Barc63 is an abbreviated version with many of the more recent texts missing. Both assumptions are wrong. A series of canons from the third book of the *Panormia* is inserted after canon 4.72 in P3876. The first is the election decree of Nicholas II of 1059: *In nomine domini dei salvationis nostri.* The text has the rubric: 'De electione et consecratione pape, archiepiscoporum et episcoporum'. The text is found in Barc63 (1.122.1, with the rubric 'De electione summi pontificis') following 3.16 of Salamanca 2644. The texts which follow the election decree in P3876 are left in a block. In Barc63 groups of these texts are redistributed throughout the collection according to subject matter. Since P3876 and Barc63 add the same texts to the original version and since Barc63 is not a copy of P3876, P3876, whose origin has not be determined with certainty, was probably compiled at the same place as Barc63—at Barcelona.

P3876 has an appendix containing 308 canons following a notation: 'Explicit liber est'. Book 5 of Barc63 contains a series of the texts from the the appendix. Canons 5.1-2 in Barc63 are canons 175 and 177 of the appendix and 5.3-33 are from the series in book 4 of P3876. Canons 5.34 to the end of book 5 are taken from the appendix and are almost all from the *Panormia*, the major exceptions being canons 5.39, 41-47 and 49, all dealing with judicial procedure and all found in the *Exceptiones Petri*.[41] The *Exceptiones* were available at Barcelona in the mid-twelfth century because they were used by the compiler of the *Usatici Barchinone*.[42]

In both P3876 and Barc63 the first canon of book 15 (the title of which in the Salamanca version gives an entirely false impression of the contents of that book) is moved to book 4 in P3876 and to the corresponding position in Barc63.

Many of the texts taken from the *Panormia* have no rubrics in P3876, which is not surprising, because the *Panormia* does not have many. The rubrics in the edition of the *Patrologia latina* are for the most part false. These texts, like all other texts, have rubrics in Barc63. This makes Barc63 particularly interesting for students of the history of ideas. The inscriptions, rubrics and text in Barc63 are better and more complete than those in the P3876.

The more recent decrees in P3876 are not missing in Barc63. The decretal of pope Paschal II, *Ex divine legis preceptis* (JL 6613), is 2.215.2. A second decree of

---

41 Peter Weimar, 'Die legistische Literatur der Glossatorenzeit', in: *Handbuch der Quellen und Literatur der neueren europäischen Privatrechtsgeschichte*, ed. Helmut Coing, Bd 1: *Mittelalter (1100-1500)* (Munich, 1973), 129-260, here 253-57.

42 Edited by Fernando [Ferran] Valls Taberner, *Los Usatges de Barcelona*, rev. edn by Manuel J. Peláez et al. (Málaga-Barcelona, 1984; 1st edn: Barcelona, 1913).

Paschal, *Post obitum uxoris* (JL 6436),[43] which is 10.130 in P3876 3.113 in Barc63. All of the decretals correctly attributed to pope Urban II in P3876 are in Barc63. A decretal of pope Alexander II adressed to the archbishop Bartholomeus of Tours, *Cenomannensem* (Dist. LVI c. 13 in the *Concordia discordantium canonum* of Gratian), which is attributed falsely to pope Urban II in the *Panormia* (canon 3.53) and in P3876 (four canons after 4.72 of the Salamanca version), is left out of Barc63. The *Britannica* and the collection in Arsenal 713 attribute the text correctly to Alexander II. The compiler of Barc63 seems to have been aware of the contradiction, having perhaps had access to notes taken from the Arsenal collection. All decretals of pope Gregory VII in P3876 are also in Barc63.[44]

There is a final lesson to be learned from the manner in which the *Caesaraugustana* was transmitted in the south of France and Catalonia. In the transmission of texts distances cannot be measured in kilometers alone. Texts travelled within orders, legal texts particularly within canonical orders. This has already been noted in regard to procedural literature by Winfried Stelzer in regard to the Augustinian canons,[45] and I have noted the same in regard to the Praemonstratensian canons.[46]

---

43 Uta-Renate Blumenthal, 'Decrees and decretals of Pope Paschal II in twelfth-century canonical collections', *BMCL*, NS 10 (1980), 27 and 19 respectively.

44 John Gilchrist, 'The Reception of Pope Gregory VII into the Canon Law (1073-1141) Part II', *ZRG KA*, 61 (1980), 209.

45 See Winfried Stelzer, *Gelehrtes Recht in Österreich* (Vienna, 1982), passim.

46 Fowler-Magerl, *Ordo iudiciorum vel ordo iudiciarius. Begriff und Literaturgattung*, Ius commune, Sonderhefte 19 (Frankfurt am Main, 1984), 45-56.

Chapter 17

Cardinal Deusdedit's *Collectio canonum* at Benevento

Robert Somerville

Deusdedit's canon law book, dedicated to Pope Victor III (1086-87), survives fully in only one medieval manuscript, Vatican City, Biblioteca Apostolica Vaticana, MS Vat. lat. 3833, which is not the compiler's original.[1] The paucity of copies and the work's specific focus on the Roman Church led Victor Wolf von Glanvell to write that it had limited circulation.[2] Fournier and LeBras went further and wrote that apparently the compilation was not of very great influence.[3] In comparison to the anonymous *Sententie diversorum patrum* (*Collection in Seventy-four Titles*), or the collections of Anselm of Lucca and Ivo of Chartres, Deusdedit's work circulated and was used less widely. Yet its diffusion and influence was not negligible. The most recent published inventory of manuscripts contains, in addition to the complete twelfth-century exemplar and an early-modern copy of it, ten witnesses under the label 'Fragments and Excerpts', and that list is incomplete.[4] Despite their reservations about its influence, Fournier and LeBras mentioned three other canonical collections which employed Deusdedit, i.e., the *Collectio Britannica*, the *Collectio Caesaraugustana*, and the *Collection in Seven Books* of Turin, Biblioteca Nazionale Universitaria, MS E.V.44.[5] That list also can be expanded with other

---

1 For basic information and bibliography on Deusdedit's work see Lotte Kéry, *Canonical Collections of the Early Middle Ages (ca. 400-1140)*, History of Medieval Canon Law, 1, ed. Wilfried Hartmann and Kenneth Pennington (Washington D.C., 1999), 228-33. For Vat. lat. 3833 see 229.

2 *Die Kanonessammlung des Kardinals Deusdedit*, ed. Victor Wolf von Glanvell (Paderborn, 1905), XVI, ' ... scheint die Kanonessammlung keine grosse Verbreitung erlangt zu haben'.

3 Paul Fournier and Gabriel LeBras, *Histoire des collections canoniques en Occident depuis les Fausses Décrétales jusqu'au Décret de Gratien*, 2 vols (Paris, 1931-2; repr. Aalen, 1972), ii, 52, 'Il ne paraît pas que le recueil de Deusdedit ait exercé une trés grande influence'. Fournier's original statement on the matter was more nuanced: Paul Fournier, 'Les collections canoniques romaines de l'époque de Grégoire VII', *Mémoires de l'Académie des inscriptions et belles-lettres*, 41 (1920), 362 (repr. in *idem, Mélanges de droit canonique*, 2 vols, ed. Theo Kölzer [Aalen, 1983], ii, 518).

4 Kéry, *Canonical Collections*, 229, to which can be added both the text to be treated in this article and also a fragment from Deusdedit in Dresden, Sächsische Landesbibliothek, MS F.168: see Claudia Märtl, *Die falschen Investiturprivilegien*, MGH Fontes Iuris Germanici Antiqui, 13 (Hanover, 1986), 103-4.

5 Fournier-LeBras, *Histoire*, ii, 52 (cf. Fournier, 'Collections', 362-3 [*Mélanges*, ii, 516-17]). Rome, Biblioteca Casanatense, MS 2010, also mentioned by Fournier as a derivative collection actually

books from the period of the eleventh- and twelfth-century papal reform which utilized Deusdedit's collection, to say nothing of items associated with the papal chancery in the twelfth century, e.g., at the time of Pope Innocent II the work of Canon Benedict of St Peter's, and the compilation of Cardinal Albinus and then the *Liber censuum* toward the end of the century.[6]

The comments which follow will deal with another trace of Deusdedit's collection. Copied into a late fourteenth-century manuscript from Benevento—now Vatican City, Biblioteca Apostolica Vaticana, MS Reg. lat. 399—is a series of excerpts which is worthy of attention on several grounds. This book contains no Beneventan script, but its origin in the region which produced that elegant hand, whose circulation Roger Reynolds has done so much in recent time to elucidate, makes it an apt subject for an essay in his honor.

Reg. lat. 399, written by a cleric in the diocesis of Benevento probably shortly after 1374, is described in detail in Wilmart's published catalogue of the *Codices Reginenses* in the Vatican Library.[7] The greatest part of the book is devoted to a *Liber provincialis* of Archbishop Hugo Guitardi of Benevento (1365-83), which presents the legislation from a provincial council held at Benevento in April 1374.[8]

---

contains a fragment of Deusdedit's work: see *Kanonessammlung*, ed. Wolf von Glanvell, XXIX; Kéry, *Canonical Collections*, 229; and Fournier-LeBras, *Histoire*, ii, 39 (with an incorrect shelfmark).

6   Fournier-LeBras, *Histoire*, ii, 53, acknowledged the use of Deusdedit's collection by Placidus of Nonantola and by these later twelfth-century works. Cf. Jörg W. Busch, *Der Liber de Honore Ecclesiae des Placidus von Nonantola*, Quellen und Forschungen zum Recht im Mittelalter, 5 (Sigmaringen, 1990), 64, and *passim* throughout the book (see 245 for references). For use of the collection elsewhere during the period of reform see: Giorgio Picasso, *Collezioni canoniche Milanesi del secolo XII*, Pubblicazioni dell'Università cattolica del s. Cuore, Saggi e Ricerche, ser.3, Scienze storiche, 2 (Milan, 1969), 172-3; Friederich Kempf S.I., 'Ein zweiter Dictatus papae? Ein Beitrag zum Depositionsanspruch Gregors VII.', *Archivum Historiae Pontificiae*, 13 (1975), 119-39, especially 132 ff.; Uta-Renate Blumenthal, 'An Episcopal Handbook from Twelfth-Century Southern Italy: Codex Rome, Bibl. Vallicelliana F.54/III', in *Studia in honorem eminentissimi Cardinalis Alphonsi M. Stickler*, ed. Rosalius Iosephus [Rosalio José] Castillo Lara, Studia et Textus Historiae Iuris Canonici, 7 (Rome, 1992), 13-24, especially 20-21 (repr. in *eadem*, *Papal Reform and Canon Law in the 11th and 12th Centuries* [Aldershot, 1998], no. XVIII, with addenda), and Linda Fowler-Magerl, 'Fine Distictions and the Transmission of Texts', *ZRG KA*, 83 (1997), 172, n. 125. For use of Deusdedit's collection in the works of Benedict, Albinus, and the *Liber censuum* see Wilhelm M. Peitz, S. J., *Das Originalregister Gregors VII.*, Sitzungsberichte der Kaiserlichen Akademie der Wissenschaften in Wien, Philosophisch-Historische Klasse, 165.5 (Vienna, 1911), 246-58, and 348-9; and *Le Liber censuum de l'Église romaine*, ed. Paul Fabre, L. Duchesne and G. Mollat, Bibliothèque des Écoles Françaises d'Athènes et de Rome, 2nd Ser., 6, 3 vols in 8 parts (Paris, 1889-1952), i (1889), 4-7, who added the work of Cardinal Boso, *camerarius* of the Roman Church at the time of Popes Hadrian IV and Alexander III.

7   Andreas [André] Wilmart, *Codices Reginenses Latini, Tomus II, Codices 251-500* (Vatican Library, 1945), 457-62. See 462 for Wilmart's comments on the book's age.

8   For Archbishop Hugo see Conradus Eubel et al., *Hierarchia catholica medii aevi*, 2nd edn, 7 vols (Münster, 1913-68), i, ed. Eubel (1913), 133. Wilmart, *Codices*, 457, gave his dates as 1365-85, but the evidence presented by Eubel appears to indicate 1383 as the end of Hugo's pontificate.

Those decrees cover sixty-one folios, and after describing them Wilmart wrote that 'Several things follow concerning maintaining discipline, added by the same copyist to fill up the book'.[9] There seems to be no thematic unity to that potpourri of added texts. They cover various liturgical and disciplinary topics and include a lengthy item about St Boniface which appears in Deusdedit's canonical collection, a fragment from the *Liber pontificalis*, selections from Bonizo of Sutri, and some excerpts which Wilmart did not identify.[10] Fo 70 treats the mass, includes texts from St Thomas Aquinas, and concludes 'Et hec de eucaristia dicta sufficiunt'.

The book's last page, fo 71, which should be bound 71v-71r, contains a set of excerpts dealing with simony and money. The following tabulation lists them in the order they were meant to be read, i.e., verso to recto. For ease of reference the texts are assigned numbers, followed by an inscription if there is one, and then the incipit, explicit, and material source.[11]

<i>   Per pecuniam [?].[12] Ex decretis Calixti pape ii. Sanctorum patrum exempla sequentes ... spe deponatur.—Pope Calixtus II, Lateran Council, March 1123, cc. 1-3; *Conciliorum oecumenicorum decreta*, ed. Josephus [Giuseppe] Alberigo et al., 3rd edn (Bologna, 1973), 190.

---

9   Wilmart, *Codices*, 458, 'Accedunt conplura, ab eodem librario addita, de disciplina servanda, ut liber perficeretur'. The acts of the council of 1374 are printed in the *Synodicon s. Beneventanensis ecclesiae*, ed. V. M. Ursinus [Orsini] (Benevento, 1695), 77-291, 2nd ed. (Rome, 1724), 66-244; cf. Mansi, xxvi, 619-20, n.1. Father Vincenzo Maria Orsini, O.P., was archbishop of Benevento from 1686 until election as Pope Benedict XIII in 1724. At the beginning of the account of the synod in 1374 he wrote (*Synodicon* [ed. 1695], 77): 'Habemus hoc Concilium in Codice veteri m.s. in pergameno in nostra Metropolitana Bibliotheca, unde summa diligentia exscribi curavimus Romae anno Domini 1691. exemplumque in eadem Bibliotheca reposuimus'. Is this a reference to Orsini's specific use of MS Reg. lat. 399? Wilmart, *Codices*, 462, saw no reason to think that the book ever was part of Queen Christina of Sweden's library, and said that it probably came to the Vatican from an Italian owner at the end of the seventeenth century. Interpreting Orsini's statement is difficult because the word *exemplum* can mean both 'original' and 'transcription', so it is unclear what he sent back to Benevento. But contrasting *codice veteri* and *exemplum*, it seems reasonable to think that the copy was returned and that the *codex*, in all probability MS 399, entered the Vatican Library (a view shared by Carmela Vircillo Franklin, to whom the author is grateful for her views on the matter).

10 Both E. Perels, the editor of Bonizo's *Liber de vita christiana*, and Wolf von Glanvell, were aware of the fragments in Reg. lat. 399: *Bonizo, Liber de vita christiana*, ed. Ernst Perels, 2nd ed. mit einem Nachwort zur Neuauflage von Walter Berschin (Hildesheim, 1998), LX; *Kanonessammlung*, ed. Wolf von Glanvell, 189-92 (bk. 1, c. 327), where variants from MS 399 are presented. See also *Le Liber Pontificalis*, ed. L. Duchesne, Bibliothèques des Écoles françaises d'Athènes et de Rome, 2nd Ser., 3, 2 vols (Paris, 1884-92 [2nd edn with 3rd vol. by Cyrille Vogel, 1955-7]), i (1884), 316.

11 The author is very grateful to both Consuelo Dutschke and Susan L'Engle for information about this last folio of Reg. lat. 399.

12 The top of this page is mutilated. It is possible that another word, e.g., *ordinationes*, once preceded *Per*. Whether the title was meant only for the following canons of Lateran I or for the entire series of excerpts is unclear.

\<ii\> Ex libro novellarum i constitucio. Non liceat dari pecunie ... consecravit episco-
       pum.—Gustavus Haenel, *Iuliani Epitome Latina Novellarum Iustiniani* (Leipzig,
       1873), 29, ll. 9-10, 15-27, and p. 30, ll. 4-6.[13]

\<iii\> Item ex libro eodem. Ante omnia illud observari ... ecclesie dare.—*Ibid.*, 148, ll.
       1-2, and 4-11.[14]

\<iv\> Item in libro eodem constitucion\<um\> ii.[15] Imperator Leo Armasio p\<refecto\>
       p\<retorio\>.[16] Si quemquam vel in ... pena comitetur. Data viii id. Marcii consulibus
       Zenone et Mauro.—*Corpus Iuris Civilis, II: Codex Iustinianus*, ed. Paulus Krueger
       (Berlin, 1914), 22 (bk. 1, tit. 3.30 [31]).

\<v\>   cxciiii.[17] Innocentius papa. Qui de proferenda accusatione ... volumus revocari.—
       This is a fragment of JE 1373, a letter sent from Pope Gregory I to Bishop John of
       Corinth: *S. Gregorii Magni Registrvm Epistvlarvm Libri I-VII*, ed. Dag Norberg,
       CCSL 140 (Turnhout, 1982), 352 (bk. 5.57), ll. 24-33.

\<vi\> cciii. Accusatum simoniacum necesse habuimus ... potuissemus addiscere.—JE
       1382 *partim*, Pope Gregory I to Maximus, *praesumptor* of the church of Salona:
       CCSL, 140.371 (bk. 6.3), ll. 7-9.

\<vii\> Nam idem. Turpe est defendere quod prius non constiterit iustum esse.[18]—JE 1794
       partim, Pope Gregory I to Leontius, exconsul: *S. Gregorii Magni Registrvm Epistv-
       larvm Libri VIII-XII*, ed. Dag Norberg, *CCSL* 140A (Turnhout, 1982), 864 (bk.
       11.4), ll. 56-7.

\<viii\> Papa Paschalis Mediolan.[19] Fraterne mortis crimen incurrit ... hereticus pro-
       movetur.—JL +6613a *partim*: John Gilchrist, 'Die Epistola Widonis oder Pseudo-
       Paschalis. Der erweiterte Text', *Deutsches Archiv*, 37 (1981), 594.

\<ix\> Item idem. Quisquis contra symoniacam et ... vobis remictatur.—*Ibid.*, 594-7.

\<x\>   Item ex registro ii Alexandri pape, inter cetera. Siquis beneficium ecclesie quod ...
       pecunia comparavit.—Cf. JL 4722 *partim* (*Italia pontificia*, iii, 389, no. 7), Pope
       Alexander II to the clergy and people of Lucca: *PL* 146.1391B.[20]

\<xi\> Anno domini millesimo xc, v kal. Martii, celebrata est Placentie sinodus ... consilii
       [*sic*] comprobata. Ea que a sanctis ... Christum dominum nostrum.—Pope Urban II,
       Council of Piacenza, March 1095, cc. 1-2, 4-5, 13-15, and concluding notice on a litur-
       gical innovation enacted at the council: *Constitutiones et acta publica imperatorum et*

---

13 The *Epitome* clearly is the material source of this text but for the inscription found in Reg. lat. 399
    see the discussion of this item in the second tabulation below.
14 See the comments in the previous note.
15 There is no way to construe this inscription to refer to the material source for the text, i.e., the
    Codex Iustinianus. See the discussion below.
16 The abbreviation here, 'pp', which could also stand for 'pape', should be expanded to yield
    'prefecto pretorio': cf. Wilmart, *Codices*, 461; and *Kanonessammlung*, ed. Wolf von Glanvell,
    XLVI.
17 For numbers found before inscriptions in this text see the discussion below.
18 Wilmart, *Codices*, 461, did not identify this text, and read the final word as 'ec[clesia]'.
19 Wilmart, *Codices*, 461, speculated that 'Ex epistola' preceded 'pp Paschalis', followed by 'ad
    archiep. Mediolanensem.', but the inscription in the left hand margin for this text does not seem to
    be mutilated.
20 The textual history of this fragment, which is not identical to JL 4722 and which may not stem
    from that letter, is a complicated issue which remains to be investigated.

     regum, 1, ed. Ludewicus [Ludwig] Weiland, *MGH Legum sectio IV* (Hanover, 1893), 561-3.

<xii> Anno millesimo lxxxviii [*sic*], idus Septembris ... congregata est apud Melfiam Apulie sinodus ... edita sunt. Sanctorum patrum sentenciis consona ... occasione presumat.—Pope Urban II, Council of Melfi, September 1089, cc. 1 and 7: Robert Somerville (with the collaboration of Stephan Kuttner), *Pope Urban II, the* Collectio Britannica, *and the Council of Melfi (1089)* (Oxford, 1996), 252, and 254.

<xiii> Preceptum est etiam ut nullus omnino laicus ... nullomodo contrahantur.[21]—Pope Urban II, Council of Benevento, September 1091, c. 4: *ibid.*, 303.

<xiv> Tolosanum consilium [*sic*] pape Calixti. Anno mcx [*sic*] id. Iulii domnus papa Calixtus Tolose ... consilium [*sic*] celebravit ... approbata sunt. Sanctorum patrum vestigiis insistentes ... careat dignitate.—Pope Calixtus II, Council of Toulouse, July 1119, c. 1: Mansi, xxi, 225-6.

<xv> Damasus inter alia. Statuta sedis apostolice et ... sit liberum.—*Vere* JK 255, c. 20 *partim*, Pope Siricius to Bishop Himerius of Tarragona: *Epistolae Romanorum pontificum*, ed. Petrus [Pierre] Coustant (Paris, 1721), 637c.

Hec dicta sufficiant.

Wilmart's catalogue provided identification for most of these canons, and noted that a number of them were included in Deusdedit's collection. What is not obvious from the catalogue, however, is that the majority of those texts are replicated in Deusdedit. Excluding the conciliar decrees from Popes Urban II and Calixtus II (i.e., nos. i, and xi-xiv), which were issued subsequent to Deusdedit's book, all of the remaining excerpts are to be found therein. Several occur in sequences in book four, and although some turn up in other works too a comparison of inscriptions, incipits, and explicits demonstrates the connection between fo 71 of Reg. lat. 399 and the *Collectio canonum*. In the listing which follows, which should be read in conjunction with the earlier tabulation, reference to Deusdedit is to Wolf von Glanvell's printed edition.[22]

    <ii> Ex libro novellarum i constitucio. Non liceat dari pecunie ... consecravit episcopum. = Deusdedit 4.288 (p. 553): Ex libro nouellarum primo, const. VII titul. XXV. Non liceat pecunie ... consecrauit episcopum.

This canon has been found only in Deusdedit, and the slightly different incipit and the different inscription given in the edition are not significant points against positing a derivation thence. The inscription in Reg. lat. 399 seems to be a clumsy abbreviation of Deusdedit's, whose formal source for this text was the *Epitome Iuliani*, where it stands as Const. 6.24 in Haenel's edition. The inscription 'Ex libro

---

21 The incipit provided is expanded since this version of the canon differs slightly from the edition.

22 The process of gathering and analyzing the information which follows has been greatly facilitated by the new *KanonesJ* data base compiled by Linda Fowler-Magerl (Piesenkofen in der Oberpfalz, 2003), to whom the author is most grateful. Reference will not be made to this program at every point that it was utilized.

nouellarum primo' refers to an early tradition in the West where the *Epitome* was divided into books.[23]

> <iii> Item ex libro eodem. Ante omnia illud observari ... ecclesie dare. = Deusdedit 4.289 (p. 554): Item ex libro eodem VI, cap. CCCCXXVIIII. Ante omnia illud obseruari ... ecclesie dare.

This canon occurs in collections beyond Deusdedit's, but nowhere else with an inscription beginning 'Item ex libro eodem'.

> <iv> Item in libro eodem constitucion<um> ii. Imperator Leo Armasio p<refecto> p<retorio>. Si quemquam vel in ... pena comitetur. Data viii <id.> Marcii consulibus Zenone et Mauro. = Deusdedit 4.290 (pp. 554-5): Item ex libro codicis constit. II. Si quemquam uel in ... et Mauro.

This canon also appears elsewhere, but none of the other inscriptions matches what is given in Reg. lat. 399 as closely as Deusdedit—it is not very difficult to imagine how 'codicis' could deteriorate in transmission to become 'eodem'—and none of those other occurrences contains the concluding *Datum*. The presence of ii in the inscription in both Reg. lat. 399 and Deusdedit is puzzling, does not fit the position of the text in the *Codex Iustinianus*, and is not been elucidated by other occurrences of the excerpt.[24]

> <v> cxciiii. Innocentius papa. Qui de proferenda accusatione ... volumus revocari. = Deusdedit 4.344 (p. 571) *partim*: CXCIIII. Qui pro deserenda [MS: deferenda] accusatione ... uolumus reuocari ... .

Reg. lat. 399 offers only part of what is found in Deusdedit, with some variation in the incipit, and an attribution to 'Pope Innocent' which is missing in Deusdedit (where no inscription occurs, although the canon is part of a chain of excerpts from Pope Gregory I). The same segment of text found in Reg. lat. 399 also is in the *Breviarium* of Cardinal Atto, without the Innocentian attribution, with the rubric

---

23 Jean Gaudemet, 'Le droit romain dans La *Collectio canonum* du Cardinal Deusdedit', in *Études d'histoire du droit médiéval en souvenir de Josette Metman*, Mémoires de la Société pour l'Histoire du Droit et des Institutions des anciens pays bourguignons, comtois et romands, 45 (Dijon, 1988), 158, and 164 (repr. in *idem*, *La doctrine canonique médiévale* [Aldershot, 1994]), stated that the *Epitome* was Deusdedit's source for this and the following canon, but does not comment on the inscriptions. For that see Max Conrat (Cohn), *Geschichte der Quellen und Literatur des Römischen Rechts* (Leipzig, 1891), 122. The ninth-century *Lex Romana canonice compta* offers a similar mode of reference: see Carlo Guido Mor, *Lex Romana canonice compta: Testo di leggo romano-canoniche del sec. IX pubblicato sul ms. parigiano Bibl. Nat. 12448*, Pubblicazioni della R. Università di Pavia, Facoltà di Giurisprudenza, A: Studi nelle Scienze Giuridiche e Sociale, 31 (Pavia, 1927), 87 ff., for cc. 1 ff.

24 Gaudemet, 'Le droit romain', 164-5, did not address this question in his discussion of the text.

'XCIIII. De accusationibus episcopi.', and with the incipit 'Qui pro deserenda'.[25] Clearly there was some textual disturbance in transmission of the incipit of this selection, but a ready explanation is not at hand for the curious attribution to 'nnocent'. There is no reason to think that Innocent was the source for Reg. lat. 399, and that Deusdedit's collection probably was is indicated by looking more closely at the number 'cxciiii'. Its meaning relates to the way in which the letters of Pope Gregory I were available in the eleventh century. A lengthy selection of Gregory's correspondence from the original Lateran Register, which had been organized according to indiction and is now lost, was made in the time of Pope Hadrian I (it is this excerpt which is generally called the 'Register' of Gregory I). The letters received numbers in groups, i.e., the texts of indiction 9 (which essentially corresponded to the first year of Gregory's pontificate), were assigned numbers 1-82, those of indictions 10-11 were numbered together as 1-104, etc.[26] These numbers were sometimes carried over into canon law collections made during the late eleventh-century Reform when Gregory's letters were cited.[27] Considering the present instance: JE 1373, from Gregory I to John of Corinth, is found numbered as 'cap. 94' in the grouping of indictions 12-15 in the 'Register'.[28] That number is reproduced in Cardinal Atto's collection, and appears in Deusdedit as CXCIIII, but undoubtedly should read 'C<ap.> XCIIII'. Reg. lat. 399 in turn reproduces the form occurring in Deusdedit.

<vi> cciii. Accusatum simoniacum necesse habuimus ... potuissemus addiscere. = Deusdedit 4.345 (p. 572) *partim*: CCIII. Accusatum symoniacum necesse habuimus ... potuissemus addiscere ... .

This same text is in both Reg. lat. 399 and Atto's *Breviarium*, where it is preceded by the rubric 'CIII. De accusato simoniaco.', and has the incipit 'Necesse habuimus'.[29] JL 1382 is numbered 'cap. 103' within the grouping of indictions 12-15 in the 'Register'.[30] This explains Atto's enumeration, and in Deusdedit's collection and in Reg. lat. 399 the number before the text should read 'C<ap.> CIII'.

25 For Atto see in general Kéry, *Canonical Collections*, 233-4, and the bibliography given there. Atto's work survives in one eleventh-century manuscript, Vatican City, Biblioteca Apostolica Vaticana, Vat. lat. 586. The text in question is on fo 112v; see the edition in *Scriptorum veterum nova collectio e Vaticanis codicibus*, ed. Angelo Mai, 10 vols (Rome, 1829-38), vi/2 (1832), 87.

26 See *S. Gregorii Magni Registrvm Epistvlarvm Libri I-VII*, ed. Dag Norberg, *CCSL*, 140 (Turnhout, 1982) IX; and also *Gregorii I papae Registrum epistolarum*, ed. Paulus Ewald and Ludovicus M. Hartmann, *MGH Epistolae 1-2*, 2 vols (Berlin, 1887-99), ii, IX.

27 Fournier, 'Collections', 292, 305, and 337 (*Mélanges*, ii, 446, 459, and 491).

28 *Registrvm epistvlarvm*, ed. Norberg, 351.

29 MS Vat. lat. 586, fo 113r; ed. Mai, 87.

30 *Registrvm epistvlarvm*, ed. Norberg, 371.

<vii> Nam idem. Turpe est defendere quod prius non constiterit iustum esse. = Deusdedit 4.344 (p. 572) *partim*: ... .Turpe est defendere, quod prius non constiterit iustum esse.

This sentence has not been found in any collection as a separate canon, and is not part of the text of JE 1373 in Atto. If the compiler of fo 71 used Deusdedit's full collection he had to reach back one canon to 4.344 for this text, after copying no. vi above from 4.345.

<viii> Papa Paschalis Mediolan. Fraterne mortis crimen incurrit ... hereticus promovetur. = Deusdedit 4.93 (p. 440): Ex epistola pape Paschalis missa Mediolani. Fraterne mortis crimen incurrat ... hereticus, promouetur.

This segment of the well-known forged letter of 'Pope Paschal' occurs in several collections, but there is no reason to think that it was taken from any work other than Deusdedit's.

<ix> Item idem. Quisquis contra symoniacam et ... vobis remictatur. = Deusdedit 4.94 (pp. 440-42): Item idem. Quisquis contra simoniacum et ... uobis remittatur.

This excerpt also is found in other collections but only Deusdedit prefaced it with 'Item idem'.

<x> Item ex registro ii Alexandri pape, inter cetera. Siquis beneficium ecclesie quod ... pecunia comparavit. = Deusdedit 4.95 (p. 442): Item ex registro II Alexander pape inter cetera. Si quis beneficium ecclesie, quod ... pecunia comparauit.

This text circulated elsewhere but only Deusdedit bears the same inscription as in Reg. lat. 399.[31]

<xv> Damasus inter alia. Statuta sedis apostolice et ... sit liberum. = Deusdedit 1.99 (p. 79): Idem. Statuta sedis apostolice, et ... sit liberum.

In Deusdedit's collection 1.99 follows a fragment of JK +245 bearing the inscription 'Reverentissimo fratri Aurelio Damasus inter cetera'. The author responsible for Reg. lat. 399 must have had an eye on that inscription and prefaced this excerpt with 'Damasus inter alia'. 'Statuta sedis apostolice ... sit liberum' has been located as a distinct canon outside of Deusdedit only in Atto's *Breviarium*, correctly inscribed there to Pope Siricius.[32]

This register shows that the page of texts at the end of MS Reg. lat. 399 is clearly linked to Deusdedit's collection of canons. In particular, the inscriptions

---

31 The author hopes to devote a separate study to this item, which also is found outside of canon law collections. See Tilmann Schmidt, *Alexander II. und die römische Reformgruppe seiner Zeit*, Päpste und Papsttum, 11 (Stuttgart, 1977), 222.

32 MS Vat. lat. 586, fo 100v; ed. Mai, 73.

and the sequences of texts demonstrate that whoever assembled these selections either had access to that compilation or used a work that had drawn on it.[33] Only a full collation will show the relationship of these canons to the surviving complete manuscript of Deusdedit (Vat. lat. 3833), yet that codex can be discounted as a direct source for Reg. lat. 399 because there is no reason to suppose that it ever was in southern Italy.[34] Eight of the nine shared items occur in the fourth book of the *Collectio canonum* (nos. ii-x above). Drawing on Book 4 would not be surprising for a group of regulations focused on simony and money because Deusdedit's third book and especially the fourth treat 'the liberty of [the Roman] Church, both of its clergy and property'.[35] The last text in the series, no. xv, appears in the first book and has nothing to do with property, but instead affirms the obligation of *sacerdotes* to obey papal decrees. Perhaps it was meant as a coda to what came before, a supposition that would be strengthened if all of the preceding excerpts had been papal in origin.

Why would a compiler in Benevento at the end of the fourteenth century assemble a page of texts on financial issues from a variety of sources, none of which was issued later than the year 1123? A clear answer is not at hand, although the concluding statement—'Hec dicta sufficiant'—suggests a contemporary compilation and not a transcription of an earlier work (cf. the similar remark on fo 70v about Eucharistic texts, which was cited above after n. 10). No connection has been discovered between the acts of the synod of 1374 earlier in this manuscript and the array of texts copied thereafter, including the *florilegium* on fo 71. The book's last ten pages could simply represent odds and ends from works which an enterprising scribe had at hand. The author responsible for this hodgepodge possessed an eclectic interest in mining nuggets from different sources, so it does not strain credulity to think that in searching out regulations on money he dug less than one folio's worth of information out of a large eleventh-century *Collectio canonum*.[36] The focus in this study is on fo 71, but it is worth a reminder that in the

---

33 It could, of course, also be supposed that Deusdedit and the scribe of Reg. lat. 399 used a common source, but that possibility seems very remote and can be disregarded.

34 See *Kanonessammlung*, ed. Wolf von Glanvell, XX, for the *fortuna* of Vat. lat. 3833.

35 Translation from Robert Somerville and Bruce C. Brasington, *Prefaces to Canon Law Books in Latin Christianity, Selected Translations, 500-1245* (New Haven, 1998), 124. Latin text in *Kanonessammlung*, ed. Wolf von Glanvell, 2: '... libertas ipsius et cleri et rerum eius tertio et maxime IIII libro euidenter ostenditur'. The second book is concerned 'de clero et rebus eiusdem ecclesie', but nothing is excerpted thence in Reg. lat. 399.

36 It is, of course, possible that an eleventh- or twelfth-century treatise on simony which had been influenced by Deusdedit was used to compile the texts on fo 71. With that possibility in mind the 'Indices auctoritatum' of the three-volume *MGH Libelli de lite imperatorum et pontificum saecvlis xi. et xii. conscripti*. were searched. That foray did not yield a work containing the texts in question, although some reappear in Deusdedit's *Liber contra invasores et simoniacos et reliquos simoniacos*. The *Liber* is found, ed. E. Sackur, in *MGH Libelli de lite*, ed. E. Dümmler, 3 vols (Hanover, 1891-7), ii (1892), 292-365.

mélange of texts between that folio and the 1374 synodal canons, as noted above at n. 10 a long fragment appears, 'Ex gestis Sancti Bon<if>atii martiris et archiepiscopi R. ecclesie'.[37] This text seems to have been preserved only in Deusdedit's collection and would thus offer further evidence for the use of that work by the compiler of Reg. lat. 399.[38]

Turning from the canons shared with Deusdedit, what can be said about a source for the conciliar decrees of Popes Urban II and Calixtus II on fo 71, i.e., nos. i, and xi-xiv in the first tabulation above? These texts show up in canon law books from the first half of the twelfth century, but only one form of a known compilation includes all of them. Three codices in the so-called 'French group' of manuscripts of the early twelfth-century Polycarpus preserve, at or near the end of the collection, a long appendix mainly of records in chronological order for synods convened by Popes Urban II and Calixtus II, i.e., Melfi (1089), Benevento (1091), Troia (1093), Piacenza (1095), Clermont (1095), Toulouse (1119), and Lateran I (1123).[39] Étienne Baluze discovered this supplement in a manuscript from Aniane which today is Paris, BNF, MS lat. 3881, a well-known book containing the *Sententiae* of Magister A preceded by the *Polycarpus*.[40] The source and purpose of the appendix are unknown, but its texts have been valued highly. Some of them are known to have occurred in Urban II's now lost papal Register, and others were cited by twelfth-century popes, indicating perhaps that they too were available from the Register.[41]

The conciliar supplement has not been found as a unit beyond manuscripts of the *Polycarpus*, but from the time of Gabriel Cossart's work on councils in the late seventeenth century the accounts therein for Clermont and Toulouse were known to have been transcribed in a copy, or copies, of the *Liber censuum*, where texts

---

37 Wilmart, *Codices*, 460.

38 See *Kanonnessamlung*, ed. Wolf von Glanvell, 189. The author is grateful to Michael Glatthaar, Universität Freiburg im Breisgau, for information about this text.

39 The bibliography on the Polycarpus is vast. Paris, BNF, lat. 3881 is one of three copies containing this conciliar supplement. The others are Vatican City, Biblioteca Apostolica Vaticana, Reg. lat. 987, and Reg. lat. 1027. See inter al. Claudio Leonardi, in *Conciliorum oecumenicorum decreta*, ed. Josephus [Giuseppe] Alberigo, et al., 3rd edn (Bologna, 1973), 188-9; Robert Somerville, *The Councils of Urban II, 1: Decreta Claromontensia, Annuarium historiae conciliorum*, Supplementum, 1 (Amsterdam, 1972), 121-4; Uwe Horst, *Die Kanonessammlung Polycarpus des Gregor von S. Grisogono, MGH Hilfsmittel*, 5 (Munich, 1980), 12; Martin Brett, 'The canons of the First Lateran Council in English manuscripts', in *Proceedings of the Sixth International Congress of Medieval Canon Law*, ed. Stephan Kuttner and Kenneth Pennington, MIC Series C, Subsidia, 7 (Vatican City, 1985), 19; Somerville-Kuttner, *Pope Urban*, 187-8 (especially 187, n. 8 for the placement of this supplement in the Polycarpus), with further bibliography; and Kéry, *Canonical Collections*, 267.

40 Baluze published conciliar texts from Paris, BNF, lat. 3881 in 1663 in his notes to Pierre de Marca's *Dissertationes de concordia sacerdotii et imperii*. See *Dissertationes* (Rovereto, 1742), 479-80, 172 (see 169), 396, 487, and 497-8.

41 Somerville-Kuttner, *Pope Urban*, 233-4.

from those synods did not normally appear.[42] It is unclear whether Cossart was referring to one or to two manuscripts when he discussed Clermont and then at a later point Toulouse. In the latter case he specified that the book in question was a Roman manuscript, but he never said that the work preserving Clermont was not, and both Clermont and Toulouse could have been added to the same copy of the *Liber censuum* which was discovered in a Roman library in the seventeenth century. Cossart pointed out that Baluze's decrees for the Council of Clermont were the same as his, and although this also was true for Toulouse it was not mentioned, an omission which did not escape Baluze's notice.[43] No decrees from Clermont are found in Reg. lat. 399, but Toulouse is represented there, along with Lateran I, Melfi, Benevento, and Piacenza. Whether those four gatherings were present in the manuscript(s) of the *Liber censuum* that yielded Clermont and Toulouse remains undetermined, but perhaps at some point a version of the '*Polycarpus* supplement' was unearthed and transcribed in toto or in part into the manuscript of the *Liber censuum* that Cossart knew.[44]

Did the late fourteenth-century Beneventan compiler responsible for Reg. lat. 399 have access to a copy of that supplement, either per se, in the *Polycarpus* or some unknown work, or from a copy of the *Liber censuum*? The *Polycarpus* is an unlikely source because none of the manuscripts which preserve the conciliar appendix are from southern Italy. Bringing the *Liber censuum* into consideration is suggestive given its link with Deusdedit which was noted at the beginning of this paper. There is, however, no evidence that the texts common to fo 71 and to the *Collectio canonum* occurred in any manuscript of the *Liber*, although someone could have amplified a copy of that important book with both the appendix and a set of items from Deusdedit on money and property.[45] Whatever its source, Reg. lat. 399's selection from the Council of Toulouse begins with an abbreviated

---

42   For the most recent summary on this question see Somerville-Kuttner, *Pope Urban*, 233. Cossart's presentations are found in *Sacrosancta concilia*, ed. Philippus Labbeus [Labbe] and Gabr. Cossartius [Cossart], 16 vols in 17 (Paris, 1671-2), x (1671), 588-90 (= Mansi, xx, 901-3), and 856-8 (= Mansi, xxi, 225-8).

43   In his unpublished notes to Labbe-Cossart's *Sacrosancta Concilia* in Paris, BNF, MS Baluze 12, fo 4r, he wrote that the account of Toulouse, 1119, was printed 'Ex libro Cencii Camerarii, cum editum a me fuerit'.

44   This author has examined a number of Roman manuscripts of the *Liber censuum* in the hope of finding Cossart's book, but without success. Cardinal Nicholas Roselli (d. 1362), also known as the Cardinal of Aragon, compiled a new edition of the *Liber censuum* in the fourteenth century: see Uta-Renate Blumenthal, 'Some Notes on Papal Policies at Guastalla, 1106', *Studia Gratiana*, 19 (1976), 69-70 (repr. *eadem*, *Papal Reform*), and *eadem*, *The Early Councils of Pope Paschal II, 1100-1110*, Pontifical Institute of Mediaeval Studies, Studies and Texts, 43 (Toronto, 1978), 47-8. Perhaps Cossart's manuscript was a copy of the Roselli recension.

45   The analyses of manuscripts of the *Liber censuum* and its predecessors given in *Kanonessammlung*, ed. Wolf von Glanvell, XXXV-XLIII, do not include a version containing the texts on the last page of Reg. lat. 399.

introductory protocol which, as opposed to Baluze's and Cossart's version, provides a correct date for the synod, i.e., placing it on 'id. Iulii' rather than 'id. Iunii'.[46]

Little more can be said at present. That the influence of Cardinal Deusdedit's canonical collection was felt at Benevento in the late 1300s seems beyond question, and perhaps the conciliar supplement known from certain versions of the *Polycarpus* also was at hand and used there. But in exactly what form either of those sources might have been available, and in what combinations, is impossible to say. Perhaps the answer remains still undetected in Benevento.[47]

---

46 'Iunii' probably is not an especially significant variant of 'Iulii' because a scribe could readily make the error on his own, without seeing it in his exemplar. For the date of the Council of Toulouse see *post* JL 6708. Cf. Baluze, *Dissertationes*, 487, and Labbe-Cossart, *Concilia*, x, 856 (= Mansi, xxi, 225-6), with the preamble of no. xiv in the first tabulation above, which reads as follows: 'Anno mcx id. Iulii domnus papa Calixtus Tolose cum archiepiscopis, episcopis, et abbatibus provincie Gotie, Guasconie, et Yspanie consilium [*sic*] celebravit et capitula hec promulgata et totius assensu concilii approbata sunt'. The text of Toulouse c. 1 in Reg. lat. 399 exhibits some shifting of words as compared with the other two accounts but nothing is missing. Collations with the editions of Baluze and Cossart have not been done for all of the conciliar texts in Reg. lat. 399. It also can be noted that the one council which was not specifically identified on fo 71 of Reg. lat. 399 is the council held under Urban II in 1091 at Benevento (no. xiii in the first tabulation)!

47 The manuscripts there which are written in Beneventan script seem to be well known, but no catalogue exists of the full holdings of the Biblioteca capitolare: see Paul Oskar Kristeller and Sigrid Krämer, *Latin Manuscript Books before 1600*, 4th revised and enlarged edn, *MGH Hilfsmittel*, 13 (Munich, 1993), 276-7.

Chapter 18

The Collection of St Victor (= V), Paris: Liturgy, Canon Law, and Polemical Literature

Uta-Renate Blumenthal

'If one looks to the canon law of the day [the Investiture Controversy], it is surprising how much canon law dealt with liturgical matters ... collections are filled with liturgical regulations and even liturgical texts and commentaries'.[1] Roger Reynolds' statement is once again confirmed by part II of a manuscript now found in Paris at the Bibliothèque de l'Arsenal, MS 721. It is composed of two distinct manuscripts: the *Margarita Martiniana* of Martin of Troppau (fos 1r-164v) and an anonymous twelfth-century canonical collection, covering fos 165r-250v, followed by three blank folios, 251-3. A later ex-libris on fo 253v, perhaps still from the twelfth century, refers to the library of St Victor: 'Decreta pontificum liber deflorata canonum. Iste liber est Sancti Victoris parisiensis. Quicumque eum furatus fuerit uel celauerit uel titulum deleuerit anathema sit'. There is no evidence when the two manuscripts were bound together, but a late thirteenth-century ex-libris on fo 1r also indicates St Victor, and just a single old shelfmark, N 13—it could not be traced—is pasted onto the verso of the present paper guard (fo A). The consensus opinion that Arsenal 721 was part of the library of the Augustinian Canons of Saint-Victor, Paris, at the latest by *c.* 1200 as first suggested by Paul Fournier seems very plausible.[2]

The subject of the following remarks is exclusively the twelfth-century canonical collection found in the Arsenal manuscript. It displays a pronounced interest in

---

1   Roger E. Reynolds, 'The Liturgy of Rome in the Eleventh Century: Past Research and Future Opportunities'. The paper read for him at the Fordham University Symposium 'The Liturgy of Rome in the Eleventh Century', held September 18-19, 1998, will appear in *Scientia veritatis. Festschrift für Hubert Mordek zum 65. Geburtstag* (Sigmaringen). I am very grateful for advice and help with this paper to Martin Brett, Detlev Jasper, Joerg Müller, and Robert Somerville. I also owe a special note of thanks to Linda Fowler-Magerl whose CD-Rom *KanonesJ* has been extremely helpful to me (see n. 2 below).

2   Paul Fournier and Gabriel Le Bras, *Histoire des collections canoniques en Occident depuis les Fausses Décrétales jusqu'au Décret de Gratien*, 2 vols (Paris, 1931-2; repr. Aalen, 1972), at ii, 261-5; Linda Fowler-Magerl, *A Selection of Canon Law Collections compiled between 1000 and 1140: Access with data processing* (Piesenkofen in der Oberpfalz, 2003), 177; Lotte Kéry, *Canonical Collections of the Early Middle Ages (ca. 400-1140)*, History of Medieval Canon Law, 1, ed. Wilfried Hartmann and Kenneth Pennington (Washington D.C., 1999), 288.

matters liturgical as well as theological/political that are harmoniously embedded in canonistic texts. While the collection can be described succinctly as dependent on the *Liber decretorum* of Burchard of Worms and the *Pseudo-Isidorian Decretals*, an analysis has revealed the use of an astonishing array of material sources and a very sophisticated treatment of the texts.[3] Given the fact that the manuscript was preserved in the library of St Victor, the suggestion of Paul Fournier, 'une pure hypothèse' he called it, that its content was possibly inspired by William of Champeaux might not be far-fetched.[4] In any case, it seems very likely that the collection reflects some of the earliest studies at the famous abbey, granted a privilege by King Louis VI in 1113 as a hermitage, a few years after it had been founded by William of Champeaux.[5] Since it has been thought that the most recent item included in the Collection of St Victor (= V) was a letter of Pope Paschal II (JL 5971, fo 221ra-va), it has been assumed that the compilation could be dated to *c.* 1110. It is not possible to date the contemporary hands found in the codex with precision, but given its punctuation and the use of capital letters after a period at the beginning of a new sentence throughout the manuscript, it would appear to have been copied a decade later. This is supported by indications that the Codex Udalrici at the very least shared a common source with V. The Codex Udalrici, a collection of poems, official records, documents and letters originally compiled by a canon from Bamberg, Germany, and dedicated to Bishop Gebhard of Würzburg in 1125, exists today only in a later recension of 1134.[6] However, Carl Erdmann argued convincingly that Codex Udalrici as well as other German pro-Gregorian letter collections still extant today originally all depended on a common ancestor which he designated 'p'.[7] As this presumed ancestor 'p' has been lost, the dependence of the Arsenal manuscript on the Codex Udalrici rather than 'p' can in no case be demonstrated with absolute certainty.[8] Nevertheless, the composition of V probably took place *c.* 1125 rather than *c.* 1110. The division of

---

3 For the most recent bibliography see Kéry, *Canonical Collections*, 133-55 (Burchard) and 100-114 (Pseudo-Isidorian Decretals); see 288 for Arsenal 721: '... A combination of the *Decretum Burchardi* with Pseudo-Isidore'.

4 Fournier-Le Bras, *Histoire*, ii, 264-5: '... la date que nous assignons à ce recueil permettrait peut-être de le croire inspiré par Guillaume de Champeaux, qui ne quitta Saint-Victor qu'en 1113'. I intend to pursue this hypothesis in the future together with the analysis of book 6 of the collection and the edition of an unidentified admonition addressed to Emperor Henry IV, inc. 'Iussu omnipotentis dei' (fos 212va-213vb).

5 *Lexikon des Mittelalters*, 9 vols (Stuttgart and Weimar, 1999), vi, 1716-17, s.v. Paris (L. Fossier) and viii, 1668-9, s.v. Viktoriner (R. Berndt).

6 An excellent brief introduction and bibliography by Timothy Reuter is found in *Lexikon des Mittelalters*, ii, 2209-10.

7 Carl Erdmann, 'Die Bamberger Domschule im Investiturstreit', *Zeitschrift für bayerische Landesgeschichte*, 9 (1936), 1-46; I. S. Robinson, 'The Dissemination of the Letters of Pope Gregory VII During the Investiture Contest', *Journal of Ecclesiastical History*, 34 (1983), 175-91.

8 A possible exception is the excerpt from the letter of Pope Alexander II (JL 4501) to be discussed below.

V into nine books, all without titles or rubrics except for book 1, is shown by large initials—two initials in the case of book 4—that are more elaborate than the simple red, green or blue initials used for many of its texts. The canons are not numbered, nor is there a *capitulatio* except for the very first two canons. Fortunately, however, inscriptions are given in the margins, and occasionally a corrector is seen at work as, for instance, on fo 199va-b, where the erroneous initial P[*iberti*] has been corrected in brown ink into L[*iberti*]. The remarks that follow constitute an initial attempt to delineate the methodology of the compiler of the collection, and in particular to identify the sources that were available to him. In the first part, I will look at canonical collections; in the second part his access and approach to German propagandist letter collections, especially the Codex Udalrici, will be considered.

Canonical Collections

The canonical Collection of St Victor (Arsenal 721, fos 165ra-250vb; = V) is written in two columns in several, closely related hands datable to the second quarter of the twelfth century. It opens after an invocation and brief capitulatio with two liturgical *ordines*: Ordo 1 for a provincial synod (fos 165v-166r) and Ordo 17 for a diocesan synod (fos 166r-168bis verso-a).[9] As customary for liturgical books particular care was taken in copying such texts; in this case red ink was used for the instructions and black ink for the prayers. The script, too, although it seems to be contemporary with the rest of V, has a very different appearance compared to the hands of the canonical collection itself. Nonetheless, the invocation leaves no doubt that these liturgical *ordines* were copied as part of the collection as is typical for canonical collections originating in houses of canons, especially in the second half of the eleventh century and in the twelfth century. And whether or not V originated at St Victor, the content leaves no doubt that the canonical collection was compiled by canons, and more precisely by regular canons who shared the concerns of Pope Gregory VII and venerated his memory, evidently sharing and exchanging materials commemorating his *gesta*, as the manuscript calls them, with their brethren elsewhere, especially in Germany.[10] This 'commemoration' of the great issues that faced Gregory VII and likewise Henry IV

9   *Die Konzilsordines des Früh- und Hochmittelalters,* ed. Herbert Schneider, *MGH Ordines de Cele-brando Concilio* (Hanover, 1996), 131-2.

10 Uta-Renate Blumenthal, *Gregor VII.: Papst zwischen Canossa und Kirchenreform,* Gestalten des Mittelalters und der Renaissance, ed. P. Herde (Darmstadt, 2001), 31-43 and 42 n. 108 for the evolution of the Augustinian Rule. The interesting question of the link to Italian circles around Countess Mathilda of Tuscany and Anselm of Lucca cannot be pursued here. For a recent discussion of the role of Anselm of Lucca and his work see Kathleen G. Cushing, *Papacy and Law in the Gregorian Revolution: the canonistic work of Anselm of Lucca,* Oxford Historical Monographs (Oxford, 1998).

is the most distinctive feature of the compilation of St Victor. The invocation and opening on fo 165r read:

> In nomine patris et filii et spiritus sancti incipiunt deflorata canonum, quorum primus liber est collectus de synodali ordine et de primatu Romane ecclesie et de ordinatione et diversa correctione episcoporum[11]

It indicates only the title for book 1 of V: 'De synodali ordine et de primatu Romane ecclesie',[12] and the *capitulatio*, more disappointing still, breaks off after giving the grand total of ten rubrics. The final two pertain to c. 1 and c. 2 of book 1 of V:

> IX. De exordio sacerdocii in nouo testamento
> X. De priuilegio beato Petro domini uice solummodo commisso[13]

These particular texts are the first non-liturgical texts of book 1 of V on fo 170ra-b (V 1.1: 'In nouo testamento', and 1.2: 'Atque hoc priuilegium'). They are probably derived from Burchard's *Liber decretorum*, 1.1-2, and are typical of the procedure of the compiler who used Burchard's work as a basic framework that is then filled with a mosaic of canons derived from multiple possible sources. The preceding *ordines*, 1 (fos 165v-166r) for a provincial synod and 17 (fos 166r-168bis verso) for a diocesan synod, have been critically edited by Herbert Schneider who included the Arsenal manuscript despite contamination by at least one other *ordo* as a late 'Sonderform' of the diocesan Ordo 17.[14] Schneider has shown that Ordo 17 was originally found in three early manuscripts of Burchard's *Liber decretorum* of German provenance which can be linked to the entourage of Archbishop Aribo of Mainz and the synod of Seligenstadt (1023).[15] The close links between Burchard and V are illustrated through all of its books. The methodology of its compiler/author remains basically the same although the frequency with which he interspersed non-Burchard texts diminishes considerably in the final books of the collection.

---

11 See *Konzilsordines*, ed. Schneider, 131, where the reading 'diversa' is followed by '(?)'.
12 The generalized remainder of the title rubric is probably a general description for the 'rest' of the collection.
13 See *Konzilsordines*, ed. Schneider, 131, for the earlier rubrics I-VIII referring to the *capitula* of the liturgical *ordines*. Rubric VI is lacking.
14 *Konzilsordines*, ed. Schneider, 80-4, 131-2 and 470.
15 *Konzilsordines*, ed. Schneider, 84-5; an early adaptation of Ordo 17 found in the pontifical of Nevers from the time of Bishop Hugh (1013-66). In Arsenal 721 Ordo 17 shows influences of Ordo 13 and perhaps even of Ordo 15.

The books cover the following subjects:

Book 1	fos 170r-175ra	Authority and privileges of the Roman Church, archbishops and bishops
Book 2	fos 175ra-192rb	Ordinations and regulations for other clergy, including canons prohibiting simony and in particular nicolaitism (fo 192v is blank)
Book 3	fos 193ra-207r	Churches, liturgy, ecclesiastical properties and possessions
Book 4	fos 207ra-222va	Excommunications and consequences
Book 5	fos 222vb-228ra	Oaths, perjury, penance (fo 228rb and 228v are blank)
Book 6	fos 229ra-239rb	Emperors, kings, princes and laity
Book 7	fos 239rb-244ra	Juridical procedures and problems
Book 8	fos 244rb-251vb	Incest and fornication
Book 9	fos 252vb-257r	Marriage

Paul Fournier already noted the equivalent books in Burchard's *Liber decretorum* covering these topics, and indicated some of the additional sources put to use by V. Besides Burchard he pointed out the *Pseudo-Isidorian Decretals*, the collection of Martin of Braga—here always with the noteworthy inscription 'Ex decretis Orientalium Patrum'—and the *Diversorum patrum sententie sive Collectio in LXXIV titulos digesta* or *Collection in 74 Titles*.[16] All of these are already represented in book 1, 'De primatu'. It will come as no surprise that selections from the latter collection are found almost exclusively in this section of V dedicated to the papal primacy. The initial sequence from Burchard, *Liber decretorum*,[17] 1.1-2, is followed immediately by two brief excerpts from Augustine and Jerome unique to V, then by several excerpts from the *Collection in 74 Titles*: cc. 8, 17, 9, 174, and 183, before the compiler returns to Burchard, *Liber decretorum*, 1.4 (= V 1.10).[18] This chapter, based on the *Pseudo-Isidorian Decretals* with the

---

16 These books depend on Burchard's *Liber decretorum*, books 1, 2, 3, 11, 12, 15, 16, 17, and 9 in this sequence; see Fournier-Le Bras, *Histoire*, ii, 262.—The use of the inscription 'Ex decretis orientalium patrum' is an idiosyncrasy of the author who uses it when his sources disagree as to derivation. Examples are V 1.14 with that inscription, when Burchard, *Liber decretorum*, 1.10, indicates 'Ex concilio Bracarensis cap. I', the collection of Bordeaux and Würzburg names a council of Orléans, and the collection in Rome, Biblioteca Vallicelliana, MS B 89, says simply 'Ex conciliis orientalium patrum'; the examples could be multiplied. See, however, V 2.24 with the inscription: 'Ex decretis Fabiani pape orientalibus missis', when its source, Burchard, *Liber decretorum*, 2.10, indicates correctly c. 20 of the *Capitula* of Martin of Braga. See n. 18 below for the *Collection in 74 Titles*.

17 I have used Burchard's work in *PL* 140.537-1065, which is unfortunately not very reliable; for this and bibliography see Kéry, *Canonical Collections*, 133-4.

18 *Diuersorum patrum sententie siue Collectio in LXXIV titulos digesta*, ed. Joannes T. Gilchrist, MIC Series B, Corpus collectionum, 1 (Vatican City, 1976). It will be cited below as *Collection in 74 Titles*. For a bibliography see Kéry, *Canonical Collections*, 204-10; and Fowler-Magerl, *Selection*, 53-7.

incipit 'Sacerdotum, fratres, ordo' and the explicit 'locum tenent', in V constitutes only the initial section of Burchard, however; unless the compiler is responsible for the abbreviation of the same chapter in Burchard, the text in this form could only have been derived from Pseudo-Isidore directly, for no other canonical collection analyzed by Horst Fuhrmann or included by Linda Fowler-Magerl terminates the well-known passage in the same manner.[19]

The composition of Book 1 of V is especially complex even though excerpts from Burchard dominate even here. But they are more frequently interrupted than in later books by lengthy selections from more 'modern' collections such as the *Tripartita* attributed to Ivo of Chartres or the *Collectio Lanfranci*.[20] The compiler worked very carefully to express his views with traditional canonistic material, seemingly weighing the meaning and validity of all he had inherited as well as of contemporary writings. V 1.41 (fo 173va), corresponding to Burchard, *Liber decretorum*, 1.67 ('Quicumque episcopus alterius episcope ... prouinciarum termini confundantur'), is yet another example. It bears the inscription 'Ex concilio arvernensi cap. xxiii', found in Burchard's work.[21] The compiler of V, however, or less likely the scribe, added in the margin a second inscription for the same text: 'De eadem re. Ex concilio toletano cap. xxxiiii'. The reference to the Fourth Council of Toledo (633) indicates the provenance of this text correctly.[22] It means that the compiler of V must have compared his Burchard manuscript with those of other contemporary canonical collections only to discover the different inscription for one and the same text. Several such collections from both north and south of the Alps could have provided the inspiration for the abbreviated Burchard text.[23] In one instance the manuscript provides evidence for a personal comment. V 1.23 (fo 172rb) with the inscription 'Ex dictis Leonis pape' reproduces what was at the time a very familiar canon in both canonistic and polemical writings: 'Qui alios ab errore non revocat seipsum errare demonstrat'.[24] This sentence from letter 15.15 (JK 412; *PL* 54.688B) of Pope Leo I to Bishop Turibius of 447 continues in V with

---

19 Horst Fuhrmann, *Einfluß und Verbreitung der pseudoisidorischen Fälschungen: Von ihrem Auftauchen bis in die neuere Zeit*, MGH Schriften, 24/i-iii (Stuttgart, 1972, 1973, 1974), iii, 950, no. 354. See n. 2 above for Fowler-Magerl.

20 See for these collections Kéry, *Canonical Collections*, 244-50 and 239-43; and Fowler-Magerl, *Selection*, 126-9 and 121.

21 Fowler-Magerl, *Selection*, 30: Vatican City, Biblioteca Apostolica Vaticana, MS Pal. lat. 585/586.

22 Hartmut Hoffmann and Rudolf Pokorny, *Das Dekret des Bischofs Burchard von Worms*, MGH Hilfsmittel, 12 (München, 1991), 175 s.v. I 67.

23 With the help of Fowler-Magerl, *Selections*, the following collections were identified with the Toledo inscription: *Polycarpus* I; Vatican City, Biblioteca Apostolica Vaticana, MS Vat. lat. 1361, the *Collection in Ten Parts*, and Ivo's *Tripartita*. The collections are described by Fowler-Magerl.

24 See, for instance, Giorgio Picasso, *Collezioni canoniche Milanesi del secolo XII* (Milan, 1969), 51 for *Ambrosiana I*, c. 80 with its bibliography. For the decretals of Pope Leo I see Detlev Jasper and Horst Fuhrmann, *Papal Letters in the Early Middle Ages*, History of Medieval Canon Law, 2, ed. Wilfried Hartmann and Kenneth Pennington (Washington, D.C., 2001), 49-59.

personal comments on an issue that was very much alive at the time of the eleventh-century church reform and evidently was still debated in the twelfth:

> Denique quod non gratis accipitur gratia non est nec recte dici potest. Symoniaci autem non gratis accipiunt quod accipiunt. Igitur gratiam que maxime in ecclesiasticis ordinibus operatur non accipiunt. Si autem non accipiunt, non habent. Si autem non habent neque gratis neque non gratis cuiquam dare possunt quod non habent. Quod ergo habent spiritum utique mendacii. Quomodo hoc probamus? Quia si spiritus ueritatis testante ipsa ueritate de qua procedit gratis non accipitur, proculdubio spiritus mendacii esse conuincitur.

This is the only example of a personal note, and the connection of the argument to the statement from Leo's letter is no longer clear. Much more frequent are brief patristic excerpts as inserts into Burchard series or, as I mentioned earlier, selections from the *Tripartita* or the *Collectio Lanfranci*. Often, of course, as Martin Brett has taught us, these two collections run parallel to each other and not a few texts in V might have either as a material source.[25] If Paul Fournier was correct in assuming that V was not only preserved in that abbey's library throughout the middle ages but also originated in France and most likely in the region of Paris, it is, for instance, surprising to find excerpts in V from the Pseudo-Isidorian collections which are found nowhere else in the same form except in the *Collectio Lanfranci*.[26]

Book 2 of V presents similar obstacles, when it comes to an analysis, although the sequence from Burchard's *Liber decretorum* is interrupted less frequently. Once again the inserts can often be found in the *Tripartita* and/or the collection of Lanfranc as well. The topic of book 2, ordinations and regulations for clergy, inspired the compiler to include as 2.106 (fo 185ra) an excerpt from an encyclical letter sent *c.* 1063 by Pope Alexander II to reinforce the decisions of the Lateran synod of 1059 (JL 4501).[27] It has been transmitted in numerous canonical

---

25 Martin Brett, 'The Collectio Lanfranci and its Competitors', in *Intellectual Life in the Middle Ages: essays presented to Margaret Gibson*, ed. Lesley Smith and Benedicta Ward (London, 1992), 157-74. V 8.36-39 and 8.41 (fo 248vb) likely depends on Ivo's *Decretum*, 9.99-102a and 9.103.

26 See V 1.33, 34 and 35 (fo 173ra), a sequence also found in Ivo, *Tripartita*, 2.53.11, 2.53.12 and 2.53.13. The last two also occur in Lanfranc's collection as 2.51.12 and 2.51.13; i.e., = V 1.34 and 1.35. Moreover, V 1.32 is found exclusively in Lanfranc as 2.51.10. Without a careful comparison of all known manuscripts it is impossible to decide which collection was in fact the material source considering that V 1.33 is documented in the *Tripartita* alone. Another example of the use of Lanfranc's abbreviation of the *Pseudo-Isidorian Decretals* is probably found at the end of book 8 of V, cc. 53-62.

27 For the use of the term 'encyclical' see Rudolf Schieffer, 'Die Erfindung der Enzyklika', in *Fortschritt durch Fälschungen? Ursprung, Gestalt und Wirkungen der pseudoisidorischen Fälschungen*, ed. Wilfried Hartmann and Gerhard Schmitz, *MGH Studien und Texte*, 31 (Hanover, 2002), 111-24. For the Lateran council of 1059 see Detlev Jasper, *Das Papstwahldekret von 1059. Überlieferung und Textgestalt*, Beiträge zur Geschichte und Quellenkunde des Mittelalters, 12, ed.

manuscripts—including the *Tripartita* for the relevant sections of text—either in its entirety or in part. Apart from the inscription: 'Ex epistola Alexandri pape omnibus episcopis missa', the partial text in V ('Preter hoc autem ... patria mereantur ascribi') corresponds to the consensus of MSS in the critical edition of Rudolf Schieffer.[28] The passage from the letter of Alexander II of 1063 which has been transcribed as a single item repeated regulations from the council of 1059 that were of the greatest of interest to regular canons. It not only prohibited priests and deacons as well as subdeacons from living with and marrying a concubine, but enforced this prohibition by ordering the laity to boycott the masses of such priests who were forbidden to say mass and were to lose their benefices. At the same time chaste clergy were exhorted by the pontiffs to live the common life.[29] What was the source of this material?

The possibility cannot be excluded that the passages in V which were excerpted as a single item of text with an individualistic inscription were derived not from a canonical collection but instead from the Codex Udalrici.[30] One reason for the assumption is the inscription found in Arsenal 721 quoted earlier. It presupposes a complete letter of Alexander II as source. The other, more weighty reason is the lack of separation within the text itself. In the *Collectio Tripartita,* for instance, the excerpts found in V constitute two decrees: 1.68.1 and 1.68.2; the same divisions are found in all of the canonical collections which were included in the critical edition.[31] Rudolf Schieffer noted that there were no divisions of the text preserved by the *Collectio Lanfranci,* but that collection cannot have been the source for V 2.106, because it lacks the initial two sentences: 'Preter hec autem ... statuit dicens'. These words introducing the excerpt are essential characteristics of the Alexander letter (JL 4501), which otherwise corresponds in the relevant passages verbatim to the text of 1059 of Pope Nicholas II (JL 4405/4406) transmitted by the *Collectio Lanfranci.* Once the canonical manuscripts have been eliminated from

---

Horst Fuhrmann (Sigmaringen, 1986); as well as Franz-Josef Schmale, 'Synoden Papst Alexanders II. (1061-1073)', *Annuarium Historiae Conciliorum,* 11 (1979), 307-38, at 317-20.

28 Rudolf Schieffer, *Die Entstehung des päpstlichen Investiturverbots für den deutschen König, MGH Schriften,* 28 (Stuttgart, 1981), 208-25, at 213 col.b-225 col. b. The text of Arsenal 721 corresponds to 219 col. b, and 221 col. b of the edition; Paul Fournier, 'Les collections canoniques attribuées à Yves de Chartres', *Bibliothèque de l'École des Chartes,* 57 (1896), 645-98, at 665 for the letter of Alexander II and the *Tripartita.* Fournier's article has been reprinted in Paul Fournier, *Mélanges de droit canonique,* ed. Theo Kölzer (Aalen, 1983), i, no. 8, 451-504, 471.

29 For a discussion of the importance of this decree in general terms see the study of Erwin Frauenknecht, *Die Verteidigung der Priesterehe in der Reformzeit, MGH Studien und Texte,* 16 (Hanover, 1997); as well as Uta-Renate Blumenthal, 'Pope Gregory VII and the Prohibition of Nicolaitism', in *Medieval Purity and Piety: essays on medieval clerical celibacy and religious reform,* ed. Michael Frassetto (New York and London, 1998), 239-67.

30 See n. 6 above and Robinson, 'Dissemination', 176-80.

31 See n. 28 above and especially the prolegomena to Rudolf Schieffer's edition of JL 4501 on 211. The text in V does not share any of the peculiarities of Schieffer's MS V2 (Vatican City, Biblioteca Apostolica Vaticana, MS Vat. lat. 3829).

consideration the Codex Udalrici emerges as the most probable source for the excerpt from Alexander's letter (JL 4501) in Arsenal 721. The texts in both Codex Udalrici and V show only a single variant apart from the inscription.[32]

German Propagandistic Letter Collections (the Codex Udalrici)

Letter collections from the late eleventh and the twelfth century are eloquent witnesses to the connections between scholar-churchmen throughout Europe.[33] It is clear that the Codex Udalrici was used at least once more by the scholarly canon in France who compiled the collection and had much sympathy for the Gregorian reforms. At the end of V 4.106 (fo 222va) the reader comes across the famous account of the death of Pope Gregory VII. Under the inscription: 'Ex gestis sancte memorie Gregorii .vii. pape' we read the brief and moving narrative beginning in V: 'Pie ac sancte memorie dominus papa Gregorius .vii. cum apud Salernum ...' with the explicit: 'morior in exilio'. The critical edition of this anonymous text, found also in the letter collection of Hildesheim, is that by Carl Erdmann on the basis of the Hildesheim text. Erdmann included variants from other transmissions: the chronicles of Montecassino and of Hugo of Flavigny as well as from Paul of Bernried's *Vita* of Gregory VII.[34] Erdmann noted, however, that he omitted from the edition the 'strongly altered recension found in Codex Udalrici' because it was without consequence for the text he edited.[35] It is precisely this maligned text of the Codex Udalrici that was transcribed in V 4.106.[36] The single most important variant differentiating the version found in the Codex Udalrici from the Hildesheim collection used by Carl Erdmann is the omission of the paragraph where Gregory VII urges the clergy surrounding his deathbed to be obedient only to a canonically elected successor. Such a request would prevent any imperial intervention in papal

32 See Philippus Jaffé, *Monumenta Bambergensia*, Bibliotheca Rerum Germanicarum, 5 (Berlin, 1869), 48-50, no. 24 (at 49-50); and the essential discussion in Schieffer, *Entstehung des päpstlichen Investiturverbots*, 84-90, with references to earlier transmissions of Udalric's form of JL 4501. Udalric's inscription reads: 'Alexander episcopus seruus seruorum Dei omnibus episcopis catholicis cunctoque clero et populo salutem et apostolicam benedictionem'. V 2.106 reads: 'Ex epistola Alexandri pape omnibus episcopis missa'. Schieffer's edition of JL 4501, here always column b on 219 and 221 gives the variants for Codex Udalrici. V follows U in all cases except for 'hoc' instead of 'hec' (219, l.99). 'Preter hoc autem' is also the reading in Gratian's *Decretum*, D. 32, c. 6, but textual variants exclude a connection between V and the *Decretum*.

33 Giles Constable, *Letter and Letter-Collections*, Typologie des sources du Moyen Age occidental, fasc. 17: A II (Turnhout, 1976).

34 Carl Erdmann† and Norbert Fickermann, *Briefsammlungen der Zeit Heinrichs IV.*, MGH Die deutschen Geschichtsquellen des Mittelalters 500-1500: Die Briefe der deutschen Kaiserzeit, 5 (Weimar, 1950), 75-6, Hildesheimer Briefe no. 35.

35 Erdmann, *Briefsammlungen*, 75, n. 1: '... Eine stark veränderte Fassung, die für den vorliegenden Text nichts ergibt, steht im Codex Udalrici ed. Eccard Nr. 166, ed. Jaffé Nr. 71'.

36 Jaffé, *Monumenta Bambergensia*, 143-4, no. 71.

elections. Its omission, therefore, indicates the collector's sympathies for the imperial cause despite his general support for the papal position, an attitude that is reflected also in V throughout, but most notably in books 4 and 6.[37] Other variants of the text common to the Codex Udalrici and V compared to the Hildesheim collection consist mainly of abbreviations and do not affect the sense of the account; Gregory's words, apart from the above exception have been carefully preserved and remain unaltered, including the intriguing final words: 'Dilexi iusticiam et odivi iniquitatem; propterea morior in exilio'.[38]

Three brief patristic excerpts (V 4.103-105)—two are ascribed to Augustine and one to Ambrose—with a focus on penance, sin, and forgiveness in keeping both with the theme of book 4 and with the tenor of the account of the death of Gregory VII at Salerno in May 1085, separate this passage (V 4.106) from a letter (JL 5971) of Paschal II (1099-1118) to bishops Gebhard of Constance and Ulric of Passau (V 4.102; fo 221rb-vb). The admonition of the pontiff, urging the two bishops and faithful Christians to remain in their posts however difficult it was to avoid contact with the excommunicated, was likewise inspired by such pastoral concerns. Paschal basically confirmed a widely known decree of Pope Gregory VII, issued at the Lenten council of February/March 1078 and also transcribed in V.[39] The letter of Pope Paschal II, now dated 1104 rather than 1110, was noted by Paul Fournier as one of the indications that the Arsenal collection was of French origin, for instead of Passau (Pataviensi), the scribe of V assumed that the bishop meant in Paschal's address was a bishop U. of Poitiers (Pictaviensi).[40] Once again it is tempting to assume that the south German Codex Udalrici furnished the text, this scribal 'amelioration' notwithstanding, for the canon at Bamberg also included Paschal's missive.[41] The texts in V and the Codex Udalrici are closely related, but

---

37 For the intellectual climate at the cathedral of Bamberg in the twelfth century see Johannes Fried, 'Die Bamberger Domschule und die Rezeption von Frühscholastik und Rechtswissenschaft in ihrem Umkreis bis zum Ende der Stauferzeit', in *Schulen und Studium im sozialen Wandel des hohen und späten Mittelalters*, ed. Johannes Fried, Vorträge und Forschungen, 30 (Sigmaringen, 1986), 163-201.

38 A full discussion and bibliography is found in H. E. J. Cowdrey, *Pope Gregory VII: 1073-1085* (Oxford, 1998), 678-82. He adds the *Vita Anselmi ep. Lucensis* to works familiar with the account.

39 See John Gilchrist, 'The Reception of Pope Gregory VII into the Canon Law (1073-1141)', *ZRG KA*, 59 (1973), 35-82, at 61, no. 11/3 and the discussion below. On the age-old problem of communication with the excommunicated see Elisabeth Vodola, *Excommunication in the Middle Ages* (Berkeley, Los Angeles and London, 1986), 16-18, as well as her article 'Sovereignty and Tabu: Evolution of the Sanction against Communication with Excommunicates, 2: canonical collections', in *Studia in honorem eminentissimi cardinalis Alphonsi M. Stickler*, ed. Rosalius Iosephus Castillo Lara, Studia et Textus Historiae Iuris Canonici, 7 (Vatican City, 1992), 581-98.

40 Fournier-Le Bras, *Histoire*, ii, 264.—For JL 5971 see *Germania Pontificia*, ed. Albertus Brackmann, 4 vols in 5 (Berlin, 1911-1935; repr. 1960), 2/i: *Provincia Maguntinensis*, 133, no. 36.

41 Jaffé, *Monumenta Bambergensia*, 253-4, no. 136. For the difficult situation at Constance and further bibliography see Carlo Servatius, *Paschalis II. (1099-1118)*, Päpste und Papsttum, 14 (Stuttgart, 1979), 162-4, and esp. 163 n. 51.

Arsenal 721 shares several significant variants with an independent transmission of Paschal's letter (JL 5971), found in the margins of fo 218r of Paris, Bibliothèque Nationale, MS lat. 11851, the autograph copy of the chronicle of the Annalista Saxo. Paschal's letter is one of twenty-six such letters and records in the Parisian manuscript as Klaus Naß has shown. Naß concluded tentatively that the Annalista Saxo did not use the Codex Udalrici for his transcription of JL 5971 but rather depended on a source common to both. That source could not be determined: 'Man wird deshalb annehmen müssen, daß der Ann. Saxo mehr als nur eine einzige Briefsammlung, vielleicht auch Einzelabschriften herangezogen hat'.[42] The same conclusion might well also apply to V for JL 5971 despite the close textual relationship to Codex Udalrici.

Paschal's letter JL 5971 in V is directly preceded by the decree of Pope Gregory VII from the Lenten synod of 1078 which Paschal reconfirmed. The decree, c. 16: 'Quoniam multos peccatis nostris', exempted certain groups of individuals from excommunications imposed automatically because of contact with the excommunicated (V 4.101, fo 221ra-b). This selection is yet another sign of the care and the attention to detail that went into the work of the compiler of V. With this excerpt he provided the proof, one might say, for the correctness of Paschal's dispensation and its attribution to Gregory VII in the letter to the two German bishops. Gregory's regulation understandably enjoyed a particularly wide reception both in canonical collections and in contemporary chronicles.[43] Much of it, including the text in V, is probably derived from the *Empfängerüberlieferung* of the text which for once has also been recorded in the register, or it depends on a contamination of both register and recipient transmission.[44] The tell-tale addition 'que dicitur Constantiniana' to describe the Lateran basilica ('ecclesia Saluatoris') that we find in V is one common indicator for a branch of transmission represented

---

42 Klaus Naß, *Die Reichschronik des Annalista Saxo und die sächsische Geschichtsschreibung im 12. Jahrhundert*, MGH Schriften, 41 (Hanover, 1996), 329-37, esp. 333, item no. 17, and 336 with the discussion of the texts which are found also in the Codex Udalrici. For the Annalista Saxo see *Lexikon des Mittelalters*, i, cols 1005-6 s.v. Arnold, Abt v. Berge und Nienburg. The chronicle known as that of the Annalista Saxo was begun at the earliest in 1139, too late to have been used in V. The propagandistic collection of letters of Gregory VII 'p' cannot have included Paschal's epistle (see n. 7).

43 John Gilchrist, 'The Reception of Pope Gregory VII into the Canon Law (1073-1141), Part II', *ZRG KA*, 66 (1980), 192-229, at 226, Table I, s.v. Reg. 5.14a, c. 16. Reg. refers to the critical edition of the register of Pope Gregory VII = *Das Register Gregors VII.*, ed. Erich Caspar, MGH *Epistolae Selectae* 2, 2 vols (Berlin, Dublin, Zürich, 1920-3; repr. 1967); for Reg. 5.14a, c. 16, see ii, 368-78, at 372-3 c. (16). For a discussion of the council see Cowdrey, *Pope Gregory VII*, 591-2; and Blumenthal, *Gregor VII.*, 185-98. The register has recently been translated into English by H. E. J. Cowdrey: *The Register of Pope Gregory VII, 1073-1085: an English translation* (Oxford, 2002); c. 16 is found on 263.

44 *Register Gregors VII.*, ed. Caspar, 252-4, esp. 253 n. c), 254-5, esp. 255-6 n. *Empfängerüber-lieferung*, reveal the outline of the complex transmission.

by the Arsenal manuscript and by Codex Udalrici.[45] The two are readily distinguished from the chronicle transmission, and it seems certain that in this selection
the French compiler relied once again on the Bamberg collection, unless, of course,
both V and the Codex Udalrici share an unknown common source for this particular text![46]

The most famous excommunication of the time, the excommunication of Henry
IV by Pope Gregory VII at the Roman Lenten synod of February 1076, also found
its place—it would seem naturally—in book 4 dealing with excommunications and
its consequences (V 4.21; fo 211va-b), again within a well thought-out sequence of
relevant texts which have been chronologically arranged (V 4.20-3; fos 211va-
213va). They will provide my final example of the multi-faceted traditions underlying V. The variants in Gregory's excommunication of Henry IV as transcribed in
the text of V (4.21) indicate a source that has been thought to have been only of
local influence: Bruno's 'Book of the Saxon War'.[47] Bruno included the letter of
Gregory VII itself (JL 4979) which publicized the text of the excommunication; V,
a canonical collection, omitted this letter in contrast to the chronicler. Nevertheless, the coincidence of variants suggest that the French compiler had access to
Bruno's book.[48]

In the light of the traditions prevalent at Bamberg in the twelfth century one
cannot be surprised that Codex Udalricus omitted Henry's excommunication. Not
so the text immediately following in V 4.22 (fo 212ra-212va), a letter sent by
Archbishop Gebhard of Salzburg to Bishop Hermann of Metz, describing in detail
the deposition and the justification for the excommunication of Archbishop Wibert

---

45 Jaffé, *Monumenta Bambergensia*, 122-3, no. 57.

46 Naß, *Annalista Saxo*, 329-30, also discusses Hugh of Flavigny: *Chronicon Hugonis, monachi
Virdunensis et Divionensis, abbatis Flaviniacensis*, ed. Georg Heinrich Pertz, *MGH Scriptores*, 8
(Hanover, 1848), 280-503, at 443, as well as Berthold of Reichenau. The long awaited critical
edition of the chronicles of Berthold and Bernold is now available: *Die Chroniken Bertholds von
Reichenau und Bernolds von Konstanz 1054-1100*, ed. Ian S. Robinson, *MGH SRG, NS* 14
(Hanover, 2003), at 355 c. III. This chronicle transmission is related to the Annalista Saxo, here
depending on *Brunos Buch vom Sachsenkrieg*, new ed. Hans-Eberhard Lohmann, *MGH Deutsches
Mittelalter/Kritische Studientexte*, 2 (Stuttgart, 1980; on the basis of the edition Leipzig, 1937),
61-2, c. 70. The place of Hugh of Flavigny relative to the lost source 'p' of letters of Gregory VII is
discussed by Robinson, 'Dissemination', 181-4.

47 See n. 46 above and Lohmann, *Brunos Buch von Sachsenkrieg*, 5 (introduction). Bruno's chronicle
was compiled in 1082; *ibid.*, 2; Robinson, 'Dissemination', 180-81.

48 The excommunication of Henry IV in 1076 has been transcribed twice in Gregory's register: Reg.
3.6*; and as part of the conciliar acta as Reg.10a, 270-71. Caspar's annotations to Reg. 3.6*, 253;
Reg. 3.6, 255-6; and Reg. 3.10a, 270 show the complicated history of the transmission of this text.
Brunos Buch vom Sachsenkrieg, 60-62, included the letter Reg. 4979 = Reg. 3.6 and the excommunication Reg. 3.6* in his narrative. The variants in V which point to Bruno as source rather than
Reg. 3.6* directly, read: 'hanc diem'; 'rapinam'; 'tibi specialiter' and 'regni teutonicorum et
italie'.—For the historical background see Cowdrey, *Pope Gregory VII*, 129-50; and for the canonistic background Vodola, *Excommunication*, 20-27.

of Ravenna who had been elected and consecrated as (anti)pope Clement III between March 21 and 30, 1084, when the Romans had opened the city gates to the army of Henry IV and Gregory VII had fled.[49] Like Codex Udalrici, the chronicle of Hugh of Flavigny—the only other known source of the letter besides now V— prefaces the letter (inc. 'Wigbertus quondam Ravennas') simply with the formal address: 'G. Salzeburgensis episcopus H. Mettensi episcopo salutem'.[50] The Arsenal manuscript, by contrast, raises the importance of the text by a double-spaced rubric in maiuscule letters:

Ordo in romana ecclesia conscriptus quomodo aut quare excommunicatus sit. Wicbertus rauennas non apostolicus sed apostata perniciosus qui digne periit ut satanas quia in angelum lucis transfigurare se presumpsit, et sedem et dignitatem magistri sui, pape Gregorii, contra leges diuinas et humanas ascendit.

This colorful introduction is not found in either Codex Udalrici or Hugh of Flavigny's chronicle. It might be an expression of strong indignation on the part of the author at this attempt to replace Gregory VII, but the additional inscription, found as usual in the margin, indicates a more puzzling and intriguing possibility: 'Ex gestis eiusdem pie memorie Gregorii VII pape', suggesting as it does that the text of the letter of Gebhard of Salzburg had been derived from some kind of dossier if not actually a vita of Gregory VII.[51] The transcription of the text of the letter, although in a few cases with better readings than those found in either Codex Udalrici or Hugh of Flavigny, unfortunately also contains certain transpositions and omissions. Thus it would be hazardous to postulate direct links to the only other known texts of Gebhard's letter. Because the letter is very rare, it is reasonably certain that the excerpt is yet again an example of a common source for Codex Udalrici and for V. The item following is an unidentified admonition, addressed to Emperor Henry IV (V 4.23; fos 212va-213vb), urging the ruler to do penance and to return to the bosom of the Church and thus softening the implications of his excommunication. It is not known from other manuscripts.[52]

The last item of this thematically linked group at the beginning of book 4 that should be included in this paper is the excerpt V 4.20 (fo 211va). It is as brief as it is noteworthy:

---

49 For the letter see Jaffé, *Monumenta Bambergensia*, 141-2, no. 69; for its dating and further bibliography Jürgen Ziese, *Wibert von Ravenna, Der Gegenpapst Clemens III. (1084-1100)*, Päpste und Papsttum, 20 (Stuttgart 1982), 63-4.

50 Hugo of Flavigny, *Chronicon*, 459-60, at l. 43.

51 I am grateful to Martin Brett who first pointed this out to me; unfortunately, the manuscript uses the terms 'ex gestis' as practically equivalent to 'ex dictis', and very loosely to boot.

52 I thank Detlev Jasper for this information. It will be published in *Scientia veritatis. Festschrift für Hubert Mordek zum 65. Geburtstag* (Sigmaringen, in print).

Ex decretis Gregorii magni pape. Decernimus reges a suis dignitatibus cadere, participatione corporis et sanguinis domini carere, qui temerario ausu presumpserint contra apostolice sedis iussa uenire.[53]

As noted earlier, the compiler of V used the *Collection in 74 Titles*. One of the more significant texts which are included in the Swabian Appendix that was attached to the collection by Bernold of Constance is the final c. 330, and like V it attributed the statement that kings were to be deposed for disobedience to Pope Gregory I. It echoes two parallel letters of Pope Gregory VII of May 1077. The first is addressed to his legates, cardinal-deacon Bernard and Abbot Bernard of St Victor at Marseilles, and the second to 'archbishops, bishops, dukes, counts and all clergy and laity faithful to Christ, rich or poor, living in the German kingdom'.[54] In these letters Gregory VII quoted a sentence of Gregory I out of context in order to justify his attitude toward Henry IV which remained judgmental despite the reconciliation of Canossa in January 1077. In the privilege of Gregory the Great for Abbess Talasia of S. Maria at Autun the threat against violators of the grant did indeed include kings, but was part of a standard penal clause.[55] Gregory VII, however, threatened to impose the sanction on kings in case they boldly dared to treat the commands of the apostolic see with contempt. The readings of c. 330 in the *Collection in 74 Titles* depend on Gregory VII, Reg. 4.24:[56]

Ex decretis Sancti Gregorii Pape Primi. Decernimus *reges a suis dignitatibus cadere et participatione corporis et sanguinis Domini nostri Iesu Christi carere, si* presumant *apostolice sedis* iussa *contemnere*.[57]

Bruno as well as Hugh of Flavigny included both the 'French' and the 'German' letter in full; the Codex Udalrici included a recension of the letter to the

---

53 See Gregory VII, Reg. 4.23, 336 ll. 6-8: '… a sua dignitate cadere, si temerario ausu presumerent contra apostolice sedis iussa venire'.

54 Reg. 4.23 (JL 5034), 334-6; the text in Reg. 4.24 (JL 5035), 336-8, at 338 ll. 10-14, reads: 'et quod beatus Gregorius doctor sanctus et humillimus reges decrevit a suis dignitatibus cadere et participatione corporis et sanguinis domini nostri Iesu Christi carere, si presumerent apostolice sedis decreta contemnere'. See n. 53 for the relevant text of Reg. 4.23 (JL 5034).

55 *Gregorii I papae registrum epistolarum*, ed. Ludovicus M. Hartmann, *MGH Epistolae 1-2*, 2 vols (1887-99), ii/2, 376-8: Reg. 13.11 (JE 1875), 378 ll. 9-11: 'Si quis vero regum, sacerdotum, iudicum atque saecularium personarum hanc constitutionis nostrae paginam agnoscens contra eam venire temptaverit, potestatis honorisque sui dignitate careat reumque se divino iudicio existere de perpetrata iniquitate cognoscat …'.

56 See n. 54 for the text.

57 *Collection in 74 Titles*, ed. Gilchrist, 196, c. 330. The term *iussa* is found in Gregory VII, Reg. 4.23, 336 l. 8. It is much stronger than *decreta* used in the letter to Germany (Reg. 4.24). Whether Bernold of Constance was familiar with both letters or decided on his own to replace the two terms cannot be determined although it is highly likely. However, Reg. 4.24 is undoubtedly the source for c. 330 as the italicized segments in the text above indicate.

German kingdom.[58] The compiler of V was certainly influenced by the *Collection in 74 Titles*. Only here do we meet the categorical attribution of the threat to Pope Gregory I, separated from the context of the letters of Gregory VII, that is also a hallmark of V. The compiler even increased the impact of the 'decree' of Gregory the Great by following up with the text of the actual excommunication of Henry IV at the Lenten council of 1076 (V 4.21), a very logical arrangement. Nevertheless, the Arsenal manuscript by no means follows the *Collection in 74 Titles*, c. 330, but instead relies on the text of Gregory's letter to the two Bernards (Reg. 4.23). The variants allow no doubts.[59] It would be pure speculation to try to decide where the compiler of V obtained his text. Both the Saxon Bruno and Hugh of Flavigny are candidates, but their place in relationship to the *Empfängerüberlieferung* in general and to each other still has to be determined.[60] The text in Arsenal 721 does allow us to assume, however, that guided by the interpretation of the letter of Gregory VII documented by the *Collection in 74 Titles*, or more precisely by that of Bernold of Constance who added c. 330, its compiler replaced its text, derived from Reg. 4.24, by the equivalent passage from Reg. 4.23 addressed to the Bernards. The purpose is unclear, unless what lay behind the change was simply a desire to show off his learning.

V is an impressive witness to the interest not only in Germany as is generally assumed but also in France in the great dispute between *regnum* and *sacerdotium* in the late eleventh and in the twelfth century. The investigation of Paris, Bibliothèque de l'Arsenal, MS 721 is an obstacle course, but Paul Fournier was certainly correct when he wrote that the manuscript 'nous a conservé une collection canonique qui mérite de retenir notre attention'.[61]

---

58 See Caspar's notes accompanying his edition of Reg. 4.24, 334-6.
59 See n. 53 for textual agreements with Reg. 4.23, 336 ll. 6-8.
60 See for Hugh of Flavigny (+ *c.* 1114) in addition to Robinson, 'Dissemination', also the bibliography in *Lexikon des Mittelalters*, v, 171 (P. Bourgain). A new edition is highly desirable.
61 Fournier-Le Bras, *Histoire*, ii, 261.

Principal Publications

Roger E. Reynolds

Abbreviations

Clerics   Roger E. Reynolds, *Clerics in the Early Middle Ages: hierarchy and image*, Variorum Collected Studies Series, CS 669 (Aldershot, 1999).

Clerical Orders   Roger E. Reynolds, *Clerical Orders in the Early Middle Ages: duties and ordination*, Variorum Collected Studies Series, CS 670 (Aldershot, 1999).

Law and Liturgy   Roger E. Reynolds, *Law and Liturgy in the Latin Church, 5th-12th Centuries*, Variorum Collected Studies Series, CS 457 (Aldershot, 1994).

In press or in preparation

'Canonical Collections of the late Fifth Century'; 'The *Collectio canonum hibernensis* and its Influence in the Early Middle Ages'; 'Derivatives of the *Collectio Dionysiana* in the early Carolingian Period'; and 'The *Collectio Anselmo dedicata* and its Influence in the Early Middle Ages'; all in *The History of Western Canon Law to 1000*, The History of Medieval Canon Law, ed. Wilfried Hartmann and Kenneth Pennington (Washington, D.C., in press).

'South and Central Italian Canonical Collections of the Tenth and Eleventh Centuries (non-Gregorian)', in *The History of Canon Law in the Age of Reform, 1000-1140*, The History of Medieval Canon Law, ed. Wilfried Hartmann and Kenneth Pennington (Washington, D.C., in press).

'The Liturgy of Rome in the Eleventh Century: past research and future opportunities', in *Scientia veritatis: Festschrift fur Hubert Mordek zum 65. Geburtstag* (Sigmaringen; in press).

'A Monastic Florilegium from the Collectio Canonum Hibernensis at Montecassino', *RB* (2004; in press).

'An early eleventh-century canonistic Florilegium at Montecassino (cod. 372)', submitted to *Mediaeval Studies*.

'An Ordinal of Christ in Medieval Catalan', submitted to *Mediaeval Studies*.

The Ninth-Century Salzburg Liturgico-Canonical Collectio duorum librorum: study and edition (in preparation).

(with J. Douglas Adamson) *The Collectio Toletana: a derivative of the South-Italian Collection in Five Books: an incipit-explicit edition with an introductory study*, Studies and Texts, Monumenta Liturgica Beneventana (Toronto, in preparation).

Introduction and Hand Lexicon for Medieval Liturgical Study (in preparation).

2003

'Amedeo Carrocci—Un Scriitor Şocant', in Amedeo Carrocci, *Eseuri* (Chişinau, Moldava, 2003) 5-8.

2002

'ОТЗЫВ', in Amedeo Carrocci, *НЕНУЖНЫЕ НАСАВЛЕНИЯ ЗАПАДА* (Chişinau, Moldava, 2002), vii-x.

2001

The Collectio canonum Casinensis duodecimi saeculi (Codex terscriptus). *A Derivative of the South-Italian Collection in Five Books: an incipit-explicit edition with an introductory study*, Studies and Texts, 127, Monumenta Liturgica Beneventana, 3 (Toronto, 2001).

'An Early Rule for Canons Regular from Santa Maria de l'Estany (New York, Hispanic Society of America MS HC 380/819)', *Miscellànea litúrgica catalana*, 10 (2001), 165-91.

'Monumenta Liturgica Beneventana: un programa superior de investigación de historia litúrgica medieval en el Pontificio Instituto de Estudios Medievales de Toronto (Canadá)', *Oriente-Occidente: Revista de Investigaciones Comparades*, 16 (1999), 101-15.

'Transmission of the *Collectio canonum hibernensis* in Italy from the Tenth to the Twelfth Century', *Peritia*, 15 (2001), 20-50.

'The South Italian *Collection in Five Books* and its Derivatives: the south Italian appendix to the *Collection in Seventy-Four Titles*', *Mediaeval Studies*, 63 (2001), 351-63.

'Sacramentarium Spalatense', in *Tesori della Croazia: restaurati da Venetian Heritage Inc.*, ed. Joško Belamaric (Venice, 2001), 164-65 (Italian and English versions).

2000

'The "Isidorian" *Epistula ad Massonam* on Lapsed Clerics: notes on the early manuscript and textual transmission', in *Grundlagen des Rechts: Festschrift für Peter Landau zum 65. Geburtstag*, ed. Richard H. Helmholz, Paul Mikat, Jörg Müller, Michael Stolleis, Rechts- und Staatswissenschaftliche Veröffentlichungen der Görres-Gesellschaft, NF 91 (Paderborn, Munich, Vienna, 2000), 77-92.

'The Drama of Medieval Liturgical Processions', *Revue de Musicologie*, 86 (2000), 127-42.

General editor with Virginia Brown and Richard F. Gyug, Monumenta Liturgica Beneventana, 2: Charles Hilken, *The Necrology of San Nicola della Cicogna: Montecassino, Archivio della Badia, cod. 179, pp. 1-64*, Studies and Texts, 135 (Toronto, 2000).

1999

Clerics in the Early Middle Ages: hierarchy and image, Variorum Collected Studies Series, CS 669 (Aldershot, 1999). Including first publication of no. I: 'Clerics in the Early Middle Ages: hierarchies and functions', 1-31; II: 'Christ as Cleric: the Ordinals of Christ', 1-50; IV: 'The Subdiaconate as a Sacred and Superior Order', 1-39, + Table (7 pp.); and VI: 'Clerical Liturgical Vestments and Liturgical Colors in the Middle Ages', 1-16.

Clerical Orders in the Early Middle Ages: duties and ordination, Variorum Collected Studies Series, CS 670 (Aldershot, 1999). Including first publication of no. XI: 'The Ordination of Clerics in the Middle Ages', 1-9; and the Addenda (1-24 + Table) to no. XII: 'The Ritual of Clerical Ordination of the Sacramentarium Gelasianum saec. viii: early evidence from southern Italy'.

'The Law of the Church in the Central Middle Ages: its creation, collection, and interpretation', in *The Contentious Triangle: church, state, and university. A Festschrift in Honor of Professor George Huntston Williams*, ed. Rodney L. Petersen and Calvin Augustine Pater (Kirksville, Mo., 1999), 111-25.

'Les cérémonies liturgiques de la cathédrale de Bénévent', in *La cathédrale de Bénévent*, ed. Thomas Forrest Kelly (Royaumont [France] and Ghent, 1999), 167-205 + 15 pls.

'Monumenta Liturgica Beneventana: New Directions', in *Sources for the History of Medieval Books and Libraries*, ed. Rita Schlusemann, Jos. M. M. Hermans, and Margriet Hoogvliet (Groningen, 1999), 311-27.

Die Konzilsordines des Früh- und Hochmittelalters, ed. Herbert Schneider, *MGH Ordines de Celebrando Concilio* (Hanover, 1996), review for *Speculum*, 74 (1999), 831-5.

Robert Somerville and Bruce C. Brasington, *Prefaces to the Canon Law Books in Latin Christianity: selected translations, 500-1245* (New Haven and London, 1998), review for *The American Journal of Legal History*, 42 (1998), 299-301.

1998

'A Homily in Beneventan Script on the Sacred Orders, Canonical Hours, and Clerical Vestments (Vat. Borghese 186)', in *Roma, Magistra mundi. Itineraria culturae medievalis. Mélanges offerts au Père L. E. Boyle à l'occasion de son 75e anniversaire*, ed. Jacqueline Hamesse, Textes et Études du Moyen Âge, 10/i-iii (Louvain-la-Neuve, 1998), i-ii, 711-24.

Ludger Körntgen, *Studien zu den Quellen der frühmittelalterlichen Bussbücher*, Quellen und Forschungen zum Recht im Mittelalter, 7 (Sigmaringen, 1993), review for *The Catholic Historical Review*, 84 (1998), 318-22.

'Corpus Christi in Agnone', *Mediaeval Studies*, 60 (1998), 307-13.

1997

'*Canonistica Beneventana*', in *Proceedings of the Ninth International Congress of Medieval Canon Law, Munich, 13-18 July 1992*, ed. Peter Landau and Joerg Mueller, MIC, Series C, Subsidia, 10 (Vatican, 1997), 21-40.

'The Visigothic Liturgy in the Realm of Charlemagne', in *Das Frankfurter Konzil von 794: Kristallisationspunkt karolingischer Kultur, Akten zweier Symposien (vom 23. bis 27. Februar, und vom 13. bis 15. Oktober 1994) anlässlich der 1200-Jahrfeier der Stadt Frankfurt am Main)*, ed. Rainer Berndt, Quellen und Abhandlungen zur mittelrheinischen Kirchengeschichte, 80 (Mainz, 1997), 919-45.

'Anamnesis'; 'Collect', in *Encyclopedia of Early Christianity*, 2nd edn, ed. Everett Ferguson, 2 vols (New York, 1997), 47-8, 268-9.

Ma. Milagros Cárcel Ortí, *La enseñanza de la paleografía y diplomática: centros y cursos* (Valencia, 1996), review for *Speculum*, 72 (1997), 797-9.

1996

'The South Italian *Collection in Five Books* and its Derivatives: Maastricht Excerpta', *Mediaeval Studies*, 58 (1996), 273-84.

'Gratian's *Decretum* and the *Code* of Justinian in Beneventan Script', *Mediaeval Studies*, 58 (1996), 285-8.

'Parerga Beneventana' (with Virginia Brown); 'Visigothic-Script Remains of a Pandect Bible and the *Collectio canonum hispana* in Lucca'; 'Utrecht Fragments in Visigothic Script'; 'A Visigothic-Script Folio of a Carolingian Collection of Canon Law'; *Mediaeval Studies*, 58 (1996), 289-90, 305-13 + 2 figs, 313-20, 321-5.

1995

'The Organization, Law and Liturgy of the Western Church', in *The New Cambridge Medieval History*, Vol. II: c. 700-c. 900, ed. Rosamond McKitterick (Cambridge, 1995), 587-621, 991-5.

'Liturgy and the Monument', in *Artistic Integration in Gothic Buildings*, ed. Virginia Chieffo Raguin, Kathryn Brush, and Peter Draper (Toronto, 1995), 57-68.

Manuel C. Díaz y Díaz, *Vie chrétienne et culture dans l'Espagne du VIIe au Xe siècles* (Aldershot, 1992), review for *The Catholic Historical Review*, 81 (1995), 639-40.

1994

Law and Liturgy in the Latin Church, 5th-12th Centuries, Variorum Collected Studies Series, CS 457 (Aldershot, 1994).

Lester K. Little, *Benedictine Maledictions: liturgical cursing in Romanesque France* (Ithaca, 1993), review for *The Catholic Historical Review*, 80 (1994), 786-9.

Fountain of Life (in memory of Niels K. Rasmussen, O.P.), ed. Gerard Austin (Washington, D.C., 1991), review for *Speculum*, 69 (1994), 105-6.

Anglo-Saxon Litanies of the Saints, ed. Michael Lapidge, Henry Bradshaw Society, 106 (London, 1991), review for *Journal of Medieval Latin*, 3 (1994), 204-9.

1993

'Baptismal Rite and Paschal Vigil in Transition in Medieval Spain: a new text in Visigothic script', *Mediaeval Studies*, 55 (1993), 257-72.

1992

'Guillaume Durand parmi les théologiens médiévaux de la liturgie', in *Guillaume Durand, Évêque de Mende (v. 1230-1296): canoniste, liturgiste et homme politique*, Actes de la Table Ronde du C.N.R.S., Mende 24-27 mai 1990, ed. Pierre-Marie Gy (Paris, 1992), 155-68.

'A Beneventan Monastic Excerptum from the *Collectio Vetus Gallica*', *RB*, 102 (1992), 298-308.

Rosamond McKitterick, *The Carolingians and the Written Word* (Cambridge, 1989); and *The Uses of Literacy in Early Mediaeval Europe*, ed. Rosamond McKitterick (Cambridge, 1990), review for *Speculum*, 67 (1992), 1003-7.

1991

'Leonard Boyle and Medieval Studies in Canada'; 'Leonard Eugene Boyle, O. P.: Publications (1946-1988)', in *Rome: tradition, innovation and renewal. A Canadian International Art History Conference, 8-13 June 1987, Rome, in Honour of Richard Krautheimer on the Occasion of his 90th Birthday and Leonard Boyle O.P., Prefect of the Biblioteca Apostolica Vaticana* (Vancouver, B.C., 1991), 23-38, 55-63.

'The South-Italian *Collection in Five Books* and its Derivatives: the *Collection of Vallicelliana Tome XXI*', in *Proceedings of the Eighth International Congress of Medieval Canon Law, San Diego, University of California at La Jolla, 21-27 August 1988*, ed. Stanley Chodorow, MIC, Ser. C, Subsidia, 9 (Vatican City, 1991), 77-92. Reprinted in *Law and Liturgy*.

(with Hubert Mordek) 'Bischof Leodegar und das Konzil von Autun', in *Aus Archiven und Bibliotheken: Festschrift für Raymund Kottje zum 65. Geburtstag*, ed. Hubert Mordek, Freiburger Beiträge zur mittelalterlichen Geschichte, 3 (Frankfurt am Main, Bern, New York, Paris, 1991), 71-92.

1990

'A Visual Epitome of the Eucharistic "*Ordo*" from the Era of Charles the Bald: the ivory mass cover of the Drogo Sacramentary', in *Charles the Bald: court and kingdom*, 2nd rev. edn, ed. Margaret T. Gibson and Janet L. Nelson (Aldershot, 1990), 241-60 + 1 pl.

'The Ritual of Clerical Ordination of the Sacramentarium Gelasianum saec. viii: Early Evidence from Southern Italy', in *Rituels: mélanges offerts au Père Gy o.p.*, ed. Paul De Clerck and Éric Palazzo (Paris, 1990), 437-45. Reprinted in *Clerical Orders*.

'The South-Italian Canon Law *Collection in Five Books* and its Derivatives: new evidence on its origins, diffusion, and use', *Mediaeval Studies*, 52 (1990), 278-95. Reprinted in *Law and Liturgy*.

'The Greek Liturgy of St. John Chrysostom in Beneventan Script: an early manuscript fragment', *Mediaeval Studies*, 52 (1990), 296-302. Reprinted in *Law and Liturgy*.

'The Ordination of Clerics in Toledo and Castile after the Reconquista according to the "Romano-Catalan" Rite', in *Estudios sobre Alfonso VI y la Reconquista de Toledo: Actas del II. Congreso Internacional de Estudios Mozárabes:Instituto de Estudios Visigótico-Mozárabes*, 4 vols, ed. R. Gonzálvez-Ruíz, Instituto de Estudios Visigótico-Mozárabes, Serie Histórica, 4-5 (Toledo, 1987-90), iv (1990), 47-69.

General editor with Virginia Brown and Richard F. Gyug, Monumenta Liturgica Beneventana, 1: *Missale Ragusinum: the Missal of Dubrovnik (Oxford, Bodleian Library, Canon. liturg. 342)*, ed. Richard Francis Gyug, Studies and Texts, 103 (Toronto, 1990).

1989

Cyrille Vogel, *Medieval Liturgy: an introduction to the sources*, rev. and trans. by William G. Storey and Niels Krogh Rasmussen (Washington, D.C., 1986), review for *The Catholic Historical Review*, 76 (1989), 107-8.

'The Civitas Regia Toletana before the Reconquista: a Mozarabic vision in the Codices Vigilanus and Aemilianensis', in *Estudios sobre Alfonso VI y la Reconquista de Toledo: Actas del II. Congreso Internacional de Estudios Mozárabes (Toledo, 20-26 mayo 1985)*, 4 vols, ed. R. Gonzálvez-Ruíz, Instituto de Estudios Visigótico-Mozárabes, Serie Histórica, 4-5 (Toledo, 1987-90), iii (1989), 153-84 + 14 figs.

1988

'An Early Medieval Mass Fantasy: the correspondence of Pope Damasus on a Nicene canon', in *Proceedings of the Seventh International Congress of Medieval Canon Law, Cambridge, 23-27 July 1984*, ed. Peter Linehan, MIC, Series C, Subsidia, 8 (Vatican City, 1988), 73-89.

'Pseudonymous Liturgica in Early Medieval Canonical Collections', in *Fälschungen im Mittelalter: internationaler Kongress der Monumenta Germaniae historica, München, 16.-19. September 1986, Teil II. Gefälschte Rechtstexte, Der bestrafte Fälscher*, MGH, Schriften, 33/ii (Hanover, 1988), 67-77 + 2 pls. Reprinted in *Law and Liturgy*.

'An Eighth-Century Uncial Leaf from a Mondsee Liber Comitis (Harvard, Houghton Library MS Typ 694)', in *Scire litteras: Forschungen zum mittelalterlichen Geistesleben [Festschrift Bernhard Bischoff]*, ed. Sigrid Krämer and Michael Bernhard, Abhandlungen der Bayerischen Akademie der Wissenschaften, Philosophisch-Historische Klasse, N. F., Heft 99 (Munich, 1988), 328-32 + 2 pls. Reprinted in *Law and Liturgy*.

'A South Italian Liturgico-Canonical Mass Commentary', *Mediaeval Studies*, 50 (1988), 626-70. Reprinted in *Law and Liturgy*.

'Pontifical'; 'Rosary'; 'Sacramentary'; 'St. Peter, Liturgy of', in *Dictionary of the Middle Ages*, ed. Joseph R. Strayer (New York, 1988), x, 30-31, 530-31, 605-6, 620-21.

'Stations of the Cross'; 'Syrian Rites', in *Dictionary of the Middle Ages*, ed. Joseph R. Strayer (New York, 1988), xi, 467-8, 567-8.

'Vestments, Liturgical'; 'York Tractates', in *Dictionary of the Middle Ages*, ed. Joseph R. Strayer (New York, 1988), xii, 397-404, 729-30.

1987

'Rites and Signs of Conciliar Decisions in the Early Middle Ages', in *Segni e Riti nella Chiesa Altomedievale occidentale, 11-17 aprile 1985*, Settimane di Studio del Centro Italiano di Studi sull'Alto Medioevo, 33/i-ii (Spoleto, 1987), i, 207-49 + 32 pls. Reprinted in *Clerics*.

'Rites of Separation and Reconciliation in the Early Middle Ages', in *Segni e Riti nella Chiesa Altomedievale occidentale, 11-17 aprile 1985*, Settimane di Studio del Centro Italiano di Studi sull'Alto Medioevo, 33/i-ii (Spoleto, 1987), i, 405-37. Reprinted in *Law and Liturgy*.

'South Italian Liturgica and Canonistica in Catalonia (New York, Hispanic Society of America MS. HC 380/819)', *Mediaeval Studies*, 49 (1987), 480-95. Reprinted in *Law and Liturgy*.

'Mass, Liturgy of the'; 'Metz, Use of'; 'Missal', in *Dictionary of the Middle Ages*, ed. Joseph R. Strayer (New York, 1987), viii, 181-97, 301-2, 437.

'Narbonne Rite'; 'Ordinale'; 'Ordinarius, Liber'; 'Ordination, Clerical'; 'Ordines Romani', in *Dictionary of the Middle Ages*, ed. Joseph R. Strayer (New York, 1987), ix, 62-4, 261, 262-3, 263-9, 269.

1986

'Kyriale'; 'Law, Canon, before Gratian'; 'Lectionaries'; 'Litanies, Greater and Lesser'; 'Liturgy, Stational'; 'Liturgy, Treatises on', in *Dictionary of the Middle Ages*, ed. Joseph R. Strayer (New York, 1986), vii, 312, 395-413, 534, 587-8, 623-4, 624-33.

1985

'A South Italian Ordination Allocution', *Mediaeval Studies*, 47 (1985), 438-44. Reprinted in *Clerical Orders*.

'The Ordination Rite in Medieval Spain: Hispanic, Roman, and hybrid', in *Santiago, Saint-Denis, and Saint Peter: the reception of the Roman liturgy in Leon-Castile in 1080*, ed. Bernard F. Reilly (New York, 1985), 131-55. Reprinted in *Clerical Orders*.

'Feet, Washing of'; 'Furniture, Liturgical', in *Dictionary of the Middle Ages*, ed. Joseph R. Strayer (New York, 1985), v, 41-42, 316-21.

'Hereford Rite'; 'Holy Week'; 'Holyrood'; 'Incense', in *Dictionary of the Middle Ages*, ed. Joseph R. Strayer (New York, 1985), vi, 187, 276-80, 281, 431-33.

Jean Mallet and André Thibaut, *Les manuscrits en écriture bénéventaine de la Bibliothèque capitulaire de Bénévent, Tome I, manuscrits 1-18* (Paris, 1984), review for *Journal of Ecclesiastical History*, 36 (1985), 487-8.

1984

'Odilo and the *Treuga Dei* in Southern Italy: a Beneventan manuscript fragment', *Mediaeval Studies*, 46 (1984), 450-62. Reprinted in *Law and Liturgy*.

'Customary'; 'Dead, Office of the'; 'Death and Burial in Europe'; 'Divine Office', in *Dictionary of the Middle Ages*, ed. Joseph R. Strayer (New York, 1984), iv, 68, 117-18, 118-22, 221-31.

Paul F. Bradshaw, *Daily Prayer in the Early Church: a study of the origin and early development of the divine office* (New York, 1982); review for *Speculum,* 59 (1984), 970.

1983

'Image and Text: a Carolingian illustration of modifications in the early Roman eucharistic ordines', *Viator,* 14 (1983), 59-82. Reprinted in *Clerical Orders.*

'Unity and Diversity in Carolingian Canon Law Collections: the case of the *Collectio Hibernensis* and its derivatives', in *Carolingian Essays: Andrew W. Mellon lectures in early Christian studies,* ed. Uta-Renate Blumenthal (Washington, D.C., 1983), 99-135. Reprinted in *Law and Liturgy.*

'Patristic "Presbyterianism" in the Early Medieval Theology of Sacred Orders', *Mediaeval Studies,* 45 (1983), 311-42. Reprinted in *Clerics.*

'Image and Text: the liturgy of clerical ordination in early medieval art', *Gesta,* 22 (1983), 27-38. Reprinted in *Clerics.*

'Bangor, Rite of'; 'Blessed Virgin Mary, Little Office of'; in *Dictionary of the Middle Ages,* ed. Joseph R. Strayer (New York, 1983), ii, 72, 273-4.

'Carthusian Rite'; 'Christmas'; 'Churching of Women'; 'Cluniac Rite'; 'Colors, Liturgical', in *Dictionary of the Middle Ages,* ed. Joseph R. Strayer (New York, 1983), iii, 118, 317-19, 382-3, 467-8, 484-5.

Christine Schnusenberg, *Das Verhältnis von Kirche und Theater: dargestellt an ausgewählten Schriften der Kirchenväter und liturgischen Texten bis auf Amalarius von Metz (A.D. 775-852)* (Bern, 1981), review for *Church History,* 52 (1983), 257-8.

1982

'Advent'; 'All Saints' Day'; 'All Souls' Day'; 'Altar—Altar Apparatus'; 'Ascension, Feast of the', in *Dictionary of the Middle Ages,* ed. Joseph R. Strayer (New York, 1982), i, 59, 176, 177, 221-5, 582.

Raymund Kottje, *Die Bussbücher Halitgars von Cambrai und des Hrabanus Maurus: ihre Überlieferung und ihre Quellen,* Beiträge zur Geschichte und Quellenkunde des Mittelalters, 8 (Berlin and New York, 1980), reviews for *The Catholic Historical Review,* 68 (1982), 118-19; and *Church History,* 51 (1982), 448.

John Gilchrist, *The Collection in Seventy-Four Titles: a canon law manual of the Gregorian Reform,* Medieval Sources in Translation, 22 (Toronto, 1980), review for *Church History,* 51 (1982), 488-9.

1981

'A Visual Epitome of the Eucharistic "Ordo" from the Era of Charles the Bald: the ivory mass cover of the Drogo Sacramentary', in *Charles the Bald: Court and Kingdom: papers based on a colloquium held in London in April 1979,* ed. Margaret Gibson and Janet Nelson, British Archaeological Reports, International Series, 101 (Oxford, 1981), 265-89 + 2 pls.

'Basil and the Early Medieval Latin Canonical Collections', in *Basil of Caesarea, Christian, Humanist, Ascetic: a sixteen-hundredth anniversary symposium,* ed. Paul Jonathan Fedwick (Toronto, 1981), 513-32. Reprinted in *Law and Liturgy.*

'The Judeo-Christian Tradition' and 'Sarcophagi of the Roman Empire', in *Ladders to Heaven: art treasures from lands of the Bible: a catalogue of some of the objects in the collection presented by Dr Elie Borowski to the Lands of the Bible Archaeology Foundation and displayed in the exhibition 'Ladders to Heaven: our Judeo-Christian heritage 5000 B.C.-A.D. 500'* held at the Royal Ontario Museum June 23-October 28, 1979, ed. Oscar White Muscarella (Toronto, 1981), 287-89, 296 + pls. 277-80; also trans. as 'Die jüdisch-christliche Tradition' and 'Sarkophage des römischen Imperiums', in *Archäologie zur Bibel: Kunstschätze aus den biblischen Ländern* (Mainz, 1981), 309, 315-16.

Antonio García y García, *Estudios sobre la canonística portuguesa mediéval*, Publicaciones de la Fundación Universitaria Española, Monografías, 29 (Madrid, 1976), review for *The Catholic Historical Review*, 67 (1981), 653-4.

The Letters of Lanfranc Archbishop of Canterbury, ed. and tr. Helen Clover and Margaret Gibson, Oxford Medieval Texts (Oxford, 1979), review for *Church History*, 50 (1981), 363.

1980

'Canon law collections in early ninth-century Salzburg', in *Proceedings of the Fifth International Congress of Medieval Canon Law, Salamanca, 21-25 September 1976*, ed. Stephan Kuttner and Kenneth Pennington, MIC, Series C, Subsidia, 6 (Vatican City, 1980), 15-34. Reprinted in *Law and Liturgy*.

'The "Isidorian" *Epistula ad Leudefredum:* its origins, early medieval manuscript tradition, and editions', in *Visigothic Spain: New Approaches*, ed. Edward James (Oxford, 1980), 251-72 + 2 pls. Reprinted in *Clerical Orders*.

Jaroslav Pelikan, *The Growth of Medieval Theology (600-1300)*, vol. 3 in *idem, The Christian Tradition: a history of the development of doctrine* (Chicago, 1978), review for *The American Historical Review*, 85 (1980), 99-100.

1979

'"At Sixes and Sevens"—and Eights and Nines: the sacred mathematics of sacred orders in the early Middle Ages', *Speculum*, 54 (1979), 669-84. Reprinted in *Clerics*.

'An Early Medieval Tract on the Diaconate', *Harvard Theological Review*, 72 (1979), 97-100. Reprinted in *Clerical Orders*.

'The "Isidorian" *Epistula ad Leudefredum:* an early medieval epitome of the clerical duties', *Mediaeval Studies*, 41 (1979), 252-330. Reprinted in *Clerical Orders*.

Patrick J. Geary, *Furta Sacra: thefts of relics in the central Middle Ages* (Princeton, 1978), review for *Speculum*, 54 (1979), 570-72.

1978

The Ordinals of Christ from their Origins to the Twelfth Century, Beiträge zur Geschichte und Quellenkunde des Mittelalters, 7 (Berlin and New York, 1978).

'Liturgical Scholarship at the Time of the Investiture Controversy: past research and future opportunities', *Harvard Theological Review*, 71 (1978), 109-24. Reprinted in *Law and Liturgy*.

'An unexpected manuscript fragment of the ninth-century canonical collection in two books', *BMCL*, NS 8 (1978), 35-8. Reprinted in *Law and Liturgy*.

Hubert Mordek, *Kirchenrecht und Reform im Frankenreich: Die Collectio Vetus Gallica, die älteste systematische Kanonessammlung des fränkischen Gallien: Studien und Edition*, Beiträge zur Geschichte und Quellenkunde des Mittelalters, 1 (Berlin and New York, 1975), review for *Speculum*, 53 (1978), 176-9.

1977

'Marginalia on a Tenth-Century Text on the Ecclesiastical Officers', in *Law, Church, and Society: essays in honor of Stephan Kuttner*, ed. Kenneth Pennington and Robert Somerville (Philadelphia, 1977), 115-29. Reprinted in *Clerical Orders*.

Horst Fuhrmann, *Einfluss und Verbreitung der pseudo-isidorischen Fälschungen von ihrem Auftauchen bis in die neuere Zeit, MGH Schriften*, 24/ii-iii (Stuttgart, 1973-74), review for *Speculum*, 52 (1977), 662-5.

Hubert Mordek, *Kirchenrecht und Reform im Frankenreich: Die Collectio Vetus Gallica, die älteste systematische Kanonessammlung des fränkischen Gallien: Studien und Edition*, Beiträge zur Geschichte und Quellenkunde des Mittelalters, 1 (Berlin and New York, 1975), review for *Church History*, 46 (1977), 237-9.

1976

'Ivonian Opuscula on the Ecclesiastical Officers', in *Mélanges Gérard Fransen*, ed. Stephan Kuttner, Alfons M. Stickler, E. Van Balberghe and D. Van den Aufweele, 2 vols, *Studia Gratiana*, 19-20 (1976), ii, 309-22. Reprinted in *Clerical Orders*.

R. H. Helmholz, *Marriage Litigation in Medieval England*, Cambridge Studies in English Legal History (Cambridge, 1974), review for *Church History*, 45 (1976), 106.

G. M. Lukken, *Original Sin in the Roman Liturgy: research into the theology of original sin in the Roman sacramentaria and the early baptismal liturgy* (Leiden, 1973), review for *Speculum*, 51 (1976), 761-3.

1975

'A Ninth-Century Treatise on the Origins, Office, and Ordination of the Bishop', *RB*, 85 (1975), 321-32. Reprinted in *Clerical Orders*.

'Excerpta from the *Collectio hibernensis* in three Vatican manuscripts', *BMCL*, NS 5 (1975), 1-9. Reprinted in *Law and Liturgy*.

'Isidore's Texts on the Clerical Grades in an Early Medieval Roman Manuscript', *Classical Folia*, 29 (1975), 95-101. Reprinted in *Clerical Orders*.

Horst Fuhrmann, *Einfluss und Verbreitung der pseudo-isidorischen Fälschungen von ihrem Auftauchen bis in die neuere Zeit, MGH Schriften*, 24/i (Stuttgart, 1972), review for *Speculum*, 50 (1975), 116-19.

Peter Partner, *The Lands of St. Peter: the papal state in the Middle Ages and early Renaissance* (Berkeley, 1972), review for *Journal of the American Academy of Religion*, June Suppl. (1975), 429.

1973

Johannes Wilhelmus Smit, *Studies on the Language and Style of Columba the Younger (Columbanus)* (Amsterdam, 1971), review for *Speculum*, 48 (1973), 179-82.

1972

'The *De officiis vii graduum*: its origins and early medieval development', *Mediaeval Studies*, 34 (1972), 113-51. Reprinted in *Clerical Orders*.

Wolfgang S. Seiferth, *Synagogue and Church in the Middle Ages: two symbols in art and literature* (New York, 1970), review for *Church History*, 41 (1972), 118.

James A. Brundage, *Medieval Canon Law and the Crusader* (Madison, 1969), review for *Journal of the American Academy of Religion*, (1972), 597.

Schafer Williams, *Codices Pseudo-Isidoriani: a palaeographico-historical study*, MIC, Series C, Subsidia, 3 (New York, 1971), review for *Speculum*, 47 (1972), 818-23.

Stanley Chodorow, *Christian Political Theory and Church Politics in the Mid-Twelfth Century: the ecclesiology of Gratian's Decretum* (Los Angeles and Berkeley, 1972), review for *Church History*, 41 (1972), 537-8.

1971

'The Pseudo-Augustinian *Sermo de conscientia* and related *Dicta sancti gregorii papae*', *RB*, 81 (1971), 310-17. Reprinted in *Law and Liturgy*.

'The Portrait of the Ecclesiastical Officers in the Raganaldus Sacramentary and its Liturgico-Canonical Significance', *Speculum*, 46 (1971), 432-42 + 15 figs. Reprinted in *Clerics*.

1970

'A Florilegium on the Ecclesiastical Grades in Clm 19414: testimony to ninth-century clerical instruction', *Harvard Theological Review*, 63 (1970), 235-59. Reprinted in *Clerical Orders*.

'The Pseudo-Hieronymian *De septem ordinibus ecclesiae*: notes on its origins, abridgments, and use in early medieval canonical collections', *RB*, 80 (1970), 238-52. Reprinted in *Clerical Orders*.

1969

'Further Evidence for the Irish Origin of Honorius Augustodunensis', *Vivarium*, 7 (1969), 1-7.

'The Turin *Collection in Seven Books*: a Poitevin canonical collection', *Traditio*, 25 (1969), 508-14. Reprinted in *Law and Liturgy*.

'The Unidentified Sources of the Norman Anonymous', *Transactions of the Cambridge Bibliographical Society*, 5.2 (1969), 122-31.

1968

'Virgines Subintroductae in Celtic Christianity', *Harvard Theological Review*, 61 (1968), 547-66. Reprinted in *Law and Liturgy*.

Index

II. General Index